COMMUNICATION

for Business and the Professions

Eighth Edition

D0470631

COMMUNICATION
for Business and the Professions

Eighth Edition

Patricia Hayes Andrews
John E. Baird, Jr.

WAVELAND
PRESS, INC.
Long Grove, Illinois

For information about this book, contact:
Waveland Press, Inc.
4180 IL Route 83, Suite 101
Long Grove, IL 60047-9580
(847) 634-0081
info@waveland.com
www.waveland.com

Contents

PART 2
INTERPERSONAL COMMUNICATION   129

PART 3
INTERVIEWING   283

PART 4
SMALL GROUP COMMUNICATION   361

PART 5
PUBLIC COMMUNICATION   451

Preface

THE BOOK'S UNDERLYING PHILOSOPHY

Without question, communication is important to any organization. Thousands of books, articles, and speeches have arrived at the same conclusion: Without communication, organizations could not exist. At present, however, a trend that is sweeping U.S. business and industry is changing the role of communication in organizations. "Participative management" in its various forms is increasingly replacing other styles of management as the preferred method of problem solving and governance in all types of organizations. For example:

- "Self-managed work teams" in many businesses allow employees to set their own work methods, select new employees and discipline current ones, monitor quality and productivity, and perform other functions traditionally assigned to "supervisors" or "managers."

- "Shared governance" systems in hospitals provide nurses with opportunities to establish their own work schedules and systems of rotation between units and shifts, to set and monitor standards of patient care, and to develop methods for improved staff education.

- Employee advisory groups provide top-level company executives with important feedback concerning pending decisions and actions, and with important advice about the perceptions and problems of employees.

- Study circles bring together groups of citizens who are concerned about community problems to interact with each other and with elected leaders and to participate in articulating solutions to complex community problems.

- Problem-solving groups composed of nonsupervisory staff identify and solve work-related problems in organizations of all types, resulting in improved efficiency and millions of dollars in savings.

As this trend continues, managers and supervisors increasingly are playing the role of "facilitators" rather than "order givers," and nonsupervisory employees are contributing their minds (as well as their hands) to the achievement of organizational goals. Along the way, it is hoped that these participatory measures will also lead to greater employee satisfaction and perhaps even to a sense of empowerment.

Such fundamental changes in the way organizations are managed have placed the challenge of communication effectiveness on individuals at all levels of the organization, not just on those in positions of leadership. For example, an employee in a typical organization can expect to:

- Collaborate on one or more group problem-solving projects
- Be asked to contribute his or her ideas for improving the job, the organization, and the way everyone interacts
- Deliver to management all or part of a presentation outlining ideas or proposals for change
- Work informally with peers and superiors in making decisions previously reserved for management alone

All of these activities require communication skills and sound judgment by organizational members at all levels. Knowing this, forward-thinking organizations are currently training their staffs in communication skills as well as recruiting skilled communicators whose values and principles are consistent with those of the organization. Now more than ever, getting and keeping a job requires excellent communication skills.

EMPHASIS OF THE BOOK

The structures and functions of communication in organizations are virtually limitless. As in the past, we have selected some of the most important types of situations students will encounter when they become part of organizational life and then have described communication strategies and skills that are widely applicable across diverse contexts. After establishing foundational principles of ethics, organizational communication and culture, and perspectives on leadership, we devote considerable attention to interpersonal communication (including verbal and nonverbal messages and conflict management), interviewing, group communication, teamwork, and public speaking. Our purpose throughout is to analyze the demands placed upon people in each situation and to present strategies and techniques by which students might meet those demands and learn to communicate effectively. Our assessment and advice are based on more than 60 years of combined experience working as consultants, teachers, and scholars.

Consistent with the previous seven editions, the eighth edition emphasizes skills acquisition in the context of organizational communication theory and research.

- We have continued our practice of including many *real-world illustrations* throughout the text, based on the testimony and experience of successful leaders whom we have known.
- As in earlier editions, *we emphasize business and industry and the professions.* We do this with the belief that the students who read this text are preparing for

diversified careers in education, law, agriculture, and the health sciences, as well as in business and other professions.

- The eighth edition, like previous editions, is ***peppered with business briefs*** that depict contemporary illustrations of communication theories, research, or principles. Each attempts to highlight or illustrate important concepts elaborated in the text. Many business briefs are new to this edition.
- Like the last edition, this new edition includes ***special features that highlight diversity, ethics, and technology.***

This edition, however, contains some new features, significant content reorganization, and several new sections.

NEW FEATURES

In addition to emphasizing the above-mentioned issues and features of continuing importance, the eighth edition adds ***a new special feature:***

- civic engagement

Based on the belief that participation in community life is an important responsibility of all citizens, regardless of their profession or work commitments, we have included significant sections throughout the book that address varied ways of becoming involved in community affairs—and we invite students to think about corporate social responsibility when choosing an organization to work for. To assist students in applying the civic engagement content added to the text, a number of end-of-chapter exercises feature civic engagement or advocacy.

Other chapters contain ***extended new sections or fully developed chapters*** on:

- effective writing
- nonverbal communication
- verbal communication

In addition, other chapters feature somewhat ***shorter sections containing new content*** on a wide variety of subjects:

- cross-cultural communication
- multinational business and ethics
- "politically correct" speech
- telecommuting and virtual work teams
- blogs as informal communication
- crisis management and 9/11
- posting resumes on the Internet
- new management philosophies
- followership
- pressure and stress in the workplace
- gossip
- swearing
- speaking assertively

- giving positive feedback
- apologizing
- feng shui
- communicating with difficult people
- study circles as a vehicle for managing conflict
- gender and leadership in groups
- deliberative dialogue
- participating in town meetings
- avoiding plagiarism
- avoiding sexist language

At the end of each chapter, some new questions for discussion and exercises are followed by new case applications. These can be used for in-class discussions, for homework assignments, or for group work.

ORGANIZATION OF THE EIGHTH EDITION

Part I explores foundational elements of organizational communication. Chapter 1 considers the ethical environment in which communicative interaction in organizations occurs, examining diverse perspectives for making ethical judgments and introducing several issues that offer ethical challenges for all organizational members. In chapter 2, we explore fundamental principles of organizational communication, including the meaning of communication, the nature of organizations, and the basic channels that people use to communicate, both formally and informally, together with challenges and guidelines for their effective use. Chapter 3 concludes this section by considering the organization's cultural environment, looking at various aspects of corporate culture, considering diverse perspectives on leadership as well as principles of followership, and examining challenging issues that confront managers in the twenty-first century.

Part II covers interpersonal communication. In chapter 4, we look at principles of sending messages, including semantics, characteristics of both negative (defensive) communication and positive (supportive) communication, as well as the elements of effective written communication. Chapter 5 is devoted to nonverbal communication—including the physical environment in which organizational members interact, as well as the ways they use their faces, bodies, and voices intentionally or unintentionally to convey messages. Taking these basic communication elements as a foundation, chapter 6 focuses on interpersonal relationships, considering ways we perceive others and sometimes stereotype them, as well as the dimensions of human relationships and how communication impacts relationship development in organizational settings. A special section of this chapter is devoted to communication strategies for improving relationships, including the role of listening in relationship development. Finally, the final chapter of part II (chapter 7) turns to conflict and its management. After examining the nature and sources of conflict, the chapter examines how conflicts develop and considers personal styles of conflict management before offering a model of collaborative conflict management. The chapter also considers how technology might be used to manage conflict.

Part III represents an applied section devoted to interviewing. This is a common form of interpersonal communication in organizational contexts. Chapter 8 discusses fundamental interviewing principles and then looks at special interviewing applications, including corrective, appraisal, and complaint-resolution interviews. In chapter 9, we offer a detailed consideration of the employment interview, including the roles of interviewer and interviewee. Interviewing is presented in a legal context, and guidance is offered on preparation, performance, and evaluation. We also give special advice on constructing resumes and cover letters.

Part IV examines organizational communication in the context of groups or teams. After emphasizing the frequency with which groups are used in the contemporary organization, chapter 10 considers the socioemotional dimensions of group work, including group role structure, status and power, group pressure and groupthink, and group cohesiveness. Chapter 11 then examines the process of group decision making, considering the advantages and disadvantages of group work, diverse ways of organizing a discussion and planning an agenda, and the ways that technology can assist group interaction. The last chapter in this part, chapter 12, focuses on group meeting management. After considering diverse styles of leadership, the chapter looks at how to handle problem participants and different ways of getting all group members involved.

Part V discusses the important elements involved in public speaking. Chapter 13 considers topic selection, audience analysis, and diverse speaking purposes (to interest, to inform, and to persuade), as well as the formulation of purpose and thesis statements, the discovery of evidence to support and develop ideas, and ways of testing evidence to determine its quality and likely effectiveness. The chapter concludes with an examination of inductive and deductive reasoning, together with reasoning fallacies to be avoided. Chapter 14 examines the organization of the speech (the introduction, the body, the conclusion, and transitions) as well as different kinds of outlines (formative, formal, and keyword). The fourteenth chapter also discusses modes and principles of delivery and the use of presentational aids. This final part of the book concludes with chapter 15, which is devoted to special persuasive speaking applications. After examining principles of persuasion (strategies of using emotional and logical appeals, as well as establishing credibility), we move to a detailed consideration of proposals and sales presentations.

The appendix focuses on the basic principles of parliamentary procedure. These principles can be helpful to those chairing meetings as well as to anyone who wants to introduce motions and get the group to take action.

OUR APPRECIATION

Many people have contributed to our personal communication effectiveness. We think it appropriate to acknowledge their contribution to our still-developing skills. The late Professors J. Jeffrey Auer, Robert G. Gunderson, and Raymond G. Smith, along with Professors James R. Andrews, Richard L. Johannesen, Dennis S. Gouran, Paul Batty, and our colleague, the late Herbert G. Melnick, taught us by word and example the techniques of effective communication. Our friends and colleagues at Indiana University and Baird/Borling Associates have shown us the pleasures and successes that good communication can bring. We would also like to thank the reviewers of this edition for their suggestions and comments. Finally, we are indebted to our spouses and our parents, whose encouragement, support, and love have been sustaining forces in our lives. To them, we dedicate this book.

Patricia Hayes Andrews
John E. Baird, Jr.

PART 1

COMMUNICATION IN ORGANIZATIONS

The unquestioned authority of managers in the corporation has been replaced by . . . the need for managers to persuade rather than to order, and by the need to acknowledge the expertise of those below.

—Rosabeth Moss Kanter, *The Changemasters*

1

Ethical Foundations of Organizational Communication

After reading this chapter, you should be able to:

❏ Explain the importance of ethics for organizations
❏ Explain how communication both shapes and reflects an organization's ethical standards
❏ Describe ethical issues involved with advertising, "service" versus "profit," social responsibility, and employee rights
❏ Explain the impact of "globalization" on the development of ethical standards
❏ Explain four perspectives for determining what is "right"
❏ List and explain four methods organizations are using to improve ethical behavior

For years, Dr. Laura Schlessinger has been talking with people who call into her radio show looking for advice on how to manage their lives. After lecturing, directing, brow-beating, or at times patronizing her callers, "Dr. Laura" used to conclude her broadcast by saying, "Now go take on the day." More recently, though, that has changed, and her concluding tag line became, "Now go do the right thing." Whatever one may think of Dr. Laura and her views regarding what is "the right thing," the most important element of effective communication within and between organizations is doing the "right thing." Developing skills to communicate effectively is extremely important, of course. But developing a moral compass that guides the utilization of those skills is even more important.

Throughout your life you will face decisions about what is "right" and "proper" and "fair." You may decide, for example, the occupation to which you will devote much of your life, the standards by which you want to raise your children, or the ways in which you want to acquire and use your material possessions. On the job, you will have to decide whether to tell your superiors things they do not want to hear, or how to promote your product or service (and indeed, yourself), or how to track and report your business expenses to your employer (and possibly the Internal Revenue Service), or how to exercise power in dealing with subordinates. All of these decisions about what is "the right thing" are *ethical* decisions.

Similarly, the organizations in which you work will struggle with ethical concerns: how employees should be treated, how products or services should be priced, how the environment should be protected, how they should fulfill their social responsibilities, and so on. And as a member of those organizations, you will need to decide how you feel about their ethical decisions and, if you disagree, what you should do about it.

In this first chapter, we will consider the nature of "ethics" in organizations and some key ethical issues organizations today are facing. After exploring the importance of behaving ethically, we will examine several different perspectives for making ethical judgments. One or more of these perspectives might guide the actions and underlie the judgments you make as an individual; they also influence the behavior and worldview of every organization with which you are or will be associated. Finally, we will consider some ways in which organizations today are trying to promote ethical behavior.

WHY "GO DO THE RIGHT THING"?

Perhaps the best answer to that question is to examine some recent situations where people in organizations have not done the right thing. Sadly, there is no shortage of such examples:

- Kenneth Lay, former CEO of the poster child for corporate corruption, Enron, was arrested on charges of helping to direct a financial conspiracy, misleading employees and stock analysts and improperly profiting from more than $90 million in hidden stock sales. Among other alleged deceptions, Lay urged Enron managers and employees to buy more company stock, while at the same time, quietly selling $24 million of his own Enron holdings. Enron's eventual bankruptcy caused the loss of 5,000 jobs and depleted savings for 20,000 pensioners.[1]

- Enron's auditor, Arthur Andersen, a onetime giant accounting firm, also was convicted of obstructing justice and no longer is in business.

- TAP Pharmaceutical Products executives were charged with conspiring to pay kickbacks and bribes to doctors and other customers in marketing prostate cancer treatment Lupron, and TAP agreed to pay a fine of $885 million while pleading guilty to a criminal charge of conspiring to bill government insurers for free samples of Lupron. Four doctors also pled guilty for their role in the scheme. Prosecutors highlighted the drug company's use of lavish gifts including Aspen ski vacations, island resort golf trips, and thousands of dollars in cash allegedly meant to entice physicians into prescribing Lupron.[2]

- Adelphia Communications Corporation founder John Rigas and his son Timothy were convicted of looting the cable company and deceiving investors by hiding its backbreaking debt. Prosecutors accused the Rigas family of using complex cash-management systems to send money to family-owned entities as a cover for stealing money for themselves.[3]

- HealthSouth Corp. fired CEO Richard Scrushy, who then was charged with leading a multi-billion dollar scheme to overstate HealthSouth earnings to make it appear the company was meeting Wall Street forecasts. Sixteen former HealthSouth executives were charged with participating in a conspiracy to inflate earnings statements; all but Scrushy pleaded guilty.

- Qwest Communications International executives were charged with plotting to help the company improperly book $34 million in revenue. Although prosecutors failed to win convictions against some mid-level executives, others pled guilty to charges of accessory after the fact to wire fraud.
- Tyco International former CEO Dennis Kozlowski and former CFO Mark Swartz were accused of stealing $600 million from the company, but a mistrial was declared and another trial was scheduled.
- WorldCom former CEO Bernie Ebbers faced federal fraud and conspiracy charges for allegedly directing an accounting fraud now estimated at $11 billion; former CFO Scott Sullivan pled guilty to fraud charges and agreed to testify against Ebbers.
- Martha Stewart was convicted of conspiracy, obstruction of justice, and issuing false statements stemming from her December 2001 sale of ImClone stock.
- Hollinger International, Inc., jarred the newspaper industry by announcing that its *Chicago Sun-Times* had been significantly overstating its circulation figures for "the past several years." The importance of circulation figures is this: the greater a newspaper's circulation, the more it can charge for advertising. Then, two days later, the Tribune Company came forward with an admission that its *Newsday* newspaper on New York's Long Island, along with its Spanish-language sister paper, *Hoy*, also had overstated circulation numbers.[4]
- Criminal charges were brought against former Symbol Technologies CEO Tomo Razmilovic, who fled to Sweden in an effort to avoid extradition to the U.S. When he was CEO of the computer company Cominvest, Razmilovic was ousted after stock exchange officials discovered accounting irregularities that resulted in reported profits being cut in half. At Symbol, authorities charged that much of the growth of the company was "fictitious," and Razmilovic was responsible for having fostered a "numbers-driven" culture.[5]
- After investigating the activities of intelligence agencies prior to the beginning of the war with Iraq in 2003, the U.S. Senate Intelligence Committee concluded that those agencies had provided false information about Iraq that served as the basis for this country's decision to wage war. Most major judgments in the October 2002 National Intelligence Estimate about Iraq's alleged nuclear, chemical, and biological weapons programs were "either overstated or were not supported by the underlying intelligence reporting," the report said, and much of the information provided or cleared by the CIA for inclusion in Secretary of State Colin Powell's February 2003 speech to the United Nations justifying war with Iraq "was overstated, misleading, or incorrect."
- On July 6, 2004, the Archdiocese of Portland, Oregon, filed for bankruptcy protection because it had run out of money after spending $53 million to settle more than 130 priest sex abuse claims dating to 1950. All of these claims stem from the actions of one priest, who is now deceased.[6]

These are but a few of the situations in which prominent people in a variety of organizations have behaved in ways that are less than ethical.

Why should we be concerned about ethics in the first place? Why is it important to behave ethically if unethical behavior might provide us with some advantage in the competitive business and professional world? Although each of us must answer these questions to our own satisfaction, recent events suggest the following:

- *Unethical behavior can have seriously damaging consequences.* These consequences can affect both the person committing the practice and the people that practice touches. In many of the cases noted above, innocent employees lost their jobs, investors lost some or all of their life savings, and some of the perpetrators lost their freedom by being sent to jail. Enron's collapse, for example, cost investors billions of dollars, put thousands of Enron employees out of work, and wiped out retirement savings for many. The company, once admired, became a symbol of corporate greed and excess.

- But beyond that, *the people and organizations* (and indeed, entire industries) *who were involved lost credibility.* And once your image is so tarnished that people no longer are willing to believe or put their faith in you and your business, failure is almost certain. Our own observations indicate that ethical missteps end careers more quickly and with more finality than any other mistake in judgment. Lying, stealing, cheating, reneging on contracts, and so on undermine the very foundation upon which organizations are built and thus are not readily forgiven or forgotten. For every newspaper headline discussing major breaches of ethics, there may be hundreds of "minor" situations where an individual is fired (or "asked to resign") for unethical behavior, or where an executive or manager is put in a dead-end career track by a company wishing to avoid a public relations scandal.

- Unfortunately, *unethical behavior by just a few can taint not only those individuals, but everyone else with whom people associate them.* For example, in a Gallup poll conducted in 2002, 90 percent of Americans said corporate leaders could not be trusted to look after their employees, and 43 percent said senior executives were in it only for themselves. Apparently, unethical behavior by a few leaders in organizations has led to distrust of organizational leadership in general.[7]

- On the other hand, *behaving ethically has important positive consequences.* Honesty in business dealings allows others to trust you and your organization, and makes you far more effective in your dealings with them. Indeed, organizations in general depend on the acceptance of rules and expectations, mutual trust, and fairness in order to exist. Simply put, ethical behavior not only is good business, it is a fundamental requirement for the existence of communities, organizations, and societies.

- In addition, *your behavior serves as a model, both to yourself and to others.* If you behave ethically and discover the effectiveness of such behavior, you are more likely to behave ethically in the future. Similarly, the people with whom you work will be more likely to engage in ethical behavior. Conversely, if you behave unethically and get away with it (or even gain some short-term profit from it), you become more likely to continue your unethical behavior and to promote such behavior by others.

- Finally, *ethical behavior is intrinsically valuable.* Knowing that you are honest, that you behave humanely in your dealings with your fellow employees, that you are fair in your evaluations of others, and that you are concerned for the welfare of the whole organization and the society it serves are important self-perceptions that truly are priceless.

WHY CAN IT BE DIFFICULT TO "GO DO THE RIGHT THING"?

Given the value of ethical behavior and the potential "downsides" of unethical actions, you might wonder why so many organizations seem to have chosen to follow the less ethical path. The Enron case provides some useful insights. The Enron scandal prompted Congress to create the Public Company Accounting Oversight Board chaired by William McDonough, former president of the Federal Reserve Bank of New York. In an interview, he was asked why unethical behavior had seemingly become so widespread. His answer was simple: **greed**. Executive compensation has skyrocketed, he said, and a significant piece of an executive's pay often is stock options. If company earnings are higher than Wall Street analysts predict, stock prices usually go up (and along with that, the executives' total compensation package); if earnings fall below analysts' predictions, stock prices usually go down, even though the company may be highly successful. Consequently, there is a strong financial incentive for executives to deceive Wall Street analysts so that their predictions are lower than the actual earnings, and, as was the case at Enron, to use accounting methods to make earnings appear higher than they actually are. The end result, McDonough said, is that "You start cooking the books big time. How many companies were cooking the books, we don't know. We know some, because they were the subjects of scandals. But it looks an awful lot as if there was a fair amount that was going on."[8]

The 2003 Business Ethics Survey, conducted by the Society for Human Resource Management in collaboration with the Ethics Research Center, found that just over half of the respondents said they felt at least some pressure to compromise their organization's ethical standards, up significantly from the percentage seen in 1997. According to Jennifer Schramm, manager of the Workplace Trends and Forecasting Program at the Society for Human Resource Management, while organizations have been put under pressure to establish and enforce ethical standards, "There still are pressures that encourage the violation of such standards. Such pressures are most likely financial but not necessarily just matters of the greed of a few corrupt individuals. Instead, there is the continued pressure for short-term profit, usually attributed to the demands of shareholders."[9]

While plain, old-fashioned greed has played a major role in the corrupt behaviors of organizations, there are other factors that may encourage unethical communication and behavior. Organizations by their very nature involve **competition**. Internally, resources and rewards are limited, so people compete with one another for the positions, promotions, pay increases, and "perks" that the organization makes available. Sometimes the desire to "win" this competition motivates people to work hard and contribute to the organization's success; sometimes, it leads to unethical behaviors as people try to "win" at any cost. Externally, organizations typically must compete with other organizations in order to survive. Companies do not last very long when customers select the products or services offered by other organizations. So to be competitive, many organizations try to offer products or services that are unique, of high quality, and priced attractively. But some organizations cheat, just as Hollinger International overstated their circulation figures in order to attract advertisers and charge them more, and TAP Pharmaceuticals bribed doctors to prescribe the drugs they manufacture.

Yet another factor that seems to be encouraging unethical practices within organizations is a growing emphasis on *scorekeeping*, with an attendant loss of focus on what the scores should actually represent. For example, why do students cheat on tests in school? Why do they pull papers off the Internet and turn them in as their own work? The answer is simple: they want a good grade. Their focus is on scorekeeping, not on learning, which presumably is the point of the educational process.

The use of employee and customer satisfaction surveys as a measure of organizational and leadership performance has become increasingly common, as a later chapter in this text describes. However, these surveys also provide opportunities for organizations to focus on scorekeeping rather than on the thing the scores are supposed to represent. For example, one of the authors bought a new vehicle recently from an automobile manufacturer renowned for its high quality and customer satisfaction. During the course of a two-hour sales experience, he was reminded eight different times by five different dealership representatives how important it would be for him to indicate on the J.D. Power survey he soon would receive that he was extremely satisfied with all aspects of his experience with the dealership. Indeed, each of the representatives said, if he intended to give the dealership anything less than a "5" on the five-point scale used by the survey to measure his satisfaction with a variety of issues, he should not return the survey at all, since doing so could "hurt our reputation" with the company. One representative even showed him what a survey marked with all 5s looked like, just in case he could not figure it out for himself. But no one asked him how satisfied he actually was with his time at the dealership—their focus was on their score, not on the customer satisfaction the score was intended to reflect. J. D. Power customer satisfaction scores can be powerful marketing tools when they are extremely high, and some auto manufacturers punish dealerships whose scores pull down the overall company average. Clearly, these representatives wanted to be sure their scores reflected well on them, regardless of how their customers actually felt.

Lastly, it is important to remember that organizations are comprised of people, and *people are not perfect*. People have biases and prejudices, and thus may be inclined to favor some groups over others. People have bosses whom they want to please and thus may be inclined to withhold negative information while passing (or even embellishing) positive information upward. People have kids to feed and rent to pay and thus may pad their resumes in order to have a better chance at getting a job. Everyone is flawed, and despite our best efforts to live and work together in harmonious, productive societies and organizations, those flaws inevitably get in the way.

CIVIC ENGAGEMENT AS ETHICAL BEHAVIOR

Organizational participation presents us with temptations that may challenge our ethical standards as well as affording us with abundant opportunities to meet each challenge with maturity and ethical responsibility. In addition, outside the workplace each of us has the chance to become actively involved in the communities in which we live, with the hope of participating as engaged citizens in a democratic society. The opportunities are seemingly infinite—we can volunteer at a soup kitchen, work on a Habitat for Humanity building project, participate in a Salvation Army toy drive, assist in voter registration, work with an adult literacy program, deliver meals to the homebound, or serve as a mentor for a disabled child. No matter our interests—animal rights, clean air, campus safety, sex education, homelessness, hate crime legislation—we can find one or more civic, religious, or educational groups that will allow us to express our views and potentially have a positive impact on the neighborhoods, communities, and states in which we live.

Yet we have not taken advantage of these opportunities in recent years. According to Robert Putnam, author of *Bowling Alone: The Collapse and Revival of American Community*, over the last generation U.S. citizens have deserted the voting booth, the church pew, the union hall, the Rotary luncheon, the bowling league, and even the family dinner table.[10] The statistics are sobering, as shown in Highlighting Civic Engagement.

These trends are critically important for the well-being of our communities. When Putnam writes about *social capital*, he is talking about community connectedness and the trust and sense of reciprocity that those connections foster. When we live in a community that is rich in social capital, we are more likely to live in a community with safe streets, economic growth, and a responsive government. When we participate in networks characterized by trust and reciprocity, we are also more likely to achieve higher levels of education and to live long, happy, and healthy lives.

Why has civic engagement declined? There is no simple cause, but among the likely culprits, according to Putnam's assessment are: first, *two-career families*—when everyone in the family is working, each is more challenged to find time to play a vital role in community affairs. Second, *sprawl* has also contributed

Highlighting Civic Engagement

Signs of Civic Disengagement

- Americans socialized one-third less each day in 1995 than in 1965.
- 77 percent of U.S. 6th graders have their own television sets, up from only 6 percent in 1970.
- Today's Americans give 39% less to charity (relative to their income) than in 1964.
- We trust strangers only about half as much as we did in 1960.
- Over the last 25 years, political engagement is down by 25%—including such activities as working for a political party, attending public meetings, making a speech, serving as a club's officer, signing a petition, running for office, writing a letter to a congressional representative or a letter to the editor.
- The Roanoke, Virginia, chapter of the NAACP, active since 1918, witnessed membership in the 1990s wither from 2,500 to a few hundred.

Source: Robert D. Putnam, *Bowling Alone: The Collapse and Revival of American Community* (New York: Simon & Schuster, 2000); and Thomas H. Sander, "The Fight against Civic Disengagement" [online]. Available: http://chorusamerica.org/voice_article_civic_engagement.shtml (accessed: May 19, 2004).

to the decline. As we live further and further away from central meeting places, we become less likely to attend public meetings, to volunteer, to attend church, or to even sign petitions. Each ten minutes of commuting cuts civic engagement by 10 percent. The longer the commute, the less engaged. The third factor is *television*. Putnam writes that those reporting "TV is my primary form of entertainment" overwhelmingly exhibit low levels of civic engagement. Television has become a giant sponge for our leisure hours; viewing increased by 50 percent between 1960 and 1998. Finally, the decline in civic engagement may be traced to *generational change*. Americans born before 1940 are now, and have always been, more civically engaged than their children or grandchildren. What Tom Brokaw calls the "greatest generation" lived through the Great Depression and two World Wars and came of age in a TV-less world—all of which contributed to their sense of self-sacrifice and commitment to civic participation. Today, many of that generation have passed away or are in their twilight years. If civic engagement is to be revitalized, it can only be because a younger generation has discovered a new or renewed sense of commitment to participate in civic life.

The links between ethical behavior and a commitment to civic engagement seem clear. In *Bowling Alone*, Putnam shows how increased social capital contributes to many positive outcomes—for children, for individuals, and for society. For example, medical research has shown that those who join groups get sick less and recuperate faster. Those who are well connected socially are also more likely to find jobs, as most people get their jobs through whom they know (not through the classified ads or even on the basis of what they know). In communities, murder and violence rates are much lower in high social capital states. An intensive study of Chicago neighborhoods, for instance, revealed that mutual trust, altruism, and the willingness of adults to intervene when they see children mistreating other children were strong predictors of why some neighborhoods exhibit far less criminal behavior than others. Finally, those who are civically engaged are more likely to feel that they are living their lives in ways that contribute to the common good; this, in turn, contributes to their sense of well-being and happiness. Putnam concludes his book with this:

> In the end . . . institutional reform will not work—indeed, it will not happen—unless you and I, along with our fellow citizens, resolve to become reconnected with our friends and neighbors. Henry Ward Beecher's advice a century ago to "multiply picnics" is not entirely ridiculous today. We should do this, ironically, not because it will be good for America—though it will be—but because it will be good for us.[11]

For additional reading on how civic engagement should be part of every college student's educational experience, see *Educating Citizens: Preparing America's Undergraduates for Lives of Moral and Civic Responsibility* by Anne Colby and others, published in 2003.

DECIDING WHAT'S "RIGHT": SOME ETHICAL PERSPECTIVES

Every day, you (and every other member of every organization in the world) must decide how to conduct yourself from an ethical perspective. For example, do you speed or adhere to the 55 mph limit on your way to work? Do you punch in yourself, even though you arrived late (perhaps you should have exceeded the speed limit after all), or do you call another employee from your cell phone and ask her to punch your card for you so it appears you arrived on time? Do you tell your boss the truth about why you were absent yesterday, or do you tell her that your grandmother passed away, again? During a meeting, do you raise an objection to a proposal the rest of the group favors (even though you are convinced that the proposal cannot possibly work), or do you keep your mouth shut lest you risk the ire of everyone in the room?

In every profession, people face daily ethical decisions that can be much larger and more far-reaching than these. Consider the following examples: (1) a doctor must choose whether or not to prescribe a drug for a patient suffering from a largely psychosomatic illness; (2) an insurance salesman tries to decide how to convince an elderly couple to purchase his company's homeowner's insurance; (3) a division head must decide how to present financial data reflecting poorly on her own department in the monthly report; (4) a teacher must determine how to handle a severe discipline problem developing in his classroom; (5) a vice president must decide which of two equally qualified employees ought to be promoted. While all of these situations have pragmatic dimensions, they all involve issues of right or wrong, good or bad, fair or unfair—dimensions of ethical significance.

How do you decide what the "right thing" is? Ethics can be viewed from several perspectives, each of which provides a different basis for making judgments. Depending on the specific perspective employed, the answer to any given ethical dilemma may vary.

In an early consideration of organizational ethics, Hosmer described three general approaches to ethical decision making.[12] *Economic analysis* bases ethical judgments on financial considerations. This school of thought holds that people in organizations always should act to maximize revenues and minimize costs, thereby making the organization as profitable as possible. Over the long term, this strategy will ensure that society gains the greatest benefit, adherents argue. This approach, however, ignores the use of questionable practices (bribes, environmental pollution, hazardous working conditions, or unequal treatment) that might improve an organization's bottom line, at least over the short term, and it is an impersonal approach that considers people a means to an economic end rather than taking into consideration the well-being of those people themselves.

Legal analysis reduces ethical judgments to a matter of law. Anything that is illegal is unethical; if it's legal, it's OK. This approach has the advantage of being simple: to make an ethical decision, one has only to investigate the law, the rule, or the regulation covering a particular behavior and then adhere to it. However, while some may take great comfort in guiding their decisions and behavior by legal standards, this perspective often leads to oversimplification and superficiality. For example, the law does not prohibit lying except under oath in a court or in some formal contracts. Moreover, the law tends to forbid negative actions but does not encourage positive ones (for example, no law requires someone to go to the aid of a drowning child). Finally, some laws in and of themselves are morally objectionable to some: until the early 1960s, some areas of the United States legally required racial discrimination, and even now laws concerning abortion, homosexuality, or religious observances in schools are repugnant to many.

The third approach Hosmer describes, *philosophical analysis*, seems more likely than the first two to provide useful guidance in making ethical decisions. However, a wide variety of such philosophical perspectives is available, including the following.

Religious Perspective

Within the framework of every world religion, there are crucial moral and spiritual injunctions that might be used to measure the ethics of a given behavior. Church leaders and some philosophers (Thomas Aquinas and Thomas Jefferson are but two examples) hold that there is an Eternal Law, incorporated in the mind of a Supreme Being, apparent in Nature, revealed in holy writings, and available to anyone who studies either nature or scriptures. Just as Jefferson claimed that certain truths are "self-evident" and people have "inalienable" rights to "life, liberty, and the pursuit of happiness" (so that everyone has an obligation to ensure those rights to others), most religions teach that "if we are loved, then we must love others," so that behaviors such as lying, committing adultery, slandering, and murdering are wrong. For instance, Christians are taught to love their neighbors as themselves, discouraging any remark or behavior of harmful intent directed toward another person. The Taoist religion stresses empathy and insight as roads to truth, de-emphasizing reason and logic.

The religious perspective provides some key ethical guidelines but leaves us with the problem of deciding which set of religious teachings we should follow. As the workforce in the United States has become increasingly diverse, many different religions have found their way into the workplace. Indeed, organizations now are prohibited from observing religious holidays (Christmas is considered a federal holiday) because observing the holidays of one religion to the exclusion of any others is discriminatory. Each religion provides moral standards for its members, and many of the members observe those standards in daily life. Nevertheless, the standards differ between groups, and it is difficult to determine which one is "right" or 'best" or "proper" for all members of society.

Utilitarian Perspective

From a utilitarian perspective, usefulness and expediency are the criteria used to make ethical judgments. Taking this approach, we would conclude that a behavior is ethical if it provides the greatest benefits to the greatest number of people. A utilitarian critic judging the effectiveness of a public speech would be mainly concerned with whether or not the speech actually got the vote, changed the belief, or positively stimulated the audience. Techniques used to achieve the speech's purpose would be judged in terms of practical results. One might evaluate the worth of an advertising campaign, an incentive plan, or a public relations program from the same perspective.

While it is probably safe to say that the utilitarian view has less intrinsic appeal as an ethical perspective, it still has great practical significance. There would be no persuasive appeals, marketing strategies, or incentive plans without some pragmatic goal in mind. Organizations must be concerned with the ultimate effects of their plans, policies, and procedures, and laudable means that fail to promote important organizational goals should be subject to criticism, just as questionable goals themselves should be scrutinized. However, ends do not always justify means, and the rights of the minority must not be sacrificed for the "good" of the majority. In addition, the focus on "scorekeeping" we criticized earlier can actually be promoted by taking a utilitarian perspective exclusively. Thus, this perspective, too, has its limitations.

Universalist Perspective

While the utilitarian perspective considers the outcomes of an action, the universalist perspective holds that because outcomes are too difficult to predict or control, we should focus on intent. In effect, the morality of an action depends on the intentions of the person making the decision or performing the act. If that person wishes the best for others, his or her actions are ethical even if, due to the person's clumsiness or ineptitude, those actions end up hurting someone. This approach holds that there are certain universal duties we have in dealing with each other (hence the "universalist" perspective), such as telling the truth, not taking another's property, and adhering to agreements, and that if our intent is to uphold those duties, we are behaving ethically.

Under this approach, people are seen as ends rather than means. They are worthy of dignity and respect, not tools to be used by us for our own purposes. Perhaps that is the greatest lesson the universalist approach teaches. On the other hand, it is difficult to determine what "intent" is (even our own motives for performing various actions may be unclear to us), and in business, people at times *do* serve as a means to an end: for example, customers are a means of making money and earning a living, and employees are a means of getting work done.

Humanist Perspective

Some writers attempt to make ethical judgments philosophically by isolating certain unique characteristics of human nature that should be enhanced. They then look at a particular technique, rule, policy, strategy, or behavior and attempt to determine the extent to which it either furthers or hampers these uniquely human attributes. Aristotle believed, for example, that truly human acts were performed by rational persons, individuals who recognized what they were doing and chose freely to do it.[13] In the case of a persuasive speaker, for example, his or her persuasive appeals and strategy should be judged in terms of their tendencies to enhance or reduce the listeners' rationality and their decision-making ability. From this perspective, we might infer that an ethical organization is one that encourages its members to communicate fully, freely, honestly, and cooperatively and ethical organizational members are people who act in ways that enhance understanding and free choice. Still, this perspective leaves unanswered a question that every organization faces every day: what should be done with people who do not choose to do what the organization needs them to do (such as, for example, their jobs)? Dealing ethically with organizational members who, with full understanding, choose to goof off is an important consideration that the humanist perspective tends to overlook.

Political/Cultural Perspective

Political systems and specific cultures provide another perspective from which to view ethical behavior. Within any given cultural or political context, there exist certain values or processes that seem basic to the well-being and growth of society. Values govern the way we behave as well as the kinds of goals we seek throughout our lives, and thus can serve as ethical standards for judging behavior.

Of course, cultural perspectives are widely diversified, and as the U.S. workforce has become more diverse, cultural diversity in organizations has become more apparent as well. Consequently, many organizations work to develop their own unique culture and values, and they ask—even demand—that organizational members adhere to the values and norms that comprise their culture.

Unfortunately, however, organizations can develop cultures that are less than optimal from an ethical perspective. Consider the case of Putnam Investments, which at the time of this writing has agreed to pay $110 million in fines and restitution to settle market timing charges but still faces other probes since it has received subpoenas and requests for information from regulators in Florida, New York, and West Virginia, among others. At the heart of its problems was a "cutthroat" work environment and rigid hierarchy that rejected change and discouraged employees from reporting problems, according to former employees, clients, and consultants. Lawrence Lasser, the former CEO, set the tone. He was known as a brash, mercurial taskmaster. Putnam employees who fell short of their goals could expect a dressing down, and Lasser was known to rebuke poor performers in public. Putnam's culture encouraged employees to try to contain problems rather than report them, a strategy that ultimately backfired. Thus, adhering to the values and conforming to the culture established by this organization seems to have produced unethical, rather than ethical, behavior among organizational members.[14]

Dialogic Perspective

An interesting viewpoint for making ethical judgments has emerged from scholarship on the nature of ethical human communication as dialogue rather than monologue. According to this perspective, the attitudes that individuals in any communication transaction have toward one another are an index of the ethical level of that communication. Some attitudes are believed to be more fully human, facilitative of self-actualization, and humane than other attitudes. According to Johannesen, for example, when people communicate from a dialogic perspective, their attitudes are characterized by honesty, trust, concern for others, open-mindedness, empathy, humility, sincerity, and directness. They are non-manipulative, encourage free expression in others, and accept others as persons of intrinsic worth, regardless of differences of opinion or belief. Communication as monologue, on the other hand, is characterized by such qualities as deception, superiority, exploitation, domination, insincerity, distrust, and so forth. Freedom of expression is stifled, and others are viewed as objects to be manipulated.[15]

In using this perspective, you would observe any behavior, advertisement, speech, managerial practice, or organizational policy and determine the degree to which it reveals an ethical dialogic attitude or an unethical monologic attitude toward its intended audience. For the dialogic critic, any communication act or attitude that promotes deception, exploitation, or domination is unethical, regardless of the situation.

Situational Perspective

Some writers are less universal in their approach to ethics, believing it impossible to set definite ethical guidelines apart from the specific situation. They believe ethical criteria vary as factors in the communication situation vary, as the needs of the listeners vary, and even as role relationships change. According to this view, receiver expectations and knowledge levels are especially critical determinants. For example, we often expect hyperbole in political speeches and filter our responses accordingly. We do not, on the other hand, anticipate exaggerations from a college professor giving a lecture or from a doctor explaining the nature of an illness. Thus, in the political context, hyperbole might be acceptable; but in the educational or medical setting, it would be taken literally and therefore should be considered unethical.

Clearly, there are a variety of approaches to making ethical judgments, and each has its advantages and limitations. Perhaps the best thing to do in any given situation is to ask oneself a series of questions designed to test an action in terms of almost all of these approaches. The questions might include the following:

- Would I want this action to be broadcast on the six o'clock news?
- Would I want my boss and top management to know I did this?
- Would I want my parents to know I did this?
- Would I want my spouse or family to know I did this?
- Would I want my customers to know I did this?

Business Brief 1.1

Finding an Ethical Organization

As you look for employment, one factor you should consider is the ethical standards of any organization you might join. Before you accept a position at a company, you might use these strategies to find out what its values are:

- *Throw out what you hear in interviews.* They're selling you on the company. You'll hear that the organization is "family friendly" and "committed to open communication." The gap between buzzwords and reality is often huge.

- *Ask clever questions to get at the truth.* Rather than asking vague questions about values, ask questions that elicit anecdotes. Ask how they handled the latest downsizing; ask about senior management turnover; ask if there has ever been a problem with an employee who had a conflict with the company's values. Get the interviewer telling stories rather than reciting stock phrases, and you'll learn a lot more.

- *Find and interview a "superstar."* Ask the interviewer to tell you about one or two superstars in the department or organization—people who have had great success. Ask these superstars if they've had to compromise their principles to succeed, or if they've had to put family and personal values on the back burner. Stress that the conversation will remain in confidence so they'll speak freely.

- *Do research in the field.* You'll never learn about a company in an interview. Ask to sit in on a team meeting. Listen carefully to how employees talk to and treat each other. See if they feel comfortable speaking freely to managers and leaders.

Source: "Pinpoint a Company's Values," *Positive Leadership* (July 1998): 11.

- Would I want my subordinates to know I did this?
- Would I want this action to be announced to my church congregation, with me present, during next Sunday's service?
- Would I do this if a police officer were standing or sitting next to me?
- Is doing this "good business"?
- Will doing this promote trust in me by others?
- Will I be able to sleep at night knowing I've done this?
- Would I want others to do this to me?

Even these questions provide an incomplete guide. For example, a professional football player who also happens to be homosexual might well answer "no" to most of these questions, not because he feels his lifestyle is unethical but because he fears the reactions of teammates, coaches, other players, his family, the public, and so on—people who have a different set of ethics. Nevertheless, if you consider a possible course of action by asking yourself these questions, and you find that the answer to many of them is "no," you should consider carefully whether this action is truly ethical.

ETHICAL ISSUES CONCERNING ORGANIZATIONAL COMMUNICATION

The concept of ethics has important implications for several topics related to organizational communication and in the following sections we will review several.

Advertising

A key element of most organizations' public relations and sales efforts is advertising. Each year, over $200 billion is spent by companies to convey information about their products or services. But the competitive nature of organizations and the vital role advertising plays in an organization's "winning" or "losing" have led to some questionable advertising practices, as was illustrated as long ago as 1957 by Vance Packard's best-seller, *The Hidden Persuaders*.[16]

The ethical complexities of advertising in turn have attracted the attention of regulatory agencies over the years. As early as 1962, the American Association of Advertising Agencies prohibited its members from knowingly producing advertising that contained: (1) false or misleading statements or exaggerations, visual or verbal; (2) testimonials that do not reflect the real choice of a competent witness; (3) misleading price claims; (4) comparisons that unfairly disparage a competitive product or service; (5) claims insufficiently supported or that distort true meaning or practicable application of statements made by professional or scientific authority; (6) statements, suggestions, or pictures offensive to public decency. These kinds of guidelines, of course, must remain flexible, and many of their major terms—such as *misleading, competent, unfairly, true meaning,* and *offensive*—are open to interpretation.

The Federal Trade Commission (FTC) has also taken an active role in ensuring that facts are available to support claims made in advertising. In 1972, for instance, in a case involving Unburn sunburn lotion, the commission took the

DILBERT

DILBERT © by Scott Adams; reprinted by permission of United Feature Syndicate, Inc.

position that not only must evidence be presented to support the advertiser's claims, but the substantiation should provide a "reasonable basis" for believing the claims are true. In other words, the quality of evidence to support the claims made by advertisers is important.

Recently, for example, the Lay's potato chip company posted a billboard at Wrigley Field in Chicago claiming that Chicagoans prefer the taste of Lay's to the taste of Jay's, a primary competitor in the marketplace. When Jay's protested to the FTC, the commission demanded to see Lay's proof of that claim. Their investigation revealed that Lay's had done a survey of a few people who may or may not have actually come from Chicago, and that the Jay's chips they were asked to evaluate were "unflavored" chips of a type Jay's denies even making. The billboard was taken down.

Over the years, the tobacco industry also has come under attack for their advertising practices. Critics have charged that the "Joe Camel" character appeals directly to teens, encouraging them to initiate a lifelong smoking habit (an irony if ever there was one, given the contradiction between long life and smoking). Moreover, critics claim, tobacco companies deliberately have attempted to hide the addictive nature of cigarettes and the harmful effects they have on users' health. Executives of the major tobacco companies in turn have denied these charges, stating during public hearings (mostly with straight faces) that their products are neither harmful nor addictive—statements that also have ethical implications, particularly in the face of the old saying that "two wrongs do not make a right." Some tobacco companies have even adopted a strangely schizophrenic advertising posture, simultaneously seeming to discourage smoking by telling the public that smoking should be done "responsibly" since it has been proven harmful to one's health, while at the same time trying to peddle their product.

Some defenders of advertising suggest that advertising should be judged by a special set of ethical standards. Advertisers recognize certain "truths" about their audience. Among them are that people expect exaggeration whenever they view advertising, that they hope to be promised effects beyond realistic expectations, and that they largely understand the rules of the game. The renowned John Kenneth Galbraith pointed out many years ago that "the merest child watching television dismisses the health and status-giving claims of a breakfast cereal as 'a commercial.'"[17]

Highlighting Civic Engagement

Good Corporate Citizenship? The Phillip Morris Web Site

- During the summer of 2004, Phillip Morris saturated both television and radio broadcasts with advertisements talking about their Web site, http://www.PhillipMorrisUSA.com, which according to the advertisements provides useful information about the potentially harmful effects of smoking and lists resources to which people can go to get help if they want to quit smoking.

- By broadcasting these "public service" announcements on TV and radio, Phillip Morris, one of the world's leading cigarette manufacturers, was able to get its name in front of the public (thereby overcoming FCC bans of cigarette advertising on TV and radio) and portray itself as a good citizen that has a strong commitment to society.

- But they continued to make the cigarettes they "warned" people against using.

But what happens when advertisers try to keep the targets of their advertising from realizing that what they are seeing and hearing is "a commercial"? Recently, a new type of advertising called **undercover marketing** has emerged where the public is exposed to a form of advertising that they do not even realize is advertising. For example, people walking into a Starbucks coffee shop might notice a young man sitting at a table playing a complex video game, but using a unique glove-like controller to run the game rather than the usual joy stick. Those who are intrigued enough to stop and talk with the young man to find out more about the glove eventually are asked to give him their e-mail address so he can send them more information. They never find out that the young man is on the payroll of the company that makes the controller glove and that he is a paid marketer.

Similarly, a young couple on the sidewalks of New York City pose as tourists and ask passersby to take their picture, using the unique picturephone/camera the couple just happens to have. If the picture takers are intrigued by and ask questions about the camera, the couple gives them information and, eventually, may get their name, address, phone number, and e-mail address to provide them more information in the future. The young couple is being paid to sell the picturephone/cameras without the targets of their sales pitch even knowing they are being marketed to.

Finally, a preteen boy goes on the Internet and visits chat rooms, talking about the terrific, fantastic cartoon movie he has just seen and suggesting to everyone he contacts that they, too, should see the movie. He doesn't mention that the movie producer has given him t-shirts, posters, and other loot to reward him for going online and pushing their product. The people he contacts have no idea that they are being subjected to interpersonal advertising.

Advertising for years has been accused of inflated claims and questionable practices that serve to deceive the targets of their communications. Now, they seem to have hit upon yet one more way to try to catch consumers "with their guard down," masking marketing as just a casual conversation with a stranger.

Business Brief 1.2

Advertising Practices

Each month, *Consumer Reports* provides examples of what it considers to be questionable advertising or marketing practices. Some examples include:

- A bottle of "TransFix Automatic Transmission Stop Leak & TuneUp" fluid from Snap Products claims to stop transmission leaks "within five minutes." But elsewhere on the bottle the claim is that the product stops leaks "within 50 miles of normal driving." Apparently, the company views driving 600 miles per hour as "normal" (*Consumer Reports,* January 1998).

- The Wine Enthusiasts "Miniature Distilling Machine" allows you to "put in your favorite wine or beer and make great-tasting, full-proof spirits." However, a note in their ad also says that under the laws of the Bureau of Alcohol, Tobacco and Firearms, use of the contraption is legal only if "it is not used for distilling" (*Consumer Reports,* January 1998).

- A package of Northwest's Finest "Chick'N Rice Soup" lists as its ingredients "brown rice, wild rice, garlic, salt, onion and herbs"; apparently, you add your own chicken (*Consumer Reports,* July 1998).

- From Time-Life Music comes an offer for a free CD or cassette stating "send no money" and face no "risk" or "obligation"—at first. The small print reveals that if you keep the CD or cassette more than 10 days, you will have to pay $9.99 plus shipping and handling, and you'll automatically start to receive more CDs or tapes that cost $14.99 to $16.99, plus shipping and handling (*Consumer Reports,* March 1998).

- The front of the package for "Aqualite" watch says "water resistant to 100 feet," but the fine print warranty on the back doesn't cover "any failure to function properly due to misuse such as water immersion" (*Consumer Reports,* August 1998).

- An ad in *TV Guide* promoted the "liquid bullet," a self-defense mechanism that sprays a high-powered stream of tear gas at an attacker. Best of all, the ad claimed, liquid bullet "can't injure kids." When asked what would happen if a child did unsnap the safety strap and twist the cap to spray position, perhaps spraying him/herself by mistake, a company spokeswoman replied that "at worst, a child would be immobilized for 30 minutes" (*Consumer Reports,* March 1993).

Service versus Profit

Most business theorists argue that good service means better profits—that maximizing the services provided to customers ultimately improves an organization's bottom line. In health care, however, that principle does not necessarily hold true.

Since the mid-1980s, agencies who pay for health-care services (such as insurance companies and the federal government's Medicare program) have become increasingly concerned about rapidly rising health-care costs. In 1983, Congress enacted the Medicare prospective payment system, which established fixed amounts that would be paid to hospitals for each of 468 different types of treatments (Medicare would pay a certain amount for appendectomies, a certain amount for tonsillectomies, and so on). Prior to that time, Medicare and Medicaid had paid hospital charges regardless of the amount. Under the new plan (which changes based on diagnosis-related groups), hospitals whose actual costs fell below the fixed levels could keep the difference, while hospitals whose costs were above the established levels suffered losses. Since 40 percent of all hospital patients on the average are covered by Medicare, this represented a significant change in health-care funding. Soon after, other private insurers implemented similar plans of their own, and then state Medicaid programs began to follow suit.

More recently, the concept of "managed care" came into being. Many health-care organizations signed contracts with insurance companies whereby those companies would pay the hospital a flat rate every year to cover all of the health-care needs of each of the payer's subscribers. Those subscribers are strongly encouraged to use the hospital's facilities for all of their health needs; and if the hospital can meet those needs for less than the insurance company pays them, they make money. Conversely, if providing that care costs more than the insurance company pays them, they lose money. In short, it is in the hospital's best interests financially to provide as little care as possible, thus maximizing the difference between what it costs to provide that care and what the insurance companies pay them per person.

Of course, similar arrangements exist throughout U.S. business. For example, school bus companies sign contracts with school systems to bus students to and from schools, and those contracts pay a fixed amount to the bus company for providing that service over an entire school year. If the actual cost of bussing students is less than the amount the school system pays, the company makes money. If the cost is greater, they lose. Similarly, janitorial services contract with real estate management firms to provide cleaning services for a certain fee over a certain time. If the actual cost of labor and materials is lower than the amount the management firm pays them, the cleaning company profits; if labor and materials cost more, the cleaning company themselves are taken to the cleaners.

As almost all organizations do under such circumstances, health-care organizations responded to financial pressures in several ways, most of which involve cutting the cost of providing care. Reducing patients' length of stay was a key element of cost reduction: for example, by reducing from five days to three the amount of time an appendectomy patient spent in the hospital, hospital administrators could reduce the cost of delivering care to that person. "Get 'em out quicker and sicker" became the motto for many hospitals. But at what point does cutting corners on care become detrimental to patients? Health-care administrators and managers thus face a variety of ethical choices: What level of care is good enough? Are RNs really needed to provide care, or can less-qualified (and much lower-paid) staff do almost as well? How much work can reasonably be demanded of hospital employees? Ultimately, answers to ethical issues like these will determine the quality and type of health care all of us receive in the future.

Social Responsibility

In response to the question "Do corporations have social responsibilities over and above their obligations to their stockholders?" most would answer "Of course!" But the scope of that responsibility remains an area of some controversy.

The impact of organizations on the environment is just one area of ethical concern. Some companies have made a genuine effort to minimize any harmful effects they or their products have on the environment; others have been less thoughtful. For example, British Petroleum pledged in 1998 to reduce by 10 percent the greenhouse gas emissions that contribute to global warming. The London-based giant intends to eliminate 4 million of the 40 million tons of carbon dioxide and greenhouse gasses it emitted in 1990, its baseline year. Its progressive stance is in contrast to that of a Chicago-based company with which British Petroleum has merged: Amoco. Along with other U.S. refiners, Amoco consistently has fought tougher environmental rules. Some analysts believe that their differing philosophies concerning environmental impact have made the merging of these two organizational cultures very difficult.[18]

Concerns about working conditions in manufacturing plants abroad also have caused pressure to be put on various company spokespersons. For example, Kathy Lee Gifford found herself under criticism because a line of clothing she endorsed was made in Asian sweatshops, and former basketball star Michael Jordan was criticized for endorsing Nike shoes made in horrendous working conditions by poorly paid Asian workers. Both were given assurances by the companies they represented that conditions in those manufacturing settings would be improved, and both in turn conveyed those assurances to the general public.

Concerns about the *globalization* of many businesses also have raised some questions concerning organizations' ethical social responsibilities, and about which societies organizations have a responsibility to. In an effort to reduce labor costs and thus increase profitability, many U.S. corporations have *outsourced* parts of their operations to countries where wages are substantially lower and benefits nonexistent. But shipping jobs overseas means workers in the United States lose their employment, which clearly is not in the interests of U.S. society. Consequently, an antiglobalization movement (illustrated by H. Ross Perot's famous description of the North American Free Trade Agreement as the "giant sucking sound" of jobs being siphoned out of the U.S.) has grown in an effort to keep jobs "at home" and force corporations to accept their social responsibility to U.S. workers.[19]

Yet not everyone agrees that "social responsibility" should be so narrowly defined. In his book *In Defense of Globalization*, Jagdish Bhagwati cites India,

Highlighting Civic Engagement

Encouraging Corporate Social Responsibility

Social responsibility by U.S. corporations has been a focus of some activists. An example follows:

- Operation PUSH, a Chicago-based civil rights group founded by, among others, Reverend Jesse Jackson, demanded that the Nike shoe company change the composition of its management and board of directors. Their reasoning: since African Americans comprise a significant portion of Nike's athletic footwear market, African Americans should hold prominent positions in the company as well.

- When Nike refused Operation PUSH's demands for detailed financial information about the company and changes in the organization's structure (and indeed, countered with similar demands for detailed information about Operation PUSH), leaders of Operation PUSH declared economic war and attempted to organize a boycott of Nike products.

- The boycott generally proved unsuccessful, but Nike nevertheless resolved to increase the diversity of their leadership.

China, and the East Asian nations as he puts forward a two-step thesis: globalization leads to growth, and growth reduces poverty.[20] He argues that reducing barriers to trade and globalizing the workforce are economically beneficial and have no negative impact on the environment, women's rights, child labor, or other issues of concern to those who oppose globalization.

Still, the question remains: to which society or societies do organizations have a social responsibility? Within that framework, there are other ethical issues. Do company spokespersons have any accountability for the conditions in which the products they endorse are made? Do organizations have an ethical responsibility to preserve the environment? Does any group have the ethical right to declare itself the spokesperson for some segment of society and make demands on manufacturers who sell their products to that segment? Relations between organizational systems and their environment will continue to raise ethical questions in the future.

EMPLOYEE RIGHTS

The treatment of employees by their employers involves a myriad of ethical issues. Most theorists imply that employees have certain basic rights and that the ethics of management's treatment of employees can be judged, at least in part, by the extent to which those rights are upheld. We will consider just a few of those rights here.

The Right to Fair and Equitable Treatment

For years, government regulations, often in the form of *affirmative action* policies, have required equitable procedures in screening, hiring, promoting, and terminating employees. Title VII is the federal law covering employers with 15 or more employees that prohibits discrimination, harassment, and retaliation based on race, color, religion, national origin, or gender. Other laws govern employer pay practices, benefit plans, work hours, and other aspects of the employee/employer relationship.

But despite the existence of such laws, situations often arise where employers are accused of treating employees in ways that violate the law and would be considered unethical. For example, more than 30 lawsuits were filed against Wal-Mart, accusing it of cheating workers out of overtime pay.[21] In a case in Oregon, the company was found to have forced employees to punch out and then return to work off the clock. A federal investigation discovered that in dozens of stores Wal-Mart used contractors that hired illegal immigrants. And in 2004 a federal judge in San Francisco ruled that a sex-discrimination lawsuit filed in 2001 by six women could proceed as a class action on behalf of all Wal-Mart's current and former female employees. With up to 1.6 million plaintiffs, it was the largest private civil rights case in U.S. history.

A variety of specific situations and charges were included in the lawsuit against Wal-Mart. For example, an 11-year employee in Wilson, North Carolina, wrote a note asking for help sorting lingerie; she got the note back with a chauvinist comment scrawled across the top. When a male colleague admitted to the deed, "instead of being reprimanded, he was promoted to assistant manager," the employee said. Investigations of Wal-Mart payroll statistics for 2001 (the most recent available to the plaintiffs) reportedly show that female workers in hourly jobs took home $1,100 less than men, while women managers earned $14,500 less than their male counterparts. In addition, 65 percent of Wal-Mart's hourly employees were female, but two-thirds of the company's managers were men. Finally, on average, it took men 2.86 years to get promoted to assistant manager, while it took women an average of 4.38 years, even though they had better performance ratings.

The company denied that it mistreated workers. But in response to the complaints, it adjusted its pay for many jobs, created an electronic job posting system to notify all workers of job openings, and created a department to promote diversity. Indeed, CEO H. Lee Scott warned that executives will see their bonuses reduced if they fail to meet diversity goals.

The tragic events of September 11, 2001, also created concerns related to employee rights and ethical organizational practices. After 9/11, the Equal Employment Opportunity Commission (EEOC), the federal agency that enforces Title VII of the 1964 Civil Rights Act, received a significant number of charges alleging discrimination against people who are or are perceived to be of Middle Eastern descent. In fact, on November 19, 2001, the agency issued a statement indicating that they will "intensify their efforts to combat discrimination based on religion, ethnicity, national origin, or immigration status in the workplace." They recommended that employers be sure that their policies are broad enough to encompass discrimination based on national origin and religion. For example, employers should not simply have policies that prohibit sexual harassment in the workplace. Such policies also should prohibit harassment based on religion, national origin, race, and color. The policies should also contain adequate complaint mechanisms that facilitate the airing of complaints of discrimination or harassment by affected employees. For example, if a supervisor is the only avenue for making a complaint and that supervisor is the alleged perpetrator, the employee is not likely to come forward; thus the employee must be provided with an alternative means of filing the complaint. Also, such policies should be well-communicated to employees, and managers should be trained to understand that the company has a zero-tolerance policy with regard to discrimination and harassment and protects all individuals, regardless of religion and national origin, the agency said.[22]

The issue of *sexual harassment* is an important consideration related to ethical communication. In 1980, the EEOC issued guidelines stating that sexual harassment is a violation of Title VII and defined harassment as occurring when:

- Submission to the sexual conduct is made either implicitly or explicitly a term or condition of employment.
- Employment decisions affecting the recipient are made on the basis of the recipient's acceptance or rejection of the sexual conduct.
- The conduct has the purpose or effect of reasonably interfering with an individual's work performance or creating an intimidating, hostile, or offensive working environment.[23]

Clearly, according to this broad definition, much sexual harassment is fairly subtle. It could be viewed as including leering, staring, or verbal harassment, such as sexual joking or referring to women as "girls," or even making sexist

---

Highlighting Diversity

Defining Sexual Harassment

Three relatively recent court cases illustrate the breadth of sexual harassment definitions:

- In the case of *Oncale v. Sundowner Offshore Services*, the U.S. Supreme Court ruled that a male roustabout working in an eight-man crew on a Chevron USA oil platform had been sexually harassed through threats, name-calling, and physical assault, even though the people involved were of the same sex. In short, they ruled, what matters is the conduct at issue, not the sex of the people involved.

- In the case of *Burlington Industries, Inc. v. Ellerth*, the U.S. Supreme Court ruled that comments made by a male supervisor to a female employee constituted sexual harassment, even though the employee did not report her supervisor's misconduct to management and did not suffer any tangible job detriment.

- In the case of *Faragher v. City of Boca Raton, Florida*, the U.S. Supreme Court ruled that eight female lifeguards had been sexually harassed by two supervisors, despite the city's argument that they had a clear policy against sexual harassment and were not aware of the supervisors' behaviors. The Court stated that an employer is liable for a pervasive, hostile atmosphere of harassment and for its supervisors' misconduct, whether or not the employer is aware of the harassment.

Source: Jennifer Laabs, "What You're Liable for Now," *Workforce* 77 (October 1998): 34–42.

---

comments such as "women are just too emotional to take the pressure." It is also important to note, however, that even though the majority of cases of sexual harassment involve *women* as victims, the EEOC guidelines apply equally to *men*, and the courts over the years have ruled that sexual harassment can involve gay workers harassing others, women harassing men, subordinates harassing managers, and outside vendors harassing customers.

The financial and human costs of sexual harassment can be immense. The financial costs include fines and other legal settlements, which can be substantial. In 1998, for example, an Iowa jury awarded $80.7 million to a former United Parcel Service employee who had sued for sexual harassment.[24] Moreover, if the employer is a contractor with the federal government, it may lose its federal contracts. The human costs of sexual harassment are equally great. Victims suffer embarrassment, intimidation, helplessness, and anger. In many cases, the victims live with these feelings rather than confront the offender, for fear of retaliation. Numerous studies have reported that some victims eventually suffer from serious psychological problems requiring medical attention because of the harassment, although more frequently, these emotional problems lead to increased absenteeism, reduced efficiency, and even resignations. Thus, even in small businesses (with fewer than fifteen employees) where EEOC guidelines are not binding, employers should still be concerned about lowered morale and productivity. In most instances of harassment, both the victim and the perpetrator ultimately suffer.

The Right to Privacy

Most would agree that employee offices or lockers, files, telephone conversations, personnel data, outside activities, and so on should not be invaded by their employers—that people have a right to privacy at work. Yet the limits of employee privacy are being pushed back almost daily. For example, employees commonly are tested in a variety of ways by their employers: for drugs and alcohol usage, for AIDS, for honesty (using polygraphs), and for job skills. Employees subjected to such tests often object that "what I do on my own time is my own business" (including, supposedly, taking drugs). Yet a few years ago, three Northwest Airlines pilots were convicted of flying under the influence of alcohol as the result of participating in a party on their own time the night before the flight. As another example, employees at a meat-packing company in Monmouth, Illinois, objected to random drug and alcohol testing conducted by their employer, despite the fact that their jobs required them to use extremely sharp knives to butcher hogs and the testing was designed to improve safety. As one company foreman said to one of the authors: "We try to protect those who are too dumb to protect themselves."

As technology has become increasingly prominent in the workplace, the need for surveillance of employee activities also has grown, at least in the view of many employers. A *Wall Street Journal* article reported a growing trend in the workplace: "using technology to make it look like you're working when you're not."[25] For example, a tech support worker in Denver installed a program on his Handspring Visor hand-held device that allowed him to manipulate the screen on his office computer from a booth at a local diner. As he lingered over a burger and fries, the tech could open windows and move documents on his office computer screen via his hand-held device, creating the impression to anyone who walked by that he had just stepped away from his desk. It may be worth noting, however, that after manipulating his computer from a nearby diner so he could take three-hour lunches, the worker eventually was fired for habitual lateness.

Psychologists call these activities *impression management*, a field whose rules have been transformed now that so many people communicate through technology. Consider the following examples:

- E-mail timers, a standard feature on Microsoft Outlook, let you send e-mails hours after you've gone to bed—a painless way to suggest to the boss that you're burning the midnight oil.

- RIM BlackBerry hand-helds allow workers to send e-mail messages that appear to have come from their office computers, but in fact could have been sent from anywhere.

- GoToMyPc.com provides download software that allows you to control your work computer screen over the Internet from anywhere.

- Yahoo! By Phone, for $4.95 per month, allows you to call in and have your e-mail read aloud to you by a computerized voice named Jenny.

- Call forwarding makes it a snap to answer your desk phone from a baseball game. SBC Communications currently offers five different call forwarding services, including one that lets you transfer your phone to different phone numbers throughout the day.

Some companies say these new tools are dangerous because they play into employees' increasing willingness to fudge the truth about their work life. An ethics survey by the Society for Human Resources Management found that 59 percent of human resources professionals said they personally observed employees lying about the number of hours they worked; some 53 percent reported that they saw employees lying to a supervisor, an eight-percentage-point jump in six years. These activities can be devastating to an organization. "If you're out playing golf, and you look like you've spent four hours in the office . . . and everybody does that, the company goes bankrupt,"[26] says Stuart Gilman, director of the Ethics Resource Center in Washington.

Even employees who come into work may be tempted to use technology for recreational purposes during paid working time. Some play video games (and develop techniques for making those games quickly disappear and work reappear on the screen whenever a supervisor approaches). Some surf the Internet and, occasionally, may visit sites that, by any ethical standard, they probably shouldn't visit. Some go to chat rooms that have replaced the traditional water cooler as the locus for employee conversation and gossip. Judi Epstein, product manager for iPrism, an Internet monitoring and blocking system from St. Bernard Software in San Diego, says her clients typically find that an employee goes online for business purposes and then gets unintentionally sidetracked, sometimes for a few hours. "At other times, it is intentional," she says. "At my last job, I worked with a woman who ran a side business on eBay while at the office—eight hours a day." All of these workers have one thing in common from their employer's perspective: they aren't working.

Employers have received help from a variety of companies specializing in helping them to keep tabs on employee activities. For example, Sapphire Technologies, an IT placement firm in Woburn, Massachusetts, installed both e-mail and Internet monitoring systems from Elron Software in Burlington, Massachusetts. The e-mail system, called "Message Inspector," uses certain triggers, such as keywords, video files, or attachments, that when detected cause an e-mail to be forwarded automatically to a senior technical analyst at Sapphire for review. The Internet system blocks pornographic Web sites and, if an employee tries to go to a blocked site, the senior technical analyst automatically is notified. Sapphire began the practice as a way of preventing potential legal problems. If one employee makes allegations about another employee's behavior, for example, checking e-mail can substantiate the charge. Three people have been fired at Sapphire for surfing adult-oriented Web sites. The company reminds its 350 employees that they are being monitored each time they log on to the network.

Bart Lazar, a partner in the law firm of Seyfarth Shaw in Chicago, says smart employers do monitor e-mail and Internet use. He was lead counsel for GeoCities in 1998 in the country's first Internet privacy suit. The Federal Trade Commission sued GeoCities, arguing that the company took consumer information collected on its Web site and disclosed that information to a direct mail marketing company. GeoCities eventually settled with the FTC. Lazar advises his clients to use filtering or monitoring systems, and many do, largely to protect computer systems from viruses and junk e-mails, some of which could be offensive to certain employees, prompting hostile work environment lawsuits. Employers also use monitoring to protect trade secrets and prevent other proprietary information from getting out.

Nancy Flynn, founder of the ePolicy Institute in Columbus, Ohio, says a company can also set up its monitoring system to alert management to suspicious behavior.[27] "If you find that someone who never works after 6 p.m. is suddenly showing up at the office in the middle of the night and going online, that should raise eyebrows. Why is this employee online? Is she downloading proprietary information?"

Fifty-seven percent of U.S. companies (and 70 percent of those companies having 1,000 or more employees) now monitor their employees' e-mail and Internet use, according to IDC, a technology research firm in Framingham, Massachusetts, and that number is expected to rise in the coming years. A recent study by the Privacy Foundation, a Denver-based organization that studies communications, technologies, and services that may pose a threat to privacy, found that 14 million U.S. workers are already subject to continuous monitoring while online.[28]

Still, not every organization believes that careful monitoring of employees' electronic activities is the answer to ensuring ethical and productive behavior. In May 2001, Federal Appeals Court Judge Alex Kozinski and other judges ordered the shutdown of software that tracked the online activities of all employees in the Ninth Circuit Court of Appeals. In an open letter to federal judges published in the *Wall Street Journal* on September 4, 2001, Kozinski likened the monitoring of judiciary employees to the treatment that prison inmates receive. "The proposed policy tells our 30,000 dedicated employees that we trust them so little we must monitor all their communications. . . . How did we get to the point of even considering such a draconian policy?"[29]

Some organizations have tried to strike a balance between close monitoring and no monitoring by helping employees monitor themselves. One service—FastTracker—puts out reports that resemble a telephone bill and allow employees to see their own usage. FastTracker analyzes its clients' traffic and sends reports back to the company for examination by both management and employees. When employees have access to their own usage statistics—where they've been and how long they were there—they become responsible for managing their own time, says Bob Silk, FastTracker's vice president of sales. "When you block sites, you treat employees like children. You don't give them responsibility. Our product makes each employee responsible for his or her actions."[30]

For useful information about your own rights to privacy and attempts by various agencies to obtain information about you that you might not want them to have, you might visit the Web site http://www.privacyrights.org.

The Right to Conscientious Objection

Despite organizational rules prohibiting insubordination, most would agree that employees should have the right to refuse orders that violate their principles (such as falsifying figures in a financial statement, giving or accepting bribes, or lying to government agencies). Yet controversy still surrounds the actions one should take when one sees an organization engaging in unethical practices. In such situations, should an employee blow the whistle on his or her employer?

The prototypical case of a *whistle-blower* involved Dan Gellert, a pilot for Eastern Airlines. He became concerned about the safety of the Lockheed 1011 airplane. In flight simulation, the automatic pilot would disengage without warning about 90 seconds before landing (or about 2,000 feet above the ground). He reported his concerns to company management, who said, "We'll look into it."

On December 29, 1972, an Eastern Airlines L-1011 crashed, killing 103 people. Gellert took his report to the top of the company, who ignored him. Then he sent his report to the National Transportation Safety Board. While his actions did prompt some needed adjustments in the automatic pilot (done quietly by the company), he was demoted and then grounded by the company. He went through grievance procedures for seven months and then sued. Ultimately, he won more than he had sued for ($1.6 million).

The movie *Silkwood* was based on Karen Silkwood's fight against Kerr-McGee to improve safety for nuclear plant workers—a fight in which she blew the whistle on the company. Other similar situations have developed since. For example, Enron's financial dealings came to light when an accounting manager, having had her concerns suppressed or ignored within the organization, brought the company's financial shenanigans to the attention of federal regulators; and President Clinton's infamous dalliances with a White House intern were brought to light by Linda Tripp, a government staff worker. Even more recently, the abuse of Iraqi inmates at Baghdad's Abu Ghraib prison by U.S. soldiers was reported by Sgt. Joseph Darby, who testified during the trial of one alleged abuser that: "It violated everything I personally believed in and all I've been taught about the rules of war. . . . It was more of a moral call."[31] Even so, he agonized for a month about disclosing what he had seen before finally contacting authorities. "These people were my friends. It's a hard call to have to make the decision to put your friends in prison," he testified.

Although the government attempts to protect whistle-blowers, they may still find themselves at risk. Enron executive Sherron Watkins testified before the House Commerce subcommittee that she was nearly fired after she warned then-Enron CEO Kenneth Lay that investors were being misled by inflated profit statements.

Government agencies gradually have developed guidelines for protecting whistle-blowers. For example, in November 1988, the Occupational Safety and Health Administration (OSHA) issued final rules outlining procedures the agency will use to investigate cases in which employees in the trucking industry allege that they were fired or otherwise subjected to retaliation by their employers for voicing complaints about health or safety conditions. New Jersey already enacted a Whistle-blower Act in 1986, and in 1990 Wisconsin enacted new employment laws under which employers would be liable for retaliating when they believe that an employee has filed a complaint, even if the employee has not actually filed. Now, most states provide legal protection to workers who report misdeeds by their employers.

Whistle-blowing is controversial because it puts into conflict two employee obligations: loyalty to the employer and responsibility to society. Some argue that employees should exhaust every possible avenue within the company before they make their concerns public. While some organizations make an "ethics and compliance" hotline available to their employees, others provide no such avenues for workers to report concerns. Because there is no one to whom an employee can "conscientiously object," he or she may be forced to go outside to a government agency or the media. And because they are eager to protect their public image, some companies try very hard to discourage this sort of public airing of their dirty laundry.

Certainly, employees have many rights beyond those discussed above: the right to (qualified) free speech (to complain, for example, but not to defame the company in public), the right to due process, the right to participate in outside activities, and so on. Each of these rights leads to important moral and ethical judgments.

Highlighting Technology

Nothing Wrong with That!

Of the 24% of 4,000 U.S. workers who responded to a survey on Technology & Ethics in the Workplace, the following percentages do *not* believe the following actions are unethical:

- Playing computer games on company equipment during office hours: 49%
- Using office equipment to help children/spouse do schoolwork: 37%
- Using company e-mail for personal reasons: 34%
- Using office equipment for personal reasons: 29%

Source: "Ethical Actions," *HR Fact Finder* 12, no. 3 (July 1998).

MULTINATIONAL BUSINESS AND ETHICS

Maintaining ethical behavior becomes particularly challenging for companies with a global presence. U.S. corporations encounter countless obstacles as they walk the fine line between the requirements of the Foreign Corrupt Practices Act—passed by Congress in the '70s to restrict unethical business practices of U.S. companies internationally—and the realities of local business culture. Corporate ethics statements often deal with gift giving and receiving, proprietary information, bribes, nepotism in hiring practices, conflict of interest, sexual harassment, treatment of racial and ethnic minority employees, and use of convict or child labor by suppliers. All of these areas are viewed differently depending on the cultural perspective. Therefore, some important issues must be considered as ethical rules are exported by U.S. businesses:[32]

- *Rules definitions*. Are rules supposed to be obeyed without question or exception as generally they are in Switzerland and Germany? Or are they merely ideals meant to be honored in the abstract but not feasible in many situations, as in some Latin American countries?

- *Exempt status people*. In companies with rigid social hierarchies and great differences in economic status, members of the elite class assume they have privileges and prerogatives others don't. Therefore, they feel exempt from the rules and standards that apply to other people—and accepting this behavior is common in the Philippines, India, and Latin America.

- *Public service norms*. The main purpose of bloated government bureaucracies in some countries is to provide jobs—mostly low-paying ones. The bureaucrats, in turn, aren't required to be very productive. Therefore, receiving gratuities for doing a task with extra speed or efficiency is considered appropriate. Such payoffs are so common in India that a local newspaper recently published a "bribe index" cataloging the bribery cost of various government services.

- *Gifts and bribes*. In Asia, gift giving has been used for thousands of years as a means of gaining access to, and favorable consideration from, important business contacts and government officials. The gifts are not viewed as bribes unless they are paid in cash to the recipient for doing something blatantly illegal or immoral.

- *Confidentiality and group identity*. In Japan and other countries where group bonds are strong, people function as parts of entities rather than as autonomous individuals. Confidentiality and shared information are essential within the group. The outsider's right to confidentiality is valued less than group loyalty.

- *Office gender roles*. Touching between female and male employees isn't seen as sexual harassment in Latin America. Slightly flirtatious behavior and somewhat provocative dress for women aren't considered out of place in many business environments. Rules to the contrary would seem unnecessarily punitive and stifling.

These are only a few of myriad cultural factors that complicate a corporation's attempt to create a global ethics standard. Worldly-wise organizations take into consideration the cultural values of the countries in which their ethics standards are to be applied. They do not assume the standards automatically will be understood the same way in all locations.

"POLITICALLY CORRECT" SPEECH

Consider this true story. The human resources director of a large urban hospital had an outstanding record for encouraging diversity in her workplace. She had instituted a "school to work" program that encouraged Hispanics and African Americans throughout the hospital's community to prepare themselves for jobs in health care. She started a program that helped people convicted of minor offenses to get back into the workforce after they had served their jail sentences. She worked hard to make sure that the leadership of the hospital was as ethnically diverse as the workforce. And most of her own department's staff members were African American and Hispanic, just as employees throughout the hospital were.

Unfortunately, she also was known for her somewhat caustic sense of humor, and that ultimately proved to be her undoing. During a meeting with her assistant director (an African American male) and a consultant (a Caucasian female), she jokingly said about a group of disgruntled staff, "What do they think they are, a bunch of [N-word]?" Both the assistant director and the consultant sat in stunned silence after she had uttered the "N-word," and after an uncomfortable moment, the meeting continued. Later, however, the assistant director called the health system's corporate ethics and compliance officer to report the incident and demand action be taken. The officer in turn called the consultant, who confirmed that the statement had, in fact, been made. A meeting was held with the director, who admitted she had made the statement but "was only kidding." The health system felt they had no choice—they fired the director.

Increasingly, organizations are actively discouraging workers from saying or doing anything that others might find offensive. Racial slurs are always unacceptable. Ethnic jokes meet disapproval. Sexist comments are discouraged, although often less strongly than racial or ethnic insults. And "just kidding" is no longer an acceptable excuse for words or actions that others find offensive.

Yet there are those who believe that organizations, at least in some cases, have gone too far in enforcing the expectation that people will not say things that offend others. For example, in their book *The Shadow University: The Betrayal of Liberty on America's Campuses*, Alan Kors and Harvey Silvergate accuse college and university bureaucrats of unjustly punishing students and faculty who don't conform to a "politically correct" ideology.[33] They argue that speech and conduct codes, sensitivity training, and other practices violate the right of free speech and that institutions hold students and faculty to a double standard.

In an interview, Kors stated, "What has built up in the last 12 to 15 years is this university that operates in the shadows, with ideologically driven orientations, judicial systems, behavioral codes."[34] When the interviewer asked Kors to explain what this ideology is, he answered: "That students are part of a racist, sexist, homophobic, Eurocentric society, that they are unaware of their status either as victims or as beneficiaries of privilege, and that the university is going to enforce a way of behaving in which the victims will be made whole and the beneficiaries will come to understand their role as privileged beneficiaries."

The interviewer then asked Kors to explain where this ideology comes from, and in response, he blamed on-campus pressure groups:

> Who causes disruption? Radical, militant students—ideologues who want to change the world. But administrators want quiet on their watch. So upper-level administrators co-opt these ideologues—people who might otherwise criticize them—make them part of the power structure by bringing them in as the dean of student life or the officer in charge of minorities.

Since, according to Kors, administrators want peace with academic radicals at any price, they trample on First Amendment rights, use double standards for different races and genders, and arrange "star chamber" trials for anyone who violates trendy taboos. The end result of all this, Kors concludes, is lingering anger:

> Suppose a kid is accused of a politically charged crime. He faces possible suspension, expulsion, legal costs. Or, he's offered a settlement. Most kids will take a settlement. And the settlement is that he undergoes sensitivity training on issues of gender, sexuality, and race. Along the way, he loses respect for all sense of fairness and due process. So what it has produced is cynics who swallow their rage but go along.

"Correct" speech over the air waves has also been an ethical concern. After years of garnering high ratings, for example, "shock jock" Howard Stern was forced off the radio because of public objections to the highly sexual nature of his broadcasts. Indeed, because public objection to the program content of Stern's show and the shows of other imitators across the country, Congress implemented standards that could lead to millions of dollars a day in Federal Communication Commission fines for radio outlets that broadcast sexually explicit content. In addition, the Supreme Court considered, but ultimately blocked, a federal law that would set up penalties for Internet transmission of pornography.

Public sentiment concerning freedom of speech versus on-air obscenity has proven to be somewhat divided. In a *Chicago Tribune* poll of 1,000 adults, 64 percent answered "no" when asked, "Should radio personalities who use implicit or explicit sexual expressions be allowed on the air?" but 84 percent answered "yes" when asked, "Should groups opposed to the war be allowed to demonstrate and protest against the war?" In addition, 58 percent said "yes" when asked, "Do you approve of heavy FCC fines of radio stations due to broadcasts they considered indecent?" and 55 percent said "yes" when asked, "Should the government restrict violence and sexual content that appears on cable television?" Fifty-two percent said "yes" when asked, "Should the government impose restrictions on information and content that appears on the Internet?" and remarkably, 20 percent said negative reporting on the war in Iraq should not be allowed, nor should critical editorials that speak out against the war.[35]

The *Tribune* reported that the results of their survey are remarkable "not for the support they display for the First Amendment rights (which was anticipated), but for the size of the group that would choose to muzzle all kinds of expression, from Stern's vulgarities to news reports on the prisoner abuse scandal in Iraq to criticism of a wartime government."

Issues surrounding "political correctness" and public "obscenity" raise a host of ethical questions. Is any statement or action that offends someone else unethical? Does the gender, race, age, sexual orientation, and other social identity attributes of the person making the statement make any difference (note that the real-life example above of the fired human resources director intentionally does not mention her ethnicity)? When does the First Amendment's guarantee of free speech take a back seat to the sensibilities of particular groups? And does a university's goal of promoting free expression and creative thought conflict with efforts to enforce codes of conduct by students and faculty?

BUILDING ORGANIZATIONAL ETHICS

As organizations have come to realize the importance of ethical behavior, they have attempted to develop a sense of organizational ethics in a variety of ways. Each of these involves communication.

Statements of Mission and Values

Many organizations try to promote ethical behavior by developing a statement of the organization's mission and values that presumably tells employees what the organization is about and what kinds of behaviors it expects. For example, Advocate Health Care, Chicago's largest health system, is cosponsored by two religious groups: the United Church of Christ and the Evangelical Lutheran Church in America. In accordance with the doctrines of those two groups, Advocate teaches their leadership, employees, and physicians their "MVP": Mission, Values, and Philosophy.

Advocate's mission makes clear its religious roots, stating that the purpose of the organization is "to serve the health needs of individuals, families, and communities through a holistic philosophy rooted in our fundamental understanding of human beings as created in the image of God." Advocate's philosophy then identifies 8 principles: (1) realize that everyone is created in the image of God; (2) respect all people; (3) assure the spiritual freedom of all people; (4) show concern for the whole person; (5) address ethical issues; (6) be guided by justice; (7) be accountable for what we do; (8) work collaboratively. Finally, Advocate's values are:

- *Compassion*. We embrace the whole person and respond to emotional, ethical, and spiritual concerns, as well as physical needs in our commitment to unselfishly care for others.
- *Equality*. We affirm the worth and spiritual freedom of each person and treat all people with respect, integrity, and dignity.
- *Excellence*. We empower people to continually improve the outcome of our service, to advance quality, and to increase innovation and openness to new ideas.
- *Partnership*. We collaborate as employees, physicians, volunteers, and community leaders to utilize the talents and creativity of all persons.
- *Stewardship*. We are responsible and accountable for all that we are, have, and do.

The decisions and actions of all members of the Advocate organization should be in accordance with the philosophy and five values that guide the entire health system.

However, mission statements are by no means an ethical panacea. In his article "Sex, Lies and Mission Statements," Christopher Bart argues that the mission statement, "the most popular management tool deployed in recent decades," represents an "organization's sex drive" and should fulfill two fundamental purposes: motivating "organizational members to exceptional performance" and guiding "the resource allocation process in a manner that produces consistency and focus."[36] So much for the sex part; now for the lies: Bart's survey of 88 leading North American corporations revealed that, despite all the time, money, and effort that goes into crafting mission statements, "the vast majority are not worth the paper they are written on and should not be taken with any degree of seriousness." Bart concludes that a statement's ability to affect organizational behavior improves "the more the various stakeholders are involved in its development . . . the more organizational arrangements are aligned with the mission . . . [and] the greater the satisfaction with the statement."

Codes of Ethics

Many companies have attempted to ensure ethical behavior by their members by establishing a code of ethics. Baxter International, a worldwide producer of medical products, distributes to its people a booklet titled "Baxter Ethics" that deals with several key ethical policies:

- *Business conduct.* Display good judgment and high ethical standards in your business dealings.
- *Legal obligations.* Do not break the law.
- *Financial records.* Keep honest and accurate financial records.
- *Company property.* Use company property for business only.
- *Conflict of interest.* Conduct personal business to avoid conflicts of interest.
- *Payments to government officials.* Do not use funds for improper or illegal activities.
- *Confidential information.* Do not use confidential information for personal gain.
- *Securities trading.* Avoid writing options on Baxter stock.
- *Customer gifts.* Use good sense when giving gifts to customers.
- *Advertising.* Sell Baxter's products fairly and honestly, stressing their value and capabilities.
- *Government requests.* Requests from national, state, and municipal government agencies should be forwarded to the corporate Law Department.
- *Antitrust.* Comply with the company's antitrust policies.

Each of these policies is explained in detail and illustrated with a series of commonly-asked questions and answers.

To support their statements of ethics, many companies have appointed formal ethics officers. The Ethics Officer Association, which started in 1992 with 12 members, grew steadily to more than 600 members representing 355 companies by 2000. After scandals broke at Enron, Arthur Andersen, and WorldCom, the association saw "a nice big spike" over a two-year period, according to Mary Zeinieh, manager of member services.[37] The association, based in suburban Boston, now has 950 members representing about 500 companies. Some of the impetus for ethics officers, codes of ethics, and ethics training sprang from the 1991 U.S. Sentencing Commission's Guidelines. Under the guidelines, fines and penalties for corporate misconduct could be reduced if employers demonstrated they had taken steps to prevent such wrongdoing.

However, Joshua Joseph, research manager at the Ethics Resource Center in Washington, states that simply having a corporate ethics code has no effect on employee behavior. Organizations must communicate what's in the code, provide training on what it means, and put systems in place, such as employee hotlines, that allow workers to ask questions and report possible misconduct without fear of reprisal.[38]

Lockheed Martin is one example of a company with a formal comprehensive ethics program. The defense contractor has a vice president of ethics and business conduct who reports to the company's chief executive officer and its board of directors. Each division of the corporation has an ethics officer whose full-time job is to promote ethics and monitor employee concerns. Every employee receives a booklet titled "Our Values" that lists the company's ethics standards and discusses why honesty, integrity, and quality are crucial. Another booklet, "Ethics in our Workplace," provides detailed discussion of a variety of topics, including ethics in cyberspace, conflicts of interest, cultural differences, and excuses for misconduct. A separate newsletter, "Corporate Legal Times," provides self-assessments and information. In addition, every year all 200,000 employees attend a one-hour ethics awareness seminar conducted by their own supervisors, and the company provides a three-inch thick binder that discusses the role of the company's ethics officers and gives realistic scenarios dealing with sexual harassment, interpersonal communication, and gifts, gratuities, and other business courtesies. A board game, called "The Ethics Challenge," reviews ethical issues in a humorous way (featuring characters from the Dilbert comic strip), and employees play the game during ethics training to spur discussion. Finally, there is a toll-free hotline that brings in more than 4,000 calls a year, and ethics officers are located at all 70 business units worldwide.[39]

Management Behaviors

Penn State researcher Linda Trevino reported in a 1999 nationwide ethics survey that too many companies rely too heavily on formal ethics programs. Although virtually every Fortune 1000 company had written ethics codes, such codes had little effect without "ethical leadership, fair treatment of employees, and open discussion of ethics in the organization." Trevino's study of more than 10,000 employees found that employees take a hard look at the motive behind an ethics program. A program perceived as merely protecting top executives in case of a legal mishap "may be worse than having no program at all."[40]

Mary Zeinieh observes that "Over the years, the ethics and compliance officers have been focused on lower-level employees, when the focus should have been at the top. They've been watching the little guy, and they should have been watching the CEOs and the board." In her view, simply announcing a code of conduct to all staff, posting the code on bulletin boards throughout the company, or having new employees sign a copy of the code as a part of their orientation will not ensure cooperation. Individual members of leadership must serve as role models of the code, and organizational rewards and punishments must be applied to encourage following the code's provisions.[41]

"Ethics must start at the top," said Marshall Schminke, who teaches business ethics at the University of Central Florida.[42]

> A person's individual moral framework is only the third most important factor in deciding what they'll do. The most important is, what does their boss do: workers look to their boss first for cues on what constitutes moral behavior. Second, they look at their peers, and finally at their moral code. . . . The boss, and by that I mean the immediate supervisor, has a huge impact on ethical behavior.

Joshua Joseph of the Ethics Resource Center in Washington makes the same point, noting that the most important determinants of ethical behavior are "what your supervisor communicates to you in everyday interactions, what your coworkers communicate in terms of 'what we do around here.'" And that can be a real problem, says Marvin Newman, who teaches ethics at the Crummer School of Business at Rollins College in Winter Park, Florida. An attorney who has been teaching for more than 40 years, Newman complains that students go to work for companies with ethics codes and formal ethics programs in place.[43]

> Then they hand these kids sales targets for the next quarter. Whoever is giving those targets out knows that without fudging, without unethical conduct like boasting about the product beyond exaggeration, they can't realistically meet the sales target. What the company says and what the company does are two different things.

As members of organizations, we must promote ethical behaviors by *serving as role models*. People emulate what they see, not what they are told. If they see unethical behaviors or tolerance for improper practices, they will cease to believe any written codes of ethics.

Carly Fiorina is chairman and chief executive officer of Hewlett-Packard, making her one of just a handful of women who head major U.S. corporations. She also is architect of the merger between Hewlett-Packard and the Compaq computer company, achieved in the face of fierce, even vicious opposition by some of Hewlett-Packard's original founders. In an interview, she was asked, "What are your principles of leadership? What's key to being a successful leader?" She answered:[44]

> The primary lesson that I have learned is that the best people are known not just for their capabilities but for their character; that as much as our world changes, there are fundamental values that never do; that responsibility still counts; that integrity still matters; and that honesty counts. . . . I think leadership takes what I call a strong internal compass. When the winds are howling and the storms are raging and the sky is cloudy so you have nothing to navigate by, a compass tells you where true north is. I think when you're in a difficult situation, a lonely situation, you have to rely on that compass to tell you if you're doing the right things for the right reasons in the right ways. Sometimes that's all you have.

SUMMARY

At the beginning of this chapter, we noted that ethics within organizations are important and involve relationships among all members of an organization and other organizations with which they have contact. Despite efforts to increase ethical behaviors, however, there seems to be a rise in unethical acts, driven in part by increasing pressures in the workplace and various organizational practices. We discussed the reasons ethical conduct is important and examined civic engagement as an extended illustration of ethical behavior outside the workplace.

Next, we considered some perspectives for determining what's "right," evaluating both organizational and communication ethics from various philosophical perspectives, including religious, political, utilitarian, universalist, dialogic, and situational. Then we looked at the areas of advertising, "service versus profit," social responsibility, and employee rights, which seem particularly relevant to ethical concerns, and we reviewed some important ethical issues related to each.

Despite these difficulties, the contemporary thrust of organizational leadership and behavior embraces a compelling appeal for a sense of ethics within the context of social responsibility. Thus, we reviewed some efforts organizations are making to improve ethical behavior, including statements of mission and values, codes of ethics, and most important, role modeling by members of the organization itself, particularly leadership.

Ultimately, however, responsibility for ethical behavior rests with each member of the organization and the greater community. Each of us must decide what the right thing to do is. And even if, like guards overseeing Iraqi prisoners, our superiors tell us to do things that are unethical, we bear the responsibility for deciding whether to carry out those orders or for "doing the right thing."

Questions for Discussion

1. Discuss the assertion that the end justifies the means. Are there any particular kinds of situations in which this position might be defensible? Elaborate with at least one example.

2. It is not uncommon for individuals to vary their ethical perspectives, depending on the precise nature of the situation in which they find themselves. Can you justify this point of view?

3. What is your view of contemporary advertising in terms of ethics? What advertising practices are problematic from your ethical perspective?

4. Why is civic engagement in a state of decline? To what extent and in what ways do you see civic engagement as a form of ethical conduct?

5. What should an employee do when he/she feels his/her immediate supervisor is doing something unethical? Outline a series of actions that an employee might take.

6. What if an employee is ordered by his/her superiors to do something unethical—what should he/she do then?

7. How would you define the ethics of an organization with which you presently are affiliated? What do their ethical standards seem to be? How do they communicate those standards? How do they enforce them?

Exercises

1. Choose any prominent persons (such as an educator, religious leader, politician, lawyer, or executive) and discuss her/his behavior from an ethical perspective. What is the apparent value system of this individual? On what is it based? From your own view, is this person's behavior ethical? Be specific.

2. Select any three advertisements. Consider their bases of appeal, operating assumptions, and general taste. To what extent is each a reasonably accurate representation of reality? How would you rate each in terms of *your* ethical perspective?

3. Choose an executive with a moderate to large organization. Arrange for an interview. During the interview, discuss his/her philosophies of management, relating them to his/her own values and those of the organization.

4. Contact several major organizations that have branches near your community. Ask them whether or not they have written procedures for dealing with discrimination and/or sexual harassment. If they do, obtain copies. Do they seem adequate? If not, how could they be improved?

5. You are the manager of a newly established realty company in a medium-sized town in the Midwest. While the organization has nationwide branches, your office is new, and you are relatively free to run it as you prefer—so long as you operate in the black. Your fifteen years of experience in the real estate business has taught you that it is a competitive, exciting, and in some senses treacherous business. Yet one of its major purposes is to serve the public.

   a. What values would influence you most in building your organization? Why?

   b. How would these values be reflected in your hiring and handling of employees, especially other real estate agents?

   c. How would your values relate to your handling of the public?

   d. What is the ethical basis for your particular values? Elaborate.

6. Imagine yourself as a fairly new employee in a rapidly growing firm. You have high hopes for rapid promotion, but your boss is a person who presents certain problems. His ideas of how to manage are very command-oriented, whereas yours are much more democratic. His political views are conservative (far to the right of Rush Limbaugh, to say nothing of conservative politicians); yours are just left of Ted Kennedy. He loves sports; you loathe sports. Unfortunately, he often asks for your views on all of the above and on other painful issues as well. What do you do? Do you articulate your true opinions? Do you pretend to agree? Do you downplay your views or simply attempt to change the subject? Is it possible to distort your position in some areas but not in others? *What is the relationship here between the ethical and the political thing to do?* What ethical perspective would you use to resolve this dilemma? Why?

7. Choose someone you respect who was born before 1940 (a grandparent or older member of your community). Talk with this person about the organizations he/she has belonged to throughout his/her life. What kinds of involvement has this individual had in the community? Now, compare and contrast his/her civic engagement with your own. Try to identify at least one cause or organization that you plan to join in the future that addresses a social issue that you feel strongly about. Why did you choose this particular organization or cause?

Case Application 1.1   Ethical Decision Making

Hospitals and Health Networks magazine created an ethically challenging scenario to which they asked a panel of five hospital chief executive officers to respond. The scenario was as follows:

Robin Wood Medical Center has posted large losses for three years in a row. It is located in a decaying neighborhood on the fringes of a large city with plenty of—perhaps too many—hospital beds available. The hospital is the largest employer in its area and serves pockets of elderly and poor residents, many of whom do not own or drive cars. The community leans heavily on the hospital, which operates an adult day-care center, a busy emergency room, and other key services. However, the number of patients using the hospital has been declining steadily.

Longtime hospital president Joan Morgan has the confidence and trust of her board of directors, who have asked her to investigate affiliations with other hospitals. MetroCare, a large health system that owns two hospitals in the area has offered to buy Robin Wood Medical Center, but for a very low price. MetroCare has also made promises to Joan Morgan, offering her a generous severance package and consulting agreement if she persuades the board to accept their offer. MetroCare has also made clear to Joan their plan to close the hospital and transfer only a fraction of its employees to other sites. They have given no assurances that the hospital's services will be continued near its present location.

Two other city hospitals also have approached Joan Morgan, but they recently have entered into their own merger talks. Executives from the two facilities have told Morgan that they cannot consider deals with Robin Wood Medical Center until those discussions come to a conclusion. Morgan worries that MetroCare's offer may be the only affiliation possible.

Source: "Ethics & the CEO," *Hospitals and Health Networks* 72, no. 2 (January 20, 1998): 28–34.

Questions

1. How should Morgan weigh the ethical issues concerning the hospital's survival versus the survival of its vital services?

2. What are the ethical implications of MetroCare's offer for the hospital versus its financial promises to Morgan? What should she do?

Case Application 1.2 Ethical Decision Making for Academic Leaders

During the past two decades, the troubled U.S. economy has put many colleges and universities into a precarious financial situation. Several private colleges have been forced to close their doors while public institutions have taken unprecedented actions to maximize their chances for survival. Many colleges have had to ask talented nontenured faculty to leave; in some extreme instances, even tenured faculty have been dismissed.

Most universities have dealt with the financial crunch by dismissing a few faculty members from different departments around the university, thus spreading the losses throughout the institution. A few universities, however, like Michigan State, the University of California-Davis, the University of Washington, and the State University of New York at Albany, have chosen to pursue a different (and in some ways unpopular) route by actually eliminating entire academic departments. This strategy is based on the argument that it is better to have an incomplete curriculum than a weak overall curriculum.

State University, a large, public institution, has just received its biannual budget from the state legislature, and the news is anything but good. Due to severe cuts in the budget supporting curriculum and instruction, the university's administrators have decided that they must phase out (and ultimately eliminate) *three departments* within the College of Arts and Sciences. Following are the departments from which they are choosing:

African American Studies, Anthropology#, Astronomy, Biology*#+, Chemistry*#, Classical Studies+, Comparative Literature, Computer Science, Criminal Justice*, East Asian Languages & Literature+, Economics*, English*#+, Fine Arts#, Folklore#, French & Italian#+, Germanic Languages+, Geography, Geology, History*#+, Linguistics, Mathematics+, Philosophy#, Physics, Political Science*, Psychology#*+, Religious Studies#, Slavic Languages & Literature+, Sociology*#+, Spanish & Portuguese, Speech Communication#+, Speech & Hearing Sciences*, Telecommunications*, Theatre & Drama, and Women's Studies.

* =   departments with a large number of undergraduate majors
\# =   departments with high national visibility (based on research)
\+ =   departments that serve other departments by offering courses that are required for the B.A./B.S. degree

Questions

1. If you were involved in making this difficult decision, what ethical perspectives would guide your choices? Why?

2. What criteria, besides national rankings, demand (number of majors), and service should be considered in making this decision? How are they related to the ethical perspectives you selected?

3. Which departments would you choose to eliminate, based on your ethical (and perhaps other) criteria?

2

Fundamentals of Organizational Communication

After reading this chapter, you should be able to:

❑ Explain how communication relates to the success of and within organizations

❑ List the defining characteristics of organizations

❑ Explain the meaning of transactional communication

❑ Define organizational communication

❑ List and explain three common shortcomings of communication in organizations

❑ Explain the purposes of formal and informal communication channels in organizations, providing examples of each

❑ List some of the problems commonly associated with upward, downward, horizontal, and external communication

❑ Explain some of the ways in which technology has impacted organizational communication

❑ Describe the major challenges associated with communication technology

T hink for a moment about success. What does success mean to you? What do you want for yourself, on both a short-term and a long-term basis? Short term, your goals may be relatively specific: obtaining an entry-level job with some organization, being promoted to some higher-level position, getting a raise, achieving a particular grade in a certain class, or graduating at a certain time. Long term, your goals may be less well defined, but definite nevertheless: financial security, happiness, status, love, the chance to make a lasting contribution, and so on. Whatever your goals—whatever success means to you, both short term and long term—two important facts hold true:

• Much of your professional success will be achieved through your participation in some organization or group of organizations.

• Your professional success will be determined to a significant extent by your skills as a communicator.

Let us examine each of these facts one at a time. First, much of your success and personal and professional fulfillment will likely come through your affiliation with one or more organizations—whether a law firm, a corporation, a small business, a college, or a volunteer organization. The reason for this is simple: our society is composed almost entirely of organizational entities. Indeed, whenever human beings gather together for the purpose of accomplishing some goal, organizations are born. Some are informal and loosely structured; most are characterized by deliberate structuring and formal divisions of power, labor, and authority. Whatever their nature and scope, however, we seldom escape their influence. As noted organizational theorist Amitai Etzoini observed many years ago, we are born in organizations, educated by organizations, work for organizations, and spend much of our leisure time in organized activities.[1]

Second, your ability to succeed will be determined largely by your skills as a communicator. This is true in a number of respects. Your ability to enter an organization in the first place depends heavily upon your communication skills. Consider, for example, the thoughts of Bill Coplin, professor of public policy at the Maxwell School and the College of Arts and Sciences, Syracuse University, and author of *10 Things Employers Want You To Learn in College*. He points out that

> surveys of employers put work ethic, communication, information-gathering and people skills at the top of the list [of things employers look for], followed by analytical and problem-solving skills.
>
> Students in technical fields, such as engineering or the physical sciences, or those destined for graduate programs, such as law or an MBA, need to pay particular attention to communication and group work. . . . Graduate-school recommendations ask more questions about attitude, commitment and people capabilities than intelligence and analytical ability. They may weigh standardized tests more, but soft skills matter.[2]

An example of this emphasis on communication skills, even among technically-oriented professions, can be seen in medical schools. Starting in 2004, U.S. medical students must pass a standardized examination on "doctoring" that goes beyond clinical knowledge. The reason is that being a good doctor requires more than simply knowing medicine. "It is also about what the patient is feeling," said Dr. Ronald Epstein, a neurology professor at the University of Rochester's Medical School who has conducted research on doctor-patient relationships.[3]

The national exam, which was first offered in June 2004, was in the making for more than a decade and was introduced as part of an effort to improve the communication skills of future physicians. Doctors and medical educators say the better the rapport between physicians and their patients, the easier it is for doctors to elicit crucial information. They also say better communication might eliminate some costly diagnostic testing and thus reduce medical bills. But there is also a suggestion that a friendlier atmosphere might reduce the risk of patients bringing a malpractice suit against a doctor they disliked or felt had not really cared.

Once you have joined an organization, your ability to perform successfully in your current job and to move to jobs with greater responsibility and status will be determined by two important elements: your technical skills and your communication skills. You perform your job well by skillfully completing your assignments and, in today's increasingly team-oriented environment, by working well with others. As others learn of your accomplishments, however, you gain prominence and begin to move up within the organization. Written reports, memoranda, and even e-mails, for example, are important "advertisements" of your identity, your achievements, and your skills as a communicator. Meetings, everyone's favorite target for criticism, also provide opportunities for you to demonstrate your knowledge and communication skills. Presentations of project proposals and progress reports give you the opportunity to make a positive impression in the minds of people holding influential positions within the organization. Certainly, doing your job tasks well is important, but communicating effectively may be even more important.

The higher you move in an organization, the more important communication becomes to your overall job performance. Indeed, some believe that communication style becomes more important than technical skill. Andrew Sherwood, president and chief executive officer of Goodrich & Sherwood Company, a human resources firm, says that

> meeting goals and objectives are quantitative measures of "what" you do on the job—"what" you're being paid for. When you begin your career, and until about age 35, "what" criteria are generally used to judge work performance. After age 35, however, when most people move into middle management or beyond, performance criteria begin to shift and style becomes more important.

After this point in your career, "how" you do your job becomes most important. The "how" criteria include such things as "how you relate to your superiors, how you interact with your peers, how you handle and motivate people, and how you communicate," Sherwood explains. "The higher you rise in your company, the more visibility you have, the more you become a public figure—the more important 'how' you do your job becomes."[4]

When one reaches the top of an organization, communication activities occupy virtually all of one's time. Several years ago, for example, the administrator of a large hospital kept a detailed record of his activities for ten consecutive workdays. Of his 5,186 minutes, approximately 70 percent was spent in oral communication, about 17 percent in writing, and less than 13 percent in activities involving no form of communication.[5] Getting to the top requires communication skills; performing effectively once you get there requires even greater skill.

Of course, organizations are changing at an unprecedented pace. Some changes have been brought about by advances in modern technology, others by developments in the economy, and still others by the increasingly global environment. The world marketplace has many participants, of which the United States is only one. Over 100,000 U.S. companies are doing business abroad; about one-sixth of our nation's jobs come from international business. U.S.-made products are increasingly rare. At the same time, jobs are changing. According to the U.S. Department of Labor Statistics, computer-related occupations will experience the fastest job growth between 2000 and 2010.[6] The typical large business will be information-based, composed of specialists who guide themselves based on information from colleagues, customers, and top managers. Even now, one out of every two Americans works in some aspect of information processing. The new technologies offer change as well as opportunity.

Preview

In this chapter we will create the foundation for developing your communication skills by offering some basic definitions of the meaning and nature of organizations, the communication process, and organizational communication. We will examine both formal and informal organizational communication channels, together with their purposes and potential problems. Finally, we will explore some of the ways in which new technologies have altered the communication landscape within and between organizations, offering both great promise and interesting challenges.

BASIC DEFINITIONS

An overarching purpose of this book is to help you develop the communication skills you will need to be successful in whatever career and organization you choose. We begin, then, by examining some of the defining elements of organizations and organizational communication.

Defining Organizations

Over the years, communication scholars have defined *organization* in a variety of ways, including: "a stable system of individuals who work together to achieve, through a hierarchy of ranks and divisions of labor, common goals";[7] "an information and decision system";[8] "the complex pattern of communication and other relations between human beings";[9] "social relationships . . . interlocked behavior centered on specialized task and maintenance activities."[10] Although diverse, these definitions share several common threads. In particular, they emphasize:

- goal-directed behavior
- coordinated actions
- information sharing
- decision making
- human relationships

These elements in turn emphasize the importance of communication in organizations. Communication is not merely an important activity in organizations; it is the lifeblood that allows organizations to exist. No human relationship could be maintained, no organizational objective achieved, no activities coordinated, and no decisions reached without communication. Perhaps Bavelas and Barrett expressed it best in their classic article on organizational communication, where they noted:

> It is entirely possible to view an organization as an elaborate system for gathering, evaluating, recombining, and disseminating information. It is not surprising in these terms that the effectiveness of an organization with respect to the achievement of its goals should be so closely related to its effectiveness in handling information.

In other words, in their view organizational success is directly tied to communication effectiveness. They conclude, "Communication is not a secondary or derived aspect of organization—a 'helper' of the other presumably more basic functions. It is rather the essence of organized activity and is the basic process out of which all other functions derive."[11]

Not surprisingly, when Peters and Waterman concluded their "search for excellence" many years ago, they said:[12]

> What does it add up to? Lots of communication. . . . The name of the successful game is rich, informal communication. The astonishing by-product is the ability to have your cake and eat it, too; that is, rich, informal communication leads to more action, more experiments, more learning, and simultaneously to the ability to stay better in touch and on top of things.

In short, the effectiveness of communication within an organization significantly shapes how successful that organization will be.

Understanding the Communication Process

Acknowledging the importance of communication is crucial. Equally crucial, however, is to understand it as a complex process. Early models of communication failed to do this. They conceptualized communication as *linear*, largely a one-way event involving the flow of information from a source to a receiver. These models also focused on channels, so that communication was viewed as a conduit through which individuals attempted to accomplish their goals. Barriers to effective communication were viewed as noise, or anything that interfered with or distorted the message's movement through the channel. Noise might involve anything from crackling telephone wires to garbage on a computer screen to the receiver's attitudes—any one of which might affect message reception and interpretation.

More contemporary models of communication are *transactional*, emphasizing communication as a two-way, reciprocal *process* of mutual message exchange. To understand the transactional process of communication, imagine interviewing for a job. In response to a question the interviewer asks, you mention that you were involved in a large number of volunteer activities while in school. The interviewer reacts with raised eyebrows, looking directly at you and saying, "Oh?" You realize that this has aroused her interest—seemingly in a positive way—so you describe in some detail the many activities in which you had been involved. However, later in the interview, you mention that while in school, you particularly had enjoyed napping during class and participating in hanging out at bars during weekend evenings. You notice that the interviewer looks down, frowns slightly, and writes something in the margins of your resume. This information does not seem to have pleased her, and you resolve to avoid any further discussion of these hobbies as the interview progresses.

Gerald Miller argued that communication is a process and

> should not be thought of as discrete events with identifiable beginnings and ends, but rather as parts of a dynamic, on-going whole which has no clearly defined temporal boundaries. In particular, process stresses the *transactional* nature of . . . communication, rather than conceptualizing it as a unidirectional, linear act.[13]

Your soon-to-be-unsuccessful employment interview demonstrates these points. The interviewer asks questions that, hopefully, shape your answers. Your answers cause her to react, and your interpretations of her reactions shape your subsequent behaviors: you elaborate on things that seem to please her and probably avoid issues that seem to cause her concern.

The transactional perspective does not distinguish between the roles of "source" and "receiver" since each person plays both, and often at the same time. Unlike the linear view, verbal and nonverbal feedback is considered central to the transactional model. How meaning is constructed is another concern. The linear view posits the notion that the meaning of a particular message resides with the sender, whose challenge is to use a message channel effectively. By contrast, the transactional view is more oriented toward the receiver and toward the construction of a message's meaning in her or his mind. In short, people grow to share meanings through mutual experiences and by negotiating shared interpretations.

Within the framework of the transactional model, then, ***organizational communication*** is that process wherein: *mutually interdependent human beings create and* *exchange messages and interpret and negotiate meanings while striving to articulate and realize mutually held visions, purposes, and goals.*

How Communication in Organizations Is Unique

All of us communicate every day, with friends, family, chat room acquaintances, and so on. And each of those communications is a transactional process involving people who are mutually interdependent to some extent, exchanging messages and interpreting meanings and trying, at least for the moment, to achieve some common goal. But communication in organizations has some unique characteristics that make it different from communication in other settings.

First, organizations have a *hierarchy*. There are bosses and workers, leaders and followers, those who are in charge and those who aren't. Most organizations have an organization chart (see, for example, figure 2.1) that shows both the horizontal level of the organization a particular position occupies and the vertical portion of the organization over which a position has authority. For example, a vice president of finance may occupy the third horizontal level of the organization and thus has less authority than the chief operating officer to whom she reports, or the chief executive officer to whom the COO reports. She has more authority than any of the directors throughout the organization on the level below her, but only the directors working in finance report to her; thus, while she has more positional authority than directors in other areas, such as manufacturing, she may not be able to tell those directors what to do (indeed, if she were to try to do so, the vice president of manufacturing to whom those directors report may well be annoyed). The hierarchy prescribes to a large degree who talks to whom about what, and who makes what decisions.

Second, organizations have *specified goals and roles*. That is, everyone by virtue of their position in the organization has a job to do, and the tasks and objectives of their jobs shape their communications with other members of the organization. People holding similar jobs with common objectives tend to find themselves working together as teams, whether or not they enjoy one another's company, because the structure and overall objectives of the organization throw them together. Conversely, people working in different departments or different

Figure 2.1   Sample organization chart

locations may never have contact with one another, other than via the e-mails they receive from each other with annoying regularity.

Third, organizations have *behavioral expectations*. As we noted in the preceding chapter, organizations use mission and values statements, work rules, policies and procedures, and, perhaps most important, behavioral role modeling to shape the behaviors of its members. Pressure to conform to those expectations, exerted both informally through peer pressure and formally through supervisory counseling or discipline, usually is strong, and people who fail to conform often are asked to leave the organization.

Fourth, organizations involve both *cooperation and competition*. Coworkers often must cooperate and work as a team in order to achieve departmental goals, but only one team member can be promoted when an opening in the supervisory ranks occurs. Thus, people working in organizations often find themselves with conflicting motives as they interact with their colleagues, depending on them to some degree for their own success while simultaneously wanting to beat them in the never-ending competition for limited rewards and resources. People whose communication behaviors are too competitive may come to be viewed as "backstabbers" by their colleagues or as "not a team player" by their superiors, and their careers may stall as a result. But people whose communication behaviors are too cooperative may be viewed as "wimps" or followers who lack the drive and "killer instinct" to move up the ranks of organizational leadership. Certainly, balancing cooperation and competition can be very delicate.

Finally, communication in organizations often involves and shapes *long-term relationships*. On a day-to-day basis, we may not think about the effects our communications have. If we offend the person in the drive-through window at McDonald's as he hands us our super-size fries, there probably are no serious consequences. But in organizations, people see each other every day, sometimes year after year, and those people often have very long memories. Consequently, when you "flame" a colleague one day with a blistering e-mail, you face the possibility that you could well find yourself needing that person's help (or worse yet, reporting to that person) some time in the future. Good luck. On the other hand, if you compliment someone one day and then need a favor a year later, that offhanded compliment could be repaid one thousand times over. The old saying, "What goes around, comes around," is never truer than in the case of communication in organizations.

As you communicate within an organization, then, you must consider not only the clarity with which your meaning is understood by those with whom you are communicating, you must consider the appropriateness and effects of your actions in terms of your own and others' roles within the organizational hierarchy, the organization's formal and informal expectations, your orientation toward cooperation and competition, and the potential effects of what and how you communicate on your long-term relationships with others in the organization. Clearly, communication in organizations can be much more complicated than communication in more informal settings.[14]

COMMON COMMUNICATION SHORTCOMINGS

During the past 20 years, the authors have consulted with nearly 1,000 different organizations. Our experiences and observations have shown that while organizations typically try very hard to communicate well, senior leaders, middle-level managers, and nonsupervisory staff often name "communication" as the one thing they feel most needs to be improved in their organization. Generally, we have found six basic causes of communication shortcomings:

1. *Communication often is activity-oriented, not results-oriented.* When consulting with hospitals, for example, it is our practice to ask the hospital administrator to show us the hospital's employee handbook. Then we ask, "Do you feel this is a good employee handbook?" Typically, the answer will be yes, followed by such reasons as it has won national awards for design and layout; it costs us a lot of money to produce; my picture is on the inside cover; and consultants helped us to develop it. We then ask, "But does it do what it is supposed to do?" Often we receive a puzzled look and a long silence in response. Communication is a tool designed to achieve some effect. Too many organizations, however, view communication as something that "ought to be done," losing sight of the impact their communications should have.

2. *There is too much communication activity rather than too little.* The most common complaint we hear about communication is not that there is a lack of messages, but that there are too many for people in organizations to deal with. Members of management particularly complain about the number of meetings they are required to attend, often with little apparent benefit. Employees at all levels of the organization complain about the number of e-mails they receive—often several hundred per day, with most of them sent by well-meaning colleagues who want to be sure that everyone is kept informed of their activities, whether or not sending this information either directly affects the sender's or the receiver's work responsibilities. When people are buried under an avalanche of communication, they become unable to sort out the important messages from the unimportant ones, and often simply start ignoring all of the communication they receive. Then they complain at how uninformed they seem to be.

3. *Communication often is one-way.* Managers frequently assume that as long as they are sending messages regularly to the rest of the organization, they are communicating. They therefore engage exclusively in downward communication, receiving little or no feedback from lower levels of the organization. As a result, they often do not know whether their downward messages were received, understood, believed, or approved of by employees, and they cannot adjust future messages to employees' needs or characteristics. In addition, they often assume that they are communicating effectively because they hear no questions and receive no objections. To be effective, communication in organizations must flow not only downward but upward and laterally.

4. *The impact of communication is not measured.* This problem is related to the preceding one. In many organizations, management receives informal feedback. However, no systematic attempt is made to measure the impact of communication in terms of the objectives or results the communication was supposed to achieve. If, for example, the employee handbook is designed to inform employees about company benefit programs and to cause them to feel positive about their organization, actual measures should be taken to determine how much information employees get and retain about benefit plans by reading that handbook and what effects, if any, the handbook has on attitudes

toward the organization. In effect, management must clearly define the results they want their communication systems to achieve and then regularly measure the extent to which those results have occurred.

5. *Communication is not responsive to employee needs.* When defining the objectives of their communication systems, managers should first ask employees what information they want or need. Then they can tailor downward messages to meet those needs. Rarely, for example, do companies ask new employees what information they would like to receive in their orientation meetings; rather, they assume that the information provided is exactly what the employee needs. When we interview incoming employees about their concerns and desires, we often find an entire body of information is needed that company orientation programs do not provide. Thus, in addition to providing information that management knows is important, organizational leaders also should ask employees what they want and what they need to know.

6. *The people who implement communication systems may lack the necessary communication skills.* Department meetings cannot be effective if the department heads conducting them lack communication leadership skills. Customer service and sales representatives cannot be expected to maintain good relations with customers if they have never been taught customer communication skills. Communication systems and opportunities are not enough; the people who use those systems must have skills as communicators.

As you may have gleaned, communication in organizations has two basic elements: *communication systems* (the meetings, electronic systems, publications, conversations, and so on in which messages are transmitted) and the *communication skills* of the people participating in those communication systems. In the remainder of this chapter, we will focus on the systems through which people in organizations communicate. In later chapters, we will discuss the skills you need to communicate effectively.

FORMAL COMMUNICATION CHANNELS

As we have already implied, communication in organizations takes two forms: formal and informal. *Formal communication* is that which follows prescribed channels of communication throughout the organization—typically, the chain of command, although team-oriented communication among peers is increasingly being emphasized by companies that encourage lateral problem solving and decision making. Often depicted on official organizational charts, formal channels provide for the structured flow of downward communication; upward communication; and, occasionally, horizontal communication.

Downward Communication

Messages flowing from upper to lower levels of an organization's hierarchy constitute *downward communication*. Through downward communication, organizations direct the activities of employees, instruct them in proper behaviors and work methods, persuade them to adopt certain attitudes and ideas, evaluate their performance on the job, solicit upward communication, and provide entertainment—all typical functions of communication in organizational settings.

In modern organizations, downward communication occurs in a variety of *written* and *oral* forms. Many instances of oral communication are face-to-face—the communicators are looking directly at each other. Both written and oral communication often include the use of *electronic technology* for convenience, speed, and the many other benefits it provides. In describing some methods used by companies to communicate their benefits plans to employees, for example, some years ago Hourihan discussed three "generations" of benefits communication: the printed materials provided by insurance companies themselves (which are written from the insurer's viewpoint using highly technical language), written communications from the employer (such as an annual computerized benefits statement for each employee), and a large meeting presentation using dual-projector slide shows and professional speakers, with a social event afterward (cocktails and dinner) at which questions about benefits programs could be asked and answered.[15] Through this description, he also illustrated a change in emphasis in downward communication, with companies moving from a traditional reliance on written messages to greater face-to-face interaction.

Since the time of Hourihan's article, however, an entirely new generation of benefits communication has arisen: *electronic messages*. Companies such as MCI, JCPenney, Paymentech, and Texas Instruments are moving human resource ser-

When employees have the opportunity to work with managers in departmental meeting contexts, to share their ideas, concerns, and constructive feedback, the organization's communication climate is likely to flourish. Meetings may serve as a stimulus for goodwill and trust-building.

vices online via intranets, which use Internet technologies to distribute information and communicate with employees over a company's internal computer network. At MCI, for example, employees can sign up for health benefits or view their paycheck stubs on an internal site if they use electronic deposit. They can check their 401(k) or stock options. Through electronic communications, companies cut mailing, printing, and labor costs, and employees seem to like the convenience.[16] Thus, as technology changes, so do methods of communication in organizations.

WRITTEN DOWNWARD COMMUNICATION

- *Employee handbooks*, given to employees when they first join an organization, summarize the mission, values, policies, and pay and benefits practices of the organization. These handbooks often are an organization's first attempt to convey its behavioral expectations to organization members.

- *Job descriptions and work procedures and protocols* typically are given to supervisors and managers to help them govern employees' day-to-day behaviors and in turn are shared with employees to clarify performance expectations. The organization's formal set of hierarchically arranged roles usually are defined via these written documents.

- *Newsletters and other internal publications* contain information ranging from social activities to important organizational decisions and events. Some organizations produce glossy, expensive newsletters that are distributed to staff every month or so. Others produce informal, one-page bulletins that are distributed to each department and placed on tables throughout the cafeteria just to keep everyone updated about day-to-day events. But as globalization, telecommuting, and job sharing change the very definition of "workplace" and make it increasingly difficult for employers to communicate with the workforce, more companies are turning to cyberpublications to communicate company news, create a feeling of unity among employees who are spread out over various locations, and get the word out during times of change.[17]

- *Digital publications* offer several important advantages as a form of downward communication. Speed of communication is much greater because electronic newsletters let breaking news be distributed in seconds rather than days, so employees can be informed of important events within the organization before they hear about them from outside sources. Cost savings are achieved because cyberpublications eliminate costs for printing, distribution, and adding copy and features. Flexibility is greater because the length of each issue can be determined by the messages that should be communicated, not by whether the issue will be in a two-page or four-page format. Customization is possible in that digital publications can be inexpensively customized for different audiences. For example, one edition can be produced for the sales force, another for research and development, and still another for engineering. While general news stories may appear in all versions, each edition could also deliver news of particular interest to its target audience.

Multimedia content can be used to spice up digital newsletters through the use of audio clips, music, video clips, and the like. Searchable archives can be set up allowing articles to be stored and retrieved efficiently, creating a digital corporate history and making it easy for employees to find previously published stories. Furthermore, interactivity is possible when digital publications encourage reader involvement and obtain quick online responses to announcements and articles. Some employers include quick surveys in their electronic newsletters, providing an instant measure of reader reactions. Integrating links into electronic stories can make it easier for readers to sign up for courses, submit applications for in-house jobs, and change benefits selections, for example.

Digital publications do have some drawbacks, however. Obviously, workers must have computer access at their jobs; those who don't will not have access to digital newsletters. In addition, digital publications are less portable; people who want to read an electronic newsletter on a bus or plane may have to print out a copy to take with them. If everybody prints out the newsletter, it can actually be more expensive than simply producing a hard-copy version to begin with. Still, for most organizations the advantages far outweigh the disadvantages of digital newsletters that are now replacing paper documents.

- *Bulletin boards* are used to post important notices (particularly those required by various governmental agencies), but are frequently ignored by passersby. Some companies use electronic bulletin boards that provide constantly changing messages and thus attract more interest.

- *Letters and memoranda* may be sent to employees' homes, distributed in paycheck envelopes, or handed out by supervisors and managers to facilitate conversation with staff. Usually, organizations send letters to employees' homes only when a very important matter is under consideration, since doing so involves considerable time and expense.

- *Electronic mail (e-mail)* is used routinely by most organizations to communicate information to management and staff, often replacing written letters and memoranda. This communication channel has the advantages of being fast, cheap, and available to virtually everyone, which unfortunately has led to the overuse of e-mail in many organizations.

- *Intranets* are internal company networks, similar to the World Wide Web, whereby individual employees can log on, check their personal e-mail, and access any information of interest to them. For example, Unified Grocers of California has an intranet for its employees on which announcements, stories about the company appearing in the media, detailed messages about current activities or future plans, job openings throughout the organization, and other information of interest to employees are listed, and an employee can peruse any or all of these messages. Since many of Unified's warehouse employees do not have computer access either at work or at home, the company also has set up kiosks with computer keyboards and screens throughout the facility, enabling employees to log on to the intranet whenever they have time.

Written downward messages offer the advantages of being relatively permanent, easily distributed, and time efficient for the receivers, who can read them whenever it is most convenient. In addition, these messages can serve as legal documentation of a company's philosophies and practices, thereby helping to defend the company (or convict it, if the messages are inappropriate) in court proceedings. However, written messages typically do not allow immediate discussion between sender and receiver, thereby hindering clarification or debate of unclear or controversial information.

ORAL DOWNWARD COMMUNICATION

- *Employment interviews* often are one of the first instances of downward communication that potential employees encounter; they can be useful for transmitting information about an organization.

- *Performance evaluations* are viewed by many organizations as an important tool for both assessing and improving the performance of their members. In most organizations, employees receive a formal evaluation from their immediate superiors once a year (and sometimes more often), possibly accompanied by a change (hopefully upward) in their rate of pay. Evaluations typically consist of a review of job responsibilities and performance quality standards, a summary of how well the superior perceives each subordinate to have performed in comparison with those standards, and development of a plan for improving performance during the upcoming year. In addition, those receiving the evaluation may be given an opportunity to offer input concerning how well they performed in the past, plans for improving performance in the future, and any objections they may have regarding the evaluation the supervisor has provided.

- *Disciplinary interviews*, often used after corrective interviews have failed to improve behavior, mete out some form of punishment in addition to advice for behavioral improvement. Depending on the severity of the discipline, the interview may be supplemented by written documentation as well.

- *Department or unit meetings* involve groups of employees and their supervisors or managers. As channels for downward communication, such meetings often discuss what some refer to as the "4 Ps": progress (how we are doing), people (what personnel moves are occurring), policy (what is unclear or changing), and points (anything that arises during the meeting). Unfortunately, the authors' experience suggests that many meetings can probably be characterized by another "P": pitiful.

- *Mass meetings* often are used by top-level executives to communicate important information to large groups of employees. Often taking the form of town hall meetings, these forums are used to make important announcements, explain significant events, initiate companywide programs or processes, and keep employees up-to-date on the organization's progress.

- *Educational and orientation programs* can be used to indoctrinate and educate new employees about companywide practices, benefits, pay procedures, and so on, or to teach employees new information and skills related to their jobs.

Recently, a variety of *electronic media* have been developed to facilitate face-to-face (or voice-to-voice) downward communication:

- *Video conferencing and presentations* often are used to present important information during large group, department, or unit meetings. In large organizations where personal visits by senior executives are impractical, for example, video-conferenced presentations can be used to communicate information to all employees at the same time. Unified Grocers of California, for example, announced their new "cultural change initiative" by setting up huge video screens in their warehouses throughout California and using satellite technology to transmit a presentation by their chief executive officer and other key executives to all employees at the same moment. For less immediate (or dramatic) messages, many companies place video monitors in high-traffic areas (such as near cafeteria entrances or in break rooms) and replay videotaped messages constantly for viewing by passersby.

- *Telephones* have been in use for years, of course, and remain one of the most frequently used channels for downward communication in organizations. *Voice messaging* (or voice mail, or V-mail) is a telephone-based system whereby callers leave brief recorded messages for the receiver. Such systems can range from relatively simple telephone answering machines to extremely sophisticated organization-wide networks. The receiver can decide when to listen to the recorded messages, although the messages typically must be listened to in the order in which they were received.

PROBLEMS WITH DOWNWARD COMMUNICATION

In most organizations, a variety of problems commonly afflict downward communication. Frequently, for example, *messages are not received*. Announcements, e-mails, or letters often are not read, meetings are poorly attended, needed corrective interviews are not conducted, and so on. But just as frequently, *information overload* occurs. Too many messages are sent by the organization, so that employees are bombarded with letters, memos, bulletin board announcements, meetings, and the like. For example, one manager reported to one of the authors that his normal practice was to start his work day by deleting all of the 250 or so e-mails he had received since the last time he checked. "If the message is really important, they'll send it again," he reasoned, never explaining how he distinguished a re-sent message from the other 249 he automatically deleted. Unfortunately, the massive use of e-mail in most organizations has led many to experience information overload and in turn has begun to limit the effectiveness of this communication tool.

Organizational bypassing often can occur as well, with top management communicating information directly to lower levels and, in the process, omitting one or more members of middle management who then must obtain the information from their staff—something that bothers many supervisors and managers a great deal, since in their view their role is to convey information to their staff, not hear it from them. *Distortion* or *filtering* can also occur as one person passes a message on to another, who in turn communicates that message to a third person, and so on. At each link in the communication chain, the message is changed and filtered slightly so that, by the time it reaches its final destination, it may bear little resemblance to the original form.

In addition, some organizations provide downward communications containing information employees don't particularly want to know while withholding information employees would like to hear. What types of information should be communicated downward? While many organizations confine their messages to "the 3 Bs" (babies, bowling, and birthdays), employees surveyed some time ago by Allstate Insurance said they want information that will help them understand the business and serve customers better; they want the "whys" behind the information they receive; and they want to receive integrated, coordinated, and reinforced messages. When asked to suggest ideas to make communication more effective, they said it should be straightforward and timely, should use supervisors and peers as key communicators, should be organized and delivered in a simple style, and should use face-to-face interactive approaches.[18]

Failure to use communication as a motivational tool is one final shortcoming typically seen with regard to downward communication. Several years ago, *Communication Briefings* suggested formally acknowledging employees' sacrifices and reminding them frequently of how much they are valued by the company, as well as involving them deeply in making decisions, offering them opportunities to learn new skills, giving them new titles or greater visibility, having lunches or coffee breaks involving upper management and employees, and providing inexpensive tangible rewards symbolic of the company's appreciation (such as pens or plaques). Such efforts can be extremely useful in organizations that simply do not have the funds to provide pay increases to all employees.[19] These principles, greatly expanded upon, later served as the basis for two top-selling books, *1001 Ways to Reward Employees* and *1001 Ways to Energize Employees*.[20]

Effective downward communication most often is achieved through a thoughtful and strategic combination of oral, written, and electronic messages. Written messages are easily distributed and consistent in form, but do not allow feedback or further discussion. Oral messages allow interaction, but may be transmitted inconsistently (or not at all) from person to person or group to group. Transmitting messages electronically often limits interaction as well and may require a certain level of skill and technological sophistication that not all organizations or employees possess. Thus, the most effective downward communication process might be written or electronically communicated announcements, followed by individual or group discussions that are then summarized in writing for permanence. For communicating particularly important messages, using a combination of written, oral/face-to-face, and electronic channels is usually most effective.

Upward Communication

Communication sent from lower to higher levels of an organization constitutes *upward communication*. Like downward communication, messages flowing upward are vital to an organization's success. Employees' ideas, concerns, reactions, and recommendations are extremely valuable resources that are tapped only when upward communication works effectively. Also, like downward communication, upward messages can be sent in writing or orally, and can be done via electronic media.

WRITTEN UPWARD COMMUNICATION

- *Employee opinion surveys* ask employees to report anonymously their perceptions, attitudes, and values so that management can determine what actions, if any, are needed to improve employees' feelings toward the organization.

- *"Write to know" or "gripevine" systems* typically allow employees to write messages, often anonymously, to management and to see their answers published in an employee newsletter or posted on a bulletin board designated for that purpose.

- *Suggestion boxes or suggestion systems* are often effective in obtaining employee input, although their effectiveness tends to wane over time. Typically, these

---

Business Brief 2.1

Effective Communication Is Central to Participative Management

Many leaders like to think of themselves as fostering an open, supportive communication climate, where employees feel free to tell them what they really think. But what should manages actually *do* to foster such a climate? Based on the University of Michigan's research on effective management, the participative manager is someone who:

- Gives subordinates a share in important decision making
- Keeps subordinates informed of the true situation, good or bad, in all circumstances
- Is easily approachable
- Trains, counsels, and develops subordinates
- Shows thoughtfulness and consideration of others
- Is willing to make changes in the way things are done
- Is willing to support subordinates, even when they make mistakes

Source: Patricia Hayes Andrews and Richard T. Herschel, *Organizational Communication: Empowerment in a Technological Society* (Boston: Houghton Mifflin, 1996), 74.

---

systems provide some recognition and reward to employees whose suggestions save money or improve operations in the organization. Interestingly, the concept of soliciting employee suggestions has been in use for a very long time. Scottish shipbuilder William Denny is credited with starting the first employee suggestion program in 1880. He realized that the people who worked for him were experienced and knowledgeable in their crafts, so he let them know that if anyone had an idea that would help build better ships, he wanted to hear about it. While he did not operate a formal suggestion system, his was the first recorded instance of employee suggestions being solicited. A few years later, the Yale and Towne Manufacturing Company hung a suggestion box in its plant. The first formal suggestion system was put into operation by the National Cash Register Company in 1896; two years later, Eastman Kodak Company implemented a program that continues today—the oldest continuous suggestion program in the United States. At present, there are estimated to be as many as 6,000 formal suggestion systems in operation, and probably even more semiformal systems.[21]

- *Memoranda, letters, reports, and e-mails* are frequent channels for upward as well as downward communication. Just as members of organizational leadership keep lower-level management and staff informed via letters, memoranda, and the like, so too do organizational members keep their superiors informed through the use of memos, letters, and full-fledged reports. Indeed, there are times when the effectiveness of downward communication is enhanced through the use of upward communication. For example, one of the authors often advises managers of organizations that the most effective method of sending a letter of recognition, which usually is a form of downward communication, actually is to use it as a form of upward communication. That is, rather than writing a letter to the employee who performed well, the manager instead writes a letter to an upper-level executive extolling the outstanding things the employee achieved and sends the employee a copy of that letter. By so doing, the manager not only expresses appreciation for the employee's efforts (the only objective accomplished by the traditional downward letter of recognition) but also makes the employee feel even better by letting her see that senior leadership is aware of her achievements, plus the manager gains some positive personal visibility with senior leadership by praising the accomplishments of a staff member. In short, everyone wins.

E-mails are often an effective way to reach higher-level management since many executives spend most of their time in meetings; this system often is the only way in which these people can be reached by others in the organization.

- *Intranets* are also used by some companies to gather employee suggestions and feedback. After reading an announcement, for example, employees can send their responses to the originator of the announcement. Indeed, some companies include a brief questionnaire at the end of each story posted on the intranet to assess employees' interest in and understanding of the information provided.

- *Complaint or grievance procedures* allow employees to express, in formal terms, dissatisfaction with a decision that has impacted their work lives. Often, companies have not only a formal grievance form but an entire procedure whereby the employees can complete the form and express their grievance. They then proceed through a series of meetings ascending through the organization's hierarchy as they seek a satisfactory resolution to the problem.

- *Performance evaluations* traditionally have been used as a tool for downward communication, but some companies are instituting upward appraisal systems as well. The use of "360-degree" evaluations has spread rapidly over the past decade; for example, in 1992, AT&T developed a 40-question survey asking subordinates to evaluate the effectiveness with which their supervisors show respect, emphasize helping customers, promote teamwork and innovation, and maintain high standards. Now, many companies ask subordinates to provide (usually anonymously) input into the evaluations of their superiors' performance. The use of performance evaluations as an upward communication tool is based on the realization that a manager's "customers" are the people who work for him or her (and thereby are the recipients of that manager's communication skills) and that an assessment of "customer satisfaction" is an important element of improving managerial performance.

ORAL UPWARD COMMUNICATION

- *Open-door policies* tell employees that they are welcome to enter any manager's office with a question or concern whenever they wish. However, managers' doors too often are not open, and employees may be afraid to walk through those doors even when they are open. Thus, a more effective policy is the "open floor" approach, whereby managers leave their offices and *manage by walking around* (MBWA) and have informal conversations with employees in their workplaces. Indeed, several organizations have adopted MBWA as a formal expectation of all of their middle-level and senior leaders, although in one organization with which one of the authors consulted, disgruntled employees claimed that MBWA in their organization stands for "managing by walking away."

- *Formal grievance procedures* give employees some recourse when they have a complaint or feel they have been treated unfairly. While initiated in writing, usually by completing a form, grievances are then processed in formal interviews and hearings. In unionized companies, shop stewards or union business agents assist employees with their grievances, which typically are presented to successive levels of management until a solution is reached or taken to outside arbitration if a solution cannot be agreed upon. Nonunion companies occasionally have trained ombudspersons to assist grievants and may use employee committees to hear and resolve grievances.

- *Department or unit meetings* should serve as effective channels for upward and downward communication, with announcements being made and employee input sought by the manager conducting the meeting. However, too often entire meetings are devoted to announcements and information disseminated by the manager, with no time left for discussion or staff input. Thus, the authors often teach clients to conduct "employee operations meetings" in which staff members are asked to identify 1–3 things that most get in the way of them performing their jobs effectively, to analyze the causes of those things, and to develop solutions that will resolve, or at least improve, those issues.

- *Individual interviews* similarly should promote both upward and downward communication. During corrective or disciplinary interviews, for example, the employee's reactions should be solicited and heard, and his or her ideas for behavioral improvement should be sought and integrated into a plan of action.

- *Advisory committees* are formal bodies of employees who provide management with information about employee concerns, perceptions, and reactions. For example, Purdue University uses its Clerical and Service Staff Advisory Council to obtain advice from employees and hear their concerns; and JFK Medical Center in West Palm Beach, Florida, makes similar use of its Employee-Management Advisory Committee.

- *Task forces and problem-solving groups* often are formed to empower employees to identify, analyze, and resolve work-related problems. Quality circles and other participative problem-solving groups typically are used within individual departments, while task forces frequently involve people from a variety of areas throughout an organization.

- *Telephone hotlines* may be used to encourage employees to express their feelings or report problems anonymously. For example, many organizations have set up an "ethics and compliance hotline" whereby employees can report, anonymously if they choose, perceived violations of company ethics occurring within their facility. In addition, during times of crisis or difficult change, companies may create a temporary hotline employees can call for up-to-the minute information.

- *Voice messaging* is used for upward as well as downward communication since many executives spend most of their time in meetings; this system often is the only way in which these people can be reached by others in the organization.

PROBLEMS WITH UPWARD COMMUNICATION

Upward communication has its share of problems in organizations. First, **upward communication is subject to substantial distortion.** Specifically, subordinates may be especially reluctant to communicate negative information to superiors, particularly when those superiors seem to prefer hearing *positive* feedback more than they do hearing *accurate* feedback. Yet even the earliest of studies conducted in organizations demonstrated that when fear of punishment is reduced and trust runs high between employees and management, the accuracy of upward communication is greatly facilitated.[22]

Second, *some members of the organization actively discourage upward communication*. Weak supervisors, for example, will perform the organizational ritual called "CYA" (cover your posterior) by attempting to block communication between their employees and other members of management. They discourage employees from participating in opinion surveys, fail to conduct departmental meetings, falsify their monthly reports, and sharply criticize employees who "go around them" by talking to management or "hang out our dirty laundry" by taking problems to the personnel department. Naturally, it is imperative that top management discover and deal with these situations as quickly as possible.

Third, *upward communication can be intimidating to some employees*. Many find it difficult to talk to their superiors, choosing instead to smile and answer "everything's fine" when asked how things are going. Entering a manager's office

---

Business Brief 2.2

Using a Speakerphone

While an entire body of literature on e-mail etiquette has grown over the years (the Yahoo! search engine devotes an entire category to "netiquette" and lists more than 100,000 World Wide Web pages mentioning the subject), a Yahoo! search on speakerphone etiquette turns up only one Web site that mentions it. Yet communication over speakerphones is a daily event for many working in organizations. Consequently, you might consider the following suggestions for those occasions when you are talking on a speakerphone:

- Don't shake a can of peanuts (this happened during one call) or anything else that might make noise, especially if you're talking at the time.
- The same goes for shuffling or crumpling paper, eating crunchy food, or popping chewing gum.
- Don't type while you're talking or start a lengthy print job at the same time you make your call. Sometimes the speakerphone will magnify the sounds and the person on the other end won't hear what you're saying.
- Don't drum your fingers on the phone or on your desk.
- If you need to pick up the handset, do it gently. That noise gets magnified, too. In fact, you might announce that you're picking up the handset just before you do.
- Don't get up and walk around the room while you're talking.
- Don't shout. Today's phones transmit normal conversations.
- If the person on the other end asks you to pick up the handset to speak privately, do it—or make arrangements to talk about sensitive subjects on a separate call.
- Don't engage in side conversations with other people in your office.
- If there are others in your office, let the person you're phoning know at the very beginning of the call. And introduce everyone. That may save a lot of embarrassment.

Source: John T. Adams, "When you're on a speakerphone, don't make noise," *HR Magazine* (March 2001): 12.

via the open-door policy is virtually impossible for them, and writing a letter to the editor of the newsletter is too challenging. In many organizations, there is a "silent majority" of employees who simply are nervous about talking to the people over them.

Fourth, since upward channels allow criticism or negative feedback from employees, some **upward communication can be intimidating to management leadership** who prefer to live by the credo, "no news is good news," rather than risk hearing information that is upsetting, embarrassing, critical, or otherwise negative. We will return to this problem when we discuss small group communication in a later chapter.

Lastly, **employees simply may not know that management wants them to communicate upward**. While employees may want to contribute their ideas, express their thoughts, or voice their concerns to management, they may believe that reprisals might be taken against them if they complain, or that management simply is not interested in their input. For example, Robinson and Schroeder argue that too often managers give employees the impression that they are only on the lookout for "home runs"—the big ideas that will leave their competitors in the dust.[23] By doing this, they miss the less glitzy employee suggestions that would actually have a greater impact on day-to-day cost reductions and improvements. Their study of the employee suggestion systems of more than 150 companies led them to the conclusion that when it comes to generating ideas, more is better than bigger: "The best employee ideas systems encourage employees to come up with small ideas—and lots of them. The more ideas there are to choose from, the more good ideas will emerge." For example, at Grapevine Canyon Ranch in southeastern Arizona, owner Eve Searle meets with employees every two weeks, and each employee is expected to show up with one idea that will improve some aspect of the ranch's operations. Innovations that have come out of these sessions include adding a step stool in the van for guests, stocking alcohol-free cider for

---

Business Brief 2.3

Soliciting Ideas

According to Robinson and Schroeder, there are some simple principles organizations should keep in mind as they solicit ideas from employees:

1. Make it easy for employees to suggest ideas—if more information is needed, you can ask the employee for it later.

2. Create a departmental "ideas board" where everyone can post problems and solutions.

3. Order pizza and discuss employee ideas over an extended lunch.

4. Encourage everyone to identify things that make their work difficult, waste money, or distract from the customer experience, and then think of ways to fix them.

5. Nix the reward systems. They run counter to the concept of working together as a team and are difficult and costly to implement. Better to do something that shows the entire group you value their ideas, such as taking them out to lunch or buying a new refrigerator for the break room with the money saved from their suggestions.

Source: Alan G. Robinson and Dean M. Schroeder, *Ideas Are Free: How the Idea Revolution Is Liberating People and Transforming Organizations* (San Francisco: Berrett-Koehler, 2004).

nondrinkers celebrating anniversaries, and adding a screen to the kitchen door to save on cooling costs. None of these suggestions can be described as a big idea, "but the cumulative effect of these small ideas over time has made it possible for the ranch to attain exceptionally high levels of productivity and customer service."

In short, upward communication works best when organizations provide systems designed specifically to promote it and then use a great deal of downward communication to actively encourage it.

Horizontal Communication

The next major formal communication channel involves exchanges of messages among individuals on the same organizational level, or *horizontal communication*. Traditional organizations discouraged horizontal exchanges between individuals in different divisions because messages were supposed to be passed vertically throughout the organizational hierarchy. The assumption was that by following vertical flows, each message would touch all appropriate points of authority. Rank-and-file workers were neither expected nor trusted to work out their own problems without the assistance of their superiors. Today, however, emphasis on teamwork, participative decision making, and the "empowerment" of everyone throughout an organization makes horizontal communication among peers vital to organizational success.

TYPES OF HORIZONTAL (LATERAL) COMMUNICATION

Progressive organizations have implemented a variety of programs designed to improve horizontal communication and teamwork. Most of the written and oral methods listed above, which include electronic channels, are used frequently for lateral communication as well, but some other methods may also be utilized:

- *Team-building seminars* often are conducted by trained specialists to improve relations among individuals or groups that interact with one another in the workplace. Top-level executives, for example, may be taken on team-building retreats lasting several days, while nonsupervisory employees may simply meet in break areas to discuss ways of working together more effectively.

- *Cross-departmental visitation* is a simple but effective method for improving lateral communication. One department manager, for example, may invite the manager of another department to visit her or his work area, talk with employees, and discuss more effective and efficient ways in which the two departments might work together.

- *Committee meetings* occur when representatives from different departments or units meet to hear announcements or discuss problems of mutual concern. Most organizations, for example, conduct department head or management meetings designed to build horizontal communication. Too often, however, these meetings are dominated by the leader and serve only as a channel for downward messages.

- *Work teams* are being used with greater frequency to manage the operation of individual units in an organization. Semiautonomous or autonomous groups of employees often meet to plan their work schedules, assign duties, review their own performance and progress, and even hire or dismiss team members. For example, Epson, a leading maker of printers for personal computers, devel-

---

Business Brief 2.4

Building Teamwork

Several methods can be used to build a sense of teamwork among organizational members. In its simplest form, team building is the guided discussion of several questions, through which the team members examine themselves and decide how their teamwork might be improved. Questions commonly considered in team building meetings include:

- What would we be like if we were an ideal team?
- What are we like now as compared to that ideal?
- How do we need to change?
- How can we change?
- How, specifically, will we change?
- What things can each of us do to help other team members more?
- What things can each of us do to support and encourage other team members to adhere to the commitments we have made?

The decisions made by the group should be written down and distributed to each member, as well as to any person to whom the team reports. When done well, the team building meeting (or series of team building meetings) will improve the relationships among team members and, in so doing, improve communication and cooperation among them.

Sources: Based on William I. Gordon and Roger J. Howe, *Team Dynamics* (Dubuque, IA: Kendall/Hunt, 1977); William G. Dyer, *Team Building: Issues and Alternatives* (Reading, MA: Addison-Wesley, 1977).

---

oped a bizarre-sounding method of developing new products called "scrum and scramble." This method, also known to company insiders as the "rugby team" approach to product development, is vastly different from the traditional "relay team" approach where a new product is passed sequentially from the design department, to the engineering department, to the production department, and so on. Under the "scrum and scramble" approach, a hand-picked, multidisciplinary team, with its members working from start to finish on the development process, "passes the ball back and forth" as they complete the entire process.

- *Virtual work teams* are formed through the use of electronic media—videoconferences, intranets, conference calls—that allow horizontal communications among groups of people who never meet one another face-to-face. As businesses become more interconnected and more global, they must learn to make faster and smarter strategic decisions and to take advantage of technological advancements. A key part of that decision making is the use of "virtual teams"—groups of people who work together, even though they may be located in different offices, different time zones, and even different continents. Virtual teams may have a global reach or involve combinations of local telecommuting members and more traditional in-house workers. Team members may deal with key players who are not only out of the country but also work for another organization, perhaps as suppliers who are on the virtual team to add information and technical support.

Highlighting Diversity

Cross-Cultural Challenges in Virtual Teams

Many companies are increasingly turning to virtual teams for all kinds of creative projects. Bakbone Software, Microsoft, and Ford all use virtual teams to do everything from developing computer chips to designing the latest model cars. Even so, when virtual teams are made up of workers from diverse cultures, challenges abound.

Here is one example: North Americans have a "need for speed" and seem to enjoy the efficiency of sparse, sometimes disjointed, prose when communicating by e-mail. They also like fast responses. Japanese virtual team members, by contrast, bring a different set of needs, customs, and work ethic to the virtual team experience. The Japanese tend to be more proper in carefully crafting their messages and responses. They also view a written message, devoid of nonverbal communication elements, as incomplete and difficult to interpret. Most believe their own English (which is usually quite good) to be flawed; as a result, they tend to remain quiet and to agree with others, rarely stating their own views.

Some scholars suggest that effectively managing organizations that use cross-cultural virtual teams is 90% reliant on people skills and only 10% on technology.

Sources: Steve Alexander, "Virtual Teams Going Global," *InfoWorld* 22 (November 13, 2000): 55–56; Jessica Lipnack and Jeffrey Stamps, *Reaching Across Space, Time, and Organizations with Technology* (New York: Wiley and Sons, 1997).

Naturally, other communication channels already described, such as e-mail, voice mail, telephone calls, memos, and letters, can carry communications between peers. As organizations continue their efforts to "flatten" their hierarchy and move toward self-managing and team-oriented organizational models, horizontal communication will continue to take on greater importance.

PROBLEMS WITH HORIZONTAL (LATERAL) COMMUNICATION

Horizontal communication should serve to solve problems, promote cooperation, and improve the overall effectiveness and efficiency of the organization. Unfortunately, *many organizations do little to encourage horizontal communication.* In fact, highly competitive organizations may even discourage it, directly or implicitly. Employees who are eager to obtain rewards for their work may not be willing to share bright ideas or coveted data with peers who are after the same, usually limited, rewards. By the same token, managers may believe that their workers will, in fact, be more productive in an atmosphere that encourages *competition* and rewards selectively. When this is true, horizontal communication usually decreases or becomes routine.

Even when organizations want colleagues to communicate freely and frequently, such a goal is not readily accomplished because of *specialization*. The highly skilled machinist uses a specialized vocabulary, as does the neurosurgeon, the corporate lawyer, the engineer, the chemist, and the accountant. Yet many large organizations bring all these specialists together under the same professional roof. While informal social chitchat may be manageable, serious exchanges of task-relevant information are far more difficult. One way of dealing with this problem is to hire employees who have a good general background of education and experience, with their specialization representing only one aspect of their

Highlighting Technology

Online Communication and the Medical Community

Joan Barber is an MD in Santa Cruz, California, who starts her day by reading her e-mail. On this particular day, the first message she reads is a critical blood test, red-flagged by a lab's computer when it was sent the night before. Dr. Barber sends a copy of the results to the referring doctor and suggests immediate follow-up. Over the next 30 minutes, she reads and sends more than a dozen messages. She approves an experimental treatment, forwards a prescription request to her assistant, and consults online with two colleagues concerning whether surgery is warranted for a patient they share.

Dr. Barber is using an Internet messaging system that links 150 doctors throughout Santa Cruz with two hospitals, a dozen labs, an independent practice association, and insurance companies. More than 160,000 patients are also registered to use the system. Unlike ordinary e-mail, all communications are coded to ensure confidentiality. "It has freed me to spend more time with my patients," Dr. Barber claims, estimating that the system saves her office hundreds of hours in paperwork and telephone calls. She even credits the system with saving the life of an 11-year-old patient suffering from acute kidney disease by getting approvals to see a specialist in just days—a process that normally can take weeks for an HMO patient. Her biggest gripe: trying to reach colleagues who aren't online. "They might as well be on the moon," she complains.

The growth of online communication among members of the medical community is increasing with incredible speed. Still, there are issues that eventually will have to be resolved.

• Can doctors be held legally responsible if they fail to answer an e-mail?

• What about privacy issues for patients using e-mail at work?

Despite concerns such as these, the future is clear: graduates from medical school will need skills in using this communication technology, as well as an effective "bedside manner."

Source: Michael Meduno, "Prognosis: Wired," *Hospitals & Health Networks* 72 (November 5, 1998): 28–35.

interests and skills. In addition, many organizations hold regular meetings that bring together individuals from different divisions. These people should take turns talking about their work, skills, and frustrations in jargon-free language that can be understood by those not familiar with their areas of specialization. Through efforts such as these, many companies are achieving noteworthy improvements in their lateral communication and teamwork.

External Communication

Increasingly, organizations are realizing that effective communication with external audiences is crucial. Certainly, communication targeted to potential customers (in the form of advertising or public relations) long has been an important element of organizational communication. Now, however, companies have come to realize that effective communication with suppliers, customers, consumers, governmental agencies, and the general public is vital to organizational success.

Communication between an organization and its environment can involve many of the same types of written and oral forms, which may include electronic channels, used for internal organizational communication.

WRITTEN EXTERNAL COMMUNICATION

- *Newspaper and magazine press releases* are distributed by an organization to communicate its message to readers.

- *Newspaper and magazine stories* written about an organization may carry either laudatory information (as when the company engages in some act of good community citizenship) or information the organization would just as soon *not* have communicated (such as an unfavorable review of the organization's products or some internal scandal the organization wished to suppress).

- *Brochures and publications* describe the products and services of the organization to prospective customers, summarize the financial achievements of the organization for shareholders and the public (in the form of quarterly or annual reports, for example), or recruit new organization members.

- *Web sites* have, for many organizations, come to supplement or even replace more traditional forms of external communication. Many companies put on their site information about the company that also appears in any published brochures they distribute. Indeed, since brochures tend to be costly, while Web site space is virtually free, most organizations put far more information on their Web sites than they do in print form. In addition, organizations may include links to key organizational offices, such as human resources (for employment inquiries), customer service (for service issues), or technical assistance (for help in working with company products). Some also include an online survey soliciting customer perceptions of the products or services the organization offers.

- *Electronic mail* can be used extensively by companies to get information from or communicate it to their environment.

Highlighting Technology

Online Learning

Electronic media make useful information available to members of today's organizations. For example, to support sales professionals' self-development efforts, Virginia-based Max-Pitch Media, Inc., launched a Web site called www.Justsell.com. The Web site's founders, two former salesmen, envision it as a sort of college of sales knowledge. "We want to create a community where people can hang out and exchange ideas about selling," said Jim Gould, cofounder along with his partner Sam Parker. The site is written with a particular bent toward the needs of small business. Recently, for example, the commentary section of the site offered a three-part, step-by-step series on how to hire a company's first sales representative, including writing a recruitment ad, structuring an interview, asking the right questions, and sifting through candidates. Other articles deal with how to target a market, size up the competition, and discover the real reasons customers choose not to buy from you. The "Sales Mine" section links readers to top stories about selling from a range of magazines and filters the best sales-related information from online sources, describing it in a one paragraph summary. Indeed, the research and self-development efforts historically undertaken by employees in libraries and college night courses now are being enhanced by online information resources done in the convenience of one's home.

Source: Mary Connors, "Go Online to Locate Tips on Salesmanship," *Crain's Chicago Business* 21 (November 9, 1998): 25.

ORAL EXTERNAL COMMUNICATION

Oral (including face-to-face) communication also can be used by organizations to communicate with their environment:

- *Tours* of company facilities, conducted for members of the general public or for the media, can be useful in acquainting the public with company operations.

Highlighting Civic Engagement and Ethics

Who Are the Best Corporate Citizens?

While we tend to associate civic engagement with individual participation, corporations too can choose to act ethically and responsibly—through the way they treat their employees, interact with the environment, and make contributions to the greater society. Beginning in the year 2000, *Business Ethics* published an issue in which they named the "100 Best Corporate Citizens" and based their scores on a corporate social responsibility index. Each company was rated in these areas:

- Environmental Stewardship
- Community Relations
- Employee Relations
- Diversity
- Customer Relations

In 2004, some of the top companies honored as "offering model business strategies in good corporate citizenship" were the following:

- *Fannie Mae,* in 2003, financed over $240 billion in home mortgages for 1.6 million minority first-time buyers. As a part of this, the company created a Native American Conventional Lending Initiative to help finance $75 million in loans on trust land for the Navajo Nation of Arizona, the Oneida Nation of New York, and the Menominee of Wisconsin.

- *Proctor & Gamble* created technology that helps people in developing nations clean and disinfect water inexpensively at home. P&G has been the most consistent civic engagement performer. In business in Cincinnati, Ohio, since 1837, it has placed in the top five for social responsibility all five years.

- *Green Mountain Coffee Company* pays fair trade prices for coffee beans from farmer cooperatives in Peru, Mexico, and Sumatra. Its CAFE (Community Action for Employees) program enables its employees to take paid time off to volunteer in their community wherever they see a need. Green Mountain volunteers also visit coffee-growing communities in Mexico and Central America where they work on projects to improve the health care and housing of coffee farmers and their families.

- *John Deere & Company* recently decided to forgo selling prime real estate to a developer, instead donating $1.5 million in land and facilities to Western Illinois University, thus allowing the university to better serve the community. In addition, since 1975, the company's lost-time injuries rate has dropped 94%.

- *Kodak* has cutting-edge antidiscrimination polices for gay, bisexual, and transgender employees. These policies have also earned the company the rare distinction of receiving a perfect score from the Human Rights Campaign, an organization working to end sexual-orientation discrimination.

Source: "100 Best Corporate Citizens for 2004: Companies That Serve a Variety of Stakeholders Well" [online]. Available: http://www.business-ethics.com/100best.htm (accessed: August 15, 2004).

- *Large group meetings* may be conducted for shareholders or for the general public. For example, when two Massachusetts hospitals—Leonard Morse Hospital in Natick and Framingham Union Hospital in Framingham—merged to form MetroWest Medical Center, the chief executive officer of the new organization used large town meetings effectively to respond to and defuse community concerns about losing their community hospitals.

- *Seminars and workshops* may be provided by organizations either as the core of their customer services (such as consulting firms specializing in supervisory and management training) or to augment their services and products (as when technicians from IBM teach customers how to use their newly purchased hardware).

- *Customer or supplier meetings* increasingly are being used to improve service, either by having customers communicate their preferences and expectations directly to groups of employees or by having suppliers meet with employees (their customers, in effect) to hear concerns and preferences regarding the suppliers' services or products.

- *Employment interviews* are an often overlooked channel of communication with the environment. For every position filled, there may be several candidates rejected. Yet those candidates' perceptions of the organization are strongly shaped by their interview experiences, making the employment interview an important channel of external communication as well.

- *Radio and television* serve as channels for advertising, for public service announcements, and for news about organizations.

- *Telephone communication* is key for most organizations; many companies provide in-depth training for employees in telephone courtesy and monitor employees' communication performance in telephone conversations with customers.

- *Voice messaging* can be used to record external messages for people who were unavailable when the call arrived.

- *Teleconferencing* via satellite is used by many organizations to conduct news conferences or to provide information to external audiences. A few organizations use this channel for internal communication as well, although it tends to be too expensive for frequent internal use.

- *Video communications* often are prepared and released to news services, customers, and other organizations in the environment as a means of communicating the organization's message in an interesting, compelling manner.

PROBLEMS WITH EXTERNAL COMMUNICATION

Communication to and from external audiences suffers from many of the same problems that afflict upward, downward, and lateral communication within organizations, such as *information overload, unreceived messages,* and *filtering and distortion.* Indeed, organizations have far less control over the distribution of messages sent to external audiences than they do over internally communicated messages, making these problems even more likely to occur.

Regardless of the external channel or channels chosen, several principles should be observed to minimize the impact of potential communication breakdowns. Communication consultant Frank Corrado claims that a formal plan for managing issues should be developed by every organization and that communication with external audiences should be carefully coordinated with internal communications.[24] In addition, the impact of external communication should be carefully and continually evaluated to ensure that the desired effects are being achieved. In this manner, then, relationships between organizations and their environment can be more effectively managed.

INFORMAL DIMENSIONS OF COMMUNICATION

Within every formal organization there also exists an informal organization in which a great deal of communication behavior occurs. Much communication in large organizations is informal, springing up whenever an individual feels a need to communicate with someone not connected by a formal organization channel. Whereas formal communication consists of messages the organization recognizes as official, informal messages do not follow official lines. Rather, informal networks often develop through a variety of factors that may not be related to organizational roles and goals, such as where people happen to be located physically in the organization, similarity of interests (as when people in various departments join the company softball team), or compatibilities of personalities. For example, employees may end up talking to each other and forming relationships simply because they have adjacent cubicles, enjoy NCAA basketball, or feel similarly about various social issues. Most employees are involved in several networks at the same time. Traditionally, many companies have viewed such communication as a "time waster" and an activity to be discouraged. Now, however, many more enlightened organizations recognize that among motivated, goal-directed employees, casual communication can do even more than formal communication to build organizational success.

As you might expect, informal communication is by far *the dominant form of oral interaction* in organizations. Indeed, in their best-selling book about corporate cultures, Deal and Kennedy suggested that 90 percent of what goes on in an organization has nothing to do with formal events.[25] Rather, the informal network, the "hidden hierarchy," is in reality how an organization operates. And the operation of informal networks is not necessarily bad. Peters and Waterman noted in *In Search of Excellence* that:[26]

> The excellent companies are a vast network of informal, open communications. The patterns and intensity cultivate the right people getting into contact with each other, regularly, and the chaotic/anarchic properties of the system are kept well under control simply because of the regularity of contact and its nature (for example peer versus peer in quasi-competitive situations).

The "Grapevine"

It is not uncommon to find writers referring to informal message behavior as *grapevine communication*. Information introduced into the grapevine travels quickly because it is not inhibited by structural constraints. Although we tend to publicly discredit information we receive through the grapevine, research has shown that it is *amazingly accurate*. Scholars have consistently reported 78 to 90 percent accuracy figures in their extensive studies of grapevine communication in organizational settings. When errors do occur, however, they are often of a critical or dramatic nature.

Probably the most negative attribute of the grapevine is that it serves as a network through which **rumors** travel. Unlike much grapevine activity, which consists of verifiable informal communication, rumors are unconfirmed; that is, they are devoid of supporting evidence or cited sources. Rumors develop in part because employees perceive the formal communication system as inadequate. Whenever there are organizational policies that foster secrecy or superiors and subordinates who regard each other suspiciously, rumors are likely to flourish. For some, participation in rumor transmission may serve as an emotional safety valve to relieve frustrations and worries.

In their classic study of rumor transmission, Allport and Postman noted that rumors spread both as a function of their *importance* and their *ambiguity*.[27] If you are up for promotion and you hear through the grapevine that a promotion decision has been made, you are quite likely to discuss this rumor with others, especially your friends. The issue is vital to you and the message is ambiguous. Who was promoted? When did it happen? Why haven't you been officially informed? Myth has it that certain people function as specialists in rumor transmission, but research does not confirm this notion. Whether or not an individual will pass on a rumor usually depends on the individual's degree of interest in the rumor, perception of others' interest in the rumor, access to others, and personal goals. Relatively few people who receive rumors actually transmit them. Those who do often tell a cluster of others, only a few of whom will send the message further. Figure 2.2 depicts a typical rumor cluster chain.

Generally, communication experts suggest that managers do several things to defend against destructive rumors, including:

- Keep employees well-informed (so that rumors do not occur to fill an information void).

- Create opportunities for employees to report the rumors that are going around (such as regular meetings where current rumors are solicited).

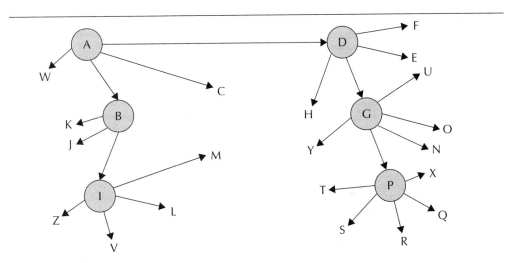

Note: Only circled letters represent active rumor transmitters.

Figure 2.2   Typical rumor transmission pattern: the cluster chain

- Pay attention to the rumors that are going around (to identify issues that are important to employees and may need official attention).
- Act promptly (before rumors spread and attitudes harden).
- Enlighten personnel (both to provide them with accurate information and to call their attention to the potential destructiveness of rumors).

The grapevine is a part of organizational reality—a natural outgrowth of humans being together. Managers who do not admit to the grapevine's existence usually have trouble. Managers who try to stamp out the grapevine with such policies as "employees must not discuss their salaries with each other" also have trouble. Policies to that effect simply tend to drive the discussions underground.

Keith Davis, who has studied grapevine communication for more than 20 years, believes that management should accept the *grapevine as an inevitable fact of organizational life*. He points out that "if properly guided, it can help build teamwork, company loyalty, and the kind of motivation that makes people want to do their best. It may weld the group together more effectively than company policy and other formal tools of the organization."[28] It is vital that managers be in touch with informal networks, participate in them, learn from them, and use them carefully to disseminate information.

Blogs as Informal Communication

One final form of informal communication that extends beyond an organization's boundaries but nevertheless can have a significant impact on the organization is the *blog*. The word blog—it works as both a noun and a verb—is short for Web log. It was coined in 1997 to describe a Web site where you can post daily journal-style scribblings about whatever you like. Unlike traditional media sources, bloggers focus their efforts on narrow topics, often becoming self-proclaimed experts. Blogs can be about anything: politics, sex, baseball, haiku, car repair. There are blogs about blogs.

Most of America paid little attention to blogs until December 2002, when during Strom Thurmond's 100th birthday party, Trent Lott made what sounded like a nostalgic reference to Thurmond's past segregationist leanings. The mainstream press largely glossed over the incident, but the blogs didn't—and Washington insiders and media honchos read blogs. Three days after the party, the story was on *Meet the Press*. Four days afterward, Lott made an official apology. After two weeks, Lott was out as Senate majority leader.[29]

Blogs have also broken stories that ultimately became big media news. On April 21, 2004, a blogger from Arizona named Russ Kick posted photographs of coffins containing the bodies of soldiers killed in Iraq and Afghanistan and of *Columbia* astronauts. The military zealously guards images of service members in coffins, but the blogger pried the photos free with a Freedom of Information Act request. "I read the news constantly," he said, "and when I see a story about the government refusing to release public documents, I automatically file an FOIA request for them." By April 23, the images had gone from Kick's blog to the front page of newspapers across the country.

Many organizations now assign one or more staff members from their marketing or public relations functions to track blogs daily, just to see what is being said informally about them, their competition, and potential customers.

Business Brief 2.5

Exploring Blogs

Here are five sites that, at the time of this writing, make it easy to find, organize, and keep tabs on your favorite bloggers:

- http://www.Kinja.com is one of the best ways to sample and automatically subscribe to a wide range of blogs, which are divided into 12 categories, from movies to politics to baseball. Click on a subject and up pops a listing of short excerpts from current postings. If you see one you like, simply click on the + button to have it added to your digest, which reads like a personalized online newsletter of new posts from your favorite blogs.

- http://www.Bloglines.com lets you organize your blogs in much the same way that your browser sorts its bookmarks. After creating a free account, you choose the blogs you want to track.

- http://www.Feedster.com is a search engine dedicated to indexing and finding the particular blogs you are after. Scanning more than 500,000 sources, it presents you with either the most recent posts or the most commented-on blogs, whichever you choose.

- http://www.Technorati.com lists the top-10 current events, books, and general news that people are blogging about.

- http://www.Blogdex.net presents the most contagious, or fastest spreading, ideas in the Web log community.

THE COMMUNICATION SYSTEM: TECHNOLOGICAL BENEFITS AND CHALLENGES

As John Naisbitt and other trend forecasters foresaw, information technology is booming in organizations today.[30] Voice mail, e-mail, teleconferencing, the World Wide Web, company intranets, cellular telephones, and laptop and handheld computers all have helped to link organizational members wherever they happen to be, whenever they wish.

Greengard reports, for example, that nearly every Fortune 200 corporation has instituted an *intranet*.[31] In turn, these electronic systems have proved extremely effective in improving efficiency and saving time. Employees at Ostram-Sylvania in Danvers, Massachusetts, now can handle their own records updates without any assistance from the Human Resources Department, and benefits information and job postings all are handled automatically online. If a manager wants a job posting to expire on a particular date, she simply enters the data into a field and the event will take place. Not only has this eliminated paper and work, it also has reduced hiring time from weeks to days. In addition, the system has saved the company nearly $150,000 per year in data collection and reporting costs, and recent employee surveys show employees are pleased with the new system.

Now, companies are beginning to take yet another step forward. This is what James Barksdale, president and chief executive officer of Mountain View, California-based Netscape Communications Corp., refers to as "the beginning of a whole new attitude in business about how to communicate—within the business, among employees and managers, as well as between the business and its external constituents: partners, customers and vendors."[32] This new development, which has been called the *extranet*, involves designing private networks so that data can flow freely between companies. A growing number of organizations have realized the value of linked databases. For example, Oracle Corp. of Redwood City, California, now conducts open benefits enrollment for more than 8,500 employees in only three weeks. Here's how it works: Oracle's intranet contains a link to pages on Aetna's Web site that have been specially designed for Oracle employees. Using a variety of electronic forms and hyperlinks, employees can step through the entire enrollment process online—even choosing a doctor

---

Highlighting Technology

Developing a Technological Vocabulary

A glossary of some useful Internet and intranet terms:

domain.   The name of a computer or a service on the Internet—referred to by the characters following the symbol @ in an online address.

download.   Receive a file from another computer.

firewall.   Hardware or software that protects a private network from an unsecured or public network.

FTP (file transfer protocol).   An Internet protocol for transferring files to and from another server over a network.

groupware.   An application that enables users to collaborate over a network.

home page.   The first page of a Web site or a group of HTML documents.

HTML (hypertext markup language).   The language in which World Wide Web documents are formatted.

hyperlink.   A linking mechanism that allows a user to jump from one Web page, graphic, or document to another.

Internet.   The world's largest computer network, which enables users to send e-mail, transfer files, participate in newsgroups, and access the World Wide Web.

intranet.   A private network that uses Internet software and standards.

Java.   An object-oriented language, developed by Sun Microsystems, that creates distributed Web applications.

newsgroup.   An electronic bulletin board on which users can post and exchange messages.

SSL (secure sockets layer).   A method of authentication and data encryption between a Web server and a Web browser.

upload.   The process of transmitting a file to another computer.

URL (uniform resource locator).   A standardized character string that identifies the location of an Internet document. Also known as a Web address.

Web browser.   Software that requests and displays HTML documents and other Internet or intranet data, such as Microsoft Outlook or Internet Explorer.

World Wide Web.   Part of the Internet; a worldwide, HTML-based, hypertext-linked information system.

Source: Samuel Greengard, "Internet/Intranet Glossary of Useful Terms," *Workforce* 76, no. 3 (March 1997): 82.

directly from insurance provider Aetna. Employees of Houston-based Compaq Computer Corp. can access their 401(k) accounts by linking directly to a financial institution's or a mutual fund provider's computer to make investment decisions or reallocate their assets.

Recruitment and Hiring

An important technological tool, the World Wide Web, has allowed corporations to improve their recruitment efforts by marketing themselves directly to college students and professionals, 24 hours a day. As resumes come in, they are automatically routed into databases. When managers need to fill a position, they can search keywords and find top prospects. Then, using videoconferencing software over the Internet, it's even possible to conduct a preliminary interview.

Many prominent companies are using the Web for recruitment. Since Silicon Graphics, a Mountain View, California, manufacturer of computer workstations, went live with its Internet site (http://www.sgi.com) it has collected 4,000 to 12,000 resumes each month. More than one-quarter of new hires now come to the organization through cyberspace. IBM's CyberBlue site (http://www.cybrblu.ibm.com) offers searchable job postings, job fair information for college students, benefits information, a resume builder, and a page that links to some of the most entertaining sites on the Web, including "The Dilbert Zone." Other companies have found that services such as WorkTree (http://www.worktree.com), Career Builder (http://www.careerbuilder.com), Job-Hunt (http://www.job-hunt.org), MonsterTrak (http://www.monstertrak.com), JobWeb (http://www.jobweb.com), and the Monster Board (http://www.monster.com) provide quick ways to get job postings on the Web without establishing their own sites. Job seekers also can set up a "personal search agent" by, for example, going to http://www.careerbuilder.com and conducting a "quick job search," then on the search results page, click on the "e-mail me jobs like these" button, and finally follow the on-screen instructions to choose which days you would like to have job postings automatically e-mailed to your in-box.

Technology now is playing an important role in employment interviews, too. A *Chicago Tribune* article described one person's experience. After New Yorker Laura McCormick did well in a phone interview with an executive at Kinko's, Inc.'s, headquarters in Ventura, California, she was invited for a second interview—at Kinko's video conference center in Manhattan. "It was very exciting," McCormick recalled. "I could see the person I was speaking to on one video monitor and could see my own face on another, so I knew how I was coming across. The interview was at least an hour and a half, and I developed a personal rapport with the person, much more than over the phone." Paul Ray, president of Ray & Berndtson, a New York-based executive search firm, said:[33]

> When doing a search, interviewing by video is often an expedient way of narrowing the prospect list to the best two or three, who you would then arrange to interview personally. At the senior levels, it's still face-to-face, but it won't be long before everybody has a laptop on their desk with videoconferencing capability.

Since resumes are easy and inexpensive to submit online, many employers receive a flood of e-mailed resumes for every opening they advertise. In addition, applicants are able to post resumes on some sites so they can be inspected by employers. In this highly competitive arena, it is important to use some tactics that help to achieve the best results, according to Dave Driscoll, director of career services for DeVry Institute of Technology in Long Island City, New York.[34]

First, be sure that all of your resume material is Internet friendly. Indeed, one common mistake is using a resume that cannot be read by computers. Driscoll suggests that "electronic resumes need to be simple in style; all content should be left-justified and you should avoid bullets, italics, boldface type and variations in font size." Rather than using formatting tricks to make your resume stand out, Driscoll suggests that you emphasize content by, for example, emphasizing activities you have been involved with, "such as projects or presentations that demonstrate 'soft skills,' like communication, leadership, or your ability to work effectively with a team." In addition, proper grammar and spelling are key: since the written word represents you, typos and misspellings are equivalent to looking shabby or having poor communication skills during a face-to-face interview.

Since many computer-based searches are keyword based, it might help to include a set of keywords at the bottom of your resume. The Occupational Information Network's database of job descriptions, O*NET OnLine http://www.onetcenter.org includes numerous examples of keywords and phrases for hundreds of jobs. In addition, if an ad for a particular job includes a particular set of keywords, you should try to include them in your resume as well, making it more likely that it will surface in the organization's computer search. For example, if an ad for a receptionist includes the phrase "Looking for someone who is able to organize, plan, and prioritize work and maintain positive interpersonal relationships," your resume might include similar keywords, such as "Kept XYZ Company work flow moving smoothly by organizing messages for staff based on time and priority" or "assisted the organization's public relations efforts by maintaining positive relationships with customers and sales staff." We will further examine resume writing in a later chapter on the employment interview.

Crisis Management

When the terrorist attack of September 11, 2001, occurred in New York, Aon Corporation, a Chicago-based international insurance and consulting firm, faced the same tasks faced by other organizations that were devastated by the fall of the New York twin towers: dealing with the immediate crisis, and then picking itself up from the devastating blow and getting its business operations up and running again as soon as possible. Aon had to accomplish those tasks in a city hundreds of miles away from its headquarters, where its surviving employees were wandering the chaotic streets with tens of thousands of other displaced workers, cut off from company e-mail, fax machines, and phones. "So we had to invent a new plan," said Melody Jones, vice president and chief human resources officer. "With everything else down, we decided to use the company Web site. That seemed like the only option we had."[35]

One major part of the challenge Aon faced was simply locating and reestablishing contact with employees who were scattered in the streets or suddenly stranded in airports around the globe. But that was just the start. They also had to develop strategies for providing employees with up-to-date information about the disaster, access to services such as health coverage and grief counseling, and assistance in getting back to work. And they had to convey messages from top executives, reassuring employees that they and the company would make it through the ordeal and work together through the stages of recovery. Lastly, they had to provide help to people who in some cases were cut off from the company's usual channels of communication.

Aon used a wide variety of communication technologies to meet these challenges. When the crisis struck, Aon quickly manned a phone bank and started calling employees' home numbers in the hope of locating them. At the same time, Aon established a toll-free number that employees and their families could use both to get information and to share it. In addition, since survivors of the attack probably didn't have their company laptops with them and thus did not have the special security software they needed to access the company's intranet, Aon used the company's Web site, with a quickly redesigned home page, as a portal for crisis communications. Two days after the attack, Aon chairman and CEO Patrick G. Ryan participated in a telephone conference call that also was Webcast, so that employees and their families could listen by using Windows Media Player. Aon also noticed another phenomenon—employees were communicating among themselves on a bulletin board at a personal Web site put up by an Aon employee.

Other companies directly affected by the September 11 attack also utilized technology to weather the crisis. Cantor Fitzgerald, Morgan Stanley Dean Witter, United Airlines, and numerous other companies utilized corporate Web sites as a key part of their crisis communications. Merrill Lynch, whose headquarters were destroyed in the attack, auto-dialed dislocated employees at home with a recorded message that directed them to a corporate Web site. This, in turn, helped them settle into temporary offices elsewhere in New York and New Jersey. Marsh & McLennan provided a Webcast of a memorial service at St. Patrick's Cathedral for employees killed in the attack, so that those who couldn't attend had an opportunity to feel they were part of the service.

Ultimately, through the careful but rapid use of a wide variety of technologies, these and other organizations were able to communicate with their workers and weather the September 11 crisis.

Knowledge Management

A relatively recent development within organizations is "knowledge management," termed by Greengard "the hottest idea spiraling through the corporate universe right now."[36] Collecting, culling, and trading information throughout organizations is nothing new, but companies now are using "knowledge management" in a thorough, systematic fashion to promote organization-wide communication. Buckman Laboratories in Memphis, Tennessee, established a series of "forums" on CompuServe so employees could share wisdom throughout the 1,200-person company. Using online forums, connected knowledge bases, electronic bulletin boards, libraries, and virtual conference rooms, employees began exchanging proposals, presentations, spreadsheets, technical specs, and more. The payoff was quick. When a Buckman sales representative approached the management of an Indonesian paper mill with a potential business deal, the

DILBERT

DILBERT © by Scott Adams; reprinted by permission of United Feature Syndicate, Inc.

plant's senior executives asked to see a detailed proposal within two weeks—a deadline that seemed impossible to meet. The sales rep went into the online forum and mentioned that he had a potential $6 million deal and needed sample proposals and information. Within two days, he had responses from other Buckman employees scattered across the globe, and he was able to go back to the customer with the proposal and make the sale.

Knowledge management uses technology to create the "learning organization" described in the next chapter and can give organizations a major competitive advantage. Thomas Koulopoulos, president of the Delphi Group, a Boston-based consulting firm, argues:[37]

> An organization's ability to quickly tap into wisdom gives it a competitive edge in the marketplace. Today, the challenge is to capture all the data, information, and interactions that occur so an organization can collectively benefit. Within many organizations, valuable knowledge too often disappears into a black hole.

Knowledge management can be categorized in three ways. First, "competency management" tracks skills and competencies throughout an organization by developing and maintaining a data bank of all employees' knowledge and skill areas. This information is used by the company to identify skill gaps and training needs that could endanger future performance, to guide decisions concerning recruitment and hiring, and to assemble cross-disciplinary teams of employees holding the knowledge and skills required for a particular project. "Knowledge sharing" is a form of knowledge management that uses intranets and online forums to spread knowledge throughout an organization, much as Buckman Laboratories uses technology to interconnect its employees worldwide. Finally, "competitive knowledge management" blends competency management and knowledge sharing. Arthur Andersen's business consulting division (now known as Accenture) established an intranet in 1996 where consultant firms posted information—work plans, methodologies, research, proposals, and resumes—so that others could tap into high-level expertise on an as-needed basis. A consultant at Arthur Andersen could log onto Arthur Andersen's intranet, fill in a search form, and instantly view the results. He or she could request information from specific functional areas, such as human resources, finance, or marketing, but could also mine for information outside the realm of individual departments.

Technology Issues

The emergence of electronic technology has not been without problems. The *Chicago Tribune* reports, "Now that we have instant communication, thanks to the new technology, some workers find it so daunting they call it 'information overload.'"[38] "Between e-mails, voice mails, and faxes, each day employees are exposed to more messages than ever before," observed Jeannie Glick, an employee communication consultant who cited a study by Pitney Bowes, Inc., showing that 71 percent of employees at the nation's top 1,000 firms "feel overwhelmed by the number of messages they receive." Another finding: 84 percent of respondents are interrupted by messages three or more times an hour. Glick concludes that "the reality is our technological ability to share information is more advanced than our human ability to process it, much less act on it."

The proliferation of technology also is straining other more traditional forms of communication in organizations, as many managers now "are trying to wrest back control of meetings from the insidious grip of wireless electronic devices that tempt participants to peek at messages, peck at keyboards, and sneak out for just one quick call."[39] For example, David Erickson, partner in charge of the security and technology practice at PricewaterhouseCoopers, conducts meetings according to this rule: for every 50 cell/PDA/Blackberry/computer-free minutes, he guarantees people a 10-minute break to use their wireless gadgets. Tom Rotherham, CEO of RSM McGladrey, Inc., a Minneapolis-based business consulting firm, fines meeting participants $50 for each violation of his no-devices-in-meetings rule. "You'd be surprised at how upset people get about paying $50," he says. In the last two years, since the company has instituted this practice, he has collected about $700 from his executive team. They used the money to take themselves out to dinner. The harsher the penalties the better, says Ann Marie Sabath, a business etiquette consultant who runs Cincinnati-based At Ease, Inc. "You have to make it hurt," she said, because "positive behavior modification doesn't work."

In addition, some organizations have applied technology inappropriately to situations that still require the human touch. Chris Serb reports:[40]

> According to a new Towers Perrin/Care Trac survey, Medicare HMO members truly appreciate plans that reach out to them via strong customer service. "If I were a Medicare HMO, I would retune my approach to the marketplace," says Stephen P. Wood, Towers Perrin's national practice leader for health plan consulting. "I would steer away from high-cost electronic media—the 'Have Betty White pitch your plan on TV' approach—and I'd get down to the physical approach, reaching out to people through visits and phone calls."

Research demonstrates that Medicare health maintenance organizations (HMOs) need to stay in touch with their members to gain a competitive advantage. But many fail to do that. Of seniors living in high-penetration managed care markets, just over a quarter received follow-up phone calls from health plans once they signed up. Yet seniors place a premium on that type of contact: 87 percent view those calls very favorably. In addition, only 36 percent of seniors in HMOs say they have received a visit from HMO sales reps, while at the same time 93 percent credit visits from a sales rep with helping them to choose their health plan. The upshot, according to the survey, is that the personal touch leads to loyalty. Phone calls, sales rep visits, and a knowledgeable support staff can give a company a competitive advantage over other health plans and traditional Medi-care. But too often, companies rely on impersonal media technologies to maintain contact with their clientele.

Clearly, knowledge of *how* to use today's burgeoning communications technology is important. But so too is knowing *when* to use it.

SUMMARY

At the beginning of this chapter, we made two assertions: first, much of your professional success will come through participation in some organization (or groups of organizations), and second, your professional success will be determined to a significant extent by your skills as a communicator. Learning to function effectively in an organizational setting requires considerable understanding of organizations, how they are structured, and the underlying principles that have influenced their traditions and contributed to their culture. The inability to communicate effectively in organizations can result in feelings of powerlessness and anonymity, and in the experience of being passed over when important committee assignments are made or promotion opportunities arise. It is not enough simply to know your stuff. You must also be able to communicate with others about your knowledge, ideas, and suggestions for change. To be able to inform others, to ask good questions, to listen carefully, and to persuade others—these are the basic elements of effective communication.

In this chapter, we have demonstrated the importance and diversity of communication within and between organizations. In writing, in communicating orally, and through electronic media, we continually exchange information, convey our ideas and opinions, render judgments, and assist in making decisions. Your future organizational experiences may take you into a business firm, a hospital, a school, or an industrial organization. You may function as a marketing analyst, an accountant, a teacher, a chef, or an executive. Whatever the organization or the specific function you fulfill, your daily activities, productivity, and pleasure will be greatly influenced by the quality of your communication interactions.

Questions for Discussion

1. Why is communication so important to success in an organization?
2. Since people already know how to talk to one another, why would formal training in communication skills be helpful for organizational success?
3. How is communication a "transactional process" in an organization?
4. How might communication serve to translate workers' abilities into job performance?
5. In your opinion, why has the amount of communication in organizations increased but the quality of communication has not improved?
6. What might cause an organization to take an "activities" approach to communication rather than a "results" approach?
7. Why might management be more comfortable with one-way communication?
8. What do you see as being some of the most serious problems with each of these modes of formal communication in organizations: downward, upward,

horizontal, and external? Offer at least one suggestion for improving the use of each channel.

9. If the grapevine is very active in an organization, should its leaders be worried? Why/why not?

10. In what ways might you consider using the Internet when you apply for your first job after college?

11. How might technology assist organizations in managing crises?

12. On balance, do you see technology as assisting or complicating organizational communication (or perhaps a bit of both)? Explain.

Exercises

1. Consider an organization with which you are very familiar. Describe the ways and extent to which this organization uses formal communication channels (downward, upward, horizontal, and external). What have been the organization's greatest challenges with these channels? In what ways have informal channels complicated or complemented the formal channels? Please provide specific examples.

2. Choose an organization of interest to you and arrange to interview one of its managers/leaders. Ask him/her about the ways in which the organization uses technology to communicate with employees, the public, customers, etc. Discuss benefits as well as challenges. If the organization has a Web site, be sure to visit it prior to your visit to help you prepare for the interview.

3. Go to the following Web site: http://www.business-ethics.com/100best.htm. There you will find information about a large number of organizations that have been named as the most socially responsible organizations over the past five years by the magazine *Business Ethics*. Choose one of these organizations, such as Hewlett-Packard, Eastman Kodak, Fannie Mae, or the St. Paul Companies. Using the Internet, investigate the company you selected. What actions and policies have led to this company being named as an outstanding corporate citizen? Can you discover any problems or flaws in the company's policies, actions, or reputation? On balance, do you feel this company deserved to be recognized for its sense of social responsibility in 2004? Why/why not?

Case Application 2.1   Communicating Difficult Information

Michael Johnston is a top supervisor in a large food manufacturing corporation. He must communicate some bad news to a number of the organization's employees (all of whom are under him in the organizational hierarchy). New, more stringent health regulations will require them to wear special caps to cover their hair, to wash their hands frequently with a special antibacterial soap, and to have two checkups per year with the company physician (instead of just one, as is the present practice).

Questions

1. Given your knowledge of downward communication, how should Johnston approach the communication of this information?

2. Should he utilize both formal and informal channels and both oral and written modes of communication? Why or why not?

3. What problems might he encounter, and what strategy might he use for overcoming them?

Case Application 2.2   Communicating Difficult Information

You are administrative assistant to the vice president for sales in a moderate-sized business firm. While your boss is extremely bright and superbly competent in her area, marketing, sales, and public relations, she tends to run a fairly authoritarian operation with minimal desire to let others assist her in decision making. She neither seeks nor is particularly receptive to feedback from anyone. While many lower-level employees are reluctant to discuss problems with *her*, they often come to *you* to complain about both task-related problems and the fact that they are frustrated with the managerial style of the vice president. You have known this woman for many years—first as a friend and only recently (for six months) as a boss. You have high regard for her as a person, but you are appalled at the lack of congruence between her general humanitarian philosophies and her conservative, rigid style of leadership.

Questions

1. Using your knowledge of communication behavior, how would you approach this situation?

2. How might your upward mobility aspirations figure into this?

3. Consider your probable feelings with regard to trust and status.

3

Organizational Culture, Leadership, and Followership

After reading this chapter, you should be able to:

❏ Explain the concept of "corporate culture" and how it is reflected in organizational communication practices and behaviors

❏ List and explain at least five organizational philosophies and their implications for communication practices and behaviors

❏ Identify at least five critical communication practices that differentiate one philosophy from another

❏ List and explain at least four characteristics of effective followers

❏ Identify which organizational philosophies seem best suited to meeting the key issues organizations face today, and explain why

In every organization, communication is of vital importance. Indeed, without it, the organization by definition could not exist. However, the forms, functions, and frequencies of communication vary from one organization to the next. In some organizations, employees are involved in making meaningful decisions and solving important problems. In others, their communication experiences are confined to receiving orders from management and complaining to one another during break times. Indeed, your experience with any organization will largely be a communication-driven experience, and the nature of those communications will reflect the organization's *culture* or underlying philosophies and practices.

Deal and Kennedy, in their ground-breaking book *Corporate Cultures* and their more recent *The New Corporate Cultures*, suggest that an organization's culture is defined by several factors.[1] First is an organization's *history*. Good organizations recognize that their histories serve as a "symbolic glue" that bonds people together. Disney's "Traditions Program" is required for all new hires, and the Hershey Corporation gives new arrivals a book about its founding years, for example. Such narratives about the past provide a foundation for the rest of the organization's cultural attributes. Second are the organization's *values*—the shared views, philosophies, and beliefs of organizational members. An organization's values establish the tone, set the direction and the pace, and suggest appropriate attitudes and courses of action.

Ritual and ceremony comprise the third element of an organization's culture. Through rituals, organizational members celebrate and reinforce their beliefs, applaud their heroes, and share their visions of the future. *Stories*, or an organization's cultural oral history, are a fourth element of an organization's culture. The stories that members of an organization tell each other carry cultural values and are an important part of everyday life. In his book *The Healing Art of Storytell-*

ing, Richard Stone notes, "After a hard day compounded by fighting traffic, one of the first things we do is tell our spouse or a friend about everything that has happened. . . . This is the mechanism through which we explain our world and come to understand who we are."[2] Similarly, we tell our coworkers about things that have happened at work: meetings we have attended, gossip we have heard, things executives have said and done, projects that are rumored to be under way, and the like. The stories people in organizations tell one another may focus on organizational heroes, dramatic employee exploits, or big mistakes. Through all of these stories, participants learn important lessons about the organization's values and goals.

Those organizational members who personify and illuminate the organization's values are *heroes,* the fifth cultural attribute identified by Deal and Kennedy. Often, these heroes occupy the top position in their organizations. Such chief executive officers as Herb Kelleher (Southwest Airlines), Donald Trump, Bill Gates, Ted Turner, Steve Jobs, or George Steinbrenner articulate and reflect their organization's vision and values. Their actions show by example the way others should think, behave, and talk. Their language is quoted often, and their way of discussing the world is imitated by others throughout the organization. Thus, they influence their organization's sense of social reality.

The final cultural attribute discussed by Deal and Kennedy is the *cultural communication network*. While rituals and ceremonies represent the ultimate form of formal organizational communication, communication networks are *informal* channels of interaction, typically used for influencing members' perceptions of reality and indoctrinating them to hold the right attitudes and behave in appropriate ways.

Bolman and Deal describe how these factors combine to produce four different types of organizational cultures that they call "operating models" or "frames," and they provide a metaphor that describes each: the structural model (factory), the human resource model (family), the political model (jungle), and the symbolic model (temple).[3] All four can manifest themselves to varying degrees over time in any given workplace, but the logic of one tends to be dominant in any one company most of the time.

- *Structural—the factory*. An office functioning at the structural level relies on a hierarchy and rules. Taken to an extreme, the structural approach can be cold, bureaucratic, and stifling. At its worst, a structural workplace can be dominated by the ego and vanity of the boss. Unhealthy structural organizations are hierarchical and autocratic; leaders think they can do no wrong. For example, a manager who sees an employee behaving uncooperatively could handle the situation in different ways. She could use her higher standing on the food chain: calling the employee in for a closed-door meeting, she might snarl, "I don't care whether you like working for me or not, just do your job or get out." Or, she might work within the structural environment more deftly, and instead of invoking her status she might arrange a meeting with the employee to talk about the behavioral changes that are needed and solicit his suggestions concerning how those changes might be made. Thus, rather than taking an "I'm the boss and you're not" approach, she could take a problem-solving, "How can we work together to get the desired results," strategy.

When employed thoughtfully, the structural approach can benefit employees, who appreciate working in a clear and universally understood system. "Structural" need not be rigid, Bolman and Deal stress—leaders can design a workplace architecture that encourages creativity.

- *Human Resource—the family*. Whereas the structural model asserts that people work to serve the organization, the human resource model turns that around: organizations exist to serve human needs. Relationships are at the center of this construct—the relationship between people in the organization and their relationship to the organization itself.

"In the human resource frame, the issue is human needs and how well we're meeting them," Deal says. "It's about listening and trying to figure out what really motivates people, and inquiring into how they're feeling about things." The structural approach could not care less about feelings, but the human resources approach tries to understand where people are coming from.

Leaders who go overboard in applying the human resources frame by trying to make everyone happy all the time may find that some employees begin taking advantage of them. They may discover that the desire to meet their staff's needs cannot be satisfied in all cases. Meeting needs is a two-way street; the organization cannot possibly succeed if it is satisfying desires that are counter to the company's interests.

- *Political—the jungle*. Bolman and Deal believe the political frame is not only a reality but often the most desirable approach.

> There's nothing wrong with being "political." In fact, we say it's absolutely essential. The fact that politics has such a bad name hurts organizations because, rather than resolving issues out in the open, they fight behind the scenes. People get mad and then they try to get even. Politics is really the art of making good deals. We believe there's a good place between naiveté and Mugger Alley.

Conflict is inevitable—the question is how to achieve resolutions all parties can live with. "Sophisticated political leaders," Bolman and Deal write, "prefer to avoid head-on demonstrations of power, looking for ways to appeal to the self-interests of potential adversaries." Ineffective politicians try to use attacks or threats to get their way; effective ones often see that power plays can fail with disastrous consequences and threats can create powerful enemies, thereby compromises and cooperation are strategically superior.

- *Symbolic—the temple*. Since 1964, two employees of the Seibu real estate and transportation company in Japan have kept an overnight vigil at the tomb of their company's patriarch, Yasujiro Tsutsumi. On New Year's Eve, the group swells to 500 or more, lined up by rank and seniority, to listen to a stern speech by the current company head. This ritual, described by Bolman and Deal, makes little sense from a structural, human resource, or political standpoint. The Seibu people are operating in the symbolic frame, in which organizations honor the beliefs, values, practices, and legacies that define their cultures.

Bolman and Deal believe that the symbolic is too seldom recognized in today's workplace. Symbols, they note, can be particularly important in an age of mergers and acquisitions. Change is often demoralizing; leaders need to find ways to allow employees to mourn and celebrate what they're leaving behind and form a kinship with the new organization. Many companies have used videos and skits to inspire a sense of their organization's special character and a bond among its people.

The use of symbols can go wrong, of course. The vice president of human resources at a private university, for example, gave t-shirts to all staff members to thank them at the annual recognition luncheon. But many of the employees, already miffed about their perceived second-class status relative to the faculty, rolled their eyes when they discovered that the shirts were all extra large. When one petite woman suggested that smaller sizes should be offered as well, the VP made a sarcastic remark about her lack of gratitude. Instead of communicating his appreciation, the VP had inadvertently reinforced the perception that these employees didn't really matter.

Bolman and Deal point out that virtually every organization has characteristics of all four models, including a hierarchical structure, interpersonal relationships, politics and the use of power, and symbols and rituals. The question is, which of these four is dominant? None is inherently better than the others; each can be either functional or dysfunctional. But all shape and are shaped by organizational communication, and all begin with the organization's leadership philosophy concerning how organizations and the individuals who comprise them should relate to one another.

Preview

This chapter takes a macroscopic view of organizations that ultimately translates into a microscopic look at day-to-day work experiences everyone in an organization enjoys or endures. By reviewing various philosophies of organizational leadership and culture and the way in which those philosophies shape organizational communication, we hope to enable you both to select the right kinds of organizations in which to participate and to develop some skills in shaping organizational cultures yourself, should the opportunity arise.

LEADERSHIP PHILOSOPHIES

Organizations are shaped by their leaders, and organizational cultures ultimately begin with the philosophies held by the people who control rewards, punishments, information, and other organizational resources. In this section, we will review some of the most prominent leadership philosophies and their implications for communication in organizations.

Assumptions about People: "Classical" Philosophies

In the late eighteenth century, Adam Smith's *Wealth of Nations* emphasized how productivity could be increased in manufacturing pins by assigning workers more specialized tasks. In addition, he laid out a philosophy concerning how leaders and workers should relate, suggesting that workers need close supervision, clear direction, and careful discipline from their superiors. Significantly, Smith's own pin manufacturing plant was led in that fashion largely because of the needs of his workforce, which consisted primarily of boys 10–14 years of age (the cheapest form of labor available at the time, short of slavery). Smith apparently discovered that, if you take a group of young boys and have them do the same thing over and over again, day after day, week after week, you have to keep a close eye on them lest they decide to do something else. Thus was born a philosophy of leadership whereby workers are not to be trusted, work does not come naturally to people so they must be forced to do it, and managers do the thinking while workers do the working.

This philosophy changed little over the next 150 years. In the late nineteenth and early twentieth centuries, the industrial revolution had taken hold. Factories were in wide use, and the assembly-line technique of production was about to be implemented in the Ford automobile plants. Because so much of the technology of manufacturing was new then and because the techniques for large-scale production were just being developed, management theorists of that age focused largely on work methods as the source of performance improvement. The view that developed at that time is now called the *classical school of organization theory,* or the *school of scientific management.*

FREDERICK TAYLOR'S SCIENTIFIC MANAGEMENT

One leader of this school of thought was Frederick Taylor.[4] Taylor's approach to organizations was highly structured and mechanistic. His famed time-and-motion studies attempted to break down each minute aspect of a given job and to match workers with the tasks they could most efficiently perform. Taylor believed in instigating a competitive spirit in organizations by rewarding workers on the basis of their individual output. Praising workers or encouraging creativity never crossed Taylor's mind as being potentially motivating. Rather, he believed that real rewards would invariably be of a monetary nature. Taylor saw no particular clash between the interests of the organization and the welfare of the workers. Rather, he assumed that if individuals could increase their own prosperity while contributing to the organization's efficiency, then everyone would be satisfied. Such a view proved unrealistic. With the growing strength of labor unions in the 1930s, both workers and labor leaders bitterly opposed Taylor's views. They witnessed jobs being eliminated because of Taylor's efficiency-training techniques. This resulted in rises in unemployment. They argued further that those workers who learned to produce with dazzling efficiency were seldom fairly compensated for their extraordinary productivity.

In organizations managed by people who adopted the classical philosophy, communication took on certain characteristics. As a rule, communication was almost exclusively downward. Executives issued general orders and plans to their managers, who in turn issued the same orders (perhaps with more specific instructions) to their employees. Upward communication was virtually nonexistent. Employee suggestions were rarely solicited. Employee complaints were rarely expressed, and those employees who did express them were often encouraged to leave. Conflicts were handled through the chain of command and usually were resolved through decisions made by the chief executive officer. In effect, a very rigid, militaristic hierarchy was maintained, with work-related communication flowing downward through the chain of command.

DOUGLAS MCGREGOR'S THEORY X AND THEORY Y

Classical organization theory provided the impetus for Douglas McGregor's first theory of managing human behavior.[5] McGregor labeled this approach ***Theory X***. In the spirit of scientific management, its central principle is one of direction and control through the exercise of authority. The Theory X manager makes most decisions alone, issues many orders and commands that flow downward through appropriate formal channels, displays little interest in acquiring suggestions and information from those near the bottom of the organizational hierarchy, and generally treats workers as economic beings who are most readily motivated through wage incentive plans and other monetary management methods.

Unfortunately, as McGregor pointed out, supervisors who manage their workers in accordance with the principles of Theory X often create climates of distrust, fear, and misunderstanding. Because so little information flows upward through the hierarchy (and the information actually reaching the top is usually filtered and considerably distorted), decision making is based on only partial and often inaccurate data.

As an alternative to this authoritarian approach to management, McGregor advocated a second management philosophy, ***Theory Y***, which emphasizes the social nature of workers. It contends that human beings can be meaningfully motivated to work productively only when organizations fulfill their higher-level needs for belonging, esteem, and self-actualization. Theory Y further argues that workers prefer self-control and self-direction over being directed and controlled by executive commands. Managers practicing the principles of Theory Y encourage the flow of messages up, down, and across the organization. They are sensitive to employee feedback and facilitate frequent, honest interaction in an atmosphere of confidence and trust.

Significantly, McGregor's Theory X and Theory Y are more theories about people than they are theories of leadership or management. Theory X leaders assume that people are untrustworthy and unmotivated, and thus must be carefully watched and controlled. Theory Y leaders assume that people are self-motivated and want to achieve company goals, and thus can be trusted to participate in problem solving and decision making and allowed to manage their own efforts to some extent. And both sets of leaders are right. Certainly, there are some people who are untrustworthy and are unmotivated, and there are others who are self-starters and do not need any supervision whatsoever. But more important, Theory X leaders tend to produce Theory X employees (thereby proving in the Theory X leader's mind that his or her assumptions were right all along), while Theory Y leaders tend to develop Theory Y employees. For instance, a leader who shares information with employees, asks their opinions, and tries to ensure that their noneconomic needs are met will more likely have a group that has high morale, works well without supervision, and is self-motivated—just as the leader assumed they would. In short, Theory X and Theory Y tend to be self-fulfilling prophesies in which the leader's own behavior ultimately causes employees to become what the leader expected all along.

RENSIS LIKERT'S FOUR SYSTEMS

Rensis Likert and his colleagues took McGregor's concept a step further, suggesting that people can be categorized more accurately in four ways rather than

---

Business Brief 3.1

The Benevolent Autocrat

One should not assume that Theory X leaders are automatically doomed to fail. Benevolent autocrats still abound, and many have achieved noteworthy success. One example was Jack Hartnett, president of D. L. Rogers Corp., a company based in Bedford, Texas, whose primary business consists of owning 54 franchises of Sonic Corp., the drive-in restaurants that dot the South. At a time when management experts preached the importance of company-wide learning and flat hierarchies, Hartnett instructed his employees to "do it the way we tell you to do it." Here are some of his management principles:

- **Show them the money.** Hartnett believes the best way to motivate people is to give them what he covets most: cash, and lots of it. "We're all money motivated," he says. "If someone tells you they're not, they've just committed one of the eight sins of this company." Those who have memorized his list of commandments know he is referring to the fourth: "You don't lie to me."

- **Share their secrets.** Hartnett believes the more he knows about his workers, the more he can help them stay focused at work and happy at home. No subject is too delicate for his ears. "There are no secrets here," he says.

- **Make them part owners.** Executives are required to buy equity stakes in the stores they run, while most fast-food chains give managers and supervisors little more than an occasional free meal.

- **Motivate through fear.** Hartnett rarely yells or screams at his managers or supervisors. He doesn't have to: So frightened are they of provoking him that they go out of their way to please him. "If you're really nice and you occasionally get upset, you'll get their attention," he says.

- **Be a commanding presence.** Hartnett tells people exactly what he expects and how to get there. "I want people to want to do what I want them to do."

- **Sweat the small(est) stuff.** In Hartnett's world, to delegate is to shirk responsibility. He's the master of minutiae. Nothing escapes his attention. He'll even rummage through a trash bin to see what customers are not eating. "If they're throwing away fries, maybe we're not cooking them right," he says.

His eight commandments include "I don't steal from you" as the first and "You don't steal from me" as the second. "I will only tell you one time" is the last.

Source: Marc Ballon, "Extreme Managing," *INC.* 20 (July 1998): 60–66.

McGregor's two.[6] Likert's four "systems" considered ways in which organizations approached a variety of key factors, such as motivation of employees, workers' sense of responsibility to the organization and its goals, amount of cooperative teamwork to achieve organizational goals, and leaders' confidence and trust in their subordinates.

- *System 1* organizations motivate workers through fear, threats, punishment, and occasional rewards; workers feel subservient and hostile toward their superiors; leaders have contempt for subordinates; strong forces (like fear and mistrust) exist that cause upward communication to be withheld or distorted, and subordinates deceive superiors; practically no cooperative teamwork to achieve organizational goals is present; superiors share a minimum amount of information with subordinates, who in turn view messages from leadership with great suspicion.

- *System 2* organizations motivate workers through rewards and some actual or potential punishments; workers are subservient toward superiors and competitive toward peers; leaders are condescending toward subordinates; many forces cause upward communication to be distorted, but there also are forces for honest communication; only a slight amount of cooperative teamwork exists to achieve organizational goals; leaders give subordinates only information they feel subordinates need; subordinates view leadership messages with some suspicion.

- *System 3* organizations motivate workers through occasional punishment and some involvement; workers have cooperative attitudes toward superiors but are somewhat competitive with peers; leaders feel positively about, but nevertheless are condescending toward, subordinates; many forces promote accurate communication although distortion occasionally occurs; a moderate amount of cooperative teamwork to achieve organizational goals is present; leaders provide needed information and answer most questions, and subordinates usually accept the information they are provided.

- *System 4* organizations motivate workers via economic rewards developed participatively, plus group participation in setting goals and improving methods, plus full recognition for achievement; mutual trust and confidence exist between and within all levels of the organization; powerful forces exist to support accurate upward communication, keeping distortion to a minimum; there is a lot of cooperative teamwork to achieve organizational goals; leadership tries to give subordinates relevant information, and subordinates generally accept what they hear and feel free to ask questions or challenge the information they receive.

Likert's research in the early 1960s found that System 4 organizations had the highest level of productivity and System 1 the lowest. He also noted that managers' personal preferences leaned toward the System 4 approach and that the most successful managers worked to develop a "supportive" climate within their organizations. Subordinates usually perceived these supportive (System 4, Theory Y) managers as friendly and helpful, genuinely interested in the well-being of each employee, and trusting in the ability and integrity of all workers. Unfortunately, however, Likert also found that most of the organizations he studied seemed to operate from a System 1 (Theory X) perspective.

While Likert's research is nearly 50 years old, examples of System 1 or System 2 organizational philosophies still can be found, and these in turn can lead to difficult organizational and ethical issues. Not long ago, the leadership philosophy of the *New York Times* led to embarrassment for the organization around the actions and falsifications of one of their reporters, Jayson Blair.[7] Several months before the entire situation became public, Metropolitan Editor Jonathon Landman had sent a memo to the *Times* leadership saying, "We have to stop Jayson from writing for the *Times*. Right now." But nothing happened. Blair took a brief hiatus, but soon was back writing for the national desk of the *New York Times*, one of the most prestigious assignments in journalism. Shortly thereafter, Blair was found to have written false stories and plagiarized materials he claimed were his own, much to the humiliation of this prestigious, even arrogant, company.

The leadership philosophy of Executive Editor Howell Raines was blamed by many as the cause of this unfortunate situation. His personal style has been described as "aloof," and his top-down, often intimidating style make it difficult for those below him on the organizational chart to question or challenge his decisions. In addition, he cultivated a star system at the *Times*, promoting stars such as the writer Rick Bragg while exiling others not in his favor. He pushed his favorites' stories to the front page, but buried reports from those of whom he disapproved.

Blair, an African American, was one of his chosen stars. At a journalism convention, Raines singled out Blair as his best single example of success with diversity at the *New York Times*. But through that public praise, he may have created a person who was untouchable—above reproach and beyond criticism by the rest of the organization. Consequently, despite numerous published corrections, warnings about poor performance, and critical memos, Blair continued to be given choice assignments. When several key officials rebuked the *Times* for Blair's inaccurate reporting, Blair did not receive yet another warning to be more careful. Instead, he got a congratulatory memo from the boss: "Good shoe leather reporting," Raines wrote. Raines also chose not to tell Blair's immediate editor about the young reporter's past problems, nor did he ask Blair to identify his anonymous sources.

Ultimately, Raines's top-down, intimidating approach to leadership—an approach that created at the *Times* the kind of System 1 organizational environment Likert described—led to the embarrassment of the company and, eventually, his own downfall.

Leadership Roles: "Task vs. Relationship" Philosophies

While some theorists have based their systems on the fundamental nature of people who work in organizations and the kind of leadership and environment they need, others have focused on the role of the leader in a group or organizational setting, identifying leadership styles as defined by the things leaders emphasize.

BLAKE AND MCCANSE'S LEADERSHIP GRID®

Robert Blake and Jane Mouton developed a management grid for analyzing leadership behaviors and organizational philosophies, which considered two basic dimensions—the *task* facing a group or organization, and the *socioemotional maintenance* of the group itself—and used concern for task as the Y axis and concern for socioemotional or relationship issues as the X axis.[8] The grid has been further refined by Blake and McCanse (see figure 3.1) but still classifies leaders and organizations as being low, moderate, or high in their emphasis on task issues; low, moderate, or high in their emphasis on relationship variables; and the combination of these results in five basic managerial styles.

The first, the *impoverished management* style, is illustrated by the manager who cares neither for people nor productivity. This leader provides no guidance for employees, avoids involvement in any conflict, delegates decision-making responsibilities to others, and prefers to leave others alone and to be left alone. Actually, this person is a manager in name only and a leader in no sense of the word.

As the name implies, the *authority compliance* manager demonstrates a low concern for people and a high concern for production and is a direct parallel to

McGregor's Theory X and Likert's System 1 managers. Thus, the authority compliance manager issues commands, cares little for employee feedback, and bases motivational strategies on "carrot and stick" concepts of rewards and punishments.

A third style represents the opposite of the managerial approach just described. Called *country club management*, it is totally *people oriented*. These managers are entirely interested in interpersonal relationships, to the exclusion of any concern for organizational productivity. They smooth over conflict, reward extravagantly, and promote good fellowship and harmony. This approach is effective for organizations whose primary purpose is social, such as, oddly enough, a country club. However, if there is work to be done, this approach can be disastrous.

The fourth style is the *middle-of-the-road* approach, emphasizing moderate concern for both people and production. Managers espousing this philosophy

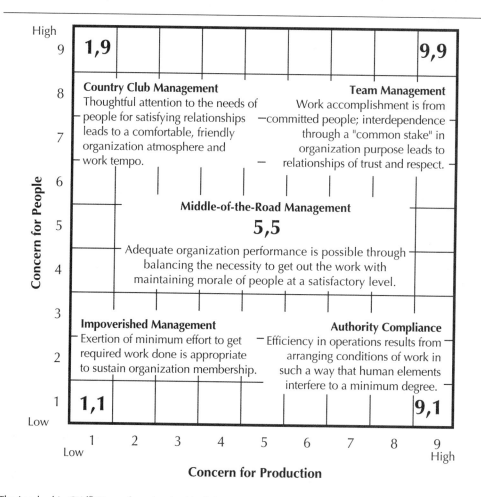

The Leadership Grid® Figure from *Leadership Dilemmas—Grid Solutions,* by Robert R. Blake and Anne Adams McCanse (formerly the Managerial Grid by Robert R. Blake and Jane S. Mouton). Houston: Gulf Publishing Company, copyright 1991 by Grid International, Inc. Reproduced by permission.

Figure 3.1   Leadership Grid®

probably fall somewhere near Likert's System 3. They generally support participation in decision making, and encourage teamwork and employer-employee interaction, but are not totally committed to either.

The fifth style, *team management*, is adopted by a person who has high concern for both people and production; thus, this leader parallels the Theory Y, System 4 managers already discussed. The team manager strives to maintain the group while accomplishing the organizational task. He or she confronts and resolves conflict, encourages consensus in decision making, and seeks candid and spontaneous employee feedback in an atmosphere of trust and mutual respect.

Probably the greatest advantage of Blake and McCanse's Leadership Grid® is the fact that it allows for individual analysis and assumes that different philosophies of management are often operative within the same organizational setting. As with McGregor's and Likert's theories, however, each manager is classified with regard to his or her basic approach, allowing little room for the adoption of different managerial styles with varying tasks and personnel.

HERSEY AND BLANCHARD'S SITUATIONAL LEADERSHIP

Like Blake and Mouton and Blake and McCanse, Hersey and Blanchard focused on two elements of leadership: managing work and managing people.[9] However, unlike other management theorists, Hersey and Blanchard do not make static assumptions about either managers or workers. In their examination of leadership styles and employee needs, they acknowledge the inevitability of some change as well as the potential for growth. Their theory of leadership affirms the need for a dynamic leadership approach in which the manager's effectiveness is determined by the ability to assess the needs and abilities of employees accurately and adjust his or her leadership strategy accordingly.

According to Hersey and Blanchard, an effective manager should begin by assessing a *subordinate's maturity*, which they define as the "willingness and ability of a person to take responsibility for directing his or her own behavior." Actually, there are two dimensions to maturity in any work environment: *psychological maturity*—the willingness or motivation to do something, the belief that responsibility is important, and the confidence to complete tasks without extensive encouragement; and *job maturity*—the ability or competence to do something and the knowledge, experience, and skill needed to carry out work without the direction of others. Hersey and Blanchard recognize that a number of important situational factors exist in any organizational environment. They remain convinced, however, that the behavior of the manager in relation to individual employees in the work group is the most crucial.

Hersey and Blanchard's situational approach to management has been labeled the *life cycle theory of leadership* in that it examines leader-subordinate interactions over an extended period of time and assumes that changes, adjustments, and growth will occur. A manager who is dealing with an individual or a group of employees whose psychological and job maturity are low begins by emphasizing task-oriented leadership. As the employees' maturity level increases, the manager decreases task behavior and increases relationship behavior until a moderate level of maturity is attained. Ultimately, with increases in maturity, the manager begins to decrease both task and relationship behavior. At this point, employees possess both job and psychological maturity and are capable of providing their own reinforcement. Hersey and Blanchard believe that when high levels of maturity are reached, employees accept the reduction in close supervision and attention as an indication of the manager's confidence and trust.

The importance of Hersey and Blanchard's approach is its recognition of employee differences and changes in maturation over time. While managers hope for highly mature employees, most work with at least some individuals who are less talented and motivated. Hersey and Blanchard's theory accepts the fact that some workers may never reach high levels of maturity. In those instances, these writers contend that the manager's task is to provide highly task-oriented leadership.

The Sharing of Power: "Participative Management" Philosophies

While early theorists focused primarily on the nature of workers and the leadership they need, or on the extent to which leaders emphasized task and/or relationship issues, more recent examinations of leadership philosophy and the organizational cultures it creates have centered around the extent to which decision-making power is vested entirely at the top or is shared with lower levels of the organization.

JAPANESE PHILOSOPHY

During the 1970s and 1980s, U.S. managers invested much time and money studying Japanese approaches to management because of the fine quality of Japanese products and the general productivity of their organizations. While the U.S. and Japanese cultures differ significantly in many ways, it is still possible to examine Japanese management and discover several relevant principles.

In his widely acclaimed book *Theory Z*, William Ouchi describes the predominance of work teams throughout Japanese industry and argues that this approach to productivity is one of the reasons the Japanese have been so successful over the past several decades. He notes that the "Type Z company is characterized by many cohesive and semi-autonomous work groups even though a Z company seldom undertakes any explicit attempts at teambuilding."[10]

Extensive studies of Japanese organizations have demonstrated that Japanese managers stress the following:

- *Bottom-up initiative.* Japanese managers believe that change and initiative within an organization *should* come from those closest to the problem. So they elicit change from below. Top-level Japanese managers see their task as creating an atmosphere in which subordinates are motivated to seek better solutions.

- *Top management as facilitator.* Japanese managers do not view themselves as having all the answers. When a subordinate brings in a proposal, the manager neither accepts nor rejects it. Rather, he tactfully and politely asks questions, makes suggestions, and provides encouragement.

- *Middle management as impetus for and shaper of solutions.* In the Japanese system, junior (middle) managers are initiators who perceive problems and formulate tentative solutions in coordination with others; they are not functional specialists who carry out their boss's directives. Because so much emphasis is placed on coordination and integration, solutions to problems evolve more slowly, but they are known and understood by all those who have been a part of the solution-generation process. Horizontal communication is stressed as essential to the coordination of problem solving efforts.

- *Consensus as a way of making decisions*. The Japanese are less inclined to think in terms of absolutes, that is, the solution (which is right) versus the alternatives (which are wrong). Rather, they recognize a range of alternatives, several of which might work and all of which possess advantages and disadvantages. When a group makes a decision, all members become committed to the chosen solution. From a Japanese perspective, that commitment, and the ensuing dedication to working to make the solution successful, is probably more important than the objective quality of the decision. The Japanese have an interesting concept of consensus. Those who consent to a decision are not necessarily endorsing it. Rather, consenting means that they are satisfied that their point of view has been fairly heard; although they may not wholly agree that the decision is the best one, they are willing to go along with it and even support it.

- *Concern for employees' personal well-being*. Japanese managers have a kind of paternalistic attitude toward their employees. Traditionally, Japanese organizations have offered their workers housing, extensive recreational facilities, and lifetime employment. The Japanese believe that it is impossible to divorce a worker's personal and professional lives. Good managers express concern for workers as persons with homes and families as well as for the quality of the products the workers produce. Managers typically work alongside their subordinates, counsel them regarding their personal lives, and encourage much peer interaction.

It is interesting that principles that are considered by many to be advantages of the Japanese system can also be viewed as problems, at least from a U.S. perspective. There is a fine line between encouraging consensus and forcing it. When groups place too much emphasis on being agreeable and conforming to organizational expectations, poor-quality decision making is a likely outcome. Moreover, the Japanese notion of taking care of employees can extend into an extreme form of paternalism with which few well-educated Americans would be comfortable. It is appropriate to protect children or others who cannot think for or look after themselves, but professionals hardly fall into these categories. Most Americans would prefer an organizational system that makes it possible for them to function as mature human beings, responsible for their own security and well-being.

The diversity of the U.S. workforce also makes it quite different from the workforce in Japan and thus can limit the effectiveness of some Japanese management principles (as automakers such as Toyota, Nissan, and others discovered when they established manufacturing facilities in the United States). Ethnic diversity is very limited in Japan—with the exception of the lowest-level service jobs, almost all of their workers are, not surprisingly, Japanese. The entry of women into the Japanese workforce has been very slow as well. Consequently, Japanese managers deal with workers who are much more homogeneous and thus more likely to think, behave, and make decisions in similar ways.

Finally, the realities of today's work environment in the United States make irrelevant some of the assumptions underlying Japanese-style leadership. For example, job security is virtually a thing of the past: every year, literally hundreds of thousands of U.S. workers lose their jobs as a part of corporate "downsizings" or "restructurings" intended to increase their organization's profitability and returns to shareholders. Concern for employees' well-being too often has been replaced by concern solely for the bottom line. As a result, employees' loyalty to their organizations has diminished significantly; and many theorists are advising employees to be loyal not to their companies but to their professions, the projects in which they are involved, and their own careers. In turn, savvy companies are recognizing the "new deal" in employment relationships and are trying to retain employees not by relying on blind loyalty, but by customizing the work environment to meet their work and personal life needs.[11]

TEAMWORK PHILOSOPHY

Increasingly, theorists have been adopting the position (long held by the Japanese) that productivity in an organization is the result of communication in all directions: upward, downward, and lateral. Such communication fosters the development of work teams. The *teamwork* and "team work" (that is, the sense of team identity and the tasks performed by the work team) achieved by these groups determines how successful the organization is.

Edward E. Lawler, in his book *High-Involvement Management*, takes the perspective that entire organizations should act as teams, with every level participating to some degree in decision making and problem solving.[12]

> No more fundamental change could occur than that involved in moving power, knowledge, information, and rewards to lower levels. It changes the very nature of what work is and means to everyone who works in an organization. Because it profoundly affects the jobs of everyone, it can impact on the effectiveness of all work organizations.

Bradford and Cohen similarly call for a "post-heroic" conception of workplace leadership, one based on "shared responsibility" to replace the "outdated and inadequate" model that had held sway for so long—the idea that "The Lone Ranger rides to the rescue."[13] They portray the post-heroic manager as someone who sees everyone as a leader, who views the leader's primary function as the building of a strong team with a common vision and mutual influence, who invites other employees to share the responsibilities of managing—thereby producing better decisions and ideas, more learning, and higher morale.

Lawler points out, however, that teams are not appropriate in every organizational context. Most agree that teamwork is most effective when a task entails a high level of interdependency among three or more people. For instance, complex manufacturing processes common in the auto, chemical, paper, and high-technology industries can benefit from teams, as can complicated service tasks in insurance, banking, and telecommunications. In most cases, simple assembly-line activities are less amenable to teamwork. As Lawler points out, *the more complex the task, the better suited it is for teams*. Presumably, when the right kind of task is matched with the team approach, the result will be greater problem-solving speed and effectiveness.

Many U.S. organizations already have instituted various team approaches to managing and communicating. Nearly all of Motorola's 57,000 U.S. employees are involved in some stage of its "Participative Management Program." Honeywell, Xerox, General Motors, and Westinghouse, among others, have publicly committed themselves to using a more participative approach to organizing and managing people. Hundreds of companies are using quality circles or some other form of group problem solving to involve employees in identifying and resolving work-related problems. Clearly, as Lawler claims, "participative management is an idea whose time has come."

Still, not every organization has seen the team philosophy succeed. As Stewart reported in her article "Teams Don't Always Work," companies from Motorola to the Ritz-Carlton hotel chain have successfully used work teams as they try to achieve optimum productivity, but others have seen productivity actually decline because of infighting and a lack of direction.[14] A particularly striking example of the difficulties involved in the team approach took place at Levi's, the jeans manufacturer. In 1992, the company directed its U.S. plants to abandon the old piecework system, under which workers repeatedly performed a single, specialized task (like sewing zippers or attaching belt loops) and were paid according to the amount of work they completed. In the new system, groups of 10 to 35 workers shared the tasks and were paid according to the total number of trousers the group completed. Levi's figured that this would cut down on the monotony of the old system and that it would enable stitchers to do different tasks, thus reducing repetitive-stress injuries. Instead, it led to a quagmire in which skilled workers found themselves pitted against slower colleagues, damaging morale and triggering corrosive infighting. Threats and insults became more common. Long-time friendships dissolved as faster workers tried to banish slower ones. "You hear so much shouting, lots of times you don't even look up from your work," recalls Knoxville seamstress Mary Farmer.[15]

Ultimately, Levi's for the most part was forced to scrap their team approach and return to a system that emphasized individual performance and individual rewards. Perhaps this situation proves Lawler's point: some tasks and processes may not be suited to the team approach.

The teamwork philosophy contains elements of McGregor's Theory Y and Likert's System 4 because it is based on assumptions about the nature of people within organizations. Communication in this sort of organization moves in all directions, including laterally in informal meetings between peers. Spontaneous problem solving is encouraged, and conflict is resolved at the lowest level possible. Opportunities are created for employees in different departments to meet and talk with one another, and formal task teams are created whenever appropriate. Above all, communication cuts across formal organizational boundaries, occurring between people directly involved in getting the work done.

SELF-MANAGEMENT PHILOSOPHY

The teamwork philosophy has begun to emphasize informal leadership in place of formal management. In an article titled "Who Needs a Boss?", *Fortune* describes self-managed "superteams" that typically consist of between 3 and 30 workers, "sometimes blue collar, sometimes white collar, sometimes both."[16] For example, teams in a General Mills cereal plant in Lodi, California, schedule, operate, and maintain machinery so effectively that no managers are present on the night shift. Similarly, after organizing its home office operations into teams, Aetna Life & Casualty reduced the ratio of middle managers to workers from 1:7 down to 1:30 (and at the same time improved customer service). Finally, many nursing units in U.S. hospitals have the nurses themselves determine their work schedules.

Responsibilities often undertaken by self-managing teams include such traditional management functions as preparing an annual budget, timekeeping, recording quality control statistics, monitoring inventory, assigning jobs within groups, training other team members, adjusting production schedules, modifying production processes, setting team goals, resolving internal conflicts, and evaluating team performance. Leadership within self-managed teams usually emerges informally. Once company managers have trained team members in basic problem-solving and group-dynamic skills, and defined for them their scope of responsibility and authority, they allow the team to develop their own procedures and relationships. Team members skilled in group communication techniques are most likely to emerge as the informal leaders.

Self-managed teams have proved extremely effective in many organizations. During their weekly meeting, a team of Federal Express clerks identified a billing problem that had been costing the company $2.1 million a year (and eventually they resolved the problem). In 3M, cross-functional teams tripled the number of new products produced by one division. Teams of blue-collar workers at Johnsonville Foods of Sheboygan, Wisconsin, helped increase production by more than 50 percent over four years.

Despite such successes, the spread of self-managed teams has been relatively slow for several reasons. First, self-managed teams require a great deal of mutual trust between top management and employees—trust that may take years to build (and only a moment to undo). Second, middle managers often feel highly threatened by the concept because they believe it will reduce their power and influence. Thus, they may openly or covertly oppose the process. In addition, implementation of self-managed teams often takes a long time (18 months to two years is common), and training employees in self-management skills can be time-consuming and expensive. Finally, like it or not, there are Theory X workers in just about every organization—people who view their employment as "just a job"—who have little or no interest in the success of their employer, and who might be best described, in terms devised by Buckingham and Coffman, as "disengaged" from their organization.[17] While Buckingham and Coffman argue that it is the responsibility of organizations to increase the extent to which workers are "engaged" in their work, their research in the Gallup organization showed that every organization has some percentage of disengaged workers—and disengaged workers do not manage themselves particularly well.

Philosophies Based on Key Organizational Concepts

The approaches to leadership and organizational culture described above focused on either or both of two components: the nature of the people who work in organizations and the actions of the leaders who oversee their efforts. However, more recent philosophies have focused on concepts external to leaders and workers and used those concepts as the basis for developing recommended leadership and communication strategies.

VALUES-DRIVEN PHILOSOPHY

Some theorists have argued that the most effective organization is one that lives according to a clear, widely supported set of values. One of the most influential theorists taking the values-driven philosophy is Stephen R. Covey, whose

DILBERT

DILBERT © by Scott Adams; reprinted by permission of United Feature Syndicate, Inc.

book *The 7 Habits of Highly Effective People* propelled him to national prominence and provided him with the funding to establish the Covey Leadership Center and the Institute for Principle-Centered Leadership. Shopping malls everywhere now are dotted with retail outlets for Covey paraphernalia, such as desktop decorations, personal planners, pictures and posters, and other accoutrements apparently vital to an effective person's work life.

In his original book, Covey noted that highly effective people are proactive, begin with the end in mind, put first things first, think win/win, seek first to understand and then to be understood, synergize, and sharpen the saw.[18] Covey then turned his attention to organizations in *Principle-Centered Leadership,* arguing that organizational leaders should apply his seven habits on four different levels:

- organizational (to achieve alignment between individual and organizational objectives);
- managerial (to achieve empowerment of others);
- interpersonal (to build trust with others); and
- personal (to achieve trustworthiness in the eyes of others).[19]

All of these things are achieved through such communication behaviors as listening before explaining; involving others to produce win/win solutions; refraining from saying unkind or negative things; and admitting mistakes, apologizing, and asking for forgiveness. As such, Covey's approach to leadership and organizational communication theory is much more behavioral and interpersonally based than the philosophies outlined above.

Kenneth Blanchard, advocate of the situational leadership philosophy, also has adopted the values-driven philosophy. In *Managing by Values,* he and coauthor Michael O'Connor argue that leaders should clarify their organization's values, communicate them thoroughly and consistently, and then build alignment toward those values through a participative "gap" identification and problem-solving process.[20] Labovitz and Rosansky discuss the need for both "vertical" and "horizontal" alignment with organizational goals and values, and incorporate the self-management philosophy in their discussion of "self-aligning" organizations.[21] Others similarly have argued that the most effective organizations are ones in which every individuals' efforts and behaviors are guided by a common set of values and a shared vision for the future.[22]

Business Brief 3.2

The Challenges of Putting Theory into Practice

While Stephen Covey has gained great notoriety and even greater fortune via his expertise in values-oriented leadership, parenting, and living, even that expertise proved insufficient when he attempted to merge his organization, Covey Leadership Center, with rival Franklin Quest in the mid-1990s. Covey initially claimed the organizational expertise of the two firms would create a model merger, but the Franklin Quest/Covey honeymoon was short-lived. "The merger has been harder and has taken longer than we imagined. It's been one tough baby," said Covey. "It's proof that the great business gurus know how to run everyone's business but their own," observed John Butman, who created fictional management expert Stephen Michael Peter Thomas and Thomas's book "The Book That's Sweeping America! Or Why I Love Business!", a parody on management consulting.

Different corporate cultures probably thwarted efforts of the two organizations to merge. Covey Leadership built its reputation catering to Fortune 500 clients on theory-inspired seminars and books. Franklin Quest offered meat-and-potatoes items such as its ubiquitous Franklin Day Planners. Even Franklin's string of retail stores, with their dark, clubroom look, seemed dated compared with the more modern stores Covey had been developing. Covey's mission-oriented leadership training and Franklin Quest's emphasis on task-skilled, time-management products clashed and caused in-fighting.

Friction emerged at several levels. Employees were polarized when most Covey workers remained in Provo, Utah, 40 miles south of Franklin Quest's Salt Lake operations. At Franklin Quest, employees made cryptic jokes that they would have to shave their heads to look like Covey. Franklin Quest's on-site fitness center and cafeteria made some Covey employees envious. Franklin's button-down conservative dress code inspired fear, underscored by internal memos suggesting Covey workers could no longer wear ultra-casual work attire. Post merger, the dress code turned "business casual."

Reward systems also differed between the two firms. At Franklin Quest, sales commissions were based on business the individual sellers generated, and a top seller could make $250,000–$300,000 per year. The Covey sales force was compensated based on team performance. Post merger, the new organization adopted team compensation, which crimped some individuals' earnings.

Remarkably, each of the two organizations subscribes to the values espoused in Covey's books. However, differences in *the ways those values were applied* in each organization thus far have made for a very difficult merger of the two.

Source: Gary Strauss, "Consultants Learn Tough Merger Lesson," *USA Today*, December 17, 1998, sec. B, 1.

The values-driven philosophy takes into account both how an organization communicates and what it communicates. Initially, communication is downward as the organization's leadership states clearly what the vision for the future is and what values are to guide employees' behaviors. In turn, the values may dictate that superiors talk with their subordinates in certain ways or that employees participate actively in making decisions that affect their work lives.

INFORMATION-DRIVEN PHILOSOPHY

An interesting combination of the classical school of organizational thought (which heavily emphasizes measurement as a guide to employee behavior) and the values-driven philosophy is "open book" leadership, which holds that employees' efforts should be guided and motivated by information. For example, Kaplan and Norton argue that organizations should use a "balanced scorecard" that measures four categories—financial performance, customer knowledge, internal business processes, and learning and growth—to align individual, organizational, and cross-departmental activities and to motivate better performance.[23] Using this principle, a large health-care system in upstate New York every three months provides its management and employees with a single page that shows charts tracking patient satisfaction, employee satisfaction, financial performance, and costs involved in delivering patient care. They assume that managers and employees will be motivated to achieve improvements in these measures (a key Theory Y assumption), and to date their experience has proved this assumption correct.

Open book management is a similar philosophy intended to encourage all the people in an organization to "think and act like business partners."[24] Based on the assumption that employees want to know about the industry in which they work and will act responsibly if they are given enough information, the open book management philosophy suggests that organizational leaders should do four things:

- make full information about the organization's performance available (create the open book);
- build "business literacy" among all employees so they understand what the information means;
- empower all employees within the organization so they can act on the information they are given; and
- create reward structures that give employees a stake in their organization's success.[25]

Like the values-driven leadership philosophy, the information-driven philosophy is heavily communication oriented. Theorists believe that workers want the same information that managers have, and that if they are provided with feedback concerning how well they and their organization are doing, they will make adjustments and improvements to do even better.

CUSTOMER-DRIVEN PHILOSOPHY

The values-driven and information-driven philosophies are combined in the customer-driven philosophy, whereby everything an organization and its members do should be guided by the goal of satisfying the organization's customers. In their best seller *Service America!* Albrecht and Zemke argued that in the new economy, organizations must perform rather than produce, and an organization's success ultimately is determined by how well each of its members handle the thousands of "moments of truth" they face each day as they provide service to their customers.[26] Albrecht's follow-up book, *At America's Service*, expanded on those ideas and claimed that the traditional pyramid of authority must be turned upside down, so that those who serve the customers—their needs, capabilities, and problems—become the central focus of management.[27]

Whiteley reports that a customer-driven company is based on several communication practices, including:

- creating a customer-keeping vision through top-down communication of the organization's values;

- saturating the company with the voice of the customer by using a wide variety of communication tools to listen to customer opinions: surveys, group discussions, informal customer-employee contacts, and so on;
- liberating "customer champions" by giving all employees freedom to make decisions and solve problems related to customer service;
- following the rule "measure, measure, measure," so that customer satisfaction information can be used to assess individual, team, and organizational performance and to motivate and guide performance improvements; and
- "Walking the talk" so that values and customer focus are exhibited by everyone in the organization—particularly top management.[28]

Wiersema similarly argues that communication and relationships with customers should guide communication and relationships within the organization, such that every organization achieves true "intimacy" with its customers.[29] In his view, organizations should be characterized by *judgment* (where everyone is sensitive and responsive to customer needs), *cooperation* (where positive teamwork among coworkers and with customers is maintained), and *learning* (whereby everyone is helped formally and informally to continuously build understanding of what it takes to achieve customer satisfaction).

Lawton incorporated both the "classical" philosophy of Frederick Taylor and elements of the Japanese philosophy by suggesting that products and processes need to be clearly defined, systematic measures of customer service and satisfaction need to be developed and implemented, and processes need to be systematically improved in order to achieve a customer-centered culture.[30]

The customer-driven philosophy is also heavily communication-oriented, emphasizing upward, downward, and lateral communications, all pointed toward a single goal: achieving customer satisfaction. However, many advocates of a customer-driven culture do not deal with some particularly ticklish issues (for example, what if the customer wants something that is immoral or unethical?) and some tend to take an overly altruistic view of organizational life, not recognizing that employee satisfaction must be achieved to some extent before they will be eager to please their customers.

"LEARNING ORGANIZATION" PHILOSOPHY

A more recent philosophy of organizational communication and leadership that combines elements of the values-based, teamwork, and information-driven philosophies initially was expressed in Peter Senge's influential *The Fifth Discipline*. Senge argued that, in order to survive, organizations must become "learning" entities characterized by five "disciplines":

- *Systems thinking.* Recognizing the interrelationships among all elements of an organization
- *Personal mastery.* Continually "clarifying and deepening our personal vision, focusing our energies, developing patience, and seeing reality objectively" to develop individual mastery of skills and the organization's values
- *Mental models.* Building "assumptions, generalizations, or even pictures or images that influence how we understand the world and how we take action" in a manner that builds organizational success

- *Building shared vision*. Creating a shared picture of the future the company seeks to create
- *Team learning*. Using "dialogue" to create teams whose intelligence exceeds the intelligence of the individuals in the teams and teams that "develop extraordinary capacities for coordinated action"[31]

Gifford and Elizabeth Pinchot extended Senge's thinking, claiming that in a complex and intelligence-intensive world economy, organizations can no longer rely solely on the thinking and intelligence of those few at the top of the bureaucracy.[32] The amount of clear thinking required to deal with the multitude of customer demands, ethnic cultures, technological advances, and diverse workforce needs makes it necessary to involve everyone within the organization. Organizations therefore must develop and engage the intelligence, business judgment, and system-wide responsibility of all members in order to respond to customers, partners, and competitors. Successful organizations will be characterized by "voluntary learning networks" composed of informal contacts among organizational members, "democratic self-rule" whereby decision making is delegated to the lowest levels of the organization, and "limited corporate government" such that centralized control is minimized in favor of decentralized thinking and action.

Central to the learning organization is communication. Downward communication and participative discussions are used to create shared visions and values; classroom training and individual mentoring are used to build skills and knowledge; lateral networks among all components of the organization share information quickly. Indeed, the ultimate learning organization might be the one featured years ago in the television series *Star Trek: The Next Generation*, "The 'Borg.'" A population of cyber-beings, the Borg are completely and instantly connected, so that the thoughts of one are shared by all and the learning of one contributes to the knowledge of all. Just as their ability to acquire and share information instantly and to make quick adjustments to their environment make the Borg a threat to the *Star Trek* universe, so does the ability to learn and adjust quickly make a more typical organization a threat to its competitors.[33]

"WINNING IS EVERYTHING" PHILOSOPHY

In sharp contrast to the thinking of most management experts is what some call the *"S.O.B." school of leadership*—an approach whereby leaders are disinterested in the affections of their followers and view people as something to be sacrificed in the interests of organizational achievement. In his book *Confessions of an S.O.B.*, Al Neuharth, founder of *USA Today* and former chairman of Gannett Publishing, attributed his success to the principle that "cream and S.O.B.s rise to the top."[34] Through such principles as "promote thyself," "build molehills into mountains," and "best the boss," he transformed himself from a "poor country kid from South Dakota" to a multimillionaire media mogul. However, careful reading of his book indicates that he achieved his success by using more Theory Y principles than Theory X.

The same cannot be said for other executives who have received recent prominence. In his article "The Hit Men," Sloan reports, "Once upon a time, it was a mark of shame to fire your workers en masse. It meant you had messed up your business. Today, the more people a company fires, the more Wall Street loves it, and the higher its stock price goes."[35] To improve profits and stock prices, massive layoffs were implemented by executives in such companies as AT&T (40,000 layoffs), Boeing (28,000), IBM (60,000), Delta Air Lines (15,000), General Motors (74,000), Sears, Roebuck & Co. (50,000), and McDonnell Douglas (17,000), among others. Employees at AT&T reportedly quipped that former chairman Robert Allen would have fired everyone but himself, and AT&T would have stood for "Allen & Two Temps."[36]

Perhaps the most prominent proponent of the S.O.B. philosophy was "Chainsaw" Al Dunlap, the former chief executive officer of Sunbeam who preferred the nickname "Rambo in pinstripes." When his picture was published in *USA Today* a few years ago, he was shown holding an automatic pistol in each hand, wearing a black headband, and bullet-laden bandoliers forming an "X" across his chest. In his first year at Sunbeam, Dunlap cut 6,000 jobs, or half the workforce, and closed 18 of 26 factories.[37] Interestingly, when *Newsweek* asked more than 50 CEOs of large U.S. companies to discuss corporate restructuring, only Dunlap was willing to talk. His comments:[38]

> When journalists and politicians spout off about corporate downsizing, it's the Al Dunlaps of the world who tend to get the blame. We're painted as villains; but we're not. We're more like doctors. We know it's painful to operate, but it's the only way to keep the patient from dying.

Dunlap also is reputed to have said of his leadership style, "You want a friend? Buy a dog." Ultimately, Dunlap was fired from Sunbeam; and shortly after his departure it was revealed that he had overstated the company's losses when he first took over, and then overstated their profits after he had been in office for a time, thereby artificially inflating the "turnaround" he had achieved.

Like basketball coach Bobby Knight, whose winning teams have allowed him to continue coaching for over 30 years despite his edgy temperament, some CEOs are known for having difficult personalities. Former CEO Robert Crandall of American Airlines' parent AMR had "mankind's biggest bladder," former employees joke, because of demanding meetings that could go eight hours without a break and were peppered with intimidation and profanity. Cypress Semiconductor CEO T. J. Rodgers liked to clip and display articles written about his rants, and he bragged about the "drooling psych face" he used when he really wanted to intimidate an employee. Sam Zell, the 132nd richest person in America as ranked by *Forbes* and chairman of Equity Group Investments, is a "Rumpelstiltskin, and he glories in it," according to former American Motors CEO Gerald Meyers. "He literally jumps up and down yelling in meetings," Meyers said. Linda Wachner, former CEO of Warnaco and a trailblazer among women breaking the glass ceiling at Fortune 500 companies, also has a reputation for being tough. She told *Fortune* magazine that she yells at people and is not ashamed of it: "We have to run this company efficiently and without a bunch of babies who say, 'Mommy yelled at me today.' It's impossible to run a leveraged operation like camp," she said. "If you don't like it, leave. It's not a prison."[39]

William George, a professor at the Harvard School of Business, notes that the business world has been plagued by scandals that have damaged the trust of the American people in the integrity of business leaders. In every scandal, he says, the cause can be traced to the failures of business leaders. In most cases, these leaders placed themselves above the institutions for which they were responsible.

Basketball Hall of Fame head coach Bobby Knight is known as a tough, demanding leader. Often called "The General," he is equally recognized for his integrity and his consistent record of running a clean basketball program with high academic standards.

Rather than recognizing that they were put in office to serve their shareholders, customers, and employees, they fell prey to pursuing their own desires. The real problem is that *organizations have been choosing the wrong leaders*, selecting them for their charisma, image, style, and ability to impress Wall Street with short-term numbers. Instead, organizations need **authentic leaders**, chosen for their character, integrity, and substance. George elaborates that authentic leaders:

- are known for their ability to create lasting value for their customers and their shareholders;

- are motivated by a sense of purpose and practice a consistent set of values, leading with their hearts, not just their heads; and

- create long-term connected relationships with their employees and customers that build trust throughout their organizations.

As a result, their organizations produce long-term results for all their stakeholders.[40]

Perhaps the perfect illustration of George's points is Putnam Investments, a company that is struggling to recover from scandals that led customers to withdraw more than $61 billion in assets and the federal government to fine the organization $110 million. As it does so, it must contend with a corporate culture that encouraged wrongdoing and kept it under wraps.[41]

Under the leadership of Lawrence Lasser, the former CEO, Putnam developed a cutthroat work environment and rigid hierarchy that rejected change and discouraged employees from reporting problems. Unlike many top industry executives who routinely meet with clients, Lasser was inaccessible. In addition, one executive perk was the eighth-floor corporate dining room with a buffet offering first-rate menu selections such as beef Wellington, Arctic char, and grilled portobello mushrooms. Executives, who dined on fine china, did not have to pay for their meals. While executives hobnobbed in the dining room, rank-and-file workers were often left out of the loop. The top-down management style and layers of bureaucracy hindered communication. In addition, senior executives tended to give speeches rather than hold open staff meetings, and employees had to submit questions in advance when meeting with senior management.

In an effort to change the company's culture, new Putnam CEO Charles "Ed" Haldeman moved his office from the executive floor to the investment floor of the building and opened the executive dining room to all employees. He has communicated frequently with the staff and encouraged employee input. "I try hard to respond to every phone call and e-mail that I receive from an employee," he says. He has also tried to encourage long-range thinking by lengthening the time horizon for evaluating investment performance, slashed the number of meetings, and given more autonomy to investment professionals. He has accompanied marketing and distribution executives on out-of-town client meetings: "When you're traveling with them, you go out to dinner with them and find out what they're thinking and what's going on," Haldeman says. Because of measures like these, Putnam has become more open and accessible. Finally, there is a new emphasis on *how* things are done, not just on financial results: "The policy that I'm trying to bring to Putnam is one of zero tolerance of unethical behavior," Haldeman says.

ROLE MODEL PHILOSOPHY

Many leadership theorists have not been theorists at all. Rather, they have produced books and programs that say, in essence: "This organization/person has been successful; do what they do." The roots of this philosophy can be traced to *In Search of Excellence*, the best seller that made millionaires of its authors, Tom Peters and Robert Waterman.[42] When the Japanese began competing effectively against U.S. business, U.S. managers' confidence began to wane and the belief emerged that "somebody, somewhere, knows how to do business—but it isn't us." This sense of insecurity led to a desire to find experts who could tell U.S. managers how better companies do it—and helped Peters and Waterman sell over one million copies of *In Search of Excellence* within the first 11 months of its release.

While Peters and Waterman used organizational role models, dozens of individual historical figures have been the subjects of books for harried business executives looking for secrets about how to manage. One of the first was *Leadership Secrets of Attila the Hun*, published in 1985 by Wess Roberts and offering such advice as, "Never allow your Huns too many idle moments. These give rise to the beginnings of discontent." In 1992 came *Lincoln on Leadership: Executive Strategies for Tough Times* by Donald Phillips. Then the floodgates opened. Do you want to model yourself after a military leader? There is *Patton on Leadership: Strategic Lessons for Corporate Warfare* by Alan Axelrod (Prentice-Hall), as well as at least two books on Robert E. Lee and two on Ulysses S. Grant. If you are looking for political models, you are most likely going to have to settle for Republicans: in addition to the Lincoln book, there is *Theodore Roosevelt on Leadership* and *Reagan on Leadership*, both by James Strock. Some books focus on literary figures, such as Shakespeare, Winnie-the-Pooh, and Goldilocks. But very few focus on female leaders; *Elizabeth I, CEO* by Axelrod (Prentice-Hall) is a rare exception. Then there are books about religious leaders: in *Moses on Management*, David Baron and Lynette Padwa describe the Old Testament prophet as "the greatest manager of all time." Richard D. Phillips draws from the Old Testament in his *The Heart of an Executive: Lessons on Leadership from the Life of King David*. In *The Management Methods of Jesus*, Bob Briner asserts that "The all-time greatest management entrepreneur is Jesus Christ." Both, though, seem to be trumped by Larry Julian's book, *God is My CEO*.

In his article "Leadership Lessons for 2004," Steve Powers decries the state of management role models:

> We know times have been tough, but we had no idea the world had run so low on role models. The industry that churns out inspirational books about business leaders—and, in the past, served up such heroes as Lee Iacocca and Sun-tzu, as well as Jack Welch and Attila the Hun—seems to be scraping the bottom of the barrel.[43]

Powers mentions two books that particularly seem to be reaching for role models: Himsel's *Leadership Sopranos Style: How to Become a More Effective Boss*, which takes as a role model leader HBO's Tony Soprano, a fictional, foul-mouthed Mafia boss, and Robbins and Finley's *The Accidental Leader: What to Do When You're Suddenly in Charge*, which espouses the philosophy "you may feel like a quivering bowl of jelly, but when you suddenly end up in charge, take the reins maturely," and cites as a role model former President Gerald Ford, the classic accidental leader.

Some books have looked for examples among other species. Book titles such as *The Wisdom of Wolves: Nature's Way to Organizational Success*, or *Flight of the Buffalo*, or even *Strategy of the Dolphin* are just a few of the works that offer guidance based on beings that presumably are wiser than we are.

Irving Rein, a Northwestern University professor who specializes in communication and popular culture, notes that "It's simply a hook. The celebrity draws attention to something relatively mundane, and that's what these books are, really mundane. They're almost all the same—five rules for this, 10 rules for that. They're formula books." Perhaps "buyer beware" is the watchword for assessing theories of leadership. As media mogul Rupert Murdoch observed, "You go to Doubleday's business section, and you see all these wonderful titles, and you spend $300, and then you throw them all away."[44]

Comparing/Contrasting Leadership Philosophies

The various philosophies of leadership differ with regard to their view of several key organizational issues:

- *The value it places on people.* Are people a commodity that is to be controlled (classical view, Theory X, System 1) or dispensed with in the interests of profits (winning is everything, S.O.B. philosophy), or are they a resource to be developed (Theory Y, System 4, learning organizations), or engaged (Japanese philosophy, teamwork approach, self-management)?

- *The extent to which it shares information and authority.* Is all power vested in centralized leadership (Theory X, classical/scientific management) or shared throughout the organization (teamwork, self-management, learning organization)?

- *The topics about which communication takes place.* Is the primary focus on profits (winning is everything, S.O.B.), productivity (classical, Blake and McCanse's authority compliance), service (customer-driven), values (values-driven), employee satisfaction (Blake and McCanse's country club), employee maturity (Hersey and Blanchard's life cycle theory), the discovery of good role models (role model philosophy), or, potentially, all of the above (information-driven)?

- *The directions in which communication flows.* Does it flow primarily downward (classical, Theory X, System 1, S.O.B.), upward, downward, and horizontally (teamwork, Theory Y, System 4), or throughout the organization and between the organization and its customers (customer-driven, learning organizations)?

Leadership and Gender

While relatively few women occupy CEO positions in major corporations, some are beginning to argue that successful leaders incorporate communication techniques that historically have been viewed as "feminine." For example, the term **metrosexual**, which emerged from the popular TV show *Queer Eye for the Straight Guy* and has come to refer to a man who pays more attention to his "softer" or "feminine" side, is moving into the workplace. The reason, according to Nancy Halpern, senior vice president of the Strickland Group, an executive coaching organization based in New York, is the huge numbers of employed women. "The impact of women in the workplace has had an enormous effect on how men are expected to behave as leaders," she said. "I have clients who say to me that not long ago if a male executive made the numbers, everyone was happy. But not now. Now, it's 50 percent numbers and 50 percent behavior." And that, she says, means being a metrosexual, which includes "fabulous communication skills, how they dress, their haircut and posture; if they are kinder and gentler, are consensus builders and have good emotional intelligence—traits traditionally associated with women. The kind of drive to get the result no matter what it takes no longer is acceptable if it translates into abusive behavior." Halpern recently wrote an in-house paper titled "The Feminization of Men" that discusses how what used to be called "soft skills" now are necessary for a man's success as a leader—and the importance of being a metrosexual to succeed.[45]

If being a metrosexual—a kind, caring, and inclusive executive—is becoming so important for men, why doesn't it also benefit the people who invented those traits—women? "Because women not only are a minority, but they also get conflicting advice," Halpern answers. "For 20 years, they've been told to be more like men—and clearly that doesn't work." Though the arrival of metrosexuals in the workplace suggests that adapting female traits may pay off for men, women's struggle to obtain equality will take much longer, she observes.

A seemingly contrasting perspective is provided by Lois Frankel in her book, *Nice Girls Don't Get the Corner Office*.[46] She argues that women sabotage themselves and fail to move into leadership positions because "from early childhood, girls are taught that their well-being and ultimate success is contingent upon acting in certain stereotypical ways, such as being polite, soft-spoken, compliant, and relationship-oriented." Consequently, they do things that disempower themselves, such as couching statements as questions, apologizing, using minimizing words, talking too fast, crying, or assuming too much responsibility (such as by allowing others to delegate menial tasks to them or doing others' work for them). On the other hand, however, one of the 101 mistakes women make is "acting like a man." She notes that "acting like a man in the workplace will inevitably get you into trouble." Rather, "Women bring a unique set of behaviors to the workplace that are needed, especially in today's climate. Our tendencies to collaborate rather than compete, listen more than talk, and use relationships rather than muscle to influence are the very same behaviors I coach men to acquire. But it's all about balance." We will return to the subject of gender and leadership in a later chapter on small group communication.

Organizational Culture and Leadership Philosophies

In her excellent summary of the ways in which leadership philosophies have been applied on a day-to-day basis, Coudron observes that the most successful companies have an organizational culture that possesses several key dimensions:[47]

- *Respect for work/life balance*. These companies recognize employees have pressures outside the office and work to ease those pressures by providing such benefits as flexible work schedules, part-time jobs, job sharing, telecommuting, sabbaticals, and on-site day care, dry cleaning, and banking. Among the leaders in this area are Deloitte & Touche LLP, Eddie Bauer, and the city of Phoenix. But some companies go even further, allowing employees to bring "life" into their work via casual dress and personalized office decor, or even by allowing them to play while at work. For example, OddzOn Products, a toy manufacturer, closed the office and took all 100 employees to a movie in the middle of a workday.

- *A sense of purpose*. Successful companies are those in which employees feel connected to the product, to the corporate mission, or to the overall vision of the industry. In such companies, employees are energized by the sense that they are making a meaningful contribution. Employees at Harley-Davidson, based in Milwaukee, Wisconsin, apparently are so excited about their product that many of them have tattooed the company's name on their bodies.

- *Diversity*. An increasingly important dimension of an organization's culture is diversity. Successful companies make employees feel safe in expressing their differences, whatever those differences may be, including gender, race, sexual orientation, work style, temperament, and opinion. Allstate Insurance, headquartered in Northbrook, Illinois, takes diversity seriously and has received extensive recognition for its work to provide opportunities to women, African Americans, Hispanics, and disabled individuals (see Highlighting Diversity). But true commitment to diversity, according to Jerry Hirschberg, president of Nissan Design International, San Diego, California, can best be illustrated by two kinds of parties: "An uncool party is one where people are invited for the sole reason of having a proper and impressive guest list. A cool party, on the other hand, is one where people are invited because they provide a stimulating and enjoyable mix, regardless of whether or not they have the right credentials."[48] Presumably, "cool" companies operate the same way.

- *Participatory management*. The most successful companies have realized that employees on the front lines often have the best ideas and that it is often counterproductive to tell them what to do. In such companies, collaboration is the norm, but it is also possible for individual employees to have an impact.

- *Learning environment.* In the best companies, employees leave at the end of the day knowing more than they did when the day started. Companies such as Motorola, based in Schaumburg, Illinois, offer massive amounts of training and education to their people.

- *Integrity.* Integrity refers to the ability of a company to communicate the truth to employees—whatever that truth may be. But it also refers to an organization's ability to care about the quality of its products and services. Companies with integrity want employees to do a great job, and not just get the job done. Companies also want employees to stand up for what they believe in. More

---

Highlighting Diversity

One Company's Commitment to Diversity: Allstate Insurance

Over the past decade, Allstate Insurance has been honored for devising many programs to foster diversity and support minority groups. Of its 50,000 employees, 52.2% are women, and women of color make up 20% of the workforce and 24% of new hires in 2003.

- Allstate's efforts were officially launched in 1993 when its president and CEO backed diversity as a "strategic imperative." Allstate's efforts center around two goals:

  — expanding career and advancement opportunities for women and minorities, and

  — fostering greater customer growth, retention, and satisfaction (especially crucial since Allstate is one of the country's largest insurers of African Americans and Hispanics).

- In June 2004, *Working Woman* named Allstate *One of the Best Companies for Women of Color.* Five other companies made the list: American Express, Fannie Mae, General Mills, IBM, and JP Morgan Chase & Co.

- *Working Woman* magazine has also recognized Allstate for 13 years as a *Top Company for Working Mothers.*

- *DiversityInc* magazine recently honored Allstate for its commitment to diversity, African Americans, and the recruitment and retention of minorities in general.

- Allstate has demonstrated its commitment to diversity by building long-standing partnerships with organizations devoted to eradicating racial injustice and promoting civil and human rights—such partners as the NAACP, the National Urban League, the Organization of Chinese Americans, and the U.S. Hispanic Leadership Institute.

- To alleviate discrimination, Allstate has partnered with Washington State to create *The Hate Free Zone*—a campaign to create spaces where individuals feel safe, secure, and welcome regardless of race, religion, or ethnicity and where acts of hatred and discrimination will not be tolerated.

- According to the Allstate Foundation, the company supports national and local organizations (through financial and volunteer efforts) in three major areas:

  — safe and vital communities

  — tolerance, inclusion, and diversity

  — economic empowerment

Visit the Allstate Web site at http://www.allstate.com to read more about specific programs.

Source: "*Working Mother Magazine* names Allstate to Elite List of Best Companies for Women of Color," press release [online]. Available: http://www.csrwire.com/article.cgi/2719.html (accessed: August 17, 2004).

recently, some companies also want employees who are interested in volunteering for worthy community projects (see Highlighting Civic Engagement).

Research demonstrates that companies that have established a corporate culture with the characteristics listed above show significantly lower rates of employee turnover and higher levels of employee morale than do organizations with less desirable cultures.

And where does such a culture come from? It starts with leadership. The value an organization places on people, the extent to which it shares information and authority, the topics about which it communicates formally, and its use of upward, downward, and lateral communication channels are all shaped primarily by people in leadership. Yet even individual organizational members at the lowest

---

Highlighting Civic Engagement

Volunteerism Encouraged by Businesses

In June 2002, eighteen CEOs from a number of prominent U.S. companies met with President Bush to discuss employee volunteerism. By December 2002, the group Business Strengthening America (BSA) had developed policies, a governance structure, a mission, and goals and had quietly recruited 100 companies to join the effort.

On their Web site, BSA writes that "all businesses—from small companies to Fortune 500 companies—can help encourage and inspire Americans to participate in service and volunteer activities that are the cornerstones of a healthy society." In particular, they ask supporters (which today number in the hundreds) to:

- incorporate volunteer opportunities on company Web sites and intranets;

- communicate to executives, employees, and prospective employees your company's support of, and *expectations for*, volunteer service;

- integrate volunteer service as a key component of employee/workforce development programs; and

- make information available to employees on how to volunteer most effectively and to record service hours and activities.

Efforts like BSA have come at a timely moment. Following the September 11 attacks and recent corporate scandals, Americans' expectations of companies' community contributions have increased dramatically.

- According to the 2002 Cone Corporate Citizenship Study, 89% of Americans say that it is more important than ever for companies to be socially responsible.

- The result is that volunteerism has become one of the most important features of any company's social investment program.

- Studies have shown that socially responsible companies that encourage their employees to give back to the community are also often highly ranked in employee satisfaction and productivity.

Although government-supported programs to assist the elderly, youth, the disabled, the poor, and the disadvantaged are perhaps more urgently needed than ever before, business involvement in/encouragement of volunteerism with these and other groups is surely a plus.

Sources: Connette Gayle, "Peer Pressure among CEOs Advances Corporate Community Involvement [online]. Available: http://www.onphilanthropy.com; "Business Strengthening America" [online]. Available: http://www.bsanetwrok.org; and "Companies Increasingly Recognize that Volunteering is Good for Business" [online]. Available: http://www.bergenvolunteers.org (all accessed: August 17, 2004).

levels of the organizational hierarchy can have some influence on their organization's culture, because it is possible for nearly any employee to provide leadership. We concur with Tannenbaum, Weschler, and Massarik, who define leadership as "interpersonal influence, exercised in a situation and directed, through the communication process, toward the attainment of specialized goal or goals."[49] By informally exerting leadership that promotes the sort of organizational culture we desire, each of us can help to shape our environment rather than simply being controlled by it.

Providing "Good" Leadership

There are many opportunities for people to assume leadership roles without having been anointed as such. Bob Nelson, author of *1001 Ways to Take Initiative at Work*, says, "anyone in an organization can be a leader. The ability to lead is not a trait formally conferred only on supervisors and managers. In fact, some might say that the most effective leaders in their organizations are informal leaders, line workers without any official supervisory or management role."[50] Michael Useem, director of the Center for Leadership and Change Management at the Wharton School, echoes that thought: "Everybody should be good at leading, whatever their level in the hierarchy." Within organizations large and small, work teams form around special projects. Leaders often are selected informally by the group, and leadership may switch from one individual to another depending on what strengths are needed at the time to move the project forward. In a small business these opportunities can groom people for future management roles as the business grows.

Prominent leadership theorist Warren Bennis claims that "character is the core competency of leadership. Everything else is perishable."[51] Character is built on three factors: ambition and drive, competence and expertise, and a well-exercised moral compass. An effective leader balances these forces. Drive without competence and integrity produces a demagogue. Competence without integrity and drive manifests a technocrat. Someone who has ambition and competence but is void of integrity is a destructive achiever. Bennis also believes that leaders and managers are not one and the same. Leaders do the right things. Managers do things right. Managers focus on the how-to, the short-term, the bottom line. Leaders build cultures that create self-esteem, generate and sustain trust, elevate the dignity of work, create community and foster open communication and, finally, encourage growth and learning.

A similar view was expressed by Richart Notebaert, who left Ameritech Corp. to take over Qwest Communications International in the midst of an accounting scandal that brought indictments against some top executives, a federal investigation, and an imminent threat of bankruptcy. He said his top priority was to open lines of communication with employees, customers, and shareholders. "I came in on a Sunday night and got the senior team together," he said. "On my first day, I met with employees from across the entire corporation and established an open-door policy. I gave everyone my e-mail address—e-mail that only I see—and I've gotten 100,000 since I've been here."

Notebaert advises anyone taking over a company to remember three things: discipline, transparency, and the newspaper test.[52]

We do better when we are open, honest and candid. People may not always like to hear the answer, but they respect you for telling the truth, straight from the shoulder. Whenever you do something, think about how you'd feel to see it printed on the front page of the *Chicago Tribune.* That takes it above the normal ethics thing.

Finally, television critic Michael Medved pointed to the similarity between successful leaders and successful television programs, noting that current programs have ensemble casts, not superstars.[53] The most acclaimed and popular programs feature an array of nicely matched but lesser-known players—as in Emmy leaders *The West Wing* and *The Sopranos,* or ratings champs such as *Everybody Loves Raymond, CSI, Friends, Seinfeld, Will and Grace, ER,* and *Survivor.* When people who had become stars in these ensemble shows tried to do shows on their own, they invariably failed. When the networks attempted to lure viewers by employing Hollywood superstars (*The Bette Midler Show* or *The Geena Davis Show*), the results proved quickly disastrous.

Medved claims that a similar principle operates in organizations. Superstar leaders consume too much energy and attention, thereby discouraging the emergence of new generations of outstanding performers. Stars also distort every organizational structure, forcing everything to revolve around them instead of fostering balanced lines of responsibility. Politics, for example, has experienced a de-emphasis on all-powerful charismatic figures. Bill Clinton was a political superstar. For good or ill, he dominated every aspect of his administration and easily overshadowed all of his colleagues. George W. Bush, on the other hand, is comfortable working with partners such as Colin Powell, Condoleezza Rice, and Dick Cheney, who effortlessly upstage him. Clinton's superstardom also proved difficult to pass on to his chosen successor, Al Gore, highlighting another chronic problem of overwhelming personalities: they tend to make potential replacements look pallid and drab by comparison. That is one reason the world of business has also moved away from a fascination with attention-grabbing swashbucklers. Investors understand that any organization that's totally dependent on such a personality is inherently on shaky ground. Even the few undeniable superstars today (Bill Gates at Microsoft, for example) are soft-spoken commanders noted for their emphasis on building a reliable team to back them up.

Participants in these "ensemble cast" organizations may feel stressed through the pressure placed on all of them to rely on one another; but without one outstanding personality ruling the roost, it's more difficult for anyone to feel superfluous or unimportant.

So how can you, as a formal or informal leader, exert influence that contributes to a desirable organizational culture? According to "The Manager's Intelligence Report," published by Lawrence Ragan Communications, if you gathered 100 experienced managers together and asked for their advice, you would hear something like this:[54]

- "Don't be afraid of the phrase, 'I don't know.'" If you don't know the answer, don't try to bluff. If you're at fault, take the blame. If you're wrong, apologize. A wise person once said, "If you always tell the truth, you never have to remember anything."

- "Never gossip." And if someone wants to gossip with you, politely say you're not interested. This old corporate adage is true: when someone gossips, two careers are hurt—the person being talked about, and the person doing the talking.

- "No task is beneath you." Don't think you're above anything. Be the good example and pitch in—especially if the job is one that nobody wants to do.

- "Share the credit wherever possible." Leaders who spread credit around look much stronger than those who take all the credit themselves.

- "Ask for help." If you think you're in over your head, you are. Before it gets out of hand, ask someone for help—most people enjoy giving a hand. Besides saving yourself from embarrassment, you'll make a friend and ally.

- "Keep your salary to yourself." Discussing salary is a no-win proposition. Either you'll be upset because someone is making more than you, or someone will be upset with you.

- "When you don't like someone, don't let it show." Especially if you outrank them. Never burn bridges or offend others as you move ahead.

- "Let it go." When you are slighted, passed over, mistreated, etc., move on. Harboring a grudge will not advance your career.

- "When you're right, don't gloat." The only time you should ever use the phrase "I told you so" is if someone says to you, "You were right. I really could succeed at that project."

In addition to these suggestions, we would add seven more:

- Make others feel important. If your goals and decisions are self-centered, your colleagues will lose their enthusiasm quickly. Ask for and listen to their input and emphasize their strengths and contributions, not your own.

- Promote a shared vision. Your colleagues need a clear idea of where you're leading them, and they need to understand why that goal is valuable to them. Your job as a leader is to provide that vision.

- Follow the Golden Rule. Treat your colleagues the way you enjoy being treated. An abusive leader attracts few loyal followers.

- Admit mistakes. If people suspect you're covering up your own errors, they'll hide their mistakes, too, and you'll lack valuable information for making decisions.

- Criticize others only in private. Public praise encourages others to excel, but public criticism only embarrasses and alienates everyone.

- Stay close to the action. You need to be visible to the members of your organization. Talk to people, visit other offices and work sites, ask questions, and observe how business is being handled.

- Lastly, to learn more about effective leadership, you could consult one or more of the books listed in Business Brief 3.3, but you also could go to two helpful Web sites that discuss leadership principles: http://www.smartleadership.com or http://www.emergingleader.com.

Business Brief 3.3

Consider Reading These Books on Leadership

While books about leadership are plentiful, but not necessarily worthwhile, a few leadership books are worthy of review, at least in the opinion of an editorial appearing in the magazine *Business 2.0*:

- *The Manual,* by Epictetus (1st Century AD). The Stoic philosopher Epictetus provided what may have been the world's first business text, offering a list of simple suggestions such as "Enter into no contest in which it is not in your power to conquer" and "Let only what is necessary be said, and in few words." *The Manual* is noteworthy for its emphasis on moral leadership.

- *The Prince,* by Machiavelli (1513). While many believe *The Prince* is a cynical description of techniques for manipulation, Machiavelli's meaning is more subtle and his emphasis on informed action and striving for virtue are worthwhile.

- *Moby Dick*, by Herman Melville (1851). An epic tragedy about a leader who fails to understand the value of leadership, the book describes how Captain Ahab uses fear as a motivational tool while pursuing his own personal goals, ultimately losing the support of his crew—as well as his ship.

- *Shackleton's Way*, by Margot Morrell and Stephanie Capparell (2001). The tale of explorer Sir Earnest Shackleton, whose ship and crew were trapped in icy Antarctic waters for two years, is one of the world's great survival stories and illustrates the leadership concepts of resourcefulness, teamwork, and triumph over adversity.

- *The Change Makers*, by Maury Klein (2003). Klein studied the biographies of 26 entrepreneurs—from Thomas Edison to Henry Ford to Bill Gates—to identify the secrets of their success. He discovered that there is no one right way to do things, but shows how creativity, failure, family, and work ethic combine to make great leaders.

Source: *Business 2.0* (September 2003): 139–140.

LEADERSHIP CHALLENGES IN CONTEMPORARY ORGANIZATIONS

Organizations and everyone within them face an ever-increasing rate of change and a set of issues that have critical implications for organizational communication. In many ways these challenges make it all the more difficult for leaders, formal and informal, to build a positive organizational culture. In this section, we will review some of the issues that are most closely related to organizational cultures and communication practices.

Pressure and Stress in the Workplace

For many workers, life in corporate America is increasingly turning into a pressure cooker with nonstop stress, long hours, and never-ending worries about the next layoffs. Workers are being asked to do more with less and at faster speeds, even as they contend with downsizing, restructuring, and outsourcing to foreign workers. In addition to wage freezes or even pay cuts, many have had to bear the cost of rising health-care premiums, and some stand to lose overtime pay thanks to proposed new government rules.[55]

"It used to be working hard meant you got a promotion," said Mitchell Marks, a San Francisco organizational psychologist who helps corporations cope with mergers and other workforce changes. "Now, working hard means staying in the same place." Marks notes that because of this stress, people are taking longer to return phone calls, and when they do call back, they are a bit ruder.

> It's not because they are bad people. . . . They are frazzled. People are running scared. . . . People can't change, change, change. People aren't machines. It's going to get worse before it gets better: this focus on speed at any cost, this focus on short-term results. The human machine is going to break.

Bruce Talgan, a workplace expert and chief executive of Rainmaker Thinking, Inc., in New Haven, Connecticut, describes the situation as the "real new economy, where employers must be ruthless to survive, and individuals must be very aggressive to succeed."

Recent research suggests that *pressure in the workplace is taking a toll*. According to a 2004 study by Randstad North America, an international staffing firm, 73 percent of employees said it is important to feel like they are part of a family at work, up from 67 percent in January 2002. Employers also said they prefer a closer-knit, familial environment at work (84 percent, up from 74 percent a year before). But while more employers and employees want a workplace "family" culture, fewer say such an environment exists in their organization. A January 2004 survey of 1,200 U.S. workers by the consulting firm Watson Wyatt & Co. found that overall employee commitment levels have dropped since 2002. In addition, a survey based on more than 2,800 telephone interviews found that while 70 percent of employees say they are loyal to the boss, only 53 percent of employers believe this is the case. Similarly, while 77 percent of bosses say they are loyal to their workers, only 41 percent of workers think the boss is loyal to them. Apparently, employee concerns about job security and employer fears about turnover once the economy improves have heightened suspicions on both sides, making those warm, fuzzy feelings both sides say they want even harder to achieve and sustain.[56]

In her article "Employees Behaving Badly," Laura Stack observes that several *economic and social trends have heightened worker sensitivity to stress*—war, a bad economy, layoffs, greater workloads, increased productivity demands, and longer hours.[57]

> Mix that with smaller, cramped workspaces that make employees feel restless and disorganized. Add office clutter, shorter response time requirements and a dash of technology to increase customer expectations. Beat out interpersonal communication. Blend with shifting responsibilities and work that is never complete, reducing time spent off work. Add a fluid, diverse, multi-generational workforce with different work process methods, and you've got a recipe for extreme stress.

According to the American Institute of Stress, 40 percent of worker turnover is the result of job stress, and some one million workers are absent each workday because of stress-related complaints.[59] In turn, extremely stressful conditions can cause employees to have short tempers and poor working relationships. In its 2000 survey of 775 workers, University of North Carolina's Kenan-Flagler Business School showed that 12 percent of workers had quit their jobs to avoid nasty people at work, and 45 percent were thinking about doing so. In addition, more than half of workers lost time worrying about irate or rude people in the office.

Because of the emergence of "desk rage" and violence in the workplace, experts suggest that people in organizations should be on the lookout for the following *stress stages* among their colleagues:

1. Physical stage: headaches, illness, fatigue

2. Social stage: negativity, blaming things on others, missing deadlines, working through lunch

3. Cerebral stage: clock-watching, errors in assignments, minor accidents, absentmindedness, indecisiveness

4. Emotional stage: anger, sadness, crying, yelling, feelings of being overwhelmed, depression

5. Spiritual stage: brooding, crying, wanting to make drastic changes in life, not relating well with people, distancing themselves from personal relationships

"Desk rage" is usually a stage 4 stress reaction when an employee "just can't take it any more." To prevent employees from reaching this stress level, or to help those who do cope with their feelings, organizations increasingly are providing *anger management workshops*, where the aim is to teach people to handle emotions without losing control. Courses lay out how to deal with anger in the moment—a strategy that promises to improve relationships and lessen the chance of blowing up.

In the past couple of years, more business and governmental organizations have enlisted anger management services, which can cost more than $2,500 for one-on-one "coaching." Postal workers, prison guards, and business leaders have taken workshops and seminars. Some medical schools, such as the University of Miami's, are putting students through special training to help them cope better with their own and their patients' anger.

Most anger management classes share basic principles of psychology—identifying and learning to control angry emotions and employing relaxation techniques to minimize the physiological responses to anger. Classes help clients decide what is worth getting angry over and what is not. But there is little research to demonstrate whether these programs work.

Effective communication also can help people manage their anger, says Robert John McCrary, a psychologist at G. Werber Bryan Psychiatric Hospital in Columbia, South Carolina. He recommends:

- Use active listening. Make eye contact and say, "I understand that you feel such-and-such." This helps calm the situation and clarify misunderstandings.

- Choose nonattacking words and use a polite tone.

- Do not let the argument expand. Stick with the current issue, not old ones. Politely repeat that you will stick to the first issue and deal with the others later.

- Resist the temptation to stop and defend yourself from personal attacks.[60]

Also, reducing noise levels in the workplace can help, even if it is just encouraging employees to take breaks or lunch or go out for fresh air, or use white-noise machines or headsets to mask constant, low-level noises like keyboards, voices, or the hum of a photocopier—all of which serve to elevate stress hormones.

Ultimately, the key to helping members of an organization cope with mounting pressure is to build a supportive, positive organizational culture, and the key to building such a culture is good communication. However, recent research also illustrates that "good" communication is in the eye of the beholder. Most of the employers in the Randstad North America study (92 percent) rated communication with employees as excellent, but only 69 percent of employees said their bosses were good communicators. On the other hand, about 30 percent of employees said their employers communicated poorly or danced around the truth.

Clearly, leaders face an increasingly challenging work environment.

Telecommuting and Virtual Teams

Computers are everywhere in organizations today, and the proliferation of computers in turn allows many members of organizations to do their work virtually anywhere. According to research by Gartner, Inc., 137 million workers worldwide were involved in some form of remote electronic work by 2003, and research by the International Telework Association and Council (ITAC), located in Washington, DC, showed that there were 23.6 million teleworkers in the United States. Gartner projects that by the year 2010, employees will spend 30 percent of their time alone, 5 percent interacting with people in the same place and time, 25 percent interacting with people in a different place and same time, and 40 percent interacting with people in a different place and time.[61]

As businesses become more interconnected and more global, a key element of their communications will be the use of virtual teams. As we noted in chapter 2, virtual teams are groups of people who work together, even though they may be located in different offices, different time zones, and even different continents. Virtual teams may have a global reach or involve combinations of local telecommuting members and more traditional in-house workers. Team members may deal with key players who are not only out of the country but also work for another organization, perhaps as suppliers who are on the virtual team to add information and technical support.

Virtual teams pose both advantages and challenges. Electronic communication allows companies to recruit talent without the constraints of location and to offer more scheduling flexibility; for example, telecommuting enables employees to work from their homes rather than going to the company's offices. It also creates the potential for follow-the-sun, 24-hour workdays and the ability to maintain close contact with customers worldwide. However, it also is difficult to manage people who must work collaboratively and interactively but may never actually lay eyes on one another. The complexities and subtleties of dealing with widely different personalities, cultures, and languages make communication far more difficult among virtual team members. Consequently, it is important for team participants, and particularly team leaders, to determine the best technology to facilitate communication and to work hard to engender trust and productivity among team members.[61]

Using the right technology can be challenging, given the vast array of electronic technologies available to choose from. A thorough understanding of e-mail, teleconferencing, and videoconferencing is vital, but knowledge of other tools, such as Webcasts, meeting managers, white boards, bulletin boards, and data sharing helps workers to develop digital environments that foster ingenuity and innovation.

For example, a manager at Nortel Networks wanted to teach her virtual team of 60 finance and legal employees basic principles of negotiation. Since team members were located around the world, the meeting was scheduled on the company's intranet calendar, and participants were invited by e-mail to attend. The team leader chose an assortment of technology tools, including one designed for group meetings called Meeting Manager. Participants were on individual PCs and also on a teleconference line, so they could talk and listen to one another. The team leader prepared charts, which team members could view on their screens, and provided an electronic white board for random ideas and scribbling. The leader obtained charts from the meeting presenters and uploaded them onto the company's Meeting Manager, which allowed for group viewing. As chair of the meeting, she was able to control the order of the meeting and the viewing of the charts. Participants posted questions on the white board, which the leader could see. She was then able to address or answer the questions on the computer screen, or pose and take questions on the phone.

Nortel Networks relies heavily on Meeting Manager, Web Meeting, and teleconferencing. When visual cues are especially important, the company uses videoconferencing, Webcasts for mass audience viewing, and very regular updates on the company's intranet so that everyone on the team has the same information.

New York-based accounting and consulting firm Deloitte & Touche LLP has 90,000 employees in 130 countries, and its far-flung clients need virtual work teams so that accurate information is available to everyone at all times. To address the issue of globally shared data, the firm created a Web-based tracking system that enables anyone anywhere in the world to check the status of company projects. The system operates like a file that contains all policy documents necessary to serve the clients, including appropriate practice tools that were developed at different locations around the world. If, for example, there is a tax decision that affects a specific region or client, it is put in the system.

Virtual teams demand some critical nontechnological skills. Managers have to trust that people will perform when they are away from direct supervision. Individual team members need to develop trust across different media, such as e-mail and telephone, which can be difficult to do. One reason developing trust is so crucial is that teams are formed to create knowledge. Problems often arise when people work across cultures and have different perceptions of projects. They have to be able to trust each other and the leader if they are going to get the job done effectively.

To help build that trust, the *leader must be explicit about the team's goals* whenever the team has a meeting, whether it is a teleconference, videoconference, or face-to-face encounter. In addition, *feedback on the group's progress is vital;* all group members need a clear, shared understanding of how far the group has come and what the group knows as a whole. Group leaders should *set up regular virtual meetings* to share expectations and debriefings. They should frame the team's objectives so members clearly understand their roles; they should emphasize the consequences of team decisions; and they should provide ongoing monitoring and honest feedback about how the team is doing. Finally, to build a sense of team spirit among team members who never see one another, formal or informal leaders should try to **keep team interactions upbeat and action oriented**, celebrate reaching targets, and if possible, create a shared space—a "virtual water cooler"—where members can interact beyond the scope of the work.

Generally, research investigating the effects of telecommuting has produced positive findings. According to data from ITAC, telecommuting reduces turnover by 20 percent on average, boosts productivity by up to 22 percent, and trims absenteeism by nearly 60 percent. However, a study of employees and managers by Boston College's Center for Work & Family in Chestnut Hill, Massachusetts, found that telecommuting can present serious disadvantages. The study found that telecommuters work more, rate their work/life balance and life satisfaction significantly lower, believe they have worse relationships with their managers and coworkers, and are less committed to their jobs. Telecommuting also causes more stress than other types of flexible work arrangements, such as daily flextime.[62]

Many leaders thus find themselves trying to provide leadership and build positive work cultures among colleagues who are scattered around a variety of locations, and even a variety of continents, making the challenges of effective leadership greater than ever.

BEING AN EFFECTIVE FOLLOWER

Just as leaders have been the focus of this chapter, so too are leaders the primary focus in most organizations. Indeed, CEO compensation has risen 1,900 percent since 1980, while the pay of those they lead has grown just 74 percent, according to the AFL-CIO. In 2003, the average CEO of a major company received $9.2 million in total compensation.[63] Similarly, a search on Amazon.com turns up 57,000 hits on leadership, while a search on followership turns up fewer than 500 hits, and a Google search for leadership turns up 19.8 million hits, but followership turns up 15,400 hits. Yet without followers, there would be no leaders, and a leader's success is determined largely by the performance and actions of his or her followers.

Some experts now are saying that the real shortage is in good followers, not in good leaders. Houston corporate governance consultant Brent Longnecker says the lack of great followers is as much to blame as crooked executives for recent scandals.[64] Followers have a duty to speak up, he says. Few do. Dennis Haley, CEO of Academy Leadership, agrees. In his book, *The Leader's Compass*, he writes that ethical and financial scandals were "at the very least enabled by yes men and yes women who adapted chameleon-like."[65]

At a leadership training camp in Delaware, Yale University psychiatry professor and leadership expert David Berg asks future CEOs to name great followers from literature and pop culture. Several are named, but Berg focuses on Tonto and Mr. Spock. The Lone Ranger and Captain Kirk could hardly have functioned without their followers. Spock and Tonto were not mindless servants. They knew their place, yet pushed their leader's boundaries. They eliminated blind spots. Spock's logic offset Kirk's intuition. The Lone Ranger's daring came from the assurance that Tonto would rescue him from tight spots.

Followership requires courage, Berg says. There is no guarantee that whistle-blowers, or even employees who speak their mind, won't get fired. "A winning team is not people who salute and march down the path. The closer you get to the customer, the more you know about where the opportunities are. All good ideas are not in the headquarters of corporations."[66]

Leaders deserve the followers' best advice, and then their unconditional commitment to the decision. "I draw the line if it's unethical or immoral," says retired Army colonel Larry Donnithorne, author of *The West Point Way of Leadership*.[67] Followers have an obligation to express strong disagreement with the leader. It's also appropriate for followers to be honest when asked about a decision they disagree with. Entrepreneur and former executive Liz Ryan offers 10 pieces of advice to followers from the perspective of a boss:[68]

- Don't take it personally when I'm abrupt. Bosses don't necessarily handle stress any better than anyone else does.
- I can't make a federal case out of every issue that's important to you. When it comes to doing battle with my own boss or other departments, please let me pick my battles on your behalf.
- I am not King Solomon. When you and a coworker both want the desk next to the window, play rock-paper-scissors.
- Don't give me a reason to watch you like a hawk.
- You're the expert on how to do your job, not me. Don't be frustrated that I don't know the details. I have a different job description than you do.
- When you're angry with me, let me know.
- Don't ask me to tell you what I can't talk about. Are layoffs coming? I like you, but not enough to jeopardize my job.
- Bring me problems as far in advance as possible. I can help you out of a jam if I have lead time.
- Give me feedback on my management style but be tactful and constructive.
- I can help you if you goof up, but don't do anything really stupid.

Following a Bad Leader

Unfortunately, however, not every leader in an organization is a sterling example of the principles this chapter has described. Bosses who treat their employees like punching bags rather than assets are not uncommon in the workplace, and you should take steps to protect yourself should you find yourself working for a proponent of the S.O.B. philosophy. Katherine Sopranos suggests:[69]

> From the beginning of your employment, keep dated records of conversations, comments, and scenarios that occurred between you and your boss. Detailed documentation is evidence of your tumultuous working conditions, and it allows you leverage if you decide to sue for emotional distress or physical harm, such as stomach conditions. Having collected this documentation, you should discuss it individually or with a group of colleagues, with Human Resources or a higher-level executive in the company, including your boss's boss. And mention that you spoke with an attorney.

Lisa Bertagnoli describes what she terms "dragon bosses" who tear down employees' self-esteem and hamstring their careers.[70] They alienate their followers to the degree that employees dream up ways to sabotage the company, not enhance its success. Although dragon bosses may initially boost productivity, usually employees end up being less productive due to the stress of working under a poor manager.

An article in the *New York Times*, "Fear in the Workplace: The Bullying Boss," describes four different varieties of bullying bosses based on interviews conducted by the Workplace Bullying and Trauma Institute. Regardless of style, each boss seeks control.

- *The Snake*—the most common type of bully, this boss is a Jekyll and Hyde who trashes you behind your back.
- *The Screamer*—less common, this boss is a fist-pounder who thrives on public displays of rage.
- *The Nitpicker*—a boss who uses insinuation and insult to chip away at an employee's confidence.
- *Gatekeeper*—cold and controlling, this boss plays favorites, allowing some workers to succeed and cutting others off from resources needed to get the job done.[71]

Anywhere from 3 to 5 percent of American bosses count as "white-collar psychopaths," said David L. Weiner, author of *Power Freaks: Dealing with Them in the Workplace or Anyplace*.[72] Power-freak bosses tend to exhibit the same characteristics. They play employees against each other, supposedly for the good of the company. While reprimanding employees, they use phrases such as "you could have" or "you should have" or "why didn't you?" Their favorite and most demeaning ploy is the double-bind, where they tell an employee exactly how to perform a task, then scream at them for having done it that way, according to Patrick Dorin, author of *The Dragon Complex: Strategies for Identifying and Conquering Workplace Abuse*.[73] A Web site, http://www.powerfreaks.com, provides a power quiz that lets you identify the extent to which you or others exhibit "dragon boss" characteristics.

Dealing with a dragon boss can be difficult and stressful. When leaving is not an option, Weiner suggests the somewhat distasteful option of becoming passive. "A lot of people think you should challenge these people. That's wrong. You have to be compliant," he says. Weiner suggests sitting as far away as possible from the boss, leaving him or her alone unless absolutely necessary, and never breaking a confidence with him or her. Also effective is admitting mistakes, actual or imagined: "Admit it and take the tantrum that will inevitably come your way," he recommends.

Dorin recommends never bad-mouthing the boss, but keeping a diary of your dealings with the person. "It's crucial to your emotional health and will be important if you ever end up in court with that person," he says. That's a possibility if the boss ever turns abusive; such behavior warrants an immediate visit to the organization's human resources department.

It is also important to stay true to yourself—and to treat your fellow employees with respect. Organizational psychologists have been studying the effects of management styles on small groups and have found that those who work for bullying, insensitive bosses tend themselves to become less sensitive and more aggressive over time. Dr. Michelle Duffy, a psychologist in the University of Kentucky Business School, notes: "It looks like if there's a strong leader in the group, then that person's behavior is contagious." And if that leader is really nasty, then "moral disengagement spreads like a germ."[74] Based on interviews with over 500 workers, Duffy also reported that while workers were delighted to receive praise from a boss, they were even more delighted when the praise was accompanied by news that another colleague was struggling. Sometimes, employees who witness a boss bully a coworker may begin to wonder if the worker deserved the treatment—if he or she messed up or was lazy—even when they have seen the boss in action before. To avoid falling into these traps, experts recommend participating in old-fashioned grousing sessions—sharing the misery with others—but to guard against substituting these informal group sessions for lodging justified formal complaints.

Ingratiation

In "The Fine Art of Sucking Up," Girard points out the value of ingratiating oneself with one's superiors.[75] To assess the value of ingratiation, Jenny Chatman, a professor at the University of California at Berkeley's Haas School of Business, interviewed 120 Northwestern University students who were interviewing for jobs. Those who told corporate recruiters what they wanted to hear (such as, "Your company has a reputation for being team-oriented, and that is something I truly value") landed jobs twice as fast as their more reserved but equally qualified peers. "Targets eat it up," Chatman explained. "People are happy to be ingratiated upon." Girard suggests several communication strategies that leaders "eat up," such as:

- Master the art of eye contact. Maintaining eye contact with a leader shows interest.

- Incorporate key ideas or slogans. Using the boss's pet phrases in meetings, reports, and memos shows you are getting the message, you respect her opinions, and you firmly grasp what she wants from you on the job.

- Be aware of your managers' interests. Those pictures on your manager's desk are there for a reason. Ask how they're doing. Talk about her, not you.

- Run ideas by managers who are most likely to hate them. This protects you from looking like a dolt later on and proves that you covet their opinion.

- Take credit for accomplishments. Send managers concise e-mails that report your accomplishments, but don't forget to credit others who helped.

- Beware of ingratiating one manager at the expense of another. Don't try to make a friend of one leader by criticizing another. You never know who talks to whom, or for whom you might end up working some day.

Girard even suggests some specific comments to make to your boss:

- "I'm really excited about your proposal. What an original idea." (leaders like supportive followers)

- "It's like you said in last week's meeting: 'the brand is everything.'" (leaders like to hear themselves quoted)

- "Thanks for your excellent advice on the revision. It made a big difference." (leaders like appreciative followers)

- "You look great. That Zone diet is really working." (leaders like compliments)

- "Got it. Great idea. I'll do it that way, and you said you want it tonight, right?" (leaders like it when you show that you have listened intently)

On their face, Girard's suggestions sound insincere and manipulative, and thus raise some potential ethical concerns. Yet many of these suggestions are the same ones offered to people who aspire to become effective leaders: run ideas by others, be aware of their interests, do not ingratiate one person by trashing another, show appreciation, give (hopefully sincere) compliments, and listen intently, for example. Therefore, the skills that make a good leader and the skills that typify a good follower may, in fact, be the same.

SUMMARY

In this chapter, we have examined how leadership and followership impact the organization's culture. Leadership philosophies have evolved significantly from the beginning of the twentieth century to the present. The earlier theories tended to stress more structure and leader control (with a task focus), while more recent theories have emphasized employee participation and empowerment (with a greater concern for human relationships as well as task productivity).

It is our view that in almost any organization, the preferable organizational philosophy, and the corresponding leadership style, is one that encourages others to participate, respects a diversity of perspectives, values listening as much as talking, and encourages everyone to exert leadership appropriately. Every organization needs employees who are capable of influencing others, completing tasks without close supervision, suggesting constructive changes, and thinking in independent and creative ways. Each of these is a form of leadership behavior that should be widely distributed across the organization rather than concentrated at the very top. Thus, the most effective leaders share leadership roles with others while remaining role models themselves. They demonstrate high expectations and goodwill toward their fellow employees, a willingness to listen to and tolerate dissent, and high personal and professional integrity.

Today's organizations face many challenges, ranging from dealing with new technologies to workplace stress. Both leaders and followers must seek new ways to work together, to develop and sustain trust, and to treat each other with mutual respect. They will have the best chance of realizing these goals if they can create and sustain organizational cultures that are characterized by a respect for work/life balance, a clearly communicated sense of purpose or mission, a respect for and commitment to diversity, an enduring commitment to integrity in policies and actions, an emphasis on employee involvement and participation, and the creation of a constructive organizational environment in which all members can learn and grow.

Questions For Discussion

1. What are the key components of an organization's culture?

2. Which three of the leadership philosophies do you prefer? Why? Briefly describe each.

3. Which ones do you find least appealing? Explain.

4. If you were asked to construct a profile of an effective leader, what characteristics would you include? Why?

5. If you were asked to construct a profile of an effective follower, what characteristics would you include? Why?

6. What are the chief contributors to stress in the workplace?

7. What do you see as being the greatest challenges and opportunities associated with the use of virtual teams in organizations?

8. What are some ways to deal with a bullying boss?

9. How do you feel about ingratiating yourself with your boss? Elaborate.

10. Based on everything you have read in this book so far, what leadership qualities will you especially seek in your boss when you interview for your first job?

Exercises

1. Think of an organization for which you have worked or with which you are very familiar. Which organizational theory seems to prevail in this organization? Cite specific examples to support your views.

2. From the business section of a newspaper, clip articles referring to any organizational practices that illustrate principles of one of the organizational schools of thought. Bring it to class to share with others.

3. Arrange to interview an individual who currently serves in a leadership position. Ask this person to describe her/his philosophy of or approach to leadership and management. How does this leader make decisions or solve problems? After the interview, write a brief essay in which you describe the theory (or theories) of management that best characterizes the leader you interviewed.

4. Find an organization that is culturally diverse. Talk to a member of that organization regarding how that diversity is managed. Share your findings with the class.

5. Talk to at least three people who have held several jobs. Ask them to describe organizational situations in which they have felt especially empowered—or, by contrast, not at all empowered. What factors contributed to these situations?

Case Application 3.1   Complaining on the Net

An interesting use for the Internet has developed recently—complaining. As Guynn reports, the traditional labor movement may have lost some of its vigor, but there is a growing worker rebellion on the Web. Hundreds of sites have popped up—serving as public forums where disgruntled workers "kvetch" and moan about their companies, jobs, and bosses. Workers say they are overworked, underpaid, mistreated, or fired for no good reason. Some sites, such as "Working for the Man," offer subversive advice, such as frown while "fake-working," randomly delete files or documents, or skimp on personal hygiene.

With the power and reach of the Web, this kind of job misery has found a lot of company. But some companies contend that people are taking their rage to extremes. And they're fighting back. The Adobe Systems legal team is working to shut down the Adobe Trouble site. And the *Orange County Register* made headlines of its own when it took legal action against a Web site, called the Orange County Unregistered Press, operated by a former newspaper employee.

Source: Jessica Guynn, "Rankled Workers Go Online," *The Valley Times*, July 24, 1998, sec. 1, 1.

Questions

1. From the perspective of an employee, what is your view of the appropriateness of the Web being used in this fashion?

2. From the perspective of a business owner, what do you think about the appropriateness of using the Web in this fashion?

3. If you were a business owner, how might you use such Web sites to your own advantage?

PART 2

INTERPERSONAL COMMUNICATION

Whether I'm selling or buying, whether I'm hiring or being hired, whether I'm negotiating a contract or responding to someone else's demands, I want to know where the other person is coming from. I want to know the other person's real self.

—Mark H. McCormack,

What They Don't Teach You at Harvard Business School

4

Verbal Messages

After reading this chapter, you should be able to:

- ❑ List and explain the semantic problems that words pose and ways to avoid them
- ❑ Write using sound principles of composition, wording and phrasing, punctuation, grammar, and spelling
- ❑ Discuss storytelling as a communication strategy and create a personal story
- ❑ List and explain rules for effectively using e-mail
- ❑ List and explain verbal behaviors that commonly produce defensive reactions
- ❑ List and explain verbal behaviors that show and elicit aggression
- ❑ Describe types of gossip and ways of keeping it to a minimum in organizations
- ❑ Discuss the disadvantages of swearing
- ❑ List and explain supportive verbal behaviors
- ❑ List and explain assertive verbal behaviors
- ❑ Describe steps for giving positive feedback
- ❑ Describe steps for giving corrective feedback
- ❑ Prepare an effective apology

Several years ago, Sullivan reported the results of research that compared characteristics of successful company presidents with those of average college graduates.[1] Perhaps not surprisingly, the study showed that company presidents excelled in several areas, including (in order): verbal skills, mathematical reasoning, logical thinking, personality (presidents were more dynamic and assertive, with more positive attitudes toward other people), energy and drive, ascendance (presidents had more leadership confidence and assertiveness), personal relations (presidents had greater ability to get along with others and, perhaps surprisingly, were kinder and more sympathetic, understanding, tolerant, and warm-hearted), and values (most presidents placed high value on gaining power and responsibility and on attaining the financial rewards that go with those objectives). The importance of verbal skills is therefore obvious; what is less obvious is that each of these other qualities manifests itself in various communication behaviors. As we have said repeatedly, your ability to succeed is directly tied to your ability to communicate.

Preview

The cues we transmit to other people traditionally have been divided into two general categories: verbal messages (those that involve spoken, written, or electronically transmitted words) and nonverbal messages (cues that convey meaning without the use of words or that modify the meaning of the words we use). Although the adage "Actions speak louder than words" is certainly true, nonverbal cues convey significantly more meaning than verbal messages in face-to-face encounters, in today's organizations verbal messages have become increasingly important. Much communication today occurs electronically, via e-mail and text messaging, so that in many cases, there are no nonverbal cues on which to rely for meaning—the entire message is verbal. In addition, written documents, such as resumes, letters, memoranda, proposals, and reports, remain at the heart of communication in many organizations, even though they may be transmitted electronically rather than put on paper. Consequently, in this chapter we will focus only on verbal messages, saving for the next chapter a consideration of the nonverbal cues that accompany our words when we interact with others.

USING WORDS: SEMANTICS

Most of this book is about words. In various chapters, we discuss what to say to influence the thoughts and actions of others, what to ask to solicit information during interviews, how to structure words so they make sense in conveying information, and how to use words to lead groups effectively. But in this section, we want to take a more microscopic view of words and the impact they have on communication within organizations.

In his editorial in *Newsweek*, Alter underscores the importance of words when he argues that "language is the most underappreciated force in politics."[2] To prove his case, he asks:

> Why does the rest of the world so dislike President [George W.] Bush? The answer is the cowboy language that Bush uses: "Axis of Evil." "Either you're with us, or you are with the terrorists." "Bring it on." The folks who work at the Arab network Al-Jazeera don't hate us for who we are. . . . They hate us— more specifically, our government—for what we say. "With words, we govern," as Benjamin Disraeli put it.

Certainly, U.S. corporations are well aware of the power of words. For example, although airline pilots are encouraged to talk to passengers frequently over the public address system, using words such as "late" or "turbulence," let alone "thunderstorm," is discouraged. Instead, according to a U.S. Airways guide, a captain should stick to stating the "new departure time," call turbulence "bumpy air," and refer to a thunderstorm as a "rain shower." Liz Harrison, who coordinates Northwest Airlines' fear of flying program, notes that pilots' careless use of words can unwittingly frighten passengers who are nervous about flying.[3] For example, when a flight hit some rough, bumpy air the pilot went on the PA and announced, "Forgive me; I'm just learning"—an attempt at humor that instead made nervous passengers even more so. Similarly, words like "terminal" (which to a fearful flier means "death," Harrison says) and even "fog" are avoided (because passengers associate airplanes crashing in the fog, presumably). Preferred words are "mist," "haze," or even "restricted visibility." At Delta, the flight crew guide advises pilots to avoid the term "aborted takeoff." According to the guide, "the word abort has a negative effect." Instead, pilots should say "We apologize for the inconvenience in discontinuing the takeoff, but there was an inconsistency between two of our instruments."

Often we hear people say something like, "It's just a question of semantics," or "We're having problems with semantics." What they mean is that they are concerned with words. And well they should be—perhaps the most imperfect part of the imperfect process we call communication is the words people send one another. Seeking to improve our understanding of language, an entire field called *general semantics* was developed several decades ago to investigate the effects words have on our everyday lives.

Semantic Problems

Through the efforts of Johnson, Korzybski, and others, several problems common to the words we use have been brought to light.[4]

- *Bypassing* is a semantic problem that stems from the nature of "meaning" and occurs when the same words mean different things to different people. Words have no meaning in and of themselves; rather, we have agreed that certain words symbolize certain ideas or things, and it is through this shared agreement that words have utility. The word "terminal" means "a place where airplanes park" to a pilot, but to a nervous flier it could mean "end of life."

- *Allness* stems from the word "is." Often we apply this word to people, noting that "She is a manager," "He is a secretary," and so on. Labels like "manager" and "secretary" pose no terrible problems; labels like "lazy," "disgruntled," and "racist" are another matter. Essentially, the "allness" principle holds that when we apply a label to someone by using the word "is," we are saying, "She or he is that, and nothing more." Thus, when a manager concludes that a certain worker is "lazy," the manager tends to see that individual only as a lazy person. As a result, the manager continually watches over the employee, often creating resentment within the worker that in turn makes him or her less inclined to work hard. Thus, the term "lazy" becomes a self-fulfilling prophecy. Since people are complex and constantly changing, treatment of a person based on an "allness" description is likely to be inappropriate.

- *Stereotyping* comes from the labels we affix to people when using the word "is." We may believe that certain categories of people typically do certain things: that all "politicians" are dishonest, that all "executives" are greedy, or that all "blue-collar workers" want to avoid hard work. Whenever a label is applied to someone, then, we tend to assume they have those characteristics. In addition, stereotypes cause us to see the same characteristics in everyone to whom a label is applied. Managers often see all line workers as being alike; professors see no difference between students (nor do students see differences among professors); racists cannot distinguish among individual members of groups against whom they are prejudiced. Racists may therefore treat all members of those groups in the same way by attributing to each group member the blanket characteristics that they apply to the entire group.

- *Time-fixing* is our failure to recognize that people change over time. When we apply a label such as "lazy" to someone, we tend to fix that person in time; that is, we assume that the person always will possess that characteristic. But the behaviors we observed may have occurred purely as a function of the situation, so we may have misperceived the individual in the first place. Since we know that people change continually, time-fixing may lead us to incorrect conclusions about them.

- *Polarization* happens when the words we use cause us to think in dichotomous or polarized terms. That is, while people and things typically occur in gradations ("shades of gray"), words may cause us to see them as being one thing or another ("black or white"). In addition, we tend to attach evaluations to these labels. A worker may feel that "workers" are good and "management" is bad; a manager may believe that "supervisors" are hardworking and "employees" lazy. Language thus encourages us to see things as opposites, both in their characteristics and in their values.

- *Signal responses* occur when we react to words not as symbols, but as things in and of themselves. Signal responses are immediate and automatic: we jump when we hear an unexpected noise; we stop the car when the traffic light turns red. A symbolic response requires interpretation and thought and thus occurs more slowly. While our responses to words ought to be symbolic, involving careful and rational thought, too often they are a signal. In Western movies, cowboys often say "Them's fightin' words." Similarly, when we hear an emotion-charged word like "racist" or "terrorist," our response typically is immediate and unthinking. When we make quick, emotional, and unthinking responses to words, we have fallen into yet another trap posed by language.

Avoiding Semantic Problems

How then can we avoid these pitfalls of language? In fact, we cannot. But we can minimize the probability of being misled by words through the use of certain techniques.

- *E-Prime language* seeks to avert problems caused by the word "is" by avoiding the word altogether. "E-Prime" language (a term coined by Bourland) is "standard English with the exclusion of the influential forms of the verb 'to be.'"[5] Writing and speaking without using any form of "to be" obviously is difficult, to say the least, but the goal of E-Prime language is laudable: to be sensitive to the difficulties inherent in "is." If we avoid using "is," substituting with "seems" or describing behaviors rather than attaching labels ("He doesn't seem to devote much effort to his job" rather than "He is lazy"), we can avoid some of the problems "is" causes.

- *Etc.* helps us to avoid the "allness" error by recognizing that people are more than labels or words can express; thus, we must mentally add "etc." to statements we make. Rather than simply noting, "She is an executive" (thus limiting her to one specific role or identity), we should think, "She is an executive, etc." We thereby recognize that we can never say everything about people or things, and that our labels consider only small parts of those referents.

- *Indexing* tries to overcome the problem of stereotyping, or perceiving as identical everyone falling into a particular category, by mentally applying a numerical index to each person about whom we speak. Rather than saying "worker," we

Highlighting Diversity

Using Words across Cultures

Imagine you have submitted a proposal to an organization that is located in a foreign country. You follow up your proposal by calling to ask whether it has been accepted, and you are given one of the answers below. What do these answers have in common?

- "If everything proceeds as planned, the proposal will be approved."
- "Have you submitted a copy of your proposal to the ministry of . . . ?"
- "Your question is very difficult to answer."
- "We cannot answer this question at this time."
- "Will you be staying longer than you had originally planned?"
- "Yes, approval looks likely, but. . . ."
- "You should know shortly."

Believe it or not, all of these answers mean the same thing, but say it politely and indirectly. The answer is "no."

Source: David C. Thomas and Kerr Inkson, *Cultural Intelligence* (San Francisco: Berrett-Koehler Publishers, Inc., 2004), 111.

should say "worker-1," thus distinguishing that person from "worker-2," "worker-3," and all other workers. In this way, we recognize the uniqueness of each individual within the category. Perhaps the best way to deal with the "allness" trap, however, is to avoid categories altogether and speak only of individuals (such as "Professor Hill," "Professor Peters," etc.).

- *Dating* encourages us mentally to attach a date to our words, helping us to recognize the changing nature of reality and people. "He was obnoxious (January 1, 2005)" demonstrates that the behavior was situational and not necessarily an unchanging characteristic of the person. Similarly, "love (2001)" is different from "love (2005)," and "anger (January)" is different from "anger (March)." By mentally attaching dates, we recognize that things continuously change and that responses that were previously appropriate now may be destructive.

Strategies for Using Words

To avoid causing misunderstandings as we use words, there are several strategies we might use to promote clear communication. *Succinctness* involves using as few words as possible, since the fewer the number of words we use, the fewer opportunities for misunderstanding there are. *Definitions* of terms and explanations of meaning also help to ensure that we are understood. We should try to anticipate potential misunderstandings and explain or define clearly our meaning. *Repetition* of key issues, difficult points, and complex ideas, done by saying the same thing but in different words, as well as the use of *analogy* to draw parallels between this and other situations (using one instance to clarify another) can help to minimize confusion.

Singularity helps promote understanding by considering only one topic at a time, taking things step by step. Finally, *structure* of the message is important: we

---

Business Brief 4.1

Annoying Verbal Behaviors

There are verbal behaviors that either annoy other people or cause them to draw unfavorable conclusions about the speaker. Among them:

- Repeated use of the same conversational closing, such as "Take care" or "Take it easy." These are impersonal and indicate a lack of creativity and thoughtfulness.

- Repeated use of the same designation (referring to everyone as "you guys"), the same modifier (calling everything "cool," "awesome," or "bogus"), the same expression ("Wow," "Good grief!" or "No kidding!"), the same cliché ("a stitch in time" or "strike while the iron is hot"), or conversational fillers such as "you know" and "like." These become annoying and show sloppy mental habits.

- Mistakes in usage, such as the *double negative* ("They can't hardly expect us to do that!"; "Irregardless"; "He never did nothing"); misuse of *do* and *did, don't,* and *doesn't* ("He don't have any right to do that"; "She admitted she done it"); misuse of *knew, know,* and *known* ("He knowed we couldn't do it"); misuse of *gone* and *went* ("I wish I had went"); misuse of *personal pronouns* ("They fired him and I"; "They did it to her and myself"); misuse of *was* and *were* ("They was going"); use of *dem* and *dose* ("I don't like dose guys").

Source: Edward J. Hegarty, *How to Talk Your Way to the Top* (West Nyack, NY: Parker, 1973).

---

can minimize misunderstanding by carefully organizing our message into a clear, coherent pattern. Generally, the topic under consideration dictates the structural pattern we should use. Some topics require a chronological sequence ("First this happened, then this, and then this"); some require a spatial pattern ("You take the first right you come to, then go two blocks and make a left"); others a procedural sequence ("First you jack up the car, then you unscrew the lug nuts . . ."). In any case, it is important that some logical structure be followed so the listener can use that structure to more accurately understand the information.

The language we use is riddled with imperfections and inadequacies, and semantic breakdowns occur all too often. By recognizing the traps language poses and using some of the techniques suggested above, however, we can minimize this barrier to communication and improve the flow of messages throughout organizations.

EFFECTIVE WRITING

Much of the communication done in organizations is written. From informal e-mails to coworkers to formal reports submitted to senior executives, workers use the written word to build relationships, achieve their job goals, and contribute to the success of an organization.

Often, readers assume that the written documents we send to them are examples of our best work: a resume we think is good enough to get us hired, a proposal we think is good enough to have our firm retained, or a report we think is a good summary of our efforts. While an audience might forgive a presentation that bombs or an interview that goes poorly by thinking "maybe he was just nervous" or "maybe he's having a bad day," no such forgiveness is granted for written documents; we had every opportunity to prepare a good piece of work, and if we failed to do so, there's no excuse. For that reason, writing effectively is extremely important.

The purpose of this section is to provide some basic suggestions for effective business and professional writing. For more comprehensive guidance, you should consult one or more of the many books that have been written on the topic.

Suggestions for Composition

- *Use the active voice*. The active voice is one in which the subject performs the action: "John committed the crime." The passive voice is one in which the subject is acted upon: "The crime was committed by John." Using the active voice makes your writing style more direct and vigorous and your sentences more concise and readable.

- *Vary sentence length*. Some teachers of business writing suggest using short sentences at all times. Our feeling, however, is that sentence length should be varied in order to keep the reader's interest and attention. Short sentences can be abrupt. They can make reading feel jerky. They are like stop-and-go traffic. They keep attention. But eventually they get tiresome. Longer sentences can get readers into the flow of the words, helping them to move more smoothly through the text and more quickly grasp your meaning. But, like a long drive, long sentences used over and over can become tiresome as well, lulling the reader to sleep. Writing is like commuting to work: the stretches where you are able to cover longer distances at higher speed give you a sense that you are actually making progress, while the short stop-and-go stretches keep your attention lest the car you are following becomes your hood ornament.

- *Delete words, sentences, and phrases that do not add to your meaning*. Do not waste your readers' time by wasting words. Rather than saying "in the majority of instances," write "usually." Rather than using "at this point in time," say "now." Banks are fond of sending letters to one of the authors that start out: "It has come to our attention that your account again has been depleted of funds." It would be much simpler if they would simply say: "You're out of money again."

- *Use a conversational style*. In speaking to a customer, you would never say "As per your request, enclosed please find three (3) copies of our proposal to provide consulting services." Rather, "here are three copies of our proposal" would be much more normal. As Blake and Bly observe, many writers in business tend to use "unconversational businessese," creating stilted wording and stiff and formal phrasing.[6] For example, "If further information is required, you may contact Mary Yott" can be restated as, "Please contact Mary Yott if you'd like more information" in normal conversation.

- *Keep ideas parallel*. Ideas that parallel one another in content should also parallel one another in form. Consider these memorable examples: "One if by land, two if by sea"; "Where there's a will, there's a way"; "I came, I saw, I conquered"; "Ask not what your country can do for you, ask what you can do for your country"; "If guns were outlawed, only outlaws would have guns." Or consider the memorable line in an old country song, "I'd rather have a bottle in front of me than have a frontal lobotomy." All of these examples illustrate parallelism in sentence construction that clarifies meaning, creates symmetry, and promotes memory. Indeed, the preceding sentence used parallel verb-noun combinations: clarifies meaning, creates symmetry, promotes memory. The sentence would have been less readable if it had said that parallel sentence construction "clarifies meaning, creates symmetry, and each idea is easier to remember."

The parallelism principle also applies whenever you create a list, whether that list is a series of short ideas or a sequence of bulleted paragraphs, like the ones above. For example, each of the above paragraphs starts with a verb: "use," "vary," "delete," and "keep." Parallelism would have been lost had the paragraphs begun with: "Use the active voice," "Sentence length should be varied," "If words do not add to meaning, delete them," and "You should try to keep ideas parallel."

Suggestions for Wording and Phrasing

- *Use small words.* Generally, the best writers prefer small words that convey ideas clearly over big words that, apparently, are intended to impress more than communicate. Indeed, there is an organization devoted to the use of small words. In 2004, The Plain English Campaign (PEC) celebrated its twenty-fifth anniversary. Based in New Mills, Derbyshire, in England, the campaign is an editing service and lobbying group that bugs bureaucrats, corporations, and others to say things more clearly. Their Web site is http://www.plainenglish.co.uk. Among the examples of grotesque jargon on its Web site is this government statement: "High-quality learning environments are a necessary precondition for facilitation and enhancement of the ongoing learning process." PEC changed it to, "Children need good schools if they are to learn properly." The PEC also bestowed its "Golden Bull" award for gobbledygook on an insurance pamphlet's 146-word opening sentence and on an office of the British National Health Service for its 229-word definition of "bed."[7]

- *Avoid repetitive wording.* Expressions such as "absolutely true," "close proximity," "current status," "present time," or "each and every" use multiple words when just one will do: "true," "near," "status," "now," or "every."

- *Avoid sexist language.* Over the past 25 years or so, organizations have become more sensitive to the problem of sexist terms and the stereotypes they tend to convey and reinforce. Effective business writers try hard to avoid sexist terms and use terms that are gender-neutral; for example, "server" rather than "waitress," "chair" rather than "chairman," "firefighter" rather than "fireman," "police officer" rather than "policeman," "spokesperson" rather than "spokesman," and "flight attendant" rather than "stewardess." Even the venerable term "secretary" has been replaced in many organizations by "assistant" or "office staff member."

- *Use strong verbs.* Sentences often seem to lie dead on the page, due largely to the weak-kneed verbs they use—particularly forms of the verb "to be." Good writing jumps off the page with vivid, active verbs. Consider this common example: "There are several advantages to this proposal." Nothing is wrong with that sentence, other than the fact that it's dull—it starts with two of the most boring words ever combined, "There are." Use something stronger: "This proposal boasts several advantages." The action-oriented verb "boasts" drives home the message that the proposal can be proud of its offerings.

- *Vary verbs.* Finding creative substitutes for common verbs, such as "say" or "go," makes your writing more interesting. When reporting what others have said or written, for example, you might use such verbs as "stated," "claimed," "declared," or "asserted" rather than saying, over and over, "he said." However, in business writing the verb "to go" is not an appropriate substitute for the verb "to say." In conversation, you may hear someone tell someone else, "And then I go, 'No way,' and he goes, 'Yeah, way, dude,' and then I go, 'No way, and don't call me dude. . . .'" In business, "goes" is what an "apprentice" does when Donald Trump says, "You're fired!"

Business Brief 4.2

"Consultantspeak"

Bierck claims that a crippling disease has been sweeping organizations across the country: Infectious Consultant Syndrome (ICS). Symptoms include "a magnetic attraction to the vague, sterile, redundant, and trendy utterances of consultants." Those who have the disease are impressed by, or worse yet, actually use, some of the terms below:

- *Granularity.* No one knows exactly what this means, but consultants use it to suggest that something is very specific, for example, "Once we do more research, we can achieve granularity on the problem."

- *Datapoint.* Seldom do datapoints have anything to do with actual data; typically these are nothing more than factoids (an equally unfortunate term).

- *Drill down.* This term again seems to denote incisiveness; that is, people "drill down" to achieve "granularity."

- *Bulletproof.* While this is apparently synonymous with "invulnerable," it is frequently used by technical consultants to describe computer systems, among the most vulnerable products on the planet.

- *End users.* These are the people who use the bulletproof systems, although one never hears of "beginning users." The equally redundant term "past history" is similar.

- *Front end and back end.* In describing an abstract process as if it were an automobile body, consultants make it seem more concrete: "We'll come out better on the back end if we put more pressure on receivables on the front end."

- *Tools.* These are used to work on the front end, back end, and everything in between. Again, the abstract seemingly becomes concrete.

- *Going forward or moving forward.* "We're going to refine this system going forward."

- *Bluesskying.* "While others are bluesskying, we are drilling down to get granularity." Bluesskying signifies endeavors that the speaker considers pie-in-the-sky.

- *Robust.* When something is not quite "bulletproof," apparently robust is the term that is used.

- *Infrastructure.* If consultants merely said structure, how impressive would this be?

- *Turnkey.* "We'll handle everything so we can charge you more."

Source: Richard Bierck, "Consultantspeak," *Harvard Management Communication Letter* 3, no. 4 (April 2000): 9.

- *Choose positive words over negative words.* Some words imply a criticism of the reader and may be interpreted as accusatory or arrogant. For example, the phrase "you claim" implies that "you say so, but I don't believe you." Similarly, "failed to" is harsh and insulting and implies incompetence, "neglected to" similarly implies carelessness, and "lack of" suggests shortcomings. Thus, rather than saying "This notice is in regard to your failure to remit payment on our invoice," it is far more positive to say, "Did you get our bill?" "You consistently fail to show up for work on time" is better said, "Please come to work at 8:30, when your shift begins."

- *Give the bad news first, followed by the good.* When you must convey both positive and negative information, present the negative first: "We don't have any openings right now, but your resume is very impressive." This leaves the reader with a better feeling than "Your resume is impressive, but we don't have any openings right now," which ruins any positive feeling the first clause creates by giving negative information at the end.

- *Avoid jargon and clichés.* Some expressions have been used so long and so often that they have lost much of their freshness and power; others are meaningless to just about anyone in polite society. Such clichés as "back to square one," "at the end of the day," "cost-effective," "few and far between," "take the ball and run with it," or "first and foremost" often are seen as trite and lacking in creativity. Similarly, every industry has its "buzz words" (itself a cliché) that may be understood by people in that industry, but not by anyone else. Ambrose reports, for example, that new terms were born during the corporate scandals of recent years.[8] Under "Lady Godiva" accounting principles, for example, companies must make full disclosure. "Leprechaun leaders" are mischievous, elusive executives who hide their millions, perhaps in offshore accounts. "Enronitis" describes a stock whose price has fallen because of suspected accounting irregularities. Finally, Peter Ricchiuti, a finance professor at Tulane University in New Orleans, mentioned on a radio program the "dead cat bounce," a temporary jump in a stock price after a steep decline. The theory is based on the premise that even a dead cat will bounce if it is dropped far enough. Animal lovers called in to complain.

Suggestions for Punctuation, Grammar, and Spelling

- *Use commas to indicate a brief pause.* There are so many possible uses for commas that, if you want in-depth information, you should consult books on punctuation and grammar.[9] A few principles to keep in mind, however, are these.

  — *Use commas to separate items in a series:* "I'm interested in investing in stocks, bonds, real estate, mutual funds, or swamp land in Florida."

  — *Use a comma to separate two or more adjectives that modify the same noun:* "It was a dark, windy night when we had our dull, time-wasting meeting."

  — *Use a comma to separate independent clauses joined by a coordinating conjunction (and, or, nor, but, yet, for), or a long introductory clause from the rest of the sentence:* "The outline was good, but the actual report stank" uses a coordinating conjunction ("but") to connect two thoughts, and thus needs a comma to signal that transition. Similarly, "After reviewing your resume and talking with your references, we have concluded that there is no chance you will ever work in this organization" uses a comma to separate a long introductory clause from the rest of the paragraph.

- *Use a semicolon to separate independent clauses not joined by a conjunction.* A semicolon is similar to a period in that it separates two clauses, each of which can stand on its own as a complete sentence. Generally, semicolons are used when the two clauses are very closely related and not connected by a conjunction: "Dozens of measures were taken to ensure safety; none guaranteed that no accidents would happen." Semicolons also can be used to separate phrases that contain commas: "We went to three cities last week: Enid, Oklahoma; Gary, Indiana; and Taos, New Mexico."

- *Use a colon to introduce a list or explanation.* In punctuation, colons indicate that something more detailed is about to follow: a list, a formal quotation, a detailed explanation, an example, etc. The paragraphs that precede this one are absolutely riddled with colons.

- *Use an apostrophe and an "s" to form the possessive case of a singular noun, but just add an apostrophe to form the possessive of a plural noun.* "The boss's desk is behind the employees' lounge" illustrates how to express that a single entity (the boss) possesses the desk, while a plural entity (employees) possess the lounge.

- *Use hyphens to unite two or more words into a single adjective that precedes a noun.* When two or more words are compounded to form an adjective, they are hyphenated: long-term employee, long-range goals, easy-to-follow instructions, year-to-date sales.

- *Use parentheses to add explanatory information that is not part of the main thought.* Parenthetical expressions add information beyond the main point of the sentence: "We received your order (which had been delayed 6 years in the mail) last week." If parentheses are used at the end of a sentence, the period goes outside the closing parenthesis: "Here are the items you requested (wrapped individually in fish scales)."

- *Use an em dash to interrupt or highlight a thought.* An em dash can act in ways similar to parentheses or commas, but in more dramatic fashion. For example, "My wife (who happens to own the company you work for) will certainly hear about the lousy service you provided" can also be written: "My wife—who happens to own the company you work for—will certainly hear about the lousy service you provided," thereby more dramatically highlighting the reader's uncertain employment future.

- *Ensure subject-verb agreement.* Singular subjects take singular verbs; plural subjects require plural verbs. However, sentence construction can make it tricky to adhere to these rules. For example, which is correct: "Neither of us are able to attend," or "Neither of us is able to attend?" Since the subject of the sentence is "neither," not "us," the correct verb is "is." Similarly, "Some employees complained, but Senior Management and the Governing Board was willing to shut down the pension plan" is incorrect because the subject, "Senior Management and the Governing Board," is two entities and thus requires the use of "were" rather than "was."

- *Properly use reflexive pronouns*. Personal pronouns combined with "-self" or "-selves" are called reflexive; for example, "himself," "myself," or "themselves." Too often, people use the reflexive form when it is unnecessary: "Mary and myself would have been a great team" should instead be "Mary and I would have been a great team." The key to identifying these situations is to leave the other person out of the sentence and see how it reads. For example, "The security guard was nasty to Bill and myself" would read "The security guard was nasty to myself" if Bill were left out. The proper statement becomes clear: "The security guard was nasty to Bill and me."

- *Avoid sentence fragments or run-on sentences*. A group of words becomes a sentence when it has a subject and a verb and expresses a complete thought. Sentence fragments do not express complete thoughts; run-on sentences express more than one complete thought. For example: "As we discussed in our meeting of November 18, 2005, which was a very cold day" is not a complete thought since it lacks either a subject or a verb—it's just an introductory phrase. On the other hand, "As we discussed in our meeting of November 18, 2005, which was a very cold day, we will go on strike as soon as the weather gets warmer however our signs aren't painted yet" is a run-on sentence because it tacks on another complete thought ("however, our signs aren't painted yet") to the thought that was just completed.

- *Avoid dangling modifiers*. A modifying phrase or clause must define or limit the meaning of a word or phrase in the sentence. If we wrote: "In its present form, the contract does not protect you from anything," the modifying phrase "In its present form" defines a characteristic of "the contract." When the phrase or clause does not modify the subject of the sentence, it is said to be "dangling." For example, in the sentence, "As a new inmate, Martha, I know you will enjoy sprucing up your cell," the subject of the verb is "I," not "Martha," so that the clause "as a new inmate" suggests that it is "I," not "Martha," who is the new inmate. More correct is the sentence: "Martha, I know that, as a new inmate, you will enjoy sprucing up your cell," since now the subject of the sentence is "you," the verb is "will enjoy," and the "new inmate" clause clearly refers to the subject, "you."

- *Avoid misplaced modifiers*. Awkward placement of modifiers can make a sentence confusing: "The list is in the car, which you should take into the store with you." If the modifier is placed too far from the word it is supposed to modify, the meaning can become unclear. Always place modifiers as close as possible to the words they modify: "The list, which you should take into the store with you, is in the car."

- *Use "spell-check," but don't stop their*. We hope you noticed the spelling error in the preceding sentence. Spell-check didn't. As far as the program is concerned, we spelled "their" just fine. The program also would have been happy if we had written, "Use 'spell-check,' but don't stop they're." To find typos, read your material out loud. That will force you to read the material slowly and make it less likely that you will overlook errors in spelling, punctuation, grammar, etc.

> ### Highlighting Technology
>
> #### In Search of Readable Documents
>
> Deloitte Consulting has created new software designed to help make business documents more readable.
>
> - Called **Bullfighter,** the software works like a spell-checker in either Microsoft Word or PowerPoint and assigns documents a score based on sentence complexity and the use of some 350 "bullwords."
> - Using Bullfighter, Deloitte found that among companies in the Dow Jones industrials, those that spoke plainly in shareholder letters and other communications outperformed those that loaded up on jargon.
> - Bullfighter is available free on CD-ROM or at http://www.dc.com/bullfighter.
> - Some of the bullwords identified by the software, along with Bullfighter's suggested translations, include *"envisioneer"* (create), *"leverage"* (use), *"re-engineer"* (change), *"synergize"* (combine), *"utilize"* (use), and *"walk the talk"* (do it).
>
> Source: "Buzz Words: Memo Matador," *Time* (August 17, 2003): A7.

Suggestions for Putting It All Together[10]

- *State your objective*. How often have you read the title of a memo or document and decided to read no further? Compare these titles: "Fourth Quarter Sales Summary" versus "Fourth Quarter Sales Up 60% Due to Business Boom in New England." Because the second title summarizes the document, it allows you to decide quickly if you need to read it. That writer has done a good job by saving you time; you should have the same respect for your readers.

  For longer, more complex documents, you may not be able to summarize the objective in the title, subtitle, or first sentence. Still, consider stating the objective somewhere in the first few paragraphs. For example, after some introductory material on the importance of employee surveys, you might say, "The purpose of this document is to propose conducting an employee survey for Company XYZ."

- *Know your audience*. Before you start writing, ask yourself, *Who will read this? What do I want them to think, feel, or do as a result of having read this? What do they want or need to know?* Then write directly to that audience.

- *Stay on topic*. One of the benefits of stating your objective up front is that you can always refer to it later. Again, ask yourself, *What does the person I'm talking to need to achieve this goal?* If you're writing extensively about anything else, you're either writing the wrong thing or you've chosen the wrong objective.

- *Put your conclusion first and your evidence second*. Many writers, especially those with science training, tend to hold off their conclusions until the end of a document. Much like an episode of *CSI*, they expect readers to stay in suspense, watching the evidence collect and forming their own conclusions to compare against the writer's. But most readers don't want to work that hard. They want you to tell them the conclusion up front, and then present the evidence to support it. If they agree with your conclusion, maybe they can stop reading after the first paragraph, saving time. If they are doubtful or surprised, they can study the evidence with a skeptical eye.

- *Use formatting techniques such as lists and subheads.* A lot of business writing looks like a gray blob of text: no title or subtitles and few paragraph breaks. Nothing jumps out. Bad formatting makes the reader's job more difficult. If your text looks like a gray blob, consider the following tricks:
  — Insert a subhead every few paragraphs.
  — Use a heading for each of the points in your outline.
  — Keep your paragraphs short.
  — Every time you use a list, make it a bulleted or numbered list.

- *Emphasize major points using boldface, subheads, and lists.* When looking at text, our eyes naturally go to vivid contrasts of black and white. Is there a key sentence you want your readers to remember? Use formatting techniques to emphasize it. Make it a heading or make it the first sentence of a paragraph. If it has to be in the middle of a paragraph, put it in boldface. Anything that's bold and/or surrounded by white space will jump out at the reader.

- *"Make the paragraph the unit of composition."* In these few words, Strunk and White capture one of the most important rules of good writing.[11] Their book, *The Elements of Style*, emphasizes three key ideas that help clarify how to create effective paragraphs.

  First, *"begin with the familiar, end with the new."* Just as a good politician begins talking to us about what we already know or have in common, good sentences and paragraphs should do the same. Save the new idea for the end. This simple device works because it respects the way the mind learns—by building on what it already knows.

  Second, *"limit the number of subjects in the sentences in each paragraph."* Typically, a paragraph will have anywhere from three to a dozen sentences. Each one of these sentences will have a subject. The second key to good paragraph construction is to keep the number of subjects to a minimum without making your writing sound like a preschool booklet. For example, take a piece of your own writing and underline all the subjects of the sentences. If there are more than three or four different subjects in the typical paragraph of average length, your writing will suffer from incoherence.

  Finally, *"make sure each paragraph has an issue, a point, and a discussion."* The issue comes first. It is a statement, in one or more sentences, of what, in general, the paragraph is about. Next comes the point, a one-sentence statement of the "takeaway," or your main comment on the issue you've brought up. Finally, add several sentences of discussion, further amplifying or defending your point with supporting evidence, and the like. You can vary this structure by putting the point of your sentence at the very end of the paragraph, but most readers unconsciously expect to find the point at the end of the issue. So vary the basic paragraph structure only for a good reason.

- *Tell a story.* People think in terms of stories, so it only makes sense to write using the same techniques. What is the essence of a good story? At minimum, we need an actor, an action, and an object that is acted on: *The terrorist kidnapped*

Highlighting Technology

The Vocabula Review

Most business writing is painful to read, and Vocabula Review is an online journal that reports on this sad state.

- The feature *"Grumbling about Grammar"* is a compilation of grammatical errors taken from publications and public figures who really should know better (such as using "conversate" instead of the word "converse" or "more preferable" instead of just "preferable," and using the phrase "sure and" in place of "sure to").

- The review also offers lists of unusual and infrequently used words to jazz up everyday writing. It's a great reminder of how to write proper yet interesting English.

- Yet another useful feature of this Web site is *"The Dimwit's Dictionary,"* which is available for purchase as a downloadable file. "The Dimwit's Dictionary" is a compilation of "dimwitticisms"—clichés, colloquialisms, idioms, etc.—that are used excessively in both spoken and written English. The entries include sentence examples taken from publications, Web sites, radio, and television and suggested synonyms to use instead.

The site is: http://www.vocabula.com/vocabulareview.htm.

the diplomat's child. That is the beginning of a (potentially) good story. The actor is the terrorist, the action is kidnapping, and the diplomat's child functions as the object.

Stories and sentences both need a simple, clear, and logical structure to work effectively. Consider the differences between the following two sentences:

> "Because we didn't know the competition, we couldn't write a competitive proposal."

> "Our lack of understanding of the competitive climate surrounding us precluded the writing of an adequate sales document."

Most people would find the first version easier to read than the second. To see why, consider the basic "story structure" of the first part of the first sentence. There is an actor: "we." There is an action: "didn't know." And there is an object: "the competition." The second half of the sentence follows the same pattern of actor ("we"), action ("couldn't write"), and object ("a competitive proposal"). Contrast that with the second version. What is the actor? It is a mouthful, something like the following: "Our lack of understanding of the competitive climate surrounding us." What is the action? A slightly pretentious verb: "precluded." And the object is similarly wordy: "the writing of an adequate sales document." So the actor and the object have become much more abstract and harder to find, and the action is weak and abstract as a result.

In addition, the first sentence works better because it gives us cause-and-effect in the structure of the sentence itself. "Because" of our ignorance, "we" were unable to write. Remember that cause-and-effect—actor, action, and object—underlie how we experience reality and how we learn. So it is an enormous help to us to read prose that brings causal relationships to the surface clearly, rather than letting us try to sort them out ourselves. The second sentence lacks the simple, clear logic of "because" and forces us to figure out a cause from the verb "precluded."

In short, good writing tells a story by conveying concepts the way we experience our lives: by describing how an actor takes an action that affects some object.

Business Brief 4.3

Creative Ways of Teaching Grammar

An approach to teaching grammar and usage that is less tedious than most is the one used by Karen Elizabeth Gordon, whose books include *The Deluxe Transitive Vampire, The New Well-Tempered Sentence,* and *Torn Wings and Faux Pas.* Gordon's books are full of winged creatures, demons, mythological beasts, and apocalyptic scenes, all of which she uses to teach basic principles of grammar.

"Most of the language that people are exposed to today comes from the popular media or the business world," Gordon observes, "and it's gradually eroding people's notions of how to use language. For example, I hate abstract language. I think businesspeople should look to create something highly visual and dramatic in their writing and that doesn't necessarily mean using esoteric words." Consider these examples taken from Gordon's books:

- To illustrate an appositive (italicized in the following example, the appositive is an element that further identifies another noun): "Wolves, *the Children of the Night,* always mate for life."

- To demonstrate how an infinitive phrase can function as a noun: "There is nothing I want of my lovers but *to loosen my mortal coils."*

- To show the proper use of a restrictive clause: "The girl *who is stroking the gargoyle* is in love." A restrictive clause, Gordon explains, is one that "restricts the meaning, zeros in on specific qualities" of the noun or pronoun you're talking about. Thus, the adjective clause *who is stroking the gargoyle* "tells *which* girl is in love; there could be a dozen other girls engaged in equally ridiculous acts, but not with gargoyles."

- To demonstrate the proper punctuation of an absolute phrase: "Her hair matted with greasepaint and her magnificent torso protruding from a negligee of green nylon, she maundered through the apartment house next to her own, thrusting her key into each astounded door." "A comma," Gordon writes, "sets off absolute phrases—phrases composed of a noun or pronoun plus a participle—that are not joined to the rest of the sentence by relationship words."

See: Karen Elizabeth Gordon, *The Deluxe Transitive Vampire: The Ultimate Handbook of Grammar for the Innocent, the Eager, and the Doomed* (New York: Pantheon, 1993); Karen Elizabeth Gordon, *The New Well-Tempered Sentence: A Punctuation Handbook for the Innocent, the Eager, and the Doomed* (New York: Ticknor & Fields, 1993).

Source: "Interview with a (Grammar) Vampire," *Harvard Management Communication Letter* 3, no. 9 (September 2000): 10–11.

STORYTELLING

Good writing tells a story, and in turn, storytelling in the workplace is a powerful verbal strategy for communicating important concepts and values to employees. Rather than merely describing a concept, philosophy, or value, storytelling brings concepts to life by providing an example that helps people understand and remember what you are trying to convey to them.

One key function of storytelling is imparting the values that underlie an organization's culture. For example, Chris Dunblazier, director of operations for the Souper Salad restaurant chain, claims that "Storytelling is the most effective way to show what happens if you don't do [something] the right way, and what happens if you do. Stories stick in a person's mind." For example, she tells this story:[12]

> Once I had a call from a general manager who told me, "You won't believe this, but our manager, John, just walked in here in full makeup, in uniform, with long red fingernails." I consulted with HR, then explained to John that he was free to wear whatever he wanted outside of work, but the restaurant doesn't even allow heavy makeup for women employees, and no restaurant employee can have long fingernails at work. I told him that anything that makes a guest look twice at the manager is not a good idea. The next day, John didn't have the nails, and had just a small amount of eyeliner.
>
> Months later, I was wearing my corporate shirt on a flight. I found myself seated on the plane beside a man who told me he'd gone into one of our stores once and an employee—he was pretty sure it was the manager—had been in full makeup. He said he'd never gone back.

When Dunblazier tells this story, she hopes that it will remind an employee to think twice about wearing a particular "look" at work. Such stories use a specific incident to teach key behavioral lessons and, ultimately, to shape the organization's culture.

Storytelling can also help to overcome resistance to change. For example, managers at TRW's Space and Electronics Group (S&EG) in Redondo Beach, California, tell the story of competing for the contract to build China's first satellite.

Southwest Airlines chairman Herb Kelleher is an engaging storyteller whose stories reinforce and illuminate such core Southwest values as common sense, love, hard work, ownership, and fun. Because Kelleher's stories are powerful and dramatic, they are memorable for the employees who listen to them.

Through their story, they demonstrate to their colleagues the value of participating in TRW's Workforce Diversity Program:

> In 1994, TRW bid for a satellite contract with the People's Republic of China's National Space Program Office (NSPO). The successful bidder would build the first Chinese satellite.
>
> Chinese-American TRW employees organized themselves into a Chinese Employee Network Group, and assumed a major role in making sure that the proposal was compliant and culturally coherent. Chinese-American employees who were skilled in speaking Mandarin, and reading and writing Chinese, took a leadership role in representing TRW to the customer. They helped develop the proposal and reviewed it before submission to NSPO. They videotaped an executive summary of the proposal, explaining that the group also would be working on the satellite development team.
>
> Well into 1995, after TRW had won the bid and was developing the satellite, members of the Chinese Employee Network Group reported that the customer's comfort with the proposal and development teams contributed strongly to the success of the ongoing project. Their achievement spurred other Employee Network Groups based on a workforce diversity variable such as country of origin.

Since that experience, TRW also tells the story of the successful bid for the Korean Multipurpose Satellite, relying on a proposal and development team that was comprised of, as you can probably guess by now, Korean Americans. By telling stories that tout successes, organizations build support for similar actions in the future.

Restaurant chain Red Robin International uses stories to teach a value set that began with a single story. While president and CEO Michael Snyder was watching his son ride a horse several years ago, his son dismounted and unbridled the animal, setting it free to run powerfully and gracefully across the field. The event inspired Snyder, who used the story to introduce the "Unbridled Philosophy" to the organization when he took over the company in 1996. Soon, stories of unbridled passion were everywhere—in internal newsletters, advertisements, and recruitment flyers. Stories of unbridled acts are even told at every meeting, large or small, to show acts going above and beyond normal duty. One such story tells of the Tacoma, Washington, Red Robin manager who drove a group of teenagers to their homecoming dance after their chaperone's car wouldn't start. Another tells of the Bakersfield, California, employee who assisted a gentleman who was out of breath by seating him, bringing him water, and retrieving his oxygen tank from his car.

As these examples illustrate, a good story is not complicated. First, the teller describes a situation: for example, the chaperone's car wouldn't start and the teenagers had no way to get to their homecoming dance. Second, he or she describes the action: a restaurant manager left his restaurant and used his personal car to drive the group to their dance. Third, the teller provides a lesson or "punch line": how unbridled actions that go beyond normal job duties are expected in this organization.

People are going to talk. By understanding and using the power of storytelling, you create a message that people will share with one another. Like throwing a rock into a quiet pool, your message triggers outwardly expanding waves that go far beyond the people you have seen.

Business Brief 4.4

Creating Stories

To create your own stories, try the following:

- Look for plots and themes in your life, such as dealing with adversity, obtaining scarce resources, or overcoming challenges.

- Look for consequences—the causes and effects of your choices. This helps derive meaning from a series of events.

- Look for lessons in your life—personal changes and developments brought about by your experiences. When you give advice about patience or persistence through a story that relates your own experiences, it's all the more powerful.

- Look for lessons by identifying the elements that were essential to the successes described in your story: timing, patience, kindness, and so on. How can these attributes apply to other situations?

- Look for vulnerability—the problems and imperfections of your human side. Failures, derailments, mistakes, and simple goofs make wonderful stories. When combined with successes, they can build credibility.

- Look to the future. We even learn from experiences we have not yet had by imagining how we might behave if we did have them.

- Look for story meanings and memories from your past. When we are able to recall surprises, lessons, inspirations, and examples, we find our story.

Source: Beverly Kaye, *Up Is Not the Only Way* (New York: Consulting Psychologists Press, 1997).

WRITING E-MAILS

Exchanging words electronically via e-mail has become an increasingly important form of communication within and between organizations. However, the informal, spontaneous nature of e-mail technology often causes it to be overused or misused, to the detriment of both the user and the organization as a whole.

Several errors commonly occur in the use of e-mail.[13] One is "hiding behind the terminal." E-mail should not be used for important, potentially sensitive communications, such as performance reviews, disciplinary actions, and resolving personal conflicts. Such reasons for communication should be handled in person. Forgetting that e-mail is permanent is another common error. While informal and convenient, e-mail also constitutes a permanent record of a written communication that can be retrieved relatively easily. Many a time, old and long-forgotten e-mails have come back to haunt their senders—often in a courtroom.

The fact that e-mail is purely verbal, with no nonverbal cues to provide additional meaning, is often overlooked. When we try to express humor or irony or sarcasm via e-mail, we often fail: the reader sees only the words, with no facial or vocal expressions to let him or her know we are only kidding. Lastly, "flaming" someone via e-mail may feel good—and is certainly easier to do than confronting that individual face-to-face—but these messages can destroy relationships and build long-lasting animosity as surely as any spoken words.

In *The ePolicy Handbook*, Nancy Flynn suggests that everyone in an organization should follow several key guidelines whenever they use e-mail.[14] First, *use a conversational tone*. Flynn says to imagine you are attending a dinner party with colleagues, supervisors, and customers. Use the same language and tone in an e-mail that you would use at this kind of event. In addition, *don't be overly rigid with grammar use*. Feel free to use contractions, end sentences with prepositions, and use pronouns like I, we, and you. If grammar is too stiff, readers won't know what the message is about. However, Flynn suggests that you *limit your use of abbreviations* and use only legitimate and recognizable ones, not your personal shorthand. An excess of abbreviations can be annoying and confusing to the reader.

Your e-mails should contain *no sexist language*. This isn't just referring to harassing or discriminatory jokes and comments but also the overuse of masculine pronouns. Given the increasing number of women in the workforce, it's important for electronic writers to avoid language that could offend clients or colleagues. Moreover, *don't incorporate jokes* into electronic business writing. Because e-mail is impersonal and lacks inflection or body language, your joke is likely to fall flat or to be misconstrued. Finally, *don't try to "warm up" your business writing with "smileys"*—also known as emoticons—using keyboard characters to represent smiles and similar facial expressions. "Smileys" are the equivalent of e-mail slang, Flynn says, and have no place in business communication.

Flynn also suggests that *organizations adopt formal policies regarding e-mail usage*, and as you send e-mails you should try to adhere to these rules as well. She says organizations should ban e-mail language that could negatively affect the organization's business relationships, damage its corporate reputation, or trigger a lawsuit, such as sexist or racist language, or even jokes. Employees should be prohibited from posting or transmitting materials that are "obscene, hateful, harmful, malicious, threatening, hostile, abusive, vulgar, defamatory, profane, or racially, sexually, or ethnically objectionable," Flynn says, and we would offer the same recommendations to you.

Companies also should *ban inappropriate Web sites*—usually those that are sexually explicit or violent or contain otherwise objectionable images or language. To conserve bandwidth, they should outlaw Net surfing for personal information, game playing online, chat rooms, gambling, shopping, and any other electronic activity not directly related to professional duties (although many employers do allow some personal use of the Web during lunchtime). Again, we believe this is advice you should follow as well.

Lastly, organizations should *provide corporate guidelines* such as how to refer to the company, how to sign off, and what kinds of salutations to use—information you should obtain from the leadership of your own organization once you begin using their system to e-mail.

DESTRUCTIVE VERBAL STRATEGIES

When we start stringing words together, they become not only sentences, paragraphs, and documents—they become verbal patterns or strategies that can help or hurt relationships with other people in organizations. In this section, we will consider some verbal strategies that are damaging to relationships.

Behaviors that Induce Defensiveness

As described many years ago by Gibb and more recently by Ellison, defensive behavior occurs when we perceive or anticipate a threat or an attack from someone else.[15] We feel that our well-being is in danger, that we are likely to lose status, that we may be rejected by the other, or that some other undesirable event will occur. Thus, we take steps to protect ourselves—we behave defensively.

There are certain behaviors that cause people to feel threatened to a degree that they act defensively:

- *Evaluative behavior.* If we seem to be passing judgment on the other person, evaluating her worth or characteristics, she naturally will tend to become defensive. There is always a chance that our judgment will be unfavorable to her, in which case her self-esteem may be damaged. Rather than take that risk, she may withdraw from us or, worse yet, launch a counterattack.

- *Control-oriented behavior.* Speech that attempts to control the other person usually provokes resistance. In essence, control-oriented statements imply superiority on our part, inferiority on the other person's. We, through our vast wisdom, know what is best for him; he is incapable of making judgments for himself. Therefore, as our statement implies, we will do him the favor of telling him how to direct his behavior. Again, by threatening his self-esteem, we cause him to become defensive.

- *Strategic behavior.* If the other person perceives that we have something sneaky in mind, or that we are up to something, he naturally will defend himself. No one likes to be tricked, so whenever we perceive that someone has hidden motives or is following some preplanned strategy we engage in defensive maneuvers.

- *Neutral behavior.* If we appear unconcerned about the other person's welfare, dealing with her as an object rather than a person, she probably will become defensive. Since we do not care about her, she assumes, we probably would harm her without a second thought. This potential threat in turn causes her to take protective measures.

- *Superior behaviors.* When we communicate to another that we feel superior in ability, position, morality, power, or some other characteristic, we arouse defensiveness (even though, in our hearts, we know we're right). No one wants to feel inferior to another, and usually people will protect themselves when they confront others behaving in superior ways.

- *Dogmatic behaviors.* If we make it clear to the other person that our point of view is right and all others are wrong, he probably will become defensive. He knows that to express his thoughts is to invite attack from us, so he simply withdraws from the interaction.

Through these verbal behaviors we usually cause others to feel threatened. This is particularly true in situations involving persons of unequal status. Since the high-power person controls to some degree the fate of the lower-power person, the subordinate probably will feel in some danger and will engage in defensive maneuvers.

What are these defensive maneuvers? Goffman lists several defensive behaviors: ***physical avoidance***, where individuals completely avoid interacting with oth-

NON SEQUITUR

The importance of writing with clarity...

Coat and Tie Required

ers who might pose a threat; *physical retreat*, in which the individual makes a gracious withdrawal before a threat materializes; *verbal avoidance*, or changing the topic to something less threatening; *verbal retreat*, where the individual simply does not mention information that might evoke a threatening response; *information control*, or engaging in ambiguous or deceptive verbal behaviors; *interaction control*, in which the potential threat is neutralized through the use of humor or some other distracter; *aggression*, or attacking the threatening person; *tactful blindness*, where the threat is ignored; *projection*, in which feelings of inadequacy are transferred to the other so he or she becomes the one who, in the view of the defensive person, is afraid; and *verbal rationalization*, where a presumably "rational" explanation is used to rationalize the threat away.[16] Each of these behaviors creates a barrier to communication. The receiver is so concerned with protecting his or her well-being that he or she fails to truly understand the transmitted message. It is important, then, that behaviors that induce defensiveness be avoided.

Aggressive Behaviors

A second set of communication behaviors that are detrimental to communication and interpersonal relationships within organizations consists of behaviors that release (and in turn often provoke) aggression. While these behaviors provide a temporary benefit to the performers by allowing them to vent aggressions and hostilities, in the long run they usually are detrimental to their relationships with others. Some of these behaviors, labeled "verbalizers" by Palmer many years ago, include:[17]

- *Arguing*. Like each of Palmer's verbalizers, arguing is a socially acceptable method of releasing aggression. The person simply waits for someone else to state an opinion and then argues with that person. On a short-term basis this strategy is extremely effective. The arguer releases hostilities while at the same time appearing knowledgeable and intellectually active to others. In the long run, however, this strategy is disastrous: others eventually get fed up with continuous arguing and simply avoid the arguer altogether.

- *Complaining*. Another method of releasing hostility is to complain. Used occasionally, this strategy is not detrimental to relationships and may provide entertainment for one's coworkers. When employees gather in a break area and gripe about their boss, their pay, their parking facilities, and everything else, they are performing a mutually useful function by giving each other a chance to express hostilities harmlessly. The person who complains constantly, however, will find it difficult to establish good relations with others—particularly the boss.

- *Martyrdom*. This strategy involves seeking sympathy from others by constantly portraying oneself as a victim. Indeed, highly skilled users of martyrdom can make people feel vaguely uneasy even when they are doing the person a favor. The strategy usually begins with the phrase, "That's OK, I'll. . . ." For example, a martyr might tell us that his car isn't working. Trying to be of help, we offer him a ride to work the next day. He responds, "That's OK, I can walk, even though my old football injury is acting up again." We repeat the offer; he still replies, "That's OK, I don't want to be any bother." Finally, after a long and bitter struggle, he lets us give him a ride. Thus, he uses this strategy to vent his aggressions by making us feel uneasy, and at the same time he reaps the benefits of our generosity (unless, of course, we conveniently "forget" to pick him up the next morning, thereby making him late for work). Not surprisingly, this strategy soon wears thin; people stop communicating with the martyr altogether.

In addition to Palmer's verbalizers, Fleishman suggests other forms of verbal aggression:[18]

- *Interrupting*. By repeatedly interrupting the statements of others, we can both vent our hostilities and control the flow of the interaction. In so doing, however, we irritate other people and may ruin our relationships with them.

- *Name calling*. This strategy involves attaching labels to people directly ("You're crazy!") or indirectly ("Only an idiot would think that!"). While this is an effective method for releasing aggression, it typically is not appreciated by the crazy idiot to whom you are speaking.

- *Challenging integrity*. Hostilities can be expressed by questioning the other person's motives, character, or behavior. Although no direct charges of dishonesty are made, such questions as "What's in this for you?" and "What are you trying to hide?" carry clear implications and place the person in a defensive posture. Not surprisingly, the other person will not find the conversation particularly enjoyable.

- *The "brush-off."* This technique involves simply ignoring the other person. When she disagrees with you or tries to explain her point of view, you simply keep talking or occupy yourself with something else—rearranging the contents of your briefcase, picking dirt from under your fingernails, looking out the window, or studying the acoustical tiles on the ceiling. A useful release of aggression, this behavior nevertheless tends to frustrate others and produces a quick end to communication.

The remedy for aggressive behaviors is simple: Avoid them. Carrying out this remedy can be more difficult, however, as it often requires changing habitual verbal behaviors. Yet the effort is worthwhile, for only by avoiding these verbal behaviors can we build good relationships with others.

Gossip

Lies, rumors, and office gossip have always been a part of any organization. Indeed, Dunbar claims that gossip serves as one of the most important parts of social interaction. "What characterizes the social life of humans is the intense interest we show in each other's doings. Language . . . allows us to exchange information about other people, so short-circuiting the laborious process of finding out how they behave."[19] Indeed, gossip and storytelling are one and the same, and they are effective for the same reasons. But if storytelling is Dr. Jekyll or Bruce Banner, gossip is Mr. Hyde or The Hulk—faster, stronger, and often evil.

In *Managing Your Mouth*, Genua distinguishes between different types of gossip.[20] "Garden-variety gossip" involves people talking about all the little incidents that happen each day. This goes on over the backyard fence, during bridge club, or during little chitchats at each other's homes. In general, garden-variety gossip tends to deal with nonthreatening subjects; however, it can (and often does) develop into "malicious gossip," which contains half-truths and lies, and tarnishes reputations. Anything that happens to a person or is found out about a person that is outside the realm of normal behavior or the norms of society is ripe for becoming the subject of malicious gossip. Many careers, and even lives, have been destroyed by malicious gossip.

Rebecca Gushe, who worked with employees and local university students to improve communication and reduce gossip in the workplace, claims that both garden-variety and malicious gossip *usually take two forms: relationship-oriented talk* (for example, which executives and managers are dating which employees) and *office politics* (for example, who is on the verge of being promoted, fired, or transferred). In some cases, she says, gossip is designed to slander or defame an individual—often for personal or political gain.[21] Simmons reports that there also are *gender differences in the use of gossip*. She believes that men often use gossip as a form of political control, while women employ it to make themselves look and feel important.[22] Both agree, however, that a lack of official information often lies at the heart of gossiping. Simmons notes that "When people aren't fully engaged in work, it creates a vacuum. And when they don't know what's going on, especially regarding promotions and layoffs, they begin to speculate."

The effects of gossip on an organization can be as destructive as the effects of gossip on the individuals it discusses. Gossip in the workplace has a strong effect on how well and how much people produce. Productivity suffers because gossip eats up work time and damages the welfare and morale of employees. Although office gossip might inflict a great deal of pain, there's an even nastier practice that runs rampant in some companies: *mobbing*. Workers gang up on another employee, including a boss, in an attempt to intimidate, bully, or humiliate and force the person out—usually through scathing verbal abuse. In their book *Mobbing: Emotional Abuse in the American Workplace*, Davenport, Schwartz, and Elliott describe the victims of mobbing: "Coworkers, colleagues, superiors, and subordinates attack their dignity, integrity, and competence, repeatedly, over a number of weeks, months or years. At the end, they resign—voluntarily or involuntarily, are terminated, or are forced into early retirement." Indeed, the authors claim that at times, "mobbing behaviors are ignored, tolerated, misinterpreted, or actually instigated by the company or the organization's management as a deliberate strategy."[23]

To *minimize the potential negative effects of office gossip*, organizations (and their members) should do several things:

- They should make an effort to *keep employees fully informed*. When people know what's going on, they are less inclined to gossip.

- They should strive to *build a culture that's supportive rather than competitive*, since the worst gossip occurs in organizations where the fight for limited rewards and resources is ruthless.

- Members of management should *let workers know that malicious, personal gossip is not acceptable*, making it clear that such talk can be very damaging and create tension, animosity, and organizational problems.

- Members of the organization also should *deal with rumors immediately;* left unchecked, rumors can spiral out of control and sap energy and productivity as workers spend time speculating rather than working.

- Individual supervisors (and even colleagues) should *confront chronic offenders*—those who start rumors and/or spend an inordinate amount of time gossiping—to let them know the behavior is not acceptable.

Swearing

All languages have swear words, and most of us have used them at one time or another. In fact, for better or worse, swearing seems to be gaining acceptance in society. For many years, four-letter words were banned from the air waves, for example, but gradually the restrictions have eased; in movies, on radio, and even on TV, foul language is commonplace.

Despite its widespread use, however, swearing is *not a desirable verbal strategy*. As Genua observes, whenever a person curses, there is a tendency among listeners to lower their opinion of that person: "the listener immediately forms an impression that portrays the user of the swear word as vulgar or, in today's vernacular, 'a low-life,'" he claims.[24]

But in today's diverse organization, there is another important dimension to cursing: *the issue of sexual harassment*. For example, if a man curses in mixed company and then turns to a woman in the group and says, "Please pardon my French," problems arise. The man may think that by saying this he is deferring to women in the group and displaying his good manners and respect for females. However, the woman may feel that he is discriminating against her. She has been singled out for special attention. That puts her on the spot, and she has to indicate somehow that she accepts the man's insincere request for pardon. With a nod or faint smile, she may have to acknowledge that "it's all right; I don't mind." But what if she does mind? And what if she minds the man's implication that, because she's a woman, she should mind?

In her column in *Newsweek*, Anna Quindlen traced the development of swearing in U.S. politics.[25] In 1962, when the *New York Times* quoted President John F. Kennedy during a dispute with the steel industry as saying, "My father always told me that all businessmen were sons of bitches, but I never believed it till now," White House officials were furious that the *Times* would report such behavior by the president. The White House press office complained, the publisher of the *Times* apologized, and the Associated Press noted that other newspapers had found the quote unfit to print.

But things have changed dramatically in recent years. Vice President Cheney's use of the "F-bomb" as he advised Senator Patrick Leahy to perform an

anatomically impossible act produced relatively little outcry and was widely pub-
licized. Rather than apologize, Cheney offered this explanation:

> He had challenged my integrity. And I didn't like that. But most of all I didn't
> like the fact that after he had done so, then he wanted to act like everything's
> peaches and cream. And I informed him of my view of his conduct in no
> uncertain terms. And, as I say, I felt better afterwards.

To Quindlen, this incident revealed much more than a declining system of
American values. To her

> the most enduring lesson of this event has more to do with what passes for a
> guy than what passes for a role model. Slinging obscenities has always been
> the verbal equivalent of towel snapping; cursing the senator . . . was the clos-
> est the Vice President could come to throwing a punch. . . . To appreciate just
> how much of this is macho, consider what the response would have been had
> Sen. Hillary Clinton used the same word. . . .

Kennedy obviously thought being seen as crude would lessen his stature. But
Quindlen observes that in today's climate, being seen as too polite or too sensitive apparently is considered weak. She concludes that "This is not particularly
useful in elevating the tone in Washington, or in trying to show kids that the
reflexive use of certain words is the last refuge of those who are neither intelligent nor thoughtful enough to plumb a more varied vocabulary. It brings out the
worst in everyone."

As a verbal strategy, swearing has little to say for it, since it has no positive
effect on anyone and it can damage your image and detract from your profession-
alism. Add to that the possibility that you may offend someone—or even prompt
a sexual harassment claim against you—and the downsides of swearing far outweigh the nonexistent upsides.

Constructive Verbal Strategies

The preceding section identified a variety of ways in which words can damage
our relationships with others. Certainly, those verbal strategies should be
avoided. However, there are ways in which words can be used to build more positive, constructive relationships within organizations, and in this section we will
consider some of those positive verbal strategies.

Supportive Behaviors

To improve interpersonal communications with others, suggests Gibb, we
should *establish a "supportive" climate.*[26] Rather than appearing to be a threat to
the listener or releasing our own feelings of aggression, we instead should demonstrate our support for that person's well-being. Just as some verbal behaviors
create defensiveness or display aggression, others seem to produce this supportive climate. Among them:

• *Descriptive behavior.* Rather than passing judgment on the other's behavior, we
  should simply describe the behavior and our reaction to it. Instead of saying,
  "You're disgusting," it would be more supportive to say, "When you put your
  bare feet on the dinner table while we are eating, it makes me uncomfortable."

Thus, the focus of the interaction is not the worth of the person but the behaviors in which that person is engaged.

- *Problem-oriented behavior.* Trying to control another person creates defensiveness; suggesting that you work cooperatively to solve a problem avoids the implicit superiority that control-oriented statements contain and instead makes the person more willing to interact. The focus on the interaction is shifted from the person to an objective problem, thus reducing the possibility of a perceived threat.

- *Spontaneous behavior.* Behaviors that are spontaneous, growing from the immediate situation, tend to avoid the defensive reactions produced by strategic behaviors. Rather than planning strategy ahead of time, it usually is preferable to let the situation dictate appropriate behaviors. Obviously, there are exceptions to this rule. Speeches and interviews must involve some planning. In everyday conversation, however, spontaneous reactions rather than strategically motivated behaviors produce better relationships.

- *Empathic behavior.* Rather than appearing neutral or unconcerned, we should demonstrate to the other person that we do indeed care about him and his well-being. Empathy involves a genuine concern for the other, which we communicate in our interaction.

- *Egalitarian behavior.* Superiority produces defensiveness; we therefore should stress equality in our interactions. Even conversations between superiors and

Highlighting Civic Engagement

Community Dialogue Encourages Supportive Communication Behaviors

In 2004, the Campus Compact Reader offered a selected listing of online resources for conducting constructive dialogues with citizens concerning an array of issues about which community members often possess sharply contrasting views. A trip to these Web sites reveals a clear emphasis on supportive communication behaviors as a way of initiating and sustaining productive dialogues and seeking consensus on complex problems. It also highlights books on dialogue and specific dialogue techniques. The following sites are especially recommended:

- *The Dialogue to Action Initiative*—a very extensive site, including short commentaries on the nature of dialogue and deliberation, but also (more rarely) funding opportunities, resources, and a regularly updated calendar of dialogue-related events: ***http://www.thataway.org***

- *Innovations in Democracy*—a compilation of over 100 Web sites on "innovative practices, ideas, experiments, organizations, and references useful for building wiser democracies that work for us all": ***http://www.democracyinnovations.org***

- *Public Conversations Project*—originally known for its early work on dialogues among those with different positions on abortion, this site "promotes constructive conversations among people who have differing values, worldviews, and perspectives about divisive public issues": ***http://www.publicconversations.org***

- *Study Circles Resource Center*—promotes and provides resources for group dialogues (study circles) on various local and national topics. Conducts workshops and training for facilitators and publishes "how-to" guides for community organizers: ***http://www.studycircles.org***

Source: "Conducting Dialogues: A Selected Listing of Resources" [online].
Available: http://www.compact.org/reader/winter04/resources2html (accessed: August 22, 2004).

subordinates may contain elements of this technique, as the superior stresses commonalties of the relationship (for example, organizational goals toward which both are working) rather than emphasizing the differences in status.

- *Provisional behavior.* Since a dogmatic "my way or the highway" attitude produces defensiveness, it generally is preferable to take a provisional attitude. Our communication should indicate that our attitudes are tentative, not cast in concrete, and that we are willing to listen to other viewpoints. By minimizing the threat of attack on others, we make them more willing to communicate their true feelings.

Assertive Behaviors

Aggressive behaviors are detrimental to organizational relationships, as we pointed out earlier in this chapter. But so too are passive behaviors: putting aside your own wants and needs and giving in to the wishes or needs of others. In fact, the two can be combined: we become "passive/aggressive" when we try to undermine someone else by doing nothing—we just sit back and wait for them to tell us what to do, and we let them take the blame when things "go south" because they didn't have our help.

Far more constructive are "assertive behaviors," whereby you stand up for your rights and the things you want and need; you express your feelings, opinions, and preferences openly, honestly, and directly in ways that show respect for yourself and others. Leebov reports that assertiveness rests on several key principles:[27]

- When we stand up for ourselves and let ourselves be known to others, we gain greater self-respect and greater respect from others.
- When we stand up for ourselves and express our honest feelings in direct, honest, and appropriate ways everyone benefits in the long run.
- When we share our true reactions with others and allow others to share their honest reactions with us, our personal relationships become more authentic and satisfying.
- Not letting others know what we think is as inconsiderate as not listening to others when they express their thoughts and feelings.
- When we repeatedly place others in positions of greater importance over us, we teach them that they can take advantage of us.
- By acting assertively and telling other people how their behavior affects us, we are able to give them the opportunity to change, and we show them that we respect their right to know where they stand with us.

Behaving assertively primarily involves the use of "I statements." Aggressive and passive behaviors involve "you statements"—attacking statements if we are aggressive ("You're an idiot!"), or compliant statements if we are passive ("Whatever you say."). Assertive "I statements" talk about your own wants, feelings, needs, reactions, and so on, and leave it to the other person to decide what they want to think or do.

There are several specific types of "I statements" you might use assertively. "I want statements" clarify what you desire of yourself and others. They tell people what you want to do or what you want them to do. If their needs conflict with yours, you can negotiate to reach a compromise. For example: "I want to know what I did to make you upset so we can talk about it," or "I'd like you to be on time when we have an appointment."

"I feel statements" let you express your feelings without trying to make others feel inferior or inadequate. "I feel grateful to you for helping me to finish the project" expresses positive feedback, while "I feel angry when you don't do the things you say you will do" expresses the consequences of the other person's actions.

"I statements" can also express mixed feelings: "I'm happy that I got a pay increase and I appreciate the recognition you have given me, but I'm still bothered that my salary is below that of the people who report to me." Such statements help others to understand any conflicts we may be feeling, and to see why we may not be completely comfortable with something that looks positive from one point of view but has shortcomings from another perspective.

A particularly important form of "I statement" is the flat-out "no." Passive communicators never use this word. They always agree. If they are passive/aggressive, they say "yes, I'll do it" and then do nothing, but they don't say "no." Assertive communication means that you state, clearly and emphatically, that you will not comply with the person's request when you don't want to do so. But before you say no, be sure that's what you mean. If you're not sure, take more time to think about it. If you need more information, get it. And if you choose to give the person a reason, fine—that is up to you. But if your answer is "no," don't just swallow it and say "OK"; just say "no."

An empathetic "I statement" shows that you empathize with the other person—you understand how he or she is feeling, even as you stand up for your own rights or needs. For example: "I know you're probably disappointed that I have said no, but that's my final answer. Can I suggest someone else who might do it

Table 4.1   Passive, Aggressive, and Assertive Characteristics and Consequences

	Passive	*Aggressive*	*Assertive*
Characteristics	wants, ideas, and feelings not expressed or expressed in self-demeaning ways	wants, ideas, feelings expressed at expense of others	wants, ideas, feelings expressed in direct, appropriate ways
You feel	anxious, disappointed with self, angry and resentful after the fact	self-righteous, superior, but sometimes embarrassed later	confident, good about self
Others feel about you	irritation, pity, disgust	humiliation, hurt, anger	respect
Outcome for you	unsatisfactory, anger continues to build	satisfactory, but at expense of others, making them hesitant to cooperate	satisfactory, often getting what you want
Payoff	unpleasant conflict, tension, and confrontation avoided	anger vented, temporary feelings of superiority but lost respect and cooperation of others	feel good, respected by others, improved confidence, increased quality of relationships

From Wendy Leebov, *Practical Assertiveness for Health Care Professionals* (Chicago: American Hospital Association, 1991), 10.

instead?" Or, "I understand that your car isn't very reliable and that causes you to be late some times. But I still need you to be here on time." Such statements show that you understand the other person's perspective—assuming that you are correctly interpreting his or her behaviors and feelings—and thus make it less likely that the person will become defensive.

"I feedback" messages are especially useful when you want to express difficult negative feelings and give other people feedback about how their actions have affected you. If handled properly, such statements help the other person reconsider, with a minimum of embarrassment or defensiveness, a behavior that is problematic for you. Since such statements involve feedback, they involve both "you" and "I" statements, and often involve the words "When you . . ." and "I feel." For example: "Bob, when you start yelling at me, I feel angry because everybody can hear and I feel embarrassed. I am very willing to listen to you, but I want you to stop yelling at me." Similarly, you might say, "When you give me the information I need at the last minute, I feel frustrated because I don't have much time to do my part of the project. I would really appreciate it if you could get the information to me more quickly so I would have more time."

Confrontational "I statements" are used when other efforts have failed. Perhaps you have made it clear to someone how you feel and what you want them to do, but no change took place. By using confrontational assertion, you clarify what was said before and what you want from the person now or in the future. For example: "You asked for my suggestions, but as far as I can tell, you haven't done any of the things I proposed. I feel frustrated when you ask my opinion but then seem to ignore it. I would like to know what, if anything, you're going to do." Problems that remain unresolved are handled in the same way: "I thought we had agreed that you would not yell at me any more, but you're doing it again. I feel angry when you yell, particularly after we had agreed that you wouldn't. I'd like you to stop, please."

Just as you are assertive with others, others are going to be assertive with you. Being on the receiving end of others' "I statements" can be uncomfortable, particularly when those statements suggest that you should behave differently. Accepting criticism can be done in a passive, assertive, or aggressive manner as well, and you are most likely to maintain positive relations with others (and gain maximum benefit from the gift of feedback they are giving you) if you follow these guidelines:

- *Listen*. Do not try to defend yourself until you hear exactly what the problem is. Breathing slowly and deeply will help you stay calm and pay attention.

- *Paraphrase*. Repeat the criticism in your own words to be sure you have accurately understood what the person is saying. This also shows the other person that you have been listening and gives her a chance to correct any misunderstandings.

- *Ask for specific examples*. If the feedback is too general for you to understand exactly what the person wants, ask for an example of what is being criticized.

- *Decide for yourself whether the criticism is valid*. Just because the other person says it doesn't make it right (a passive perspective) or wrong (the aggressive stance). Decide for yourself whether it seems reasonable and focuses on something you want to correct.

- *If the criticism seems valid, don't make excuses.* Instead, think of ways you can act differently, or ask the person, "What would you like me to do instead to correct the problem?"

- *If the criticism seems unfair, start with an "I statement."* "I feel my actions may have been misunderstood," or "I don't feel I can do what you're asking me to do." Avoid argumentative "you statements," such as "you don't understand" or "you're being unfair." These accuse and possibly insult, leading to hard feelings and an argument.

- *If you feel yourself becoming angry or defensive, suggest postponing the rest of the conversation.* "I appreciate your feedback and I really want to hear what's on your mind, but I'm feeling myself getting upset. How about if we get back together a little later when I'm a little more calm?"

Giving Positive Feedback

One of the most powerful motivational forces is feedback. Consider, for example, a survey that was done for American Express that looked at what workers most want from their employers.[28] The survey found that the number one desire, listed by 46 percent of all respondents, was personal feedback. This compares with the 32 percent who said they most wanted financial rewards. In turn, such feedback can have an impact on productivity and morale. A survey by Menlo Park, California-based staffing service OfficeTeam found 66 percent of respondents believe performance review sessions have a favorable impact on job motivation. And particularly powerful is positive feedback. For example, newspaper columnist Dale Dauten reports that more than 20 years ago, Walter Vaux was a young chemical engineer working in a lab when his boss walked in. "You're doing a wonderful job," he remembers the supervisor saying. "I'm so glad you're part of the department." It was just a few words, but the input was such a valuable motivator that Vaux, now retired, still talks of the lesson he learned: it takes more than cash to buy loyalty.[29]

In his weekly newspaper column, Dauten invited readers to send in workplace compliments they have seen or heard. He received dozens, many of them describing events that happened many years earlier. The letters led him to conclude that "When you put a person's talent on display in such a way that everyone can admire it, you make a person better, give him or her something to rise to. This doesn't make you a flatterer but a futurist."

In our view, however, there is a difference between a compliment and meaningful, positive feedback. A compliment simply says you feel positively about some aspect of the person to whom you are speaking: "Nice tie," or "What a cute baby!" Typically, the compliment isn't intended to focus on and/or influence the person's behavior—you aren't trying to suggest to the person that he wear the same tie again tomorrow, nor that she should have another baby. Rather, it simply shares your positive feelings with the other person, and in the process you probably make him or her feel positive as well.

Positive feedback, on the other hand, *focuses on behavior*. Done properly, it motivates the recipient to repeat the behavior that prompted the positive comment, but too often we miss opportunities to give motivating positive feedback by giving general compliments instead. We say, "You really did a nice job on that project" rather than telling the person exactly what he or she did well: "You got the project done ahead of schedule, and with zero defects." The "nice job" compliment makes the person feel good; the "ahead of schedule, and with zero defects" feedback both makes the person feel good and conveys how the behavior is valued. That feedback in turn is likely to cause behavior deserving of more positive feedback in the future.

The keys to giving positive feedback, then, are these: First, *be specific*. State exactly what the person did that, in your view, was good. Second, *tell the person why that behavior is important*. For example: "You got the project done ahead of time, and with zero defects; that made our client really happy, so they are more likely to use us again." This teaches the person organizational values that may guide him or her even when you are not around to give positive feedback. Lastly, *express your personal appreciation*. "Thanks so much; I really appreciate what you did."

Positive feedback is *best delivered in person*, not electronically. As Cottrell and Harvey point out in *The Manager's Communication Handbook*, "Employees want to know that managers recognize their contributions, and they want to hear it in person. . . . A handshake and a look in the eyes to say 'thank you' have a far greater impact than any message on a computer screen."[30] The same principle applies when you are giving positive feedback to a coworker; personal contact is much more powerful than any e-mail or text message.

Giving Corrective Feedback

Sometimes, we face the need to give people feedback they may not want to hear. Nevertheless, when our colleagues make mistakes, do things that are detrimental to the organization, or even do things that hurt us personally, we have to give them feedback intended to correct their behaviors.

Giving corrective feedback isn't easy. For example, even though managers are paid to correct inappropriate employee behaviors, many don't. In *Managing Workplace Negativity*, Gary Topchik argues that only one manager in four does a good job of confronting negative employees.[31] Many "don't have the skill, time, or patience to deal with negativity," he says. Yet those who fail to deal with negativism find their workplaces smitten by a negativity "virus that spreads rapidly from one person to another." This virus takes a heavy toll on the organization by hiking error rates and customer complaints and fostering employee tardiness, absence, and turnover.

There are four keys to giving corrective feedback. First, as Solomon suggests, *"Blame the method, not the motive."*[32] Often, we think we know why someone did something we don't like; however, when we start making accusations about the person's intent, emotional conflict quickly ensues and the argument focuses on *why* he did something, not *what* he did. The *why* is unimportant; the *what* is the issue.

Second, *describe the problematic behavior specifically*. Just as a general compliment serves only to make a person feel good, a general criticism just makes her feel bad; the person learns nothing about what needs to be changed or improved. "Your report really stinks" is no help. "Your report left out how much the project ended up costing" tells the person exactly what your concern is. In addition, be sure to focus on the behavior, not the person. Saying "you're a lazy slob" is both general and insulting and is unlikely to produce a change in behaviors. Saying "you have been wearing the same outfit for three consecutive weeks, and you sleep in front of your computer screen" makes it clear what behaviors are causing your discontent.

In addition to describing the behavior, you also need to *indicate the impact of the behavior*. This makes it more likely that the person will change the behavior, and it also makes it less likely that the person will think you're just being "picky" or personal in your criticism. "Your report left out how much the project ended up costing. That's really important, because cost containment is one of the major concerns that senior leadership has." Or, "When you come in late, everyone else has to cover for you, and their workloads already are heavy. So, people are getting pretty annoyed."

As you provide feedback, *maintaining respect and dignity (yours and the other person's) is absolutely vital.* Being criticized in public can be humiliating, so give corrective feedback in private whenever possible. But as you deliver feedback, be careful not to generalize ("You always foul things up this way!"), accuse ("You're just trying to get my job."), stereotype ("You people are all alike."), or threaten ("If you keep this up, I'll tell the boss."). Calmly describe the behavior you observed, how the behavior impacts the situation, and your personal concern about the situation.

Throughout the conversation, *start with and maintain the philosophy, "I want you to succeed."* By showing that you are interested in the person's well-being and success, you convert the conversation from an adversarial position of you criticizing into a cooperative position of you working to help the other be successful. For example: "You have been late every day this week, and everyone else has had to cover for you. Their workloads already are heavy, so they're getting pretty annoyed. Personally, I want you to be successful here, but to do that you need to get in on time." If you clearly have the person's best interests at heart, he or she is much more likely to view you as an ally rather than an adversary.

Finally, *ask the person for suggestions* rather than simply saying, "Do this to improve." By asking, "What could we do to make sure you get here on time?" you encourage the person to come up with the solution rather than allowing him or her to sit back and let you do the thinking. But regardless of the solution the person devises, one thing must remain clear: the behavior needs to change. We will return to the subject of the corrective interview later in the book.

Apologizing

Sometimes we goof up. When that happens, the best verbal strategy is a simple one: *say you're sorry.* But what seems like a very simple strategy has proven very difficult for some public figures. Jonathan Turley, a law professor at George Washington University and a criminal defense attorney, describes the apologies of three prominent people.[33] First, the *empty apology* offered by Martha Stewart:

> Today is a shameful day. It is shameful for me, for my family and for my beloved company and all of its employees and partners. What was a small personal matter became over the last 2½ years an almost fatal circus event of unprecedented proportions, spreading like oil over a vast landscape, even around the world. I have been choked and almost suffocated to death during that time.

Turley contends that Stewart took no responsibility for her actions despite the fact that her trial left little doubt as to her guilt. Indeed, the "small personal matter" she referred to was actually a series of federal crimes, including lying repeatedly to federal regulators. Rather than focusing on her own actions, she seemed to portray herself as the victim.

Former President Bill Clinton provides an example of what Turley calls the *nonapology:*

> Mere words cannot fully express the profound remorse I feel for what our country is going through and for what members of both parties in Congress are now forced to deal with. . . . I understand that accountability demands consequences, and I'm prepared to accept them.

In Turley's opinion, Clinton spent a lifetime perfecting the nonapology apology: speaking in hushed, even emotional tones, while not actually admitting anything.

Finally, the *perfect apology,* as executed by former President Ronald Reagan:

> I take full responsibility for my own actions and for those of my administration. . . . As disappointed as I may be in some who served me, I'm still the one who must answer to the American people for this behavior. And as personally distasteful as I find secret bank accounts and diverted funds—well, as the Navy would say, this happened on my watch.

Reagan knew how to apologize. At the height of the Iran-contra scandal, he went on the airwaves to apologize. Of course, he was not admitting any guilt since he insisted that he knew nothing about the widespread criminal conspiracy operating out of the White House. Nevertheless, he conveyed a sense of remorse that Martha Stewart, Bill Clinton, and dozens of others failed to express.

Saying "I'm sorry; I'll try not to do it again" is *rarely seen as a sign of weakness or failure*. In fact, most people recognize that it takes some courage to say "I was wrong" and resolve to improve. Repeated apologies lose their charm after a time, of course, but as an initial verbal strategy, we highly recommend the apology.

SUMMARY

Words are the basic building blocks of interpersonal communication in organizations, and as electronic communication has removed the nonverbal element of interaction between organizational members, words themselves have taken on increasing importance. Moving from a microscopic view of words (the thoughts of the general semanticists, for example) to a more macroscopic perspective (broader verbal strategies that hurt or help organizational relationships), we reviewed a variety of ways in which your skills in using words might be improved.

After examining some problems of semantics (and how to avoid them), we addressed the fundamentals of effective written communication—offering suggestions for sound composition, wording and phrasing, punctuation, grammar, and spelling before turning to some tips on how to create unified, well supported statements in letters, memos, and other fully developed documents you might compose in professional settings. Since so much interpersonal interaction occurs via e-mail, we then offered some guidelines for communicating effectively in that medium.

In the final section of the chapter we considered some issues surrounding the use of destructive verbal strategies (including gossiping and swearing). We next discussed such positive verbal strategies as communicating supportively and assertively, giving positive feedback, offering corrective feedback in a constructive manner, and even apologizing. In the next chapter, we will move to the actions that speak even louder than words.

Questions for Discussion

1. Using principles of semantics as the basis for your answer, what specific words can you list that serve to divide organizations and impair their success?

2. Why is telling stories such a powerful element of communication in organizations? What stories have you heard in your own organizations?

3. What are some behaviors that cause people to become defensive? Why do they cause people to react that way?

4. What effects on other people do aggressive behaviors have? Why?

5. How can gossip be harmful in an organization? How can it be helpful?

6. How can swearing be harmful in an organization? How can it be helpful?

7. Why is it hard to say "no" at times?

8. If someone makes a mistake, how should the person apologize? Should the person apologize? Explain.

9. When you read a memo or letter that someone has written, how do you judge the quality of the writing? Discuss.

10. What are some of your pet peeves about the way others communicate with you via e-mail?

Exercises

1. List some "fighting words" that mean different things to different people. In what situations would such words be acceptable?

2. Write a paragraph describing how you spent your day yesterday, implementing the "suggestions for composition" provided in this chapter; underline at least one example in your paragraph of each of the five suggestions.

3. List every verb you can think of that could replace the verb "say" or "said."

4. Imagine global warming is about to cause a worldwide flood that will wipe out all life—except a handful of people who will be floating in a large boat being built by the United Nations. Write a proposal that you should be included among the boat people.

5. Write a brief story that illustrates something in your life that taught you an important lesson; describe the event and the lesson you learned.

6. Identify something positive your course instructor has done, and provide him/her with positive feedback following the steps outlined in the chapter.

7. Identify something your course instructor has done that could be improved, and provide him/her with corrective feedback following the steps outlined in the chapter.

8. Apologize to your course instructor.

Case Application 4.1

Consider this true story. In a large Chicago company, an African American supervisor found herself having to take disciplinary action against one of her employees, who also was an African American female. She met with the employee and reviewed the situation: the employee had been late several times during the past three weeks, despite the verbal warning the supervisor had given her almost a month before. Consequently, the supervisor had to give the employee a written warning that would go into her personnel file.

During the entire session, the employee said nothing, but simply sat with her arms folded, glaring at the supervisor. When the supervisor had finished her description of the employee's unsatisfactory behaviors and the disciplinary action she was taking, she asked the employee if there was anything she wanted to say. The employee thought a moment, and then said with her teeth clenched: "Just one thing. You're white."

Questions

1. From the perspective of general semantics, what problems are involved in the employee's use of the label "white"?

2. If you were the supervisor, what would you say in response?

5

Nonverbal Messages

During a typical day, people in organizations spend much—and often, most—of their time meeting and talking with other people. Although words are a key component to these interactions, as the last chapter described, equally important are the imagery, place, and movements that surround and accompany the verbal exchanges. Images, settings, and physical and vocal actions are not just the "supporting cast" for the words; they carry messages as well, and sometimes they *are* the messages.

Many books have been written about nonverbal communication—some so technical that they are almost beyond comprehension, and others so simplistic as to be misleading. The most simplistic among them offer a single translation for many facial expressions and body postures. For example, arms crossed against the chest "means" that the listener has closed her or his mind to what the speaker is saying. This kind of simplistic interpretation is an unfortunate misuse of the scholarly research on nonverbal communication. No gesture has a single, unvarying meaning—the meaning of any gesture depends on cultural norms, personal style, the physical setting, what has gone before, and what both parties anticipate for the future.

Five aspects of nonverbal communication that seem particularly important, as summarized by Elgin in *The Gentle Art of Verbal Self-Defense at Work*, are these:[1]

• For American English, about 90 percent of all emotional information, and more than half of all information whatsoever, is carried not by your words but

169

by the body language that goes with those words—particularly intonation and tone of voice.

- The most powerful mechanism for body language is not your body, it's your voice: its volume, pitch, quality, tone, and how those things are applied to words and parts of words.
- There is a grammar of body language, just as there is a grammar of words and sentences. You know that grammar but may not be aware of what you know.
- Any words can have their meaning cancelled by body language, but not vice versa; there are no words that can cancel the meaning transmitted by body language.
- Because your nonverbal communication has powerful effects on other people— effects that can literally cancel the words you say—you must take responsibility for your body language.

Daniel Goleman's work on "emotional intelligence" has demonstrated the link between ability to understand how others are feeling and success at the highest reaches of the business world. No matter how expert you are at your job, his research shows, if you don't develop the skill of understanding others' emotional lives, you will never succeed in an organization.[2] Since 90 percent of emotional meaning is conveyed nonverbally, the importance of being able to perceive and correctly interpret nonverbal cues becomes obvious.

Preview

Like Latin, mathematics, and accounting, nonverbal communication is a language that can be learned. With intelligent practice, for example, a person can learn to read and to speak "place"—that is, to understand the symbolic, territorial, and behavior-influencing aspects of physical settings. Again, nonverbal messages rarely provide definitive information, but they do provide a way of knowing what is not available through words. In this chapter, then, we will consider a variety of forms of nonverbal communication. After reviewing the roles nonverbal cues can play in relation to words, we will look at ways the environment can shape interaction among people within organizations, and then examine specific aspects of our behavior that accompany the words we say.

ROLES OF NONVERBAL CUES

To understand nonverbal cues as they operate in human communication, we need to consider the roles they play when people interact. These roles become most apparent when we consider nonverbal cues as they relate to verbal messages. To see nonverbal messages in action, consider this hypothetical situation: you go into the company president's office to ask him to give you a raise. During the encounter, the nonverbal cues you receive perform the following roles:

- *Framing*. The environment creates a context that in turn shapes the interaction that occurs within it. The president's office is huge, with wood paneling and expensive artwork; the president himself seated behind an enormous desk. The room is rather dark, although the window behind the president is open and bright sunlight is coming from directly behind him.

- *Repeating*. "Sit down," the president says, pointing to a chair in front of his huge desk. His nonverbal cue, a hand gesture, serves to repeat the message he has spoken. "Want a cigar?" he asks, holding a box out toward you. Again, his gesture repeats his words.

- *Contradicting*. "You know," he begins as you light your cigar, "I'm a simple man. I've always been satisfied with little things." His office with its wood paneling, leather-upholstered furniture, deep-pile carpet, and teak desk contradicts his words. "Now, I've always been happy to talk to people who are eager to improve their lot in life." He kept you waiting nearly an hour in his outer office and now speaks to you with a scowl on his face. His nonverbal cues thus suggest that he is anything but happy to see you.

- *Substituting*. "And I wish the company had enough money to give everyone the raise they deserve. But. . . ." His voice trails off, and he shrugs and shakes his head. These gestures substitute for words. He does not have to say, "We don't have enough money to give everyone a raise, so you're out of luck." His nonverbal gestures have said it for him.

- *Elaborating*. Suddenly, the president bursts into tears. Between sobs, he manages to stammer, "I hate having to do this. You can't know how bad I feel about not being able to give you a raise. Sometimes this job is hell!" His words express his feelings, but his actions elaborate on them, showing us just how much he means what he says.

- *Accenting*. Slowly, the president rises from his chair, struggling to regain his composure. "Dang it!" he explodes, pounding his fist on the desk. "Dang it, I'm going to give you that raise, even though we can't afford it. It won't be as much as you asked for—three cents a week, in fact—but we need to do something for employees as faithful as you." His fist pounding serves to accent his "dang its," and his rising out of his seat likewise accents both his dominance and his generosity.

- *Regulating*. "I'm glad you came in," he concludes, extending a clammy hand. "We need to talk like this more often." He then sits down, turns away, and resumes reading the *Wall Street Journal*. The role of these last behaviors is to regulate or control the interaction. In essence, he is saying, "Our conversation is now over. No further communication is desired. Please leave."

Thus, **the roles of nonverbal cues are determined largely by their relationships to spoken messages**. Nonverbal behaviors may produce or change meaning by repeating the verbal message, contradicting it, substituting for it, elaborating on it, accenting parts of it, or regulating it. Each of these functions is important, as our example demonstrates, and each of them shows the crucial nature of nonverbal communication in our everyday interactions.

THE PHYSICAL ENVIRONMENT

The physical setting in which communication occurs constitutes the environmental element of nonverbal communication. As you might suspect, the work environment is important, particularly from the viewpoint of those within that environment. Indeed, a study done several years ago by the Buffalo Organization for Social and Technical Innovation showed that satisfaction with work space created an extra $1,600 of productivity annually in white-collar workers.[3] On a 1999 survey conducted by the American Society of Interior Designers, employees ranked the look and feel of their work spaces as their third most important consideration, after salary and benefits, in deciding whether to accept or decline a job. "People, knowledge, and technology need to be integrated and supported by the physical environment to achieve success," says David P. Secan, workplace development consultant and principal of Elkins Park, Pennsylvania-based Secan Associates. "People represent a company's largest and most important asset. But corporate real estate and facilities represent the second."[4]

Contributions of the Environment

According to Steele, the physical settings in which people work promote five key elements of any organization.[5] The first, and possibly most important, is *task instrumentality:* the appropriateness of facilities for carrying out tasks. This element of the physical environment considers specific settings and tasks, such as the soundproof room needed for taping records, the locations of groups that work together, the presence of equipment, and sensory conditions. While physical environments affect interaction, perceptions of status, and the like, it is important to remember that they are constructed to get work done. Offices are arranged in ways that theoretically will enhance productivity; production lines are similarly set up to promote work. Traditionally, industrial engineers and architects have concerned themselves only with the task instrumentality of the environments they design, working to create a workplace that ensures work will flow efficiently. Only recently have they begun to focus on the impact of environments on the relationships among the people working within them.

A second important environmental factor is the sheer *pleasure* a place gives to those who use it, such as the views employees enjoy from the sixtieth floor of the Sears Tower in Chicago. This factor includes the absence of unpleasant stimuli (noise, smells, uncomfortable temperature) and the presence of pleasant stimuli (furniture, music, colors, artwork, and other visual stimuli). Consider, for example, Gap Inc.'s, headquarters in the San Francisco Bay area. On the campus are walking paths that wind through oak groves to invite outdoor conversations. The building has a roof covered with native grasses and wildflowers that provides thermal and acoustic insulation, and increases energy savings year-round. Indoors, there is an entrance granting access to a lobby and commons area that includes a teleconference center, meeting rooms, and a café. Downstairs, there is a full-service fitness center (featuring an aerobics studio and lap pool) that provides on-site amenities for Gap Inc.'s 500 headquarter employees. Workers even receive smog-free air: fresh air is drawn into the building, blown across the concrete decks, and then fanned into the offices' interior via adjustable grilles located on the floor. "The environment our employees work in is all part of what makes the Gap's formula creative and innovative," said Mickey Drexler, former president and CEO of Gap Inc. "Frankly, it's what makes us feel good about our jobs every day."[6]

Noise in the work environment is detrimental to having a pleasant atmosphere and of workers' ability to do their work effectively. Not every company needs a work space so quiet that employees can hear a pin drop, but good office acoustics are vital to preventing distractions. That's especially true for open-plan offices, which eliminate most private offices. "In an open-plan office, you're willing to hear someone else's voice, but you don't want to understand it," says Al Shiner, president of Shiner & Associates, Inc., a Chicago-based acoustic consult-

---

Highlighting Civic Engagement

Understanding the Power of the Physical Setting

The thoughtful citizen is one who thinks critically about the impact of the messages, both verbal and nonverbal, that she or he is exposed to. Political speakers may attempt to manipulate the speech setting to influence the way listeners respond. In Kathleen Hall Jamieson's account of Reagan's First Inaugural Address, she notes:

- In his first rhetorical act as president, Reagan demonstrated his fluency in the grammar and syntax of television. He began, "This is the first time in our history that this ceremony has been held, as you've been told, on this West front of the Capitol."

- That location enabled Reagan to use television to underscore the central claim of his address, that heroism is both part of America's past and of her future. As he spoke of the national monuments, the cameras "lovingly transmitted them" to the living rooms of America. He said, "Standing here, one faces a magnificent vista, opening up on this city's special beauty and history. At the end of this open mall are those shrines to the giants on whose shoulders we stand."

- While other presidents used words to assert a connection with the "venerated past," Reagan invited the cameras *visually* to meld his presidency into those of his great predecessors. He shows, as well as tells, as he pays tribute to each one—for example, "Directly in front of me, the monument to a monumental man, George Washington, father of our country. A man of humility, who came to greatness reluctantly."

- He then pays tribute to those heroes who have given their lives—pointing to the "sloping hills of Arlington National Cemetery, with its row upon row of simple white markers bearing crosses or Stars of David. . . . Each of these markers is a monument to the kind of hero I spoke of earlier."

- Finally, he moves to the roll call with which the country identifies the victories of its past. "Their lives ended in places called Belleau Wood, The Argonne, Omaha Beach, Salerno, and halfway round the world on Guadalcanal, Tarawa, Pork Chop Hill, the Chosin Reservoir, and in a hundred rice paddies and jungles of a place called Vietnam."

- Jamieson concludes: "Having roused our disposition to assent by visually and verbally invoking one non-controversial symbol after another (e.g., Washington, Jefferson, the Declaration of Independence, the cemetery, and a litany of battles), Reagan rehabilitates the Vietnam War by including it. Relying on television's irresistible impulse to show and capitalizing on its disposition to argue by visual association, Reagan . . . transformed a body of revered national symbols into *an extended visual aid.* The panorama invites our respect for the founders, freedom, heroism, and the Vietnam War. At the same time, these visual symbols visually bracket his speech, functioning as the set on which he introduces his presidency."

Source: Kathleen Hall Jamieson, *Eloquence in an Electronic Age: The Transformation of Political Speechmaking* (New York: Oxford University Press, 1988), 119–120.

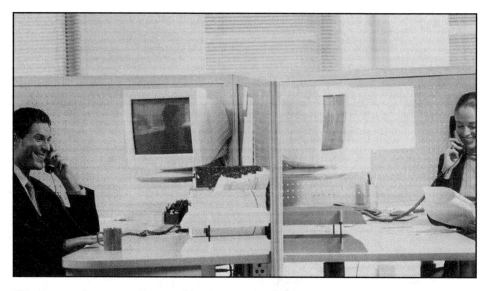

Whether employees are distracted by the sounds of those working in adjacent cubicles will largely depend on the kind of work they are doing, and may also be influenced by how well they like each other. Even when relationships are good, however, distracting conversations may well hamper concentration and resulting productivity.

ing firm that works with interior designers and architects, offering expertise in such areas as choosing the right wall and ceiling materials and layout of ventilation systems to minimize building noise.[7]

Common strategies for controlling noise include careful layout (such as avoiding putting a noisy break room or cafeteria right next to a conference room used for teleconferencing), putting partitions between workers' cubicles, and hiding speakers that emit "white noise" in the ceiling. For example, when Blue Cross/Blue Shield Association of Illinois moved to new offices, they switched to an open layout: getting rid of the walls, both physical and social, that had been in their old offices was consistent with a new strategic plan that called for better communication and collaboration between employees. The design team brought in Shiner & Associates to deal with acoustical issues, and ultimately they implemented a variety of measures to reduce noise, including installing sound-masking speakers to generate white noise, ceiling tiles that absorb ambient noise, indirect lighting that doesn't interfere with the performance of the ceiling tile, modular furniture with sound-absorbing panels, and carpeting that absorbs sound. All of this was done, at considerable expense, to provide an environment that is both pleasant and conducive to concentrating on tasks.

Open space also is a major feature at NextMonet.com, an online gallery that offers original contemporary artwork for sale on the Internet. Even with the open space, phone calls are rarely a problem; because NextMonet is an Internet company, much of the business is conducted online. Here, too, aesthetics serve to inspire and motivate the employees. The walls are decorated with original artwork that changes every other month. And because the warehouse is located near the local flower mart, desks often are adorned with fresh sunflowers, lilies, amaryllis, and daisies.

Business Brief 5.1

Music in the Environment

While organizations typically strive to provide their members with a pleasant work environment, it is important to remember that pleasure is an individual thing; conflicts over what stimuli are pleasurable sometimes occur among organizational members. A particular source of conflict often is music. Many companies—particularly those where employees work out of the view of customers, such as in production or warehouse environments—broadcast music into the workplace in an effort to make the environment a bit more pleasant. But tastes in music vary: some employees want country and western, others prefer jazz, still others prefer salsa, and one or two want classical. Thus, no matter what music is played, a portion of the population wants to hear something else.

To resolve the issue, organizations have tried a variety of approaches. Some have created employee committees, asking them to come up with ways to provide music their colleagues like. Others have conducted surveys, trying to identify the most popular choices. Many rotate music types, playing country on Mondays, salsa on Tuesdays, and so on. A few allow workers to wear headsets or use ear buds to listen to their own music, although not when this could create a safety hazard.

The Chicago Cubs dealt with this issue when conflict between their players developed in the clubhouse and locker room over the music players blared on their boom boxes. Home run slugger Sammy Sosa strongly preferred salsa music, and his boom box blared louder than anyone else's. Others had different preferences—notably first baseman Mark Grace, who grew tired of salsa and demanded that other music be played instead. Cubs management thought long and hard about this issue, and eventually arrived at a decision. Sammy Sosa was a superstar and his preferences were honored.

Interestingly, however, when Sosa's skills began to fade and he no longer was a dominant player, he ceased to be dominant in the clubhouse as well. His boom box continued to play, but he was told by management to "turn it down."

Work environments also should provide *security and shelter*, offering protection from harmful or unwanted things, such as a roof keeping out the rain or thick walls keeping out sounds. Such protection can include both physical and psychological security; privacy, for example, may be provided or prevented by the physical surroundings. The tragic events of 9/11 caused security to be stepped up significantly in many organizations, for example. Access to many facilities now is strictly limited, and visitors must check in with security guards before they are allowed to go into company offices. Security cameras typically are placed throughout buildings and are monitored 24/7. Areas of the organization that are potentially vulnerable to terrorism, such as parking areas located underneath office buildings, are carefully controlled. All of these measures are taken both to make building occupants safe and to make sure they feel safe.

An important aspect of this environmental factor is the concept of *territory*. Animals mark off the range of their territory and defend it against intruders. People do the same thing. Fences, doors, and boundary markers of all sorts separate what belongs to one person from what belongs to everyone else, and people defend against unwanted intrusions. In Chicago, for example, after a heavy snow fall people in some neighborhoods will shovel out parking spaces and then mark these as their own by placing furniture (frequently old dining chairs) in their spot. Woe to the person who moves one of those chairs and tries to park there.

The importance of place as territory shows up in the office as well. When a boss and an employee meet, where does the conversation happen? The purpose of the meeting should decide that question. If the meeting requires the boss to be "the boss" (such as in a disciplinary action or a performance review), the boss should hold the meeting in his or her territory. On the other hand, if the boss wants to talk informally with the subordinate, or even solicit any concerns or complaints the person might have, he or she should use the "MBWA" philosophy described in chapter 3: manage by walking away from his or her office and going to the territory of the employee, who is more likely to be comfortable in that setting.

McCaskey tells the story of a manager who used the concept of territoriality to his advantage.[8] Just before the start of a tough negotiation session at another manager's office, this manager managed to sit in the other's big, ostentatious chair. He joked about sitting in the other person's chair by commenting on how it felt as he swiveled from side to side, but he refused to budge. The chair owner was sufficiently thrown off balance by this tactic that he lost the "home-court advantage" he had for the meeting, and ultimately lost out in the negotiations.

Just as animals mark their territories and Chicagoans mark their parking spots, so too do members of organizations establish their territories, usually through the use of various personalized decorations. In a large office building, every desk inside of every cubicle may look the same, but closer inspection reveals a variety of things people use to make their cubicle and desk their own: pictures on the desk or hanging on the walls, small carpets, unique pen or note-

Highlighting Ethics

Workplace "Decorations" and Sexual Harassment

Court rulings regarding sexual harassment have consistently upheld the principle that the alleged harasser's intentions are irrelevant. Whether the words or deeds were meant to be offensive is not the point; the point is that at least one reasonable man or woman was offended by them. This often is the hardest part of the law to understand, because people find it difficult to believe that what they *meant* to do is of little or no legal significance. For example, an accounting professor who uses *Playboy* centerfolds as the background for PowerPoint slides may truly be doing that only because he honestly believes it will get the students' attention and help them learn. But if the students are offended and if a court considers them reasonable men and women, it's sexual harassment all the same.

This principle applies to office decorations as well. If a male employee puts up a picture that a female employee finds offensive, such as a "pin-up" calendar, he has helped to create a "hostile" work environment and thus is responsible for that action. Similarly, if he is looking at pornographic pictures on his computer screen and another employee happens by, sees the pictures, and is offended, he still is considered guilty of sexual harassment, even though he said nothing to the passer-by and may not even be aware that the pictures were seen.

The implications seem clear: when you mark your territory by personalizing your work area, use only socially acceptable, nonoffensive decorations. Put another way, if you wouldn't want your mother to see it, don't put it up.

pad holders, cartoons cut from newspapers ("Dilbert" is a particularly popular source of this material), calendars, and the like. Most large corporations have policies governing what can and cannot be displayed as personalized decorations, but those policies tend to be enforced only in the most flagrant cases of abuse.

The physical environment also shapes *social contact* among organizational members by determining to some extent who talks to whom. Factors driving social interaction include locations of people in relation to one another, physical arrangements that permit or promote social interaction (such as the water cooler around which people accidentally come into face-to-face contact), and the degree to which the environment encourages people to move around and have contact with one another. Some locations in the environment are high-contact (such as desks near doorways), while others are low-contact (desks in a back corner of a room). The presence or absence of central gathering places (such as break areas or coffee machines) also is influential in promoting or discouraging communication.

In 1997, Nortel Networks, a Canadian-based global telecommunications giant, moved its global headquarters to Brampton, a northern suburb approximately 15 miles outside of downtown Toronto. Before the move, its 3,000 headquarter employees were scattered between three different locations. "We weren't very productive," said Roy Dohner, a Nortel executive. "Our initial motivation for the move was to get people into one location so they'd run into each other."[9]

But not everyone was thrilled with the move. Many employees had worked in an office located in downtown Toronto, and they liked being able to walk the city streets during lunch or after work. Therefore, when Nortel leadership bought an old factory as their new headquarters, they spent $50 million remaking it into a horizontal office building/cityscape complete with color-coded neighborhoods. Like ancient Roman cities, Nortel Brampton Center has a recognizable plan. Its two main arteries—Main Street and the Colonnade—form the heart of the city grid. Smaller "streets" provide access to the color-coded "neighborhoods"—the company's various departments. The city within a company also includes seven indoor parks, a Zen garden, a full-service branch of the Canadian Imperial Bank of Commerce, fitness centers, basketball and volleyball courts, a physiotherapy area, a dry cleaning service, a café, and the "Docklands"—a shipping and receiving area that features a 20-foot tall graffiti mural created by 12 local street artists. There is even a "spirituality room" where employees of various religious beliefs can pray and meditate—and even wash their feet, if they're Muslim.

On a smaller scale, the physical environment influences the amount and type of interaction among people. Many years ago, Thomas Allen at MIT studied communication patterns in research and development offices and found that, beyond a distance of 25 or 30 yards, personal interaction dropped off significantly.[10] This finding suggested that organizations should physically locate together people who have the greatest need to talk to each other, or that if a department is starting up a new team, it should locate core members close to each other.

Physical settings can have other effects on interactions among people. A buyer for an electronics company housed in a building that lacked an elevator deliberately located his office on the third floor. A salesperson coming to the reception desk on the first floor would invariably be told that the buyer "could see you immediately." The salesperson would then climb three flights of stairs to the buyer's office and, while still out of breath and somewhat disoriented, be greeted by the buyer, who then would proceed to start negotiating a price. In this case, physical setting was designed to control the interaction, creating an advantage for the buyer and a disadvantage for the salesperson.

Finally, Steele argues that the physical environment provides *symbolic identification*, communicating messages that tell someone what a person, group, or organization is like or what his, her, or their position in the organization is. Companies will select arrangements, furniture, and so on to project a certain image or corporate culture both to their employees and visitors. For example, Systek Corporation in Oak Brook, Illinois, selected teak furniture for all its sales staff because wood has greater warmth than steel, and company executives wanted to emphasize that Systek is a warm, people-oriented company.

In many organizations, the relative status of individuals, groups, and entire departments is communicated by the arrangement of the physical environment. Some portions of a facility are available to only a select few, such as reserved parking places, executive dining rooms, or the organization's board room. In addition, in large buildings, individual floors often express the dominance implicit in the hierarchy. The corner offices on upper floors are occupied by senior executives or department heads. Middle offices are occupied by executives of lesser status. The most powerful executive has the largest office with the most windows and best view. Middle management personnel have one-window offices. Employees on the lowest rungs—clerks, secretaries, typists—work together in a large, open room.

Similarly, accessibility is inversely related to status. Presidents often have two or three assistants and two or three waiting rooms one must go through to get to them. Lower-level managers have one assistant and no waiting area. Even in the open areas, there are status differences. Recently we observed one large room housing a personnel manager, the personnel assistant manager, and several support staff members. As figure 5.1 shows, the manager had a corner cubicle, the assistant manager had a corner desk with two screens that people had to go around to see him, and their administrative assistants had desks close to the managers' officers. The secretaries' desks were in the center of the room, and the low-status clerk-typists had desks in the front of the room nearest the door. Thus, the more important you are, the more difficult it is to see and communicate with you.

This odd characteristic of organizations, incidentally, is one communication-related problem with important implications. The people who must be involved in organizational communication are the executives. The more important an executive is, the more crucial it is that that leader be tied in to the communication network. Yet organizational arrangements work to produce the opposite effect. Important executives are inaccessible, while clerk-typists are a part of virtually everything. It is small wonder, then, that studies of organizations repeatedly have found executives to know far less about organizational matters than do lower-level assistants and clerks.

Furniture arrangement is another important element of the environment. Figure 5.2 illustrates three office arrangements, each exerting a different level of dominance. In the first arrangement, power is minimized. The visitor sits next to the desk, making him or her virtually equal to the occupant and forcing the occupant to assume a relatively uncomfortable position to talk to him or her. In the

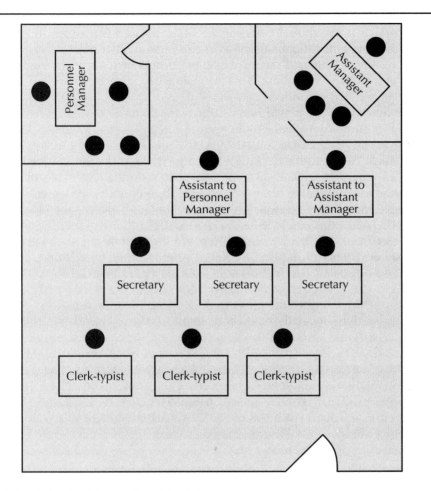

Figure 5.1   Accessibility as related to status

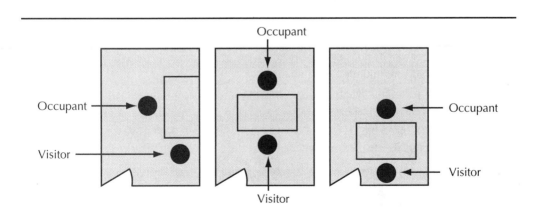

Figure 5.2   Furniture arrangement as part of environment

second arrangement, the occupant is more powerful, sitting regally behind the desk, which is interposed between the occupant and the visitor. But the third arrangement is most dominant of all. The visitor sits with his or her back to the wall, occupying minimal space, while the occupant has the remainder of the office in which to move about. This, coupled with the interposed desk, makes the situation the most domineering.

Hollywood movie mogul Harry Cohn was said to have been a master at using office furniture arrangement to emphasize his power and influence. One end of his office was higher than the other, so that in effect one had to step up onto a small stage to get to his desk. But while his desk and chair sat regally on the stage, the chairs in which visitors sat were down on the lower level of the office. In addition, he had sawed one quarter-inch off of one leg on each of the visitors' chairs, so that people meeting with him would be unable to stop wobbling back and forth. All of this combined to make meeting with Harry very intimidating.

Some organizations are trying to move away from the status symbols the physical environment implies. At Nortel's new facility, for example, most executives do not occupy formal offices. They sit at desks attached to their assistants' cubicles. When they have paperwork to do, they work at that given spot. If they have an online meeting, they connect their laptops into convenient docking stations located somewhere in the facility. Otherwise, they may be working at home or out in the field. Space at Nortel isn't based on privilege, but function. The same principles are followed at NextMonet.com. Mary Kwon, director of marketing, reported, "Our open space encourages collaboration, and it's also egalitarian. No one has a better spot than anyone else." Indeed, the company's CEO, Myrna Nickelsen, has a desk that is the same size as her employees' L-shaped work stations and is situated along a side wall in view of her entire staff.[11]

Business Brief 5.2

Basic Concepts of Workplace Design

Some key aspects of worksetting design, according to two experts in the field:

- Use visibility as a communications tool.
- Build for change and expect to change it.
- Build in some slack for spontaneity.
- Make great places for informal contact during the workday.
- Speed up group development by giving teams a place.
- Create a true center for a facility.
- Make a big deal out of having food and beverages available in central spots.
- Encourage workplaces that are more like home.

Source: Franklin Becker and Fritz Steele, *Workspace by Design* (New York: John Wiley & Sons Publishing, 2002).

Feng Shui

Only a few years ago, very few U.S. businesspeople had heard of *feng shui*. Then, during a television interview with newscaster Connie Chung, Donald Trump revealed that he had applied its 4,000-year-old principles to redevelop his Manhattan commercial properties. Since that time, interest has skyrocketed.

By definition, feng shui (pronounced *fung schway*) means wind (feng) and water (shui). In practice, it refers to the Chinese science and art of creating harmony between inhabitants and their environment. The fundamental premise of feng shui is that everything in your surroundings, down to the smallest detail of furnishing and décor, can work either for or against you. By understanding subtle currents of energy that flow through everything in the universe, you can arrange living and working environments in helpful ways.[12]

NON SEQUITUR

NON SEQUITUR © 2001 Wiley Miller. Dist. by UNIVERSAL PRESS SYNDICATE. Reprinted with permission. All rights reserved.

Implementation of feng shui principles in an organization often involves looking at building materials (wood, brick, stone, and glass all affect the flow of chi energy differently), examining entrances (the location of the front door defines the kind of chi energy that enters the building), reviewing locations where revenues are collected, and even studying electromagnetic levels (since it is important to balance electrical radiation from various pieces of electronic equipment, such as computers and printers, with more natural chi energy). Feng shui enhancements may include better use of light, space, color, natural landscaping, position of furniture, office ergonomics, and aesthetics. Even the shape and composition of your desk is important: a round or oval desk usually is preferable to a square or rectangular one, since it is more relaxing to work at for long periods of time and avoids the risk of having sharp corners cut chi, and a wooden desk promotes a natural flow of chi energy, making you feel more at ease. Softwoods like pine give a more relaxed, casual feel; darker hardwoods like teak and mahogany add formality.

PROXEMICS

Proxemics is the placement of individuals relative to other individuals—their physical closeness—as well as the way they communicate through interpersonal space and distance. Some of this is determined by the physical environment, as we saw in the previous section. However, some of it also is determined by culture, as the distance we stand or sit from one another when we communicate is to a large extent culture-bound. Researchers have identified four basic distances for interaction:

- *intimate space* (touching to 18 inches apart)—a distance reserved for physical contact or intimate encounters
- *personal space* (18 inches to 4 feet apart)—a distance reserved for close interpersonal relationships or more private discussion topics
- *social space* (4 feet to 12 feet apart)—a range of distances used for informal social activity, business consultations, and other relatively impersonal encounters
- *public space* (12 feet and beyond)—a space reserved for highly formal encounters, platform presentations, and interactions with public figures[13]

While most conversation in U.S. organizations is conducted within the personal space boundaries, however, there are **significant differences across cultures**. Research shows, for example, that while the English and Germans stand farther apart than North Americans when talking, Arabs and Japanese stand closer together.

Suppose you are a North American native speaker of English and you encounter a coworker from the company's Sao Paulo, Brazil, office in a hallway. As you talk, your colleague seems to you to be too close, and you back up a bit. To your colleague, it now seems that you are too far away, and he moves toward you to correct the mismatch. That, in turn, causes you to back up—which causes him to move toward you, so that you back up again, trying to reestablish a comfortable space. Before long, you may find yourself standing with your back to a wall at the end of the hallway, with your coworker, who at last feels that you are at "talking distance," standing right in front of you and you feeling very uncomfortable because he is "too close for comfort" and "in your face."

As the workforce becomes more diverse, you may need to interact with people of many different cultures and subcultures, and you may have no way of knowing what they view as comfortable conversational space. To function effectively in such settings, you have only to use the "process" nature of communication to adjust to the situation. Simply choose a location from which to talk, and begin. If you see the other person moving toward or backing away from you, just stand still until the individual has established the difference with which he or she is comfortable. When the person stops, it means that he or she has chosen a comfortable location—his or her preferred personal space. Respect it.

In addition to culture, the **nature of the work** also shapes the space between people. In general, people tend to sit close together when they are involved in a group and working on a common problem. But if the same group members are given individual tasks to work on for a few minutes, they will tend to move farther apart. Overall, groups perform better, more persuasively, and more cooperatively at close, face-to-face distances (18 inches versus 36 inches). But if the group describes itself as "crowded," these positive characteristics begin to disappear.[14]

Gender differences have been found in reactions to group density. North American women tend to sit closer together in groups than do men. All-male groups sit farthest apart, mixed-sex groups at an intermediate distance from one another, and all-female groups closest together. It has been argued that women in groups are more likely to develop warm, close relationships than are men. In general, men have been found to prefer meeting in large rooms and to give each other higher ratings in that setting, while women prefer smaller meeting rooms. Several studies have concluded that dense environments have a more adverse effect on males than on females.[15]

The *seating arrangement* of a group of people is particularly important in proxemics. A great deal of evidence suggests that seating has a significant impact on patterns of communication. Research indicates that people seated directly across a table from one another communicate most often and that people seated at the end of the table communicate more with the entire group than do people seated in any other position. These effects on interaction in turn have an effect on group leadership; people seated at the ends almost always emerge as group leaders by virtue of their easy access to all the other members.[16] Our physical proximity to other group members, then, influences our ability to influence them.

Again, some organizations are taking this into account. One company got rid of little four-person round tables in the company dining room, and replaced them with army mess tables—long, rectangular ones. Their belief was that, at the little round tables, four people who already knew each other would sit down and eat lunch together day after day. With long mess tables, strangers would come in

---

Business Brief 5.3

Nonverbal Communication and Tips

Research by W. Michael Lynn found that servers consistently received larger tips from their customers when they:

- Introduced themselves by name
- Squatted down next to the table when introducing themselves
- Gave big, open-mouthed smiles
- Wore unusual ornaments or items of clothing
- Entertained customers with jokes or puzzles
- Practiced suggestive selling (that is, encouraged patrons to order more expensive items, thereby increasing the total amount of their bill)
- Repeated customers' orders back to them
- Touched customers briefly on the arm or shoulder
- Forecast good weather (in fact, tips were higher when it was sunny)
- Wrote "thank you" on the bill
- Drew a smiley face on the bill (effective only for female servers, however)
- Used tip trays embossed with credit card logos
- Called customers by name
- Gave customers after-dinner candies (one piece of candy brought only a .5% increase, while two pieces brought a 2.5% increase—but when the server gave one piece of candy and then generously offered customers a second, tips increased 3%).

Source: W. Michael Lynn, "Increasing Servers' Tips," Cornell University Center for Hospitality Research [online]. Available: http://www.hotelschool.cornell.edu/chr/research.com.

contact, so that scientists might start talking with marketers or manufacturers from some other division. The hope was to cause interaction among people who normally didn't see one another.

ARTIFACTS

Those things with which we decorate our bodies also are important in communication. In most organizations and in society as a whole, clothing seems to be a strong indicator of status. The implications of this clothing-status relationship become apparent when we consider a classic study conducted 50 years ago by Lefkowitz, Blake, and Mouton, who observed the conformity behavior of pedestrians in a large city.[17] An accomplice wandered about the city violating the "Don't Walk" sign at street corners while the experimenters watched the behavior of other pedestrians to determine whether they followed his example. This was done on two consecutive days. On the first day, the accomplice wore a high-status outfit—a suit—and carried an attaché case. On the second day, he was dressed in a low-status janitor's outfit. The results were startling. When the accomplice was well dressed, several people followed him across the street; but when he was poorly dressed, no one followed him. The researchers concluded that status, as shown by one's clothing, has an impact upon one's ability to influence other people.

A variety of works have been published dealing with the impact of clothing upon success in the organization. *Dress for Success* has been widely read, although many others also are on the market.[18] Our own observations, however, indicate that the rules suggested by *Dress for Success* and other such works do not hold in today's organizations. Rather, a variety of factors determine which "uniform" is most appropriate in a particular company.

In recent years, **organizational dress codes generally have relaxed**. Initially, some companies instituted "casual Friday," allowing staff to wear "business casual" instead of typical business attire. Then some organizations instituted "dress-down summer." By the summer of 1999, a number of staid investment banks, including JPMorgan Chase & Co. in New York and BancBoston Robertson Stephens in San Francisco, began allowing employees to dress down all week. At public relations firm GCI Group in Atlanta, some employees have such a relaxed sense of dress that Vice President Bill Crane says he knows who has bellybutton rings.[19]

Not all organizations are supportive of this trend, however. Eric Webber, director of communications for GSD&M Advertising in Austin, Texas, observed that when you dress down "your guard tends to be down." At his company, women often wear no panty hose and men have shown up in western shirts with the sleeves sheared off. "In suit jobs there are barriers because you put on a uniform and are in work mode," he says. Informality of dress has promoted an informality in relationships that at times is not sufficiently business-like.

To give direction, Sears, Roebuck & Co. installed two mannequins in its cafeteria, one modeling appropriate dress and the other inappropriate. Federated Department Stores issued a terse memo warning employees at its Cincinnati headquarters that jeans, sweat shirts, and athletic caps are never appropriate. Fashion freedom has also brought managerial headaches. "The men managers want to know, 'Can I say something to Janie about her dress and compliment her?'" says Freda Klein, an organizational development consultant in Cambridge, Massachusetts. "Yes," she adds, "if the praise is very broad. It's fine to say, 'You look great,'" but not something more specific, such as "'I never knew you had such a great body under all those suits.'" Another issue is how to tell an employee not to wear something provocative without having the comment misconstrued as sexual in nature. John Feray, vice president and controller at Haggar Corp., confronted this recently when a female colleague came to work in a backless sundress. He delicately said, "That's probably not the best dress. Sleeveless is enough." Emily Woods, chairman of J. Crew Group, Inc., worries about some of her employees' office attire—even as her company adds spandex to their men's dress pants and shirts and touts them in their catalogs as suitable office wear. "As a woman heading this company, I don't want sex to be an issue here," says Woods, who wears chinos, a t-shirt, and loafers most days. "That means no underwear showing, no cleavage," she says. "And I don't want to see hairy chests in the office."[20]

Some companies now are experiencing, or even encouraging, *a backlash against casual wear* at work. Some are insisting that men wear ties and are outlawing blue jeans, t-shirts, and any revealing clothing worn by either gender. Rather than becoming increasingly relaxed, many organizations are becoming stricter in their requirements concerning the clothing employees choose to wear to work.

The authors of *Business Etiquette for Dummies* suggest that the best approach to workplace dress is KISS: "keep it simple and sophisticated."[21] They suggest initially that you memorize five colors: navy blue, charcoal gray, black, khaki, and white. These are the fundamental colors of every business wardrobe. Then, in the "suit world," start with basics: a navy blue wool suit and a charcoal wool suit, white shirts, black shoes, black belt, and black leather briefcase/notebook computer case. In the casual world, go with khaki pants or skirts, white shirts, black or brown shoes and belt, and a black or brown leather or ballistic nylon briefcase/notebook computer case. But definitions of "casual" can vary. Business casual usually means khaki pants or skirt, a plain shirt or blouse, sometimes a sport coat or blazer, and brown leather shoes. But "Friday casual" can be all these things, or jeans and tennis shoes in some offices.

The *Business Etiquette for Dummies* authors note that "The basic etiquette principle of not calling too much attention to yourself applies to clothes, too." Toward that end, they suggest avoiding several fashion mistakes:

- Avoid excessive use of bright colors and wild patterns.
- Avoid excessive jewelry and jewelry that signals your arrival with tiny clinking sounds.
- Your shoes do not need to "match" your blouse.
- Spiky, strappy sandals in metallic colors or with rhinestones aren't appropriate for most businesses. Nor are open-toed shoes.

The authors also note that perfume and aftershave or cologne should be used sparingly so that it neither precedes you nor lingers after you.

Piercings and tattoos are increasingly common in the workplace, but not always welcome. In some environments, they are perfectly acceptable; in a professional setting, however, neither tattoos nor piercings should be visible, particularly to customers. Certainly, pierced ears are commonplace, for men as well as women. But pierced lips, tongues, noses, and other even more exotic places generally are frowned upon. As a rule, if an onlooker is likely to see your piercing and think, "Eeeww, I bet that must have hurt," it probably isn't appropriate for a professional setting.

Most important to remember is that *every organization has its norms for appearance*. By adhering to those norms, and perhaps developing an appearance just slightly "better" than that expected by the organization, you can enhance your own credibility to some degree. However, by violating the norms and dressing to either extreme (too casual or too dressy), you may harm your image in the organization and even be subject to disciplinary action. It is also important to dress in a way that makes you feel good about yourself. Research has shown that those who feel inappropriately dressed often exhibit hostility, withdrawal, or aggression. However, those who feel positive about the way they are dressed tend to be more outgoing, friendly, happy, and relaxed, and they report feeling more confident.[22]

KINESICS

The category of kinesics includes general body movements—postures, gestures, facial expressions, and eye behavior. Each of these has been found to be influential in communication. In studies of body posture, Mehrabian found a close relationship between *posture* and liking for the other person.[23] For example, when confronting someone they intensely dislike, women tend to look away from the other person as much as possible. If they like the other person, they vary their direction of face, sometimes looking squarely at that person and sometimes looking away. When dealing with a total stranger, they tend to look directly at that person. No consistent results were obtained for males. For both sexes, however, leaning forward seemed to indicate liking for the other, while leaning backward seemed to convey negative feelings. Experts on nonverbal communication agree that our posture communicates much about our moods and emotions. We judge whether others are happy, sad, confident, or determined based on the way they carry themselves. In general, wider, more open body postures result in more perceived credibility and persuasive power, whereas narrower postures (legs and arms held close together) reduce status.[24]

As often is the case, however, there are cultural differences in the meanings of body postures. A Samoan job applicant in the office of a North American senior manager would want, as is the norm in Samoa, to show respect by being at a physically lower level than the manager. But this behavior easily could misfire, since to North Americans sitting down when others are standing is a sign of disrespect. Most North Americans feel it is polite to wait for others to sit down before they do, and they show respect by rising from their seats when others enter the room. Again, the way people position themselves has meaning in all cultures, and it is hard to draw up any hard-and-fast rules.

Another common body-position issue is adopting a position that makes one's body look big—a rigid, angular stance to denote aggression—or that makes one's body look small—a curled-up and cowering posture to indicate submissiveness. Bowing to show deference is common and understood across many cultures, but in some places its use is extreme. For example, in Japan some stores employ people especially to bow to customers, but the (unwritten) rules about who should bow to whom and how exactly they should do it are complex, subtle, and difficult for even a culturally sensitive outsider to master. In fact, people experienced in communicating with Japanese colleagues know that bowing in this manner is a custom best reserved for native Japanese and that trying to mimic it is at best humorous and at worst offensive.

The use of *gestures* is so closely tied to speech that we use gestures even when talking on the phone or when the person we're talking to has her back turned. People who are blind from birth use gestures even though they've never seen them.[25] Researcher Susan Goldin-Meadow found that gestures expand on what we say, providing important clues to unspoken thoughts and meanings.[26] When combined with speech, gestures tend to be spontaneous rather than structured, but they do build on what we say. For example, a speaker may report going "up the stairs," but if she winds her finger in a spiral as she says it, she communicates that she ascended a spiral staircase. If you tell a tourist a restaurant is one mile down the street, he or she knows which direction to go only by the way you point.

Gestures can also reflect the brain's visual imagination in a way speech doesn't. For example, a speaker recalling a distant memory may throw his hand over his shoulder (or sweep it forward, with the back of the hand turned outward) while saying, "That was a long time ago." The gesture may suggest that he is sweeping the memory aside or throwing it away—that it is no longer relevant, in her mind.

Gestures and speech can convey different messages. For example, in one experiment, a researcher poured all of the water from a tall, narrow glass into a short, wide one, and then asked children whether the amount of the water had changed. Many incorrectly answered yes, citing the different heights of the two containers. But some of these children made two C-shapes with their hands around the wider container, even though they were talking about its height. These gestures suggest that the children had the key to the correct answer—the width of the container—even though they got the question wrong. Such "mismatches," as Goldin-Meadow and McNeill call them, show up in numerous other problem-solving exercises, and reflect a child's openness to learning a new fact of task. "Gestures can reveal thoughts we don't even know we have," she writes.[27]

Hand and arm movements are often used simply as physical accompaniments to words, to supplement them or to provide a visual illustration of what is being said. Often gestures are meaningless without the verbal commentary, other than as a general statement of the person's state of mind. But there are also gestures that carry established meanings, for example pointing to indicate direction, hands held up with the palms facing upwards and outwards to indicate defensiveness, and a shrug of the shoulders to indicate incomprehension or lack of interest. Other more complex signals vary across cultures. Because some gestures that are positive, humorous, or harmless in some cultures are considered hostile, offensive, or obscene in other cultures, it generally is wise to avoid explicit gestures in other cultures until you know *exactly* what they mean.

Research has provided some insight into the factors that underlie a person's gestural behavior. Mehrabian and Williams observed that people trying to be persuasive show more gestures and head nods and fewer postural shifts than others.[28] O'Connor and Baird found that emergent group leaders tend to show more positive head nods and gesticulations of the shoulders and arms than do nonleaders.[29] When gestures are tied to the rhythm of our speech, they appear to help listeners follow our remarks. People who are relaxed as they communicate tend to use more gestures and to use gestures that are more natural and conversational. Highly nervous speakers may use no gestures at all, too many repetitive gestures, or touch themselves (for example, by playing with hair or jewelry)—all of which are perceived as signs of nervousness or discomfort.[30]

We may also use kinesic communication to control or regulate interpersonal communication. One example is *turn-taking*. We may signal the end of our turn by stopping or by relaxing our hand movements. We may shift our heads or eye position, or change our posture. Most important, we can signal our desire to talk by leaning forward and/or using gestures prior to speaking. In group settings, dominant persons are often seen leaning forward and using gestures to maintain the floor, preventing interruptions from other group members. Some scholars believe that it is largely kinesic behavior that determines who talks when and for how long. Listeners' kinesic movements are also important to observe since they provide clues as to who really is being listened to and whose opinions are valued. Listeners typically turn their bodies toward someone they want to hear. By not turning toward someone who is speaking, they communicate the opposite attitude.

FACE AND EYES

Facial expressions and eye contact are particularly important in communication. Paul Ekman has studied movements of the face for many years and conducts training with law enforcement personnel, medical professionals, and others. His research suggests that facial expressions show various emotions in the following ways:[31]

- *Anger*. One of the first and most subtle but reliable signs of anger is when the red margins of the lips narrow and tighten. There is also a lowering of the eyebrows simultaneous with the upper eyelid so that a glare starts to appear. When anger gets very intense, the mouth becomes square and tight.

- *Contempt and disgust*. Both are shown primarily by the mouth. Ekman claims that contempt is feeling morally superior, which means the other person is morally inferior. Contempt is the only emotional expression that's asymmetrical—only one side of the mouth tightens or moves. There is a slight tightening of one corner of the lips, which looks like a lopsided smile. Very often, we enjoy being contemptuous, Ekman says. So if you see something like a smirk along with that tightening of one corner of the mouth, "then you know the person's getting a kick out of feeling contempt." Disgust is being repulsed, which is not a constructive emotion, either. When someone's disgusted, you'll see a rise of the upper lip, akin to what you would do to show the dentist your upper teeth, and wrinkling of the nose, which raises the nostrils. "Nobody on the receiving side enjoys seeing these. It puts distance between you and the other person," Ekman concludes.

- *Fear*. This is most obvious when the white part of the eye above the iris begins to show, which happens with very few of us in our normal gaze. When someone is surprised, you start to see a little of that whiteness. As the person moves closer to fear, it increases. Another sign of fear is a subtle stretching of the lips horizontally, as if there were a rubber band in each corner pulling them toward the back of the head slightly. Only 10 to 20 percent of the population can do that voluntarily, Ekman says. Because it's nearly impossible to do deliberately, a raising and coming together of the eyebrows so they appear high and straight across is a powerful sign of fear.

- *Deception*. This is particularly difficult to spot. "We don't have Pinocchio's nose," Ekman notes. "There's no sign of lying itself; there are signs of emotions that don't fit what a person is saying, and there are signs of concealed emotions. If I'm furious and trying to hide it, it might appear in micro expressions—that's the closest to any direct sign of lying."

- *Positive emotions*. These range from amusement to contentment, gratitude, and relief, yet they share a single expression: *the smile*. And it's not just movement of the lips but the muscle that orbits the eye that contracts and "smiles" too. "The way we know which enjoyable emotion someone is feeling is by the sound of voice," Ekman says. "The face tells us something good is happening; the sound of the voice tells which one of the good things it is."[32]

Goleman's work on *emotional intelligence* also emphasizes facial expressions, and he lists eight communication lessons concerning the unspoken language of face.[33] First, he claims, *it pays to be good looking*. Research has shown that babies look at an attractive adult face longer than a plain one. This bias toward the merely pretty extends throughout life. Judges are not more likely to find ugly people guilty, but they do give good-looking people easier sentences. Attractive people earn more than plain ones in comparable jobs and rise higher in their careers. It literally pays to be good-looking.

Goleman also suggests that, to increase your appeal to others, *blink less*. Contrary to folk wisdom, blinking is not necessarily a sign of guilt or nervousness. It is an indication that the mind of the blinker has wandered to something else. We blink more when we talk than when we listen and, in fact, use blinking to control the ebb and flow of conversation; one study found that we blink in order to signal that we wish to interrupt. Actor Michael Caine was so convinced of the importance of blinks that he trained himself not to blink at all in order to increase the power of his close-ups (when his eyes might be 20 inches across on the wide screen) and to decrease the likelihood that the director would cut away from him to some other actor. As Caine realized, people like to be paid attention to—and not blinking at them increases their sense that you care about them, and you therefore are attractive to them.

Women are more facially expressive than men, Goleman concludes. Surprisingly, men's faces are more mobile than women's, but that effect covers only minor muscle movements. Women's facial muscles are, on average, smaller, so that small motions and twitches of the face don't show up as readily. Even so, women are more facially expressive. They report themselves as feeling stronger emotions than men while being more accurate in matching facial expressions with the emotions they are expressing. The business implication is that men may need to work harder to express emotions in their faces—and read others' facial gestures—if they are going to succeed at the upper levels of the business and professional world.

Remarkably, Goleman found that people of all cultures respond similarly to certain facial features—and that those responses often are inaccurate. We all imagine that high foreheads are a sign of intelligence, for example, though research has shown they are not. We equate facial signs of aging—retreating hairlines, smaller eyes, and broader faces—with dominance, even though there is no necessary connection. We also equate signs of anger—lowered brows and narrowed eyes—with power and authority. Large eyes and high eyebrows, on the other hand, convey kindness and warmth to us. None of these connections have a factual basis. But advertisers use baby-faced spokespeople to generate trust and older-looking faces to generate authority because they know that most people believe these correlations to be true.

Goleman also found that, *universally, people recognize a basic group of emotions*. While researchers differ on the precise number, there is fundamental agreement on enjoyment, anger, fear, surprise, disgust, and sadness. Perhaps not surprisingly, these correspond to the basic movements of the eyes, eyebrows, and mouth. We widen the eyes to show interest and narrow them to show negative emotions like anger and disgust. We raise the eyebrows to show surprise and interest and lower them to show anger and sadness. We smile and frown, raising and lowering the mouth to show good and bad feeling. This is the basic repertoire of the face, and it is understood around the world.

Real facial expressions are fleeting, as Goleman, Ekman, and many other researchers have observed. For example, genuine expressions of anger and surprise last only for a second or two at most. One sign of insincerity, then, may be a facial expression that lingers for an unnecessarily long period of time. Possibly the best revealers of deception, though, may be the eyes. Very few people are able to control the widening and narrowing of the eyes and pupils that indicate signs of pleasure and displeasure, anger and happiness. The muscles around the mouth may not move, but the eyes cannot hold still for long.

People are extraordinarily sensitive to staring, Goleman noted. We don't like being stared at, and when we can't avoid it, we try to escape. In one study, researchers stood on street corners and stared at drivers stopped at traffic lights. The stared-at drivers accelerated on green faster than those the researchers ignored. Similarly, stared-at pedestrians walked away faster than those left alone. Students in college libraries who are stared at leave earlier, on average, than those not so persecuted. You can use this insight to help make colleagues more comfortable (by not staring) or, in situations where you want a library table all to yourself, to make them more uncomfortable (at the risk, however, of being admonished in the library parking lot later on).

Lastly, Goleman assures that no matter how attractive or plain we may be, *there are ways we can use facial expressions to make ourselves more attractive*. When we are attracted to someone else, it is the eyes that attract us first. Widened eyes and pupils in response are a sign that the interest is mutual. After that, researchers have identified the following universal attributers of beauty: wide cheekbones, broad smile, wide eyes, eyes set far apart, high eyebrows, narrow cheeks, wide nostrils, high-placed eyes, large pupils, small nose. What is interesting about this list is how much we can control. Physically, we can widen our smile, our nostrils, and our eyes and raise our eyebrows. Makeup can effect changes in all the other areas, and while the use of makeup has been traditionally confined to women and actors, even that is slowly changing.

Other researchers have found that people do seem to use facial expressions to attempt to make themselves more attractive and influential. Rosenfeld noted that people seeking approval seem to smile more frequently, and Mehrabian and Williams observed that people trying to persuade others also showed an increase in facial activity.[34]

Eye Contact

Studies of eye contact in human communication have identified the situations in which we seek or avoid eye contact with others. Generally, we will seek eye contact with others when we want to communicate with them, when we are physically distant from them, when we like them, when we are extremely hostile toward them (as when two bitter enemies try to stare each other down), or when we desire feedback from them. Conversely, we avoid contact with others when we wish to avoid communication, are situated physically close to them, dislike them, are trying to deceive them, or are uninterested in what they have to say.

Given the generally positive functions of *eye contact*, we should find that it *improves communication*—and indeed it does. Some investigators have found that messages accompanied by eye contact were more favorably interpreted by observers than were messages sent without eye contact. Indeed, aversion of eye contact in a group setting is sometimes perceived by others as an indication of disinterest, apathy, rudeness, shyness, nervousness, or even dishonesty or deceit. Eye contact also seems indicative of status—researchers noted that high-status individuals usually receive more eye contact from other group members than do individuals of low status.[35]

Again, there are *major cultural differences*. Arabs, Latinos, Indians, and Pakistanis all have conventions of longer eye contact, whereas Africans and East Asians interpret eye contact as conveying anger or insubordination and avoid it. The situation is further complicated by the fact that most cultures have different conventions about eye contact depending on the gender, status, and other attributes of those involved.

Among Caucasians in the United States, the general rule is that the *speaker* in a conversation should find a way to break eye contact and look away. The *listener* shows attention by spending relatively more time looking at the speaker. Because it makes it harder for the speaker to continue, communication difficulties arise if the listener looks away too often. Thus, when a manager wants to hear what a subordinate has to say, he or she should take care to provide the encouragement of eye attention, head nodding, and occasional "uh huhs" as the other is speaking. Even without saying words, the manager is sending nonverbal messages about the level of her attentiveness and understanding.

Among other ethnic groups, different rules apply. A young Caucasian executive learned this lesson in his first year of managing a factory with a predominantly Hispanic workforce. He was reprimanding a stock clerk named Raphael for repeated mistakes, but as he talked, Raphael kept looking away. Eventually, the executive became angry and yelled (as many of our mothers did years ago), "Look at me when I'm talking to you." The young clerk tried to establish eye contact, but he could not maintain it for very long. To the executive, the clerk's eye behaviors showed disrespect and possibly defiance. But for the clerk, it would have been a sign of disrespect to maintain eye contact with a boss who was reprimanding him. It was only later that the executive realized that Raphael's behavior was not meant to communicate disrespect.

Crying

For many years, crying was considered appropriate for women, but not for men. As recently as the 1980s, a man who cried in public suffered loss of face, even when there was an obvious reason for the tears. Now, this seems to have changed; men today, even professional athletes, congressmen, presidents, and television anchormen, are allowed to become weepy when a good reason for tears is available.

Elgin observes, however, that women in the 1980s faced a paradox: although it was acceptable for them to weep all they liked in private life, the rule for women in public life was the same as it was for men.[36] Crying was not allowed. Consider the reaction to Congresswoman Patricia Schroeder's tears when she announced that she would not be running for president in 1988:

- "I got back to New York just in time for Pat Schroeder's three-Kleenex declaration she wouldn't be going to run."
  —James Brady, in *Advertising Age*, October 12, 1987

- "Schroeder's tears got her more media attention than anything else she said or did during her campaign. While many women were sympathetic, others were embarrassed by her crying, feeling that it gave credence to men's worst fears about women."
  —Mindy Schanback, in *Executive Female*, May/June 1988

- "Yet even Mrs. Schroeder's friends said they wished that she hadn't cried—at least as much as she did. Perhaps a tear or two—but not the weeping."
  —Bernard Weinraub, in the *New York Times*, September 30, 1987

No one said that it was all right for Mrs. Schroeder to cry because she was a woman. Weinraub's *New York Times* article—which was titled "Presidential Politics: Are Female Tears Saltier than Male Tears?"—observed that

> former Senator Gary Hart grew tearful on a campaign stop when he visited his birthplace in Kansas to talk about his roots, Governor Michael S. Dukakis of Massachusetts brushed tears from his eyes at the dedication of a park in honor of President Kennedy, and President Reagan has choked up on numerous occasions, including the funeral service for the crew of the space shuttle *Challenger*. It seems perfectly appropriate, at least nowadays, for men to be tearful. . . . But what about Patricia Schroeder? Perhaps a tear or two.

Elgin argues that crying is never OK:

> The problem with crying is that you can't talk while you cry, nor can you carry out the other aspects of language interaction that are included in "talking," such as listening and observing body language. When you cry—more than a tear or two—you can't talk; when you can't talk, you can't negotiate; when you can't negotiate, you're vulnerable. Crying in public strips you of all power in American society today in almost precisely the same way that being naked in public would—the only difference is that public crying is not forbidden by law.

Our own observations support Elgin's view. In U.S. society, publicly shedding tears now is allowable for both sexes, but it does not increase one's credibility. Indeed, Elgin dramatizes the point when she concludes that

> knowing that Congresswoman Schroeder couldn't keep from crying on such a public and important occasion struck fear into the hearts of the voters, who translated their uneasiness into the murky sentence, "She didn't seem very presidential."

TOUCH

Touching is perhaps the most primitive aspect of nonverbal behavior. Even in the womb, the child can be stimulated by touch. As a form of communication, touching is very important. Montagu argues that a person's social and psychological development is hampered if he or she receives too little touching from others early in life.[37] Although touching can serve many different functions, including sexual expression, from an organizational perspective, two are especially important: expressing supportiveness and communicating power or dominance.

Touching in a supportive way can take many forms—putting our arms around other people, patting them on the arm or hand, holding their hands in our own. Generally, we do not touch people we dislike (unless we are fighting with them), so the act of touching someone communicates a general message of liking and support. Through touching we can communicate consolation, empathy, liking, and varying degrees of commitment.

In organizational settings, a common form of touching is *the handshake*. While it is a seemingly minor act, the handshake can convey a variety of meanings and create many different initial or final impressions. Career salesman J. T. Auer points out that there are several common types of undesirable handshakes, including a limp, flabby handshake, a handshake that squeezes the life out of the other person's hand, a handshake that allows the other person only to grab your fingers (most commonly seen among women), a "jackhammer" handshake that pumps the persons arm vigorously, a "prison" handshake that refuses to let go, or a quick handshake that gives the impression you'd rather be holding a live snake.[38] Worse than all of these, of course, is refusing to shake hands, which in the United States is a clear form of rejection and extremely insulting. To shake hands appropriately, extend your hand and grip the other person's hand so that the web of your thumbs meet. Shake a couple of times, firmly, and then end the handshake after three or four seconds. Maintaining eye contact while shaking hands is also an important element of this ritual.

Some management theorists have warned about appropriate uses of touching. Blanchard and Johnson, in their popular book *The One Minute Manager*, point out that managers should touch others only when they are communicating something positive, such as encouragement, reassurance, or support.[39] They view negative touching, associated with criticizing, admonishing, or disciplining, as quite inappropriate.

One of the reasons that Blanchard and Johnson offer this advice to managers is because of *the power/dominance function of touching*. That is, it is the high-status person who has the power to touch. It is the police officer who touches the accused, the teacher who touches the student, the doctor who touches the patient, and the manager who touches the employee. As Nancy Henley points out in *Body Politics*, it would be a breach of etiquette for the lower-status person to touch the person of higher status.[40] Henley further argues that in addition to indicating relative status, touching also demonstrates the assertion of male power and dominance over women.

Whether or not Henley's assertion is true, much research has examined sex differences in touching. Mothers have been found to touch children of both sexes and of all ages a great deal more than fathers do. Women touch their fathers more than men do. Female babies are touched more than male babies. And women reportedly have a greater desire to be held than do men. In general, more touching reportedly occurs among opposite-sex friends than among same-sex friends. However, since our culture has traditionally frowned on same-sex touching, perhaps people have not felt comfortable acknowledging the extent to which they touch those of the same sex.[41]

Whatever gender differences exist, cross-cultural differences are more apparent. Kissing another person's cheek is common between men as well as women in France but much less so in the United States. In New Zealand the Maori greeting is the *hongi*, a firm pressing together of noses. In one study, students from the United States reported being touched twice as much as did students from Japan. In Japan, there is a strong taboo against strangers touching, and the Japanese are especially careful to maintain adequate distance. Another obvious cross-cultural

---

Highlighting Diversity

Cross-Cultural Differences in Nonverbal Communication

As U.S. corporations hire increasing numbers of immigrants, cross-cultural misunderstandings will occur with greater frequency. For example:

- In the United States, calling attention to oneself (particularly one's professional achievements) is considered a sign of self-respect. Many Asians, however, think that calling inordinate attention to oneself is rude and unprofessional. In an employment interview, this cultural clash could result in a Vietnamese applicant's being viewed by a U.S. interviewer as "lacking self-esteem."

- While direct eye contact is valued in the United States, other cultures avoid eye contact as a sign of respect or deference. An applicant from such a culture probably would be viewed as "unassertive" or "untrustworthy."

- Rather than risk losing face or ridicule for misusing an English word, some foreign speaking workers will simply remain silent. Their U.S. managers often assume they simply have no suggestions or ideas to contribute.

- In parts of Asia, the Hispanic countries, and much of Europe, to initiate even the simplest task without being told specifically to do so is considered a defiance of authority. From the U.S. viewpoint, this "lack of initiative" may be interpreted as laziness or a lack of self-confidence.

- As the U.S. workplace becomes increasingly multicultural, we must improve our skills in perceiving people. Rather than interpret others' behaviors in terms of our own cultural norms, we must communicate more carefully and more thoroughly to ensure that we understand what others do.

Source: Sondra Thiederman, "Communication: Overcoming Cultural and Language Barriers," *Personnel Journal* 67 (December 1988): 34–40.

difference is in the Middle East, where same-sex touching in public is extremely common. Men will walk with their arms on each other's shoulders, a practice that would not be comfortably received in the United States, except in specific situations, such as locker-room celebrations.[42]

These cross-cultural nonverbal differences can cause real problems when people from different countries and cultures attempt to interact effectively. The Japanese, for instance, may be perceived as distant or aloof, while southern Europeans may be viewed as pushy or aggressive. An awareness of and sensitivity to cultural differences in touching behavior are crucial as people from different cultural backgrounds try to work together in organizations.

VOCALICS

For a clear demonstration of the power the human voice has in shaping the meaning of words, you might try an exercise used in many university departments of theater. Say just two words: "you monster." Say those words to express the following emotions: anger, love, admiration, terror, surprise, disgust, sadness, and disappointment. Have someone else listen to you, with his or her back turned, and guess the emotion you are trying to convey. Typically, listeners are able to identify each of these emotions without difficulty—and by so doing, illustrate the power of the voice in conveying the true meaning of the words we speak.

One key judgment that is based on vocal cues is *speaker recognition*. On the basis of vocal cues alone, we can accurately recognize the identity of the person to whom we are listening (provided, of course, we already are acquainted with that person's voice).[43] On the basis of voice we also may be able to recognize personal characteristics of the speaker, such as age, sex, or ethnic background.[44] And as we have seen, vocal cues give us hints about the emotional state of the speaker—whether he or she is happy, sad, angry, or pleased.

Perhaps *the most important function of vocalics is modifying our verbal messages*. For instance, researchers have identified at least two dozen ways of saying yes.[45] There are definite yeses and wishy-washy yeses, happy and sad ones, seductive, confused, and assured ones. When we interact with others, they will believe our vocal meaning over our verbal meaning whenever our verbal and vocal messages are at odds.

Besides our tone of voice, there are other aspects of vocalics that are important. For example, different cultures vary in their norms concerning *how much* and *how loudly* one should talk. North Americans are notorious for talking a lot and talking loudly. The use of pauses and silence also is important. Silences can have a whole range of meanings, driven in part by the communicator's motives and culture. Negotiators often use them as a tactic to close a sale or to seek agreement by waiting until the other person is uncomfortable enough to give in or make some concession. Japanese negotiators particularly use silence as a means of controlling negotiating processes. Used another way, a pause in the conversation can be a valuable gift that allows the other person time to consider carefully his or her thoughts and feelings. Finns use it as a way of encouraging a speaker to continue. In Malaysia, silence can be used to show respect. Watching the other nonverbal cues a person gives off during periods of silence can help you to interpret that person's motives, but cultural awareness also is key.[46]

One special type of pause is the *filled pause*, in which the speaker uses a sound such as "um" or "uhhh" to fill the spaces between words. Filled pauses often are used to show that the speaker is in the process of completing his or her reply, while mustering up the right words. In effect, a filled pause is a signal that preserves the speaker's right to talk since it says, in effect, "Don't interrupt. I'm still talking."

Such filled pauses are very different, however, than **verbal nonfluencies**—words that are inserted as filler but add no meaning to the statement: "Like, you know, I'm trying to get this thing done, see what I'm sayin'? Dude, it's just too hard, you know, to like get it done, you know?" The repeated insertion of "you know," "see what I'm sayin'," "like," and other filler words can be distracting to the listener and, ultimately, reduce the credibility of the person doing the talking.

Accents are another vocal characteristic—the ways you pronounce the things you say. By listening to the ways people pronounce their words, we often can determine whether English is their first language (and whether that English is American, Australian, British, or Canadian), and if so, what part of the country they come from.

Unfortunately, accents can trigger within listeners a variety of stereotypes about the people who use them. A particularly dramatic example occurred during the Clinton administration, when President Clinton was accused of sexual harassment and having inappropriate relationships with female coworkers and an attempt was made to impeach him for lying, under oath, about one of those relationships. Two of Clinton's accusers were Kathleen Willey and Paula Jones, both of whom claimed they had been sexually harassed by Clinton while he was governor of Arkansas. There were dramatic differences in how each was treated in the press. Willey was described in the press as "a convincing, classy woman" and as having appeared on *60 Minutes* "in all her high-cheekboned, Virginia gentry poise."[47] Paula Jones, by contrast, looked and sounded like the stereotypical poor white female. Her accent was rural, Ozark English, and this apparently did not make her an appealing figure when she came forward with her accusations. She was ridiculed and demeaned by the press, particularly concerning her social background. The class prejudice evident in the musical *My Fair Lady*, where Henry Higgins tries to teach Eliza Doolittle how to sound like a person of culture, still is strong in U.S. society, and the accents with which people speak may trigger those prejudices more strongly than any other nonverbal cue.

Getting rid of a regional accent can be very difficult, but there are other more simple ways to improve your use of your voice. Mary Thomas-Sala, a professional voice and speech coach in Los Angeles, offers several tips.[48] First, **breathe deeply**. Supporting your voice with breath can immediately improve the quality of your voice, and it also has a calming effect. Before speaking, take deep breaths, as if you were smelling a flower. Second, **add depth to your voice**. As researchers have shown, the general pitch of your voice can communicate authority and wisdom—or youth and inexperience. Develop depth by taking a full breath and humming "mmmmm" in a lower pitch of your voice for 5 or 10 seconds.

Vocal variety also is very important for maintaining listeners' interest. People who speak in a monotone quickly are tuned out by their listeners. Radio and television personalities work hard—sometimes too hard, it seems—at developing vocal variety that helps listeners to pay attention. Turn on the television and tune in a local news broadcast. Close your eyes and just listen to the newscasters' voices; pay no attention to the words they are saying. Focus on *how* they are speaking. Then, as they talk, try humming. As you do, attempt to match the pitch changes the newscasters make. This may help you to develop some comfort with varying the pitch of your voice as you talk.

Finally, *how you use the telephone* is also an important aspect of nonverbal communication and your use of voice. Nancy Friedman, president of The Telephone Doctor, a St. Louis-based company that conducts telephone etiquette seminars and sells phone etiquette training kits, suggests that good etiquette is important for phone conversations.[49] She suggests that you speak clearly and avoid "yeah" or "uh-huh" or "huh-uh"; say "yes" or "no." In addition, you should give the person on the other end of the line your complete attention—no tapping out e-mails or playing computer solitaire while you're on the phone; the other party can usually hear it. If you have to speak to someone else nearby during a phone call, put the caller on hold rather than putting your hand over the receiver and shouting across the room.

Voice mail also introduces a potential set of problems. Friedman lists what she calls "frustrating voice-mail phrases." High on her list are the lines that have become so standard that most people don't even hear them anymore, such as "I'm not at my desk right now" or "your call is important to us." Another common problem is the way people give phone numbers in the voice-mail messages they leave: some say their number so quickly that the person called has to replay the message multiple times in order to write the number down. When leaving your number for a call-back, give it slowly, and at least twice.

If you're prone to babbling when leaving voice-mail messages, prepare a script before you place the call. When you leave a message, explain why you're calling if the recipient isn't familiar with you.

Highlighting Diversity

Nonverbal Methods of Helping ESL Speakers

When conversing with people whose first language is not English, there are some nonverbal and verbal strategies you should use to ensure that they are able to understand what you are saying:

- Speak clearly and slowly, enunciating carefully.
- Avoid using slang or unusual expressions.
- Use active verbs and avoid long compound sentences.
- Use visual restatements such as pictures, graphs, tables, and slides.
- Hand out written summaries of your verbal presentation.
- Pause more frequently, and do not jump in to fill silences.
- Take frequent breaks and allow more time.
- Check for understanding and comprehension by encouraging listeners to repeat concepts back to you.
- Avoid embarrassing listeners, but encourage and reinforce their participation.

Source: David C. Thomas and Kerr Inkson, *Cultural Intelligence* (San Francisco: Berrett-Koehler Publishers, 2004), 109.

Using a *speakerphone* should be reserved for those occasions when other people in your office have to join you on the call; don't just put all of your calls on speakerphone (as some particularly annoying executives tend to do) so that you can do other things or roam your office while you talk. Conducting a one-to-one conversation over speakerphone implies that you have more important things to do while you're talking with the other person. When you use (appropriately) a speakerphone, always ask the person you're calling if he or she minds being on a speakerphone. If the person does mind, suggest a conference call where everyone is on their own phone.

TIME

Imagine going to the office of a person with whom you have an appointment. When you arrive at her office, her assistant says, "She'll just be a moment; please have a seat." So you sit, and you wait. And you wait some more. Five minutes passes. Ten minutes. Now, it's 15 minutes after your appointment was scheduled. How are you feeling? You check your watch—it's now 30 minutes past your appointment time. Finally, a door opens, and the assistant says, "The dentist will see you now."

Time is a precious organizational resource, and how you manage that resource is a key element of nonverbal communication. Lateness is almost always frowned upon. Coming in late to work repeatedly is cause for termination. Arriving late for meetings or appointments, thus forcing others to waste their time as they wait for you, is considered insulting; the implication is that you do not consider their time important enough to arrive when you should. Starting meetings late because the meeting leader is waiting for late-comers to arrive is an insult to those who cared enough to arrive on time. Indeed, people will quickly learn that if they arrive on time, they will sit for 10 or 15 minutes while the group waits for late-comers, so they will become late-comers as well. Knowing that, some executives have a policy that, at the appointed starting time, the meeting room doors are closed and locked and late-comers cannot attend (some also fine those who do not attend a nominal amount, just to add injury to the insult).

Time marches on, of course. But your use of words and nonverbal cues can manage perceptions of time. To have others feel that you are interested in them and they are important to you, it is important to give the impression that you have all the time in the world for them, even if you really only have a few minutes. Nonverbally, two key things you can do are *sit down while you are talking with someone*, and *avoid any movement that makes you seem to be checking on how much time has passed* (for example, glancing at your watch or a clock on the wall). If you check your watch repeatedly or, worse yet, stand by the door with your hand on the doorknob, seemingly poised to flee, you give the impression that you have little time for them. When the interaction is over, if the conversation was spent sitting down, people will feel you spent a lot of time with them; if the conversation was spent standing up and checking your watch, they will feel you spent very little time, even though the same amount of actual minutes was spent during the meeting.

The words you choose also affect others' perceptions of time. Avoid the words "only" or "just," as in "I only have ten minutes" or "we just have an hour for our meeting." If you announce how much time you can devote to the meeting, do so as if you are amazed at how much time you can actually spend: "Wow, I actually have ten minutes—let's talk!"

Dentists are taught to tell their patients, "Now this might hurt a little, and it will take a few minutes. But if you tell me to stop, I will." This makes the patients feel that they are in control of the time spent on the procedure, and they often will think "I can take this just a little longer" and put off telling the dentist to stop. In addition, the actual time will seem shorter. Key to this perception of time is *having the feeling of control*. Similarly, you might announce to someone that you have ten minutes for the meeting, "but if you need more time than that, just say so." People will almost always stay within the ten-minute time frame, but they will leave feeling that you offered them an ample amount of your time.

Across different cultures, there are huge differences in perceptions and management of time.[50] North Americans are much more obsessed about punctuality than are people from many Latin American countries, for example, so that businesspeople from the United States often are impatient with their "always-tardy" colleagues, who in turn are put off by the "pushy" Americans. Similarly, the timing of communication events can vary. In the United States, for example, people "get down to business" right away, keeping small talk to a minimum out of a respect for the other person's time. In other countries, however, establishing relationships comes first. Consequently, people may meet multiple times, both at work and over dinner, without ever talking business, as they decide whether they like and trust one another before they decide whether talking business is a valuable use of their time. As always, sensitivity to these issues is key.

SUMMARY

Our purpose in this chapter has been to consider the second of two fundamental building blocks of communication and relationships within the organization's social system: nonverbal cues. If there are discrepancies between what we say with our words and the messages we convey nonverbally, others will believe how we act, rather than what we say.

Every culture has its norms pertaining to nonverbal communication. In many Western cultures, people who have higher status, for example, will sit at the head of the table, occupy a greater amount of space, and get away with arriving late to meetings. Cross-cultural differences also exist in perceptions of silence, the meaning of time, and the distance one should stand from another while having a professional conversation. In addition, some research points to nonverbal differences between men and women in facial expression, touching, and perceptions of space. While it is important to learn one's own cultural norms for nonverbal communication, it is equally important to be sensitive to and respectful of areas of difference across cultures.

To communicate effectively with others, then, we need to choose our words carefully, but even more important are the ways we use physical space, our proximity in relation to others, the artifacts with which we decorate ourselves, our bodily movements, touch, and our voice, both face-to-face and electronically. If we employ nonverbal cues appropriately, we are likely to build and sustain healthy and productive relationships with those with whom we interact in organizational settings.

Questions for Discussion

1. Choose an organization with which you are familiar. How does its physical environment communicate what that organization is like? How does the environment promote or inhibit the personal interaction of its occupants?

2. Choose another organization you know well. How does that organization's physical environment show status differences? How does it control who talks to whom?

3. What dress code seems to apply to people working in any organization with which you are familiar?

4. Should someone go into work with bright purple hair? Why, or why not?

5. What effect might wearing glasses have on how someone is perceived?

6. Since the judgments we make about people are driven largely by their nonverbal characteristics and actions, what are some common biases or prejudices people have based on nonverbal cues?

7. If someone from a culture that differs from your own behaves strangely in a professional setting (for example, by refusing to establish eye contact, by arriving late for a meeting, or by standing too close to you), how will you react (what will you say and do)?

8. The actor James Earl Jones has had his voice heard in many popular movies. Choose one or more of those movies—how did his voice contribute to his character and the movie over all?

Exercises

1. Think of the most obnoxious, unpleasant person you know. Then list all the nonverbal behaviors that person does that you find offensive. How might these habits be overcome?

2. Stand closer to a friend than you normally would. What does he/she do?

3. Choose an organization of interest to you. Contact a manager and ask permission to observe a staff meeting (tell him/her you are interested in studying communication). As you observe the meeting, make note of how the participants interact with a particular focus on nonverbal communication. Be sure to note how the physical environment and artifacts seem to influence the meeting. Do you notice any differences in nonverbal behavior that might be traced to gender or cultural differences?

4. Identify someone whose sense of style you find attractive. List the things he/she wears or uses that create a favorable impression for you.

Case Application 5.1   Managing the Environment

On Chicago's far South Side, George Pullman built, not only a factory in which his employees would work to build luxury train cars, but a town in which they would live. When "Pullman Village" opened in 1881, it was saluted as the epitome of modern town planning. The homes reflected the standing of the occupants within the company: on the corners, big substantial homes were built for executives and managers; in the middle of the block, the smaller row houses and apartments were for ordinary workers. Only one church was provided for the community, however. Pullman reasoned that, if industry could use standardized, interchangeable parts, so too could the various religious denominations. He allowed no taverns in Pullman, although visiting dignitaries could drink in the Florence Hotel, the centerpiece of the town.

Not everyone was happy with the arrangement, however. Some argued that, since every last stick within the town was owned by Pullman, his employees could never realize the American dream of home ownership. "We were born in a Pullman house," one worker told a newspaper reporter, "fed from a Pullman shop, catechized in the Pullman church, and when we die we shall be buried in the Pullman cemetery and go to a Pullman hell."

When a depression drained the company's business, Pullman cut his workers' wages. He insisted, though, that the same rents be subtracted from their paychecks, which often meant they had only a few pennies left with which to feed their families. As a result, 3,000 workers went on strike. While the strikers eventually were forced back to work, the company's victory was short-lived: The Illinois Supreme Court ruled in 1898 that Pullman Village should be sold off because a company town was "incompatible with the theory and practice of our institutions." George Pullman died three years after the strike, his name synonymous with management hostility toward workers. Marking his passing, a Chicago newspaper noted that he had built a fatal flaw into his model city: He could not understand how deeply the ordinary worker wanted to become a homeowner.

Much of Pullman Village still stands and can be toured by visitors.

Source: Ron Grossman, "Pullman Village Was No Utopia for Its Working Inhabitants," *Chicago Tribune*, December 9, 1998, sec. 5, 1.

Questions

1. How would you have felt about living in Pullman's company town?
2. How might communication have helped to make Pullman's plan more successful?

Case Application 5.2   Furniture and Personality

The Herman Miller Company in Zeeland, Michigan, has developed a computer program designed to match workers to an office space tailored to their personality types:

- "Visionaries" are long-term planners who tend to be scholarly and work through new ideas logically. Their offices need ample storage space and various surfaces for working on several projects at once.
- "Catalysts" tend to make decisions based on personal values rather than logic, to work in spurts of energy, and to need interaction with others. Their offices should include a table and chairs for meetings or a conference room nearby and lots of work surfaces to handle their clutter.

- "Cooperators" thrive on personal communication, and they value comfort over privacy. Their offices should have low panels and counter space to provide easy contact, a table and chairs for meetings, and plenty of in-and-out boxes.

- "Stabilizers" do everything by the book and believe organizations run best when everyone follows written policy. Their offices should have high walls and doors for privacy, they should have plenty of storage space, and they should have a cockpit-like work area with telephone and computer in easy reach.

From Jose Martinez, "Can You Be Categorized as Visionary or Stabilizer?" *Chicago Tribune*, March 15, 1992, sec. 7, 7.

Questions

1. From these four choices, what sort of office would you choose for yourself? Why?

2. Imagine there was a fifth category called "Slackers." How should their offices be set up?

6

Building and Sustaining Relationships

After reading this chapter, you should be able to:

❑ Describe the three stages of perception

❑ Explain the kinds of information we use in perceiving others, and describe the process by which perceptual judgments form

❑ List and explain ways in which perception can be improved

❑ Discuss the major dimensions of interpersonal relationships in organizations

❑ Explain the impact of situations upon attraction, dominance, and involvement

❑ Explain how attraction, dominance, and involvement impact one another

❑ Describe some ways in which communication can be used to improve relationships within organizations

❑ Discuss the reasons why listening to others is important in building effective interpersonal relationships in organizations

❑ Explain the "HEAR" formula for improving listening

❑ List and explain ways of relating to at least five types of difficult people in organizations

$\mathbf{A}$s organizations become more technologically sophisticated and more and more communication takes place electronically, often with no face-to-face interaction, you might expect that relationships among members of organizations might become less important. Surprisingly, however, the reverse is true, as was predicted more than 20 years ago by John Naisbitt in his best seller, *Megatrends: Ten New Directions Transforming Our Lives*. He argued that people have a need to be together.[1] Even when most work is done by computer and people have the choice of working in their own homes, he says, "very few people will be willing to stay home all of the time and tap out messages to the office. People want to go to the office. People want to be with people, and the more technology we pump into the society, the more people will want to be with people." To be successful in tomorrow's organization, you will need to establish and maintain good relationships with others.

The trend toward shared leadership and working in teams has accentuated the importance of relationships in organizations. In *The Myth of Leadership*, Jeffrey Nielsen argues for what he calls "peer-based" versus "rank-based" organizations.[2] Rather than having leadership exerted by a few people who are elevated over the majority, in a peer-based organization rankings do not exist and everyone is considered to be of equal importance and worth. In such an organization, "personal involvement and mutual respect would lead to a sharing of responsibilities" so that everyone would perform the needed functions of "leadership." The organization would have three management vehicles: peer-based leadership councils that make decisions and provide cross-functional coordination, task forces that are chartered by the peer councils to deal with specific problems, and the senior executives who, "in an advisory role," set the general direction of the organization, act as consultants to the councils and task forces, ensure that "the right questions are asked," and help to create a context where the task forces can be innovative and successful.

To us, it seems unlikely that "rank-based" organizations will disappear any time soon. Indeed, we suspect that many people actually prefer having an element of "rank" and its attendant privileges in their organizations. Nevertheless, both Naisbitt and Nielsen point to the same conclusion: relationships within organizations have always been important—with changes in technology and leadership philosophy, they are becoming even more so. In his editorial "The Layered Lives We Lead," Jonathan Alter observes, "It used to be that only people in professions like politics, show business, and sales dealt with scores of people each day. Now anyone with e-mail does. And because Americans frequently change jobs, they are constantly selling themselves—just like politicians."[3] Again, the ability to establish and maintain relationships with many different people is becoming increasingly important in today's organizations.

Preview

In many respects, this chapter builds on the preceding two. Through verbal and nonverbal communication behaviors, we interact with other people in organizations, and as we interact we form relationships with them. The choices we make, verbally and nonverbally, shape the quality of those relationships and, to a large degree, our own success. Thus, we will consider the perceptual processes that happen when we first encounter people—processes that determine what our relationships with them are likely to be like, or whether we will have a relationship with them at all—and then turn our attention to the major dimensions of relationships in organizations. We will then consider some communication strategies you can use to improve each of those dimensions, plus one of the most important communication skills of all, effective listening. We will conclude by addressing the challenges of interacting with difficult people in organizations.

FUNDAMENTALS OF
INTERPERSONAL RELATIONSHIPS: PERCEPTION

Basic to the formation of our relationships with others are the conclusions we draw from our encounters with them—our perceptions. Haney defines perception as "the process of making sense out of experience."[4] That is, we encounter environments, experience them through our senses, and then try to sort out experiences so that they become meaningful to us. While all our experiences necessarily involve perception, the most important ones are those that demand perception of people. Therefore, the process of person perception will occupy most of our attention in this section.

Stages of Perception

Although complex, the perception process seems to involve three successive stages: selecting the things to which we pay attention, sorting those things into categories or groups that are meaningful to us, and then interpreting what all of this means.

STAGE 1: SELECTING

The first step of perception, **selecting** the things to which we pay attention, involves both involuntary and voluntary choices. The world presents an infinite array of message stimuli, so that to attend to all of them is utterly impossible. We must make some choices concerning which stimuli we will attend to and which we will ignore. Actually, to some degree these choices are made for us.

Our **physical location** is one factor determining our perceptions. By making certain stimuli available to us, our location limits the experiences we can have and hence the things that we can perceive. Similarly, in an organization, we perceive the parts with which we come into contact, but know little (other than what the rumor mill tells us) about people or parts of the organization we do not encounter. While this principle seems simple and obvious, it has important implications. The number of relationships you are able to form is a function of the number of people you communicate with. If you hide in your office day after day, week after week, there's a good chance you won't get to know many people; just as importantly, few people will get to know you—often a career and opportunity-limiting problem. Later in this chapter, we'll talk about overcoming shyness as you strive to maximize the number of contacts and potential relationships you have in an organization.

Some positions within organizations are expected to have contact with a large number of people. Senior executives, for example, are expected by employees to be "visible": to be out and about, greeting employees, and seeing how things are going. In our experience, executives who do this are well-liked by management and staff, who in turn are more loyal and often more committed to their work. Conversely, executives who are never seen are often resented by staff who think, "If they really cared about us and what we do, they'd come out and see us." Indeed, the principle of "management by wandering around" is based on this entire concept—the more you get around, the more your physical proximity allows you to perceive.

Our own physical capabilities also shape our perceptions. No one, for example, hears sounds below 20 or above 20,000 cycles per second, or sees more than about one-seventieth of the light spectrum. People who are hearing or sight impaired perceive even less, although other senses, and hence their ability to perceive via those senses, may become more acute.

The **characteristics of the stimuli** we encounter also can catch our attention. Intense sights and sounds, such as loud noises or bright lights, naturally get our attention. So too does a change in the stimulus. If you are reading and see movement out of the corner of your eye, you naturally will look toward that movement; if you are listening to music and the volume suddenly drops, it will get your attention. Things that are unusual also get attention. Someone wearing a bathing suit on the beach blends in; that same person wearing that same bathing suit during a corporate board meeting probably would draw a lot of attention.

Once our location and physical abilities allow us to perceive something, there still is some selecting that goes on. Particularly important is *psychological comfort*. Just as we seek to be comfortable physically, we also select information that makes us psychologically comfortable. To a lesser degree, we avoid information that creates psychological discomfort. We tend to seek information that reinforces views we hold and to avoid information that implies we are wrong. The reason for this behavior seems to lie in our need for self-esteem or in the need to think well of ourselves. Agreeable information implicitly tells us that we are right or that our ideas are good ones. Disagreeable information tells us that somehow our ideas or beliefs are defective and that we are in need of change. Reinforcing information makes us comfortable about ourselves; conflicting information may make us uncomfortable.

For people in organizations, this principle can be deadly. The reason "yes people" are so popular with some executives is that they tell the executives what they want to hear, such as "everything is fine," "you're doing a fabulous job," "looks like you've lost weight." On the other hand, the tradition of "shoot the messenger" may be applied to the people who convey bad news—things an executive would rather not hear. So while our natural tendency is to attend to information we find comforting and ignore information we find disconcerting, it often is in our best interests to do exactly the opposite: downplay the information we like to hear and give particular attention to the information that makes our stomach hurt.

Our own interests also drive our selection decisions, as we attend to those things that are interesting or important to us and ignore things that are not. For example, if you are at a party where groups of people are standing around talking, try saying softly the name of one of the people in an adjacent group. Even though that person probably has not heard anything you said before that point, he or she almost certainly will hear his or her name. The reason is simple: a person's name is the single most interesting (important) word in the world to that person.

The same principle applies in organizations. People pay most attention to information they find interesting or important and ignore or overlook information of lesser interest. A CEO with a background in sales, for example, often will focus carefully on the organization's quarterly sales figures while giving little attention (possibly too little) to other key indicators of the organization's success, such as quality, productivity, or employee turnover. To expand your realm of experience, sometimes you have to make a conscious effort to devote attention to things you may not be as interested in, recognizing that over time interest may develop.

Past experience also shapes our perceptions, so that at times we perceive what we expect to perceive. Consider the triangles presented in figure 6.1.

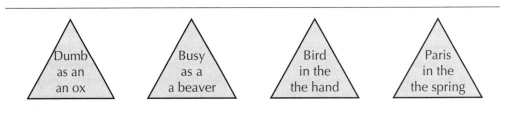

Figure 6.1   An exercise in perception

Quickly read each of them aloud. Usually, these figures are read as "Dumb as an ox," "Bird in the hand," "Busy as a beaver," and "Paris in the spring." If you saw them that way, look again—you missed something. Unfortunately, this phenomenon of seeing what we expect to see also occurs when we observe people. If we have found certain people to be annoying in the past, we may expect them to be that way the next time we talk with them—and thus we're more likely to see them as annoying again, even if they behave differently.

Figure 6.2 presents another example of past experience shaping our perceptions. There you will find a square consisting of three rows having three dots each. Your task is to connect all nine dots using only four lines and never lifting your pencil from the page. Simple, right? Try it a few times. Unless you have seen this before, you probably will have some difficulty figuring it out. Blame it on past experience. We are used to seeing the world in certain ways, and in this instance, we tend to perceive the figure as a square. Thus, we operate within the limits of the square, trying to find some way to draw four lines. As long as you let perceptual habit confine you to the square, you will be unable to solve the problem. You have to go beyond the square to solve it successfully—indeed, the buzzword expression "thinking outside of the box" came from this very example.

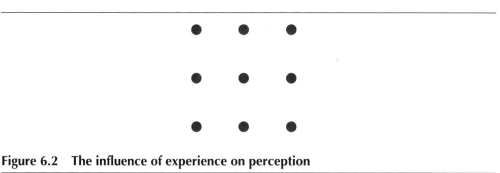

Figure 6.2   The influence of experience on perception

STAGE 2: SORTING

After we have completed the selection stage of perception (determining which stimuli we will and will not attend to), we move to the second stage, *sorting*. We do not perceive things to be random, unrelated occurrences. Rather, we tend to organize our perceptions into coherent patterns and groupings.

This process of organizing our perceptions involves several principles. For example, we tend to group together things that are located in close *proximity*. In figure 6.3, column A presents eight lines. Although no special relationship exists between any of them, we tend to group them into four pairs simply because of their physical location.

The same principle applies in our perceptions of people, as illustrated by the old saying, "birds of a feather flock together." When a few people are seen together, not just once but a number of times, others start to perceive them to be a group. Unfortunately, however, they also can start to attribute the same characteristics to each of the group members, whether warranted or not. If one group member is generally viewed as a "troublemaker," for example, the entire group could quickly come to be seen as "malcontents" or people management should watch closely. On the other hand, if one or more group members are powerful organizational figures, others will often try to be seen with them in an effort to be viewed as powerful (or at least, "near-powerful") by the rest of the organization as well.

Column B of figure 6.3 illustrates a second principle that governs how we sort our perceptions, which is *closure*. We tend to fill in incomplete figures, perceiving the entire figure as though the complete object was there. Thus, in column B, we group the lines differently, tending to see three rectangles with single lines at the top and bottom of the column.

We do the same when we encounter people. On the basis of a few bits of information, for example, we infer other characteristics about a person in order to develop a complete, although often inaccurate, view of that particular individual. A job applicant with a pierced lip and tongue, spiked electric blue hair, and wearing a leather motorcycle jacket is someone we probably would infer to be a nonconformist, unsophisticated in the "game" of employment interviewing, and in all likelihood, not at all suited to the position of Republican Party Chairperson we are trying to fill.

We also group together objects that are *physically similar*. Someone with gray hair, facial wrinkles, and a stooped posture probably would fall into our mental category of "old person." Many organizations create physical similarity by having their employees wear uniforms. Thus, in a hospital, someone who enters a patient's room wearing scrubs doesn't have to say to the patient, "I work here." The patient knows by the uniform.

STAGE 3: INTERPRETATION

When we have selected and sorted stimuli into some coherent pattern, we move to the third stage of perception, *interpretation*. Here, we finally make sense of the things we have experienced. Again, several principles seem to govern the interpretations we form. We interpret people and things in terms of their *context*. For instance, our perceptions of people may change from one context to the

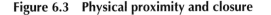

Column A   Column B

Figure 6.3   Physical proximity and closure

next; what we feel is appropriate in one context may not be appropriate in another. Talking loudly at the company picnic is expected in that context. Talking loudly during a team conference may be interpreted as pushy, aggressive, or hostile. The behaviors are the same, but what is judged "appropriate" has changed with the context.

When we encounter people, we also tend to interpret them in terms of our perception of their *intent*. Indeed, our natural survival instincts probably cause us automatically to look at the motives of each person we encounter; we are alert to any possible threat. In organizations, perceived intent is key. As you look to achieve your own work objectives and, hopefully, advance in the organization, you naturally are wary of people who seem uncooperative or out for their own gain, whereas you grow to trust colleagues who seem cooperative and willing to help you. Indeed, the way people are viewed within organizations probably is shaped more by the motives others perceive them to have than by any other factor. Marginally skilled workers will be tolerated if they seem cooperative and helpful; work superstars will be shunned and even terminated if they are perceived to be "backstabbers." Managing others' perceptions of your motives thus is extremely important and is a topic we will consider later in this chapter.

Projection also shapes our interpretation of other people. Essentially, we tend to project onto other people our own characteristics, but with this twist: we tend to attribute positive characteristics of ourselves to other people whom we like, and we tend to attribute our undesirable characteristics to people we dislike. The phrase "love is blind" relates to this principle. We overlook the faults of people we like, and instead perceive them to be more like ourselves than perhaps they really are. On the other hand, people we dislike may have many good characteristics, but we tend to overlook them and focus on their undesirable characteristics—which often are characteristics we have as well, even though we may not know it. This principle becomes most clear if you listen to people gossiping or complaining about someone else. Invariably, the characteristics they criticize most in that person are characteristics they themselves have. But don't point that out to them during the gossip session—otherwise, you won't be invited to participate in the next one.

The *labels* we attach to people also shape the conclusions we draw about them. For example, before we meet someone, we might be told "he's a real jerk" or "she's one of the nicest people you'll ever meet." These labels shape our expectations of the individuals, and we are more likely to feel negatively or positively toward them as a result. Similarly, if we are told that "Anne's an accountant" we might automatically assume that, like many accountants we know, Anne is detail-oriented, a workaholic, humorless, and dull. Using the perceptual principle of closure we discussed earlier, we take a little bit of information and from that construct in our minds a whole person—a person who may be very different from the funny, outgoing, personable accountant who is really there. When perceiving people, we are well advised to rely on our own observations, ignoring as much as possible the labels with which other people provide us and the stereotypes those labels can trigger.

The final source of interpretation is *familiarity*—the one saving grace in the perceptual process. While context, intent, projection, and labels all tend to lead us astray because they are all based on something other than the thing being perceived, familiarity considers the extent to which we have developed an acquaintance with the object. As a rule, the more familiar we are with something, the more accurately we are able to perceive it.

Perceiving People

The terrorist attacks of September 11, 2001, significantly heightened the nation's concern for security. At airports, this concern took the form of a very controversial practice called *profiling:* people having certain characteristics are singled out and scrutinized very carefully, presumably because they are more likely to be terrorists and thus pose a threat. The specific characteristics used to construct a profile of a suspected terrorist are carefully guarded secrets, lest the real terrorists learn how best to disguise themselves and elude security. However, several of the characteristics have come to light: buying a one-way ticket at the last minute, paying cash, and being a young male of Middle Eastern descent, for example.

Many people argue that such profiling is unfair—that people should not be categorized and judged in this manner. Yet, all of us do exactly the same thing with everyone we meet. When we encounter people, we naturally sort them into the different mental categories we have developed. Often we categorize others on the basis of appearance; in other cases we might consider their language, accent, vocabulary, or physical actions. We quickly notice race, gender, and age, for example, and categorize the people we meet accordingly. We also notice people who are different and thus stand out from those around them. For example, while traveling in Japan, we quickly would spot any other Westerner we encounter.

Once we form a mental category, we tend to perceive its members to be similar to each other. However, we continue to see differences between members of the groups to which we ourselves belong. For example, for many North Americans there is one category, "Asians," to which they assign every Asian-appearing person they encounter. To an Asian, however, there are very clear differences between Japanese, Chinese, Korean, Laotian, and other groups within the "Asian" category. The old and objectionable saying "they all look alike to me" unfortunately is true for many people, but they certainly don't all look alike to each other.

Stereotyping occurs when the ways we categorize people in turn shapes our attitudes about and expectations of them. We tend to perceive everyone in the group as having particular characteristics and similar behaviors. For example, we may expect Japanese to be polite, Irish to be outgoing, Scots to be frugal, and Brits to be proper with a "stiff upper lip." These stereotypes are not necessarily negative, but they often are; when stereotypes carry negative attitudes and expectations, they often lead to negative behavior or prejudice. Indeed, one of the most common types of prejudice is racism, which comes about in part because it is relatively easy to categorize others based on race.[5] Stereotypes similarly can be applied to other, often readily identifiable groups as people are sorted by gender, body shape, apparent sexual preference, and so on.

Beyond observation and interpretation of others based on perceived characteristics, we often make inferences about *why* people might behave as they do. This process of **attribution** is extremely important in our perceptions of others, particularly as it relates to "internal attributions"—in which behavior is attributed to factors associated with the person himself or herself (for example, "he

Highlighting Diversity

Cross-Cultural Differences and Interpersonal Communication Tensions

With advancing globalization, people with diverse ethnic backgrounds are finding themselves working together on all sorts of projects. How successfully they interact will depend, in part, on the extent to which they are sensitive to and respectful of the differences they bring to the table. Here are some dimensions along which cultures are likely to vary:

- *High Context vs. Low Context*—a low context culture (United States, Canada, northern Europe) is one in which ideas, plans, and courses of action are explicitly spelled out. Communication emphasizes what is actually said or written. By contrast, in a high context culture (Japan, Middle East, France) those interacting assume common knowledge and views—leading to more indirect, implicit communication, and a greater reliance on nonverbals.

- *Future vs. Present Orientation*—past-oriented societies (China, Britain, Japan, and most Latin American countries) are concerned with traditional values and ways of doing things. Future-oriented societies, such as the United States, have a great deal of optimism about the future, thinking they can understand it and shape it through their actions.

- *Perceptions of Time*—in some cultures like the United States, time is seen as a commodity—something to be valued, spent, saved, or wasted. Because time is so valuable, it must be used productively. In other cultures (such as India or Latin America), time is perceived as plentiful—so there is no problem with arriving late to meetings or making people wait. Time-plentiful cultures tend to rely on trust to do business. But in time-limited cultures, people often don't have or take the time to develop trust, hoping instead to move directly to the task as quickly and efficiently as possible.

- *Individualism vs. Collectivism*—in individualistic cultures (e.g., Anglo), individual uniqueness and self-determinism are valued. A person is viewed as all the more admirable if he or she shows independence and individual initiative. By contrast, collectivist cultures (e.g., Asian) expect people to identify with and work well in groups that protect them in exchange for loyalty and compliance.

- How can these differences lead to communication breakdowns? Here are a few examples:

  — The Japanese may see Westerns as offensively blunt, while Westerns may find the Japanese to be secretive, devious, and bafflingly unforthcoming with information.

  — The French may feel that Germans insult their intelligence by explaining the obvious, while the Germans may view the French (especially managers) as providing no direction.

  — In an Asian country, a meeting may begin with an extended period of time to establish social rapport (ranging from hours to several meetings) before even mentioning the task—a practice that North Americans will likely find frustrating.

  — Arabs consider drinking coffee and chatting with a colleague as doing something whereas most North Americans see it as doing nothing.

Sources: Michelle Baron, *Bridging Cultural Conflicts: A New Approach for a Changing World* (San Francisco: Jossey-Bass, 2003); and John G. Oetzel and others, "Cross-Cultural and Intercultural Work Group Communication," in *Small Group Communication: Theory and Practice,* 8th ed., ed. R. Y. Hirokawa and others (Los Angeles: Roxbury, 2003), 239–252. For additional reading see: William B. Gudykunst, *Bridging Differences: Effective Intergroup Communication,* 4th ed. (Thousand Oaks, CA: Sage, 2003); Larry A. Samovar, *Intercultural Communication: A Reader* (Belmont, CA: Wadsworth, 2002); Everett M. Rogers and Thomas M. Steinfatt, *Intercultural Communication* (Prospect Heights, IL: Waveland Press, 1999); and Brenda J. Allen, *Difference Matters: Communicating Social Identity* (Long Grove, IL: Waveland Press, 2004).

yelled at the employee because he's mean")—versus "external attributions," in which the behavior is perceived to be caused by external factors ("he yelled at the employee because the employee was late").

Consider this real example. A female, African American vice president in a large Chicago company had several directors reporting to her, two of whom were white. She noticed that these two did not seem to agree with her decisions as readily as the other directors did, and she also heard via the rumor mill that these two had criticized her "behind her back" in discussions with other directors. Speaking with a consultant who was working with her company, she observed, "I think we've got racial issues here." When she was asked to elaborate, she reported: "These two directors are trying to undercut me because they're racists." In fact, the consultant had already met with the two directors and found that they objected to the vice president's decisions not because they were racially biased, but because they did not like her autocratic, heavy-handed style of leadership and felt some of her decisions were flat-out wrong. Indeed, two other directors, both of them African American, also felt the same way but were too afraid of the vice president to speak up. Thus, the consultant said to the vice president, "I don't think they're racist; having talked with them, I think it's your leadership style that's at the heart of this problem." The vice president thought for a minute, then looked at the Caucasian consultant and said, "I'd say you have some racial issues, too."

When categorization and associated stereotypical expectations are combined with attribution, some significant problems can arise. The conclusion that "they are undercutting me because they are white, and whites are prejudice against African Americans" is an example of this kind of thinking.

How can we improve the accuracy with which we perceive people we encounter? Although there is no simple method, we can suggest four techniques that may prove helpful.

1. *Consensual validation* involves seeking the agreement or consensus of other people concerning the nature of "reality." In essence, you simply ask others what they think. There are some dangers here, such as the chance of asking people whose perceptions are as strange as our own or the danger of making ourselves vulnerable to manipulation by those whom we consult. But for the most part, consensual validation is a useful means of determining whether or not we perceive others accurately.

2. *Repetitive validation*, observing the person several times, allows us to determine whether our first impressions were correct. This method may not solve the problems posed by stable stereotypes and prejudices, but it may aid us in the selection and organization stages of perception.

3. *Multisensory validation* involves the use of other senses to confirm what one sense has received. A desert mirage seems real only as long as we look at it. When we try to touch it, it disappears. People may present themselves in a certain way, causing us to derive a perceptual conclusion about them, but if we listen to them we may discover that they are not the way they look at all. Thus, we ought not to rely on just one sense when perceiving others.

4. *Comparative validation* gives us some indication of perceptual validity by comparing a new perception with experiences of the past. Using this technique, we

---

Highlighting Diversity

Cultural Intelligence

In their book *Cultural Intelligence*, Thomas and Inkson suggest some techniques for improving our perceptions of others, particularly when we encounter people from other cultures. They suggest:

- Be aware of our own assumptions, ideas, and emotions, as well as the selective perception, attribution, and categorization that we and others adopt.
- Notice what is apparent about the other person and tune in to their assumptions, words, and behavior.
- Use all of the senses in perceiving situations rather than just relying on, for example, hearing the words that the other person speaks.
- View the situation from several perspectives, that is, with an open mind.
- Attend to the context to help interpret what is happening.
- Create new mental maps of other people's personalities and cultural backgrounds to assist us in responding appropriately to them.
- Create new categories and recategorize others into a more sophisticated category system.
- Seek out fresh information to confirm or disconfirm our mental maps.
- Use empathy—the ability to mentally put ourselves in the other person's shoes—as a means of understanding the situation and their feelings toward it from the perspective of their cultural background rather than ours.

Source: David C. Thomas and Kerr Inkson, *Cultural Intelligence* (San Francisco: Berrett-Koehler Publishers, 2004), 52.

---

might ask ourselves, "Does the behavior I am now seeing fit with the behaviors I have seen from this person in the past?" The answer to this question has important implications for our judgments of this person. If the behavior is consistent, perhaps we are in a position to make a judgment about the individual's traits; if the behavior is inconsistent, we may need to find out why.

Although any of these four methods may prove useful in increasing perceptual accuracy, the main point is: rather than accepting the things we perceive at "face value" (forming judgments immediately on the basis of what we perceive at the moment), we need to check our perceptions before we judge and act. If we take care in forming perceptions, or if we resolve that we are going to suspend judgment until we have made all the observations we can, we will have done much to improve our perceptions of the people we encounter.

THE DIMENSIONS OF HUMAN RELATIONSHIPS IN ORGANIZATIONS

Your perceptions of other people in organizations ultimately serve as the basis for relationships with them, and as noted before, those relationships are the web that creates an organization. Several theorists have identified the dimensions that make up our relationships. Although they have used different methodologies to arrive at their conclusions, nearly all have said the same thing: relationships consist of "affection" (the extent to which each person likes the other), "dominance" or "control" (the extent to which each person is "in charge" and makes decisions the other persons follow), and "inclusion" (the extent to which people identify and interact with each other).[6]

If you think about the various people with whom you have relationships at work, you probably will see the validity of these dimensions. From an "attraction" perspective, you feel differently about each person: some you like a lot, some a little, some you dislike, and some (hopefully not many) you despise. Some you may not care about one way or another, probably because they are acquaintances with whom you really do not have a meaningful relationship. Similarly, from a "dominance" perspective, each relationship probably is different. Some may be higher up in the organizational hierarchy than you are—your boss, for example—and thus be more in control when you are together at work. Others, such as any people who report to you, may have less control in the relationship than you do. Even with your peers, some (probably the "pushy" ones) are more dominant and in charge, while others hang back and tend to be followers.

What some theorists call the "inclusion" dimension, we instead call "involvement." This dimension considers the depth of a relationship. With acquaintances you see occasionally in the hallways—and to whom you only say "hi"—your level of involvement is relatively low. With colleagues you see and talk with every day, sharing both personal and work-related information, your level of involvement is much higher.

To these three dimensions we would add a fourth: "situation." This dimension considers the physical, social, and task environment in which we communicate with people, since all three have some impact upon relationship development.

Attraction

The first dimension considers the degree to which the participants feel positively or negatively about one another. Many factors influence the extent to which we are attracted to someone else. The first of these is *physical proximity*—the sheer accident of physical location determines to a large degree those we will be attracted to. Employees working in the same department, for example, see one another relatively often and relationships between them are likely to form as a result. But we need to emphasize that while contact produces feelings about others, those feelings are not necessarily positive. That is, to dislike someone intensely, we would need to see that person frequently as well. Thus, physical proximity simply causes us to come into contact with others, giving us an opportunity to form opinions about them and develop attraction toward (or repulsion from) them.

Although society tells us that we should not judge a book by its cover or judge people by their appearance, research indicates that we do exactly that. Indeed, *physical attractiveness* seems to be the second major determinant of our attraction to someone else. People who find one another physically attractive, regardless of their sex, are more likely to talk with one another and form friendships. Conversely, people who are extremely unattractive have fewer social contacts and, as a result, fewer friendships.

Business Brief 6.1

The Importance of Positive Relationships

A study conducted by Christine Pearson, management professor in the University of North Carolina-Chapel Hill business school, illustrated the impact of rudeness in the workplace. In her study of business professionals:

- 12% said rudeness from a colleague has caused them to decrease the quality of their work
- 22% said their work effort declined
- 28% lost time at work trying to avoid the rude person
- 52% lost time from worry about the situation
- 26% thought about changing jobs
- 12% actually took new jobs to escape a rude person

Source: "The Cost of Rudeness," *Motivational Manager* (November 1998): 9.

Third, attraction is influenced by *interpersonal similarity*.[7] A substantial body of research demonstrates that we prefer the company of people who are like ourselves. Similarity in attitudes, values, socioeconomic status, and background determines to some extent the degree to which people are mutually attracted.[8] In organizations, this tendency has been shown to be related to satisfaction with supervisors—employees who were similar in important respects to their immediate supervisors were more satisfied with supervision than employees who were significantly different from their supervisors.[9] In employment interviews, the interviewers gave more positive evaluations to applicants who were similar biographically to themselves.[10] Clearly, we are more attracted to people we perceive to be similar to ourselves.

In turn, this attraction principle brings to mind the old saying we saw earlier in this chapter: "Birds of a feather flock together." We do, in fact, prefer to flock with people who are like us, so that the perceptual principle of assuming that people who are together share common characteristics is, in fact, true in many cases.

Two final determinants of attraction are *status* and *personal rewards*. People holding a status higher than our own are more attractive to us, while people of lesser status tend to be less attractive. Ambitious middle-level managers thus scramble to get offices close to those occupied by senior executives and to associate with them as much as they can. Similarly, people who provide us (or potentially can provide us) with personal rewards are more attractive, while those who will not or cannot reward us are less attractive. And even in organizations, those rewards often are not monetary; for example, research shows that we are more attracted to people who evaluate us positively or give us praise and less attracted to people who criticize us.[11]

Dominance

The ability of one person to exert some control or influence over another seems to be a product of three things: the characteristics of the person trying to exert influence, the characteristics of the person receiving the influence attempts, and the influence strategies employed by the person trying to dominate.[12]

In order to exert influence or dominance in a relationship, you need to have one or more of several characteristics. First, it is helpful to *want to exert influence*. Generally, people who try to be influential or exert control (those "pushy" people we mentioned earlier) are more likely to do so than are those who hang back and do nothing. This principle is true even for people who hold leadership positions: supervisors who do not try to supervise (called by some theorists "laissez-faire" or "let-it-be" leaders) probably exert little if any influence over the people who report to them. Indeed, many organizations have supervisors who are "pushed around" by their employees.

Your ability to exert influence also is shaped by *the expertise you have* concerning the topic or task at hand and *the expertise others perceive you to have*. That is, if you are an expert but no one knows it, you probably won't be very influential. Conversely, if you know relatively little but sound authoritative, you probably can exert influence effectively by convincing others of your expertise (and you probably have a promising career as a consultant ahead of you). Of course, it's easier to convince people that you are an expert when you actually are.

If you have *communication skill*, you are also more likely to be influential. In a later chapter, we discuss some principles of effective persuasion; at this point, we simply note that people who are good at communicating logical, clearly reasoned arguments and appeal to their listeners' emotions are more likely to be influential, while those who lack these skills as persuaders are much less likely to exert influence.

Lastly, in organizations *status is tied to dominance*. The higher you are on the organization chart, the more formal authority you have, and thus the more potential for exerting influence you possess. Again, however, there are leaders who do not use their position to influence others, either because they are unskilled as leaders or because they deliberately choose a participative or democratic style of leadership.

Characteristics of the other person in the relationship—the recipient of influence—also shape how dominant or influential you are able to be. If that person likes you, for example, he is more likely to be influenced by you. Also, if that person wants something from you, such as obtaining some reward you control or avoiding some punishment you could dish out, he is more likely to allow you to exert control and have greater dominance. If he is by nature submissive—shy and retiring rather than pushy and persuasive—then the nature of that person's personality makes him more inclined to accept your direction. Lastly, if the person is convinced that you are right, possibly because of the expertise you demonstrated or your skills as a communicator, then he is more likely to agree with your conclusions or recommendations and thus be influenced by you.

Influence strategies comprise the final component of dominance. As you try to get someone to do something, there are a variety of influence methods from which to choose.

- One is the use of *threats:* "do it or I'll beat the stuffing out of you." Actually, unskilled supervisors use threats as an influence strategy a lot, largely because they have never been taught anything else: "do it or I'll write you up." Often, threats are effective in getting people to comply, but just as often, they cause resentment to build in the recipient of the threat and undermine another relationship dimension, attraction.

- Others use *promises* as a strategy of influence: "do it, and I'll give you something" (such as a raise, a positive performance evaluation, or some other coveted prize). Again, such influence attempts can be successful, but they are limited in that people do what is asked not because they feel it is the right thing, but because they want the reward—and they will continue to comply only so long as a desired reward is available.

- Some resort to the use of *positional authority:* "do it because I say so, and I'm the boss." Often, supervisors use this in a shortened form—"do it"—expecting that their subordinates know who's the boss. Usually subordinates will comply (often because they know a threat will be forthcoming if they don't), but sometimes they comply without much enthusiasm.

- Still others use their *relationship with the person* as a potential influence tool: "look, we've been friends for a long time; won't you just do it for me?" If the person likes you and values your good will, they may say "sure," and do what you've asked. If they don't like you so much, they may say, "you know, I've really never been that crazy about you." Then you're left to find another influence strategy.

- *Appealing to agreed-upon principles or rules* as the basis for your recommendations can also be effective: "do it because it's consistent with our corporate values and goals," or "do it because it says so in the policy manual." You may need to make the connection between your request and the agreed-upon principle clear, and you have to count on the person actually agreeing with the value, policy, or rule you cite, but often this approach is effective in exerting influence.

- *Your own expertise* can be an effective influence strategy: "I've dealt with this issue for 25 years, and trust me, I know what works; so do it my way." For motivating performance in an organization, this strategy is better than the others in that your credibility leads people to believe that what they are doing is the right thing. Thus, rewards, punishments, positions, relationships, and other factors external to the desired action are irrelevant; they do it because they agree it should be done. Of course, the recipients of your influence may not simply take your word for it; you may have to share your expertise with them, teaching them the information you already know so that they can see how your recommended course of action is, in fact, the right thing to do.

- Lastly, an effective strategy can be *giving the person a choice*, much as crafty parents do with their children: "would you rather eat your carrots first, or your broccoli?" By involving the other person in the decision-making process you help to motivate her to take action, and by letting the person choose the action, you increase her commitment to seeing it through. Participative management is based on these principles. Employees are given guidelines within which their decision must be made, and then they are allowed to make the decision on their own.

Involvement

A third relationship dimension considers the degree to which we are involved with someone else, or the breadth and depth of our relationship with him or her. Some relationships are rich and intense, while others are quite superficial. Social psychologists Altman and Taylor suggest that relationships develop in increments, moving from superficial to more intimate levels.[13]

As two individuals learn more about each other, largely through observing each other's behavior and through self-disclosure, their relationship grows in importance. The number of topics discussed (breadth) and the depth of information shared suggest whether the relationship can be defined as casual or intimate. With casual relationships breadth is often high, but depth is low. The most intimate relationships have high breadth and depth. As individuals disclose information that is central to the relationship, depth increases.

Altman and Taylor's model is useful in understanding the nature of the involvement dimension. *The larger the number of topics you discuss with someone and the more personal the information you share, the more involved you are.* Consider, for example, someone you see in the break room at work every day. You know her name, and you know she works in another department on the same floor. But that's it. Every day, the conversation is the same: "the weather's nice/

Highlighting Diversity

Changing Roles of Men and Women in U. S. Society

In U.S. society, the roles of men and women at work and at home have changed. As women have moved into the workplace, the role of fathers also has changed. According to a study reported in *Time* magazine:

- "The majority of men today are vastly more involved in the rearing of their children and maintenance of their households than their fathers ever were."
- In turn, this may be changing their life values: when asked to choose how they measure success:
  — only 3% of men said through their work;
  — 31% said through their faith in God;
  — 26% said through being the best person possible;
  — 22% said through their network of family and friends;
  — 17% said through maintaining a balance between home and work.
- Indeed, most showed a clear preference for family life over work.
  — 72%, including survey respondents who are single, said they would sacrifice advancement at work to spend more time at home;
  — 66% said they would risk being perceived poorly by a supervisor to ask for a month's leave.
- But despite all that, men are not necessarily cutting back on their work hours:
  — nearly 68% work more than 40 hours per week;
  — 62% work weekends.
- Finally, acceptance of diversity in the workplace seems to have increased among working men:
  — 55% said they have no preference for a male or female boss;
  — 9% said they actually would prefer a woman.

Source: Michele Orecklin, "Stress and the Superdad," *Time*, August 23, 2004, 38–39.

lousy today" and "how about those Packers." Obviously, this is not a very intimate or involved relationship. But over time, the nature of the information might evolve through the exchange of more personal information. For example, you notice one day that she has a cast on her right foot and you say, "Gee, what happened?" She answers, "Oh, I broke my foot kicking my husband and his dog out of my house over the weekend." You might follow up with an invitation to share more personal information, such as, "I didn't know you had a dog." Or, you might ask something even more sensitive than that. The key is that the relationship evolves from superficial and relatively uninvolved into a more personal, intimate, involved interaction. Thus, to increase involvement, increase both the depth and breadth of the interaction.[14]

Situation

The fourth human relationship dimension existing between people is the *situation*, which considers environments in which communication occurs. Three aspects of the situation seem particularly influential in interpersonal relationships. First, as the previous chapter described, the *physical environment* influences interaction among the individuals.[15] Such things as office furniture arrangement can influence the dominance dimension of interpersonal relationships, while the attractiveness of the surroundings may influence interpersonal attraction. Second, the *social environment* affects interaction.[16] The number of persons present, the role behaviors expected of the participants, and the social hierarchy have some impact upon relationships. Finally, the *tasks and purposes* present in the encounter affect relationship development. This aspect of the situation takes into account both the observable goals of the individuals and the motivations underlying their behaviors.

From the preceding description of situation, it might seem that all relationships are situationally determined. However, the *distinction* must be made *between long- and short-term situations*. In the long term, the president of an organization is higher in dominance than the manager of employee relations. When discussing actions that should be taken during an employee strike, however, the employee relations manager may be dominant by virtue of her expertise and relationship to the task. Employees presenting their recommendations to top management are dominant during that particular meeting, although their long-term status is much lower than that of the people to whom they are speaking. Finally, while everyone attending a meeting may hold the same job in the organization, the person who, by luck or design, is seated at the head of the long conference table often will exert the most dominance during that meeting.

To understand more deeply the effects of the situation, consider a phenomenon that used to be called the "bus rider syndrome," but now probably should be referred to as "the airline passenger syndrome." Long ago, researchers noted that there is a tendency for people who have never met before and are likely never to meet again to share intimate details of their lives with one another. Thus, someone sitting next to someone else on a long bus ride (or today, a long plane flight) would tell deep, personal secrets to that person, knowing that he would never see that person again and the secrets he shared thus would never come back to haunt him. Are these two people involved? The depth of the information being shared is maximum: secrets are being told that they probably would not want any of their friends or family to know. But the very reason why the information is shared is that they are not truly involved, as we define the concept. They share personal information because this is a one-time event, and they can get things off their chest without risk—there is no potential threat to the relationship simply because there is no relationship. The situation therefore promotes the sharing of information that normally would lead to greater intimacy and involvement precisely because the situation guarantees that no involvement will occur.

From a relationship perspective, the *organization itself* must be considered a situation that influences attraction, dominance, and involvement. Someone who is dominant at work because he is the CEO might be less so at the country club, where he is viewed as a lousy golfer. A manager who is in charge at the office may not be in charge at home, where both spouse and offspring exert far more control than the manager does. If, in a scene out of the movies, a group of coworkers should find themselves stranded together on an island, the survival skills of each member would cause a shift in the relationships whereby someone with the lowest status in the company could become the group leader because of her skills in building fires and trapping food. Thus, as we examine relationships in the organizational context, it is important to remember that this is just one of an almost infinite number of relationship-shaping situations in which people can find themselves.

Interrelationships among Relationship Dimensions

Last, it is important to realize that the four dimensions do not operate independently. They interact so that changes in one of them often produce changes in others. For example, attraction and dominance interact to make high-status individuals more attractive than low-status individuals.[17] And this interaction makes people of lower status have more desire to communicate with individuals of higher status than vice versa. Attraction and involvement also are related. Mutually attracted people are more likely to share personal (involving) information about themselves, and this sharing, in turn, seems to increase attraction.[18] We have already seen that situations produce changes in both attraction and dominance, and that physical and social surroundings influence people's tendencies to become involved with one another. Thus, human relationships represent a complex network of mutually influential dimensions.

COMMUNICATION SKILLS FOR IMPROVING RELATIONSHIPS

To this point, we have reviewed the dimensions of human relationships and the elements of perception that allow those relationships to exist. In this section, we turn to some strategies for improving relationships in the organizational setting.

As we saw earlier, your relationships with others in organizations consist of three basic dimensions: attraction, dominance, and involvement. These three vary according to the situations in which you encounter these people, and these dimensions influence one another. Nevertheless, we will consider each of them again briefly, noting some ways in which each might be strengthened in any organizational setting.

Highlighting Technology

Paying Attention to Others

Jeffrey Pfeffer, the Thomas D. Dee II Professor of Organizational Behavior at Stanford University's Graduate School of Business, argues that paying attention to other people is both the best way to learn from them and one of the most powerful means of influencing them, but people in organizations today are distracted by all of the communication messages and stimuli around them.

> At board meetings I attend, one director invariably hauls out his BlackBerry and thumbs out e-mails. At dozens of companies I've visited, I've seen bosses shuffling papers while talking to their employees, or workers sifting through e-mails during phone conversations. It's as if a new form of ADD has overtaken the workplace, and the habit of focusing on one thing or one person at a time seems merely quaint.

People who take phone calls and send e-mails while meeting with their colleagues send a clear message: those colleagues are not as important as the next e-mail or phone call. "And that's the worst signal you can send: if officemates seek anything from each other, it is to be taken seriously and to command respect."

Building effective relationships thus stems from first paying attention to the other person: "turning off your cell phone in meetings, resisting the urge to interrupt, setting aside e-mail for an hour." By investing 60 seconds to pay attention to someone, you can make a colleague a lifelong ally.

Source: Jeffrey Pfeffer, "How to Turn on the Charm," *Business 2.0* (June 2004): 76.

Attraction

How do you make yourself more attractive to others in an organizational setting? Many years ago, Dale Carnegie set out to answer this question with his book *How To Win Friends And Influence People*, which was so successful that it spawned an entire industry of personal development—businesspeople continue to undergo "Carnegie training" today. Carnegie's suggestions are as relevant today as they were when he wrote them more than 60 years ago.[19]

1. *Act as though you like the other person*, since we tend to be attracted to people who seem attracted to us and to avoid people who do not seem to like us. For example, acknowledge people when you encounter them. A friendly greeting, accompanied by eye contact and a warm smile, indicates to them that you feel positively toward them and encourages them to feel the same way toward you. On the other hand, if you pass someone in the hallway and say nothing, staring at the floor as you hurry along, the person is likely to think, "What's with her?" feeling somewhat less positively toward you as a result. Similarly, as you talk with someone, eye contact and a smile convey positive feelings toward that person, encouraging her to feel the same way toward you.

2. *Do not speak badly of other people.* Insulting them to their face certainly works against building mutual attraction, but so does saying bad things about them to others. The phrase "what goes around, comes around" is, you'll discover,

one of the certainties of life in an organization. If you say something unkind or critical of someone, that person is virtually guaranteed to hear about it and will feel some resentment toward you in return. In organizations, this principle is particularly important when applied to the relationship between you and your boss. While chatting with your peers, attention naturally will turn to the person you all report to. Human nature being what it is, discussion may well focus on your boss's many shortcomings—a very entertaining topic, no doubt, but there's a good chance that someone in the discussion may try to gain a competitive advantage by repeating to the boss what the others had to say. If you want your boss to feel positively toward you, say positive things about her.

3. *Communicate sincere appreciation to other people.* Empty flattery quickly becomes evident for what it is, and flatterers generally are regarded with suspicion in organizations. However, if you can identify things a person has done well and characteristics that allow that person to contribute to the team and the organization, expressing appreciation for those efforts and characteristics helps the person to feel better about himself and encourages him to continue doing those things you have praised. Typically, people are attracted to and want to communicate more with those who give them feedback that makes them feel good, while they tend to avoid people who provide negative feedback that hurts their self-esteem. Sending someone a brief note recognizing the person's efforts and achievements, or even just saying "thank you," can be important attraction-building tools.

4. *Show genuine interest in others.* Rather than talking constantly about yourself—no matter how fascinating your life may be—ask others about their lives, and then listen to their answers. Ask about the projects they are involved in, about their commute to work, or about how they spent their weekend. Then, using some of the listening techniques provided later in this chapter, pay attention to what they tell you; don't act as though you can't wait for them to finish talking so you can tell them about your projects, commute, or weekend. Most people like getting attention from others; if you provide that attention by showing a genuine interest in them and their lives, they will be more attracted to you in return.

5. *Use the person's name.* Carnegie claimed in 1936 that "a man's name is to him the sweetest and most important sound in the English language," and one assumes that today the same principle also applies to women. As we noted earlier, your name gets your attention, and most people like having their name remembered and said by others. In our consulting experience, we have found this particularly to be true in organizations. For example, the senior executives held in highest esteem by employees invariably are those who say "hello" to employees when they encounter them, and call them by name. On the other hand, employees are most resentful toward people in leadership who ignore them in the hallways or seem not to think that their name is particularly important. A supervisor in a Chicago manufacturing plant, for example, was widely despised by many of her staff because she never called them by name. Rather, she used pet names or nicknames she invented, calling each employee "sweetie," or "honey," or "darlin'." These employees quickly came to the realization that she did not have the foggiest idea what their names were, and con-

cluded that she didn't care enough about them as individuals to learn their names. Consequently, their morale and performance plummeted.

When using the other person's name, however, there are two important rules to keep in mind: ***don't overuse the person's name***, and ***use his or her name appropriately***. Often, it is easy to spot a graduate of the Dale Carnegie course: they use your name over and over, saying it at least once in every sentence. Very quickly this "sweetest and most important sound" becomes very annoying. In addition, inappropriate use of the person's name can give offense. For example, many restaurants encourage their servers to use customers' names in an effort to develop a more warm and friendly environment. Accordingly, when the customer has given the server his credit card and the server returns with the card and bill for the customer to sign, the server may use the customer's name (which he now knows by having looked at the credit card) by saying, "Thanks, *John*, for coming in this evening." Some customers view this informal form of address as inappropriate, thinking "when did we become first-name-basis friends?" A more formal, "Thanks, *Mr. Baird*, for coming in . . ." would be far more appropriate to the customer/server relationship.

Leebov adds the concept of "respect" to building positive relationships.[20] She suggests that, even though we may naturally be attracted to people we perceive to be similar to ourselves, we must ***be sure to respect others' differences***. Since diversity in gender, cultural background, race, religion, nation or origin, age, life experience, and the like tends to separate people in organizations, we need to make a particular effort not just to tolerate differences, but to understand and gain from them. Again, careful listening and working to see things from others' viewpoints lies at the heart of this concept.

Moreover, we need to respect others' time and priorities. In today's workplace, virtually everyone is under pressure, with a large number of things that need to be done, soon. Respecting their need to concentrate, trying not to distract them needlessly or keep them from doing what they need to do is important to their own success and the organization's. If you initiate a conversation that starts as a short interruption but turns into something more lengthy, be sensitive to cues that your colleague is anxious to get back to work. By the same token, you may have some task that needs to be done *right now*, but demanding that a colleague drop everything she is doing to work on your task ignores the fact that she also has tasks that need to be done *right now*. Consideration and respect for the other person's time and priorities are cornerstones to positive relationships in organizations.

Hegarty claims that certain verbal behaviors prevent the development of good relationships in organizations.[21] One such behavior is complaining. While occasional complaining may bring people together for periodic gripe sessions, constant complaining becomes irritating to everyone—particularly one's superiors in the organization. An occasional complaint among friends may promote group cohesiveness; continual complaining, Hegarty argues, brings about social isolation. ***Avoidance of complaining*** and maintenance of a generally positive attitude will enhance your success on the attraction dimension.

Finally, both Hegarty and Leebov stress ***showing the right attitude***. This consists of such specific behaviors as speaking as if you like your work; taking a cooperative ("What can we do to solve this problem?") rather than an authoritative ("What are you going to do to solve this problem?") approach to problem

Highlighting Ethics

Desk Rage

Desk rage in the workplace is becoming increasingly common. Academics and industrial psychologists use a number of terms to describe the phenomenon:

- workplace incivility
- counterproductive behavior
- workplace aggression
- personality conflict
- workplace mistreatment
- interpersonal deviance
- bullying
- mobbing

"There are so many terms, I'm keeping a running list," said social psychologist Loraleigh Keashly, an associate professor of urban and labor studies at Wayne State University. Joel H. Neuman, director of the Center for Applied Management at the State University of New York at New Paltz, said research he has conducted during the past four years indicates that workplace aggression rises:

- when budgets are reduced;
- when workforces become more diverse;
- when management changes;
- when computers are used to monitor worker productivity;
- when pay cuts are planned;
- when companies hire more part-time workers and fewer full-time workers.

Some experts attribute the problem, on occasion, to interpersonal conflict. Behavior one person may perceive as cold or brusque, another may view as a no-nonsense, competent, or efficient manner.

Workers of different cultures or backgrounds may react very differently to the same behavior. Thus, as the workplace becomes more diverse, the potential for misunderstandings or unintended offenses may multiply.

Source: Kirstin Downey Grimsley, "Rudeness on Job Can Bruise Profits as well as Feelings," *The Sunday Times*, July 19,1998, H1.

solving; and treating others as equals by taking the attitude that your subordinates work *with* you, not *for* you. All of these things demonstrate your liking for others and increase the likelihood they will regard you positively in return.

Dominance

In an organization, the dominance dimension is determined both by organizational rank and by situational variables dictating who is in control at the moment. There are several methods for influencing others' behaviors. First is use of *simple force*—threats or physical actions—to gain compliance. Since this method tends to produce resistance, hostility, or resentment and is unjustifiable from most ethical perspectives, it is the least desirable influence method.

We can also *control rewards and punishments*. We know that people want to satisfy their needs. Thus, we can suggest to them that by doing what we recommend, they can satisfy needs presently unsatisfied, satisfy needs that now are only minimally satisfied, or continue satisfaction of needs now threatened. Conservationists employ the threatened-needs strategy, telling us, "Sure, everything is fine now. But watch out for the future. Unless we conserve fuel, land resources, and clean air, we will be in serious trouble soon." In other words, needs are satisfied now, but unless we make some change the satisfaction will stop in the near future.

Still another influence strategy involves *obligation*. In our society, there exists a norm of "reciprocity," which tells us that we ought to respond in kind to behaviors we receive. If someone rewards us, perhaps by doing us a favor, then we feel obligated to reward him or her in return. As communicators, we may use an obligation strategy by reminding others of benefits they have accrued or rewards they have experienced and suggest that they now have a chance to show their appreciation by, for example, making a financial pledge or voting for a particular issue.

Controlling the environment is yet another influence strategy. Instances of this sort of influence are rather common. Confronted by several rowdy students, a teacher may put them all in the front row of the classroom so that they may be more easily intimidated, or may scatter them throughout the classroom so that they are removed from one another's influence. Similarly, on perceiving a group of troublemakers, the production line supervisor may place them on different shifts or scatter them throughout the assembly line.

Some individuals point to the positions they hold as a strategy for getting others to comply. Thus, *legitimate power* lets an individual exert influence simply because the recipient believes that person has the right to do so. The father who answers his child's "Why?" with "Because I told you to" exerts power of this sort. He has only to tell his child what to do. His position as parent gives him the authority to exert influence without question. Similarly, an organization's hierarchy confers legitimate power to people of high status. They command and their positional power causes their subordinates to obey.

We can also exert influence through *reason*. If we can convince someone that our point of view is correct, then he or she will willingly accept our influence. In our view, this influence strategy is most desirable, producing compliance for the best possible reason—because it is believed to be right.

As we repeatedly have indicated throughout this text, managerial effectiveness in today's rapidly changing environment depends on influence, the ability to get things done through people over whom one has no formal control. Jane Carroll Jackson, vice president of the Forum Corporation, outlined the results and implications of research by her company on influence as a process and as a management tool.[22] Based on data obtained from 4,000 individuals, Jackson defined a three-part model of effective influence behavior.

1. *Building influence*. This involves a core practice of being supportive and helpful to others. In effect, you first must develop good personal relationships with other people (relationships with high degrees of attraction and involvement), and then you can exert influence without giving orders or relying on your positional authority.

Business Brief 6.2

Communicating for Success

John R. Graham, president of Graham Communications, suggests that if you want to be considered a "star" performer, you should never say the following things:

- "They didn't get back to me" or "They are getting back to me." Expecting someone to get back to you stops the action. Take the initiative.
- "I thought someone else was taking care of that." Excuses indicate a roadblock to action. Always ask questions to keep things moving.
- "No one ever told me." This statement suggests to others that you operate in a tunnel of your own, oblivious to everything that is going on around you. Go get the information you need.
- "I didn't have time" or "I was too busy." Neither of these statements suggests competence or effective time management skills.
- "I didn't think to ask about that." An inability to see down the road may indicate that you lack the ability to understand and grasp relationships.

The message in business today is clear. The only measure for success is performance. Whatever the roadblocks, it is your job to take the initiative to remove them. If not, you'll be perceived as one of them.

Source: "Never Say These Things," *Communication Briefings* 15 (1998): 1.

---

2. *Using influence.* Jackson claims that sharing power is the core practice that allows for trying new ideas and working through alternatives. While the manager remains the dominant person in the situation, she asks for input from subordinates and involves them in making the decision.

3. *Sustaining influence.* In this element, trust forms a basis for gaining consensus and demonstrating openness. Even when the decision has been made, the dominant individual remains open to suggestions and criticisms, and subordinates feel enough trust in their superior to speak their minds without fear of reprisal.

Involvement

The key to developing involved relationships with others is to have contact with them in the first place. Since physical proximity shapes who talks and forms relationships with whom, we can increase the number of relationships we form by increasing the contacts we have throughout the organization. However, for some people increasing the number of contacts they have is difficult. Bernardo J. Carducci, professor of psychology and director of the Shyness Research Institute at Indiana University Southeast in New Albany, claims that between 40 and 43 percent of adults believe they are shy.[23] Unfortunately, Carducci observes, this puts them at a significant disadvantage: "They get promoted later, they make less money. One of the best predictors of career success is verbal skills. If you are too shy to demonstrate those skills, it will hold you back. You move along—it just takes you longer." The inability or reluctance of shy people to have contact with and begin relationships with others thus is something that needs to be overcome.

Several communication skills can be helpful. One is to use *quick talk*. A common mistake a shy person makes when at a business gathering is to find someone with whom he or she is comfortable and latch onto that person for the duration. With "quick talk" you speak to a lot of people for a brief period of time. That lets other people know that you're the kind of person who's willing to talk to a variety of people, and it makes them more likely to seek you out in return. Carducci suggests that you develop a repertoire of small talk that you can draw from during these brief conversations, using such opening lines as, "What did/will you do this weekend?" and graceful conversation closers as, "Let's do lunch/coffee/drinks" or "I'll let you go," both of which serve to end the conversation but imply a positive relationship between the participants.

Volunteering for committees or projects also helps, as does *participating in recreational or social activities* the organization conducts. Such participation makes people more aware of your skills and is an effective demonstration that you are willing to go beyond the basic requirements of your job. In addition, *volunteering within your community* is another way to get involved and to make a contribution that goes beyond the boundaries of your job and organization. If you take along a buddy from work, you may discover mutual interests and values, which in turn may enhance your professional relationship and ability to work well together.

Practicing social niceties can give you a reason to talk with someone and help you to make a positive impression as you do so. For example, if you're going to get a cup of coffee, you might offer to get one for a colleague; if you're going to a supply closet, ask others if they need anything. This puts you in contact with these colleagues and shows that you are interested in their needs.

Also, *preparation* can be beneficial: if you find it hard to speak up during meetings, advance preparation can help. Before you go into a meeting, take a pad of paper and write down what points you want to make and read them to yourself. After that, rewrite them as succinctly as possible. When you get to the meeting, put the pad down in front of you and just say you have a point you'd like to make. Having it written down will help you explain it clearly, rather than rambling.

During conversations, a method for increasing involvement is *leveling with the other person*—communicating with him or her openly, candidly, and honestly. As Stagnaro reports, some organizations have adopted leveling as a corporate practice.[24] The ROLM Corporation has adopted communication norms designed to promote leveling. One is the use of tactful phrasing, such as, "You might consider this," "This might be helpful," or "We have a problem," to show employees the manager is on their side and is willing to listen to their viewpoint. Another is the use of the "I perceive" technique, in which managers report to employees how they are coming across to them: "This is how I see you," stated honestly and specifically. Such statements provide employees with important feedback on how others in the organization see them. Note, however, that leveling can have unpleasant results. Occasionally, people are unable to take criticism constructively, and conflict or hurt feelings can result. Before adopting leveling as a general practice, then, an organization and an individual must consider the risks involved.

Earlier, we noted that perceptions of motives or intent are extremely important. In organizations, one of the first things people ask about others is "what's she up to?" Misperceptions of motives can be extremely destructive; consider, for example, the African American vice president who perceived the disagreeing directors to be racists because they did not support her decisions. Therefore, "leveling" about why we do what we do is extremely important. In chapter 4, we suggested that supervisors deliver disciplinary action by telling their employees "I'm doing this because I want you to succeed." Thus, they help employees to understand how supervisors look out for their best interests, even though the supervisors are administering discipline. You should almost always use the same principle: tell a colleague at the very beginning why you are asking her to do something; explain to a superior why you disagree with a decision; describe to subordinates the reasons behind the actions you have decided they should take.

Highlighting Civic Engagement

Civic Participation Organizations

If you are not sure where to start volunteering within your community, you might begin by checking out some of these organizations whose mission is to encourage civic involvement:

- *American Civil Liberties Union*—nonprofit, nonpartisan, 275,000-member public interest group devoted exclusively to protecting basic civil liberties of all Americans and extending them to groups that have traditionally been denied them.

- *Commission on Presidential Debates*—nonprofit, nonpartisan corporation established in 1987 to ensure that debates are a permanent part of every general election. The CPD sponsored presidential debates in 1988, 1992, 1996, 2000, and 2004.

- *Communitarian Network*—a nonpartisan coalition of individuals and organizations who seek to support and enhance the moral, social, and political environment. Founded by distinguished sociologist Amitai Etzioni of George Washington University.

- *James MacGregor Burns Academy of Leadership*—an organization that fosters principled leadership through scholarship, education, and training, with special attention to advancing leadership of groups historically underrepresented in public life.

- *League of Women Voters*—nonprofit organization that promotes an open government system that is representative, accountable, and responsive; that assures opportunities for citizen participation in government decision making; and that preserves public health and safety through gun control measures.

- *National Association for the Advancement of Colored People (NAACP)*—the nation's oldest, largest, and strongest civil rights organization—founded in 1909. It's primary mission is to protect and enhance the civil rights of African Americans and other minorities.

- *National Issues Forum*—a nationwide network of educational and community groups that conduct deliberative discussions of national problems through local forums and issues reports on citizens' deliberations to elected officials and others in positions of authority.

- *Public Agenda Online*—nonpartisan, nonprofit organization founded in 1975 to help citizens understand critical policy issues, to enable them to make informed and thoughtful decisions, and to help leaders understand the public's point of view on major policy issues.

- *Stateline.org*—sponsored by the Pew Center of the States, this resource helps journalists, policy makers, and engaged citizens become better informed about innovative public policies, such as welfare reform, taxes and budgets, health care, and education.

Source: "CivicMind: Gateway to Civic Participation" [online]. Available at http://www.civicmind.com/orga.htm (accessed May 21, 2004).

Do not let people simply infer why you are doing what you are doing; often, those inferences will be wrong.

Rossiter and Pearce discuss at length the concept of *"honest" communication*, in which one person reveals his or her true and innermost feelings to another.[25] Culbert terms this strategy *self-disclosure*, which he defines as "an individual explicitly communicating to one or more others some personal information that he believes these others would be unlikely to acquire unless he himself discloses it"—that is, the disclosure of personal information, or of hidden secrets, to someone else.[26] According to Luft, people possess four types of information about themselves: things unknown to both themselves and others; things known to them but hidden from others; things known to both themselves and others; and things known to others to which they themselves are blind.[27] In self-disclosing, the individual reveals things once hidden, to self, to others, or to both.

It is important to note, however, that *in organizations self-disclosure is risky*. Since the information is personal, we make ourselves vulnerable to several undesirable consequences by presenting it to others. We risk rejection—a devastating experience. When we are presenting a front or playing some social role, we can always rationalize away rejections when they occur. For example, we might conclude: "They didn't really reject me, just my front." But if we present our true selves and are rejected, there is no place to which to retreat—our very essence has been deemed unacceptable. Fortunately, this sort of rejection occurs infrequently. People are usually accepting and understanding when we open ourselves up to them. Nevertheless, the risk of rejection is a real problem that we must consider when deciding whether or not to disclose our true feelings to someone else.

Self-disclosure also is risky because of the possibility that the information we disclose might be used against us. Chester Burger, a management consultant in New York, tells of a corporate vice president who disclosed his job anxieties to a colleague at lunch one day.[28] In so doing, he destroyed his image of invulnerability and self-confidence and encouraged the other man to try to take his job—as he soon did. This negative experience reinforces an important point: Self-disclosure must be based on trust to minimize the risk of having information you reveal used against you.

Another risky aspect of self-disclosure is that it may force us to confront our own weaknesses, thus discovering things about ourselves we may not like very much. Discovering that we are inadequate in some way is painful. Finding that we are not all we could have become is disappointing. Thus, self-disclosure poses the danger of revealing characteristics we might rather ignore. If self-disclosure is so risky, why should we try it? The answer is the second characteristic of *self-disclosure*: it *produces better, more involved, more satisfying relationships*. Studies have repeatedly shown that we need relationships based on self-disclosure if we are to be happy and fulfilled.[29] Despite its risks, then, self-disclosure is an important means for establishing more involved personal relationships with others.

Having seen the benefits of self-disclosure, our next concern is how it might be accomplished. In general, there are five rules to observe when we express our personal feelings to other people:

1. *Self-disclosure should be as immediate as possible*. We should report our feelings as they occur rather than waiting until some later time to discuss them.

2. *Self-disclosure should be voluntary and natural.* We should not reveal personal information because we feel forced to do so. Rather, revelation should naturally grow out of a relationship that has developed some degree of trust and supportiveness.

3. *Self-disclosure should be self-descriptive.* Good self-disclosure is purely descriptive, noting one's emotions and how they relate to the other person's behaviors. For example, we might describe our feelings by saying, "When you yell at me, I feel angry and resentful."

4. *Self-disclosure should strive to improve the relationship.* If the relationship is likely to be harmed in the long run, perhaps because our true feelings might make the other person feel defensive or hurt, then we probably should not disclose. If, on the other hand, we think disclosure will help the relationship, then it probably is appropriate. It is crucial here to make a distinction between immediate and long-range effects. It may be painful for the other person to discover that she has made us feel hurt or angry, but if, through our self-disclosure, she can grow to understand how that feeling resulted, perhaps a better relationship can evolve.

5. *Self-disclosure should be as specific as possible.* When reporting our feelings to someone else, we should try to avoid generalizations and speak as specifically as we can about how we feel and why. What incidents have made us feel upset? Are there patterns we can perceive? Why do we react as we do?

While self-disclosure is one useful method of increasing involvement, we still face the problem of encouraging disclosure by the other person. To do so, we must find some means of minimizing the risk that disclosure poses to the other person. One useful method of accomplishing this is through *supportiveness*. That is, we should listen to people in ways that create a climate of support and trust so that the other person feels secure enough to self-disclose to us.

Highlighting Diversity

Age and Self-Disclosure

A recent study revealed some noteworthy age differences among men concerning their willingness to self-disclose. When asked "How comfortable do you feel discussing your personal problems with others?" the response breakdowns were as follows:

- Ages 18–24: 62% comfortable, 39% uncomfortable
- Ages 25–34: 53% comfortable, 43% uncomfortable
- Ages 35–49: 50% comfortable, 47% uncomfortable
- Ages 50–64: 41% comfortable, 53% uncomfortable
- 65 and Over: 37% comfortable, 55% uncomfortable

Clearly, there are generational differences concerning comfort with and, thus, willingness to share personal information openly.

Source: Michele Orecklin, "Stress and the Superdad," *Time*, August 23, 2004, 39.

EFFECTIVE LISTENING

Stephen Covey, in his best-selling book *The Seven Habits of Highly Effective People*, suggests that one habit effective people develop is to "seek first to understand, then to be understood."[30] The cornerstone to understanding others is effective listening. In organizations, *listening is crucial for several reasons*. First, it *provides us with information*. To do an effective job at work, there are things we must know: what our job is, how it interacts with other jobs, what our superiors expect of us, and what is going on throughout the company. In business, this sort of information is rarely published. Usually, it is given to us orally, either in formal meetings or informal conversations or interviews. If we listen well, we will assimilate the information we need to succeed. If we do not, we probably will find ourselves in trouble. In addition, listening *allows us to think critically*. By comparing and analyzing what we hear, we can arrive at conclusions that are more likely to be correct. From these two benefits comes another: *good listening makes us better message senders*. If we correctly interpret what people say to us, we are more likely to respond to them in appropriate ways. To a significant extent, then, our success in organizations depends on our ability to listen well to the things others say to us.

Some communication contexts encourage us to listen effectively. When a speaker of higher status or one who possesses vital information speaks to us, we attempt to listen very carefully. The doctor who reports on the results of some sensitive medical tests is likely to encounter an attentive audience.

Remarkably, research also suggests that *we gain some physiological benefit* from listening to others. James J. Lynch directed a clinic for patients with high blood pressure at the University of Maryland School of Medicine and conducted blood pressure research by putting patients on 24-hour heart monitors.[31] Although his interest was not in communication behaviors, he found that patients' blood pressure rose when they talked and fell when they listened. Follow-up research confirmed these findings, as the researchers found that although blood pressure rises much more steeply when speakers are emotionally involved, it also rises during the most uneventful speech. The same effect was found to occur during signing by people who are hearing-impaired. Lynch ultimately was able to teach people with high blood pressure to moderate it just by changing their communication behavior.

Lynch and his researchers found, however, that the beneficial effects of listening—not only a lower blood pressure, but also a slower pulse and improved chemical regulation of body processes at every level—occurred only during *real* listening. If patients were rehearsing in their minds what they were going to say next, or sitting on the edge of their chairs eagerly awaiting their turn to speak,

---

Business Brief 6.3

Listening Exercises

Once you learn how to listen to others, you'll get better feedback, communicate better, and solve more problems. Here are some exercises that will improve your listening skills and help you get the most out of each meeting with a colleague:

- *Clean off your desk.* If there are loose papers on your desk, you'll unconsciously start to fiddle with them—and may even start to glance over them. Clear your desk for every conversation with a colleague so you can focus your attention on what he or she is saying.

- *What is the color of the person's eyes?* Train yourself to notice eye color at the start of every conversation. It ensures that you'll make significant eye contact—which leads to more productive conversations. However, don't focus so much on eye color that you don't listen to what is being said.

- *Train yourself to ask questions rather than make statements.* Don't say, "Joan, don't forget that the Anderson report needs to be in by Monday morning." Rather, ask, "How is the Anderson report coming along, Joan? Any problems with making the deadline?" By asking questions you'll start a dialogue and you never know what you might learn.

- *Learn to "lubricate" conversations.* Phrases such as, "Yes, I see" and "I understand" do two things: (1) they show that you're listening and encourage the other person to keep talking; and (2) they keep your attention focused.

- *Don't blurt out questions as soon as the other person is finished speaking.* It looks as if you were formulating your reply rather than listening. Before you ask a question, paraphrase the person's words. For example, "So what you're saying is . . ." Then ask your question: "Well, let me ask you this. . . ." This cuts down on miscommunications.

- *Don't smile the whole time.* Some people do this because they think it sends a friendly message. It can, but people also often mistake it for mental absence or a sign that you're not taking them seriously. Save smiles for humorous remarks.

Source: "Train Yourself in the Art of Listening," *Positive Leadership* (July 1998): 10.

the benefits did not happen. Only when they gave the speaker their full attention did the physiological benefits come about. Elgin thus concludes:

> Listening, therefore, is not only crucial to effective communication, it is a major component in personal stress management—right up there with meditation and biofeedback and massage and many expensive trendy processes. Listening is not something you should consider because it constitutes being nice. Listening is in your own self-interest. Listening is good for your physical and your emotional health, and is actively and directly therapeutic.[32]

Research shows that the average person on the job spends 40 percent of his or her time listening, 35 percent talking, 16 percent reading, and 9 percent writing.[33] However, research also shows that, on average, people only are about 35 percent efficient as listeners. This lack of effective listening often results in missed opportunities to avoid misunderstandings, conflict, poor decision making, or a crisis because a problem wasn't identified in time.

Madelyn Burley-Allen contends that listening can be divided into three levels, which are characterized by certain behaviors that affect listening efficiency.

- *"Level 1" listening is the most effective.* When listening at that level, we look for areas of interest in the speaker's message and for new information that might be useful; we are aware of our personal biases and try to avoid making unthinking judgments about the speaker or being influenced by emotionally-charged words; we suspend judgment and empathize with the other person's feelings; we notice

---

Business Brief 6.4

Guidelines for Empathic Listening

To use level 1 rather than level 2 or level 3 listening, you should do the following:

- *Be attentive.* Through your nonverbal behaviors, such as eye contact, an open, relaxed posture, a friendly facial expression, and a pleasant tone of voice, you can appear alert, attentive, and relaxed, thereby helping the other person to feel important and more secure.

- *Be interested in the speaker's needs.* Level 1 listening means you listen with understanding and mutual respect.

- *Listen from a caring attitude.* Assume a nonjudgmental, noncriticizing manner that helps the speaker feel free to bounce ideas and feelings off of you. Don't ask a lot of questions right away since this can make the person feel like he or she is being "grilled."

- *Act like a mirror.* Reflect back what you think the other person is feeling. Summarize what the person said to make sure you understand.

- *Don't let the other person "hook you."* Try to stay relatively objective; getting personally involved in the speaker's problem may cause you to become angry or to jump to conclusions prematurely.

- *Use vocal and verbal cues.* Acknowledge the person's statement using brief expressions such as, "hmm," "uh-huh," "I see," "right," or "interesting." Encourage the speaker to reveal more by saying, "tell me about that," "I'd like to hear what you're thinking," or "I'd be interested in what you have to say."

Following these guidelines will help you be a successful "level 1" listener.

Source: Madelyn Burley-Allen, "Listen Up," *HR Magazine* (November 2001): 115–120.

nonverbal cues; since we think faster than most people talk, we use that time to mentally summarize what they have said and think about what they have said.

- **"Level 2" listening is less effective, as we listen to the words that are spoken but miss much of the true meaning the speaker conveys.** By paying attention only to the words, we fail to get messages that are expressed nonverbally through tone of voice, body posture, gestures, facial expression, and eye movement—all of which add meaning to, or even change the meaning of, the words we hear. Consequently, level 2 listening can lead to misunderstanding, incorrect actions, loss of time, and a variety of negative feelings. In addition, since listeners appear to be listening by nodding their heads in agreement and not asking clarifying questions, the speaker may be lulled into a false sense of having been listened to and understood.

- **"Level 3" listening is the worst and occurs when we tune out the speaker,** daydream, think about what we're going to say next as soon as the person stops talking, or fake attention while thinking about unrelated matters. This kind of listening damages relationships, creates conflicts, and disrupts decision making.

Barriers to Effective Listening

Unfortunately, there are **several barriers to listening** that affect all of us and make level 1 listening a challenge. Many years ago, Campbell identified several sources of systematic error that seem to inhibit listeners' understanding, including:[34]

- *Length of the message.* Listeners tend to shorten, simplify, and eliminate detail from the messages they receive, thus losing information and accuracy. The longer the message, the greater the loss.

- *Middle of the message.* Dispute continues among communication scholars over whether listeners best remember the first or the last things they hear. But everyone agrees on one thing: listeners tend to forget the middle of the message.

- *Rounding off the message.* Listeners tend to tailor messages to suit their own needs or beliefs, thus distorting the messages' actual content. For instance, an eager employee proposes some bright idea to his boss, who responds with, "That's an interesting idea. Let me give it some thought." Because of his need to feel that the boss responded with affirmation and enthusiasm, the employee may round off her message and "hear" that the boss has endorsed the idea.

- *Expectations.* In some situations, we are confident we know what the source is going to say. As a result, no matter what that person says, we hear what we expect.

- *False agreement.* When confronted with a source we respect or admire, we often modify her message so that it more closely coincides with our own attitudes and beliefs. Knowing that someone with high credibility possesses views that differ significantly from our own can produce tension. One way of avoiding this tension is to simply "hear" a higher level of agreement than actually exists.

- *Dichotomous listening.* We have a tendency to polarize the world, to create dichotomies in which things are either one way or the other—right or wrong, good or bad, beautiful or ugly. Most speakers express ideas falling somewhere between these extremes, but we are inclined to assign those ideas to one category or the other.

Other factors can lead to what Goffman called "alienation" in communicative interactions. Each interferes with effective listening:[35]

- *External preoccupation*. Whenever we give our attention to something or someone other than the person speaking to us, we are allowing external preoccupation to become a problem. Preoccupations can take many forms—suddenly becoming aware of how long someone is talking (and perhaps glancing at our watches), thinking about a dreaded meeting we have to attend later in the day, or becoming aware of how cold it is in the room.

- *Self-consciousness*. Occasionally, we become overly focused on ourselves—perhaps preoccupied with our appearance, our grammar, or how we are coming across. For instance, in a job interview, we may become so preoccupied with the sort of impression we are making that we have to ask the interviewer to repeat a question. We simply did not hear it.

- *Interaction consciousness*. At times, we may become too preoccupied with the progress of the interaction, neglecting the messages and concentrating only on keeping talk going. Hosts and hostesses suffer from this type of alienation. They don't care what people say, as long as they say something.

- *Other consciousness*. Another source of distraction may be the person speaking. We can become so involved with the speaker emotionally that we are unable to deal objectively with what he or she is saying. Or the speaker's physical appearance may be distracting. In either case, we become too preoccupied with the speaker to really listen to what is being communicated.

Still more potential barriers to listening are suggested by other writers:[36]

- *Wasting thought power*. We listen and absorb ideas at a rate much faster than people talk. On average, most of us can talk at a rate of 125 words per minute, while we can think at 400 to 500 words per minute. Unfortunately, this difference in thought and word speed is responsible for many mental tangents; that is, instead of concentrating on what the speaker is saying, our minds wander off onto other things.

- *Listening only for specific facts or details*. Too often we concentrate only on details or facts and lose sight of the overall message and feelings of the other person. Effective listening occurs only when the big picture is kept in mind; you have to maintain a focus on the overall structure and purpose of the conversation.

DILBERT

DILBERT © by Scott Adams; reprinted by permission of United Feature Syndicate, Inc.

- *Throw-in-the-towel listening*. When the going gets tough or when it becomes clear that the other person simply is not offering a supportive response to what we said, some of us simply give up and mentally check out. Instead, we should listen even more intently, trying to discover from the other person's words things we can use to further the conversation.

- *Faking attention*. Many listeners become skilled at pretending to pay attention. They mutter "uh-huh" while the speaker speaks, they sit with glazed eyes and fixed smiles during conversations, and they generally ignore everything going on around them. In effect, they just go through the motions of listening and do not really communicate.

- *Tolerating or creating distractions*. Poor listeners are easily distracted by other things, or they may even create distractions themselves. For example, the sales representative who attempts to listen while flipping through product information sheets provides a distraction for the customer and, in so doing, probably discourages further communication.

Strategies for Improving Listening

To overcome these many barriers and achieve the level 1 listening we described above, there are several techniques that are useful. One is called the **HEAR formula**. "HEAR" is an acronym formed by the first letter of the four words you should remember when trying to listen to someone: Helpful, Empathic, Attentive, and Responsive.

- To be *helpful* when you listen to someone, you should make it easy for that person to talk with you. One way to do this is to minimize the waiting time and maximize the meeting time for that person. In other words, when someone comes to talk with you, you should not keep that person waiting while you do something else. This communicates to the person that you have more important things to do and that listening to her is not among your priorities. Instead, you should try to convey the impression that you have all the time in the world—that nothing could be more important than that meeting with that person. This means avoiding glances at your watch or the clock on the wall, not fidgeting, and not giving the impression that you need to get this meeting over as quickly as possible. Even if you are pressed for time, you must always try to convey to the other person the feeling that the time you do have is all his.

  Helpfulness also is improved by making the environment as attractive and informal as possible, because attractive and informal settings encourage interaction. You should eliminate potential distractions (take the phone off the hook or move to a private location), and when the meeting is over, you should thank the person for talking with you and invite her to meet with you again some time soon. All of these things help people to talk with you—an important element of being an effective listener.

- To be *empathic* you need to show the other person that you truly understand how he feels and that you care about those feelings. This is very different from sympathy, in which you simply feel sorry for the other person. Most people want empathy; they may resent sympathy. To improve the empathy dimension, you first should ask about the person's well-being—show you care about him as a person, regardless of the topic in question. Then, while the person is talking to you, you should occasionally use "active listening" techniques, such as paraphrasing the things he has just said or reflecting back to the person the feelings he seems to be experiencing.

- *Attentiveness* means demonstrating to the other person that you are indeed listening to her point of view. To improve the attention you show, first suspend your reactions; do not react until you have heard everything the other person has to say. To the greatest extent possible, withhold judgment and emotions; when you react, do so as logically and calmly as possible. When you disagree, show you understand the other's points before you begin to present your own. Paraphrase or summarize the person's ideas and let her know that you did, indeed, understand what was being said. Then present your ideas. Finally, you might periodically summarize the points the other person has just covered ("Let me see. You said that Bill first went to . . . and that he then. . . . Is that right?"). You should always avoid distractions or directing your attention somewhere else when someone is talking to you.

- Finally, your listening should be *responsive* as you show that you are not only paying attention but you are actively interested in the person and the topic. Maintain eye contact by looking at people most of the time they are talking to you. Use nonverbal reinforcement (such as nodding your head occasionally and sitting up straight, leaning slightly toward the speaker) to show responsiveness, or use vocal prompts such as "uh-huh," "um-hmm," and "OK." When appropriate, ask questions to display your interest and to get useful information. Avoid giving advice unless you are explicitly asked to do so. And above all, let the other person do the talking.

A key to improving your listening efforts is using some of the techniques of active listening.[37] *Active listening* consists of responding, verbally and nonverbally, to the person who is talking to you. These responses should encourage the

---

Business Brief 6.5

Effective Listening: The HEAR Formula

To be Helpful:	Minimize waiting time.
	Act unhurried.
	Make the environment attractive.
	Eliminate potential distractions.
	Invite future interactions.
To be Empathic:	Show that the other's feelings are understood.
	Show that the other person is cared about.
	Use active listening techniques.
To be Attentive:	Suspend your reactions.
	Show understanding before disagreeing.
	Paraphrase and summarize.
To be Responsive:	Maintain eye contact.
	Use nonverbal reinforcement.
	Ask questions.
	Let the other person talk.

other person to tell you more, show that you understand the person's words, and indicate that you empathize with her feelings. When you listen actively, you may respond to the content of the other person's words, to your perception of her feelings, or to important nonverbal cues.

As a listener, when you respond to something the speaker has said (that is, to the message content), one goal you may have is to **demonstrate your attention and understanding**. You might do this by **paraphrasing**, where you state in your own words what you think the speaker has just said; by **prodding**, where you give short vocal and nonverbal cues that signal you are listening and encourage the speaker to continue talking; or by **accepting**, where you state your approval or acceptance of the speaker's expressed views.

Another way of responding to the speaker's remarks is to **request further input**. You might do this by **encouraging**, that is, requesting that the speaker give you more information about what happened, what caused a particular problem ("Could you give me a little more background on what happened right before George became department head?"); by **delegating**, where you place responsibility for solutions or ideas back on the speaker, thus involving that individual in the solution ("What ideas do you have that I might pass along?" or "How do you think we might solve that problem?"); by **reconstructing**, where you ask the person to recall or imagine the events that led to the topic you are discussing ("How was that decision originally made?"); or by **reversing**, where you ask for an opposite point of view ("You've discussed a number of problems with the new word processing software. Have you found any advantages to it?").

Yet another goal you may have as you listen actively to a speaker's verbal messages is to **cause him or her to think critically**. You might, for instance, try **testing**, where you ask the speaker to consider the possible results of a problem, solution, or proposed course of action ("How do you think our regular customers would react if we switched to a cheaper vendor?"); or you might try **confronting**, where you challenge the validity of what has been said ("You say that we are charging too much for those microcomputers, but sales have never been better!"). These techniques, of course, will be effective only if they are used with sensitivity and tact.

A final goal you may have in responding to a speaker's ideas and suggestions is to **demonstrate interest and offer help or guidance**. You might do this by **offering**, where you suggest possible alternatives or solutions to a problem; or by **elaborating**, where you build on what the speaker has just said, communicating understanding, involvement, and approval ("You're right about the importance of the company getting involved with community service projects. I like the ones you've mentioned, especially the blood drive. We might also consider working with the group that's trying to solve the PCB problem.").

Perhaps more difficult than responding to the speaker's expressed view is responding to your perceptions of his or her feelings. To do this, you observe reactions that seem to indicate that emotions are present and then tell the speaker what you have noticed and what you tentatively interpret your observations to mean.

As a general rule, **you should respond only to fairly obvious feelings**. Your goal is not to "psych out" the speaker, but to grow to understand that person's emotions and build a better relationship with her. By being responsive to another's feelings, you not only show concern for the individual but promote rational discussion by minimizing emotional problems that can get in the way. Therefore, when strong emotions seem evident, you might ask such questions as, "I get the feeling you are really upset about something. Would you like to talk about it?"; "You seem really sad today. Is anything wrong?"; or "You sound pretty depressed. What has got you down?" By taking the time to encourage the speaker to share her feelings, you show your concern and begin to build a better understanding, which should lead, ultimately, to improved communication.

Finally, as an active listener, you may need to *respond to the speaker's nonverbal cues*. In some instances, these cues will reinforce the verbal message. On other occasions, they will contradict what is being said. Often, the nonverbal cues will give you insight into the speaker's true feelings. In chapter 5 we discussed nonverbal behavior in considerable detail, but a few examples of the kinds of nonverbal cues that you might see while listening may be useful here. For instance, a frown in response to a comment you make may indicate confusion or disagreement; folded arms and sitting back after a comment may suggest anger or withdrawal; rapid hand movements or shifting on the chair may indicate anxiety or nervousness; a smirk on the face may denote an attitude of superiority or disgust; and a variety of other facial expressions may reveal confusion, anger, distrust, or resistance.

Whenever you observe a speaker's nonverbal behavior that seems unclear, or appears to contradict what is being said, you might ask about it with such questions as, "I know you said yes, but you look kind of puzzled. Are there some questions you still have on your mind?" When you make observations about a speaker's nonverbal cues, make your evaluations as tentative as possible. Nonverbal cues can be ambiguous. They may reveal underlying feelings that the

---

Business Brief 6.6

Avoiding Malpractice Suits through Communication

Doctors have more control over malpractice suits than they think: A good bedside manner may mean the difference between being repeatedly hauled into court and never getting sued in the first place. In a University of Chicago study, researchers audiotaped routine office visits with patients of 124 family practitioners and surgeons in Oregon and Colorado. They found that doctors who had never been sued tended to laugh and joke more with their patients, to have longer office visits, and to tell their patients what to expect—when the exam would take place, when tests would occur, and so on. They were also good listeners and encouraged patients to talk.

The researchers concluded that handling patients in this fashion is effective because doctors who carefully explain what will happen during the visit make the patient feel less awkward. In addition, they may be less likely to sue a doctor with whom they enjoy two-way communication, thus creating an atmosphere where the patient feels engaged and involved.

A good way for doctors to sharpen communication techniques, the researchers offered, might be to tape office visits and listen to them afterward—or even team up with a colleague to critique one another.

Source: Sue Ellen White, "Best Defense Is No Offense," *Hospitals & Health Networks* 71, no. 11 (November 5, 1997): 70.

speaker is unaware of or not yet ready to acknowledge or discuss. But if you can approach the subject tactfully and patiently, you may be able to help the speaker become aware of how he is coming across to others and help clarify his own reactions. But let the speaker do the interpretation.

Taken together, the ability to ask good questions and the skill and willingness to listen actively will do much to help you become an effective listener in a wide variety of communication contexts.

WORKING WITH DIFFICULT PEOPLE

Forming good relationships with others in organizations is something you can control, but only to a point. Relationships take two people, and as charming and delightful as we may be, sometimes the other person is just a jerk. Thus, we find ourselves having to devise strategies, not for building positive relationships with others, but for simply coping with them. In this final section, we will consider some of the more problematic personality types found in today's organizations.

Types of Problem People

When we participate in organizations, from time to time we have experiences with difficult people. Sometimes they are bosses; other times they are coworkers or subordinates. They surface in all kinds of organizational settings—businesses, hospitals, volunteer organizations, law firms, and even classrooms. While most colleagues will be pleasant, professional, and cooperative (at least most of the time), the "bad apples" in organizations can make life tough.

THE BRICK WALL

As Josefowitz notes, in many organizations there are people who are unreachable, stubborn, and impossible to convince and with whom it is difficult to maintain a conversation.[38] As the saying goes, talking to these people is "like talking to a brick wall." These people "switch to automatic and become immune to input from the outside"; they are "unwilling or unable to see the possibility of another way of looking at an issue." They demonstrate their unreachability through lack of eye contact, fidgeting or rigid body posture, apparent interest in other activities or frequent interruptions, yawning, looking at their watches repeatedly, giving "yes, but . . ." responses, or not responding to the topic under discussion. In effect, they are the level 3 listeners we described earlier. Josefowitz suggests three strategies for getting through to the unreachable person.

1. The direct approach confronts nonresponsiveness directly, saying such things as, "It upsets me when you don't pay attention to me" or "I don't feel you hear me, and I don't know what else to do." Usually, this will alert the person to her own behavior (and to the speaker's awareness of that behavior), and it will cause the unreachable person to let his or her defenses down, at least for the moment.

2. The preventive approach can be taken at the beginning of a conversation. The speaker might say, "I know you have had trouble listening to me in the past, but would you please try to hear a different point of view?" Again, the person's behavioral pattern may be broken.

3. *The therapeutic approach* encourages the person to examine both her own behavior and the reactions it produces. The speaker might say, "You seem to have difficulty focusing on the discussion and often retreat behind a wall. This really frustrates me because I feel I can't reach you. What can we do to solve this problem?"

THE TIME BOMB

Some colleagues have a hard time controlling their tempers. Often they are embarrassed by their bad tempers and, after blowing up for about five minutes, apologize profusely. A few, however, use their explosiveness as a device for intimidation: if they blow up every now and then, they think people will be afraid of them and they will get their way.

The way to deal with an explosive colleague often is to *allow the blow up but try to make it as private as possible*. Suggest that the person vent in his office. This may not be well-received by the colleague, however, since he may want an audience. If your skin is thick, offer to listen to the colleague; if not, tell the person that you're sorry, but you'd prefer that he not let off steam in your presence. This won't always work, but at least you'll have said what you need to if, when it happens again, you leave the room.

Moving to a private setting may not be possible if the person blows up in a group meeting. In such a situation, you may have no option but to listen to the person rant for a while. *Try to maintain objectivity*—for example, you might pretend that you're watching a play and are not involved directly. This can be difficult, especially if you're the object of the rant, but it helps you avoid becoming emotional as well. You may also want to take notes about the things said during the rant, just in case you need support if you go to the person's supervisor to complain about his or her actions, or if you decide to file a more formal complaint accusing him or her of abusive behavior.

THE BACKSTABBER

Office gossip is unavoidable and, for the most part, not particularly harmful. People naturally are interested in other people; in an organization where people socialize, gossip about others is not only inevitable, it's an enjoyable part of the social environment that causes people to want to be together. Trying to avoid gossip entirely is probably a bad idea; you do not want to be perceived by everyone else as aloof and standoffish. On the other hand, you don't want to be labeled a gossip, either. So, although you can be receptive to it, it's not in your best interest to spread negative or potentially damaging information about other people.

The rumor monger takes gossip to the extreme: he lives on gossip and uses it to "stab others in the back," presumably advancing his own career (or at least improving his self-esteem) by undermining theirs. He is potential trouble because he can easily pull others into his circle of character-assassination, turning them into gossip-mongering backstabbers as well, and he can make you the target of his verbal daggers.

There are two ways to deal with backstabbers. First, *avoid* them—don't become part (or become perceived by others to be part) of their vicious social circle. Eventually, their actions will catch up to them; remember, "time wounds all heels." Second, if you learn that your back has recently been stabbed, *confront* him. You're under no obligation to confront him if the gossip is about someone else, although you may wish to come to the defense of a friend or a colleague. But if it's about you or yours, confront the backstabber politely and publicly—politely, because you do not wish to embarrass him, and publicly, because you want to ensure that others hear him recant.

Remember, backstabbers are not particularly courageous people. Otherwise, they would be frontstabbers. Confronting them publicly forces them to be accountable for the things they say and most will back down.

THE GLORY GRABBER

The glory grabber tries to take credit that is due others. Many managers, for example, present reports to upper-level executives by saying, "here's what I have done" rather than acknowledging the efforts and contributions of their subordinates. The best leaders share credit, or even make a point of telling others "they did this, not me." Fortunately, savvy executives know who really did the work, and they tend to take a dim view of managers who try to hog all the credit but hold in high esteem managers who insist on giving the glory to their employees.

Dealing with a glory grabber can be tricky, particularly if the grabber is your boss. Still, the key is to ensure that you get the credit you deserve. *Providing regular updates of your progress* to a relatively wide audience is effective, unless your boss insists you update only him. Brief e-mails sent to people throughout the organization who might be interested in or affected by your project appears considerate and can be an effective form of personal advertising. Catching someone "on the fly," such as in a hallway or in the cafeteria, and providing a very brief update can have the same effect, particularly if that person is higher in the organization than your boss. And certainly, you want to be sure that your boss is kept apprised of your activities so that he has a chance to brag about your efforts to others in the organization, should he choose to do so.

THE BULLY

Bullies try to threaten you into doing things you don't really need or want to do. For example, one vice president of an East Coast hospital was famous for her Friday afternoon phone calls to directors who had displeased her during the week. Using their voice mail, she would demand that they have a detailed report on her desk first thing the following Monday morning. Often, these poor individuals would work all weekend to produce the demanded report only to walk into her office on Monday morning, say "Here's the report you wanted," and have her answer, "What report?"

The only way to deal with a bully is to *stand up to the person on the first occasion and to continue standing up to him thereafter*. However, maintaining a *pleasant, nonconfrontational attitude* is key. When someone tells you on Thursday to get those reports ready by the end of the day Friday or you're toast—and you know that the reports really aren't needed for another week—reply that you can't do that because rushing such an important project means you won't meet your own standards for providing high-quality work. Then couple that politely phrased refusal with an offer to start working on the reports first thing next Monday and to have them completed by, say, Wednesday.

The bottom line is, *do not allow yourself to be flustered* by bullies. They rely on your discomfort to get their way. Always be ready with a calm and polite response that offers some compromise between what they want and what you're willing to do. Still, if you have the misfortune to work for an unrelenting bully, look for another job; things will not get better.

THE MANIPULATOR

Manipulators try to use people the same way chess players use pawns, rooks, knights, and bishops: to them, everyone is just a board piece to be moved in whatever ways serve the manipulator's interests. Manipulators lie, tell half-truths, conceal information, and tell you only what they think is useful to reveal. They try to create conflicts between their colleagues, and they try to trick people into doing things they don't really want or need to do.

Trying to out-trick or out-manipulate a manipulator usually is wasted effort; most are very good at manipulation, or they would have been found out and fired long ago. In addition, communicating directly with a manipulator often is a waste of time, or possibly even dangerous; anything you say can and will be used against you. Rather, the best defense against manipulation is to **communicate thoroughly with others**. Think of the way crafty children try to manipulate their parents, telling Mom "Dad said it was OK" while telling Dad "Mom said I could." Through good communication and teamwork, parents avoid being manipulated. Similarly, through good communication colleagues can avoid being pitted against each other or misled about each other.

Also, view with suspicion and respond with caution to any comment or request manipulators make. **Refuse their offers of help;** everything they do for you will come with strings attached, as they will expect you to do things for them in return. If a manipulator tries to tell you to do something because it's required by policy, check the policy first; don't just take her word for it. Without trust, an organization cannot exist; however, some people within organizations simply are not trustworthy.

THE MALCONTENT

These are people who, when you say "Good morning," will answer "Just what the heck do you mean by that?" For them, the glass is always half empty (or worse), everyone is out to get them, and life generally stinks. Some malcontents can be extremely entertaining—particularly if their gripes are expressed creatively—and they may attract a crowd at break time. Generally, they are harmless, although you do not want to be identified as one.

Happily, most **malcontents are not a threat** and do not require that you do anything other than continue to be your usual charming and delightful self. They can be as unhappy and paranoid as they wish. If they transition into bullying, backstabbing, or manipulation, action may be required. But generally, malcontents are best ignored.

THE POWER JUNKIE

The power-hungry colleague wants power, and nothing else. Usually, this person is smart, calculating, and tenacious and will throw you under a bus if that's what it takes to get what he wants. You're either a stepping stone to be trod on, an obstacle to be crawled over, or a potential power source to be cultivated—until you, too, become a stepping stone.

Generally, the best strategy is to **stay far, far away from power junkies**. Most of them self-destruct anyway; their obvious self-centeredness ultimately will alienate the wrong person, and they will free-fall out of the organization or find themselves pigeonholed in some innocuous position—where they probably will transition into festering malcontents.

Of course, you can't always stay away. Some people have a power junkie as their boss; some have no choice but to work with one. These are among the most difficult relationships you'll encounter. If the power junkie is your boss, just know that there will be no participative leadership; he will have all the power, all the time. If you find this unacceptable, you should look for another job.

If you can't avoid working with a power junkie, you will have a struggle. You will not want to give in to this person's every demand and always do what he wants, but fighting the power junkie at every turn probably will be a losing battle. Sometimes the best you can do is to protect yourself politely; use the assertiveness techniques we discussed in chapter 4 to stand up for your rights and try to enlist help and support from others.

THE ENERGY VAMPIRE

Some colleagues will suck you dry. They'll sit back and let you do all the work but criticize what you've done when you're finished. They'll interrupt you with mindless gossip when you're trying to finish a project quickly. They'll bring rumors to you that they know you'll find upsetting, and then they'll enjoy watching you become hurt or angry. In short, they'll cause you to expend emotional, intellectual, and physical energy in ways that are not productive, and they'll gain enjoyment and be energized themselves by watching you do so.

Time spent with energy vampires is best kept to a minimum. To deal with these coworkers, you need to **develop polite ways of disengaging yourself** from them, in effect avoiding the involvement that usually is a key part of positive relationships in organizations. Statements like, "Bob, I'd really love to stop and chat with you, but now's not a good time; I'm up to my ears in this project right now" send a pretty clear message that you don't want to talk. If Bob persists, something more concise might be required: "Bob, I said, not now. Later." Eventually, you may have to tell Bob to go away. Certainly, you want to avoid allowing him to hand his work off to you: "Bob, I'd really love to help you with your project, but I've got one of my own. Good luck."

Self-Control

Ultimately, there are hundreds of things that happen each day that could annoy you. One person could pass you in the hallway and fail to say "hello," thereby making you feel snubbed. Another could fail to give you the credit you deserve for your efforts, making you feel unappreciated. Still another could put his shoes up on your desk, making you feel disrespected. And someone else could interrupt you as you are talking during a meeting, making you feel ignored and shoved into the background. You could be annoyed by the person who drums her fingers on her desk, the person who slurps her soup during lunch, the person who talks loudly on the phone, and the person who snorts when he laughs. Surrounded by all of this, what can you do?

Ultimately, **you can control all of these things**. You feel snubbed, unappreciated, disrespected, ignored, or annoyed only if you allow yourself to feel that way. And these feelings become problematic only if you act on them by lashing out against the offenders or behaving in ways they perceive to be hostile. Others *will* irritate you. Deal with it. Remember what Marcus Aurelius, an emperor of Rome, said every morning: "Today, I will be surrounded by people who irritate me. I will not demonstrate my irritation." When someone does something that really annoys you, try one or more of the following:

- Look away and count to ten . . . and repeat as often as necessary until you calm down.
- Excuse yourself from the situation to get a drink of water.
- Imagine that you're in your favorite place, doing what you enjoy most.
- Remind yourself that, in just a few hours or minutes, you'll be on your way home.
- Return to your desk or office, sit quietly for a few minutes, and plan your revenge. Don't do it—just plan it.
- If you're in a situation where there is no escape and you have to respond to an incredibly annoying comment, be polite but assertive.

When none of these things work, remember one last principle: **do no harm.** Whatever you do in response, do not make the situation worse. You do harm when you take an already bad situation and make it worse by your own actions. Here, being civil can be far more effective than any evil reprisal you might dream up. If you've developed a habit of replying in a polite, dignified, calm manner, always taking other people's concerns into consideration, you will be viewed with respect throughout the organization and, as a result, develop relationships that have the levels of attraction, dominance, and involvement you want, need, and deserve.

SUMMARY

Our purpose in this chapter has been to consider a fundamental element of the organization's social system: human relationships. So much about human relationships is influenced by the way we perceive and respond to each other. We began, then, by examining the nature of our perceptual processes—looking at how we select, sort, and interpret the surroundings and individuals that we encounter—as well as acknowledging problems commonly associated with perception (such as stereotyping) and strategies for improving the accuracy with which we perceive.

In examining the nature of human relationships, we concluded that they consist of four basic dimensions: attraction, dominance, involvement, and the situations in which persons interact. Among the factors that influence these dimensions are physical proximity and status (attraction), communication skill and expertise (dominance), the depth and breadth of interaction (involvement), and tasks and purposes (situation). We can develop communication practices that allow us to deal effectively with each of these dimensions and their interrelationships. For example, self-disclosure, although potentially risky in organizational settings, remains an important means for establishing more involved personal relationships with others. Fundamental to our effective communication skills is learning to listen to others so that we both learn from them and are perceived as good listeners. Although many barriers to effective listening exist in organizational settings, listening can be improved if we strive to be helpful, empathic, attentive, and responsive as we attempt to listen—thus, practicing basic principles of active listening.

We concluded the chapter by examining the challenge of working with difficult people—ranging from brick walls to energy vampires. While we offered tips for dealing with each type of problem behavior, we concluded by advocating self-control and offered some insights concerning how to maintain a sense of calm, dignity, and civil behavior—all of which will go far in helping you gain and maintain positive relationships with those and for whom you work.

Questions for Discussion

1. If, as many futurists project, more people begin to work at home using computers, what effect will it have on organizational relationships?

2. Describe some important factors influencing perception in organizational settings. In your view, which are the most important? Why?

3. What aspects of an organization with which you are very familiar serve to shape the dominance dimension of human relationships? Be specific.

4. What are some factors that influence the sorts of people you are attracted to as coworkers? What factors stand in the way?

5. Describe some specific ways that relationships can be improved in organizational settings. Offer concrete suggestions.

6. What are some ways (verbal and nonverbal) in which we can be Helpful as listeners? How can we be Attentive? Empathetic? Responsive?

7. What are some of the dangers associated with open, honest communication? In light of these, how do you view the risks associated with self-disclosure?

8. After examining the list of types of "difficult people" in organizational settings, to what extent do you think the strategy of self-control will work with each of them?

Exercises

1. Select an organization with which you are very familiar. Describe how the attraction factor is shaped within that organization; that is, how do proximity, attractiveness, and so on play a role in interpersonal attraction and relationships building there?

2. Choose an organization you know well. How does that organization's physical environment show status differences? How does it control who talks to whom?

3. Think of someone who has some control over your life. Then think of one example of each kind of influence (force, rewards, punishments, and so on) that person uses.

4. Suggest principles related to the dominance dimension of human relationships that you might use to be a better supervisor. How would you use them, generally, if you were supervising the work of five others in the fast-food industry?

5. Make a list of the greatest listening challenges you have faced when others have been talking to you in a professional setting. Now make a list of the ways you will attempt to improve your listening in the future.

6. Think of people you have found annoying over the years. List specifically the things they said or did that you found annoying. Knowing what you know now, what might you have done differently to deal with each of them?

7. Read the following story: A North American took a trip to Japan and was working with a Japanese airline clerk on taking a flight from one city to another. When the passenger asked the clerk about the flight options, she replied, "Perhaps you would prefer to take a train." The North American responded directly with, "No, I want to fly." The clerk replied with, "There are many other ways to go." Again, the passenger clarified his position by saying, "Yes, but I think it would be *best* to fly," to which the clerk said, "It would be very difficult." Eventually, it was revealed that there were no flights between the two cities.

   a. How would you characterize the communication behavior of the passenger and the clerk?

   b. How might cultural differences help explain the way each communicated?

   c. What are some strategies for improving their interpersonal communication?

Case Application 6.1   "Buildings Without Walls"

In parts of corporate America, private offices are becoming as scarce as typewriters and cubicles are shrinking as companies increasingly rethink the traditional workspace. Gone are floor-to-ceiling walls, windows for executives, and even elevators. Now workers—including CEOs—ride escalators to "neighborhoods" of small workspaces and meet in "teamwork" rooms and even kitchens. The changes are aimed at dragging old offices into a new world of work—where rank has few privileges, teamwork rules, and privacy is a rare commodity. Yet taking down the walls is both liberating and painful. Communication between coworkers rises, but so do distractions. To limit distractions, companies ban speakerphones except in meeting rooms, pipe in special white noise, and issue "protocols" on keeping voices low in public spaces. The savings can be significant: Xerox expects to save $10 million annually by going to smaller individual workspaces, where some managers now sit in small glass-walled windowless offices (often half the size of their old domains) and other managers work in brightly colored cubicles surrounded by their staff. Meetings occur in "teaming" rooms or kitchen-like "commons areas," and phone booths are available for personal calls.

In Pittsburgh, Alcoa will abolish all private offices—even for its chief executive officer—in its new $60 million headquarters building.

Source: Maggie Jackson, "Thinking Outside the Box," *Chicago Tribune*, June 14, 1998, sec. 6, 1.

Questions

1. What effect do you think this approach to improving organizational communication would have on each dimension of interpersonal relationships?

2. Would you want to work in an organization having this philosophy? Why, or why not?

People care deeply about their titles. "Your self-concept depends on what you do and what you're called, and even if you simply change the title it affects your ego. It affects your personality," said Patrick Lennahan, director of the Career Center at Roger Williams University in Bristol, Rhode Island. Many people would rather have a prestigious title than money, probably because a title boosts job satisfaction, he found. Much of the reason is how coworkers react to the person with the higher title. People defer more readily to a vice president—no matter how incompetent—than a manager, and so on down the line. "How long somebody will wait for you, whether you can be put on hold on the telephone or not—those are things that people aren't always thinking about but something people do without thinking," Lennahan said.

"Some progressive companies experiment with new 'organic' structures and have shed the title system as a holdover from the 'hierarchical' days," says Frank Shipper, professor of management at Salisbury State University in Maryland. One such company is Newark, Delaware-based W. L. Gore and Associates, makers of Gore-Tex fiber for active wear, which calls its top two executives president and secretary-treasurer. The other 5,000 or so employees all answer to "associate," a title meant to make them feel like members, not just replaceable employees. The founder, William Gore, believed that titles get in the way of communication. Shipper says, "If people need to talk to somebody, they should talk to them as people with expertise rather than people with a certain title." In the future, corporations will not organize permanent departments but temporary task forces, he predicted. According to Shipper, "The title you have today is obsolete tomorrow, just like your product is."

Source: Claudia Coates, "Take My Desk, My Raise, Not My Title," *The Sunday Times*, July 19, 1998, H1.

Questions

1. How do you feel about this effort to eliminate traditional corporate "labels"?

2. What effect would this approach have on the dimensions of interpersonal relationships?

7

Managing Conflict

After reading this chapter, you should be able to:

❑ Explain the concept of "conflict"

❑ List ways in which conflict can benefit or damage an organization

❑ Explain how various organizational philosophies might view the desirability and management of conflict

❑ Describe how study circles can be used to manage conflict productively in community settings

❑ List the major settings in which conflict occurs

❑ Identify at least five common causes of conflict

❑ List and explain behaviors that escalate and deescalate conflict

❑ Describe five styles of conflict management

❑ Discuss techniques involved in collaborative conflict management

❑ Explain the concepts of "arbitration" and "mediation"

❑ Illustrate how technology may be used to resolve conflicts

❑ Describe how labor-management conflict is changing in philosophy and practice

Someone once observed that "life is just one damned thing after another." In most organizations, those "damned things" are conflicts of various sorts, for all too often corporate life seems to be one conflict after another. Indeed, organizational conflict perhaps is inevitable. Throughout this text, we stress the interdependence of organizational members and the continuing need for them to behave cooperatively. Yet this interdependence, this continuing necessity for interaction among people, makes conflict unavoidable. As Bernard points out, stress and conflict will occur in organizations because they are "inherent in the conception of free will in a changing environment."[1]

Berelson and Steiner define social conflict as "the pursuit of incompatible, or at least seemingly incompatible, goals, such that gains to one side come about at the expense of the other."[2] Herbert provides another view of conflict, defining it as occurring "whenever the attainment of a goal is hindered."[3] While these definitions disagree in some minor respects, both imply that conflict involves the simultaneous presence of two or more incompatible elements.

As we shall soon see, conflict is not in and of itself bad. Indeed, in many situations some conflict is necessary for the organization to function at maximum efficiency. The key is how conflict is managed and how the energy conflict generates is channeled. If some conflicts remain unsolved or if they are managed poorly, the organization as a whole will suffer.

Preview

In this chapter, we turn our attention to identifying, analyzing, and managing conflict. Communication to manage conflict comprises a complex set of strategies involving both informative and persuasive elements. In an effort to understand these strategies, we will consider the role of conflict in organizational and community contexts, noting attitudes toward conflict and the settings, causes, and consequences of organizational disputes. We will examine different styles of conflict management, as well as how technology may assist with conflict management and resolution. We will then examine several methods by which organizational conflict may be managed. In so doing, we hope to develop communication strategies by which conflict may be managed for the benefit of everyone involved.

THE ROLE OF CONFLICT IN ORGANIZATIONS AND COMMUNITIES

As we saw in chapter 3, a great number of changes have occurred in the thinking of organizational theorists during the past century—thinking that has important implications for communication within organizations. Some of that thinking concerns the nature and role of conflict. Historically, conflict has been viewed as negative, something to be avoided or downplayed, or, at the other extreme, as inevitable and possibly even beneficial.

Philosophies Regarding Conflict

Philosophers taking the Classical or Theory X view of people would see conflict as an undesirable thing, particularly since the desires of employees (avoiding work at all costs) conflict with the objectives of the organization. In addition, conflict would suggest disagreement to those taking an autocratic view of management, and since management's wishes should be followed at all times in such organizations, conflict should be avoided or stamped out.

Other schools of thought concerning organizations would advocate avoiding conflict for a very different reason. Someone adopting a high-relationship, low-achievement style, for example, would feel that the key to organizational functioning is the maintenance of satisfactory social relationships. Since conflict seems to indicate a breakdown in human relationships, such philosophers would feel the success of their organization rests on management's ability to prevent conflicts from ever occurring. Managers adhering to such philosophies thus spend considerable time and energy making sure everyone is happy and no one is arguing. Workers in such organizations spend an equal amount of time and energy hiding conflicts from their managers lest they be reprimanded for engaging in antisocial behavior. As a consequence, conflicts are swept under the rug, not managed, so that while they disappear temporarily, they often reappear some time later, bigger and more difficult to handle than before. By stressing conflict avoidance, high-relationship managers, like very autocratic managers, do not succeed in truly avoiding conflict. Rather, they create frustrations and conflicts that are far greater than the original problem.

More recent views of organizational conflict happily have been somewhat more realistic. Evan typifies these views in his characterization of attitudes about conflicts:[4]

- Conflicts always occur because of disagreement about expectations or organizational goals.

- Conflicts can be good or bad for both the organization and the individual.

- Conflicts legitimately can be validly minimized in some types of organizations, such as those geared toward crises (the armed forces) or those that perform routine tasks (many manufacturers), but in other types of organizations (those stressing knowledge or technology) conflict should actually be encouraged.

Thus, theorists and practitioners in organizational development all have arrived at the realization that conflict in organizations not only is inevitable but may be beneficial. Some advantages conflict can provide include:

- Clarifying thought and generating better solutions

- Improving group cohesiveness and performance

- Clarifying dimensions of organizational relationships—particularly power

- Defusing more serious conflict

In fact, some organizational leaders take the view that creating conflict *can* be a useful strategy for achieving organizational change. Many managers constantly are fighting inertia. If no tensions are felt, the status quo is likely to continue. That's why some leaders create conflict: to demonstrate, for example, how organizational values are not reflected in employee behavior, how advertising is false or misleading, or that supervisors have standards for their employees that are different from the standards they have for themselves. The tension generated by conflict typically leads to some attempts to reduce or eliminate the tension level—and that means that the conflict must be confronted. With effective leadership, it will be confronted and managed in an appropriate way. But to manage conflict effectively, one must know something about the settings, causes, and consequences of conflict. We turn now to these matters.

Business Brief 7.1

Conflict Management as a Tool for Diversity Training

Some believe that the best sort of diversity training emphasizes conflict management. For example, diversity training at Harvard Pilgrim Health Care includes a heavy dose of real-life case studies. Participants are presented with quandaries like this one: A patient, an elderly white man, comes into a health center for a blood test. When a black clinician appears to give the test, the patient balks. Does the office manager bow to the patient's wishes or politely assert the company's right to say only the black employee will draw the blood?

Source: Kenneth Labich, "Making Diversity Pay," *Fortune* 134, no. 5 (September 9, 1996): 177–180.

Conflict Settings

Whenever resources are limited and individuals must compete for them, the potential for conflict emerges. As a result, conflict may involve individuals, groups, communities, or entire organizations.

CONFLICT WITHIN INDIVIDUALS

Two conflict forms, frustration and goal conflict, occur commonly within individuals in organizations. *Frustration* is the simpler of the two, occurring when one's ability to attain a goal is hampered by the imposition of some barrier. For example, we may have a strong desire to perform in a superior fashion, yet because of some limitation (limited ability, inadequate education, or a supervisor who does not like us) our performance evaluations consistently are "average." We then might try somehow to improve matters, perhaps by working harder, taking evening courses at a local college, or trying to obtain a transfer to another department. If these measures fail, frustration results and less productive behaviors are likely to follow.

More complex than frustration is a second sort of conflict within individuals, *goal conflict*, where the attainment of one goal excludes the possibility of attaining another. Three principal types of goal conflict can be identified.

- *Approach-approach conflict.* The individual is caught between trying to decide on one or another of two attractive goals that are mutually exclusive. The college graduate with excellent job offers from Johnson & Johnson and Eli Lilly and Company confronts this kind of goal conflict.

- *Approach-avoidance conflict.* The individual has both positive and negative feelings about trying to attain a goal because the goal possesses both attractive and unattractive characteristics. A job offering, an excellent salary, and advancement potential in a company that may not exist in the future (and, worse yet, is located in Boringtown, U.S.A.) poses these kinds of mixed advantages and disadvantages.

- *Avoidance-avoidance conflict.* The individual must choose between two mutually exclusive goals, both of which are unattractive. The college graduate who receives job offers from companies located in Butte, Montana, and College Station, Texas, two of his least preferred locations, encounters conflict of this sort.

CONFLICT BETWEEN INDIVIDUALS

Conflict between organizational members also takes two forms: *individual versus individual* and *individual versus group*. Examples of the first are infinite: two managers competing for the same promotion, two women vying for a tennis championship, two executives advocating a particular solution to a problem they face. Although competition may even be enjoyable to the participants (such as players in a tennis match), uncontrolled conflict of this sort is often destructive to the organization.

On occasion, conflict also occurs between an individual and a group. As we will discuss later in the book, some groups demand absolute conformity by their members, so that a "rugged individualist" who happens to join that group might find him- or herself in conflict with other members. Or an individual who is particularly eager to promote his or her own interests may do so by breaking group

NON SEQUITUR

THE IRRESISTIBLE FORCE MEETS THE IMMOVABLE OBJECT

THE FACTS AS THEY ARE

THE TRUTH AS I SEE IT

WILEY 5-16

NON SEQUITUR © 1997 Wiley Miller. Dist. by UNIVERSAL PRESS SYNDICATE. Reprinted with permission. All rights reserved.

norms. Work groups, for example, typically have informal but rigidly enforced production limits such that anyone outproducing the other group members is labeled a "rate buster" and pressured to conform. Although under some circumstances those who depart from group norms may create constructive conflict and cause the group to think carefully and thoroughly, on other occasions sustained conflict between the individual and the group will lead to painful consequences, especially for the individual.

Conflict situations within groups are commonly classified as either *distributive* or *integrative*. A distributive situation is one in which a person can only win at someone else's expense, such as in a poker game. In an integrative situation, however, group members integrate their resources toward a common task or goal, such as developing a joint grant proposal. The distributive approach is associated with many problems, including the development of a "we-they" orientation, inflated self-evaluations accompanied by a diminished regard for the contributions of others, and perceptual distortions leading to a false sense of having responded adequately to each other's concerns. By contrast, integrative conflict can reap many group benefits that include genuine exploration of individual differences in opinions and values and identification of common ground where mutual goals can be achieved.

CONFLICT BETWEEN GROUPS

Much of our organizational and community life is spent in groups: work groups, decision-making groups, social groups. Often these groups come into conflict with one another. Two particular types of intergroup conflict deserve mention. *Functional conflicts* occur when business functions are divided up into departments that often have entirely different perspectives of organizational processes. Manufacturing divisions tend to have short-term perspectives and seek to maximize their own goals of long production runs and standardized products to meet unit cost goals. Marketing divisions tend to have long-term perspectives, to evaluate products and services from the perspective of the consumer, and to endeavor to customize and provide many options to suit each customer individually. Conflicts between these groups are common and managers must seek means for their resolution.

Line and staff conflicts represent a second type of intergroup conflict, as staff groups are responsible for measuring, monitoring, analyzing, and projecting the

Highlighting Diversity

Free Speech

For nearly 150 years, Speakers Corner in London's Hyde Park has attracted diverse orators eager to practice free speech in peace. Speakers have included tourists and locals; Jews, Christians, and Muslims; Marxists, environmentalists, and self-proclaimed Jedi knights. But the atmosphere turned violent in the summer of 2004 as Speakers Corner became a ground for fierce religious debate. Jay Smith, a 50-year-old Christian missionary from Pennsylvania who has lived in London for 12 years, was physically assaulted after making derogatory speeches about Islam.

In response, Smith decided to go on the attack—although not physically. He holds a weekly workshop for Evangelical Christians, whom he trains to heckle Muslim speakers. He urges them to quote controversial Qur'anic passages—for example, one that allegedly endorses wife beating—in order to "create a paradigm shift" in the way Muslims think about their own culture. While Smith admits that a small minority are to blame for the violence he experienced, his crusade may actually worsen the tensions. "They just attack, attack, attack," said 65-year-old Abu Yassin, a Speakers Corner regular. "They come here with an agenda, so many times we just ignore them."

Source: Sarah Sennott, "Free Speech: Cornered Speakers," *Newsweek*, August 30, 2004, 9.

---

work and results of the organization, while line groups are concerned only with the actual execution of the work. Line may see staff as being impractical, overeducated, inexperienced, or abstract; while staff may view line as dull, narrow, inflexible, or unimaginative. Perceptual incongruities such as these are virtually guaranteed to produce conflict between line and staff groups.

CONFLICT BETWEEN ORGANIZATIONS

While individuals and groups within organizations often are embroiled in conflicts, the organizations themselves usually are involved in disputes as well. For example, consider some of the organizations with which an automobile manufacturer comes into contact. General Motors buys automotive parts from Borg-Warner. Although these two corporations are acting cooperatively to build automobiles, they are also in conflict: Borg-Warner wants to get the highest possible prices from General Motors for the parts it supplies, while General Motors wants to pay the lowest possible prices. Similarly, advertising agencies handling the General Motors account want to charge the highest possible prices, while General Motors wants to keep its advertising budget as low as possible. Executive recruiting firms are eager to charge high fees for finding new executives to staff General Motors, while GM wants to keep recruiting costs low. The United Auto Workers want as many union members as possible to be employed by General Motors (since those people must pay dues to the UAW), and they are eager to have their members well paid by General Motors. General Motors wants to keep its labor costs down. The federal government imposes regulations concerning safety and pollution that are supposed to reflect the public interest. General Motors tries to keep manufacturing costs minimal. The automobile-buying public wants quality cars at low prices, while General Motors wants to make a profit. In all of these instances, partial conflict (but also a partial sharing of goals) exists between each group. Yet, only by overcoming these conflicts can each group have its needs met to some degree.

Causes of Conflict

Implicit in our discussion of different settings for conflict is the notion that such conflict can be traced to diverse sources. In this section we will discuss some of the more common contributors to organizational conflict.

- *Competition for rewards or resources*. Every organization offers a limited number or amount of rewards to its members. Individuals compete for promotions, raises, and status symbols; departments compete for budget allocations; organizations compete for a larger share of the market; nonprofit organizations compete for the attention and assistance of volunteers and donors. These situations are called "win-lose" or "zero-sum." What one competitor wins, another loses, so that if the amount won and the amount lost are summed, they add to zero.

- *Interlevel incompatibilities*. The organization is composed of many levels of hierarchy. Some research suggests that as we move from one level of the hierarchy to the next, our perceptions of the organization tend to change. For instance, Likert discovered that top staff, supervisors, and line workers all felt that they understood other people's problems but were themselves misunderstood, and in fact he discovered that none of them shared congruent perceptions of what the others' problems were.[5] Labor unions for decades have operated under the assumption that what management wants (maximizing profits, in part by keeping employee pay and benefits to a minimum) is inherently in conflict with what employees want (maximizing their pay and benefits). Indeed, some believe that cooperation between union and company representatives is in conflict with the adversarial role unions should have with management.

- *Differences in values and goals*. Production and sales units often conflict in this way since sales is more geared toward rapid production for high volume and speedy delivery, while production prefers a slower pace that emphasizes quality. When "speed" as a value and "quality" as a value clash (as they often do when the sales division puts in a rush order or when production slows down), conflict is likely to result. Similarly, individuals may have incompatible personal goals that cause them to come into conflict.

- *Misinformation, misunderstandings, or communication breakdowns*. An important message may not be received; a supervisor's instructions may be misinterpreted; decision makers may arrive at different conclusions because they used different databases. Conflicts based on missing or incomplete information tend to be straightforward in that clarifying previous messages or obtaining additional information generally resolves the disputes. Since value systems are not being challenged, these conflicts tend to be easily addressed by dealing directly with the information deficiency.

- *Specialists versus generalists*. As jobs have become increasingly complex and science has made technology more intricate, the need for specialists to perform those jobs and use those technological innovations has become more and more pressing. Yet management functions typically require generalists to perform them. Most organizations are constructed so that a large number of specialists must be governed by a small number of generalists, which creates a host of potential conflicts. The generalist manager often knows less about the job than does the specialist worker, so that the worker may find it frustrating or nonproductive to communicate with his or her boss. The worker may "short-circuit" the organization's formal lines of communication, often to the dismay of the supervisor. Or there may be conflicting loyalties. Among professionals, loyalty to a discipline often conflicts with loyalty to the organization, as when a researcher feels himself a chemist first and a member of the organization second.

- **Role conflict.** Occasionally, the job behaviors (termed one's organizational "role") expected of an individual provide a source of conflict. Generally, these sorts of conflicts fall into three categories. First, **intrarole conflict** occurs when an individual occupying a single role is subjected to stress. Organizational supervisors often are subjected to contradictory expectations, as when management expects them to represent management interests during negotiations, while labor expects them to act as representatives of labor.

  Interrole conflict, on the other hand, occurs when someone is expected to simultaneously perform two different roles. Killian reports an instance of this sort of role conflict in his study of the disastrous Texas City fire.[6] When oil refineries caught fire and the blaze threatened the entire town, police were confronted with competing role demands: to play their "police" role by trying to protect the town's populace or to undertake their "father" role by looking after their own families. In every case except one (a policeman whose family was out of town), the policemen chose the role that was more important to them and tended to their families. They experienced role conflict and resolved it by selecting the role they judged most important. Finally, **interpersonal role conflict** occurs when two or more individuals have overlapping roles that cause them to do the same things in different ways at the same time. Parents disciplining a child in different ways are an example of this type of role conflict.

- **Status conflict.** An important element of any organization is status, or the ranking of roles in the organization according to importance. Organization members usually seek increases in status, which are achieved through promotions and accompanied by an increased number of status symbols: a bigger office, perhaps with a window; a larger desk; a personal parking space; or a key to the executive washroom. However, an item symbolizing status may be not only a source of motivation, but a source of conflict. In past years, new members of an organization have entered at the bottom of the hierarchy and "worked their way up the ladder." With the advent of new technologies and an increased emphasis on expertise and specialization, highly qualified and trained, young specialists now are superseding older organizational members, much to the latter's dismay. Working for someone who is younger and has less seniority produces a great deal of status conflict among older subordinates in modern organizations.

- **Personal incompatibilities.** Individuals may simply not like one another. Individual differences in background, education, socialization, age, and expectations can produce different needs, perceptions, and goals. As noted above, if those differences stem from differing attitudes and values, the resulting conflicts can be severe. In communication involving individuals who are personally incompatible, discussions can become highly emotional and take on a moral overtone.

Business Brief 7.2

The Importance of a Global Mindset

As companies "go global," the frequency and importance of cultural conflict are growing. According to Doug Ready, founder and CEO of the International Consortium for Executive Development Research (an alliance of 30 global companies and 20 leading business schools that swaps information and conducts research on doing business globally), a "global mindset" is the "capacity to appreciate the beliefs, values, behaviors, and business practices of individuals and organizations from a variety of regions and cultures." Many North Americans are not particularly good at this: according to the Centre for International Briefing, roughly 25% of North American managers fail overseas, which is three to four times higher than the failure rate experienced by managers from European and Asian companies. For example, at a business meeting in Tokyo, business cards were exchanged. The Japanese go through a very elaborate ritual when exchanging business cards, but the North American executive simply threw some of her business cards across the table at the stunned Japanese executives. One of them turned his back on her and walked out. Needless to say, no deal went through and the North American manager was called home.

Source: "Don't Be an Ugly-American Manager," *Fortune* 132, no. 8 (October 16, 1995): 225.

- *Environmental stress*. Things taking place around an individual, a group, or an organization can cause worry or stress among people, leading to increased conflict. Over the past few years, for instance, many large organizations have been downsizing, resulting in many people losing their jobs. In turn, this has caused many workers to worry about their own job security, even if no layoffs have occurred in their organizations. When people feel their jobs are threatened, and especially if there is much uncertainty about the rules by which the organization is operating, they will likely respond with frustration, hostility, and increased competitiveness. Memos threatening employees with termination if they fail to carry out management's orders contribute to this sort of environmental stress.

- *Disagreements*. Frequently, conflict is simply a matter of disagreement over any number of things, such as facts (What is right or wrong?), methods (What is the best way to do things?), goals (What are we trying to accomplish?), or values (What is the "right" thing to do?).

- *Cultural differences*. As workforces become more diverse, the likelihood of "culture clashes" increases. Differences in background, education, socialization, age, and expectations can produce different needs, perceptions, and goals. Employees from the United States, for example, may have a very different set of practices and expectations regarding giving and accepting gifts than employees in Japan; employees from some U.S. cultures (such as Native Americans) may have very different interpretations of eye contact than do the white Anglo-Saxon males running their organizations. These differences in expectations and practices can and often do produce misinterpretations that, in turn, may lead to open conflicts. If those differences stem from different values, the resulting conflicts can be severe. In communicative exchanges involving individuals who are personally incompatible as well, discussions can become highly emotional and take on moral overtones.

Finally, there are some *factors that contribute to the escalation of conflict*, making it more difficult to manage or resolve:

- *Righteousness*. Most conflicts begin simply as a disagreement. As conflict continues, one party might begin to feel he is completely, morally right while the other is entirely wrong. This may lead him to begin making personal attacks on the other's values or morality, moving the conflict from one that is over an issue to one that is more personal.

- *Not listening*. Communication is needed to arrive at a joint decision. When one party stops listening, the other is likely to become angry or frustrated, seeing that party as unreasonable and uninterested in arriving at a solution.

- *Threats*. When one party becomes frustrated with the other's refusal to agree, she may resort to threats in order to get compliance. This shifts attention away from the issue to a struggle over who has the most power to hurt whom.

- *Intentional hurt*. When one person feels sufficiently angry or hurt by the other's behavior, he may resort to insults, embarrassing examples, or other tactics in a deliberate effort to hurt that person's feelings. At this point, the relationship between the conflicting parties may become irreconcilable.

Highlighting Diversity

How Cultural Differences Can Lead to Conflict

Roger Axtell's work on cross-cultural differences in verbal and nonverbal communication points to several areas of potential conflict. In particular, he notes the "seven deadliest sins" of international misunderstanding: local color, jargon, slang, officialese, humor, vocabulary, and grammar. Some examples follow:

- When interacting with someone of another culture, avoid speaking too rapidly or too slowly. Fast talk is difficult to comprehend, while speaking too slowly can be viewed as condescending.

- Be cautious about using words and phrases that may be well understood within your corporation but may be misunderstood by outsiders.

- Anticipate differences in modes of greeting. Anglo-Americans tend to prefer a firm handshake and direct eye contact, those from the Middle East prefer a limp handshake, and Asians avoid direct eye contact during greetings.

- Arabs tend to use elaborate and ritualized forms of communication, especially during greetings. Wide gestures and animated faces may come across as boisterous, loud, and unprofessional to Americans.

- While the Japanese are very comfortable with silence, and may even close their eyes when they are deeply concentrating, Arabs perceive silence as a sign that something is wrong.

- The *way* we talk may also be remarkably different. In Latin American cultures, somewhat exaggerated variations in pitch convey that the speaker is actively engaged in what he or she is saying. By contrast, those from Asian cultures prefer to speak in monotones, which communicates self-control and respect for the other person.

Sources: Roger E. Axtell, *Do's and Taboos around the World: A Guide to International Behavior*, 3rd ed. (New York: Wiley & Sons, 1993); and Richard D. Lewis, *When Cultures Collide*, rev. ed. (London: Nicholas Brealey, 2000).

- *Violating social rules*. As hostility increases, concern for proper social behavior may decrease. "Scenes" may be created and other normally "unthinkable" actions initiated or tolerated. Physical assault may be the end result.

Certainly, escalators such as these are to be minimized or avoided when conflict situations occur—yet they occur in organizations every day.

Before examining some potential ways of managing conflict, we now turn our attention to conflict in community settings, together with some implications for the practice of democracy in public life.

Conflict in Communities

Conflict is a fundamental reality of public life. It is difficult to imagine living in a real community or a diverse society in which there are no differences of interests or opinion. In fact, the freedom to express our differences is fundamental to a democratic society. Through the ages, democratic ideals have revolved around finding participatory ways to live with, work through, and resolve our conflicting ideas and interests. Making conflict productive is an essential aspect of a democratic society.

Yet, conflict is also at the heart of what we often disdain about public life. Some say that conflict denigrates our public life to the point of exhaustion, exclusion, and indifference. It is the very thing that people name when they say they are turned off to "politics as usual." Yet, the problem is not conflict itself, but with how we handle it (or don't handle it). Historically, we have failed to create democratic arenas in which everyday people can engage in a productive exploration of differences and learn to work together.

There are a number of ways that conflict is typically managed and portrayed in U.S. political life. In almost all cases, the idea of conflict that is promoted is detrimental to a participatory public life. Conflicting ideas are not honestly expressed and examined in their complexity. Instead, conflict is often experienced as a rhetorical battle in which advocates of all stripes use confrontational rhetoric to define the parameters of an issue or win converts. As a result, ordinary people often feel sidelined. Feeling patronized, they may simply opt out of the conversation. In addition, they may come to expect all public conversation to be the verbal equivalent of war, or come to believe that those on the "other side" of an issue are misguided, stupid, or immoral.

Public conflict is often treated as a zero-sum game, in which a win for one side means an automatic loss for the other. Antagonism overshadows our willingness to search for common ground and decreases the potential for collaboration. We may also grow to underestimate the ability of the community and society as a whole to constructively solve public problems. The media, too, play a role—covering public concerns as arenas of intractable conflict and often reporting on extreme positions. The nuances and areas of ambivalence are frequently ignored in favor of what will make a good story.

Often in these situations there is little room or reason for citizen involvement. Instead of involving large numbers of people in addressing an issue of shared concern, a few people who have an exceptional zeal for the issue and are brave enough to enter into the public debate do battle for their side. Others may see the issue as important but may feel ambivalent about it and uncertain about how best to proceed. As a result, many are left out of the conversation about such critical public issues as education, poverty, jobs, youth issues, immigration, and much more.[7]

One avenue that holds great promise for managing public conflict productively is the *study circle*, a face-to-face participatory process for involving large numbers of people from all walks of life in addressing public issues. Many communities are organizing study circles to replace a negative conflict that discourages participation with a productive conflict that invites everyone to take part in the conversation and work for the good of their community. In these structured discussions, community members have the opportunity to better understand others' perspectives and concerns. They discover common ground and enhance their ability to work together as individuals, as members of small groups, and as voters and members of large organizations in the community.

Each study circle (of about eight to twelve people) meets several times and provides a safe, nonthreatening, structured environment where citizens can speak honestly about their concerns and views. Difference is treated as a normal, essential component of community life. Unbiased facilitation and nonpartisan discussion materials help to ensure that a wide range of views are aired. Disagreements are about *ideas* rather than personalized conflict. Instead of glossing over differences, participants have the chance to face them and consider reasons for disagreement.

Highlighting Civic Engagement

Study Circles in a Nutshell

What is a Study Circle?

- A voluntary small group of 8–12 participants who are guided by an impartial facilitator
- A group that considers many perspectives, rather than advocating for a particular point of view
- A group that uses ground rules to set the tone for a respectful, productive discussion
- A group that meets over multiple sessions and moves from personal experiences to examining diverse points of view to devising creative strategies for action
- A group in which members are often reminded that they *can* make a difference

What is a Community-wide Study Circle?

- It is organized by a strong cross-sector coalition and begins with a large public kickoff.
- It involves individuals and organizations from different sectors of the community, such as the chamber of commerce, the faith community, the media, local government, the United Way, youth groups, the police department, the YMCA, the local community mediation center, the Urban League, and neighborhood associations. Each brings unique tools, knowledge, and grassroots connections to the partnership.
- This is an inclusive program, designed to invite the whole community to get involved in public dialogue and problem solving. Many study circles meet at the same time across the community.
- It wraps up with an action forum, where the small groups come together to give participants a chance to talk about common concerns, get involved in community projects, and connect with community organizations and public officials.

Source: Catherine Flavin-McDonald and Martha L. McCoy, "What's So Bad about Conflict? Study Circles Move Public Discourse from Acrimony to Democracy Building" [online].
Available: http://www.studycircles.org/pages/artabout/conflict.html (accessed: July 20, 2004).

Because study circle participants meet over several sessions, they have the chance to build trust and relationships that help them see the world through someone else's eyes. Though study circle participants don't have to come to agreement, they do have the chance to seek common ground. They also have the opportunity to realize that solutions are as complex and multifaceted as is the issue and that there are abundant opportunities and resources for making a difference. By discovering a range of possible workable solutions, the community can begin to find ways to get beyond a win-lose orientation to public life.[8] See Highlighting Civic Engagement for more information about study circles.

Conflict in public life has provoked people to create better ways to work together on public issues. For their comprehensive study, *Bridging the Racial Divide: A Report on Interracial Dialogue in America*, DuBois and Hutson interviewed scores of people involved in interracial dialogue programs, many of whom participated in study circle programs. These researchers found that "fifty percent of interracial dialogues began in the past five years, prompted by alarm over racial polarization triggered by [such events as] the Rodney King police beatings and the O. J. Simpson murder trial."[9] Around the country, forward-looking community leaders are responding to divisive incidents by making grassroots dialogue and action a priority. See Highlighting Diversity for examples of how study circles have aided communities in addressing racial and other diversity issues.

Now that we have introduced some methods that have been used in community settings to address potential conflict, we return our focus to conflict in organizational and professional settings and some approaches to its management.

Highlighting Diversity

Study Circles Success Stories

- *Washington, DC*—a diverse working group has created the Multicultural Community Service Center that organizes study circles as a counterpart to their mediation program. The center operates in four neighborhoods. As an outgrowth of one of the organizations involved, the Center for Dispute Resolution (CDS), five study circles on violence are going on in Bell Multicultural High School.

- *Las Vegas, Nevada*—the Neighborhood Justice Center has joined the Anti-Defamation League, the NAACP, the county government, and a group of multicultural educators to organize a community-wide study circle program on racism and race relations.

- *Indianapolis, Indiana*—a project called "Family Circles" has given residents a way to get to know each other and work together to solve neighborhood problems. Since 2000, 780 people have participated in 92 family circles in 30 Indianapolis neighborhoods. Through partnerships with the Mexican Civic Association and St. Patrick's Catholic Church, for example, community centers recruited Latino participants. As a result, a neighborhood child-care center hired a Hispanic teacher's aide and the enrollment of Spanish-speaking children increased.

For additional illustrations of success stories, see Gloria F. Mengual, "Making Connections: 'Family Circles' Build Thriving Neighborhoods in Indianapolis, Indiana" [online]. Available: http://www.studycircles.org/pages/success/indthriving.php (accessed: July 20, 2004); Lori Crawford, "The Color of Understanding" [online]. Available: http://www.studycircles.org/pages/suc.html (accessed: August 6, 2004).

MANAGING CONFLICT

Conflict is helpful to organizations only if it is managed effectively and the energy it produces is channeled constructively. At the outset, it is clear that conflict management and resolution are more likely when:

- there is a "we-versus-problem" rather than a "we-they" attitude;
- there is a focus on all gaining rather than win-lose;
- there is an effort among conflicting parties to see others' viewpoints;
- there is an emphasis on goals, values, understanding motives, and building long-term relationships, not just on getting to a quick solution;
- there is open communication that promotes input and feedback;
- there are organizational rewards for cooperation rather than competition;
- there is an effort to achieve a solution that is both acceptable to everyone and of high quality.

Thus, resolving conflict often involves attempting to build on any of these conditions if they are already present, or to create them if they do not already exist.

Communicating to Resolve Conflict

Just as some conditions and behaviors serve to escalate conflict, so do other behaviors help to reduce conflict and make it manageable:

- *Listening and trying to understand.* Most conflicts are resolved, not when one side gives in, but when one or both sides begin to reexamine their positions in the light of new information. Trying to understand the other side shows a willingness to consider new information, an interest in cooperation, and an effort to establish an atmosphere of reason.

- *Concern for feelings.* When "sensitive" issues arise, they often can be defused by showing concern for the other's feelings and by being careful to avoid points or phrases that could aggravate him. Tact is important in resolving most conflicts.

- *Appeals to deescalate.* Many times escalation of conflict happens when people do not stop to think about the consequences of their actions. Sometimes this can be reversed by drawing attention to what is going on and pointing out the consequences: "This kind of talk isn't getting us anywhere and is just making us mad. Let's both calm down and get back to the real issues."

- *Goodwill gestures.* Trust and goodwill sometimes can be built by making symbolic gestures—perhaps as concessions or favors to one another. This is most likely to be effective when one person announces her intent to rebuild goodwill, encourages the other to reciprocate, and then responds positively to the other's goodwill gestures.

- *Airing feelings.* When hostility and hurt have become strong factors in a conflict, they probably will have to be aired before the conflict can deescalate. If the people experiencing these feelings have a chance to get them off their chest, the feelings will lose their intensity and both sides may be better able to focus on the real issues. In order for this to happen, however, the two sides must accept and listen to one another's feelings. If they ignore the feelings or respond defensively, the conflict will continue to escalate.

- *Finding alternatives.* Frequently conflict escalates because neither party can suggest alternative solutions. Without options, they feel boxed in and expend most of their energies on holding their positions. A constructive effort to generate alternative actions or solutions can build cooperation and lead to a position acceptable to everyone.

By initiating communication behaviors such as these, one side may be able to encourage the other to become cooperative, stop escalating the conflict, and move toward cooperation.

Kare Anderson offers a three-step procedure that she terms "triangle talk" as a means of handling conflict effectively. In her view, the tendencies most people have to either fight back or withdraw from conflicts can best be overcome by:

- *Knowing exactly what you want.* By asking yourself "What do I want in this situation?" you can gain greater control and focus.

- *Finding out what the other person wants and making him or her feel heard.* Knowing the other person's objectives provides a basis for negotiations.

- *Proposing action in a way the other person can accept.* This helps create the top of the triangle—the common ground between the two sides.

These three steps are best achieved by asking questions, Anderson contends. Vague, general questions should be used initially (such as "What do you think about this situation?"), but more specific questions should be used as negotiations continue ("Exactly what would make this proposal work better for you?").[10]

Finally, some specific communication skills seem useful in handling conflict among team members:

- *Ask those who disagree to paraphrase one another's comments.* This may help them learn whether they really understand each other.

- *Ask each member to list what the other side should do.* Exchange lists, select a compromise all are willing to accept, and test the compromise to see if it meshes with team goals.

- *Have the sides each write 10 questions for their opponents.* This will allow them to signal their major concerns about the other side's position. And the answers may lead to a compromise.

- *Convince team members they sometimes have to admit they're wrong.* Help them to save face by convincing them that changing a position may well show strength.[11]

All these communication techniques should be considered in situations where the management and resolution of conflict are needed.

Styles of Conflict Management

Researchers have discussed different conflict management styles since the mid-1960s. Among the first were Blake and Mouton, whose five-category conflict management grid was soon replicated and refined by others.[12] Blake and Mouton conceptualized conflict style as a characteristic mode or a habitual way that a person handles a dispute. Style can also be viewed as an orientation toward conflict or conflict tactics and strategies (either planned or enacted). The styles studied generally emanate from a five-category scheme based on concern for self (or task) and concern for others. The five conflict styles are depicted in figure 7.1.

The first conflict style is *avoiding*. Although aware of conflict at a cognitive level, the person using this style may withdraw by removing him- or herself (psychologically or physically) from the conflict situation, refraining from arguing, or simply failing to confront. If the conflict is over serious or complex issues, avoidance behaviors may contribute to frustration, deny others' feelings, and generally aggravate the problem. Moreover, at a practical level, in organizational settings where interdependent tasks are commonly addressed, long-term avoidance is probably not an achievable strategy.

At the other extreme of managing conflict is *forcing*. Those who employ this style rely on coercion rather than on persuasion or collaboration. They use assertiveness, verbal dominance, and perseverance. When all else fails, they resort to their position power or formal authority, ordering others to comply simply because they are in charge. Less direct, manipulative forms of forcing are also possible, however. For instance, a manager with a forcing style might manipulate the composition of a committee so that the solution the manager prefers emerges through a "democratic" process. Although forcing may be effective in some situations (where, for instance, quick action is required), when repeatedly used as a conflict style it tends to breed hostility and resentment.

The third conflict style is *accommodating*, an approach that glosses over differences, plays down disagreements, and generally trivializes conflict. In the ultimate sense, those who accommodate simply give in, setting aside their own concerns and surrendering to those of others. Those who smooth over conflicts

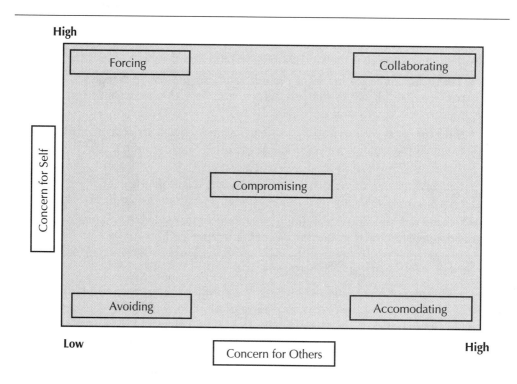

Figure 7.1   Conflict management styles

basically accommodate others, often with the goal of maintaining pleasant inter-personal relationships. Occasionally, accommodating is used strategically when someone sets aside his concerns on a particular issue with the hope that the next time there is conflict the other person will "owe him one." Whether or not this strategy is effective depends on whether the terms of the accommodation are understood, as well as the standards governing the other party's actions. Accom-modating is most appropriately used when the person who chooses to accommo-date truly perceives the issue as trivial.

As an evenhanded approach to conflict, the *compromising* style carries con-siderable appeal. Compromising involves searching for an intermediate position, splitting the difference, and meeting the opponent halfway. Thus, for both par-ties, partial satisfaction is achieved. Unlike the first three approaches, compro-mising appears fair and requires considerable effort and interaction (presumably involving both persuading and listening). The difficulty with compromising as a typical conflict style is that it is, above all, expedient. When used consistently, it sends the message that the individual is more interested in resolving the conflict than in actually finding an excellent solution to the problem. Moreover, no one is ever fully satisfied. While there are no real losers, neither are there any real win-ners. The feeling of accomplishment that can grow from working through a prob-lem to consensus is never realized through compromise.

Finally, the preferred conflict style in many organizational or community con-texts is *collaborating* or *problem solving*. This style calls on the disputants to face the conflict openly and directly and to seek, by working together, an integrative solution. Collaboration grows from a trust-building process. It encourages every-one to express themselves assertively while reinforcing the value of listening to others and approaching the problem constructively. Consistent with notions of supportive communication behaviors and attitudes discussed earlier in this book, the collaborative approach demands a focus on the problem and its thoughtful analysis rather than on placing blame. It works best in organizational environ-ments that foster openness, directness, and equality. With collaboration, the integrative approach to problem solving (as defined earlier) must prevail, wherein the "pie" is expanded by avoiding fixed, inflexible, incompatible posi-tions. For complex, important issues the collaborative approach is preferable, both in quality of the outcome achieved and in the feelings of empowerment that grow from people having successfully exercised their problem-solving skills in addressing a significant issue.

While the collaborative approach is consistently hailed as effective in man-aging conflict, it is not always the most appropriate conflict management style for every situation. For instance, collaboration is not appropriate when the con-flict is trivial and quick decisions are required. Avoidance may be quite effective for handling less important and highly volatile issues, and forcing may be appro-priate for crisis situations or for moving forward with unpopular courses of action. Problem solving or collaboration generally works well in situations where parties are interdependent, where supporting and implementing the solu-tion is required, and where the conflict stems from ambiguity or inadequate shared information.

The limited or inadequate use of the collaborative style in managing conflicts has resulted in considerable speculation. Some argue that problem solving is not

Some of the best decisions are made by groups who use the collaborative approach to managing their differences over matters of genuine importance—especially when they have the time for careful problem exploration. Collaboration encourages assertive opinion sharing paired with respectful listening.

taught by our society as a way of life. Instead, the emphasis is on obeying authority figures, such as teachers and parents. When children mature and eventually become authority figures, they may expect to be obeyed or to dominate others. This power-oriented view inhibits the individual's ability to choose problem solving or collaboration as a natural conflict management style. Moreover, in comparison with any other style, collaboration requires a greater degree of time, energy, and commitment. Thus, the combined problems—lack of skill in constructive confrontation and an unwillingness or inability to expend the necessary time, energy, or commitment—serve to diminish the extent to which collaboration is used in conflict situations.

Whatever the conflict style or strategy chosen, its effective implementation will depend on the disputants' ability to adapt to the situation, their fairness and objectivity in approaching the conflict, and the way in which they communicate. There are many different ways of forcing, for instance, ranging from soft, persistent argument to unpleasant, loudly projected references to one's power and authority. Others will react differently, depending on the specific verbal and nonverbal communicative behaviors that make up the overall conflict style. Moreover, timing is important. Executives report that early intervention is critically related to effective conflict management—the longer the delay, the more likely it is that the conflict will escalate, perhaps out of control.

Collaborative Conflict Management

Ideally, individuals, groups, and organizations are able to manage their own conflict through negotiation and bargaining rather than having to call in third parties. Effective outcomes are more likely to be realized when individuals voluntarily solve their own disputes than when leaders or other third parties are asked to intervene. Thus, developing an understanding of productive collaborative approaches to managing conflict is crucial.

All groups experience conflict at one time or another. In decision-making ventures aimed at building consensus, for example, actions taken or decisions made will clearly not meet with everyone's complete approval. Consensus is difficult to reach since most of us find it difficult on occasion to compromise our views. To help us make progress, we may choose to adopt external ground rules or guidelines to structure our group interactions with the goal of approaching our tasks more positively and productively. For instance, Hall and Watson's guidelines might be used to help minimize conflict.[13] These guidelines instruct group members to:

- Avoid arguing for your own evaluation. Approach the task on the basis of logic.

- Avoid changing your mind only to avoid conflict. Support only solutions with which you are somewhat able to agree.

- Treat differences of opinion as indicative of an incomplete sharing of relevant information.

- View differences of opinion as both natural and helpful rather than as a hindrance in decision making.

Where it is possible and desirable to approach conflict from a problem-solving perspective, several integrative negotiation strategies have been shown to foster collaboration. First, and perhaps most important, is *establishing superordinate goals*. The parties involved in the conflict should begin by focusing on what they share in common. As individuals become aware of the salience of their shared goals—for example, greater productivity, a safer community for everyone, lower costs, a fairer evaluation system, or improved working relationships—they tend to become sensitized to the merits of resolving their differences so that these mutual goals will not be jeopardized. When consensus on common goals is achieved, the disputants can begin to examine their specific differences. Once established, superordinate goals must be referred to throughout the deliberations. Some researchers have cautioned, however, that superordinate goals are more likely to reduce perceived rather than underlying conflict.[14] Whether or not superordinate goals are helpful depends on the group's ability to develop a culture for mutual understanding and constructive interaction patterns.[15]

Another important collaborative behavior involves *separating the people from the problem*. Having defined the mutual benefits to be gained by successfully resolving the conflict, attention must be directed to the real issue at hand—solving a problem. Negotiations are more likely to result in mutual satisfaction if the parties depersonalize the discussions. The participants might benefit from viewing each other as advocates for differing points of view rather than rivals. They may need to suppress their desire for personal revenge or one-upmanship. From a communicative perspective, a person would refer to "an unreasonable argu-

---

Business Brief 7.3

Negotiation Skills Move to the Fore

The importance of effective conflict resolution techniques is illustrated by the Harvard Business School's replacement of its traditional course in managerial economics with a course titled "Data, Decision, and Negotiation." A focus on negotiating skills stems from important changes in the workplace, according to Professor Robert Robinson:

- *The move away from permanent work groups.* Temporary work teams assembled for specific tasks cannot use traditional bureaucratic methods to resolve conflicts and must instead depend on effective communication and negotiations.

- *The increasingly global marketplace.* Negotiations across different cultures and legal systems require greater skill than ever.

- *The increasingly diverse workforce.* Employers now must take into account the often conflicting interests of the workforce when dealing with such issues as family and medical leave, granting same-sex spousal benefits, or establishing work schedules.

- *The changing nature of information technology.* E-mail, faxes, voice mail, and other electronic technologies all must be used effectively for handling conflicts and can muddy issues by creating information overload.

Source: From Marcie Schoor Hirsch, "New Ways to Negotiate," *Working Woman* (December 1993): 25–26.

---

ment" rather than calling his or her counterpart "an unreasonable person." In general, it is crucial to avoid loaded language, such as labeling others' ideas as stupid, crazy, naive, or "Nazi."

In situations involving conflict, *identifying and using criteria for determining the quality of alternative solutions* to a problem is crucial. No matter how many goals are shared, some interests are bound to be incompatible. Rather than seizing on these as opportunities for testing wills, determining what is fair is far more productive. This requires that both parties agree on how fairness should be judged. As objective criteria are discussed and agreed on, individuals begin to shift their thinking from "getting what I want" to "deciding what makes most sense"—fostering an attitude of reasonableness and open-mindedness.

Also related to the open-minded pursuit of solutions is *focusing on interests, not positions*. In bargaining and negotiation settings, positions are thought of as bottom-line demands the negotiator makes. By contrast, interests constitute the substructure of the evidence and reasoning underlying the demands. Establishing agreement on interests is easier because they tend to be broader and multifaceted. Achieving agreement, however, even on interests, involves a fair measure of creativity in redefining and broadening the problem to make it more tractable. For instance, once a problem has been defined, there are a variety of ways to enlarge, alter, or replace it. If a problem such as sagging productivity has been defined in a specific way (for example, worker laziness), other contributing causes exist and can be articulated. Thus, one way to proceed is by generating at least two alternative hypotheses for every problem discussed. The strategy is to broaden the problem definition by thinking in plural rather than singular terms. The questions should be phrased, "What are the problems?"; "What are the meanings of this?"; "What are the results?" Another possibility is to reverse the problem's definition by contradicting the currently accepted definition to expand the number of perspectives considered. For instance, a problem might be that morale is too high instead of too low or that a work environment is characterized by too little rather than too much structure. Opposites and backward looks often enhance creativity. When a variety of interests and problem definitions are examined, individuals are better able to understand each other's points of view and place their own views in perspective. The integrative question is "Can you help me understand why you are advocating that position?"

Another negotiation strategy requiring creativity is *inventing options for mutual gains*. Here, however, the creativity is focused on generating unusual solutions. While some negotiations may necessarily be distributive, negotiators should never begin by adopting a win-lose posture. By focusing both parties' attention on brainstorming alternatives toward mutually agreeable solutions, the negotiation dynamics naturally shift from competitive to collaborative. Moreover, the more options and combinations there are to explore, the greater the probability of reaching an integrative solution. Both goodwill and creativity are required as the parties ask, "What can we do that we haven't tried before?"

Several small group techniques discussed in later chapters might prove useful, both in defining interests and problems and in generating solutions. Brainstorming (where ideas are tossed out without evaluation) is one potential technique. In addition, the nominal group procedure might be used, in which each participant brainstorms on paper and then the ideas are collected, shared, and discussed. Finally, group support systems allow for computer-assisted brainstorming, encouraging creativity and preserving anonymity. Whatever approach to brainstorming is employed, those who participate in the process are basically asking, "Now that we better understand each other's underlying concerns and objectives, let's brainstorm ways of satisfying both our needs."

It is important to note, however, that during group meetings, conflicts may surface as ideas are generated, explored, consolidated, and evaluated—in other words, throughout the decision-making process. In an idea generation activity, for example, the brainstorming process can create polarization effects since each individual learns, perhaps for the first time, how other group members view the issue being discussed. In some cases, a particular group member may assume, before the meeting, that others support the same job candidate, course of action, or policy that she does. As views are expressed during a meeting, however, the group member may learn that she is wrong. When brainstorming is used to generate ideas, McGrath recommends that groups adopt techniques designed to:[16]

- Make sure that the creativity of each individual is not stifled by social influence processes that often operate in groups. Fear of social embarrassment, conformity pressures, and status systems that inhibit participation by low-status members should be actively discouraged.

- Take maximum advantage of whatever creativity-enhancing forces may operate in groups. Social support, reinforcement for contributing, and cross-stimulation of group members should be promoted.

Finally, the parties' approach to the notion of "success" is critical. Maintaining a realistic, optimistic attitude means that *success can be defined in terms of gains, not losses*. The employee who seeks a 12 percent raise and receives an 8 percent raise can choose to view that outcome as either an accomplishment (that is, a gain over the present situation) or as a disappointment (in that expectations were not realized). Whichever interpretation, the objective outcome is the same, but the employee's satisfaction is likely to vary significantly. Individual reactions to an outcome are greatly influenced by the standards used to judge it. Thus, the agreed-upon criteria are especially salient and should be called on to judge the value of the proposed solution or outcome. The question to be asked is, "Does this outcome constitute a meaningful improvement over current conditions?"

Perhaps the best summary of the collaborative approach to conflict resolution is provided by participants in the Harvard Negotiation Project, who suggested an alternative to traditional "positional" bargaining between labor and management they called "principled negotiation" or "negotiation on the merits."[17] This problem-solving approach can be summarized in four points:

1. *People*. Separate the people from the problem. The participants should see themselves as working side by side, attacking the problem rather than each other.

2. *Interests*. Focus on interests, not positions. Rather than focusing on people's stated positions, the object of a negotiation should be to satisfy their underlying interests.

3. *Options*. Generate a variety of possibilities before deciding what to do. Searching for one "right" solution inhibits creativity and narrows vision. A designated time should be set aside to develop a range of possible solutions that advance shared interests and creatively reconcile differing interests.

4. *Criteria*. Insist that the result be based on some objective standard. Developing a set of criteria whereby possible solutions might be judged (such as market value, expert opinion, custom, or law) ultimately will help to arrive at a fair solution.

Certainly, focus on these four factors would help to achieve conflict resolution collaboratively.

Third-Party Intervention

When the conflicting parties are unwilling or unable to arrive at a resolution to their situation, they may resort to calling in a neutral third party for assistance. In this way, they extend or elaborate on the negotiation process. The third party could be a supervisor (in conflicts between employees), an upper-level manager (in conflicts between two departments), the chief executive officer (in conflicts between divisions), a government-appointed mediator (in labor-management disputes), or a judge in a courtroom (in conflicts between organizations). Some companies establish a formal position for a person whose job it is to help resolve conflicts. Often this person is called the "employee ombudsperson."

A third-party intervener can play one of two roles: an *arbitrator* who, after hearing both sides of the issue, makes a decision that both parties must live by, or a *mediator*, who tries to facilitate communication between the parties so that they can work through their problems and arrive at a decision of their own. Although both arbitration and mediation rely on communication to manage information and exert social influence, mediation is a type of facilitation that hinges almost exclusively on communication for its success.[18]

The mediator's task requires sensitivity. Assisting with the logical, decision-making part of the conflict is only a small part of the mediator's role. Because conflicts have usually escalated before the mediator becomes involved, the mediator often finds that the parties are no longer particularly logical. Thus, the mediator will have to deal with a number of nonrational postures shaped by hurt feelings, a preoccupation with settling old scores, defensiveness, and distorted perceptions. Mediators, however, also have an advantage in this task. Because they are not as emotionally involved as are the disputants, they are usually much better able to maintain a proper perspective.

Mediators use varied tactics, including directive, nondirective, procedural, and reflexive techniques. *Directive tactics* allow the mediator to exert substantive control over the negotiation by recommending proposals, giving opinions about positions, assessing the costs associated with demands, and occasionally enforcing compliance. In general, directive tactics are more effective in the latter stages of mediation than in early meetings. *Nondirective tactics* capitalize on the mediator's role in securing information for the disputants and in clarifying misunderstandings. Thus, the mediator may act as a conduit by passing information between the parties or as a clarifier by paraphrasing messages and narrowing topics for discussion. As *procedural tactics*, the mediator may organize separate or joint sessions, establish protocol for the sessions, regulate the agenda, and establish deadlines. Finally, mediators may use *reflexive tactics* by influencing the affective tone of the mediation—developing rapport with participants, using humor, and speaking the language of both sides. Effective mediators use a combination of these tactics, although they report that reflexive tactics are more effective than directive and nondirective ones in facilitating joint collaboration. Clearly, communication is central to the mediation process. As Kolb points out, mediators are like the directors of a drama, who set the scene, manage impressions, orchestrate the script, and maintain dramatic inquiry throughout the process.[19]

Technology and Conflict

In other chapters, we have seen how technology might be used to facilitate communication, team building, leadership, and organizational change. However, technology can also contribute to conflict by depersonalizing individuals or groups and thus making it easier for them to deal with one another in stereotyped, hostile ways. E-mail, for example, removes the sender from the receiver, making it easier for the sender to "flame" the receiver in ways he or she might hesitate to use when in the presence of the other. In addition, it provides only verbal messages with no nonverbal context, making misinterpretations and misunderstandings more likely.

On the other hand, some technological approaches to resolving group conflict are showing some promise. Computer systems, particularly group and negotiation support systems, can act as intervention mechanisms specifically to address issues related to group conflict management.

Group support systems (GSS) use software and hardware to promote and enforce these conditions. GSS act as a group process intervention by:

• imposing process-related structure on the meeting;

• providing an electronic meeting channel that can improve communication among group members;

• delivering a structured heuristic to analyze the problem or task.

As we will discuss further in a later chapter, GSS allow anonymous input and parallel and simultaneous processing, encouraging group member participation since views can be aired without inhibition or constraints. GSS also facilitate the imposition of decision-making heuristics and meeting agendas. These can help keep groups on track while allowing them to systematically work through conflict. And the ability of GSS to provide an electronic record of the meeting can help group members share a common understanding of what has transpired in their meetings.

Researchers Poole, Holmes, and DeSanctis conducted one of the first and the most extensive studies designed to test the impact of GSS on group conflict management.[20] In their study, they compared groups using GSS to groups using only paper and pencils and to groups using no support at all. Discovering mixed results, the researchers concluded that GSS do not necessarily directly determine conflict interaction or outcomes. Rather, they argue, the way groups *use* the technology is what mediates its impact. They found, for instance, that some GSS groups used the structure better than others.

Despite their mixed findings, Poole, Holmes, and DeSanctis remain confident that GSS can provide a number of benefits for conflict management. Because of the anonymity feature, GSS can distance people from ideas, thereby depersonalizing and sometimes defusing difficult conflict situations. GSS make conflict management procedures salient to group members, bringing order to group meetings. In addition, procedures such as voting can surface hidden conflicts.

The impact of GSS on conflict management likely depends on the nature of the GSS and how the group applies it. Poole, Holmes, and DeSanctis note that the GSS used in their study had no specialized conflict management capabilities. Moreover, a facilitator was not used in these GSS sessions. In all likelihood, a facilitator might have been able to help more groups adapt GSS in a manner conducive to productive conflict management. Users of any technology are influenced by expectations. How GSS is explained to users and the level of training they are provided will surely influence how they will use the technology in conflict situations.

Another technology available for groups to use in resolving conflicts is *negotiation support systems*—decision support technologies that specifically focus on providing computerized assistance for situations in which group members strongly disagree on factual or value judgments. Negotiation support systems are interactive, computer-based tools that are specifically intended to support negotiating parties in reaching an agreement. These systems focus on enhancing the prospect of consensus with the intent of making compromise possible.

Negotiation support systems may include decision support software with modeling capabilities, such as decision trees, risk analysis, forecasting methods, and multiattribute functions, as well as software supporting structured group methods, such as electronic brainstorming, nominal grouping, and delphi techniques. Some of these systems even include artificial intelligence to help groups define and solve problems. Many commercial software products are available (including GSS) that encompass some or all of these features.

Ironically, computer systems themselves have been a source of conflict in employee-management relations. Savage points out that many labor unions were once vociferous in their crusade against office automation.[21] They felt, with some justification, that technology threatened a loss of jobs for their members. However, many unions have come full circle and now offer training in computer use to enhance their members' development and advancement opportunities. Instead of simply using technology training to retrain members whose skills are being passed by, Savage notes, many unions have embraced technology to further their goals and to keep members abreast of computer skills. For example, the Air Line Pilots Association, whose pilots are already computer literate, has established services enabling members to access information about new technologies as well as services that facilitate communication and negotiations with their employers.

Labor-Management Conflict

Perhaps the best illustration of how philosophies concerning the use of communication in managing conflicts are changing is the arena of labor-management bargaining. Traditionally, labor-management relations in the United States have been largely adversarial. However, rising competition from foreign firms has forced labor and management to adopt a more cooperative approach to contract negotiations: *win-win bargaining*.

Among the earliest users of win-win bargaining were the United Paperworkers International Union Local 264 and the Waldorf Corporation's St. Paul, Minnesota, facility. Both sides also adopted a set of ground rules concerning the contract talks:

- Discussion was to focus on issues, not personalities.

- Everyone was to be permitted to speak, not just the spokespersons for each side.

- Both sides would work at all times to maintain a "positive relationship."

- Agendas would be developed and followed for each bargaining session.

- Notes concerning each meeting would be kept jointly and approved by the participants at the next session.

- Information would be shared and disseminated to employees through a jointly sponsored hotline and bulletin board communications.

The resulting contract was ratified by the membership almost unanimously in 1973 and with far less turmoil than had been the case three years earlier. Participants in the process also reported much higher levels of satisfaction both with the process itself and with the contract it produced.

More recently, Chrysler Corporation and the United Auto Workers (UAW) worked cooperatively to develop a more effective, less acrimonious approach to contract negotiations. A key element of that effort has been the development of *modern operating agreements (MOAs)* for some Chrysler plants.

The MOA concept evolved in 1986–87 as a joint effort between Chrysler management and the UAW to improve quality and productivity on the assembly line. The objective of the MOAs was to create a more democratic work environment. MOAs eliminated superficial labor-management distinctions and inefficient practices; reduced job classifications, supervisory personnel, and union representatives; and established self-directed work teams and a pay system that rewards workers for their job-related knowledge.

Each MOA has a team that participates in daily audits, assists in developing work assignments, corrects minor and reports major tooling and maintenance problems, provides input regarding production standards, assists in planning work methods, monitors and controls performance, coordinates overtime work, arranges vacation schedules, and performs various other tasks.

Generally, MOA plants have reported reduced operating costs, lower turnover, fewer grievances, and lower absenteeism. All of this has been a direct result of the realization that the company and the union share common interests and that working together rather than as adversaries more effectively serves those interests.

Finally, an approach to improving contract negotiations between labor and management that is gaining increasing acceptance is *interest-based bargaining*. The approach is designed to find the common ground between negotiating parties, to build relationships, and to eliminate the adversarial elements of traditional collective bargaining. One dramatic example of such bargaining occurred when the Salt River Project (SRP), a public electric and water utility based in Phoenix, Arizona, faced a growing stalemate with the leadership of the International Brotherhood of Electrical Workers (IBEW), who represented SRP employees. The Federal Mediation and Conciliation Service (FMCS) was invited to assist the union and company management in developing a more effective approach to settling on a contract.

Initially, about a half-dozen representatives from each side participated in a FMCS-conducted seminar titled "Partners in Change." The seminar focused on building participants' brainstorming and consensus-building skills and was designed to improve their effectiveness in working in committees, overcoming individual differences, and working toward a mutually beneficial settlement. A few weeks later, 20 more participants (10 from each side) attended a two-day seminar about interest-based bargaining, again facilitated by the FMCS. Then the bargaining began.

During negotiation sessions, negotiators sat intermingled rather than in segregated groups or on opposite sides of the table. Everyone became involved because the process would fail if only a few strong personalities dominated. In addition, both sides shared information about their interests and concerns. They created a menu of possible solutions to their concerns and worked to achieve a solution that best met everyone's needs. As the talks continued, more people were called in as committees were formed to address various issues. The FMCS commissioners monitored the progress of the talks, but insisted on remaining in the background.

Initially, the progress seemed slow and laborious. Yet the negotiating parties were able to make a tentative agreement nine days before the old contract expired—quite a feat, considering how past negotiations had always extended well beyond the expiration of previous contracts. In addition, one participant's comments were particularly telling: "In the past, once we reached a settlement, both sides were eager to get away from each other. This time, after we reached a settlement, a majority of the participants went out for a happy hour."[22]

SUMMARY

Conflict is a controversial subject. Even among those who herald its virtues, ambivalence persists. In organizations, however, the reality of interdependence, competition for scarce resources, and the necessity of coping with change while working together on all sorts of tasks create conditions where conflict is inevitable. The types and sources of conflict are numerous, perplexing, and often tenacious. Even so, individuals at all organizational levels can learn under the appropriate circumstances to approach conflict cooperatively and collaboratively. There are several different conflict management styles that individuals may choose to use: there are strengths and weaknesses associated with each.

Within community settings, conflict must also be managed. The more inclusive and respectful the contexts are for addressing and discussing issues over which community members disagree, the more likely the results are to be positive and productive. Study circles have emerged as one useful tool for engaging such potentially divisive community issues as race relations, educational priorities, and the use of public funds.

On occasion, technology may function as a source of conflict, but it also offers new and ever-changing tools for groups to use in managing conflicts. With conflict comes the opportunity for growth and change, for innovation and empowerment, for problem solving and consensus building. Those who learn to confront their differences openly and honestly, to communicate about their differences with sensitivity and integrity, can contribute to a constructive and satisfying organizational and community climate.

Questions for Discussion

1. What are some ways in which conflict can be good for an organization or community and some ways that it can be bad?
2. What are the key features of study circles, and how are they helpful in managing conflicts in public life?
3. In what settings can conflict occur? Briefly, give an example of each.
4. Compare and contrast approach-approach, approach-avoidance, and avoidance-avoidance conflict.
5. Describe three types of role conflict.
6. When does increased communication fail to reduce conflict?
7. How effective is avoidance in resolving conflict? Why?
8. Compare and contrast the five styles of conflict management discussed in this chapter.
9. Describe some of the key steps in collaborative conflict management.
10. How can technology be used as a tool in managing conflict?
11. Under what circumstances might a third party be needed to address conflicts?
12. How have win-win bargaining, modern operating agreements, and interest-based bargaining impacted labor-management negotiations?

Exercises

1. Think of an organization to which you now belong or to which you belonged in the past. List one instance of each conflict setting that occurred in that organization and how it was (or should have been) resolved.
2. You have been chosen to be a mediator to work with the National Basketball Association (NBA) Player's Association and the NBA Owner's Association to

help them resolve their long-standing feud over players' salaries and the right not to be traded without the player's consent. What points would you present when the meetings begin?

3. Think of a time in your life when you experienced some conflict, preferably in a job-related situation. In a brief essay, describe the nature and extent of your conflict, the contexts in which it occurred, and the methods you and others used to manage the conflict. To what extent did you resolve the conflict? What other methods would you have tried if you had to do it over again?

4. Choose a nonprofit organization of interest to you and arrange for an interview with someone in a leadership position. As you interview this individual, address some of the following issues:

a. In what ways has this organization experienced conflict?

b. What kinds of issues are the most likely to generate conflict? Why?

c. How are conflicts typically resolved? How satisfied are you with the way they are handled?

d. Do you see conflict as being beneficial in any way? If so, how? If not, why not?

Case Application 7.1   Grappling with Globalization

Many contemporary writers have pointed with alarm to the rapid decline of U.S. businesses in an increasingly global environment. On the plus side, globalization brings an expanded market for products and services. The potential threats, however, are numerous. To be competitive, U.S. businesses are increasingly seeking the lowest possible labor costs, often turning to less expensive workers from other countries. These practices are beginning to affect white-collar as well as blue-collar employees. In many instances, U.S. businesses are closing their operations at home and moving abroad. Here is one example: A plant in northern California makes steel irons used in the home for pressing clothes. It employs approximately 800 production workers whose average wage is $10.50 an hour. This plant is owned by General Electric. GE announced that it would be closing the plant and moving production to Singapore where, instead of the metal irons, a plastic iron will be manufactured.

The shutdown of the plant will have a serious economic impact on the local community. Jobs at the plant were highly sought after. Workers would wait three to four years in hopes of securing a job at the GE plant because wages and benefits were superior to those elsewhere in the community, and workers believed that job security at the GE plant was quite high.

The plant's closing has outraged the union. Workers are bewildered, feeling they have been cheated. GE management points out that wages in Singapore are $1.10 an hour. Moreover, in Singapore, government policy basically precludes the formation of unions. Management alleges that over the years the California union has been responsible for restrictive work rules that, in addition to decreasing efficiency and increasing costs, have been a continuing source of labor-management strife.

The union reports a willingness to negotiate givebacks, including reduction of wages. But union leaders and many of the workers say that they are unwilling to give up everything they have fought for over these many years. Management, in turn, has pointed out that there is no way the California plant can compete with a plant in Singapore, with its $1.10 an hour wage, or, for that matter, with plants in Mexico where wages are about $2 an hour. The union charges that GE is calloused and is interested only in profit.

Questions

1. What instances of conflict do you see in this situation?
2. What principles of conflict management might be helpful in dealing with this complicated situation?

Case Application 7.2   A Cross-Cultural Success Story

In 1982, the General Motors automobile plant in Fremont, California, was the model of the United States in decline. With an absentee rate that hovered at about 20 percent, wildcat strikes were not uncommon. There were typically about 5,000 grievances outstanding, or about one per employee. GM decided to shut Fremont's doors, and later turned it over to Toyota as part of a joint venture called New United Motor Mfg. Inc. (NUMMI).

Over the next few years the Fremont plant underwent an amazing transformation. NUMMI's Japanese bosses set up a typical Toyota production, with just-in-time delivery and a flexible assembly line run by teams of workers in charge of their own jobs. They hired back most of the former United Auto Workers members who wanted work—even the militant leaders. NUMMI's 2,500 employees assemble 240,000 cars per year, roughly equal to what it took 5,000 or more people to produce under GM. Absenteeism runs under 2 percent and grievances have virtually disappeared.

Analysts who study these Japanese transplants (others exist in Ohio and Tennessee) point to the Japanese managers' adroit handling of U.S. workers. The Japanese approach to production, emphasizing flexible teams and attention to quality, demands extremely high employee loyalty. To cultivate this loyalty in the United States, Japanese management has learned how to translate Japanese methods to fit the U.S. values of equality and individualism. Japanese managers elicit loyalty by presenting themselves as equals. At NUMMI, there are no privileged parking lots for executives. Top executives eat in the employee cafeteria. Employees are called "associates" and help decide how their jobs will be set up—and they often find faster ways to do things. For instance, in the old GM plant at Fremont, the person who installed windows on right front doors had to walk from his toolbox to each car three times as it moved along the assembly line. Now, because of a rearrangement of the equipment, the worker can go to the car just once, and can follow along as it passes. The job now requires 11 steps rather than 23.

Questions

1. What possible sources of conflict existed in this situation?
2. What methods did the Japanese use to avoid or resolve conflict?

PART 3

INTERVIEWING

Except for conversations, interviews are perhaps the most frequently occurring form of communication . . . in an organization. . . . Interviews are so common that they are taken for granted.

—David A. Whetten and Kim S. Cameron,
Developing Management Skills

8

Fundamentals of Interviewing

After reading this chapter, you should be able to:

❏ Explain how interviewing differs from casual interpersonal conversation

❏ List and explain considerations that are important in planning for an interview

❏ Describe how to open an interview effectively

❏ Distinguish open, closed, and probing types of questions

❏ Develop strategies for coping with inadequate responses

❏ List and define types of question sequences

❏ List and describe three different types of interviews commonly encountered in organizational settings

❏ Plan and conduct an interview using effective interviewing strategies that are in keeping with ethical interviewing practices

While dyadic encounters are frequent in all human interactions, both personal and professional, in organizational settings no form of dyadic communication is more significant or more frequent than the interview. It is in the employment interview that we are initially accepted or rejected by the organization. Subsequent interviews will inform us of our progress, promise, and problems in our daily work activities. In the context of the interview, we will likewise complain and be counseled, provide and receive information, and be praised and disciplined. We will participate in problem solving and persuasion. Often, before we retire from or leave the organization, we may reflect on our accomplishments, disappointments, defeats, and triumphs in final exit interviews. Clearly, interviewing pervades all organizational activity—serving a multiplicity of functions, operating at numerous levels within the organizational hierarchy, and continuing throughout the lives of each organizational employee.

Preview

In this chapter, we will examine the unique nature of interviews as communicative events. Taking the perspective of the interviewer, we will consider the nature of interviews in general and some specific purposes for which interviews are used in organizational settings. Then we will examine some types of interview questions and suggest sequences by which those questions might be organized. Finally, we will turn our attention to several of the most commonly encountered kinds of interviews in professional settings: appraisal, corrective, and complaint resolution interviews. We conclude the chapter with a brief commentary on ethical interviewing.

THE MEANING AND IMPORTANCE OF INTERVIEWS

Like all interpersonal communication, interviewing normally consists of face-to-face interaction (although telephone interviews are increasingly common) between two parties (interviewer and interviewee) who take turns acting as sender and receiver. However, some other characteristics make interviewing a unique form of dyadic communication. First, interviews are *purposive:* they are conducted to achieve some specific objective. Informal interactions may have underlying purposes as well, but in an interview, the purpose is more clearly stated and understood by the participants. Second, interviews are more *structured* than informal conversations: The interviewer usually has some preestablished agenda that is followed during the conversation. Implicit in this characteristic is a third: Interviews are more carefully *prepared* than informal conversations. Typically, the interviewer prepares carefully for the interview before it is conducted. Often, the interviewee prepares just as carefully (as before an employment interview). Finally, the *sequence* of the interview is more predictable: The interviewer selects topic areas and asks questions, for the most part, while the interviewee offers responses. In summary, then, interviews are prepared, structured interactions between two or more parties in which questions and answers are used to achieve relatively specific and mutually understood purposes.

Knowledge of interviewing is important, both for short-term and long-term reasons. In the short term, it is likely you will experience these interviews as an interviewee. To participate effectively, you need some knowledge of how interviews function and what the interviewer has (or should have) in mind. In the long term, you may achieve supervisory or management status in an organization. As a supervisor or manager, your success may be determined to a significant extent by your competence in conducting various types of interviews. Your immediate and long-term professional success, therefore, rests to some degree on your understanding of and skill in various forms of interviews. In addition, if you choose to volunteer in nonprofit organizations in your community you will likely need a variety of interviewing skills. See Highlighting Civic Engagement for some relevant examples.

BASIC CONCEPTS OF INTERVIEWING

Although interviewing is a common organizational activity, it is not necessarily an easy one. Perhaps Stewart and Cash put it best when they wrote:

> If you think interviewing is simple and basic skills come naturally, recall some of your recent experiences: the inept company recruiter who kept answering her own questions or who was uninformed about the position . . . the professor who got very defensive as soon as you started talking about a course requirement or a grade; the pollster who asked leading questions or who became agitated over your answers; or the computer salesperson who could not answer your questions about a system and who could only talk in computerese.[1]

To avoid the kinds of problems mentioned by Stewart and Cash, we will examine some interviewing techniques and strategies that apply to all interviewing situations. Specifically, we will discuss the preliminary planning that interviews require, some strategies and questions for interviewing, ways of probing

---

Highlighting Civic Engagement

The Place of Interviews in Volunteer Organizations

At the Shalom Community Center (a resource center and daytime shelter for the impoverished and homeless in Bloomington, Indiana) volunteers often use interviews to assist and assess the guests who come there for guidance, meals, and other resources. For example:

- Job Links counselors interview guests to determine their background, educational achievements, and work experiences before helping them prepare resumes and examine employment postings in the newspaper and on the Internet.

- Social workers interview guests to determine their life needs and to help them make connections with community resources.

- Ministers conduct interviews with Shalom guests with the hope of discovering what their spiritual needs might be and discerning how those needs might be met through the local church network.

- Psychologists conduct counseling interviews to assess the sorts of emotional challenges some guests may be experiencing and to offer them insights and guidance.

- Every time a Shalom job becomes vacant, the board of directors conducts interviews with the goal of finding excellent candidates for such positions as executive director, volunteer coordinator, and kitchen manager.

The kinds of interviews portrayed in these examples are diverse. They include counseling, informational, problem-solving, and employment interviews. Those who play the role of interviewer are typically volunteers who may or may not have formal training in interviewing.

Source: The information contained in this feature is based on the current volunteer experiences of one of the authors.

---

for additional information, coping with inadequate responses, acting as listener and respondent, and closing the interview.

Preliminary Planning

While there is no certain way to create a climate for ideal interviews, *careful preliminary planning* can assist you in establishing a constructive interviewing setting. If you have been selected by any organization to serve as an interviewer, ideally you will receive some training in the interviewing process. Through training you will learn methods for structuring interviews. Too many untrained interviewers approach each interview without a specific strategy. Yet, research has shown that interviews that are systematic and structured are more valid than those that are unstructured and without design or system.[2]

Most interviews are conducted on the premises of the organization. Many are carried out in the interviewer's own office. When this is the case, it is the interviewer who is responsible for creating the best possible interviewing environment. To begin, each interview should be conducted under circumstances that promote *comfort and privacy*. Comfort involves such physical considerations as room temperature and seating comfort, as well as matters related to psychological comfort. The physical distance between interviewer and interviewee is important, as is the arrangement of the furniture. In U.S. culture, physical distances of two to five feet seem to be the most psychologically comfortable for conversation. You may want to review chapter 5's discussion of the role of proxemics in nonverbal communication. Other potential barriers to communication include chair arrangement, the presence or absence of a desk, note taking, and tape recording. If you plan to take notes or record the conversation, mention the fact directly and indicate the reasons for the practice. In each instance, you should give careful consideration to the kind of climate you wish to create and attempt to use space, distance, and other verbal and nonverbal factors to enhance the interview setting.

The interviewee's psychological comfort will also be enhanced if you do all you can to ensure that the interview remains a private exchange. Although privacy is absolutely mandatory in the context of counseling and corrective interviews, nearly all interviews benefit from a private communication environment. Your secretary should not dash in with urgent messages or put calls through to you. If you must interrupt the interview to deal with some critical issue, apologize to the interviewee.

Depending on the kind of interview you are conducting, you will probably need to *plan the basic approach you want to take*, the kinds of questions you want to ask, and the kind of information you need to share. If you are conducting an employment interview, you should plan a core of basic questions, read the applicant's resume in advance, and bring information about the job's critical requirements. With a corrective interview, you must decide how to describe your perception of the problem and how and when to encourage the interviewee to respond. In the context of a work appraisal interview, you should study your written comments, prepare to make positive comments as well as suggestions for future improvements, and decide how to encourage the interviewee to join you in setting future goals. The kind of planning you do will depend on the purpose of your interview.

In short, then, effective planning for an interview should focus on identifying your objectives as an interviewer and choosing the basic approach you want to take, creating a communicative context that ensures physical and psychological comfort and privacy, and doing all you can to remove or minimize barriers to an productive exchange of information and ideas.

Opening the Interview

The way you open the interview will set the stage for all that follows. Although individual interviewers vary in their interpersonal styles, communicating a sense of warmth (seasoned with professional restraint), interest, and genuine personal concern for the interviewee is generally a good way to begin.

• Both verbally and nonverbally, you will want to welcome the interviewee—through a handshake, a smile, and a word of thanks for his or her presence at the interview. The goal is to *establish rapport* by creating a climate of trust and goodwill. One traditional approach to putting the interviewee at ease is to engage in initial small talk. Some brief exchanges concerning sports, weather, families, and so forth may enhance rapport. But excessive small talk may backfire and cause the interviewee to be anxious and eager to settle down to the serious business of participating in the interview.[3]

Highlighting Diversity

Gender Differences

During the early moments of any interview, both verbal and nonverbal behavior will play a key role. For example, Lillian Glass has catalogued 105 differences in the communication behavior of women and men in the United States. As examples, she found that, in comparison with women, men were likely to:

- touch others more frequently;
- avoid eye contact or fail to look directly at the other person;
- sound less approachable, more abrupt;
- give fewer compliments.

Source: Lillian Glass, *He Says, She Says: Closing the Communication Gap between the Sexes* (New York: Putnam, 1993), 45–59.

- Soon after the initial greeting, you should make an *orientation statement*. In some types of interviews, both parties know essentially why they are there. Even so, it is often helpful to state your perception of the purpose of the interview. In many interviews, the interviewees are tense, uncertain, and perhaps overly aware of the status and power of the interviewer. This is especially so in appraisal, employment, corrective, and grievance contexts. To assist in overcoming this problem, you might make some early statement expressing your view that the purpose of the interview is for both you and the interviewee to exchange information so that *both of you* might make a wise decision concerning employment, performance, and other factors. This kind of orienting remark not only clarifies the purpose of the interview but also may serve to relax the interviewee.

- Next, you may want to *preview* the kinds of topics you hope to discuss. Previewing can provide some sense of direction for the interviewee, increase interpersonal trust, and improve the overall efficiency of the interviewing process. Once again, it is extremely important to be sensitive to the needs of the person being interviewed. For instance, if this is the interviewee's first-ever job interview, and you know it, you will likely offer more detail in walking him through the planned interview; but with a veteran interviewee, only a brief preview would more than suffice.

Since the early moments establish the tone and framework for the remainder of the interview, it is important to be mindful of ways in which participants' perceptions, communication styles, and cultural backgrounds may differ.[4]

Basic Interviewing Strategies

Each interview must have a goal, and the interviewer usually formulates an overall design that will theoretically lead to that goal. Many interviewees will have their *own* strategies and goals, some of which will complement and others of which will conflict with your goals as an interviewer. In an employment interview, each of you may have as a mutual goal the discovery of whether or not you

Highlighting Diversity

Intercultural Considerations

In their best-selling book on interviewing, Stewart and Cash point to some important cultural differences that may impact the opening moments of any interview. They note:

- While Anglo-Americans tend to share similar rules for greeting others, these rules are not always shared by those from other cultures.
- Shaking hands is a Western custom. While a firm handshake is valued in U.S. society, it means nothing in Japan.
- Anglo-Americans are taught to smile in response to a smile, but this is not so in Israel.
- Anglo-Americans expect others to look them in the eyes as a way of exhibiting trust, openness, and sincerity, while other cultures consider this kind of eye contact to be impolite or even insulting. Africans, for example, are taught to avoid eye contact when listening to others.
- Anglo-Americans prefer to maintain a greater personal distance with other parties than do those from the Middle East or Latin America. Many Arabs and Latin Americans see North Americans as distant and cold, while North Americans see the others as invading their personal space.
- In the United States, touching another on the arm, hand, or shoulder is usually only considered appropriate when both parties have an established or close relationship, but those from Italy or Latin America are quite likely to touch another as part of an opening greeting.

Source: Charles J. Stewart and William B. Cash, *Interviewing: Principles and Practices,* 9th ed. (Boston: McGraw-Hill, 2000), 37–62.

should become professionally associated. To achieve that goal, however, both of you may hope to spend a maximum amount of time gathering information from the other. Clearly, these goals are not compatible, given the reality of time constraints. Thus, both interviewer and interviewee must be prepared to adjust to the needs of the other as the interview progresses.

From your perspective as an interviewer, there are two basic strategies you can adopt. The first is *directive*. Using a directive strategy, you establish the purpose of the interview and strive to control the pacing of the interview and the subjects covered during it.[5] This approach is highly structured. It is particularly applicable when you believe you know the desired goal of the interview and the precise steps for getting there. The directive strategy takes the form of probing specific topics in a particular sequence with some flexibility in follow-up questions. It is especially efficient for acquiring large quantities of information.

As we mentioned earlier, highly structured interviews tend to have high validity. Nevertheless, the directive strategy has some potential weaknesses. Using a structured, familiar interview format is somewhat akin to playing the same role in a play over and over again: You must labor to make each appearance seem fresh, original, and interesting. No interviewee should leave the interview feeling that he has just been exposed to the organization's assembly line! Yet, it is not uncommon for interviewers to use the directive strategy when interviewing a number of individuals in a row (as might be the case with employment or appraisal interviews).

The second basic interviewing strategy is *nondirective*. When you choose a nondirective strategy, you allow the interviewee to control the purpose, the topics to be covered, and the pacing of the interview.[6] Nondirective interviewing was developed by therapist Carl Rogers and is most commonly used in counseling situations.[7] Even though this approach allows the interviewee to explore whatever areas he wishes with only minimal structural constraints, it is not without some interviewer control. Your role is one of empathic, nonjudgmental listening while permitting the interviewee to structure his own thinking with flexible and subtle guidance.

The obvious advantages of the nondirective approach are flexibility and the opportunity to explore interesting subjects in depth. By using this method, interviewer and interviewee can begin to establish an ongoing relationship. Moreover, with this approach, the interviewee has every opportunity for self-expression. Nondirective interviews are not without their disadvantages, however. They are less efficient than directive interviews and can be very time consuming. Because the interviewees choose most of the topics to be pursued, each interview is likely to cover entirely different ground. Thus, as an interviewer, you cannot really compare interviewee responses across several interviews. Nondirective interviews require considerable interviewer sensitivity and excellent listening skills.

While the directive strategy is more commonly used by interviewers than the nondirective approach, many interviewers use a *combined approach*. They may plan several major questions in advance (or areas they want to be sure to cover), but they allow for considerable flexibility in the ways these questions are pursued by interviewees. They also provide substantial time for interviewee questions, comments, and insights. This combined approach is practical and enables the interview, while somewhat structured, to remain a shared communicative experience.

Asking Questions

A key communication tool used by interviewers is the question. Whatever your overall design, you will ask many questions as a primary means of collecting the data you need to plan and make decisions. You may choose to use one of two basic types of questions: open or closed.[8] *Open questions* are broad in nature and basically unstructured. Often they indicate only the topic to be considered and allow the interviewee considerable freedom in determining the amount and kind of information she will provide. When you pose open questions, you are letting the interviewee know that you are interested in her perspectives, attitudes, and value system.

Some questions are extremely open ended, with virtually no restrictions, such as:

- "Tell me about yourself."
- "What do you know about General Motors?"
- "How do you think this organization can be improved?"

Other questions are more moderately open:

- "Why did you major in marketing?"
- "What can be done to improve this organization's productivity?"
- "What do you know about General Motors' newest product designs?"

Open questions allow the interviewee to talk with relative freedom. Because there are so many different ways to respond to them, they are not very threatening and tend to reduce interviewee anxiety. Open questions also give the interviewer insights into the interviewee's prejudices, values, and commitments. On the other hand, open questions can be time consuming, and they may elicit a lot irrelevant information. In addition, they may require several follow-up questions, and the responses may be difficult to evaluate or categorize following the interview. Most important, any interviewer who poses many open questions needs to be an excellent listener.

On the opposite end are *closed questions*. These are structured and restricted, and they often include several possible answers from which to choose. Thus, potential responses are limited. On occasion, a closed question will probe for a brief bit of specific information, such as:

- "When did you last study Spanish?"
- "How many years did you consult?"
- "What starting salary would you anticipate with this job?"

Others are even more closed, requiring the interviewee to select the appropriate response from among those you provide, such as:

- "What brand of toothpaste do you presently use: Crest, Colgate, Aquafresh, or Pepsodent?"
- "Where would you prefer being located with our company: New Orleans, New York, San Francisco, Chicago, or San Antonio?"
- "If you could win one of these cars, which would you choose: Buick LeSabre, Volkswagen Jetta, Ford Explorer, or Chrysler Jeep?"

The most extreme form of the closed question is the *yes-no bipolar question*. Usually the interviewee is allowed to respond only with yes or no, or possibly "I don't know." For example:

- "Do you smoke?"
- "Do you think the U.S. should have gone to war against Iraq?"
- "Have you heard about our community's new adult literacy program?"

Inexperienced, unskilled interviewers have a tendency to rely heavily on this type of questioning in spite of the fact that it requires maximum questioning effort and generates only small amounts of information per question. Occasionally a yes-no question is appropriate, but long series of such questions should be avoided.

In general, closed questions save time, increase the probability of obtaining relevant responses, are efficient, and are relatively easy to tabulate following the interview. By using closed questions, the interviewer maintains substantial control over the flow of the interview. On the other hand, closed questions generate limited information and often cause interviewees to respond less accurately (since their views may not fit precisely into any one of the offered alternatives). They decrease interviewee talking time and increase the number of questions the interviewer must generate. Finally, they fail to explore the reasons behind attitudes and opinions and stifle the offering of valuable, but unanticipated, information.

PROBING: A SPECIAL KIND OF QUESTIONING

Sometimes an interviewee will respond only partially to a question, answer it inadequately, or make a provocative point that causes you to desire additional information. When this occurs, you may attempt to stimulate discussion by probing for further information. *Probes* may request exploration, elaboration, or justification. Some examples are:

- "What do you mean by that?"
- "Why did you feel that way?"
- "Could you give me an example?"

Research by Tengler and Jablin suggests that probes are frequently used and needed by employment interviewers to obtain substantive responses to open questions.[9]

There are several kinds of specialized probes. Two commonly used in employment interviews are hypothetical and reactive probes. The *hypothetical probe* places the interviewee in a situation, not unlike one he might encounter on the job, and asks how he would handle the situation. You might say, "Suppose you had been working here for a few months and one day you heard a rumor that drastic layoffs were impending. How do you think you'd react to that?" Hypothetical probes can be useful for determining basic attitudes or approaches to problem solving, but they also encourage a certain amount of second guessing, where the interviewee gives the ideal response (that is, the one he thinks you want to hear) rather than an honest response.

You may also choose to use *reactive probes* in which you make a statement simply to get the reaction of the interviewee. Perhaps you ask the interviewee to agree or disagree with a stated position or issue. For example, a high school principal used a reactive probe in interviewing a young woman for a teaching position when he asked the following question: "There are many teachers who believe that most major corrective problems should be brought to the attention of the principal, while others prefer to handle these matters without administrative assistance, except in the most severe instances. How do you feel about dealing with discipline?"

In a sense, hypothetical and reactive probes are similar in that they provide a frame of reference and set the stage for the interviewee's response. But the reactive probe focuses on real rather than hypothetical cases. By using such probes, you can gain some insights into applicants' views on pertinent, real-life issues without in any way challenging their ideas.

Another method for obtaining follow-up information is the use of *restatement* (sometimes referred to as the "mirror" technique). With this technique, you do not directly request that the interviewee provide additional information. Rather, you restate part or all of the person's comments in such a way that it encourages her to continue. In this manner, you can communicate genuine interest, indicating that you are "with" the other person. Restatement does not demand additional information; it simply provides the opportunity for elaboration and deeper examination. Compare the following interviewer responses, one using a probe and the other restatement:

- Interviewee: I left my job at the small accounting firm because I found it unchallenging. It was just plain dull.
- Interviewer (using a probe): How was it dull and unchallenging?
- Interviewer (using restatement): You felt it was dull and unchallenging?

Restatement is a technique particularly useful for allowing people to clarify their ideas and listen to their own language without in any way commenting on or evaluating them.

QUESTION BIAS

Still another method by which types of questions can be distinguished is based on the extent to which the question reveals the attitudes of the questioner or suggests the sort of answer that the respondent is supposed to give. For example, "How do you feel about labor unions?" suggests little about the thinking of the questioner. "You don't like labor unions, do you?" suggests quite a bit more. "You wouldn't join one of those anti-American labor unions, would you?" is so loaded that it clearly reveals the feelings of the questioner and practically dictates the appropriate response. When *biased questions* are used accidentally, they place the interviewee in a difficult position; when used carefully, however, they *can* reveal much about the respondent.

As with other types of questions, unbiased and biased inquiries range along a continuum from very biased to completely neutral. Most of the examples we have offered in this section have been unbiased. For example, "How well do you feel you performed this past year?" says nothing about the feelings of the interviewer and leaves interviewees free to answer as they please without fear of being trapped by the question. Somewhat more biased or leading is the question, "You like working with machinery, don't you?" At the most biased end of the scale is, "Are you going to improve your output next month, or should I start a search for your replacement?" Because these three questions vary in their revelations of the interviewer's feelings, they exert different degrees of pressure on the interviewee to respond in a particular fashion.

In deciding whether to use biased, moderately biased, or completely neutral questions during the interview, you first must take into account your purpose. If you are seeking the interviewee's true feelings or attitudes, you probably should avoid biased questions. If, however, you are trying to persuade the interviewee, biased questions may be useful. Research on attitude change suggests that if we can encourage an individual to state a certain opinion, he is likely to adopt that opinion as his own. Thus, if an interviewee initially had no intention of changing the behaviors for which you were disciplining him, you might persuade him through a sequence of questions, such as:

- "You understand that we have to have people here at work in order to maintain our responsiveness to customers, right?"

- "You know that absenteeism hurts our ability to get the product to customers when they need it, don't you?"

- "You realize that when someone is late for work, we have to move everyone around to cover for him?"

- "You know that just as we promise to provide you with pay and benefits, so you promise to come to work regularly and on time?"

- "So what are some concrete steps that you will take to improve your attendance record?"

The yes answers produced by the first four questions will hopefully lead to a constructive plan of action in response to the final question, while at the same time

---

Business Brief 8.1

Listening: The Key to Effective Interviewing

Key to effective interviewing is effective listening. Chapter 6 discussed some techniques for effective listening. Here are more tips for listening effectively during interviews:

- *Realize that you could do better:* Some experts claim that 50% or more improvement in listening can come about simply from realizing that you have bad listening habits and can do better.

- *Practice.* Catch yourself not listening and try not to let it happen again, making a conscious effort to use good listening techniques.

- *Rephrase what you're hearing.* Adopting the practice of periodically restating what you just heard is an important "reality check" to ensure you understand—emotionally and intellectually—what the other person is saying, forces you to pay attention, and is a good test for your listening effectiveness.

- *Conquer fear of silence.* While the urge to fill silence can be almost irresistible, the practice of letting some silence occur after the other person has stopped talking and before you begin your reply allows you time to give a more thoughtful response and may encourage the other person to add more information.

- *Take notes.* This shows the other person that you care so much that you are going to write down what he or she says; it keeps you occupied so you can't talk so much; and it allows you to conclude by saying, "Now, let me review my notes to be sure I have accurately captured what you said."

Source: David Stauffer, "Yo, Listen Up: A Brief Hearing on the Most Neglected Communication Skill," *Harvard Management Update* (July 1998): 10–11.

---

leading the interviewee to an understanding of the necessity of good attendance. Thus, biased questions produce the same effect that a lecture or series of commands would achieve, but in a more palatable manner.

Finally, biased questions also can serve to test an interviewee. We can use them to determine how independent workers are or how likely workers are to provide socially acceptable responses. For example, if we asked, "Are you biased against moving women into managerial positions?" most male executives would say no. However, if we asked, "Do you think that women are often too emotional to take the daily stresses of management positions?" a "closet sexist" would be much more likely to reveal his true feelings. However, we must use biased questions with care. At times, their use can be deceptive and unethical, especially when questions are loaded and emotional. Their implications may make the interviewee suspicious, angry, or skeptical of our own opinions or judgment. For the most part, then, we are much safer in using neutral questions and relying on the openness created by other interviewing skills to elicit honest answers from the interviewee.

Coping with Inadequate Responses

Unfortunately, not all questions asked in interviews elicit the kinds of responses sought. Interviewee answers may be inadequate in many ways and for many reasons. Sometimes the interviewer's question is not clearly understood because of content, language, or structure. On occasion, an interviewee may not know how to respond appropriately because of inadequate knowledge or a misunderstanding of the interviewer's expectations (that is, she is uncertain how much detail and elaboration is expected). Finally, the interviewee may be naturally reticent or may feel that the interviewer is asking for irrelevant or overly personal information.

Whatever the reason, as an interviewer you will encounter many inadequate responses from interviewees. Each will challenge your wits and require you to respond creatively to the interpersonal communication difficulties posed by such interviews. Some responses, for example, are *oververbalized*. They are often the product of compulsive talkers who go on and on, seemingly indefinitely. As we have pointed out, the use of open questions encourages more elaborated responses. When you perceive that you are dealing with a compulsive talker, you would do well to alter your strategy to a more directive one, using closed questions to limit the response range.

Interviewers quite often encounter *partial* responses or even *nonresponses*. Both are inadequate because they provide little or no information. Interviewees who consistently respond "Yes," "No," "I don't know," or "I don't think so," or who only partially and superficially answer questions, provide a great challenge for interviewers. If the interviewee's response is incomplete or hesitant, you might nudge her by saying, "I see,"; "And then?"; "Yes?"; or "What happened next?" Superficial responses might be followed by, "Why do you think you felt that way?"; "Tell me more about your reasons for doing that"; or "How did you react when that happened?" Vague answers could be greeted with, "What do you mean when you use the word 'liberal'?"; "How are you using the term 'participation'?"; or "I'm not sure I understand."

In general, a useful strategy with any reticent interviewee is to phrase all questions in an open manner so that it becomes impossible to answer them sensibly with one-word responses. Nontalkers often lack confidence or are highly anxious about the interview. Thus, the best initial approach is one of extended rapport building and orientation. It is also imperative that the first question or two be easy. If a highly anxious person is asked a difficult question initially, she may never be able to relax and communicate fully and effectively.

Question Sequences

Another important element of effective interviewing is the order in which questions are asked. While a virtually infinite number of sequences could be identified, we shall consider five types, distinguishable by their use of open and closed questions.

1. *Funnel sequence*. This sequence begins with open questions and builds on them with questions of increasing specificity. The funnel sequence is particularly appropriate when interviewees are quite familiar with the topic and feel free to discuss it or when they are emotionally charged and need a chance to express feelings. We might begin by asking a general question about the interviewee's attitudes toward work and then become increasingly specific by focusing on particular aspects of the interviewee's position. If, for example, the interviewee formerly was an effective worker but recently has let her per-

formance slip, we might begin the interview with general questions about the interviewee's morale and overall job satisfaction. Then we would move to her performance over the past several years and become even more specific, considering her most recent performance level. Finally, we could deal with precise elements of her job, such as attendance or amount of work produced, and try to determine those factors that may have caused these elements to go downhill. Of the question sequences used in all types of interviews, the funnel sequence (illustrated in figure 8.1) is one of the most common.

2. *Inverted funnel sequence.* This is the reverse of the preceding sequence. As demonstrated in figure 8.1, the interviewer begins with specific, closed questions and gradually moves to more general, open questions. This approach may be useful if the interviewee is reluctant to talk at all. While open questions might get no response, specific questions (such as, "Did it take you long to find this place?" or "How long have you been working here?") may be an effective way to motivate the interviewee to respond freely. Once he is talking, the interviewee may be encouraged to deal with more open questions, demanding greater depth of response. One recent study of employment interviewing suggested that most interviewers use the inverted funnel sequence.[10]

3. *Diamond sequence.* This sequence begins with closed questions; moves to open ones; and then narrows again to specific, closed inquiries using a combination of the first two sequences. When counseling an employee who seems to have a drug or an alcohol problem, we might begin with specific questions about others in similar situations, then move to more open questions about the employee's own life and work performance, and then center again upon her own problems and concerns. We begin with a relatively easy topic of discussion (someone else's problems), move to something a little more personal but still not too difficult to discuss (her life in general), and then arrive at the most difficult and the most specific portion of the interview—her own problems and

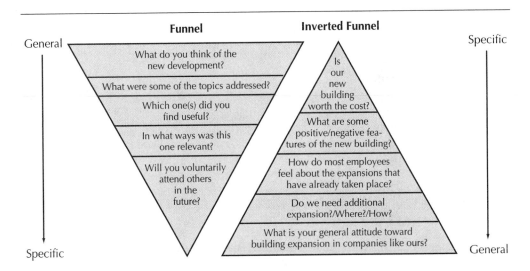

Figure 8.1   A comparison of two basic questioning sequences

what to do about them. This questioning sequence is often useful in dealing with potentially painful topics or difficult problems.

4. *Hourglass sequence.* This sequence also uses a combination of the first two sequences. It begins with open questions, moves to closed questions, and then becomes open once again. When conducting a performance review with a supervisor who has been steadily criticized by his own workers, for example, we might begin with a discussion of people and how motivated they are in very general terms, then move to specific questions about his situation, and encourage him to develop his own supervisory action plan by asking increasingly open-ended questions toward the end of the interview. Such a sequence of questions might include:

- "What do you think makes people want to work?"
- "How do you think they get these things from work?"
- "Does the supervisor play a role in providing these things?"
- "Does this apply to your staff as well?"
- "Do you provide the things they want or need?"
- "What are some things you might do more of as a supervisor?"
- "What will you try to accomplish during the next year?"

This sequence is much shorter than the entire interview would be, but it illustrates the open-to-closed-to-open procedure found in the hourglass sequence. This sequence is especially useful if you want to begin by establishing some general principles, then move to a specific application (closer to home), and finally go on to examine some action strategies for the future.

5. *Tunnel sequence.* This sequence uses questions that are all of the same degree of openness. Interviews conducted in shopping centers by market researchers who stop shoppers at random and ask them a series of questions typically follow this pattern. Very specific, factual questions are asked in a rapid sequence to gain maximum information in a minimum amount of time. In contrast, some psychotherapists use exclusively open questions in their counseling interviews with patients. Their goal is to cause the patients to talk and so arrive at solutions to their own problems.

Your selection of a question sequence, then, is based largely on your purpose in the interview and your knowledge of the interviewee's state of mind. A reluctant respondent may require use of an inverted funnel. A disagreeable interviewee may be persuaded through a diamond sequence. An uninformed or uneducated interviewee may be taught to apply general principles to his own situation through an hourglass sequence. Interviewers must carefully assess their purpose and the nature of the interviewee and then carefully plan their overall questioning strategy.

Closing the Interview

Perhaps the interviews you conduct will be subject to external time constraints; there may be only 20 or 30 minutes available. Usually you will be in a more flexible situation that allows you to decide when prolonging the interview would not be profitable. One interviewing researcher points out that in every communication encounter, there are *"crucial junctures*—those moments in an interview when the next response . . . will determine whether its continuance will be productive or not, whether vital data will be elicited, or if tangential information will be forthcoming."[11] Your ability to recognize critical junctures will improve with experience. What is important to remember is that you should terminate an interview whenever you feel that your mutual goals have been accomplished.

The end of the interview is as important as the beginning, and failure to attend to it may result in undermining earlier accomplishments. To thank an interviewee for her participation in an interview and to mumble something about "being in touch" is not an adequate conclusion. In general, the tone of the closing should be similar to that of the rest of the interview—*appreciative* of the interviewee's participation and *showing interest in her as a person.* You should encourage the interviewee to ask questions and devote the remainder of the interview to exploring the procedure to be used next. In other words, there must be some *orientation toward the next step.* If the interview has been a selection situation, you should tell applicants what will happen next: who will contact them and when the contact will be made. Or you may make the decision to hire or not to hire right then and inform each applicant accordingly. At the end of an appraisal interview, you and the interviewee should agree on what the interviewee will strive to accomplish during the next few months and discuss how you will keep track of her achievements. To close a counseling interview, you might discuss when your next appointment will be. To close a sales interview, you should ask for the sale. In each case, the closing should reflect the purpose of the meeting and should emphasize the things you want to happen as a result of the discussion. And above all, this closing should be prepared every bit as carefully as the rest of the interview. You should not simply assume that the momentum of the interview will carry you automatically into an effective closing.

Types of Interviews in Organizations

As one of the most common and important types of communication that occurs daily within every organization, interviews can take many forms. Among them:

- *Information-giving interviews* often occur during periods of orientation and training in organizations. In the context of information-giving interviews, employees are trained, instructed, and coached in particular behaviors. Orientation interviews assist new employees in adjusting to an unfamiliar work environment. Early interviews in organizations provide a structured opportunity for managers to explain job requirements, explicate procedures, and answer questions.

- *Information-seeking interviews* can take many forms—for example, legal settings in which a lawyer interviews a client in an attempt to obtain a clear account of the client's view of the case; medical settings where doctors or nurses seek patients' medical histories and descriptions of current disorders; business or government settings in which an executive calls in a staff assistant to be briefed on a particular subject about which the assistant is especially knowledgeable; and journalistic research settings where press conferences and private interviews provide the context for interviewers to elicit facts and opinions from a person of special interest or expertise, often a celebrity.

Medical professionals commonly conduct both information-seeking and information-giving interviews. After gaining an understanding of their patients' complaints and gathering information about their medical history, doctors often devote a few minutes to explaining their diagnoses and providing treatment-related instructions. As in all interviews, both parties must strive to listen attentively.

- *Persuasive interviews* occur informally among organizational members all the time, but some employees function primarily in the specific context of persuasive interviews. The most common example of this type of interview is the sales transaction, in which a salesperson attempts to sell a specific product to a prospective customer.

- *Counseling interviews* usually are directed toward personal considerations. Organizations are increasingly recognizing the impossibility of disassociating an employee's personal and professional life. Personal problems can, and often do, create and intensify problems at work. While counseling interviews are seldom appropriate for rehabilitating employees suffering from such problems as alcoholism, depression, marital difficulties, and the like, they are often used to obtain valuable preliminary information and to encourage workers to obtain professional assistance.

- *Exit interviews* occur at a time of change in an employee's organizational affiliation. Finding good employees is never easy, and the expense of training new ones increases every year. Thus, many organizations conduct exit interviews to learn why employees leave their jobs.

Much of the information discussed earlier in this chapter applies to information-seeking interviews, and later chapters will discuss techniques for giving information. Thus, in the sections that follow, we will review techniques necessary for effectively conducting three other common interview types: appraisal, corrective, and complaint resolution.

Appraisal Interviews

The director of the Medical Records Department at St. Luke's Hospital, Nancy Walserbock, had a reputation for being one of the toughest managers in the hospital. She disapproved of socializing among the Medical Records employees, constantly emphasized that they should get as much work as possible done as quickly as possible, and closely watched everyone's activities at work. Productivity in the department was extremely high, and very few errors were made by the employees. On the other hand, morale among employees was not particularly good, and conflicts between Medical Records personnel and the physicians and nurses working in the hospital were common.

Mary Straton had worked in Medical Records for eight years, making her the second-longest-term employee in the 24-person department. She did not particularly like working for Nancy but needed the job and, in fact, took some pride in the quality of her work. Her annual appraisal interview was scheduled soon, and she expected to receive good ratings and a substantial raise.

The date for Mary's appraisal came and went. In fact, four weeks passed and she had heard nothing. One day, however, Nancy walked up to Mary's desk and said, "Mary, I'd like to see you for a minute." "Sure," Mary replied. Nancy handed her three sheets of paper. "Here are three copies of your performance review. I've already filled them out, so read them and sign them, and then give them back to me. I didn't give you much of a raise; your attitude hasn't been good lately, and you were late coming to work last week. Try to improve." Nancy walked off before Mary could reply.

This appraisal interview, such as it is, illustrates almost everything that commonly is done wrong in interviews of this type. The interview was late. No notification was given to the employee. No review of job requirements occurred. No review of performance standards or measures happened. The "recency" effect prevailed. No strengths were noted and no plans for improvement made. Small wonder that Mary filed a grievance that same afternoon and that Nancy eventually was removed from the directorship of the department.

Few situations create more discomfort for both managers and employees than performance appraisals. McGregor undoubtedly was correct when he observed that "managers are uncomfortable when they are put in the position of 'playing God.'"[12] He probably could have added that employees are equally uncomfortable about having their bosses enact that role. Yet, performance appraisals are a necessity if employee performance is to be evaluated and rewarded.

PURPOSES

While there is no substitute for good day-to-day communication between supervisor and employee, the formal yearly (or semi-yearly) performance appraisal serves some specific functions.[13] Ideally, such an appraisal should:

- Tell the employee where she stands—how the supervisor judges that employee's performance to have been during the review period.
- Give the employee guidance for doing a better job in the future by clarifying what is expected of him.

DILBERT

DILBERT © by Scott Adams; reprinted by permission of United Feature Syndicate, Inc.

- Plan developmental and growth opportunities for the employee and identify specific areas in which the employee needs to improve her knowledge and skills.
- Give the employee an opportunity to express his feelings about performance-related matters.

PROBLEMS

Research has revealed a number of common failings in performance interviews. Lahiff found that appraisal interviewers have a *tendency to dwell on* the individual's *negative characteristics*. This is a highly destructive approach, as is indicated by Kay, Meyer, and French's discovery that the more weaknesses the manager mentions during the interview, the poorer the worker's performance becomes, and the lower he rates the organization's appraisal system.[14]

A second common fault is the *halo effect*, a term first used in 1920 to describe the tendency people have to see one positive trait in someone and then to attribute to that person a variety of other positive traits. Thus, we mentally place a halo around the head of that person. If an employee arrives early and leaves late every day, we probably will be impressed. However, if this causes us to overlook the poor quality and quantity of the employee's work or his inability to get along with peers, then we have fallen victim to the halo effect.

The *central tendency effect* is yet another common problem. We may tend to classify others as "average" and not do the hard work necessary for spotting gradations. If we assign the same average rating to everyone, then we do not have to think very much about the characteristics that distinguish their performance levels. Similarly, the *leniency effect* occurs when everyone is given an equally high rating. The *critical effect* takes place when no employee can measure up to the supervisor's standards, so that all of them are judged deficient. The *recency effect* occurs when we allow more recent events to outweigh past history. A recent mistake by an employee may, psychologically, cause us to erase from the record the many previous occasions on which the employee did well.[15]

The question thus arises: How can we avoid all these problems and use appraisal interviews in ways that maximize their effectiveness as analytic and motivational tools? Our own experience suggests that effective appraisal interviewing is a result of two things: careful preparation and skillful procedures. We will consider each of these in turn.

PREPARATION

You should do three things as you prepare for an appraisal session. First, you should *review the requirements of the employee's job*. Much evidence suggests that supervisors and subordinates have quite different perceptions of the employee's job and that supervisors' rarely are able to provide accurate descriptions of their employees' written job duties as expressed in job descriptions.[16] It is vital that you review the tasks that the employee ought to have performed and that you decide in your own mind which of them is more important than the others. If you have conducted past appraisals for this employee, you should also review those to remind yourself of any plans for performance improvement that the two of you developed in previous meetings.

Second, you should *obtain input from the employee concerning her level of performance*. Using a written questionnaire (perhaps similar to the preappraisal form in figure 8.2), the employee should describe for you those objectives she felt were achieved, the behaviors she was to perform, the strengths and weaknesses of the performance, and her short- and long-range career objectives. Remember, superiors and subordinates typically have different perceptions. By obtaining this sort of information, you are able to review the employee's perceptions before your interview begins.

Third, you should *complete the performance review form*, if any, that your organization requires. These forms are important, for they provide a written record of the decisions you and your employee make about his performance.[17] As such, they may serve as the basis for future personnel decisions (such as promotions, transfers, or discharge), or they may protect you from action taken against you by an employee.

When completing the review form before the interview, you must make one final decision: Will the ratings you provide serve as the final appraisal of the employee, or will they simply be a worksheet that you will use to guide the inter-

---

Instructions: In the space provided below, answer the questions posed.

1. Since your last interview, how well do you think you have performed? Give specific examples, details, information, and so on that indicate why you feel as you do.

2. Looking toward the future, in what ways do you think your performance can be improved, and how can your supervisor help you to achieve those improvements?

3. What long-term goals for personal development or achievement do you have? How can your supervisor help you achieve them?

4. What long-term objectives for personal and professional development do you have? How can your supervisor help you to achieve them?

5. What additional comments, if any, do you have concerning your performance during the past year, your future objectives, or your upcoming performance appraisal?

Figure 8.2   Employees' preappraisal summary

view, which you will revise when the interview is over? Strong arguments can be offered for each alternative. If your ratings stand, then you will not be persuaded by employees who are not good workers but who are good salespersons. More than once we have seen good workers suffer because they are not very skilled interviewees and poorer workers come out well because they are good at "slinging the bull." If your rating is to be final, then the principle of cooperative problem solving is violated. Thus, you may want to take a compromise approach: Use the rating forms to provide your final rating of the employee's performance (perhaps taking into account the self-perception information you have obtained in advance), and use the interview to communicate those ratings to the employee and then to cooperatively develop a plan for future improvements in his performance.

PROCEDURES

While a number of approaches to the appraisal interview are available, one of the most reasonable systems is that suggested by Brett and Fredian.[18] They suggest a seven-step model for performance appraisal. The first step is to *get to the point of the interview*. The appraisal should begin with a statement of the purpose of the meeting and a brief overview of the structure that the interview will follow.

The supervisor next should *describe specifically the important elements of the employee's past performance*. The supervisor should talk about criteria that both of them understand (amount of work, quality of work) and should give both good and bad examples of the employee's performance. These specifics are important. The employee learns nothing if she is simply told, "You are doing a good job." The discussion should focus on work-related matters and should deal only with performance areas that are really important. Perhaps the best way to ensure these things is to state the specific job requirement and then provide specific indications of performance. For example:

"Pat, part of your job is to write monthly summary reports of employee relations activities in each production plant and to have those to all members of top management by the fifteenth of the next month. In 5 of your 12 reports, you were more than one week late in getting those reports out. I want to discuss this with you."

This statement indicates the job requirement, provides specific information, tells Pat what is important to the supervisor, and indicates that he will have a chance to discuss the matter before any final decisions are reached. This is far superior to simply saying, "Pat, your ER reports are often late."

Third, the supervisor should *provide employees with a chance to give their own observations*. As you invite them to describe their performance, you perform step 4 in the appraisal process: *listen*. Using the techniques reviewed in earlier chapters, actively and attentively listen to the employees, both encouraging them to talk and retaining the information for use in the last portions of the interview.

When we have analyzed past performance, the fifth step is to *lay out future plans and goals*. Here, we need to take the problem-solving approach—improving performance weaknesses from the past and assessing new objectives or goals to be accomplished in the future. What does the employee feel she should do to achieve her goals, and how does the employee feel you should evaluate the quality of her performance in doing them? Naturally, you have your own ideas about the

---

Business Brief 8.2

Key Questions for Performance Appraisal

Performance evaluations can help people to reach their potential when they include such questions as:

- What are five key projects or goals you have here, and how can I help to support them?
- Does our company need you? What do you want to do here? What are you planning to do to reach your goals?
- What will you do in the coming year to develop the three highest-potential people who work for you?
- What are your personal plans for continuing education and development for the coming year?

Source: "Performance-Review Questions," *Communication Briefings* (February 1993): 6.

---

employee's goals and objectives, so you will need to work together to arrive at an action plan for next year's performance. Finally, just as the employee commits to achieving certain goals, so too must the supervisor commit to providing any assistance the employee might need. Part of the performance action plan, therefore, should include the assistance and resources that the supervisor is to provide.

The last two steps of the procedure make up the interview's closing. First, to make sure that both parties understand what decisions have been reached, *the employee should be asked to summarize the discussion*. Second, supervisor and subordinate should *agree on some follow-up procedure*. Rather than waiting until the next annual review, they should schedule meetings for progress reports and feedback, enabling both of them to adjust their behaviors as necessary. If performance problems arise, they can correct them quickly rather than waiting for the entire year to elapse.

Typically, all these things are put in writing, signed by both parties, and placed in the employee's permanent file. Again, this sort of record keeping is important to the employee, the supervisor, and the entire organization.[19]

TIPS FOR THE APPRAISEE

When you are being appraised, you should communicate in ways that help your boss to appraise you more effectively and that protect your rights as an employee. Briefly, you always have a right to know the standards by which you are evaluated, to discuss points that are unclear to you, to dispute things you feel are unfair or untrue, to have some input in determining your future goals and performance objectives, and to know what the final outcome of the appraisal will be. With these rights in mind, you should do the following:

- *Keep track of your own performance.* Be sure to maintain your own performance file by keeping copies of memos, letters, achievements, shortcomings, comments from other people, and so on that help provide a clear picture of how you have performed.

- *Know what the performance standards are.* If your company has a performance evaluation form, be sure you get a copy of it (ask for one from your supervisor). If there is no such form, ask your supervisor to spend some time with you outlining his priorities and expectations. This information should be obtained whenever you go to work for a new boss.

- *Encourage your boss to talk about behaviors, not personalities.* Statements like "You are lazy," "You are irresponsible," or even "You are very pleasant with others" tell you little about what you did or should do. Always ask for specific examples of behaviors to be sure you know what your boss means.

- *Ask your boss to suggest methods of improvement,* both in your short-term performance and in your long-term professional growth. Part of the plan coming out of your evaluation should deal with things you will do to improve yourself over time and possibly ways in which your boss will help that improvement.

- *Ask for a copy of the appraisal in writing,* just to keep for your own records. If the appraisal has an effect on your raise, ask what that will be.

- *If you disagree, do so in a way that stresses the facts and is not argumentative.* Give examples to support your opinions, but recognize that, in the end, your boss probably will be "right."

- *If you feel the appraisal is unfair, say so* (in a matter-of-fact, nonaccusatory way) to your boss and ask what your next step should be. Most companies have a grievance procedure through which unfair evaluations can be protested.

- *Between evaluations, ask your boss for feedback.* If you do not know how you are doing during the year, it is too late to correct performance problems when the time for performance evaluation arrives.

Corrective Interviews

Corrective interviews are a necessity in every organization. Organizations must have behavioral expectations for their members, and often those expectations are stated in the form of rules, policies, and procedures. In turn, people occasionally may violate these expectations. When such a violation occurs, it becomes the responsibility of the interviewer (often a supervisor or manager) to determine why it occurred and to motivate the violator not to do it again. All of this should be achieved through corrective interviews. In this section, we will consider the pitfalls surrounding corrective interviews and suggest procedures whereby such interviews can be used to improve performance while respecting others' rights.

PURPOSES

Most managers would prefer to avoid having to discipline or correct the behavior of their subordinates. Even so, the corrective interview is aimed at achieving a number of important goals.

- It attempts to correct behaviors that violate the expectations of the organization. The keyword is "correct." The goal of discipline in an organization is not punishment—it is correction.

- Corrective interviews also serve as a notice to other employees that rules are enforced and that violations of those rules are simply not ignored. When it becomes clear that violations of rules, policies, and procedures are confronted and corrected, employees will take greater care to abide by those rules.

- Protection of employees is another purpose of corrective interviews. Many organizational rules relate directly to employee safety. Rules against horseplay, drinking on the job, using drugs, theft, sabotage, and failing to follow established work procedures are all designed to protect employees from other employees or even from themselves.

Corrective interviews should preserve justice and fairness. They should ensure that everyone is treated equally and that the rights of all employees are respected and preserved. This is perhaps the most important purpose of corrective actions.

PROBLEMS

A virtually limitless number of problems occur during corrective proceedings. For example, as Alpander notes, supervisors generally are *reluctant to criticize* or *discipline* in the first place.[20] Lacking the knowledge they need to discipline constructively and desiring popularity with their people, they simply avoid taking action against employees at all. The opposite problem is *overcriticism*—angrily bawling out the employee in front of others. In such situations, the employee usually is taken by surprise, is embarrassed in front of others, and is given no opportunity to respond or react.

Still *other problems stem from procedural matters*—failure to document corrective action so that appropriate records are retained and the supervisor is protected against charges of bias or discrimination, failure to take action promptly, failure to learn all the facts before taking action, failure to follow written policies concerning corrective proceedings, failure to discipline in privacy, failure to develop a positive plan of action. Many of these failures are similar to the problems encountered in appraisal interviews; indeed, there are many parallels between these two interview types.

Business Brief 8.3

One Approach to Discipline

While formalized procedures for taking disciplinary action with hourly employees are relatively common, corrective action for salaried professionals tends to be done much more haphazardly. One company, HR Textron in Valencia, California, has attempted to implement a four-step policy specifically designed for salaried employees. These steps include:

1. A formal, documented discussion between the employee and his or her supervisor, with the supervisor keeping the paperwork generated by this discussion

2. Another formal, documented discussion, with the paperwork being placed in the employee's personnel file along with the write-up from the first step

3. A third documented discussion that may involve a probationary period or some time off from work, along with a warning that continued behavioral problems will lead to termination

4. Termination

All supervisors and managers were trained to implement this procedure effectively, and legal changes associated with discipline of professional staff dropped dramatically.

Source: Martin Levy, "Discipline for Professional Employees," *Personnel Journal* 69 (December 1990): 27–28.

Unfortunately, there is one important way in which corrective interviews and appraisal interviews differ. When appraisal interviews are done badly, they adversely affect the performance of the employee, but they do not typically lead to spectacular consequences. Not so with corrective proceedings. If an employee feels he has been wronged through corrective action, the employee may file a grievance. In unionized situations, this grievance may be accompanied by union demands for redress or management action against the offending supervisor. If such action is not forthcoming, strikes or work slowdowns could result. In non-union settings, the employee may take his grievance to an outside arbitrator, who may rule against the organization. In cases of dismissal, for example, this may result in the employee being reinstated and given back pay. Either way, the supervisor is caught up in a swirl of controversy and often is sorry he took the action in the first place. Fear of such consequences only makes other supervisors more hesitant to discipline their employees.

Briefly put, corrective procedures can be dangerous to the supervisors who invoke them. Nevertheless, discipline must be invoked on occasion, and if the supervisors know what they are doing, the corrective interview can be an effective way of correcting behavior and improving performance. Our purpose in the following sections is to suggest ways to minimize the risks of disciplining and to maximize the utility of those encounters.

PREPARATION

Corrective interviews depend heavily on thorough preparation for their success. Before initiating a corrective meeting, you should do a number of things.

1. Identify and analyze the problem. Identify specifically what has been happening and determine why it has happened. Be sure a problem exists that calls for corrective action before you confront the interviewee.

2. Check the interviewee's work record. Determine whether she has been corrected before and, if so, for what. Determine whether she has been a good, dependable worker in the past and whether the present situation represents a continuation of bad behaviors or a sudden change in behavior. While you must be consistent in the way you administer the organization's rules, you also must adapt your own behavior to the individual case.

3. Review the organization's corrective rules. In most organizations, work rules have been developed that specify the types of punishable infractions and perhaps the severity of the action to be taken in each case. Repeated lateness, for example, is typically handled by an oral warning, while theft and sabotage are handled by immediate suspension or dismissal. You need to know what the appropriate action is.

4. Examine your own attitudes and motives. The relationship that exists between you and the employee has a significant impact on the corrective interview that is about to take place. You must be certain that your actions are based on objective facts and behaviors and not on your personal biases or feelings about the employee.

PROCEDURES

The first step is to *notify the interviewee that you want to meet* with her. Obviously, you should not confront the employee in front of her peers and publicly

---

Business Brief 8.4

Offering Criticism with Tact and Sensitivity

Here are 12 guidelines to remember the next time you have to tell someone that he or she has done something wrong.

1. Identify the behavior that you want to criticize. Direct your criticism at the action, not the person.

2. Make criticisms specific. Not "You always miss deadlines," but "You missed the March 15 deadline for your report."

3. Be sure the behavior you're criticizing can be changed. Foreign accents, baldness, and other things tangentially related to some business dealings cannot always be changed.

4. Use "we" and "us" to stress that you want to work out the problem together, rather than making threats.

5. Make sure the other person understands the reason for your criticism.

6. Don't belabor the point. Keep your remarks short and sweet; don't lecture.

7. Offer incentives for changed behavior. Offer to help the person correct the problem.

8. Don't set a tone of anger or sarcasm. Both are counterproductive.

9. Show the person you understand his or her feelings.

10. If you're putting your criticism in writing, cool off before writing the critical letter or memo. Be sure only the person it is intended for sees it.

11. Start off by saying something good.

12. At the end, reaffirm your support for and confidence in the person.

Source: Blue Cross and Blue Shield of Michigan, *Highlights,* reprinted in *The Working Communicator* (October 1998): 2–3.

---

embarrass the employee by yelling. The interview should be held privately and after any emotions or anger have cooled down, and it should be done as soon after the infraction as possible (again allowing time for the preparation described above).

When the employee arrives (and the door is closed), **get directly to the point.** Engaging in small talk to relax the interviewee would probably be counterproductive. The way in which you state the point, however, is crucial. Under no circumstances should you begin by condemning or accusing the employee. The most certain way to make the employee defensive and to stop two-way communication is to begin with statements like:

- "Karen, what are you trying to do to this department (or me)?"
- "Ralph, I'm fed up with you always being late to work."
- "You've goofed off for the last time, Maria. I'm writing you up."

Generally, corrective interviews should be **treated as problem-solving sessions.** You and the interviewee have a mutual problem, and the two of you need to arrive at a solution. The best way to begin the interview is to define that problem by stating two things: (1) the behavioral expectation (such as the applicable rule or job requirement) and (2) the information you have about the person's behavior. For example:

"Jim, you know that shop rules prohibit drinking on the job. When people drink, their own work suffers, and they become dangerous to everyone else. Now, I've been told by three different people that you've been seen drinking during break periods. I'm concerned about that, and that's why I asked you to come in. What can you tell me about this?"

Through this statement, you have posed the problem, and you have asked the person for input. You have not said, "What do you have to say for yourself?" which would create a trial-like atmosphere. Instead, you've simply indicated a desire for information from the interviewee.

Your next task is to **listen**. By letting the person talk, and by asking questions when necessary, you should determine what, in the interviewee's view, actually took place. You should also obtain his explanation of why it happened, and you should ask the person to explain the appropriate rules to you.

You then face two tasks: First, you must *tell the person what corrective action is to be taken against him*. This action may range from a written warning placed in the employee's file to a suspension from work to outright termination. Then, if termination is not the action, you should work with the interviewee to determine how he will improve in the future. Through two-way, cooperative communication, the two of you decide what the person is to do, how he is to achieve that, and what you might do to help. Then you set some sort of follow-up schedule whereby you meet again to determine what progress, if any, has occurred.

When the interview has been completed and a behavioral action plan has been agreed to, the *proper documentation must also be completed*. Most organizations have forms for this purpose, and the supervisor is required to indicate the actions taken, reasons for discipline, and plans for future improvement. The supervisor then signs the form, as does the employee, and the completed paperwork is sent to the supervisor's immediate superior or to the personnel department. Since most organizations have corrective policies that say that subsequent offenses receive more severe punishment, this record will guide future corrective actions for this employee.

TIPS FOR WHEN YOU ARE DISCIPLINED

It is hoped that you never will be on the receiving end of a corrective interview. Still, if you find yourself being disciplined, there are some things you

---

Highlighting Ethics

Avoiding Lawsuits Through Honesty

- How well employees are treated when being fired or laid off may determine whether they sue their ex-bosses, Ohio State University (OSU) researchers found.

- The school also found in a study of nearly 1,000 fired Ohio workers that they were more likely to sue if they weren't given a full explanation of why they were being let go.

- Jerald Greenberg, a professor of management and human resources at OSU's Fisher College of Business, estimated companies could save at least $13,200 per termination by being honest with fired workers.

Source: "When Firing Workers, Courtesy Pays Off," *San Francisco Examiner*, July 19, 1998, sec. J, 1.

should do both to protect your rights as an employee and to ensure that you avoid similar corrective actions in the future.

- *Be sure you know what the work rules and policies are.* Often, corrective actions come about because employees unknowingly broke some rule or policy. Whenever you go to work for a new boss, ask her to discuss the rules and policies for your department.
- In a corrective interview, *listen calmly to everything your boss has to say.* Hear her out before you react. Often, quick and angry reactions from employees being disciplined cause these situations to escalate out of hand.
- *Encourage your boss to focus on specific behaviors.* Statements like "You're always breaking the rules" and "You're always late" are too general to tell you what specifically happened. Ask your boss to report what you did, when and where it happened, and so on.
- *If there are circumstances that need to be explained, give them.* Do not offer excuses, however; simply explain any factors that might cause your boss to take a different view of what happened.
- *Express your desire to avoid this kind of thing in the future.* Ask your boss to help you develop some sort of action plan that will improve your performance or work-related behaviors. Also ask for frequent feedback from your boss that will help you do better.
- *Be sure you understand the corrective action being taken.* Determine whether this conversation counts as an oral warning or a written warning and what the next step in the corrective process is if this happens again.
- *If you feel the action is unfair, say so calmly and in a matter-of-fact way.* Give your reasons. Then ask your boss what additional steps or channels are available to you. Typically, there is a grievance procedure through which corrective actions can be protested.

Above all, you should try to maintain a problem-solving attitude throughout the proceedings. Obviously, your boss must think there is a problem; otherwise, you would not be having this conversation. Your task is to determine why your boss feels a problem exists, and then to lay out a personal action plan whereby similar problems can be avoided in the future. By asking for the most complete information you can get and for assistance in improving your behavior, you encourage your boss to be helpful rather than punishing.

Complaint Resolution Interviews

Occasionally, interviews will be initiated not by the interviewer, but by an interviewee who has a particular issue in mind—a complaint, a problem needing resolution, or even a formal grievance. While these situations often allow little or no preparation by the interviewer, taking a systematic approach to complaint resolution interviews helps to turn these potentially inflammatory conversations into positive, constructive experiences.

PURPOSES

Since the interviewee initiates this type of interview, it is important to consider first some purposes she may have in mind, such as:

- "blowing off steam" by getting a problem off her chest;
- reporting misbehavior on the part of another person;
- conveying information to the interviewer just to keep her informed;
- bringing a problem or concern for discussion and resolution.

Before deciding how to proceed with the interview, the interviewer often must first determine why the interviewee has come and what her expectations are. Trying to engage in constructive problem solving when the interviewee just wants to blow off steam, for example, is likely to be unproductive and could even create greater frustration. From the interviewer's perspective, several purposes might be achieved, such as:

- demonstrating to the interviewee a genuine interest in her concerns;
- determining what the interviewee would like to see done with regard to her issue;
- if appropriate, developing an acceptable solution and plan for action that resolves the interviewee's concern;
- establishing clear expectations for follow-up after the interview.

By achieving these objectives, the interviewer can both resolve the issue at hand and, long term, build a better relationship with the interviewee.

PROBLEMS

When a complaint is brought to us, our reaction determines to a large extent how successful this interview will be and how likely it is the interviewee will bring another problem to us at some later time. Unfortunately, there are many common reactions that make complaint resolution interviews less than successful. For example, *reacting defensively* serves to stifle conversation rather than enhance problem solving. Yet, if we perceive the complaint to be a potential attack on our competence, character, or intent, we are likely to respond by surrendering, retreating, or counterattacking. On the other hand, *jumping to a solution* may appear positive (since the interviewer evidently is attempting to resolve the interviewee's issue), but may be unsuccessful because the solution does not adequately consider the actual nature of the problem. And finally, *taking responsibility for the other person's issue* allows the interviewee to delegate the burden of problem solving to the interviewer and may even allow the interviewee to play "critic" and shoot down every potential solution the interviewer suggests. Generally, it is far better for the interviewer to put responsibility for developing potential solutions squarely where it belongs: on the shoulders of the person raising the issue in the first place.

How can we avoid these inappropriate reactions and react in ways that maximize the problem-solving and relationship-building effectiveness of complaint resolution interviews? Research and experience suggest that effective complaint resolution comes about through the systematic application of information-gathering and problem-solving skills.[21]

PREPARATION AND PROCEDURES

When an employee makes an appointment to see you, you may not always know precisely what is on his mind. However, if you *do* have some inkling of an issue or problem, you may want to do a little preliminary homework. You may also choose to inquire (or have your assistant inquire) about the basic purpose of the meeting. To prepare for the interview, you may want to pull the employee's file and look over it for basic information about his tenure with the organization, as well as employment and salary history. If you know that the complaint pertains to a particular organizational policy, such as affirmative action, sexual harassment, or employee safety, you may also want to review the policy in question.

Once you are talking with the employee during the complaint resolution interview, there are a number of constructive actions you can take. *Begin by listening*. Hearing both the intellectual *and* the emotional content of the interviewee's concern is a crucial first step toward arriving at a workable solution. Moreover, in many instances the interviewee simply wants to blow off steam and wants nothing more than an attentive hearing.

Next, *ask exploratory questions*. To develop a thorough understanding of the issue (and to help the interviewee fully express his concerns), ask questions that encourage further elaboration of the issue: What happened? Where did it happen? When did it happen? Why did it happen? Who was involved? By asking these questions, you both gain a more thorough understanding of the problem and you demonstrate to the interviewee your interest in his concern.

Summarize what you think you have heard. To be sure you have understood the interviewee correctly (and to illustrate your desire to understand), state for the interviewee what you think you have heard and observed. You should report in summary form what the situation seems to be, of course, but you also might report your observations concerning how the person is feeling: "You seem to be really angry about this," or "I can see this really has you concerned."

Next, you might *ask for the interviewee's suggested solutions*. Often, the interviewee already has in mind what he would like to have done in response to his concern. Rather than attempting to guess the interviewee's preferred solution, it often is most effective to ask, "What do you think ought to be done about this?" If the interviewee cannot or will not suggest a possible solution, discontinue the interview until some specified later time and date and ask the interviewee to think about possible solutions and bring them to the next session.

Once some approaches to resolving the issue have been listed, the next step is to *evaluate each solution* in terms of its desirability. Will the suggested solution actually solve the problem? Will it have any undesirable side effects? Could it create any new problems?

Growing from your assessment of possible solutions, *develop a plan for action*. When a solution acceptable to both has been devised, a specific plan of action should be developed that answers the questions "Who will do what, when, where, and how?" Obviously, the more specific the plan, the more likely it is the actions will be taken and the better able both parties will be to track the success of their solution.

At this point, it may be tempting to implement the action plan and hope for the best. But you will need to assess the plan to see if it is working. The next stop, then, is to *develop a schedule for follow-up*. An appointment should be made for another interview, one in which discussion will focus on how successful the agreed-upon action has been in resolving the interviewee's concerns. This follow-up conversation will allow both parties to evaluate how pleased they are with the progress that has been made and to make whatever adjustments are necessary in the initial action plan.

Finally, *thank the interviewee*. Although it can be uncomfortable (at least initially) to have a complaint brought to you, such interviews are important. Problems cannot be resolved if they remain hidden, and trust cannot be built if risks are not taken. Therefore, the interviewer should express sincere appreciation to the interviewee for having raised the issue and should encourage the individual to bring similar issues to the fore in the future.

By making a habit of this sort of systematic approach to handling problems and complaints, we can overcome the lack of preparation time such interviews typically allow and use to maximum advantage these communication opportunities.

TIPS FOR INITIATING A COMPLAINT

Sometimes, those who are in less powerful positions in organizations are reluctant to initiate complaints. They may fear that complaining will lead to a poor performance appraisal, reduced chances of promotion, a diminished income, or even termination. Of course, depending on the organizational culture and the particular employer you are dealing with, articulating a complaint can be risky business. Yet, if you are unhappy or feel that you have been treated unfairly, you may not be able to remain a productive employee if you are not able to air your concerns. You will be more likely to receive a fair hearing if you follow these guidelines:

- *Choose your battles selectively.* No one wants to be seen as a nag or whiner. No manager has time to deal with an employee who is always complaining about something. So, ask for a meeting to discuss a complaint only when you feel that the issue is serious and merits a focused conversation.[22]

- *Establish rapport.* Thank your boss for taking the time to meet with you. If you have enjoyed working for this organization, if you genuinely like your job, say so. Make it clear that you value your relationship with your manager and with the company as a whole.

- *Show that you have attempted to work within the system.* Let us say that you are unhappy because you have been given a new office mate with whom you feel you are completely incompatible. When you talk to your boss about the situation, you will want to show that you have demonstrated patience, have modified some of your own behaviors, and have taken specific steps to be accommodating.

- *If possible, support your claims with evidence.* For instance, let us say that you are complaining because one of your coworkers is sexually harassing you. If others have witnessed the harassment and they are willing to testify, tell your manager that others can support your perceptions. Or, if you have kept a journal, show your manager the entries that describe specific behaviors, dates, and locations.

- *Monitor your nonverbal communication.* Initiating a complaint can be stressful. If we are not careful, our nonverbal behaviors will communicate that we are uptight, frustrated, or angry. It's important, then, to avoid such negative communicative behaviors as speaking rapidly, speaking in a high pitch, self-touching, poor eye contact, and nervous mannerisms, such as playing with a pen or tapping our fingers on the table.

- *Anticipate interrupting questions.* Your boss will likely have questions for you; and she may well interrupt you to ask them as you go along, rather than waiting until you are finished. You may be asked for clarification, for dates, for examples, for a more detailed explanation, and so forth. Don't be put off by these interruptions. Your boss may simply want to ask something while it is fresh in her mind.

- *Be prepared to offer possible solutions*. Sometimes managers are sympathetic to a complaint, but may not know how to address it. Since *you* are the one with the issue, chances are you have given a great deal more thought to it than has anyone else. You can be helpful to your boss if you show that you have considered the problem as constructively as possible and can offer some suggestions of ways the situation can be improved. Anyone can point to problems, but truly valued employees are those who are able to generate solutions.

- *Be prepared to wait*. In all likelihood, your boss will want to mull things over before taking any action. Don't be frustrated by this. You may have been living with a problem for weeks, months, or even years, but your boss has only just become aware of it. Wise managers will not want to act impulsively. They may need to solicit other perspectives or check out evidence. They will need time to think, especially if your complaint pertains to a truly serious issue.

- *Make sure you know what to expect next*. Many complainants become frustrated because they don't understand what will happen once the interview is over. They may think they will hear something the next day; but a week later, they are still sitting in their offices wondering what's going on. Clarify the boss's time frame before you leave the office.

- *Conclude with a word of thanks*. Your boss's time is valuable. Conclude as you began by thanking him for taking the time to meet with you and listen to your concerns.

Remember, the *way* you handle yourself during and following the complaint resolution interview may well influence the outcome.

THE ETHICS OF INTERVIEWING

In a sense, conducting an interview is no different from engaging in other forms of organizational communicative interaction, in that ethical behavior is important. But being an interviewer places a special emphasis on the need for ethics. Almost by definition, interviewers are individuals with authority. In most cases, the interviewer has the ability to make some decision affecting the fate or well-being of the interviewee. In employment interviews, the interviewer can eliminate the applicant from further consideration. In corrective interviews, the interviewer can choose the terms of the punishment or the nature of the contract employees must fulfill if they wish to remain with the company.

In any interview, the interviewer officially represents the organization, and his conduct reflects on the standards, values, and ethics of the organization. The interviewer who asks offensive or illegal questions, who speaks rudely or condescendingly to a fellow employee, or who refuses to listen to the interviewee's explanations or ideas not only reveals himself as insensitive or unethical, he also suggests that the company condones such behavior. One of our former students was interviewed by a personnel manager who represented a major U.S. manufacturing company. This woman was initially quite pleased when she received the opportunity to interview with this company. During the interview, however, the

Highlighting Ethics

Performance Evaluations

Why must performance evaluations be conducted appropriately and ethically? Consider these cases:

- A marketing manager received excellent ratings but was demoted because she refused to stop dating a salesman from a competitor. She resigned, then sued her employer, claiming that she had in effect been fired. The court reviewed her evaluation records and concluded that the employer was guilty of wrongful discharge. The company was fined $300,000.

- Appraisals of an engineering department manager showed steadily declining performance and indicated he had become increasingly sarcastic and disruptive in meetings. But when he was fired, he sued, claiming that after 23 years on the job, he did not believe the warnings he had been given could lead to discharge. The court found that since his evaluations did not indicate he could be fired, the manager should be reinstated and paid more than $60,000 by the company.

Careful communication and documentation during performance evaluations are becoming increasingly important as employees show greater willingness to take former employers to court.

Source: James M. Jenks, "Do Your Performance Appraisals Boost Productivity?" *Management Review* (June 1991): 46.

interviewer asked her several personal (and illegal) questions, focusing in particular on her fiancé's attitude toward the prospect of her traveling all over the country. Not only did this woman leave the interview with a feeling of disgust, she decided that she wanted no further dealings with this organization. Even when she received a letter inviting her to visit the company for a second interview, she declined.

Illegal interviewing practices are always unethical. But unethical interviewing occurs whenever interviewers treat interviewees with disrespect, use their authority to make employees feel powerless or threatened, or refuse to listen or even to give an interviewee the chance to speak. By contrast, the ethical interviewer:

- shows concern for the interviewee and his or her feelings;
- is interested in finding out what the interviewee thinks;
- genuinely listens;
- communicates respectfully with the interviewee;
- plans the interview time so that information exchange can, in fact, occur;
- is familiar with the law and other organizational rules to be sure of operating within a legal framework;
- is knowledgeable concerning the organization's code of ethics, either formal or informal;
- is sensitive to power and authority differences in the interview setting and seeks to minimize their potentially negative effects.

Behaving ethically as an interviewer is a matter of knowledge, common sense, goodwill, and hard work.

SUMMARY

In this chapter, we have acquainted you with the types and functions of interviews in organizations. We have pointed out the pervasiveness of interviewing activities, as well as the critical communication functions served by interviews, such as information giving and seeking, persuading, and problem solving. In the interviewing context, we hire people, evaluate them, counsel them, discipline them, sell things to them, solve problems with them, gain information from them, and occasionally fire them. We also commonly play the role of interviewee as we are appraised, counseled, persuaded, and so forth. Our ability to function effectively in each of these contexts will contribute to our personal and professional success.

More than any other single factor, the key to successful interviewing is preparation. As we saw in this chapter, whether the interview is aimed at appraisal, correction, or complaint resolution, we must first analyze our own purposes, and we must consider the attitudes, knowledge, behaviors, and characteristics of our interviewee. Then we must carefully plan the opening of the interview, the types of questions we will ask and the order in which we will ask them, and the way in which we will close the encounter. Moreover, we must take care to listen and react to the interviewee, so that we can make modifications in our interview game plan as needed. Above all, we must resolve to treat the interview as a problem-solving situation, one in which both participants have their own needs and priorities and in which they will work together (in keeping with ethical interviewing practices) to develop action plans whereby each set of needs can be met. By taking this sort of approach, we significantly enhance our chances for success as an interviewer.

Questions for Discussion

1. How would you distinguish an interview from other kinds of dyadic encounters?

2. What are some of the types of interviews commonly encountered in all types of organizations?

3. From the interviewer's perspective, describe the planning necessary for conducting effective interviews.

4. How might cultural or gender differences complicate the way individuals interact and react to each other in interviews?

5. Compare and contrast the following, giving examples of each:

   a. Directive versus nondirective strategy

   b. Open versus closed questions

   c. Probing versus restatement

   d. Hypothetical versus reactive probes

6. Discuss the concept of question bias. How can biased questions be used effectively? Are they ever unethical? How?

7. Compare and contrast the following questioning sequences: funnel, inverted funnel, diamond, hourglass, and tunnel.

8. Under what circumstances might a corrective interview be held?

9. What are some specific ways that you can prepare for and conduct a successful corrective interview?

10. How might you conduct yourself if you are ever in the position of being disciplined?

11. Why are appraisal interviews important?

12. What are some common problems associated with appraisal interviews?

13. How might you best prepare for and conduct an effective appraisal interview?

14. When your performance is being appraised in an interview, how will you conduct yourself?

15. What goals are served by complaint resolution interviews?

16. How can you best prepare for and handle yourself if one of your employees schedules an interview to discuss a complaint?

17. What are the critical characteristics of an ethical interviewer?

Exercises

1. Choose a local organization and make an appointment to meet with someone in a leadership position. Carefully plan an interview, with the goal of discovering what kind of appraisal system the organization uses. If there is a written form, ask if you can have a copy of it. If appraisal interviews are held, find out how often and the types of procedures used. Then, write a 1–2 page report in which you assess the strengths and weaknesses of their appraisal system. Be sure to comment on how the system might be improved.

2. Think of an organization you might like to work for in the future. Obtain a copy of that organization's corrective policy or work rules. How would a supervisor in that organization deal with an employee who was repeatedly late to work? Be specific. Come to class prepared to discuss your findings with your classmates.

3. One of the most common kinds of complaints that surfaces in academic organizations is the grade complaint. During class, pair up with one of your classmates. One of you will play the role of the professor and the other will play the role of a student who has received a C- on a recent assignment. For about 10 minutes, hold an interview in which the student complains to the professor about the grade. Follow the guidelines in this chapter. Then, when the interview is over, discuss how well you think you and your partner conducted yourselves. What would you change, if you had to do it over again?

4. Look around your campus community and identify a nonprofit organization that you would like to learn more about (such as Girls Inc., Habitat for Humanity, Boys and Girls Club, the Humane Association, or a local soup kitchen). Contact someone in a leadership position, such as the volunteer coordinator, and arrange for an interview. Prepare for this informational interview by planning how you will open the interview, structure it with a series of open-ended questions (with follow-up probes), and bring it to a courteous conclusion. As a result of your interview, what did you learn about the mission

of this organization? Programs? Priorities? Need for resources and volunteers? Write a short (2–3 page) paper in which you profile this organization. Based on what you learned from the interview, will you consider volunteering with this organization in the future?

Case Application 8.1   Harried Harry

A medium-sized business recently hired a new manager, Frederick Vine. Although Fred viewed his new position as a definite step up, in that this company was more prestigious than the one for which he had previously worked, he was extremely unhappy with his new secretary, Harry. Harry preferred to think of himself as an "administrative assistant" rather than a secretary. He was quite active in the clerical union and spent many hours (during the workday) discussing union-related activities on the telephone. Harry also had a bad back and severe allergies and often called in sick. Fred perceived him as lazy, irresponsible, and uncooperative.

When Fred first arrived, he simply tried to go with the flow and adjust to his new secretary's habits. This proved difficult, however, because he found Harry's habits very offensive. At his previous company, in contrast, he had had an ideal female secretary who was sharp, motivated, and hardworking. After a short time, Fred decided he had to do something.

Fred began by summoning Harry to his office and sharing with him a lengthy document he had written on office procedures. He explained to Harry why they were important. He noted that although his predecessor had not articulated such procedures, he simply could not operate without them. The procedures specified a number of work rules that affected all members of the staff—with a particular emphasis on the secretaries. Fred asked if Harry had any questions, and Harry responded negatively. Fred assumed, therefore, that he had made himself clear and that things would improve.

Fred was soon proved wrong. Harry's behavior did not change. In fact, about a week after he received the new set of rules, he e-mailed Fred that his back was really in bad shape and therefore he couldn't come to work that day. The next day he had a close friend call another secretary in the department and leave Fred a note indicating that Harry's back was so bad that he would probably not be in for the rest of the week.

Fred was furious. He decided to take additional, more aggressive action. He began by interviewing several members of his department to discover their perceptions of the situation. He was informed of several specific examples involving instances of what he considered to be unprofessional behavior on Harry's part (like playing computer games nearly every day from 4:00–5:00 PM). Upon Harry's return, Fred began to keep a careful log of all Harry's peculiarities, noting how they deviated from the new office procedures. Predictably, he accumulated quite a list. After several weeks, he consulted with the director of personnel to make sure he wasn't violating any company rules. Then, he wrote Harry a stern three-page letter in which he listed all his deficiencies in specific detail. He left this letter on Harry's desk so that he encountered it first thing on a Monday morning, and then busied himself with other tasks.

Later in the day, Fred called Harry in to ask if he had made himself clear. He asked if Harry understood the changes he needed to make if he were to remain gainfully employed. With teeth gritted, Harry said he did. He offered a few comments on how difficult it was to adjust to Fred's style of leadership—a style that stood in stark contrast to his previous boss's. Harry mentioned the fact that he was 45 years old and had legitimate health problems. During the conversation, Fred interrupted him several times to inquire about other sorts of issues, such as how soon Harry thought he would be able to master some newly acquired software—a mail merge program. As Harry attempted to respond to his questions, Fred tipped back in his chair and quietly watched him. Harry couldn't help noticing that Fred occasionally tapped his fingers on his chair arms with a subtle air of impatience.

Questions

1. Using the information about corrective interviews and performance appraisals presented in this chapter, how would you evaluate Fred's communication behavior?

2. How might Fred have communicated with Harry more effectively?

3. What role (if any) did the choice of communication modes (face-to-face, written [the procedures and the letter], telephone, and e-mail) play in affecting this situation? How might the varied modes have been used more effectively?

9

The Employment Interview

After reading this chapter, you should be able to:

❑ Understand the role and significance of the employment interview in the selection process

❑ List and explain the steps involved in preparing to interview applicants

❑ Discern appropriate ways to conduct an employment interview

❑ Understand the steps involved in initiating a job search

❑ Prepare the written materials necessary for a successful job search

❑ Discuss the communication and attitudinal qualities that lead to a positive self-presentation during an employment interview

❑ Prepare for and conduct an employment interview, playing both roles—interviewer (employer) and interviewee (applicant)

Every year, in colleges and universities across the nation, seniors work through their campus placement agencies as they prepare to meet prospective employers. They prepare resumes, write letters of application, and sign up for interviews. Most participate in a number of interviews—preliminary screenings that will determine who will be invited to the company for more in-depth interviews. These are exciting and potentially anxiety-producing moments for most. They know that how well they perform in their 20-minute or longer interview will determine what doors are opened to them, where they will live, with whom they will work, and how smoothly they make the transition from college to professional life.

The employment interview is a culminating experience. The applicant must find a way to prepare—to pull together his or her years of study, of cognitive and social development, of life and work experiences, and to communicate about them effectively and persuasively. For the employer, the interview is also critical. How discerning he or she is in screening prospective recruits determines the future of the organization. So, careful preparation and effective performance during the employment interview are important for both parties.

Preview

In this chapter, we focus on the employment interview from the perspective of the employer and the applicant. Understanding both roles is important to effective performance in each. We trace the preparatory steps for the interviewer-employer. We also look at the process of initiating the job hunt from the perspective of the applicant-interviewee. For both roles, we focus on how to perform

323

effectively during the interview itself. When both parties know what they are doing and do it well, the interview's outcome is more likely to be satisfying for everyone concerned.

THE FUNCTION AND IMPORTANCE OF THE EMPLOYMENT INTERVIEW

In the preceding chapter, we discussed the fundamental principles of interviewing and examined a few special interviewing applications, such as the appraisal interview. By definition, formal interviews are important. Yet, of the many functions interviews can serve, none is more important than the employment interview. For the supervisor or manager, this interview determines the quality of his employees, and this in turn determines how successful he will be as a manager.

For the interviewee seeking employment, the interview is equally important. In beginning a career, selecting the right job is of particular importance. Raelin claims that "the characteristics of a person's first job are important in explaining their later employment success."[1] His research suggests that jobs that provide challenges, opportunities for growth, and independence improve one's attitudes toward and aptitudes in work, thus enhancing chances for success in the future. Therefore, first-time job seekers should choose very carefully what positions they accept: their future could depend on making the right choice.

As we noted above, we will examine the employment interview from two perspectives: that of the interviewee seeking a position and that of the interviewer looking for qualified candidates. Only when both parties are skilled in their own roles and each has an understanding of the other's role can the employment interview be maximally effective.

THE ROLE OF THE INTERVIEWER

As the person seeking a new employee, the interviewer must be involved in a number of processes. These include understanding the interview's legal environment, defining the job, recruiting, prescreening applicants, and interviewing. We will consider each of these processes in turn. First, however, it's important to be aware of some common mistakes that interviewers have made in the past so that they can be avoided.

Common Problems to Avoid

Everyone expects the novice interviewer to make some mistakes, but often even those with years of interviewing experience may go awry. Interviewers may believe that when they sit down and look applicants in the eye, they will instinctively "know" which ones are best qualified. But, without adequate preparation for the interview and vigilance during the interviewing, many things can go wrong.[2] Here are some things to guard against:

- *Failing to know what the job requires*. If those who are interviewing applicants do not understand (and agree on) the job's critical requirements, they will be hard pressed to make a good decision, or even to be able to agree on whom to hire.

- *Neglecting to read the applicant's materials before the interview*. Some interviewers only look over the resume, references, and other materials a few seconds prior to the interview (or even during the interview). When this happens, chances are they will ask for information they already have and fail to pursue more interesting and fruitful lines of questioning.

- *Failing to formulate key questions before the interview*. Sometimes interviewers rely on the inspiration of the moment to think of a good question. When that happens, some questions may be poorly worded, some may be illegal, and critical applicant experiences may be ignored.

- *Making a hasty decision*. Research has shown that interviewers often make accept or reject decisions very early in the interview—often within the first four or five minutes![3] When this happens, the rest of the interview is wasted time, and applicants are evaluated during the precise time when they are most likely to be nervous.

- *Treating applicants you like differently from those with whom you are less impressed*. Interviewers may inadvertently show more enthusiasm, ask more animated questions, or simply "look" more interested when they are interviewing a promising applicant. Yet, everyone must be given an equal opportunity throughout the interview. Verbally and nonverbally, the interviewer must treat all applicants the same.

- *Discriminating against applicants for any reason*. Historically, applicants have been discriminated against because of their sex, sexual orientation, ethnicity, age, race, and physical attractiveness. It is critically important that the interviewer knows the laws that prohibit such discrimination and follows them faithfully.

Fortunately, these and other problems can be avoided or minimized through conscientious preparation. The foundation for an effective interview is doing your homework, knowing what you're talking about, and being committed to treating all applicants fairly. Let's begin by considering the laws that govern interviewing.

Knowing the Employment Laws

Equal Employment Opportunity (EEO) laws have been on the books for decades; yet, some employers who are involved with interviewing either ignore them or are ignorant of them. Even if an employer unknowingly asks an illegal question, he or she can still be held accountable. *The courts are not interested in interviewers' intentions—only in their behavior*. If an applicant can show that she has been asked an illegal question, or has been discriminated against in any way, then she can take the employer to court. Failure to comply with the law can be costly.

Nearly all organizations must comply with EEO laws. These federal laws pertain to all organizations that deal with the federal government, have more than $50,000 in government contracts, have more than 15 employees, and engage in interstate commerce.[4] See Highlighting Ethics for a list of key EEO laws. In addition, there are state laws and these may be more stringent than federal laws.

Although the laws may look abundant and somewhat intimidating, complying with them is not that difficult. In general, there are three rules to follow:

1. *Avoid asking questions out of general interest or curiosity*. It may seem natural to ask some personal questions about, for example, an applicant's spouse—not because one intends to discriminate, but simply because one is genuinely interested. Whatever the intention, however, such curiosity-driven questions are usually illegal.

2. *Ask the same questions of all applicants*. Of course, you will ask some resume-specific questions of each applicant, but in general, the major questions planned and posed should be asked of everyone. Those who ask certain questions only of female, disabled, older, or minority applicants are undoubtedly asking unlawful questions.

3. *Ask only questions that pertain to the job's critical requirements*. These critical requirements are called *bona fide occupational qualifications (BFOQs)*—the knowledge, skill, ability, talent, and so on that are essential for performing a particular job. BFOQs usually include work experience, training, skills, education, or personality characteristics that have a direct bearing on an interviewee's ability to perform the job effectively. BFOQs usually exclude sex, sexual orientation, age, race, religion, marital status, physical appearance, ethnicity, disabilities that are irrelevant to the job, citizenship, family ties, and arrest records.

Highlighting Ethics

Staying within the Law: Key EEO Laws to Remember

- *The Civil Rights Acts of 1866, 1870, and 1871.* Generally prohibit discrimination against minorities.

- *The Equal Pay Act of 1963.* Requires equal pay for men and women who are performing similar work (requiring similar levels of skill, etc.).

- *The Civil Rights Act of 1964.* Prohibits the selection of employees based on race, color, sex, religion, or national origin, and requires employers to be proactive in discovering discriminatory practices and eliminating them.

- *The Age Discrimination in Employment Act of 1967.* Bars discrimination against people because of age.

- *The Equal Employment Opportunity Act of 1972.* Extends the 1964 Civil Rights Act to public and private educational institutions, labor organizations, and employment agencies.

- *The Americans with Disabilities Act of 1990.* Prohibits discrimination against individuals with mental or physical impairments that limit or restrict the condition, manner, or duration under which they can perform one or more major life activities and requires reasonable accommodation by employers.

- *The Civil Rights Act of 1991.* Caps compensation and punitive damages for employers, provides for jury trial, and created a commission to investigate the "glass ceiling" for women and minorities and to reward organizations who offer opportunities for minorities and women.

- *The Family Medical Leave Act of 1993.* Provides an extended time (12 weeks within any 12-month period) for the birth of a child; the care of a sick child; or the care of a seriously ill spouse, child, or parent that prevents the employee from performing the functions of the job.

To ensure that your interviewing practices are consistent with legal require-ments, you should become familiar with the American Psychological Association's Principles for the Validation and Use of Personnel Selection Procedures and with the Uniform Guidelines on Employee Selection of the Equal Employment Opportunity Commission (EEOC).[5] Under current regulations, it is **unlawful** to ask an applicant:

- If he has **ever worked under another name**, unless the applicant previously worked for your organization under another name. However, if the applicant is female, you can usually request that she indicate her maiden name.

- For his **birthplace or the birthplace of his parents, spouse, or other close relatives**. This could reveal the national origin or race of the applicant.

- For her **birthplace or age**. However, you may ask if the applicant is over 65 or under 18.

- For his **religious affiliation, church, or the religious holidays he observes**.

- If she is a **naturalized citizen**. This could easily establish race or national origin.

- **How he acquired the ability to read, write, or speak a foreign language**. This could easily determine ethnic background. If the ability to speak French is a BFOQ, however, asking about the applicant's ability to speak it is quite acceptable.

- **To provide names of relatives other than father, mother, husband, wife, or minor-age dependent children**. This may reveal national origin, race, creed, or ethnic background of the applicant or spouse.

- For the **names of all clubs, societies, and lodges to which she belongs**. This could reveal the individual's ethnic background and color. However, the applicant can be asked to indicate membership in organizations that are not based on ethnic origins or religious membership practices.

- **To include a photograph** with the application for employment.

- **To reveal the number of his dependents**.

- **To indicate whether she has ever been treated for a mental disorder**. This would reveal past mental health problems and the applicant is protected by the Amer-icans with Disabilities Act (ADA).

- **If he will need a braille keyboard due to his limited vision**. Under the ADA, the employer must be willing to make "reasonable accommodations," which would include such a keyboard.

- **How a woman's husband would feel about her having to travel so much**. The question reveals a gender bias and would rarely be asked of males.

- **If he has ever been arrested**. Many innocent people are arrested. So long as one has not been convicted, an arrest has no bearing on qualifications for the job.

Although some questions can be identified as clearly illegal, keep in mind that the legality of many questions can be judged only in relationship to an understand-ing of the job's critical requirements. Those who apply for modeling jobs should expect to have their appearance judged. And again, many questions regarding weekend travel and child and elder care are often asked only of women. They are unlawful primarily because they are not asked of all applicants. Highlighting Tech-nology offers information on how to learn more about the EEOC, with additional insights concerning discriminatory interviewing behavior and how to avoid it.

Highlighting Technology

Exploring the EEOC

To stay up to date on employment laws, it might be a good idea to visit the U.S. Equal Employment Opportunity Commission's Web site at http://www.eeoc.gov. This Web site has links to such important topics as:

- *Federal EEO Laws and Discriminatory Practices* provides an overview of the major laws and gives examples of practices that are considered discriminatory.

- *Types of Discrimination* defines and explains such types as age, disability, equal pay, national origin, race, religion, and sex.

- *Employers and EEO* discusses EEOC investigations (describing what to do if charges are filed against you), mediation procedures, and notes special issues for small businesses.

- *Statistics* on employment, enforcement, and litigation are organized according to statute.

- *Training and Outreach Programs* provides information about some presentations and programs that are available at no cost and presenters can be scheduled as part of company meetings. Many presenters are bilingual. For a fee, the EEOC will train employers to educate their managers and employees.

- *How to Contact the EEOC* provides the phone number (202) 663-4900; mailing address; and fax number. It also provides information on the Freedom of Information Act and on the history of the EEOC.

- *For the Employee,* there is also information on jobs at EEOC and (should the unfortunate situation arise) information on how to file a charge of discrimination.

Source: "EEOC: U.S. Equal Opportunity Commission" [online]. Available: http://www.eeoc.gov (accessed: June 27, 2004).

Knowing the Job's Requirements: Developing an Applicant Profile

Once you feel comfortable in your understanding of the laws governing the selection process, you must next determine the nature of the position to be filled and the corresponding qualifications that a potential applicant must possess. This information should be the basis for recruiting and selecting people for the available position. Among the qualifications you should consider are education, experience, knowledge and skills, physical demands of the job, integrity or trustworthiness, contact with other people, and any other special requirements (such as odd working hours or unusual working conditions).

By identifying these requirements and creating an *applicant profile,* you achieve a number of things. First and foremost, you identify the BFOQs that *must* serve as the basis for your selection decisions. As noted above, EEO laws state that such personal factors as age, sex, race, religion, ethnic origin, and veteran's status cannot be involved in hiring decisions unless a BFOQ necessitates incorporation of that factor. For example, if the job is "men's room attendant" in a hotel, sex becomes a BFOQ, and you are allowed to exclude women from consideration. In most instances, however, you must give equal consideration to all applicants without regard to their demographic characteristics, and you must base your hiring decisions in every instance on the requirements of the position itself.

Constructing an applicant profile also points to the sorts of applicants you need, the places in which you should recruit for applicants, the information you should look for when reviewing resumes or application forms, and the information you should seek during the selection interview.

You can construct an applicant profile in several ways. You may talk with managers and human resources personnel, you may observe skilled employees doing the job for which you will be recruiting, and you can talk with coworkers to see what traits they most value in their coworkers. Whatever approach you use, make sure you check your perceptions against others'—and especially those others who will be interviewing applicants along with you. If you and your fellow interviewers can agree on the job's critical characteristics, you will find yourselves far more likely to agree on which applicants are most qualified following your interviews.

The applicant profile, then, is what you and others will use to guide you as you prepare for and conduct each interview. You will use the profile to plan questions, to examine resumes and cover letters, and to assess each applicant after the interview is over.

Recruiting

When looking for potential applicants, you should consider a number of sources. First, look at **sources in your own organization**. In almost every organization, it should be a policy to promote from within whenever possible. This policy shows employees that they have a chance to grow within the organization and that the quality of their performance will be rewarded by upward movement.

When additional candidates are desired, **employee referrals** should be solicited. Often, employees know people who might be qualified, and they know the organization well enough to have an idea of the type of candidate who would fit the organization.

Advertising in newspapers, on radio, and occasionally on television is another common recruiting technique. Professional journals, trade association newsletters, and other written media sent to specific types of employees are also commonly used. These sources must be used carefully, for the law prohibits advertisements that may discriminate on the basis of age, sex, veteran's status, or some other characteristic not related to the job.

Public and private employment agencies can provide job applicants. Headhunters have become the most common source for recruiting executive-level applicants, and many recruitment firms handle lower-level positions as well. Most trade schools, business schools, junior or community colleges, high schools, and colleges and universities have placement offices and counselors who refer students or graduates. Some schools have internship or work-study programs that are excellent sources for part-time employees and, ultimately, experienced help.

Former employees who left the organization on good terms may refer potential applicants, or they may even fill in as temporary help. In some cases, changed family situations (for example, a child now old enough to be cared for by someone else) may make a former employee available for work again.

Electronic sourcing can also be used to locate skilled applicants. Most major newspapers can be accessed via the computer, but there are many databases available as well. Here are a few examples: Employers' Job Net Electronic Bulletin Board (609-683-9191), Skill Search (800-252-5665), Ki Nexus Employer and Student Listing (800-828-0422), and Job Bank U.S.A. Pre-Qualified Resumes (800-296-1USA). The Internet is also a potential source, but resume accuracy can be a problem.

Screening

When the recruiting sources have produced a group of applicants, the next task is to sort out those who clearly are unsuited for the job. Typically, several pieces of information are used to screen out unqualified candidates—a resume (or application form), references, and often a cover letter. In some instances, you will also have the results of preemployment testing.

Cover letters typically accompany resumes. By reading them, you can get a sense of the applicants' writing quality and style and the sorts of skills or qualifications they emphasize. You may get a sense of why they are applying for this particular job. No two cover letters look alike, and sometimes comparisons are difficult. But, if a letter is poorly written, if the applicant doesn't appear to have a realistic sense of the job, and/or if the skills highlighted are less than impressive, the wisest course may be eliminating him or her from further consideration.

For every applicant, you will obtain a *resume or application form*, which presents basic information about educational and work history, personal references, and short- and long-term goals. Review the information that the applicant has provided and assess the implications of this information. The things you should look for include:

- *Time gaps*. Are there any time periods unaccounted for? Might these gaps be important? Why?

- *Education*. Imagine this individual is applying for a position in sales. How would you evaluate his educational background? How would you verify it?

- *Incomplete information*. Are there any instances where more information should have been given? Could the omissions be important? Why?

- *Employment history*. Does this record show success? Stability? What can you infer from the information given?

- *Salary*. Is consistent progress shown? What can you infer about the applicant based on her salary history?

- *References*. Are the right people listed as references? Do important people seem to be missing? What can you infer?

- *Appearance of the application*. Is it neat and easy to read? Grammatically correct? Professional looking? The care with which application forms or resumes are prepared often provides insight into the care with which the applicant would do his work.

The references provided by the applicant provide the other source of information you should use during the screening procedure. Typically, you would contact references only for those applicants whose written materials have kept them in contention for the job. The purpose of such reference checks is to get more in-depth information about the applicant and to verify the accuracy of the information provided on the application form or resume. When properly done, a reference check may provide information about the employee's motivation level, attitudes and personality, relations with others, judgment and common sense, resourcefulness, integrity, energy level, ability to handle pressure and meet deadlines, and leadership and responsibility levels. Obviously, this information goes far beyond that provided on the application form, and it allows you to make a far more accurate judgment concerning the suitability of a candidate.

As a rule, you should *seek several* such *references*. Work-related references are best, although personal references may be appropriate, particularly for younger applicants who have little work experience. Consider the total information accumulated during your reference checks when you decide whether or not to pursue the candidate further. That is, one slightly unfavorable reference should not outweigh two or three favorable ones. However, a single, strongly unfavorable reference may be a signal that you should investigate the applicant more thoroughly.

In some cases and for certain kinds of searches, you will have *letters of recommendation* as part of the applicant's application package. Some employers are skeptical of letters of recommendation—assuming that the applicant will only ask for a letter from those who will offer praise rather than from those who will write a "bad" letter. While those perceptions are usually true, it is still possible to glean some valuable insights from letters of recommendation. For instance, a discerning reader can usually tell how well the letter writer knows the applicant and whether the writer is *extremely* impressed by the applicant or simply happy with his or her work. Detailed letters that provide specific examples of the applicant's accomplishments, work habits, and exhibited attitudes (rather than offering broad generalizations) can really help the employer get a picture of the applicant as a person.

Sometimes you will also have *the results of preemployment tests* to guide your screening (although in some cases, such tests will be administered only *after* applicants have passed through an initial screening). In the 1970s and 1980s, for example, polygraph tests (lie detectors) were commonly used to screen applicants. Later, most states outlawed the use of such tests because of problems with their accuracy and potential misuse. More recently, however, organizations use honesty tests to help assess the honesty of applicants, especially those applying for positions that involve handling large sums of money. While some of these tests are believed to yield valuable insights into the honesty of those tested,[6] their results ought to be considered in a broader context (including other relevant performance and attitudinal qualities, reference checks, and performance during the interview itself).

Job skills testing of applicants for non-white-collar positions (such as clerical or secretarial jobs or work on production lines) is also increasing. Of the companies surveyed in an American Management Association study, 22.5 percent tested applicants for nonmanagement jobs.[7] Tests of applicants for management positions were far less frequent. Skills testing is more common in some kinds of organizations than others. For instance, insurance companies often give tests to assess sales skills and believe them to be accurate. Again, skill test results should be taken in context; and if they are to be useful, they should be validated on a cross-section of the population and meet EEOC guidelines.

As an interviewer, it is important that you be fully aware of your organization's testing policies and practices. In addition, you should be sure that all applicants for a position take the same tests: selective application of tests has been found to be evidence of discrimination. Of course, organizations vary in the nature and extent of their screening practices. Business Brief 9.1 provides an unusual illustration of one organization's approach to screening and hiring.

Upon completion of the preliminaries, you will have concluded the screening portion of the employment process. At this point, you should have eliminated applicants who clearly are unsuited for the position. Now you are ready to undertake the interviewing process.

Business Brief 9.1

One Company's Screening and Hiring Practices

An unusually exhaustive hiring process is used by Toyota Motor Manufacturing U.S.A. in Georgetown, Kentucky:

Step 1: The Kentucky Department of Employment Services has applicants complete application forms and view a one-hour videotape describing Toyota's work environment and selection system.

Step 2: Applicants take the Situation Judgment Inventory, which tests their interpersonal skills and ability to work in a team environment. The test is administered and scored by the Kentucky Department of Employment Services.

Step 3: Applicants participate in four hours of group and individual problem-solving and discussion activities conducted at Toyota's assessment center. In addition, applicants for assembly-line jobs participate in a five-hour assembly simulation, with other candidates playing the role of manager.

Step 4: A one-hour group interview is conducted by Toyota with several candidates, allowing their group communication skills to be assessed.

Step 5: Applicants undergo 2 1/2 hours of physical and drug and alcohol tests at an area hospital.

Step 6: New hires are closely monitored and coached on the job for their first six months at work; those unable to perform acceptably are immediately discharged.

Source: Gary Dessler, "Value-Based Hiring Builds Commitment," *Personnel Journal* 72 (November 1993): 98–102.

The Interviewing Process

Despite the many refinements that have been developed in recruiting and screening methods, the interview is still considered the most vital part of the selection process. The interview offers the prospective employee and the employer the opportunity to obtain information, form impressions, and make observations that would not be possible otherwise. Normally, the objectives of the employment interview are:

• to allow the interviewer to obtain enough knowledge about the applicant to determine whether she is suitable for employment in a particular position;

• to provide sufficient information about the organization and the particular job to enable the applicant to decide whether to accept or reject the job, if offered;

- to treat the applicant in a manner that will create and maintain goodwill toward the organization.[8]

Achievement of these objectives requires careful planning.

PREPARING FOR THE INTERVIEW

The first step is to *prepare*. Like other kinds of interviews, the foundation of a good employment interview is preparation. Here are some guidelines:

- *Review again the applicant profile* (detailing the job's critical requirements).

- *Carefully examine the information about each applicant* that you have obtained through written materials and reference checks.

- *Plan a core of questions that you will ask of each applicant*, following the guidelines for question construction discussed in chapter 8.

- *Prepare some questions for each applicant that are resume specific*, allowing you to probe each one's particular qualifications. In planning all questions, work within the framework of BFOQs and plan with time constraints in mind.

- *Assemble information about the organization and the position to share with the applicant.* The interview is, after all, an opportunity for you to share as well as gather information.

- *Take care to eliminate potential distractions* (such as telephone calls or unexpected visitors) *and to make the surroundings as comfortable as possible.*

Having done all these things, you are ready to meet the applicant.

CONDUCTING THE INTERVIEW

The hours of planning finally culminate in the actual interview—where a great deal must be accomplished in a relatively short period of time.

Opening the Interview: Setting the Stage

- *Greet the applicant by name, shaking his or her hand.* Engage in a little small talk, but don't get carried away. The interview time is precious. The applicant will appreciate knowing how you intend to proceed with the interview.

- *Gaining rapport* is an important first step in the interview. As interviewer, you should be courteous, show sincerity, express interest, and give complete attention to the interviewee's remarks. First impressions are particularly important in an employment interview from both perspectives, and your appearance, conduct, and attitude will influence the applicant just as much as his appearance and conduct will influence you.

- *Providing an orientation to the interview is helpful.* Simply tell the applicant what you will do first, let her know that you'll be glad to provide information and respond to questions a bit later, and mention the time available for the interview. Then you are ready to move to the first question.

Questioning: The Key to Effective Interviewing

As you question each applicant, your continuing concern should be to use the time wisely, to ask good, substantive questions, and to avoid poor questioning practices often associated with interviews. The types of questions to avoid asking include:

- questions that can be answered with a simple yes or no (and thus reveal little about the interviewee's abilities in self-expression);

- run-of-the-mill questions for which the astute applicant has long since prepared ready-made answers;
- leading questions that suggest the "proper" answer to the applicant or asking questions already answered by the resume;
- questions not related to the task at hand;
- unlawful questions.

What kinds of questions *should* you ask? What substantive areas should you probe? You, of course, will want to frame your own questions, but there are certain question areas on which you will likely want to focus your attention. These include:

- *The applicant's work experience*. A person's work experience is important and is a natural and easy place to start the interview. Some key questions might include:

"One of the things we want to talk about today is your work experience. Would you tell me about your present job?"

"What are some of the things on your job you feel you have done particularly well or in which you have achieved the greatest success? Why do you feel this way?"

"What are some of the things about your job that you found difficult to do? Why do you feel they were difficult for you?"

"Most jobs have pluses and minuses. What were some of the minuses in your last job?"

- *How the applicant feels about people*. The way the applicant feels about people—his coworkers and supervisors—has an important part in determining job success. Here are the kinds of questions that will help you explore this important area:

"What do you feel were your supervisor's greatest strengths?"

"In what areas do you feel your supervisor could have done an even better job?"

"What kind of people do you like working with? What kind of people do you find most difficult to work with?"

- *The applicant's job objectives*. The interviewer needs to know what the applicant's job objectives are in a job or career—what she is looking for or wishing to avoid. Here, again, proper questions can be of great help in obtaining such information. For example:

"What are some of the things in a job that are important to you?"

"What are some of the things you would like to avoid in a job, and why?"

"What is your overall career objective? What are some of the things, outside of your job, that you have done or that you plan to do that will assist you in reaching this objective?"

"What kind of position would you expect to progress to in five years? Ten years?"

Besides the kinds of core questions we have just suggested, you will want to use many of the other questioning techniques we discussed in chapter 8. Whenever your initial question does not elicit the kind of information you had hoped to obtain, you should follow it up with some kind of probe.

Although interviewers spend a considerable amount of time asking questions, they must also give applicants the opportunity to pose questions. As interviewers share organizational practices, policies, and values, they serve as a powerful source of information that may have a significant impact on the applicants' perceptions of the organization and its desirability as a place of employment.

Providing Information

When you have obtained all the information you need from the applicant, you will want to make sure that there is an ample amount of time to share information not uncovered in the previous segments of the interview.

- *Be sure that the applicant has a chance to ask questions.* The quality of questions the applicant asks may tell you a great deal about his thinking, the extent to which the applicant investigated the organization or position ahead of time, and his familiarity with the field of work.

- *Provide complete, accurate information* so applicants can make informed, correct decisions about you and your organization.

- *Present a positive impression of your organization*, without exaggerating. Applicants are usually interested in the company's reputation and stability, what a typical workday is like, and avenues for advancement.

- *Share with the applicant information that distinguishes your organization from others*—such as a corporate philosophy that emphasizes self-management, teamwork, or diversity. In fact, a number of forward-looking organizations are striving for a more diverse workforce, and this philosophy influences their hiring practices and organizational culture in a variety of ways. See Highlighting Diversity for a review of some of the reasons why many organizations are promoting workforce diversity.

Highlighting Diversity

Arguments for Cultural Diversity in Organizations

- *Cost Argument.* As organizations become more diverse, costs of poor integration will increase. Companies that are able to integrate a culturally diverse workforce will realize considerable cost savings over those companies that cannot or choose not to do so.

- *Resource-Acquisition Argument.* Companies develop reputations as good places for women and minorities to work. Those companies with the best reputations will be able to attract the best people. As the labor pool shrinks and changes in composition, this advantage will become more important.

- *Marketing Argument.* For multinational organizations, the insight and cultural sensitivity that employees with roots in other countries bring to marketing efforts should improve the effectiveness of such efforts. This reasoning also applies to ethnic groups within the United States.

- *Creativity Argument.* Diversity of perspectives and less emphasis on conformity and adherence to past practices should improve the level of innovation and creativity among employees.

- *Problem-solving Argument.* Heterogeneous decision-making and problem-solving groups are likely to produce better solutions because they allow critical analysis from multiple perspectives.

- *System-Flexibility Argument.* Organizations that are able to manage multicultural diversity effectively will necessarily become less standardized, more open, and more fluid within. This fluidity should create greater flexibility to react to environmental changes.

- *Empowerment Argument.* Individuals who work in organizational environments characterized by sensitivity and respect for diverse talents and perspectives grow to feel more valued and empowered, to relate better to coworkers, and to gain greater satisfaction from their jobs.

Source: T. Cox and S. Blake, "Managing Cultural Diversity: Implications for Organizational Competitiveness," *Academy of Management Executive* 5 (1991): 45–56.

Concluding the Interview and Following Through

After all the applicant's questions have been answered, your final task is to *outline the next steps, if any.* If you have reached a decision and have the power to extend an offer at that time, you may choose to do so. Similarly, if you have decided that the employee is not suited to the job, you may also inform him of that decision. If you are not in a position to make a decision at that point, tell the applicant what will happen next: when the decision will be made and how it will be communicated. Then follow through.

After the applicant has departed, take a few minutes to note your impressions of the applicant. It is imperative that you not mark on the resume, application form, or any other materials that are part of the applicant's file. Instead, make your own notes. Better still, use an evaluation form to quickly record your impressions before going on to interview other applicants. See figure 9.1 for a sample interview evaluation form.

THE ROLE OF THE INTERVIEWEE

Much of the preceding section is also of interest to the job applicant. When seeking a job, you should be aware of the needs and strategies of employers; and

INTERVIEW EVALUATION FORM

Applicant: _____   **Position:** _____

Interviewer: _____   **Date:** _____

Scales should be interpreted as follows: 1 = poor; 2 = fair; 3 = average; 4 = good; 5 = excellent

Interest in the Position	1	2	3	4	5
Knowledge of the Company	1	2	3	4	5
Education/Training	1	2	3	4	5
Work & Life Experiences	1	2	3	4	5
Communication Skills	1	2	3	4	5
Ability/Intelligence/Readiness to Learn	1	2	3	4	5
Motivation to Work	1	2	3	4	5
Maturity	1	2	3	4	5
Character	1	2	3	4	5
Community Commitment	1	2	3	4	5

Comments:

1. What are the applicant's greatest strengths?

2. What are his/her weaknesses?

Overall Assessment: Negative   1   2   3   4   5   Positive

Figure 9.1   Interview evaluation form

you should use that awareness to prepare for your interviews. In this section, we will consider the specific principles that employment interviewees should follow—principles that significantly enhance the likelihood that you will obtain the position of your choice (provided, of course, that you possess the qualifications that the position demands).

Initiating the Quest for Employment: The Self-Inventory and Job Assessment

Many people assume that when they think they are ready to look for a job, they should begin by going to a placement service. However, before seeking external assistance with employment, you must begin with an internal assessment by thinking about who you are, what you know, what skills you possess, and what you value in a job and in life.

The first step then, in initiating any employment quest, is to make a thorough *self-inventory*. Your college major is important, as are work experiences, volunteer experiences, and other kinds of activities you have participated in. They are important especially because they indicate something about your values, interests, attitudes, ambitions, and skills. Often we take stock only of our obvious and relatively superficial aspects. We assume, for example, that without a college degree in a specific field, we should never seek employment in that area of specialty. Yet, consider the example of the man who, as vice president for development, saved a small private college from financial disaster. His educational background was in counseling, speech communication, academic affairs, and the ministry. He had never studied development, fund-raising, or grant solicitation. His formal knowledge of annual giving programs, capital campaigns, and deferred giving was minimal. Even so, he succeeded in his position because he possessed the skills that allowed him to understand people and their needs and interests, to have compassion for them, and to move them persuasively to support causes in which they believed. Thus, his skills were transferable from his academic background and professional experiences to the business of fund-raising. It is important that you *identify and list those skills and personal attributes you possess that might be attractive to a prospective employer.*

Once you have conducted your self-inventory, you should move on to a thoughtful consideration of the kind of job you would be most comfortable in and the sort of organization you would really like to work for. Some jobs pay well, but are accompanied by high stress levels. Some require extensive travel. Others require the ability to work alone, without much human contact, in contrast to still others that necessitate teamwork for most major projects and extensive human interaction. There is nothing necessarily "good" or "bad" about any of these kinds of jobs. What is critical is knowing what *you* want, what you would find appealing and motivating, and then trying to match your skills, values, and interests to the job and the organization. *Taking some time to consider the things that you most value in a job is the second step in initiating the employment quest.*

As you think about organizations you might want to work for, you may want to give some thought to some of the ethical issues we raised in chapter 1. For example, to what extent do you value working for an organization with a firm commitment to socially responsible behavior? Would you consider working for less money if you believed you were making a true contribution to society? The Center for Integrity in Business at Seattle Pacific University is aimed at encouraging and facilitating an ongoing dialogue between business people, academics, and theologians about how business should work. The center publishes a newsletter and posts stories on its Web site about individuals and organizations who are committed to making a genuine impact on various social problems. Highlighting Civic Engagement features one of these stories.[9]

The Employment Quest: Where to Look for Jobs

Once you are satisfied with your self- and job-assessments, you are ready to start looking for specific jobs that are available. A detailed study of job hunting in the United States revealed that the greater the number of auxiliary avenues used by the job seeker, the greater her success in finding a job.[10] The traditional routes include, first, *friends, relatives, and former employers*. These individuals can provide the names of people to contact in the organization. You can then address letters of inquiry to specific individuals, avoiding the impersonal "Dear Sir." Positive internship experiences can lead to employment opportunities. In this situation, you know the company, the company knows you, and you know exactly whom to contact.

Highlighting Civic Engagement

The Story of Athena Water and the Race for the Cure

- *Background on the company and the product.* Trish May, a former Microsoft marketing executive with an MBA, is also a breast cancer survivor. In December 2002 she decided to wade into the $3.5 billion-a-year bottled water market, going up against such giants as Coca-Cola Co. and PepsiCo Inc. (who respectively own Dasani and Aquafina—the nation's two biggest brands of bottled water).

- *Company funded solely by personal investment.* May's goal was to create a product that people use every single day. Something healthy. She chose the name Athena, the Greek goddess of wisdom and of war, as the name and logo of her bottled water. After incorporating Athena Partners six months earlier, she introduced Athena Bottled Water to consumers in July 2003. By October, Athena was already being sold at more than 110 Safeway stores and 79 QFC stores in western Washington. Other deals are in progress.

- *The company's vision.* May's goal is for the Northwest to "become the number 1 place in the country for women's cancer research." The state of Washington had the highest incidence of breast cancer in the nation from 1996 to 2000, according to the American Cancer Society. A pink banner on every Athena bottle (which is purified with added minerals) promises, "100 percent net profits to find a cure." Volume is essential. May estimates that selling 100,000 cases will help her break even and begin donating money.

- *The owner's story.* May's story is very personal. Once a manager at Microsoft who worked 60 hours a week, where she marketed the MSN network and developed the vision that became PowerPoint software, she reordered her priorities after finding a cancerous lump in her breast and undergoing successful treatment (including a lumpectomy, six months of chemotherapy, and 45 straight days of radiation).

- *The move to civic engagement.* May began volunteering with the American Cancer Society. She joined the board of the Fred Hutchinson Cancer Research Center. She offered money and expertise to nonprofit organizations as a member of Social Venture Partners. May looked to Newman's Own, Paul Newman's food business (which has given more than $125 million to charities since 1982). She took Athena to women's health events, from walks to runs to fashion shows and golf tournaments. There, she gave the water away, hoping to create customers by giving them a taste—and a sense that they too could make a difference. May hopes it's an easy choice to make: Buy a water that benefits a company, or one that pays for research on women's cancers.

- *The future.* May estimates that if she could capture 5 percent of the bottled water market in the Northwest, she could donate $1 million a year to women's cancer research. At that point, she'll think about going national.

- *For more information.* Athena Partners has created an extensive Web site of women's cancer resources, with more than 250 links: http://www.athenapartners.org.

Source: Kristin Dizon, "Athena Is a Business Built for the Cure," *Seattle Post-Intelligencer* [online]. Available: http://www.seattlepr.nwsource.com/business/143726_athenawater14.html (accessed: June 26, 2004).

Placement agencies are a second common starting place. College and university placement services are often free or involve a nominal fee, and they provide students with job contacts and interview opportunities. Some colleges have a course associated with their placement services; in this course, you learn how to prepare a job portfolio, assess your skills, develop a resume, and interview. You may also have the chance to hear prospective employers give job talks or informational presentations about the organizations they represent. Based on what you hear at these talks, you can better decide which jobs and organizations you want to pursue.

Other placement agencies demand fees and are often affiliated with professional organizations for management, communication, accounting, and teaching. General placement agencies find jobs for individuals for a specific fee, often a certain percentage of the first month's or year's salary. In general, these services should be approached with caution.

You may also want to consult various **publications**. Don't overlook newspaper classified advertisements. Consult the *Wall Street Journal*, an excellent source of openings around the country. Visit the library or campus placement service for other useful sources. For instance, *Jobs 95* is published annually and provides addresses, toll-free numbers, and industry groupings. In addition, Career Communication Incorporated publishes a number of useful sources, including *Job Hunters Yellow Pages*, which lists more than 15,000 employment agencies and services.

Finally, you might want to explore the **Internet**. Many organizations are beginning to advertise positions through the World Wide Web. Among the Internet sources you might consult are: Careerbuilder.com, Monster.com, and EmploymentGuide.com.[11]

Researching the Organization and the Field

Once you have identified some potential jobs, it's time to look seriously at the organizations in which those jobs are embedded. Bolles, an expert on job hunting, believes that **organizational research** should be a major focus of each person's preliminary employment strategy.[12] At the very least, you should learn the location of the organization's plants, branches, and offices; the age of the company; the kinds of services it offers; and its growth and future potential. Other questions might include:

- How does the organization rank within its field?
- Is the organization family-owned? If so, does this influence promotions?
- How innovative is the organization?
- What kind of image does the organization have in the mind of the public?
- What kind of staff turnover does it have?
- What is the attitude of current employees?
- Does the organization encourage its employees to further their education?
- Is there evidence that the organization is "family friendly" (through child and elder care policies, etc.)?
- To what extent is the organization committed to diversity and to the support of women and minorities?

• In general, how does communication flow within the organization? Is decision making highly centralized, or is it spread throughout the organization?

Sources of information on organizations are numerous and include the following: Better Business Bureau reports on the organization, chambers of commerce, college libraries, and the organization's annual reports. Other sources include:

Business Week
The Career Guide: Dun's Employment Opportunities Directory
Dictionary of Occupational Titles
Dun and Bradstreet's Middle Market & Million Dollar Directories
Fortune Magazine
Fortune's Plant and Product Directory
Guide for Occupational Exploration
Moody's Industrial Manual
Standard and Poor's Industrial Surveys
Standard and Poor's Register of Corporations, Directors, and Executives
The One Hundred Best Companies to Work for in America
Thomas's Register of American Manufacturers
The Wall Street Journal

As with other areas of research, there are a growing number of databases about organizations. Many are on CD-ROM, such as American Business Disc, Company ProFile, and Dun's Electronic Business Directory.

Never overlook or minimize the value of people sources. Talk with anyone affiliated with the organization—college alumni, friends, brokers, and certainly employees—who can provide helpful insights. It's always good to talk to employees whose positions are similar to the one you are interested in. If possible, chat with those in lower-level positions, such as clerical workers. Learning that they are happy in their jobs bodes well for the entire organizational climate. Ask your sources to describe their best and worst experiences; urge them to be specific. The more stories you gather about the organization, the better able you will be to interpret the more statistical and factual information you gain through other sources.

Finally, as you do research on the organizations you are interested in, ***learn as much as you can about your chosen field***—its trends, history, leaders, challenges, current and future problems, and employment opportunities. Try to think about a typical workday in accounting, sales, marketing, or public relations. Develop realistic expectations. Those who interview you will be interested in discovering how much you know about your field and how mature and realistic you are about what will be expected of you. Doing internships, visiting and observing, or volunteering for short stints can provide further insights.

Learn everything you can. This will help you narrow and focus your interests and will assist you in developing your cover letter and resume and presenting yourself well during the interview.

Presentation of Self in Writing

For many job seekers, the initial contact with the organization is through writing. Dozens of books exist that provide comprehensive guidelines for writing cover letters and resumes.[13] The following discussion focuses on only the essentials of both forms of written communication.

THE COVER LETTER: THE POWER OF THE FIRST IMPRESSION

Most of the time when we think of first impressions, we think of the interview itself. But it's important to recognize that the employer's first impression of you will come from the letter and the resume you prepare. If these documents are not favorably received, there may never be an interview. Typically, your *cover letter* will be the first thing the employer sees—accompanied by your resume. The cover letter is important. One study reported that this letter may have even more impact than the resume in affecting hiring decisions.[14] Following are some guidelines for writing the letter of application:

- *Send each prospective employer an original cover letter.* Each letter should be specifically adapted to the organization and position you are seeking.

- *Follow proper business letter writing format.*

- *Address your letter to the specific person who will be actively involved in the recruiting process.* Avoid the impersonal: "To Whom It May Concern," "Dear Recruiter," or "Dear Sir."

- *Keep it short*—usually no more than one page.

- *Make sure that your letter is neat, well written, and checked for spelling.* The employer will look at your letter as a writing sample. If your cover letter is well written, the employer may infer that you will also approach your job responsibly and with care.

- *Immediately state the position you are interested in and how you found out about it.*

- *Briefly describe your areas of interest, special skills, knowledge, and experience.* Do not simply reiterate information contained in the resume, but creatively amplify it.

- *State your reason or reasons for selecting this particular position and organization.* Show the employer that you have done your homework, and help him to see that you and the organization are a good match.

- *In the final paragraph, indicate your times of availability for interviewing and how you can be reached to arrange for an interview.*

Figure 9.2 presents a sample cover letter.

The cover letter is typically accompanied by a *resume* (also referred to as a personal fact or data sheet). According to one extensive survey, 98 percent of all organizations prefer to receive both as part of the initial contact.[15] Like the cover letter, resumes should be reasonably brief (one to two pages)[16] and should include the following basic information:

- *Personal information.* Work and home phone numbers and addresses, and e-mail address.

- *Professional goal or job objective.* The goal or objective should recognize the employer's needs, as well as those of the applicant; for example, "salesperson with an innovative firm where self-motivation and discipline are encouraged."

- *Educational background.* Majors and minors in college, knowledge acquired, degrees received, and dates associated with each.

- *Work experience.* Jobs held, responsibilities associated with and skills developed in each, and dates and places of employment.

- *Awards and honors.*

February 15, 2004

208A Clark House—Read Center
Indiana University
Bloomington, IN 47405

Mr. Phillip Johnson, Director of Recruitment
Ameritech
1633 North Meridian Street
Indianapolis, IN 46208

Dear Mr. Johnson:

Earlier this month, I met with Tim Schick, your regional Ameritech representative who works here in Bloomington. He told me that you were looking for a college graduate who is interested in working in public relations and encouraged me to write to you. I have always admired your organization because of its commitment to quality and its strong stance on environmental issues. I am very excited about the prospects of doing public relations work for Ameritech.

As you can see from my resume, I am about to graduate from Indiana University with a double major in public relations and organizational communication. The public relations major at Indiana is competitive and rigorous, and I performed quite well (graduating in the top 10% of my class). Besides my formal education, I also have worked in a variety of organizations doing public relations and advertising. I have designed company brochures, written news releases, and made speeches at social and business functions. I consider myself an excellent writer and speaker—and have won awards for both. I love a challenge. I consider myself to be a good team player, but I'm also very happy working on my own.

My interest in your organization grew from last summer's internship. I worked at Ameritech's Bloomington branch. It was a wonderful experience! I reported directly to Tim Schick, and he gave me many opportunities to further develop my skills and expand my knowledge of public relations. During the summer, I wrote several news releases that were published throughout the state (one on Ameritech's commitment to preserving the rain forests), and I helped design an ad campaign (the "Ameritech for the Year 2005" series) that aired on Channel 4 this past September. Even as an intern, I was sent to two training programs. This commitment to continuing education, together with ongoing opportunities to show initiative and creativity, are very attractive to me!

Would it be possible for us to meet for an interview? I am available every day after noon. You can reach me at (812) 337-4697, at the above address, or by e-mail at echenson@indiana.edu. I'd be delighted to travel to Indianapolis at any time that is convenient for you. Thank you so much for your consideration.

Sincerely,

Emily C. Henson

Emily C. Henson

Figure 9.2 Sample cover letter

- *Activities*. Memberships in organizations and offices held in college, community, and volunteer organizations.
- *Special skills or talents*. Computer skills or fluency in a foreign language.
- *References*. References may be listed as "available upon request" or may be listed with specific names, positions, and contact information.

Grades may be listed as part of educational accomplishments or referred to indirectly under "Honors," such as, "Dean's List every semester of college." Many employers will ask for a copy of your college transcript, to be attached to the resume or provided following the interview.

Your resume should be thoughtfully developed and designed with your particular credentials and the employer's interests in mind. No two resumes should look alike. If you are applying for more than one kind of job, you may want to develop a different resume for each—emphasizing the things that will make you most attractive for each.

THE RESUME: HIGHLIGHTING STRENGTHS AND EXPERIENCE

There are many different ways of organizing and presenting resume information. For instance, you may prefer a more standard, *chronological approach*, as is illustrated in the resume appearing in figure 9.3. The advantage of the chronological resume is that it presents your credentials in a straightforward, step-by-step manner. The categories are fairly standard, and the employer can easily see what you have been at each step of your educational and work experience. Present information in reverse chronological order, so that you emphasize your most recent activities and accomplishments.

You can also organize your resume using a *functional approach*. Some functional resumes include few dates, so that the reader gets little sense of chronology. Emphasized, however, are skills, talents, and relevant learning and work experiences. Most functional resumes combine some dates and traditional categories with categories that highlight skills. In the Mary Kelly resume shown in figure 9.4, for example, you will see that the objective and education categories are fairly traditional. Next comes a "qualifications summary," followed by four sections that emphasize Mary's skills and experiences: training, organizational, recruiting, and technical. Other skills often emphasized on functional resumes include: communication, computer, leadership, teamwork, problem solving, and so forth. Some believe the functional resume encourages more creativity and allows the applicant to better present himself or herself as an individual. Others worry that the functional resume may be perceived as less complete than the chronological resume—and perhaps more difficult for employers to compare to the resumes of other applicants. What's critical is to choose wisely, making a decision based on your objective, the job, the employer, and the information you plan to present. For your first job you may choose a chronological resume; later, when you have held several positions, you may want to switch to a more functional format. Over many years and many positions, chronological resumes can become very long.

Whatever structure you choose, each resume should be carefully planned, checked for spelling, and presented in an attractive way. Some bulleting and highlighting is desirable. Make sure your resume is easy to read and error free. It should look professional and should be printed on off-white or light beige bond paper. In short, your resume should create a first impression of you as an interesting individual—with unique skills and contributions to offer.

EMILY C. HENSON

Present Address:
208A Clark House—Read Center
Bloomington, IN 47405
e-mail: echenson@indiana.edu
(812) 337-4697

Permanent Address:
1706 Maple Avenue
Elkhart, IN 46207
(317) 695-7422

Professional Goal:	To obtain a public relations position in a corporate setting where creativity, motivation, and community commitment are stressed.
Education	***B.A. in Public Relations and Organizational Behavior***, Indiana University, May, 2004. • GPA: 3.5; GPA in public relations major: 3.8 • Completed minors in communication and Spanish

Work Experiences

Sept. 2002–present	***Editorial staff of* Indiana Daily Student** • Researched and wrote over 50 news stories • Assisted in design of IU's *Alumni Magazine*
Summer, 2003	***Public Relations Internship, Ameritech, Bloomington branch*** • Wrote news releases • Designed brochures • Helped design TV advertising campaign
Sept. 2001–May 2002	***Part-time Assistant to the IU Director of Alumni Affairs*** • Organized and conducted alumni telethons • Made speeches to alumni groups
Summers, 2001 & 2002	***Staff Writer for the* Elkhart Tribune** • Wrote articles focusing on women's issues

Awards and Honors

• Outstanding Intern, Ameritech, 2003
• Outstanding Journalist, *Indiana Daily Student*, 2003
• First Place, Rotary's State Public Speaking Contest, 2002
• Dean's List, Indiana University, 2001–present
• Outstanding Young Women of America, 2001

Activities

• Alpha Chi Omega, vice president, 2003–04; member, 2001–02
• Women in Business, chair, public relations committee, 2002–04
• Student Speaker's Bureau, IU, 2002–04
• Big Brother's and Big Sister's Program, Bloomington, 2002–04
• IU Foundation, chair, telethon, 2003–04; member, 2001–02

References: Furnished upon Request

Figure 9.3   Sample chronological resume

Mary E. Kelly

409 S. Ramble Road
Cincinnati, OH 45201
(513) 794-6308; kellym@sprynet.com

Objective

Human Resource Specialist. To use my graduate education, knowledge of training, recruitment, and performance appraisal to develop highly trained, motivated, and productive employees for a progressive organization.

Education

Indiana University Graduate School, Bloomington, M.A. Organizational Communication, 2004
- M.A. Thesis: Conflict Management and Performance Appraisal, GPA 3.9/4.0
- Awarded Indiana University Arts and Sciences Full Fee Scholarship

Indiana University, Bloomington, B.A. Telecommunications, 1999, GPA 3.4/4.0
- Kappa Alpha Theta Women's Fraternity: Pan-Hellenic Representative and Rush Counselor

Boston University, London (England) Journalism Internship Program, August–December 1997

Summary of Qualifications

- Developed and taught courses for the Indiana University Department of Speech Communication and School of Business. Emphasized management theory, interviewing, and group decision making.
- Developed and presented workshops on conflict management, briefing techniques, and diversity.
- Recruiting experience in both academic and business environments.

Skills

Training

Trainer, Executive Services Corps, Atlanta, *2004–present.*
U.S. Defense Intelligence Agency, Washington, DC, *July 2002.*
Bloomington (IN) Department of Human Resources, *2001–2002.*
- Design, develop, and facilitate training on diversity, briefing techniques, and conflict management.

Associate Instructor, Indiana University, *2000–2002.*
- Designed a the fundamentals of business and professional communication.
- Received 2001 Arts & Science Excellence in Teaching Award.

Entertainment Supervisor, Kings Island Theme Park, Cincinnati, OH, *Summers 1994–1996.*
- Trained and supervised crew of forty people, managed entertainment facilities.

Organizational

Account Executive, WBWB FM Radio Station, Bloomington, IN, *1999–2000.*
- Consulted with clients regarding advertising needs, budget, development of advertising campaign, and production of commercials.
- Managed over eighty accounts.
- Recognized by corporate president for having tripled productivity of accounts within first six months.

Guest Relations Manager, Kings Island Theme Park, Cincinnati, OH, *April–August 1997.*
- Addressed needs of park guests through problem solving and advising park management.

Recruiting

Masters Faculty Representative, Indiana University, *2000–2001.*
- Interviewed candidates applying for faculty positions.
- Polled graduate students and presented results to faculty.

Recruiting Assistant, Management Recruiters, Cincinnati, OH, *Summer 2000.*
- Matched human resource needs of client organizations with suitable applicants.

Recruiter, Indiana University Admissions Office, *1998–1999.*
- Traveled with admissions staff, made presentations to prospective I.U. students and parents.

Technical

Proficient in WordPerfect 10.0, Microsoft Word, and Web site design.
Experience in Audio and Video Production.

References

Furnished upon Request

Figure 9.4   Sample functional resume

In addition to preparing a traditional resume, you may also want to prepare a resume that can be read by computer, a so-called *scannable resume*. This is a resume from which a computer can extract information. Recruiters and managers access resume databases; they can search for your resume in particular, or more likely, they will search for applicants with specific experiences using keywords to guide their search. See Highlighting Technology for some tips for preparing a scannable resume.

Highlighting Technology

Preparing a Scannable Resume

New technologies are providing new ways of presenting your credentials to prospective employers. One of the newest is called "electronic applicant tracking," and many leading organizations are beginning to use it to locate qualified applicants.

If you use the latest technology, your resume can be scanned into a computer system and kept active for years. The computer can search for all sorts of things in your resume. You may discover that you are qualified for all kinds of jobs that you never even knew existed.

When you prepare a resume for the computer to read, it must be "scannable." That means it's "clean" so that the scanner can pick up and reproduce an exact image.

Formatting Tips

- Use white or light-colored 8 1/2 × 11 paper.
- Provide a laser-printed original if possible.
- Do not fold or staple.
- Use standard typefaces, such as Courier, Times, Universe, and Futura.
- Use a font size of 10 to 14 points.
- Don't condense spacing between letters.
- Use boldface and/or all-capital letters for section headings.
- Avoid fancy features, such as underlining, italicizing, and shadowing.
- Avoid two-column format, as well as horizontal and vertical lines.
- Place your name on the top of the page on its own line.
- Use a standard address format below your name.
- List each phone number on its own line.

Content Tips

- Use enough specific words to define your skills, experience, education, etc. (maximizing the number of "hits").
- Describe your experience using concrete words (for instance, "supervised a sales force of 15" versus "responsible for supervising sales staff").
- Be concise and truthful (as on any resume).
- Use as many pages as you need; the computer can handle it.
- Use jargon and acronyms specific to your business or field.
- Increase your keyword list by including specifics (e.g., list the specific languages you speak).
- Use common headings, such as "education," "honors," and "experience."
- Describe your interpersonal skills, traits, and attitudes.

Source: Based on information provided by Texas Instruments; available: http://www.ti.com/recruit/docs/resume_tips.html (accessed: May 20, 2004).

Planning for the Interview

In a sense, everything you have done so far—assessing yourself, researching the position and the organization, preparing your cover letter and resume—all have prepared you for the interview. Only a few more things remain. First, try to *anticipate* the kinds of *questions* the employer is likely to ask you and think about how you will respond to them. Nearly every interviewer will ask you to describe your strengths and weaknesses, for example. Think also about how you will elaborate on your assertions. For instance, if you say you have good teamwork skills, you'll have to explain what you mean, what your experiences and successes have been. Practice responding to key questions aloud.

You should also *plan questions that you will ask* the interviewer. Nearly every interviewer will give you some time to pose questions near the end of the interview. It's important to have good questions to ask, to show that you are knowledgeable about the company but still interested in learning more. As you listen throughout the interview, other questions may occur to you, but you'll want to have tentative questions planned in advance.

Read widely about current events. Knowing what's going on in the nation and the world is always important. Employers are increasingly looking for employees who are good citizens, interested in their community and country, and committed to solving world problems. Subscribe to a good newspaper, such as the *Wall Street Journal* or the *New York Times*, and read it regularly as part of your interview preparation.

Finally, *anticipate what you will do if you are asked an inappropriate question*. Reread the section on the laws governing the employment interview. Know that some interviewers, regardless of the law, will ask unlawful questions. If you are a woman or a minority, you will want to be especially vigilant. If you are uncomfortable in the interview, you might not be comfortable working in the organization either. The interview is a two-way street in terms of decision making, each of you (interviewer and interviewee) must decide whether you want to work together in the future.

Behavior during the Interview

Just as it is important for the interviewer to establish rapport early in the interview, it is also critical for the interviewee to make a favorable initial impression.

THE INITIAL IMPRESSION

As we noted earlier, too many interviewers make their decisions during the first four or five minutes of the interview. Thus, what you do and say during that time is crucial.

Arrive on time for the interview. In U.S. culture, *punctuality* is indicative of good manners and interest in the forthcoming interaction. Secure the name of the interviewer and use it as you greet him or her. Walk confidently over to shake hands. Look *pleasant, yet professional*.

An important part of the initial impression will be determined by your *appearance*. Dress professionally—in a way that is consistent with the kind of attire commonly worn by those in the position for which you are interviewing. Each interview should be approached with intelligence and common sense regarding the sort of image you wish to convey (casual versus formal), the sort of job for which you are interviewing, and the kind of organization represented by the interviewer (industrial firm, elementary school, or artistic organization). In general, you'll want to dress "up" a bit; avoid clothing, jewelry, and other artifacts that call attention to themselves and serve as a distraction. If there is some doubt regarding the most appropriate attire, it is best to err on the conservative side.

COMMUNICATING EFFECTIVELY: NONVERBAL AND VERBAL STRATEGIES

Throughout the interview, you will communicate both verbally and nonverbally. Through the use of body, voice, and language you will articulate ideas and, perhaps more subtly, express attitudes and reveal values. Many aspects of *nonverbal communication* that apply to any communication encounter were discussed in chapter 5. In the interview context, you will be evaluated by the manner in which you:

- *Walk*. Slovenly, aimlessly, purposefully?
- *Shake hands*. Limply, warmly, vigorously?
- *Sit*. Slumped, rigid, comfortable?
- *Express yourself facially*. Darting eyes, full open-eye contact, animated, or expressionless?
- *Move*. Animated, inert, tense, or relaxed?[17]

The ***use of your voice*** is also important. Vocal quality, pitch, audibility, intelligibility, and expressiveness all count, and so does language usage—especially vocabulary and grammar. It is usually best, for example, to avoid slang and to speak clearly, fluently, and grammatically. It is also vital that you articulate your views persuasively. Avoid speaking in a monotone, sound interested and enthusiastic throughout the interview.

Several studies have revealed that the applicant's communication effectiveness has a profound impact on how she or he is rated by the interviewer and on whether or not she or he receives a job offer.[18] Research has shown that various ***verbal communication strategies*** are commonly associated with successful interviewing.[19] Here are some guidelines that grow from that research.

- ***Show how you and the position are a good fit***. In discussing your skills and abilities, try to relate them to the specific position for which you are interviewing. Specify how and why you think you are well suited to *this* job. By so doing, you demonstrate your knowledge of the position and match the demands of the job with your talents.

- *Compliment the organization*. Tell the interviewer why you want to work for this particular organization—what attracted you to this particular job. This goes beyond knowing the job's requirements: Here you are showing that you know a lot about the company and you are impressed with what you've learned.

- ***Substantiate your self-assertions with evidence***. Whatever claims you make about your positive qualities, abilities, or skills, always provide support. It is not enough to say, "I'm really motivated." You need to support that assertion with examples of situations in which you demonstrated motivation or quote the testimony of others who have endorsed your abilities.

- *Accentuate the positive; don't dwell on the negative*. The interview is, among other things, an opportunity for you to present yourself in the best possible light. Don't

DILBERT

DILBERT © by Scott Adams; reprinted by permission of United Feature Syndicate, Inc.

hesitate to show what you know, to stress what you have accomplished and what you can do. You needn't sound boastful, but you must sound confident and convinced that you can do the job. If you are confronted with some negative aspect of your record, *briefly* explain it (e.g., low grades during your first year of college); take responsibility for the problem (not blaming circumstances or others); and quickly move to the present and the future, stressing learning and improvement.

- **Develop your responses adequately.** Some interviewees give terse, underdeveloped responses, forcing the interviewer to probe endlessly. Research shows that successful applicants talk more than do those who are interviewing them—not the reverse.[20]

- **Speak fluently.** Many applicants do not convey clear messages because their sentences are punctuated by vocalized pauses ("uh"), verbal fillers ("you know"), and other disfluencies. This is where "what is said" and "how it is said" begin to interact. Practicing aloud before the interview can help you communicate more articulately.

- **Communicate honestly.** We have emphasized positive self-presentation during the interview. However, the interview, if it is to be successful, *must* be based on a candid exchange of information. Neither interviewer nor interviewee should exaggerate the truth, make unjustified claims, or intentionally mislead the other in any way. No one wants a job for which he is not really well qualified. No one wants to work for an organization in which she feels out of place. Honesty is a must in the interview, for the good of all concerned.

Attitudes to Reveal during the Interview

As we saw in chapter 2, there are many qualities interviewers look for during an employment interview: oral communication skills, motivation, initiative, and so on. Your behavior during the interview must exhibit these characteristics. During the interview, you should reveal the qualities and behavioral characteristics that are indicative of these desirable traits.

One behavior that is desirable during an interview is **directness**. Directness is revealed, in part, through appropriate eye contact, posture, and other mannerisms. An applicant who is withdrawn will often shrink back into his or her chair, will seldom gesture, and usually avoids eye contact with the interviewer. Equally important, however, is verbal directness. As an interviewee, you should never evade questions but respond to them thoroughly and directly. Avoid starting your statements with such phrases as, "Well, I could be wrong, but . . ." or "I guess I think this would work. . . ." Instead, phrase your ideas decisively and clearly.

Closely related to directness is *responsiveness*. The interviewer should not feel that she is "prying" information from you. After all, an important purpose of the interview is for the employer to gain additional information from you. Thus, you should approach the interview with an expectation of participating actively.

Interviewers also expect interviewees to be *mentally alert*. This, of course, is not synonymous with brilliance but is related to one's comprehension of questions and one's articulateness in responding to them. Preparing carefully for the interview and getting a good night's rest the night before can also contribute to mental alertness.

Alertness should be matched by general *emotional control*. Occasionally, interviewers will ask a question that is designed to put the applicant on the spot and to see how he reacts to stress. Remember: there's nothing wrong with an interviewer doing that, so long as the ability to handle stress (or think quickly under pressure) is a crucial part of the job—and so long as the question is asked of all applicants.

Certainly not the least important of the qualities to be demonstrated during the interview is your *character*. Ethical judgments are never easy to make. Sometimes information regarding personal integrity and responsibility can be gleaned from your credentials. For example, any existing history of financial responsibility or testimony provided in letters of recommendation may serve as evidence. For the most part, however, character will be judged on the basis of the personal behavior you exhibit during the interview—particularly in relationship to openness, honesty, and balanced self-assessment.

Business Brief 9.2

Group Interviews

Tom Murray, executive director of Career Transitions Center, a nonprofit organization based in Chicago, notes that "today, there's a focus on team play and consensus opinions, and that's why the use of multiple interviewers has increased. It's challenging because if you turn even one person off you might not get the job, but there's also more opportunity to show all the things you can do by responding to the different approach of each interviewer."

Murray offers some suggestions for handling the group employment interview:

- While it's impossible to please everybody, don't antagonize anyone.
- Establish eye contact with each interviewer and talk to only one person at a time.
- Remain calm; multiple interviews can be stressful, particularly when they are a surprise.
- Listen carefully to each question; because of the multiple interviewers, the interview may be somewhat disjointed rather than having the natural flow of questions a one-on-one interview usually has.
- Answer the person doing the asking, but then look at everybody, inviting everyone to participate.

And remember, "If you do well, you will impress a lot of people quickly."

Source: Carol Kleiman, "Group Interviews Pose Challenges and Opportunities," *Chicago Tribune*, June 22, 2003, sec. 6, 1.

The Interview: Closing and Follow-Up

At the conclusion of the interview, you should *pose any questions you have not yet had an opportunity to ask*. It is imperative that you know what to expect next. The interviewer should provide this information. In the event that he or she does not, you need to find out where you stand and when and how the next communication is to occur.

Immediately following the interview, *you might send a note to the interviewer*, thanking the person for his or her time and reiterating the fact that you will be pleased to hear from the organization soon. It is also appropriate to offer to send

---

Business Brief 9.3

Handling Trick Questions

Many organizations now use various kinds of trick employment interview questions designed to force applicants away from any canned answers they have developed and to think on their feet. For example: "Why are Coke cans tapered?" "How would you weigh the world's fattest man without using a scale?" "How many tennis balls are in the air in New Zealand right now?"

When they ask these questions, interviewers aren't actually looking for the "right" answer. They want to see how you think. So, consider these suggestions:

- *Accept that whatever you think of first will be wrong.* The answer that immediately pops into your head is almost never right. If it were, the question would not be very tricky. Thus, the best approach is to start your running narration immediately, but to introduce the first idea you think of with a note of skepticism: "Well, the obvious solution would be. . . ." Then examine exactly why it fails and work out your answer aloud. This not only fills the dead air while you take some time to think, but also shows the interviewer how you approach a problem.

- *Memorize a few key figures.* Many of these questions ask for information you couldn't possibly know: How many piano tuners are there in the world? How many Ping-Pong balls can you stuff into a 747? Rest assured that the interviewer doesn't know the answer either, and doesn't much care. The hidden agenda is to see how well you can outline a logical procedure for estimating the answer. Still, it can't hurt to brush up on algebra and geometry, which are basic tools for working out these sorts of problems. In addition, it could be useful to have a rough idea of the population of the world (6.3 billion), the United States (290 million), and the city in which you are interviewing. Those figures determine the size of markets, no matter what business you're in.

- *Give a novel answer.* When a question has more than one "good" answer, you can gain points for originality. For example, an interviewer at Microsoft once asked job seekers to design a spice rack for blind people. One applicant described a counter-level drawer that alleviated the need to feel for a wall-hung rack. This ergonomic issue hadn't occurred to any other candidate, and the applicant was hired on the strength of that answer alone.

- *If the question is brief, your answer shouldn't be.* Puzzles like "Why do mirrors reverse right and left but not top and bottom?" often call for long, involved responses. Be sure to include all the logic behind your reasoning, since you may be penalized for leaving out an important part of the answer.

Source: William Poundstone, "Why Are Manhole Covers Round? (And How to Deal With Other Trick Interview Questions)," *Business 2.0* (July 2003): 118.

any additional information the interviewer might desire. A sample "thank you" letter follows in figure 9.5.

March 15, 2004

208A Clark House—Read Center
Indiana University
Bloomington, IN 47405

Mr. Phillip Johnson, Director of Recruitment
Ameritech
1633 North Meridian Street
Indianapolis, IN 46208

Dear Mr. Johnson:

Thanks again for taking the time to meet with me last Tuesday. I really enjoyed the time I spent with you, and I left the interview even more convinced that I could make a positive contribution to Ameritech.

During the interview, you indicated that you are looking for two things: practical experience and an ability to be flexible. In both areas, I feel I have a great deal to offer. My work on the editorial staff of the *Indiana Daily Student*, with the Ameritech public relations office, and in the Director of Alumni Affairs office at I.U., all have given me the firsthand experience that is so important to success in any organization. And in each of these positions, changing deadlines, priorities, and events in the community taught me flexibility. No one could have survived in those positions without being able to adapt almost instantaneously!

You asked me to provide some references. May I suggest you contact the following:

Mr. Robert Jordan	Richard L. Markus, Editor	Mr. Timothy A. Hudson
Faculty Advisor, *Indiana Daily Student*	*Elkhart Tribune*	Director, Public Relations
Indiana University	12 Terre Haute Ave.	Ameritech
Bloomington, IN 43703	Terre Haute, IN 42802	Bloomington, IN 43703
(812) 855-8713	(812) 242-7751	(812) 339-8487

Each of these individuals would be able to give you their perceptions of my work performance and my ability to adapt to changing priorities.

Again, I appreciate your having taken the time to meet with me. Please feel free to contact me if you need any additional information.

Sincerely,

Emily C. Henson

Emily C. Henson

Figure 9.5   Sample "thank you" letter

The Interview as a Problem-Solving Session

There is one overriding problem that, more than anything else, contributes to poor employment interviewing: the natural desire on the part of each participant to be wanted by the other. As a result, each participant tries to sell the organization or self to the other; neither participant provides the other with complete, accurate information, and each participant concentrates too much on making a good impression on the other.

To avoid this pitfall, **both parties must take a problem-solving approach to the interview**. As an applicant, you have a problem: finding a compatible, interesting, rewarding job. As an interviewer, you also have a problem: finding a qualified, productive, and—it is hoped—satisfied new employee. Really, these two problems are one and the same. Rather than trying to sell each other a product, the interviewer and the applicant should work toward the resolution of a common problem: determining whether the position's requirements and the applicant's qualities are compatible.

The problem-solving perspective is the key to success in employment interviewing, both as an applicant and as an interviewer. Only by exchanging information can each of you educate the other to the extent that both of you can make the best possible decision. So be prepared, make a good impression, ask good questions, and follow up after the interview. Above all, be open and honest as you communicate with representatives of the organizations with whom you interview.

Summary

This chapter has focused on the employment interview from the perspective of both interviewer (employer) and interviewee (applicant). Those who participate in interviews should understand both roles. If an applicant is able to anticipate the sorts of questions interviewers are likely to pose, for example, it puts him or her in a better position to prepare well for the interview.

For the interviewer, knowing the laws that govern the employment interview is essential. Asking unlawful questions is not only unethical, it can lead to costly lawsuits and to the loss of one's job. The interviewer should also prepare for the interview by studying all written materials provided by applicants (cover letters, resumes, letters of recommendation, etc.). The primary communication tool of the interviewer is the question. Good questions must be prepared in advance—with a core of questions to be asked of all applicants and some resume-specific questions to be asked of each applicant. The interviewer should welcome the applicant and set the stage for the interview by providing a brief overview of how the interview will be conducted. As the interviewer poses questions, he or she must be ready to listen very carefully (taking notes to assist in accuracy) and to probe when the applicant's responses are inadequate in some way. At the conclusion of the interview, the interviewer must specify what will happen next and record impressions of applicants as soon as they depart.

For the applicant, careful preparation for the interview is equally vital. The first step in any employment quest is self-assessment. The applicant then considers what is really important to him or her in a job and an organization. Once job interests have been identified, the applicant's next task is to study the organizations where the attractive jobs are located—learning everything possible about each organization's history, practices, stability, and values. The next step is to prepare a resume and write a letter of application. Both should be carefully developed and adapted to the specific job and organization. Many options exist for arranging and developing resumes; the choice of resume structure is a strategic one. Before the interview, the applicant should anticipate questions, practice responding aloud, and plan questions for the employer. During the interview, the applicant must present himself or herself well, both verbally and nonverbally.

The employment interview is always an important communicative encounter for both parties. Its outcome determines whether applicants gain employment and whether companies make good decisions in selecting those who will thrive, or rejecting those who will be less successful. Careful preparation, skillful communication, and judicious decision making by both applicant and employer are essential if the interview is to be a success.

Questions for Discussion

1. Why is the employment interview important, yet complicated?

2. What is a BFOQ? How are BFOQs related to your preparation, as an employer, for interviewing a pool of applicants?

3. Why are there so many laws to govern the interviewing process? What are some laws of special importance? Why are they important?

4. How would you initially screen out the clearly unqualified candidates, leaving only those who seem better suited for the job?

5. How will you plan the questions you will ask of each applicant?

6. What are major question areas on which you should focus your attention during an employment interview? Why are these appropriate areas to probe?

7. What other responsibilities do you have as you conduct the interview?

8. As an applicant, how will you go about assessing your skills, knowledge, and so on, as you plan for your first interview? Why is such self-assessment important?

9. What are some things that you will look for as you do research on jobs and organizations? How are these things consistent with your interests, values, and priorities?

10. What do you see as being the advantages and disadvantages of the chronological and functional resume? Which do you prefer, and why?

11. What are some guidelines you will attempt to follow in communicating verbally and nonverbally during the interview?

12. What are some important attitudes and personal characteristics that an interviewee should possess? How, as an interviewee, might you demonstrate these qualities to an interviewer?

Exercises

1. Select a specific job that interests you. Then, as precisely as you can, list all the sources you would consult if you were a personnel manager, a recruiter, or an employer seeking someone to fill that job. In addition, list all the qualifica-

tions you would look for as you sought potential candidates. How would you go about determining those qualifications?

When you have completed your research, construct a one-page applicant profile that could be used during an interview.

2. Imagine you are interviewing for a job and the interviewer asks you your age, your religion, whether you have ever been arrested, or how your spouse feels about your traveling on weekends.

Then assume that regardless of the interviewer's behavior, you really want this job. In a brief paragraph, sketch out your response to one of these questions.

Now assume that you have other options and you are less concerned about landing this particular job. Now sketch out your response to the same question.

3. Create a resume and a cover letter that you might use if you were applying for the job you researched in the first exercise.

4. Now, place yourself in the role of interviewer and develop an evaluation form that you would use if you were interviewing applicants for that same job.

5. Identify an organization that you believe to be ethically responsible in terms of the way it treats its employees, customers, and community. Then, do some research. In what ways and to what extent does your research support your initial impressions of this organization? For example, are there specific policies (such as family-friendly policies) that you especially admire? Did you find evidence of the organization's commitment to social justice, environmental, or other community concerns? Come to class prepared to discuss in very specific terms the organization you researched. How have your initial perceptions been altered (positively or negatively)? Is this a company you might consider working for some day?

Case Application 9.1 Applying for a Dream Job

For most of her life, Holly has been fascinated by Disney. Now, as she is about to graduate from Indiana University with her PhD in hand, she discovers an opportunity to work at Disney University! She immediately does careful research on the organization, considers her skills and knowledge, and decides that the fit is perfect.

Following are the cover letter and resume that Holly sends to Disney University. Read them carefully and respond to the questions that follow.

14 December 2004

3061 East Amy Lane
Bloomington, IN 47408

Disneyland Resort Professional Staffing
P.O. Box 3232
Anaheim, CA 92803-3232

To Whom It May Concern,

From my earliest memories to my current taste in art, Disney and its characters have been a part of my life. Every time I go to a mall or drive by a Disney store, my friends and family instinctively know that they will be asked, pleaded, and politely encouraged, well, perhaps threatened is a better word, to stop and browse. I was browsing the Disney web page and decided to look at career opportunities and was thrilled to learn of an opening as the Director of Disney University WOW.

While I may not have current hospitality experience, I do have an extensive knowledge of Disney's business, resorts, and practices. In addition, my life-long love of Disney, my proven ability to learn new concepts quickly, and my enthusiasm for taking on challenges would more than compensate for this. While it may appear initially from my enclosed resume and application that I only have experience teaching, this is certainly not the case. While I do have a passion for university-level teaching, what I have taught shows my diversity and flexibility. I have taught business management majors the essentials of interviewing, public and professional speaking, diversity and conflict management, and how to create and present professional proposals using the newest technology available. In addition, teaching has perfected my interpersonal and organizational skills and made me an expert in conflict resolution. My educational background and advanced degrees in Communication and Human Resource Management have honed my skills in analytical and strategic problem solving, quantitative research methods, and developing appropriate communication strategies to deal with every situation imaginable. Finally, my dissertation research strengthened my skills in managing focus groups, designing training and development programs, and effectively dealing with the stress of producing high-quality work under tight deadlines. In addition, working for a company such as Disney would be tremendously exciting and would offer me constant challenges to grow and improve my skills in the aforementioned areas.

While my resume can illustrate my qualifications, it cannot show the sheer enthusiasm, motivation, and dedication with which I approach every aspect of my life. I hope you will give me the opportunity to demonstrate these qualities in an interview, as I feel my exceptional communication skills, creativity, and energy would be an asset to Disney. I can be reached at (812) 339-6965 or at hcbaxter@indiana.edu. I look forward to meeting with you in the near future to discuss the possibility of becoming a member of the Disney team.

Sincerely,

Holly Carolyn Baxter

Holly Carolyn Baxter

Holly Carolyn Baxter
3061 East Amy Lane
Bloomington, IN 47408
(812) 339-6965
hcbaxter@indiana.edu

CAREER OBJECTIVE

Seeking a position that would allow me to utilize my exceptional communication skills, passion for teaching, and in-depth knowledge of diversity issues and human resource management, while allowing me to continue to broaden my knowledge in each of these areas.

EDUCATION

Indiana University, Bloomington, May 2004, PhD (Major: Organizational Communication; Minors: Organizational Behavior and Human Resource Management). Dissertation Title: "A Comparison of Diversity Training Methods on Perceptions of Individuals with Physical Disabilities in the Workplace."

Indiana University, Bloomington, June 1997, M.A. (Major: Organizational and Interpersonal Communication)

University of Dayton, Dayton, OH, May 1993, B.A. summa cum laude, departmental honors (Major: Communication with a concentration in Public Relations; Minors: Political Science and Criminal Justice)

PROFESSIONAL EXPERIENCE

Course Director, Business and Professional Communication, Department of Speech Communication, Indiana University, Bloomington. January 2003–present.

- Manage staff of six instructors.
- Responsible for all administrative duties, including scheduling of classes, developing syllabus, and refining course requirements.
- Use skills gained as a mediator to resolve conflict-related issues and settle disputes to the satisfaction of all parties involved.

Internship in Human Resource Management (Training and Development), Deloitte & Touche, Indianapolis, IN, Spring 2002.

- Designed an instrument for evaluating the effectiveness of a leadership-training program.
- Refined quantitative research skills in SPSS and Excel.

Internship in Human Resource Management (Selection Systems), Otis Elevator, Bloomington, IN, Fall 2001.

- Helped to develop a competency model for First-line Supervisors.
- Polished interviewing and evaluation skills.

TEACHING EXPERIENCE

Managing Workforce Diversity (V452), School of Public and Environmental Affairs, Indiana University, January 2003–present (one section, 20 students). Will prepare students majoring in management to deal with diversity issues in the workplace. Focus on legal and ethical issues as they relate to selection topics, training and development, issues between coworkers, and termination decisions.

Business and Professional Communication (S223), Department of Speech Communication, Indiana University, 2001–present (six sections taught, 24 students per section). Prepare students for professional communication, such as resume and cover letter writing, interviewing, small group theory and communication, and development of professional proposals.

Representative Americans: People with Disabilities (A201 a), Division of Extended Studies, Indiana University, July 2002 (Correspondence course). Responded to questions and evaluated assignments while appointed instructor was on a leave of absence.

Interpersonal Communication (S122), Department of Speech Communication, Indiana University, 1999–2002 (ten sections taught, 35 students per section). Taught fundamentals of interpersonal communication theory and basic conversational analysis skills.

Public Speaking (S121), Department of Speech Communication, Indiana University, 1997–1998 (seven sections taught, 26 students per section). Taught basic fundamentals of Public Speaking; helped students deal with and overcome fear of public speaking.

AWARDS AND HONORS

- Indiana Speech Tradition Award for Excellence in Teaching, Indiana University, 2003.
- Faculty Award for Academic Excellence in Communication, University of Dayton, 1997 (awarded to the graduating senior with the highest overall and major grade point average).
- Golden Key National Honor Society, inducted 1997.
- Deans List, University of Dayton, every semester 1994–1997.
- University of Dayton Leadership Award, University of Dayton, 1997 (awarded for outstanding academic achievement and leadership skills).
- Beavercreek Jaycee's Scholarship, Dayton, OH, 1995 (awarded for academic excellence and community service).

SERVICE ACTIVITIES

- Department of Speech Communication, Peer Mentor for new Associate Instructors, Indiana University, 1999–2004.
- Disabled Student Services, Volunteer, Indiana University, 1997–2004.
- Dayton Mediation Center, Certified Mediator, Dayton, OH, 1996–present.
- Faculty and Staff for Student Excellence (FASE), Mentor for first generation college freshmen, Indiana University, 2000–2002.

PROFESSIONAL PRESENTATIONS

- Designed and presented; "Workshop for Associate Instructors on using electronic media in teaching," Indiana University, October 2002.
- Presented and facilitated group discussion; "Workshop on interpersonal communication and listening skills for high school Mentors for Children," Monroe County Library, Bloomington, IN, September 2002.
- Designed and presented; "Legal ramifications and diversity issues in the workplace as related to the Americans with Disabilities Act of 1990," Department of Business Law, Indiana University, May 2001.

REFERENCES

Available upon request.

Questions

1. What are some of the ways that Holly presents herself positively in her letter of application?

2. How effectively does she compliment Disney and show the match between her, the organization, and the position?

3. What criticisms do you have? How might she further improve her letter?

4. Describe how Holly organizes her credentials on her resume. Does her chosen structure seem effective? What are some other options she might consider?

5. What are the greatest strengths of Holly's resume?

6. How might her resume be further strengthened? Be specific.

Case Application 9.2   The Nightmare Interview

Linda was interviewing for a job with a large consulting firm. She very much wanted the firm to hire her: the pay they were offering was nearly double the amount she was making as a corporate EEO specialist, and her fiancé already worked for the firm. As a part of the interview process, she met with Herb, the president of the consulting firm, a man in his middle fifties who had a national reputation for the kind of work he did and a reputation within the firm for being a kind, generous, and much beloved leader.

After Linda and Herb had exchanged some information about the firm and Linda's employment history, Herb asked, "So, are you married?" Linda paused a moment, then answered, "No." "Do you have any kids?" Herb asked. Again Linda paused, and then answered, "No." "Planning on having any?" Herb asked. Linda thought a moment, and then said, "No, but I do have to ask you, why are you asking me these questions?" Herb answered, "Well, there's a lot of travel involved in the job, and it can be hard on families to have people gone all the time. We've particularly seen that with the female consultants we've hired."

Questions

1. What problems, if any, do you see with the questions Herb asked?

2. If you were Linda, what would you do or say?

3. How might Herb have handled this situation better?

PART 4

SMALL GROUP
COMMUNICATION

Groups, like individuals, have shortcomings. Groups can bring out the worst as well as the best in man. Nietzsche went so far as to say that madness is the exception in individuals but the rule in groups.

—Irving Janis, *Groupthink*

10

Group Functions and Socioemotional Variables

After reading this chapter, you should be able to:

❏ Understand the importance of small groups in organizational communication settings

❏ Distinguish the different kinds of groups that function in organizational and community life

❏ Explain how socioemotional variables impact small group interaction and performance

❏ Discuss the ways that pressure for uniformity, role structure, status and power, and cohesiveness affect group functioning and effectiveness

Throughout our lives, each of us participate in countless formal and informal small groups. Professionally, we put in hundreds of hours attending staff meetings, departmental meetings, subcommittee meetings, and unit gatherings. As we interact in these groups, we learn from each other, form friendships, and contribute knowledge and skills vital to the task of enhancing the organization's image and improving its productivity. In civic settings, we participate on panels, attend committee meetings, and work on task forces designed to tackle the community's problems. Participating in a group is not the same kind of experience as dealing individually with one other person or solving a problem alone. A group is both dynamic and complex. These qualities may lead to long-term, productive relationships and inspire innovative decision making or, by contrast, contribute to prolonged tensions and delayed action-taking.

The frequency with which you participate in small groups is in itself reason enough to make the next three chapters important ones. We must also emphasize one other point: Your success in any organization is influenced significantly by your performance in group settings. Every meeting represents an opportunity for you to impress your superiors, have your ideas adopted, assert positive influence over others, and demonstrate your capabilities for greater responsibility. On the other hand, we have seen careers stalled because of group participation. Employees who frequently arrive late or unprepared, fail to talk during meetings, behave disagreeably or discourteously, or otherwise perform poorly in the group setting rapidly develop a bad reputation among their peers and superiors—one that is virtually impossible to overcome. Moreover, organizations are increasingly placing emphasis on participative problem solving at the lowest levels of the hierarchy, so the opportunities for you to perform well or poorly in a group are increasing. In some countries, such as the Scandinavian nations, workers are required by law to participate in industrial decision making. In U.S. organizations, labor and management groups come together to attempt to keep companies open, to increase productivity, and to fight competition from foreign producers. Finally, the more involved you become as a citizen in your community, the more frequently you will work in groups to deal with such critical issues as improving the educational system, eliminating domestic violence, and creating a safe and healthy environment for everyone. Your ability to contribute constructively to these groups will surely impact their chances of successfully resolving these serious problems. For all these reasons, then, developing skill in group participation is vital to the short- and long-term well-being of you, your organization, and your community.

Preview

In this chapter, we discuss the reasons small groups are such an important part of contemporary organizational functioning. We begin by overviewing the basic functions and types of groups, highlighting teams and quality circles in professional settings and civic groups in community settings. Then we briefly discuss group meetings that occur in public settings. Finally, we focus on critical socioemotional variables—pressure for uniformity, role structure, status and power, and cohesiveness—that profoundly influence the experience of working together in groups.

SMALL GROUPS: THEIR MEANING AND SCOPE

Before going further, it is important to examine the concept of a *small group*. It is quite possible for several individuals to be together for some period of time, yet not really be considered a group. Patients waiting in a dentist's office, students sitting in a classroom on the first day of the semester, or a dozen travelers snoozing in the airport gate area waiting to catch a midnight flight are all examples of small groups of people, but not in the sense we are using the term here.

Defining the Small Group

For small groups to exist, it is essential that group members perceive themselves as something other than a collection of independent individuals. Bales was among the first to point to the importance of group members developing a *psychological relationship,* a sense of a mutual awareness and interdependence.[1] The creation of this mutual psychological awareness rarely occurs all at once. Rather, it develops over some period of face-to-face interaction. Members' relationships are furthered by repeated encounters, normally accomplished through communicative exchanges.

Communication facilitates interaction and, by doing so, helps to define the psychological relationship that develops within the small group. Small group members also have some degree of shared interest. Often this interest is expressed as *a goal on which there is mutual agreement*. When small groups form to meet the personal needs of group members (such as the Starbucks coffee-break group), the goal may grow naturally from the group itself. Group members may meet to provide mutual support, listen to one another's complaints, or provide some diversion from routine work. Other small groups form in response to a formal assignment. You may be assigned to a group whose task is to develop a new public relations campaign or to draft a sexual harassment policy. These groups are largely task oriented and are often asked to make decisions or solve problems.

The size of the "small" group can vary, usually ranging from as few as three to as many as twenty. In general, the larger the group, the more complex the patterns of interaction and the more formalized the procedures necessary to handle the group's functioning. Studies of committees have revealed the most common group sizes are five, seven, and nine.[2] For the most part, however, most experts agree that face-to-face interaction, the presence of a bond or psychological relationship, and some significant degree of common interests or goals are the critical characteristics of the small group, rather than the specific number of group members.

Groups in organizations do not exist as isolated units. They are, instead, embedded within the larger organizational system. Moreover, each individual typically belongs to multiple groups and is often subjected to conflicting pressures. If nothing else, the demands of time can make group participation a tough balancing act—as you move from departmental meetings, to task forces, to production groups, to community group meetings after work. Finally, organizational groups operate within formal hierarchies and normally function with appointed leaders.[3] In professional settings, teams and quality circles are two of the most prominent kinds of groups.

Teams

We have already discussed the teamwork philosophy of organization theory as well as the use of self-managing teams as a current application of human resources management (see chapter 3). The Center for Effective Organizations at the University of Southern California conducted a survey of Fortune 1000 companies and found that 68 percent of these companies use self-managing teams.[4] As small groups within organizations, teams generally consist of either project or work teams.

Project teams have existed for many years in organizational settings. Typically consisting of employees representing an array of specialties (such as marketing, sales, and engineering), they coordinate the successful completion of a particular project, product, or service. Project teams have been part of the space program for many years and are common in electronic, computer, and other research-based industries. These teams typically work quickly to clarify goals, roles, and responsibilities. They often possess little history, are likely pressured by deadlines, and may have difficulty establishing mutually satisfying working relationships. Nevertheless, cross-functional project teams are potentially valuable in that they keep individuals from different organizational divisions communicating with and educating each other, while reminding them of the importance of customer needs and satisfaction.

The other, and most innovative, kind of team is the **work team**. Wellins, Byham, and Wilson define the work team as "an intact group of employees who are responsible for a 'whole' work process or segment that delivers a product or service to an internal or external customer."[5] Work teams have become increas-

---

Business Brief 10.1

Teamwork in Action

In an effort to improve quality and productivity, many companies are attempting to shift from classical organizational thinking (specialized jobs and narrowly defined tasks improve performance) toward a broader, team-oriented approach (a more flexible, multiskilled workforce performs best). Even traditionally unionized companies have improved morale, speed, and efficiency by loosening job classifications and developing a more flexible workforce through intensive cross-training and job rotation. For example:

- Motorola dissolved six pay categories at its Arlington Heights, Illinois, cellular phone factory. Now all workers are in the same category, and their pay increases are based on learning new skills while maintaining high work quality.

- Lechmere, Inc., a 27-store retail chain, bases pay raises on the number of jobs employees learn: cashiers are encouraged to also sell products, salespeople are taught to drive forklifts, and so on.

- AT&T created nearly a dozen cross-functional teams to participate in developing a new cordless phone and through cross-training and employee involvement was able to cut development in half.

Source: D. Keith Denton, "Multi-Skilled Teams Replace Old Work Systems," *HR Magazine* 37 (September 1992): 48–56.

---

ingly popular and are used in such diverse organizations as 3M, General Electric, AT&T, and Corning. Each of the companies that has won the Malcolm Baldrige National Quality Award (such as Motorola, Westinghouse, and Xerox) fostered teamwork among employees as a crucial component of its improvement efforts.[6]

Katzenbach and Smith studied 50 different teams in over 30 organizations.[7] Based on their observations, they believe that the critical factor in establishing successful teams is to assemble a small number of people with complementary skills who share a commitment to a common purpose and who adopt a set of performance goals for which they hold themselves mutually accountable. They argue that teams develop direction, momentum, and commitment by working to shape a meaningful purpose. Team members then translate their common purpose into specific performance goals, such as reducing the rejection rate from suppliers by 40 percent or increasing the math scores of graduates from the 60th to the 80th percentile. Moreover, when team members work together toward common objectives, trust and commitment follow.

Can teams be empowering? Indeed they can, under the right circumstances.[8] Dumaine argues that the best teams "are truly empowered to organize their work and make decisions."[9] And mutual accountability is also a key ingredient. As Katzenbach and Smith put it:

> This sense of mutual accountability... produces the rich rewards of mutual achievement in which all members share. What we heard over and over from members of effective teams is that they found the experience energizing and motivating in ways their "normal" jobs never could match.[10]

There is an important distinction between being held accountable by one's boss and being accountable to oneself and one's team. Another determinant of a team's success may depend on how well the group manages cultural diversity, as discussed in Highlighting Diversity.

There are, however, no guarantees. Sometimes teams are "set up" to fail.[11] They may get launched in a vacuum, with little or no training or support, no changes in the design of their work, and no new technologies like e-mail to foster communication within and between teams.[12] Managers must make a commitment to empowerment by demonstrating a willingness to give teams the actual authority to get the job done. This means providing access to resources, information, and technical assistance while allowing the teams to make decisions about how to proceed, how to delegate responsibility, and so forth.

Whether or not a team is effective, then, depends on members' skills, mutual trust, sense of purpose, and commitment to objectives—as well as factors external to the group. When managers are truly committed to empowerment through teamwork, however, and are willing to put aside constraints associated with the traditional hierarchy and to think in fresh, creative ways, work teams can serve as true vehicles of empowerment. In its Statement of Aspirations, Levi Strauss & Company defines empowering leadership as that which "increases the authority and responsibility of those closest to our products and customers. By actively pushing responsibility, trust, and recognition into the organization, we can harness and release the capabilities of all our people."[13] Not surprisingly, work teams are an intrinsic component of the Levi Strauss culture.

Highlighting Diversity

Acknowledging Communication Differences in Culturally Diverse Groups

Cultural diversity in small groups is both a source of creative energy and potentially unproductive conflict. Here are some issues to consider:

- Melding different perspectives *can* encourage people to understand problems in new ways and to develop creative solutions.
- Homogeneous groups are more likely to experience defective decision making, including groupthink and shared biases.
- Research has found that groups composed of members from diverse cultural backgrounds tend to perform better and produce higher-quality decisions than groups that are homogeneous.
- Cultural differences can cause barriers to goal achievement. Such differences include:
  - Group members from Western (individualistic) cultures tend to have a direct verbal interaction style that is "I" or "me" oriented. They are more likely to be talkative and to promote their own ideas and accomplishments.
  - Group members from Eastern (collectivist) cultures use an indirect style that is more "we" or "us" oriented. They tend to be less talkative, feel comfortable with silence, attend to status differences in the group, and downplay their own contributions and accomplishments.
- Failure to recognize or acknowledge these differences in communication styles can result in misunderstandings and miscommunication among group members.

Source: "Culture and Small Groups," published by McGraw-Hill, 2000 [online]. Available: http://www.mhhe.com/socscience/comm/group/students/diversity.htm (accessed: July 2, 2004).

Quality Circles

One approach to organizational problem solving and employee participation is the use of *quality circles (QCs)*. These are small groups of people who meet voluntarily to define, analyze, and solve work-related problems. Typically these people come from the same department or work group, or at least perform similar job functions, so that the problems they discuss are familiar to all of them, and each member can contribute to the development of solutions.

At a general level, quality circles meet to analyze and solve the organization's problems. More specifically, however, their functions are often detailed and diversified. Among the things quality circles do are:

- Improve the quality of services or products
- Reduce the number of work-related errors
- Promote cost reduction
- Develop better work methods
- Improve efficiency in the organization
- Improve relations between management and employees
- Promote participants' leadership skills
- Enhance employees' career and personal development
- Improve communication throughout the organization

Although the concept of quality circles originally developed in Japan, they are increasingly common in the United States. Ninety percent of Fortune 500 companies reportedly use quality circles.[14]

Quality circles have been used with reported success in many organizations; even so, QC groups may experience problems. Case studies by Meyer and Scott

---

Business Brief 10.2

Self-Direction Through Teamwork

Many employees dread Monday mornings, the start of another work week. Not so for Al Reynolds and Amanda Dunston, employees at Northern Telecom's Morrisville, North Carolina, repair facility. "I now look forward to coming to work. I don't *have* to go to work, I *get* to work," claims Reynolds. Dunston adds, "I enjoy the challenge. Every day, I'm learning something new."

Both are part of a set of self-directed work teams recently formed by their company. As team members, they are involved in ordering materials, tracking and scheduling overtime work, calculating and monitoring productivity, reviewing budgets, and interviewing prospective team members. Soon, they will also be conducting peer performance reviews and taking corrective action when their peers do not perform adequately.

The key to successful implementation of self-directed teams at Northern Telecom was top-level management involvement. All members of supervision and management participated in intensive workshops designed to change how they think about worker-management relations and how they manage on a day-to-day basis. But not all managers were able to make the transition: company statistics indicate that about 25 percent of its first-line supervisors left after the team approach was adopted.

Source: Jana Schilder, "Work Teams Boost Productivity," *Personnel Journal* 71 (February 1992): 67–71.

suggest that quality circles may be no different from other committee meetings in some organizations in that supervisors may dominate them; the groups may lack a sense of clearly defined purpose, stray from problem solving, and get bogged down in never-ending problem analysis; and group members may be unequally committed to the group tasks.[15] Equally critical is the fact that for many organizational members there are simply no tangible rewards associated with participating in quality circles. Supervisors themselves may send mixed messages, inviting criticism and open discussion during quality circle meetings, but rarely asking for suggestions or criticisms in other contexts.[16]

In spite of potential problems, quality circles continue to thrive in many organizations when participation in them is voluntary.[17] By helping build employee problem-solving and communication skills, as well as management leadership and communication skills, and by creating a formal structure for ongoing communication throughout the organization, the QC system has the potential to develop a more goal-oriented and team-centered management climate. With an effective QC program, many positive outcomes are possible.[18]

Community Groups and Civic Engagement

Regardless of the types of organizations for whom we work, everyone of us has the opportunity to participate in groups within our communities. Sometimes these groups are associated with other organizations to which we formally belong. For instance, let's say you are an active member of the United Methodist Church. You attend church every Sunday where you worship with several hundred others who are also a part of the congregation. On the first Monday evening of each month, you attend a book discussion group (a group of about 12–18 who meet monthly to discuss all sorts of books with implications for contemporary social issues, ranging from *Nickel and Dimed* by Barbara Ehrenreich to *A Farewell to Arms* by Ernest Hemingway). Each Friday, before going to work, you join another group from the church to prepare breakfast at a local homeless shelter. You are also on a steering committee who is organizing a Habitat for Humanity build that is to be a special "United Methodist" build. In addition, you belong to the Caring Ministry—a group who visits nursing homes, hospitals, and homebound church members and prepares meals for those who have recently experienced a death in their families. Finally, you have just joined an ecumenical group of individuals from many churches across the community who are addressing the community-wide concern of hate crimes. So, growing from your membership in *one* church, you are an active part of *five* small groups who are working, in diverse ways, to address issues of poverty and homelessness, to provide support and comfort to those in need, and to grapple with the problem of safety, civility, and peace (from the community to the national level).

This extended illustration demonstrates the abundant opportunities that each of us has for becoming engaged citizens through our voluntary participation in small groups. Of course, the groups *you* join will grow from *your* interests in government, politics, city planning, entrepreneurship, the educational system, the environment, or animal rights (to name a few). The opportunities are great in number and rich in diversity. Like other small groups, these will invite face-to-face interaction and will be goal directed. Their success will depend on the level

City council meetings present an engaging arena for civic engagement. In the meeting pictured here, over seventy citizens packed the city council meeting room at the city hall in Jackson, Illinois, for an open workshop meeting on rural fire protection. This kind of robust involvement with community concerns is a central part of voluntary group participation in a democracy.

of commitment that each member brings.[19] What we get out of our voluntary group involvement will be directly related to the time, effort, and commitment we bring to our work. No one is going to pay us. If we are promoted, we will assume greater responsibility, but not necessarily greater status. We may choose to put our volunteer activities on our resumes, but doing so will not necessarily strengthen our resumes or lead to greater rewards at work, unless we are fortunate enough to be working for a company that encourages volunteerism.[20] Our rewards, then, must be based on our intrinsic belief in the value of the project, the issue, or the mission that we, together with others, have set forth to accomplish. See Highlighting Civic Engagement and Diversity for a model of deliberative dialogue that may enhance democratic participation in civic affairs.[21]

Group Discussions in Public Settings

Most of the time, communication taking place in small groups in organizations occurs in private settings. On occasion, however, we will be called on to participate in a small group discussion for the benefit of an audience. Public discussions often bring together representatives from several different organizations, all of whom share some expertise on the discussion topic, but individually possess a different perspective. For example, a community forum on poverty in Bloomington, Indiana, brought together the executive directors of five local agencies: Martha's House (a transitional housing unit for the homeless), Mother Hubbard's Cupboard (a food pantry for the poor), the Community Kitchen (an agency that provides free daily dinners to anyone in need of a hot meal), the Shalom Community Center (a daytime shelter and resource center for the poor and homeless), and the Hoosier Hills Food Bank (a food pantry that provides most of the food used by the agencies that feed the poor). Each director made a brief presentation, followed by an extensive question-and-answer period with the audience.

Highlighting Civic Engagement and Diversity

Expanding Civic Engagement through Deliberative Dialogue

The *Study Circles Resource Center (SCRC)* was created by the Topsfield Foundation in 1989 to advance deliberative democracy and improve the quality of public life in the United States. Its goal is to develop communication tools to involve a large number of people, from every background and way of life, in face-to-face dialogue and action on critical issues.

- The process of ***dialogue*** can bring many benefits to civic life—an orientation toward constructive communication, the dispelling of stereotypes, honesty in relaying ideas, and the intention to listen and understand each other.

- ***Deliberation*** brings a different benefit—the use of critical thinking and reasoned argument as a way for citizens to make decisions about public policy.

- In the SCRC model, diverse small groups ***meet in study circles***—meeting simultaneously all across a community to address an issue of common concern. The groups contain people of all races and ethnic backgrounds, men and women, and people of all income levels. In each group, participants:
  - — share their concerns and their personal connections to the issue;
  - — listen to each other, form relationships, and build trust;
  - — determine what is important about the issue facing them;
  - — identify some common ground (recognizing that they will always disagree in some areas);
  - — find ways to address the issue;
  - — decide how they want to get involved to make a difference.

- After several small group meetings, they ***come together as a whole community***. In this context, they:
  - — learn how others are working to make a difference;
  - — discern how their contribution fits into the larger picture;
  - — may decide to join forces and work together with other groups (although some will choose to remain independent);
  - — engage in a give-and-take of ideas with public officials and other community members about public policy and discover ways to collaborate.

- Such opportunities create environments that foster all forms of ***civic engagement***—connecting a diverse group of citizens to each other, to the issues, to community institutions, to policy making, and to the community as a whole. This kind of engagement leads to active participation, a feeling of power and effectiveness, and real opportunities to have a say and make a difference.

Source: Martha L. McCoy and Patrick L. Scully, "Deliberative Dialogue to Expand Civic Engagement: What Kind of Talk Does Democracy Need?" *National Civic Review* 91, no. 2 (Summer 2002) [online]. Available: http://www.ncl.org/publications/ncr/91-2/ncr91-2_article.pdf (accessed: May 19, 2004).

Public discussions can occur in several different formats or patterns of discussant interaction. A *panel discussion* is a format in which the participants interact directly and spontaneously with the guidance of a moderator. No participant has a planned speech. Instead, each speaks briefly, rather frequently, and within the realm of courtesy whenever he or she desires. A more formal mode of public discussion is the *symposium*, in which discussants prepare brief speeches representing their viewpoints. Each group member speaks in turn without interruption or interaction. As the panel moderator, the symposium leader usually introduces the group members and provides a summary at the end of the discussion. During the actual discussion, however, there is no need for moderator intervention or guidance—except for providing transitions between speakers. The poverty presentation described above is an example of a symposium. Both the panel discussion and the symposium are usually followed by a *forum period* during which members of the audience are encouraged to ask questions and express opinions. The forum is generally guided by the moderator, and questions may be directed to individual members or to the group as a whole.

Public discussions in organizations take a similar variety of forms and are conducted for a variety of "publics." As the need for a consumer-oriented corporate culture grows, an increasing number of organizations are holding symposia, panels, and forums for community groups, stockholders, customer groups, and others. One large manufacturer of hospital supplies, for example, has begun conducting seminars on "Managing Hospital Resources" across the country for hospital executives. During the seminars, those attending listen to short speeches by experts in many areas of management, watch as these experts discuss with one another, and then ask questions related to their own concerns. Similarly, many companies have started conducting such meetings for their own employees, to increase the visibility of their executive group and to promote interaction among employees and management. Our own observations indicate that public meetings, both inside and outside the organization, will become increasingly common.

KEY SOCIOEMOTIONAL VARIABLES IN GROUPS

At the beginning of this chapter, we pointed to the existence of a bond or psychological relationship among members as one of the small group's defining characteristics. The development of this relationship may be influenced by the kind of task the group is confronted with accomplishing as well as the cognitive functionings of group members in relation to that task. But it is largely socioemotional factors that contribute to the development of interpersonal bonds within the group. Chief among these are pressure for uniformity, role structure, status and power, and cohesiveness.

Pressure for Uniformity

The phenomenon of social influence has long fascinated scholars in a variety of disciplines. In the field of organization theory, researchers of the human relations school were the first to recognize the potent influence of small, informal work groups on the behavior of individuals. As early as 1911, however, Taylor noted the presence of group norms that appeared to affect industrial productivity.[22] Over the past half-century, the collective efforts of social scientists have identified the small group as one of the major contexts in which social influence or pressure for uniformity may be most potent.

The classic social influence investigation was conducted by Asch, who performed a series of experiments involving simple line discrimination tasks.[23] In fact, the perceptual task of matching one of three comparison lines with a test line was so easy (as illustrated in figure 10.1), that Asch discovered any individual with normal vision could make the correct match nearly 100 percent of the time. Asch subsequently coached a group of confederates to make deliberately erroneous judgments on the same perceptual tasks. When a naive individual was placed among Asch's group of confederates and asked to listen to the judgments of others before stating his own estimates, the results were radically skewed in the direction of the majority. Approximately one-third of all estimates made by the subjects were identical with or in the direction of the distorted majority estimates. *Only one-fourth* of the naive subjects *remained completely independent* over a series of trials.

What is especially provocative about these findings is that the individuals were not acquainted with one another before their brief encounter. Moreover, the confederates made *no overt attempts* to influence the behavior of the naive individual. Finally, the line discrimination tasks had no real intrinsic importance to the subjects, to their future relations with others, or to the fate of anyone in the room.

We have mentioned *norms* several times in the preceding discussion. Schein defines a norm as "a set of assumptions or expectations held by the members of a group or organization concerning what kind of behavior is right or wrong, good or bad, appropriate or inappropriate, allowed or not allowed."[24] Those who conform are acting in ways they perceive as consistent with those group norms. Norms may be either *implicit* (not actually articulated, but known and understood) or *explicit* (formally stated either orally, in writing, or both). Organizations often provide explicit norms in the form of rules, regulations, and other codes of conduct. These norms may include such varied items as personal appearance (hair length, cleanliness, appropriate attire), language usage, length of lunch and coffee breaks, and strategies and procedures to be used in committee meetings. Implicit norms are even more potentially diverse, dealing, for example, with our political views, the make of car we drive, and those with whom we socialize.

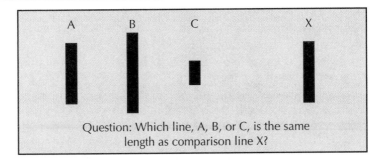

Question: Which line, A, B, or C, is the same length as comparison line X?

Figure 10.1   A line discrimination task typical of Asch's research

Whether or not we adhere to the norms of our group or organization depends on a variety of factors. Chief among them is the *degree to which we value our membership and identify strongly with the group or organization*.[25] In addition, people possess different motives for conforming. In some instances they may listen to other group members' arguments and actually become convinced that the group is right. By contrast, others may simply find it easier, less stressful, or more politically astute to mouth their agreement, even though they privately disagree.

By interviewing his subjects after the experiment, Asch discovered that only a small percentage of the yielding subjects really believed the majority estimates were correct. In most cases, the group's judgment had been accepted publicly while private views remained the same.[26] In actual organizational settings, compliance may be ingratiating, strategically aimed at increasing the worker's attractiveness in the eyes of his or her boss, or it may reveal the subordinate's fear of open discussion.

Failure to conform to the group can be psychologically uncomfortable. Or, conformity can be viewed as strategic. One organizational leader recently disclosed that he always "cooperated" with others on issues that he saw as insignificant in the grand scheme. He laughingly noted that when he voted with others, he always made them aware of it, sometimes by joking that they "owed him." However, he actually viewed the situation as demanding that others would reciprocate. He had scratched their backs, and he fully expected others to extend the same courtesy to him. Implicit in this approach to conformity is the idea that individuals might conform when an issue is not of central importance to them, while remaining quite independent on issues about which they care deeply.[27]

For years, scholars debated whether the tendency to conform should be viewed as a personality characteristic. For the most part, however, *situational factors* seem to most influence the individual's tendency to conform.[28] In general, individuals appear to be more likely to conform when they are in situations:

- that are ambiguous or confusing;
- where the members of the group are unanimous;
- where the group contains those of higher rank;
- where the group is highly cohesive;
- when a state of crisis or emergency exists that seems to demand uniformity (e.g., jury deliberations).

Groups exert pressure for uniformity in a variety of ways. Human relations researchers noted the verbal and nonverbal methods informal work groups used to get deviates "back in line." Tactics such as teasing, ridiculing, punching, and shoving were not uncommon in factory settings. Schachter's laboratory research pointed to increases in the quantity of communication as a major pressuring tactic.[29] Subsequent research by Taylor found that the verbal behavior of majority group members was characterized by reasonableness, dominance, and hostility.[30] More recently, Thameling and Andrews described the communication behavior of majority group members as being cooperative, opinionated, and emotional.[31] Finally, Wenburg and Wilmot have identified five sequential steps taken by most groups as they attempt to influence opinion deviates:

1. *Delaying action*—Doing little overtly and hoping the deviate will conform without pressure.

2. *Chatting among themselves*—Perhaps involving joking with the deviate.

3. *Ridiculing the deviate*—Overtly recognizing his behavior as different and unacceptable.

4. *Engaging in severe criticism*—Possibly including threats.

5. *Rejecting the deviate*—Ignoring and isolating him and prohibiting future interaction with the group.[32]

This is only a rough model and does not take into account unique group characteristics (e.g., level of cohesiveness) or the relationship between the deviate and the group.

One of the most critical variables affecting a deviate's treatment is her *position or status within the group*. In general, groups tolerate more deviant behavior from those of high status.[33] There are, however, exceptions. The high-status person may be treated more harshly by other group members if she commits an act perceived as extremely serious or damaging. In general, however, high status permits greater freedom.[34]

How does one respond to group pressure? Both individual and situational variables play a role. For instance, some tend to "go with the flow" in most situations, preferring to fit in with the group rather than being perceived as "making waves." Others may change their minds and begin to agree with the group's perceptions—because, in fact, they are genuinely persuaded or because they have forced themselves to deny the validity of their own views or senses. Of course, some respond to group pressure by refusing to yield. Challenging the group's authority in this way may result in a variety of outcomes. For instance, if the group or organization is threatened by the deviate's act, they may punish him or her severely. Tompkins recounts the story of Roger Boisjoly, one of the engineers who unsuccessfully argued against launching the space shuttle *Challenger*. Boisjoly subsequently "deviated" further by going against the advice of management and reporting his reservations to the Rogers Commission, which was investigating the disaster. Tompkins notes:

> He [Boisjoly] then lost his job at Thiokol. Residents of the town he lived in, who had once elected him mayor, now began to shun him and his wife . . . and many members of his own church refused to speak to him. A dead rabbit was placed in his mailbox. On several occasions while taking long walks near his home, he said, vehicles swerved as if to hit him.[35]

Boisjoly's situation was complicated in that his unwillingness to conform also served to blow the whistle on a group of very important people with a very great deal to lose.

More common instances of deviation can also lead to unpleasant consequences, especially under circumstances in which those in positions of power are intolerant of dissent. One woman recently challenged her boss during a departmental meeting. She had just learned that he had withheld important information from the group and had also misrepresented the truth with regard to some important recruiting in which the department was engaged. When she challenged his version of affirmative action at the meeting, he told her (in a loud and forceful voice) that she was "out of order." Then, giving her a cold, shark-like stare, he told her that he would not forget what she had said during the meeting. The next day, she found a note on her desk informing her that she had been removed from two important committees (one of which she had founded) and reassigned to a task force whose mission was largely to plan social events. Although many of her coworkers were sympathetic (and sent her e-mail messages, cards, and flowers in support), none stood with her in opposing this department head. Apparently, they feared retaliation. Behind the boss's back, however, they began to refer to him as "Hitler," and some exchanged cartoons making fun of tyrants.

In a healthier organizational climate, expressions of disagreement or dissent may be more positively received. One study demonstrated, for instance, that an intelligent, articulate deviate might exert considerable influence on the views of the majority, particularly on topics about which the deviate knows much and the other group members know little.[36] However, when it is the group members composing the majority who are better informed, the deviate's influence is lessened. Similarly, the minority member's *behavioral style*, particularly in terms of his or her consistency, may significantly impact how the majority reacts to his or her arguments.[37]

Considered by themselves, pressure for uniformity and conformity behavior are neither good nor bad. They are simply facts of group and organizational life. Every group has norms—some of which are quite constructive and empowering, such as tolerating and encouraging the exploration of diverse points of view, being supportive of others, and so forth. Groups must examine their norms with vigilance. Whenever majority members attempt to pressure opinion deviates into publicly complying, they run the risk of suffering depleted morale and impaired decision making.[38]

Group Role Structure

The norms that develop in groups typically suggest (or require) appropriate modes of conduct for all group members. At the same time, however, groups need considerable role diversity among their membership to function effectively. Group members perform different, although often interdependent, functions as they work together on varied tasks. (Refer to Highlighting Diversity for some unusual insights into group role diversity.)

DILBERT

DILBERT © by Scott Adams; reprinted by permission of United Feature Syndicate, Inc.

Conceptually, roles include behaviors and how those behaviors function within the group. For instance, a group member may use humor during a meeting. Her humor, however, may function in diverse ways—to relieve tension, to diminish someone else's ego (especially if the humor is sarcastic), to get the group off track by distracting members from the task at hand, or to build group cohesiveness. Clearly, some of these are more functionally related to group goal accomplishment and maintenance than others. Similarly, asking a question can function as a simple request for information ("Do we have projected trends for next month yet?"); as a strategy for changing the subject; as a vehicle for introducing a new topic; or as a put-down or challenge ("What would you know about working in a factory?"). Thus, *roles are behaviors that perform some function in a specific group context*. The individual's enactment of a role will depend on his or her interpretations of a given situation.

Highlighting Diversity

Group Roles: A Lesson from *The Secret Life of Bees* by Sue Monk Kidd

Kidd recounts this exchange between August, the beekeeper, and her young friend, Lily. It is Lily's perspective from which the conversation is shared.

August said, "Every bee has a secret life we don't know anything about."
I loved the idea of bees having a secret life, just like the one I was living.
"What other secrets have they got?" I wanted to know.
"Well, for instance, every bee has its role to play."
She went through the whole thing. The *nest builders* were the group that drew the comb. I told her that the way they created hexagons, they must be the ones who could do math in their heads, and she smiled and said, yes, nest builders have true math aptitude.

Field bees were the ones with good navigation skills and tireless hearts, going out to gather nectar and pollen. There was a group called *mortician bees* whose pitiful job it was to rake the dead bees out of the hive and keep everything on the clean side. *Nurse bees*, August said, had a gift for nurturing, and they fed all the baby bees. They were probably the self-sacrificing group, like the women at church socials who said, "No, you take the chicken breast. I'm just fine with the neck and gizzard, really." The only males were the *drones* who sat around waiting to mate with the queen.

"Of course," August said, "there's *the queen* and her attendants."
"She has *attendants?*"
"Oh, yes, like ladies-in-waiting. They feed her, bathe her, keep her warm or cool—whatever's needed. You can see them always circled around her, fussing over her. I've even seen them caress her."

August points out that all the queen does is lay eggs all day, which surprises Lily. August continues:

"Egg laying is the main thing, Lily. She's the mother of every bee in the hive, and they all depend on her to keep it going. I don't care what their job is—they know the queen is their mother. She's the mother of thousands."

Source: Sue Monk Kidd, *The Secret Life of Bees* (New York: Penguin Books, 2002), 148–49.

Various classification schemes have been developed to describe the roles or behavioral functions that group members enact. Typically, these roles fall into one of two main categories: group task roles and group building and maintenance roles.

Task roles involve the communication functions necessary for a group to accomplish its task, which often involves problem solving, decision making, information exchange, or conflict resolution. Based on the classic work of Benne and Sheats, these roles include:[39]

- *Initiator.* Proposes new ideas, procedures, goals, and solutions; gets the group started.

- *Information giver.* Supplies evidence, opinions, and related personal experiences relevant to the task.

- *Information seeker.* Asks for information from other members, seeks clarification when necessary, and makes sure that relevant evidence is not overlooked.

- *Opinion giver.* States her or his own beliefs, attitudes, and judgment; is willing to take a position, although not without sensitivity to others' views.

- *Opinion seeker.* Solicits the opinions and feelings of others and asks for clarification of positions. Ideally, those who give opinions will be equally willing to seek opinions.

- *Elaborator.* Clarifies and expands the ideas of others through examples, illustrations, and explanations. This role is valuable so long as elaborations are task-relevant.

- *Integrator.* Clarifies the relationship between various facts, opinions, and suggestions, and integrates the ideas of other members.

- *Orienter.* Keeps the group directed toward its goal, summarizes what has taken place, and clarifies the positions of the group.

- *Evaluator.* Expresses judgments about the relative worth of information or ideas; proposes or applies criteria for weighing the quality of information or alternative courses of action.

- *Procedural specialist.* Organizes the group's work, suggests an agenda, an outline, or a problem-solving sequence.

- *Consensus tester.* Asks whether the group has reached a decision acceptable to all; suggests, when appropriate, that agreement may have been reached.

Although early discussions of group task roles treated them as being part of a single dimension of group behavior, the contemporary view suggests that two different task dimensions may be represented by those roles: those that focus on the substance or content of the issue being discussed (such as giving information) and those that deal with procedural matters (such as orienting and organizing the group). These two dimensions may function in tandem if, for example, someone initiates the discussion (a procedural act) by tossing out an idea (a substantive move).

The second major category of group roles is *group building and maintenance roles*. These roles build and sustain the group's interpersonal relationships. Discussants playing these roles help the group to feel positive about the task and to interact harmoniously. By reducing the competition between individual group members and their ideas, these behaviors nurture an enhanced sense of cooperation. These roles include:

- *Supporter.* Praises and agrees with others, providing a warm, supportive, interpersonal climate.
- *Harmonizer.* Attempts to mediate differences, introduce compromises, and reconcile differences.
- *Tension reliever.* Encourages a relaxed atmosphere by reducing formality and interjecting appropriate humor.
- *Gatekeeper.* Exerts some control over communication channels by encouraging reticent discussants, discouraging those who tend to monopolize the discussion, and seeking diversity of opinion.
- *Norm creator.* Suggests rules of behavior for group members and challenges unproductive ways of behaving; gives a negative response when someone violates an important group norm.
- *Solidarity builder.* Expresses positive feelings toward other group members; reinforces sense of group unity and cohesiveness.
- *Dramatist.* Evokes fantasies about persons and places other than the present group and time; may test a tentative value or norm through hypothetical example or story; dreams, shows creativity, and articulates vision.

Although these roles are presented as largely desirable and constructive, they must be evaluated as they are enacted in a specific group context. For instance, establishing and maintaining norms is quite valuable so long as the norms are sound. If the group is committed to encouraging dissent, for instance, and someone attempts to stifle a minority view, reminding the group of its norm (tolerance for diversity) would clearly have a positive function. However, helping the group maintain an attitude of intolerance would, by maintaining that norm, be counterproductive. Moreover, stereotypically, roles in the building and maintenance category are associated with pleasant, harmonious social interaction. However, enacting some of them could readily produce tension and conflict, such as discouraging those who are dominating the discussion or challenging someone who is behaving unproductively. This suggests that if groups are to maintain themselves over time, they will of necessity go through moments of conflict and norm testing.

As noted earlier, most group members will perform diverse roles, and often the roles can be grouped together to form broader role clusters (see figure 10.2 for examples of three role clusters). Thus, those who function largely as opinion leaders, for instance, likely give their opinions rather frequently—but they also seek the views of others, evaluate everyone's views, support ideas they like, and occasionally offer procedural guidance by giving information, integrating the ideas that have been presented, and initiating a plan of action. Similarly, the supportive role cluster might involve everything from supporting others to relieving tension to building solidarity, while also offering information and opinions to create balance and harmony among group members.

Finally, not all roles function constructively in groups. To be avoided are those roles that tend to further self-interests over group interests and goals. The *self-centered roles* include:

- *Blocker.* Constantly objects to others' ideas and suggestions, insists that nothing will work, is totally negative; may also repeatedly bring up the same topic or issue after the group has considered and rejected it.
- *Aggressor.* Insults and criticizes others, shows jealousy and ill will.
- *Storyteller.* Tells irrelevant, often time-consuming stories, enjoys discussing personal experiences.

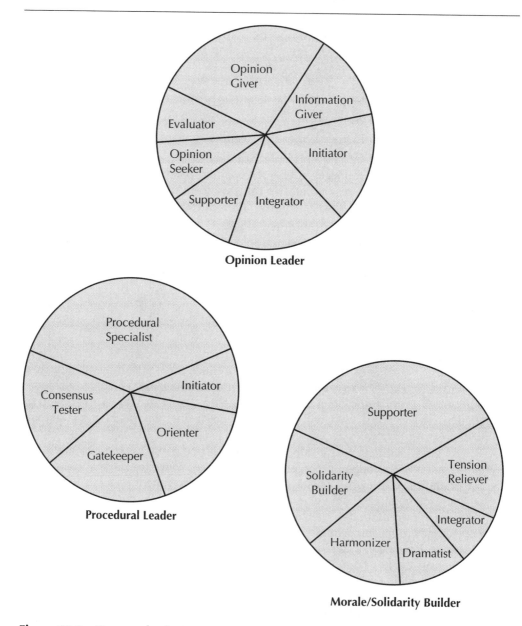

Figure 10.2   Group role clusters

- *Recognition seeker.* Interjects comments that call attention to his achievements and successes.
- *Dominator.* Tries to monopolize group interaction.
- *Confessor.* Attempts to use the group as a therapeutic session, asks the group to listen to her personal problems.
- *Special-interest pleader.* Represents the interests of a different group and pleads on its behalf.
- *Noncontributor.* Is reticent and uncommunicative; refuses to cope with conflict or take a stand; fails to respond to others' comments.[40]

In general, when positive roles are enacted and shared in groups (with negative roles minimized), positive group outcomes, such as enhanced morale and sound decision making, are more likely.[41] Moreover, from a functional view, those who perform the positive task and building and maintenance roles are actually serving as group leaders insofar as their behaviors assist the group in accomplishing its goals.

While much research on group roles has been conducted in laboratory settings, enacting roles in actual organizations is more complex. When individuals participate in committee, team, or quality circle meetings, they do so with the potential constraints and complexities associated with whatever formal organizational role they play (department head, secretary, new recruit). In organizational groups then, individuals bring with them *role perceptions* (notions of what their

Highlighting Diversity

Traditional Sex Role Expectations

Expected Behaviors:
- Women will ask many questions.
- Women will talk less than men.
- Women will listen attentively and supportively.
- Women will mostly perform group building and maintenance roles.
- When offering their opinions, women will express an air of tentativeness. ("I'm not an expert in this area, but I think we might. . . .")
- Men will play mostly task roles in groups.
- Men will dominate the conversation by talking frequently and at length.
- Men will interrupt everyone, but especially women.

Negative Implications of These Expectations:
- Those who violate traditional expectations may be viewed as "deviant"—and may even be punished.
- The group as a whole suffers because individuals are not encouraged to make the unique contributions they are capable of making.
- Turn-taking norms are violated; dominance by a few is likely.
- Women are less likely to be allowed to function as group leaders, even if they are highly qualified.

role should consist of) and *role expectations* (their understanding of what others expect of them). Weighing and balancing those, individuals choose how to enact their roles, a process to be negotiated and renegotiated over time.

Status and Power

So long as the concept of hierarchy prevails in organizations, issues of status and power will remain potent variables affecting small group and organizational behavior. Most of the time, persons who occupy positions of high status in the organizational hierarchy also possess considerable power. Thus, the two concepts are practically associated but conceptually quite distinct. Specifically, *status* is the value, importance, or prestige associated with a given role or position. *Power,* on the other hand, focuses on the opportunity to influence or control others. Throughout organizations of all kinds, individuals occupy positions that are highly valued by others (that is, high-status positions); yet, in fact, they have little opportunity to influence the behavior of others (that is, they possess little power). The vice presidency of the United States is a classic example of a position of considerable importance and prestige that carries minimal power.

Just as the concepts of power and status differ, the types of power vary from situation to situation. French and Raven distinguish seven types of social power, or power base, and designate them as follows:[42]

1. *Reward power.* The ability to elicit a desired response from another by providing the other with positive reinforcement. A realtor may show houses to prospective clients each evening, working long hours in hopes of gaining a large sales commission when a house is finally sold.

2. *Coercive power.* The ability to elicit a desired response by means of potential punishment. Besides hoping for a monetary reward, however, the realtor in the example above may also toil for fear that his employer will fire him if he doesn't make a significant sale soon.

3. *Referent power.* It functions most potently when a person strongly identifies with another, holding him or her in high esteem and respecting the individual's judgment on appropriate behavioral standards. Small, informal work groups within organizations are often potent sources of referent power. Individual workers within these groups may increase or decrease their productivity, not in accordance with the formal reward and punishment system of the organization, but simply because other members of their small informal work group are doing it (and, in this manner, indicating it to be the appropriate way to behave).

4. *Legitimate power.* Focuses on recognized authority. Individuals responding to this type of power do so, not because they anticipate a specific reward or fear some punishment, but simply because they believe that the person requesting the response is fully authorized to make the request. People holding organizational status higher than our own are often accorded this sort of power. The manager of some other department, for example, probably does not have direct power to discipline or fire us; yet when she makes a request that we provide her staff with some information, we probably will comply simply because we believe she has the right to make such a request.

5. *Expert power.* Based on a person's recognized competence in a certain area, others will follow the directions or take the advice of another who has in-depth knowledge about a topic or expertise in a particular field (e.g., a medical doctor). An intelligent supervisor or manager, in fact, makes much use of this sort of power, not by exerting it but by being influenced by it. The most effective executives surround themselves with expert advisers, frequently ask those people for advice, and use the advice when making decisions. They recognize that their advisers know more than they themselves do about marketing, engineering, sales, the law, and so on, and they allow the advisers to exert expert power by acting on the adviser's advice. Of course, by increasing your own expertise in a specific topic or area, you increase your own ability to exert expert power over others.

6. *Informational power.* The power to control the availability and accuracy of necessary information. If we can control the flow of information someone receives, we can control his or her behavior to some degree (again, consider the powerful secretaries who significantly influence organizational functioning by determining what information their bosses receive). Similarly, we all want to do the correct thing; thus, we are influenced by information we perceive to be accurate. People who can supply such information are likely to be influential for us. Figure 10.3 depicts these bases of power.

7. *Connectional power.* Of all the power bases, this is the most political, based on social psychologists' notion that every exercise of power involves some form of social exchange. Connectional power is the influence that leaders have as a result of who they know and the support they have from others in the organization. In general, connectional power is associated with a person's general connections with others whose knowledge, ideas, support, cooperation, and resources are needed for effective leadership. More than the other power bases, connectional power is based on a norm of reciprocity. Anyone who wields power from this base should be prepared to cooperate with and support others.

In comparing the effects of different types of power, it is important to remember that these categories are not mutually exclusive. The same persons can have, and often do have, several sources of power, particularly in organizational settings.

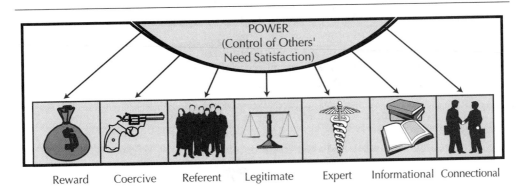

Figure 10.3   The bases of power

Individuals in organizations often belong to small groups composed of members with varying power and status. In these groups, persons do not communicate as equals, a fact that is often an obstacle to effective interaction and decision making.[43] Several studies have shown that those possessing high status are treated with more deference by fellow group members than are those of low status. High-status members are also less likely to be held personally responsible for behaving in ways normally viewed as inappropriate by others.[44] Communication directed to those possessing high status is also distorted in certain important ways.

A number of studies have investigated the nature of **upward-directed communication distortions**.[45] In general, in communicating with someone of higher status, one is likely to communicate supportively and cautiously, to attempt to seek approval, to downplay "bad" news, and to act deferentially. Of course, much depends on the nature of the relationship between the parties. If the boss is someone who truly values accurate feedback and insists on hearing the bad news along with the good, subordinates are better able to communicate openly and accurately. When trusting and supportive communication climates exist within groups and organizations, the distortions often associated with upward communication may virtually disappear.

In every organization, there are many persons who possess considerable status and power. Not all of them use their positions and influence in the same manner, however. A powerful organizational executive can stifle opinions that are contrary to his or her own and encourage superficial analysis of problems and explorations of solutions. But the same person can wisely recognize the difficulties that attach to speaking with one's superiors, reward accurate, honest expressions of opinion, and elicit the articulation of divergent points of view.

In the film *Effective Decisions*, Peter Drucker tells the story of Alfred P. Sloan, who for years was the brilliant chief executive of General Motors (GM). On this particular occasion, the executive board of GM was considering a proposal that sounded innovative, interesting, and financially sound. Not one member of the board raised an objection. Sloan asked each one, "Do you see anything wrong with this proposal?" Each one responded negatively. Sloan wisely commented, "Well, I don't see anything wrong with it either. For that reason, I move that we postpone its consideration for one month to give ourselves some time to think." Drucker reports that the proposal was soundly defeated one month later. A poor proposal was appropriately rejected in this instance because a wise manager believed that those in power had the obligation to ensure that dissenting views were voiced, and he insisted on hearing conflicting views before he would act.[46]

All group members must be concerned with the effectiveness of the group's problem-solving ability. By virtue of their power or status, some group members are in strategic positions for greatly influencing the quality of the group's decision-making process. The judicious use of authority to encourage the free expression of ideas and to reward initiative and innovative thinking can go far in eliminating the doubts and skepticism of less powerful group members.

Cohesiveness

A final significant socioemotional variable affecting group interaction is *cohesiveness*. As a small group characteristic, cohesiveness is related to solidarity, the group's "stick-togetherness," and its ability to maintain itself over time and through crisis.[47] Not surprisingly, cohesiveness and conformity are related in that the highly cohesive group usually clings to its norms, attitudes, and values. Those who are part of such groups feel a strong sense of belonging, are proud of their group affiliation, and develop close friendships with other group members.

As a socioemotional variable, cohesiveness often has a positive effect on group functioning. The sense of "we-ness" in cohesive groups often transcends individual differences and motives.[48] High cohesiveness and high group member morale are often closely associated. Studies of decision-making conferences reported a close relationship between high cohesiveness and groups members' satisfaction with the meeting experience. In addition, members of cohesive groups like each other. They rate each other highly with respect to attractiveness, motivation, and performance.[49]

While it is clear that the atmosphere in highly cohesive groups is pleasant, we often erroneously assume that these groups will therefore make superior decisions or be extremely productive. Yet, research has demonstrated that cohesiveness neither increases nor decreases group productivity.[50] Instead, it serves to heighten the susceptibility of group members to mutual influence. Thus, if a highly cohesive group establishes a standard of low productivity, group members are likely to conform to the norm and produce little.

Sometimes cohesiveness can have an even darker side. Consider psychologist Irving Janis's account of events occurring a few days before disaster struck the small mining town of Pitcher, Oklahoma, in 1950. Janis reports that the local mining engineer had warned the town's citizens to leave immediately because the land the town sat on had been accidentally undermined and was in danger of caving in at any moment. But the day after the warning was issued, at a meeting of leading citizens belonging to the Lions Club, the members joked about the warning and "laughed uproariously when someone arrived wearing a parachute."[51] Complacency, born of cohesiveness, caused these men to reason that disasters of this sort just couldn't happen to fine folks like them in a nice little town like theirs. Within a few days, this flawed reasoning cost several of these men and their families their lives.

Although this incident occurred in the mid-twentieth century, it is illustrative of a common, ageless phenomenon. Groups and organizations often make poor decisions—in part because their cohesiveness contributes to a mindset that discourages dissent and the rational examination of alternative courses of action. The tragic decision to launch the *Challenger* was clearly influenced by the inability of those near the bottom of the organization to freely and fully express their skepticism to their superiors about the wisdom of launching the shuttle in extremely cold temperatures.[52] Moreover, when the space shuttle *Columbia* exploded on February 1, 2003, killing all seven astronauts aboard, investigators drew a number of parallels between the *Columbia* and the *Challenger* disasters.

As noted earlier, pressure for uniformity often occurs in groups characterized by high cohesiveness. This pressure serves to reduce the range and quality of information and opinions presented and diminishes the advantages of having groups rather than individuals make decisions. We have already discussed some of the general problems associated with pressure for uniformity. In cohesive groups, group pressure can also gradually shift the group toward the position

---

Business Brief 10.3

The NASA Culture and the *Columbia* Disaster

According to the *Columbia* Accident Investigation Board, NASA has done little to improve shuttle safety since it lost the shuttle *Challenger* in 1986. The Board charged that NASA's organizational culture had as much to do with the accident as the foam did (referring to debris that struck and damaged *Columbia* soon after its launch on January 16, 2003). The report highlighted several cultural traits that contributed to the tragedy. Among them were:

- Reliance on past success as a substitute for sound engineering practices.

- Organizational barriers that prevented effective communication of critical safety information and **stifled professional differences of opinion.**

- The evolution of an informal chain-of-command for decision-making processes that operated outside the organization's rules.

- Inability of lower-level team members to report concerns to higher-level members. Despite top shuttle management's determination that there was no danger (due to the foam damage), **low-level engineers worried that the damage might prove fatal** and were unable to (or didn't) convey their concerns to the top.

- Lack of openness to new information. Had NASA known the probable extent of the damage to *Columbia*, another shuttle might have been dispatched on an emergency mission before the *Columbia* crew ran out of air.

Source: Richard Stenger, "Panel Criticizes NASA Culture for Shuttle Loss" (August 26, 2003) [online]. Available: http://www.cnn.com/2003TECH/space/o8/26/sprj.colu.shuttle.report.1940/index.hmtl (accessed July 2, 2004).

---

taken by the majority or by its most vocal members. Since such shifts depend more on intragroup pressures than on the quality of argument and information available, the group may end up making "extreme" decisions—ones that mindlessly continue existing policies or are inordinately risky.[53]

One of the most extensive investigations of the potentially negative impact of cohesiveness on a group's ability to make intelligent decisions was conducted by Irving Janis.[54] Janis examined the decision-making processes leading to several historic military and political fiascoes, including the decision to cross the 38th parallel in Korea, the decision to invade the Bay of Pigs, the choice to escalate the war in Vietnam, and the decisions surrounding the Watergate cover-up. To explain how poor decisions were made in each of these instances, Janis introduced the concept of *groupthink*, which he originally defined as "a model of thinking that people engage in when they are deeply involved in a cohesive in-group, when the members' striving for unanimity overrides their motivation to realistically appraise alternative courses of action. . . ."[55] Later, Janis modified the groupthink construct to focus on "premature concurrence seeking," stressing the notion that although most groups strive for agreement over time, those who are caught up in "groupthink" seek consensus so swiftly and relentlessly that full and free discussion of alternative courses of action simply never occurs.[56] Janis goes on to identify eight negative qualities that commonly lead to groupthink:

- An *illusion of invulnerability*, which creates excessive optimism and encourages excessive risk taking

- *Collective rationalization* to discount warnings that might lead members to reconsider their assumptions
- An **unquestioned belief in the group's inherent morality**, causing members to ignore the ethical consequences of their decisions
- *Stereotyped views of opposition leaders* as either too evil to warrant genuine attempts to negotiate or too weak or stupid to be a viable threat
- *Direct pressure exerted on any member who expresses dissenting views*, making clear that such dissent is unacceptable
- *Self-censorship* by group members, attempting to minimize the importance of any doubts they might have
- A *shared illusion of unanimity* concerning opinions conforming to the majority view
- The *emergence of self-appointed "mindguards,"* members who protect the group from conflicting information that might shatter their shared complacency[57]

Janis does not argue that all highly cohesive groups fall prey to groupthink. Rather, he points out that strategies exist for counteracting it. Janis believes that the group's leader is in a position to insist on the open-minded pursuit of alternative courses of action. Specifically, he suggests that the group's leader should:

- Assign to everyone the role of critical evaluator
- Avoid stating personal views, particularly at the outset
- Bring in outsiders representing diverse interests to talk with and listen to the group
- Play and ask specific others to take turns playing the devil's advocate
- Let the group deliberate without the leader from time to time
- After a tentative decision has been made, hold a "second-chance" meeting, at which each member is required to express as strongly as possible any residual doubts[58]

When leaders insist on and groups endorse these kinds of norms, cohesive groups should function extremely effectively. Cohesiveness need not doom a group. On the contrary, with appropriate vigilance, cohesiveness can contribute to constructive, satisfying group communication and outcomes.

SUMMARY

As members of organizations, we spend considerable time interacting in small groups. Some groups are informal and exist primarily to satisfy personal needs. Others are more formally structured and focus on the accomplishment of specific tasks, often involving decision making and problem solving. Group discussions occur in both private and public settings, within the community, as well as within the organization, and involve participants from many organizational levels or walks of life.

Many socioemotional variables affect the functioning of small groups, including pressure for uniformity, role structure, status, power, and cohesiveness. For instance, groups often insist that their norms be upheld. Sometimes, an individual group member may not agree with the norm or may not accept the majority viewpoint. Groups exert pressure in varied ways, and individuals respond to this pressure in different ways, depending on the situation, the issue, and the personalities of those involved. In some situations, deviant group members can influence the majority, but doing so requires considerable communication skill.

Healthy groups are structured so that members play multiple and diverse roles. There are various ways of making constructive contributions to the group's effort. Some individuals perform task roles while others help the group feel positive and appreciate each other's efforts. Self-serving roles should be avoided—those that advance individual interests over those of the group.

In organizational settings in which groups are embedded, power and status differences are common. Those differences can lead to distorted communication, but they need not impede the group's ability to interact effectively—especially if the members with greater power encourage others to share ideas openly and honestly. Power can grow from many sources, including one's position, the ability to reward or punish others, one's level of information or expertise, and the ability to provide political connections for others.

Finally, groups vary in their levels of cohesiveness. When group members are strongly bonded, they may function very productively; or they may fall prey to "groupthink," which leads to impaired decision making. The leader of a cohesive group can set the tone for the group's interactions by insisting that diverse opinions be expressed and by not allowing the group to make a hasty decision.

Taken together, these socioemotional variables play powerful roles in determining the climate in which group members interact, make decisions, and carry out their other responsibilities.

Questions for Discussion

1. How would you distinguish a collection of individuals from an interacting small group?

2. Compare and contrast organizational teams with quality circles. Describe their relative advantages and disadvantages.

3. How do study circles (as a form of small group) work to encourage deliberative dialogue and civic engagement in community settings?

4. Compare and contrast a panel discussion and a symposium.

5. Discuss your understanding of norms. What are some examples of established norms in specific organizations with which you have had experience?

6. What are some of the personal, group, and situational variables contributing to conformity behavior? How do groups exert pressure for uniformity? How do deviates respond to social influence?

7. What types of roles do individuals play in small groups? What, in your view, is the relative significance of each role?

8. Why is it important for groups to be characterized by role diversity?

9. What is the difference between status and power? Provide an example from your own group experience that illustrates the difference.

10. Discuss the seven bases of power, providing examples of each. What combinations of power are most common in your experience? Most effective? Least effective?

11. What are some of the positive and negative factors associated with highly cohesive groups?

12. What are the defining characteristics of groupthink?

13. What can leaders and other group members do to discourage groupthink?

Exercises

1. Think of an organization to which you now belong or to which you belonged for some length of time in the past. Make a list of several norms (both implicit and explicit) operating within this organization. Then think of a time when some member (possibly you) deviated from one of those norms. How did the group treat the deviate? What was the deviate's response?

2. Break into groups of five to seven members and discuss a controversial question of the group's choice. After 20 minutes, terminate the discussion and analyze the role behavior of each group discussant. Some, for example, serve as information givers or seekers, others as clarifiers, others as facilitators, and still others as blockers. Which roles seemed most useful to your particular group? Why?

3. Suzanne Martin has been hired recently as a sales representative of a prestigious women's clothing store in New York. The job is extremely important to Suzanne, as she hopes to rise first to the position of assistant buyer and ultimately to the position of buyer. In this particular organizational setting, there is great potential for advancement, and Suzanne is thrilled with her new job. There is, however, one problem. Every Friday at the close of the workday, all seven of the sales personnel in Suzanne's division visit a nearby cocktail lounge and chat informally for some time. The chatting invariably involves organizational gossip, rumor transmission, and speculation. Suzanne finds the custom distasteful, but has been warned that those who fail to "be sociable" often have trouble getting along with coworkers on the job, and that upward mobility becomes difficult for them.

   In a well-developed 250-word essay, respond to the following questions:

   a. What norm (or norms) are operating in this situation?

   b. Are these norms implicit or explicit?

   c. What are the advantages of conforming?

   d. What are the disadvantages?

   e. What would you advise Suzanne to do in this situation? Why?

4. Consider the following brief description of an organization and some of its members:

   - Michael Carr is a lower-level manager in Organization ABC. He is young, assertive, extremely bright, and particularly innovative in his approach to problem solving. Among his subordinates, he is known as "the brain."

   - Richard Walls is vice president in charge of sales in the same organization. In terms of the organization's chart, he is two levels above Carr. Walls is an autocrat who rewards liberally and punishes only occasionally. When he does punish, he often does so by firing.

- Peter Arden is president of Organization ABC. Near retirement, he has an impressive record with the company, but lately he has grown relatively out of touch with the cutting edge of the organization.

In a well-developed 150-word essay, respond to the following questions:

a. Discuss the relative status of each of these individuals.

b. What kind of power base is each operating from?

c. If the three gave conflicting orders, which one would most workers obey? Which would you obey? Why?

Case Application 10.1   Self-Managing Teams: Hope or Hoax?

When Pete became head of a major department in a large bank holding company, he thought he had arrived. He was proud of his title and rank, and his department was responsible for determining policy for hundreds of bank branches and those who managed them (viewed by Pete as "superclerks"). Pete was in charge of hiring his own staff, and he sought the brightest and the best—mostly MBAs from prestigious schools. He offered them excellent salaries and the chance for quick promotions.

Then the world began to fall apart. For the first time in recent memory, the bank lost market position and decided to emphasize direct customer service at each of its branches. The people Pete considered clerks began to depart from Pete's standard policies and to tailor their services to local market conditions. The branches moved to the team concept, with self-managed teams working together to come up with ideas for improving customer service. As these teams considered their options and went about collecting data, they actually demanded services and responses from Pete's staff, and the results of these requests began to figure into performance reviews of Pete's department. In an attempt to cooperate with the branches, Pete's people began spending more and more time in the field with the branch managers and clerks and with their self-managed teams.

To further complicate matters, the bank's strategy included a growing role for technology. Pete felt that because he had no direct control over the information systems department, he should not be held accountable for every facet of product design and implementation. But fully accountable he was.

He had to deploy people to learn the new technology and figure out how to work with it. In addition, the bank was asking product departments like Pete's to find ways to link existing products or develop new ones that crossed traditional categories. Pete's staff soon became involved in their own self-managing teams and were often away working with one of these cross-departmental teams just when he wanted them for an important internal assignment.

Caught between upper management's high expectations and the turbulence and uncertainty of the chaotic environment over which he supposedly presided, Pete felt confused and resentful. His superior said that what was important was "leading, not managing," but Pete wasn't sure what that meant—especially since he seemed to have lost control over his subordinate's assignments, activities, rewards, and careers. Pete felt as if he had lost power and status, both of which were very important to him.

Source: Based on an illustration given in Rosabeth Moss Kanter, "The New Managerial Work," *Harvard Business Review* 67 (1989): 85–92.

Questions

1. What are some of the potential problems with self-managing teams revealed in this case?

2. What are the implications of Pete's boss's comment about "leading, not managing?"

3. If you were in Pete's position, what constructive moves might you make to improve the situation, both for yourself and for your subordinates?

11

The Process of
Group Decision Making

After reading this chapter, you should be able to:

❑ Describe the positive and negative aspects of working together in groups

❑ Understand the steps involved in preparing for participating in decision-making or problem-solving meetings

❑ List and distinguish among the different kinds of discussion questions that organizational groups typically address

❑ Become familiar with key research on group problem-solving patterns

❑ Distinguish the characteristics of effective from ineffective decision-making groups

❑ Understand different ways of organizing a meeting agenda

❑ Explain the role that technology can play in assisting group decision making, as well as strengths and weaknesses

❑ Describe effective small group communication behaviors and practice them in a group meeting

Committee work abounds. Yet, anyone who has spent more than a few minutes in a committee meeting knows that being in a small group can be a frustrating experience. Groups often get off the track, bicker among themselves, and consume seemingly endless hours. With new technologies offering computer support for group endeavors and unprecedented ways of linking individuals within and across organizations and communities, group work is likely to become increasingly common and diversified. As Harvard psychologist J. Richard Hackman writes, "Almost every time there is a genuinely important decision to be made in an organization, a group is assigned to make it—or at least to counsel and advise the individual who must make it."[1]

Preview

In this chapter, we examine the process of group decision making. Every group participant must understand how to prepare for group meetings in terms of content and attitude. Groups address diverse issues, and identifying the underlying discussion question being considered in those meetings is an important preliminary step. Equally vital is knowing how groups typically structure their deliberations and understanding options for organizing group meeting agendas. Technology, and especially group support systems, also can play a role in facilitating group deliberations. When group members bring such qualities as open-mindedness, excellent preparation, careful listening, and ethics to the meetings they attend, those meetings are more likely to have positive outcomes. However, there are clearly liabilities as well as assets associated with group work, and we begin by considering those.

PROS AND CONS OF GROUP WORK

First, let's consider the possible negatives. At the top of the list is the simple fact that *groups take time*. A person making a decision alone doesn't have to take the time to listen to others or deal with interruptions or group morale. As a result, he or she is usually able to reach a solution fairly efficiently. In organizations, time and money are interdependent. When an executive who makes $100 an hour takes four hours to consider a problem and make a decision, that decision costs the company $400. But if five executives making $100 an hour meet to make a decision about the same problem, even if they take only the same amount of time, that decision costs the organization $2,000. If they take longer, which would be typical, the decision could become very expensive indeed.

Besides the time-cost factor, *many people lack training in group discussion skills*. As a result, group meetings are often poorly organized, and members come unprepared, expecting others to carry the major burden. This can be a particular problem in community settings where group members are volunteers. *Some group members are overly talkative* and dominate the discussion, while *others remain mute*. As we discussed in chapter 10, *cohesive groups may fall prey to groupthink*, resulting in impaired decision making. In the United States, group members are eager to find solutions, and *they often rush through the analysis of the problem*. Finally, *some leaders do not really allow groups to make decisions*. Instead, they use the meeting as an arena to sell their own ideas. Still others listen (or pretend to listen) to the group and then go off and quietly make the decision alone.

Given these potential liabilities, the obvious question is: *Why bother with groups?* Researchers who have pursued this question have found some rather encouraging results.

- There is some evidence to suggest that *certain groups are superior to individuals*. Groups who reach decisions through a process of cooperative deliberation do, in fact, generate more ideas and produce better-quality decisions than do individuals who work on problems alone.[2]

- *Some discussion techniques*, such as brainstorming, nominal grouping, and the use of idea-generating agendas, *can stimulate creativity*.[3]

- *Group members* often *possess considerable knowledge and information*, typically more than any one member working alone would possess.

- In groups, there exists *a greater diversity of perspectives*, and this diversity can serve to discourage the thinking ruts that often characterize the problem-solving attempts of individuals.[4]

- Besides the quality of the decision itself, people who help make decisions understand how and why they were made. Participating in decision making *increases group members' commitment to decisions and generally improves their morale*.[5] We may give our time to committee work grudgingly on occasion, but in the long run, most of us feel more useful, more productive, and more valued as professionals and citizens when we have a chance to share in making significant decisions.

Most of the so-called liabilities we discussed are not inherent to small group deliberations. Rather, they tend to occur when group members are ignorant of group processes and are poorly informed regarding sound decision-making procedures.

Group decision making offers significant advantages to organizations. It is important to remember, however, that skill in decision making is equally important to individual group members. As management becomes more participative and more team-oriented, employees become more involved in making decisions that affect them and the organization directly. Good decisions improve the employee's own working life and the success of the organization as a whole; poor decisions adversely affect both. And, as we have seen, those who are skilled in group decision making are much more likely to be held in high esteem by others, to achieve upward mobility, and to make genuine contributions to their communities.

As you approach working with others in small groups or teams, you might want to think of decision making as *a process* rather than a procedure. As with other processes, the operative elements are interdependent and delicately balanced. A personality clash among members not only disrupts interpersonal relations but also affects the problem-solving ability of the group. Besides, groups are far from static. As you interact with others in your group, you will be affected by them and they by you. The mood, balance, and focus of the group may shift from moment to moment. It is impossible, therefore, to point to a given procedure that ought to be followed in all decision-making groups. Rather, being aware of critical group variables, knowing how best to prepare for group meetings, and understanding the ways groups develop over time can help you adapt appropriately to each new group context.[6]

PREPARING FOR GROUP PARTICIPATION

In organizational settings, you will find yourself working in decision-making groups for three basic reasons. First, you will acquire some group memberships simply by joining the organization. You will participate in department or unit meetings, for example, and you will attend companywide meetings, employee training sessions, and other meetings directly related to your responsibilities. Second, you will be assigned other group memberships. Your boss may ask you to work with a task force comprised of people from several departments, or your turn to be your department's representative on a fund-raising committee may come up. Finally, you will become part of groups whose membership you seek. Quality circles, for example, consist only of employees who volunteer to participate; when you join groups who are tackling local problems or planning events in your community, you are clearly joining on a voluntary basis.

No matter how you obtain group membership, your initial responsibility to the group will be to prepare carefully. Often, your assignment or appointment to group membership is based on expertise you happen to have; however, even in those situations, you will gather and organize information that you can contribute to the group's functioning. As we have already suggested, failure to prepare adequately for a group meeting is one of the most common causes of poor performance.

Highlighting Civic Engagement

Vermont's Town Meetings

- On the first Tuesday of March, citizens in Vermont towns (as mandated by the state's constitution) hold a Town Meeting to conduct the annual business of their community. They are proud of their tradition of civic engagement, which allows each citizen the opportunity to voice her or his opinion and vote on important issues.

- In small towns all over Vermont, the votes are usually taken by voice with a yea or nay, but any citizen can request either a standing vote or a paper ballot vote.

- When the meetings break for lunch, neighbors, who only half an hour earlier were arguing vehemently over a particular issue, sit down together and enjoy a homemade lunch.

- In Weston, Vermont, the Vermont County Store (a family-owned business established in 1946) uses the concept of the Town Meeting to hold their own annual meeting. At this meeting:

  — Every employee has the chance to bring forth issues, concerns, and ideas for discussion.

  — According to the proprietor, Lyman Orton, great "stuff" comes from these meetings, as "our people know they can speak their truths about what's going on at VCS and indeed they do!"

  — Although some might think that holding such a meeting is a risk, Orton believes that "the risk lies in not doing it."

Source: "Vermont's Town Meetings Provide Civic Engagement" (Spring, 2001) [online]. Available: http://www.vermontcountrystore.com/corp/editorials/Vermont_Town_Meeting.asp (accessed: May 21, 2004). For specific information on how to plan, organize, and conduct a town meeting, see The Civic Engagement Project, "Planning an Interactive Town Meeting" [online]. Available: http://www.democracy2000.org/meetingplan.htm (accessed: May 19, 2004).

Discovering and Analyzing Information

The first step in preparing for a group meeting is to *take a personal inventory* of the ideas, information, and other relevant data already in your possession. As we noted earlier, most decision makers in organizations would not belong to the group exploring a particular problem unless they were viewed as possessing some useful information, perspectives, or insights. In the classroom setting, discussion groups are usually free to select the subjects they wish to consider, with only reasonable restrictions. Thus, choosing a topic for group exploration is probably based on some shared interest in topics, such as the parking problem on campus, how the community should dispose of PCBs, the most recent tax law, or academic dishonesty. When you join a community group, you will likely do so because of your interest in/concern for the issue. In professional organizations, topics or tasks are more likely to be assigned.

Initially, then, group members should take stock of their existing attitudes, opinions, and knowledge. In fact, it is often useful for some members of the group to meet prior to the actual meeting to assess the nature and quality of the members' collective knowledge. The deficiencies that are found in this store of existing information suggest guidelines for subsequent research. If you know how you feel about a problem but recognize that these feelings are based largely on some specific personal experiences, then perhaps the most productive strategy for you

Preparing for a problem-solving meeting requires careful, thoughtful research. Since information gathered needs to be critically assessed, on some occasions it may be helpful to work collaboratively with others prior to the meeting in an effort to determine the information's accuracy and reliability.

is to read widely regarding the issue or problem, attempting to be as open-minded as possible.

Once you have completed your self-inventory, you can identify your information gaps. At that point, you will go through a *research process* that follows the steps you would take if you were giving a speech on the problem or issue to be discussed. (Refer to chapter 13 for a thorough discussion of where to go for information.) As part of your research, you may need to interview individuals, go to the library, read local or national newspapers, and explore the Internet. Approach your research with a spirit of open-mindedness and a desire to be as knowledgeable as possible prior to the group's meeting.

Just as important as collecting information is *assessing it to determine its quality*. Several criteria should prove useful in evaluating the quality of the information you have assembled:

- How accurate is it? Can the information be verified?

- Is the information current? Data such as statistics are particularly time sensitive.

- How complete is the information? Are there identifiable gaps in what you have been able to learn?

- To what extent are your sources reliable? Do the sources have credibility with other group members?

In most cases, using these criteria will allow you to make judicious decisions about the basic quality of the evidence and information that you have identified. (Refer to chapter 13 for a detailed discussion of how to evaluate evidence and information.)

Keeping an Open Mind

A final critical preparation factor is approaching the decision-making discussion with an *attitude of open-mindedness*. Avoid jumping to conclusions or deciding on preferred solutions. There is a strong tendency for group members to reach definite conclusions about the best solution to the group's problem *before* the discussion.[7] They then enter the discussion as advocates of a given position. This prevents the group from exploring the problem together and instead creates a situation in which a number of adversaries attempt to convince each other of the superiority of their points of view. Obviously, such a confrontation is more like a debate than a decision-making discussion.

To discourage this confrontational sort of situation from developing, it is important to recognize that the *group* has been asked to reach a decision. While each person's contributions are both solicited and appreciated, no one individual should attempt to dominate the group's effort. Only when diverse perspectives are explored open-mindedly can any small group hope to reach a judicious decision, one that demonstrates the value of collective decision making.

Business Brief 11.1

The Pegasus Procedure

Meetings are notorious time wasters in most organizations. To conduct meetings more effectively, G. Laborde Associates, a communication consulting firm in Mountain View, California, recommends use of the "Pegasus" procedure:

P—present desired outcomes for meetings—make the goal of the meeting crystal clear.

E—explain evidence so that anyone can hear, see, or feel proof that the meeting accomplished its goals (that is, what should people experience if the meeting is successful?).

G—gain agreement from each person concerning the goal of the meeting.

A—activate sensory acuity—be perceptive to others' nonverbal cues.

S—summarize each decision after all decisions have been reached.

U—use a relevancy challenge—ensure that all points brought up during the meeting fit the meeting's objective.

S—summarize the next step and report back on it—make sure any required follow-up is clear.

Source: Gary M. Stern, "Here's a Way to Stop Wasting Time at Meetings," *Communication Briefings* (April 1991): 8a–8b.

DISCUSSION QUESTIONS

Although several patterns of organization may be used to structure the communication activities of decision-making groups, these patterns should be approached with flexibility and open-mindedness. One important determinant of an appropriate organizational strategy is the kind of question the group is addressing. Underlying each discussion topic or issue is a fundamental question of fact, conjecture, value, or policy. Knowing which question is at the heart of the issue you are discussing helps you and the group know how to plan and organize the discussion.

Questions of Fact

Factual questions concern matters of truth or falsity. They can be answered affirmatively or negatively without consulting the beliefs or attitudes of group members. The correct answer to the question of fact is a matter of actual events, particular properties, or specific states of affairs, not simply *perceived* truth. Here are some examples of questions of fact relevant to decision making in organizations: "Is this organization meeting the antipollution standards established by the federal government?"; "Is this hospital meeting the health-care standards recently established by the AMA?"; and "Is this company equipped with facilities to accommodate the needs of disabled employees?"

Of course, agreeing on the response to a factual question does not necessarily make it true. But, the group's assessment of the question is more likely to be sound if critical terms are defined and understood by all participants. In the question about disabled employees, for instance, your group would need to reach a common understanding of such terms as *equipped, facilities,* and *disabled.* The group defining a disability primarily in relation to employees confined to wheelchairs might reach quite different conclusions from a group that conceives of it as involving blindness, deafness, and certain learning disabilities.

Questions of Conjecture

Similar to the question of fact is the **question of conjecture**. However, instead of dealing with the present, this kind of question focuses on the future. Organizations must live with (and perhaps learn from) mistakes made in the past. The only events they can influence, however, are those that lie ahead. Since questions of conjecture focus on events as yet unseen, in discussing them, your group must base its conclusions on probabilities. Even so, it is often possible to base an intelligent prediction of the future on a substantial knowledge of the past.

In essence, the discussion of a question of conjecture demands the same knowledge and intelligent analysis as the question of fact. Examples of questions of conjecture include: "Will the demand for product X increase in the coming months?"; "Will the demand for mathematics teachers increase in the years ahead?"; and "Will our community be able to create sufficient transitional housing for the homeless over the next decade?"

Questions of Value

Not unlike questions of fact or conjecture, the **question of value** can usually be answered affirmatively or negatively. But value questions deal with neither truth nor probability. Rather, the beliefs, attitudes, values, and motives of the members of your group are sought in discussing value questions.

Values are formed in various ways, and, once established, they tend to endure. Because values cannot be "proved," questions of value should never be treated like questions of fact. When your group discusses value questions, you must recognize that it is simply *approving* the conclusions reached, not demonstrating them irrevocably. Examples of questions of value are: "Is living together before marriage a good idea?"; "Is teaching the most important mission of this university?"; "Is training our employees in communication skills worth the cost?"; and "Is ordaining women consistent with our church's doctrine?" Value-related issues underlie many contemporary problems confronting professional and nonprofit organizations.

Questions of Policy

The kind of question most frequently discussed in organizational settings is the *question of policy*. In discussing this, your group will be involved in determining the most appropriate course of action to be taken or encouraged. Underlying almost every question of policy are one or more questions of fact, conjecture, and value. As your group makes judgments about the most suitable course of action to be taken in a specific situation, it will be confronted continually with factual and conjectural questions, as well as issues related to the opinions, attitudes, and motives of individuals within the group. Thus, the policy question is the most complex. Examples of questions of policy include: "Which presidential candidate should this newspaper support?"; "What should be the stand of this church regarding the acceptance of homosexuals as members?"; "Should we use drug testing as part of our applicant screening process?"; and "Should we use the grant money to build a day-care center?"

Notice the diversity of subsidiary questions that might logically arise within these discussions. The policy question relating to homosexuality, for example, might include the discussion of factual questions, such as "What is the present stand of the church regarding homosexuals?" and "What is the attitude of church leaders regarding this question?" Conjectural issues might also be raised, including, "What will be the reaction of the average church member if this church grants membership to homosexuals?" Finally, questions of value include "Is homosexuality immoral?" and "What are our personal reactions to this issue?" Because the policy question is so inclusive of other question types, it is often seen as the most complex.

Characteristics of Good Discussion Questions

Regardless of the specific kind of question discussed, your group should make every effort to phrase the question appropriately. The three most important criteria for determining the quality of any discussion question are simplicity, objectivity, and controversiality.[8]

- A simple question is one that is clearly worded and that avoids unnecessary ambiguity or complication. *Simplicity* should not be confused with simple-mindedness. Rather, through careful wording and the avoidance of unnecessary jargon, simple questions avoid the pretentiousness and confusion associated with more ambiguous questions.

- Discussion questions should also be phrased objectively. While complete *objectivity* is never possible, your group should make every attempt to remove highly subjective language and phrasing from the discussion question. Objective questions are free of loaded language and implied premises. Consider, for example, the question, "What should be done in this community to stop the spread of drug abuse?" The subjectivity in this question resides in its assumption that drugs are being abused in the community and that the abuse is *spreading*. Further, it is assumed that the correct solution must involve halting such drug usage. A more objective way of phrasing the question would be, "To what extent are drugs used in this community?" This kind of phrasing does not preclude the discussion of drug abuse, but it does not begin with the assumption that abuse exists.

- Finally, discussion questions should be characterized by *controversiality*. This is not to imply that all discussions should be full of argumentativeness and emotional confrontations. There should be, however, at least two points of view for which support can be gathered. The discussion of a question lacking in controversiality is really not a discussion but a simple meeting to confirm previously existing and agreed-upon beliefs. When a question is controversial, however, group members can then discuss their differing views and share in finding common ground by exploring conflicting information and reaching a consensus that reflects their diversity.

Highlighting Diversity

How Different Cultures Perceive Space

When we cross cultures, we may encounter some very different ideas about polite space for meetings, conversations, and negotiations. The way we have been socialized within our culture may affect the way we behave and feel as we come together in interacting groups. Here are some examples:

- North Americans tend to prefer a large amount of space, perhaps because they are surrounded by it in their homes and the countryside.
  - Some research suggests that U.S. women are more comfortable sitting in a crowded meeting room, while men prefer more space for their meetings.
  - As U.S. groups grow to know and like each other better, they tend to move closer together.
- Europeans tend to stand close to each other when talking and are accustomed to smaller personal spaces.
- The difficulty with space preferences is not that they exist but with the judgments that often accompany them.
  - If individuals are accustomed to standing or sitting very close when they are interacting with others, they may see the others' attempts to create more space as coldness, condescension, or a lack of interest.
  - Those who are accustomed to more personal space may view attempts to get closer as pushy, disrespectful, or aggressive.
  - Neither perception is correct—they are simply different.

Notice, too, that differences in the way space is perceived and used may be related to gender, as well as to ethnic differences. In addition, preferences may change over time and depend on intragroup relationships and changes in group membership.

Source: Michelle Le Baron, *Bridging Cultural Conflicts: A New Approach for a Changing World* (San Francisco: Jossey-Bass, 2003).

ORGANIZING DECISION-MAKING DISCUSSIONS

There are many different ways of organizing a discussion. Depending on the kind of question being addressed, the amount of time available for the meeting, and the goals of the participants, different approaches may be more or less appropriate. Before we explore some of these approaches, it may be helpful here to review what is known about the ways groups typically go about making decisions and solving problems. How do groups develop? How do they approach their decision-making tasks?

The manner in which a group discusses a problem is definitely related to the group's success.[9] Early research by Bales and Strodtbeck identified three clearly discernible stages of analysis in successful problem-solving groups:[10]

- *Orientation*. Group members coordinate relevant information—exchanging, repeating, and confirming information and orienting themselves to the task.

- *Evaluation*. Group members exchange opinions, ideas, and information in an attempt to reconcile their differences over questions of fact and the appropriateness of proposed courses of action.

- *Control*. Group members exchange suggestions, consider alternative courses of action, and express both agreement and disagreement in arriving at a commonly accepted solution.

Another linear model of task group development was proposed by Tuckman and Jensen. Their group stages include:[11]

- *Forming*. Group members seek to establish their relationships, to get to know one another, and to form some sense of group spirit.

- *Storming*. Group members begin to react to the demands of the situation. They may question the group's charge and the authority of others in the group, articulating some assertions of differences and independence.

- *Norming*. The group agrees on rules of behavior, criteria for decision making, and ways of doing things.

- *Performing*. The group really examines the task or problem; information is shared; ideas are explored; questions are raised.

- *Adjourning*. As group members' time together draws to a close, they strive for closure on both task and relationship issues, moving toward adjournment.

This model is as much focused on relationship development as it is on task accomplishment; as a result, it is most appropriately applied to newly formed groups.

Process Models of Decision Making

As early as the 1960s, some small group researchers challenged the linear, phase-oriented view of group decision making. Scheidel and Crowell, for instance, proposed a *spiraling model* in which group members bounce ideas back and forth as they move toward consensus.[12] Far from being a linear progression, their decision-making model focused on group members' testing ideas, circling back, and then retesting them.

More recently, studies by Poole suggest that groups develop according to a *multiple sequence model*.[13] That is, the groups he studied tried to implement logical, orderly problem-solving sequences, but frequently other factors, such as lack of information, task difficulty, and conflict, interfered. Moreover, periods of idea development and exploration were often broken by periods of integrating activity, such as joke telling, sharing personal stories, and mutual compliment passing. In general, groups went through periods of disorganization that appeared to be unpredictable. Taken as a whole, Poole's research suggests that group development may not be as orderly as earlier models proposed.[14]

Distinguishing Effective from Ineffective Groups

There is nothing magic about making decisions in groups. Some groups work quite effectively and consistently make pretty good decisions, while others flounder. For years, researchers have attempted to compare effective and ineffective groups, trying to distinguish their behaviors and communicative activities.

In her long-term field study of eight project teams, Gersick reported that each team developed its own approach during its early meetings and tended to stick with that approach until they reached a midpoint in the time available for completing the project. At this midpoint, each group experienced a transition, or a "powerful opportunity" to alter its way of doing things.[15] Depending on whether or not the transition functioned constructively, the teams' final products or outcomes varied in quality. *Successful groups* tended to use the transition time to examine and possibly change their basic operating assumptions and procedures. Unsuccessful groups tended to ignore the opportunity for self-examination and plowed ahead using the same, often self-defeating, patterns. In general, Gersick's studies suggest that groups need to monitor their own interaction patterns and progress and be willing to make changes if they grow to believe that they are not interacting constructively or productively.

In a series of laboratory studies that spanned more than two decades, group task effectiveness was also studied by Hirokawa (and, during some of the phases, his colleagues). His work suggests that *effective groups* can be distinguished from less effective groups by:[18]

- *The way in which group members attempt to evaluate the validity of opinions and assumptions advanced by fellow discussants*. Evaluations tend to be more rigorous in effective groups.

- *The careful, rigorous manner in which groups try to evaluate alternatives*, measuring them against established criteria.

- *The kind of premises on which decisions are made*. Effective groups are more likely to use high-quality facts and inferences, whereas ineffective groups rely more on questionable facts and assumptions.

- *The sort of influence exerted by prominent group members*. In highly effective groups, leaders are more supportive and facilitating and less inhibiting. They ask appropriate questions, challenge invalid assumptions, clarify information, and keep the group from going off on irrelevant tangents.[16]

- *Whether the group begins the meeting by seeking to understand the problem*. Successful groups tend to begin their discussion by attempting to analyze the problem before trying to search for a viable solution; unsuccessful groups tend to begin the discussion by immediately trying to search for a viable solution.[17]

- *The attitudes group members bring to their deliberations*. When group members take the task seriously, when they are *vigilant* in their critical thinking, and when they weigh different alternatives carefully and judiciously, they are far more likely to make sound decisions. Thus, the spirit with which the problem is tackled significantly influences the quality of the group's work.

Problem-Solving Patterns: Some Pragmatic Considerations

Some writers are skeptical of any approach to decision making that is based on the premise of rationality.[19] For instance, in Cohen, March, and Olson's *garbage can model*, decision making is seen as a garbage pail in which people, problems, alternatives, and solutions slush around until there is sufficient contact among these elements for a decision to emerge. According to these theorists, groups will attempt to make their decisions *seem* rational retroactively through rationalization, but the decisions are really due to chance. They argue that the effectiveness of a decision should be judged according to group members' abilities to implement it and make it work rather than on the intrinsic effectiveness of the decision itself.[20]

While acknowledging that decision making is scarcely a completely rational process, most experts believe that groups can benefit from discovering and adopting procedures that minimize the widely acknowledged weaknesses associated with group interaction, such as looking at solutions before understanding the problem.[21] For example, Nutt reviewed 76 cases of organizational decision making and reported that in 84 percent of them a solution-centered process was used.[22] An initial focus on solutions may lead to a cursory consideration of alternatives. Even more serious, real problems may go unidentified in favor of problems that fit existing solutions. When this happens, the group actually formulates and attempts to solve the wrong problem.

THE REFLECTIVE-THINKING SEQUENCE

In an attempt to address some of the challenges associated with group problem solving and to encourage groups to examine problems more thoroughly and systematically, several writers and researchers have offered problem-solving patterns for groups to use. One of the most popular of these is John Dewey's *reflective-thinking sequence*. Particularly useful with questions of policy, this pattern consists of several questions:[23]

- How shall we define and limit the problem?
- What are the causes and extent of the problem?
- What are the criteria by which solutions should be judged?
- What alternatives can we identify?
- What are the strengths and weaknesses of each?
- What solution can be agreed upon?
- How can we put the solution into effect?

The value of the reflective-thinking sequence is its emphasis on careful problem assessment, a thoughtful consideration of the criteria to be used in evaluating the competing solutions, and its insistence on asking the group to grapple with the particulars of solution implementation.

QUESTION-AGENDA MODEL

Earlier in this chapter we discussed the kinds of questions appropriate for decision-making groups. We suggested that different kinds of questions should be approached from different perspectives for a maximally productive discussion to occur. Gouran has outlined several different agendas that he believes are conducive to structured and yet reasonably spontaneous interaction among discussants. The agenda selected depends upon the kind of question being discussed, as follows:[24]

- *Agenda for Discussions on Questions of Fact and Conjecture*
  - — What evidence do we have to support an affirmative position?
  - — What weaknesses, if any, exist in this body of evidence?
  - — What evidence do we have to support a negative position?
  - — What weaknesses, if any, exist in this body of evidence?
  - — Have we accumulated enough information to reach a decision?
  - — In light of the evidence examined, what position on the question appears to be most defensible?

- *Agenda for Discussions on Questions of Value*
  - — What are our individual positions on the question?
  - — On what bases have we arrived at these positions?
  - — Which of these bases for our respective positions are sound, and which are questionable?
  - — Are there positions other than those represented in the group that we should explore?
  - — Which of the bases for additional positions are sound, and which are unsound?
  - — Has our evaluation led to any changes in position?
  - — Is there one position we can all endorse?

- *Agenda for Discussions on Questions of Policy*
  - — What problems, if any, exist under the status quo?
  - — What are the alternatives among policies that we could endorse?
  - — What are the relative strengths and weaknesses of each of the alternatives?
  - — On the basis of our analysis, which policy shall we endorse? (Note, the policy agenda is similar to Dewey's reflective-thinking sequence.)

These suggested agendas are proposed only as tentative models, as potentially fruitful structures for the discussion of each kind of question. The advantage of using a different agenda for each type of question is that it is virtually impossible to neglect the nature of the question under consideration. Using these agendas, for example, your group is more likely to treat value questions as ones involving attitudes and motives and factual questions as ones necessitating the collection of considerable evidence before the discussion.

PROBLEM-SOLVING STRATEGIES EMPHASIZING IDEA GENERATION

Groups are notorious for making judgments about the quality or feasibility of members' ideas too early in the discussion. As a result, some researchers have proposed problem-solving strategies that encourage the generation of a maximum number of ideas without premature interpretation or analysis. For instance, some have advocated *brainstorming*, whereby ideas are proposed and listed without any type of judgment or criticism. This procedure has been shown to produce fresher, better-quality ideas than more ordinary problem-solving procedures.[25] A related approach, the *nominal group procedure*, gives each group member an opportunity to brainstorm privately on paper. An appointed clerk then collects the lists of ideas and compiles a master list. Ultimately, group members vote on the items they consider most important.[26]

Research comparing brainstorming groups with nominal groups has found that the nominal group procedure is more effective than brainstorming for groups composed of highly apprehensive members; it also appears better than brainstorming in terms of idea generation.[27] Its disadvantage (other than logistics) is that since the brainstorming is private, group members cannot be stimulated by

---

Business Brief 11.2

Hot Groups

Scholar Harold Leavitt argues that companies sometimes need groups that managers can't control. He calls these groups "hot groups"—lively, high-achievement, dedicated groups, usually small, whose members are turned on to exciting and challenging tasks.

- The defining characteristics of hot groups are:
  - Total preoccupation with the task at hand
  - Intellectual intensity, integrity, and exchange
  - Emotional intensity
  - Fluid role structure
  - Usually small size
- Hot groups are most likely to pop up under these conditions:
  - When organizations permit openness and flexibility
  - When leaders encourage independence and autonomy
  - When organizations put people first—hiring great talent and then giving individuals plenty of elbow room
  - When the organizational culture is committed to truth seeking
  - When a state of crisis or keen competition with other groups exists
- Members of hot groups are usually connective individualists—independent individuals who are also team players.
- Three key roles are prominent:
  - *Conductors*—who lead the orchestra—obvious movers and shakers
  - *Patrons*—who support it—working behind the scenes to protect, coach, listen, offer suggestions
  - *Keepers of the flame*—who sustain the group through time—nourishing new ideas, new solutions, and new partners in a long chain of hot groups

Source: Harold J. Leavitt and Jean Lipman-Blumen, "Hot Groups," *Harvard Business Review* 73 (1995): 109–16.

hearing the ideas of others. Of course, Groupware, also known as Group Support Systems (GSS), allow groups to function as nominal groups by allowing members to brainstorm, organize, and evaluate their ideas anonymously using computers.[28]

USING TECHNOLOGY TO FACILITATE GROUPS

Group Support Systems, interactive, computer-based systems, are rapidly being adopted and used by more corporations. GSS meeting rooms (see figure 11.1 on p. 406) incorporate the use of a local-area network, individual personal computer (PC) workstations, and GSS software to support such traditional meeting activities as idea generation, idea consolidation, the evaluation of alternatives, and decision making.

GSS Features

Originally, GSS were designed with several specific features intended to enhance group interaction.[29] First, GSS *enable parallel communication*. Because group participants brainstorm, consolidate ideas, and vote using their networked PCs, GSS allow each participant to contribute simultaneously; therefore, no group member need wait for another to finish "speaking."

In addition, GSS *facilitate group memory* by recording all typed comments electronically, allowing participants to withdraw from the group process to think or type comments and then rejoin the group discussion. At the same time, these systems enable participants to contribute to the group anonymously, thus reducing the pressure to conform and diminishing both communication and evaluation apprehension.[30] Since ideas typed into the computer do not reveal the identity of the contributor, participants can evaluate the ideas' merits on the basis of their content rather than their contributor.

Finally, GSS can be used to *provide structure and channel group behavior to maintain the group's focus on the task*.[31] Ventana Corporation, maker of GroupSystems™, argues that these features help meeting participants contribute more fully, keep meetings on track, complete projects more rapidly, and develop consensus.

Pros and Cons of GSS

Although there are clearly advantages associated with the use of technology like GSS, some losses are also possible. Advantages and disadvantages must be thoughtfully weighed.[32] For instance, typing comments into GSS PCs takes more time than speaking, thus potentially reducing the amount of information available to the group. On the other hand, the group benefits in that reading is faster than listening.

Because GSS anonymity separates the identity of the participants from their comments and votes, individuals are depersonalized—and thus presumably better able to express their true opinions. At the same time, however, this condition may also promote "deindividuation"—a loss of self- and group-awareness that is associated with "flaming," in which feelings (especially negative sentiments) are expressed quickly and without reflection. Moreover, keyboarding may actually inhibit socializing, resulting in reduced group cohesiveness and satisfaction.

One important GSS feature, group memory, allows participants to pause and think during the group keyboarding activity without missing information being

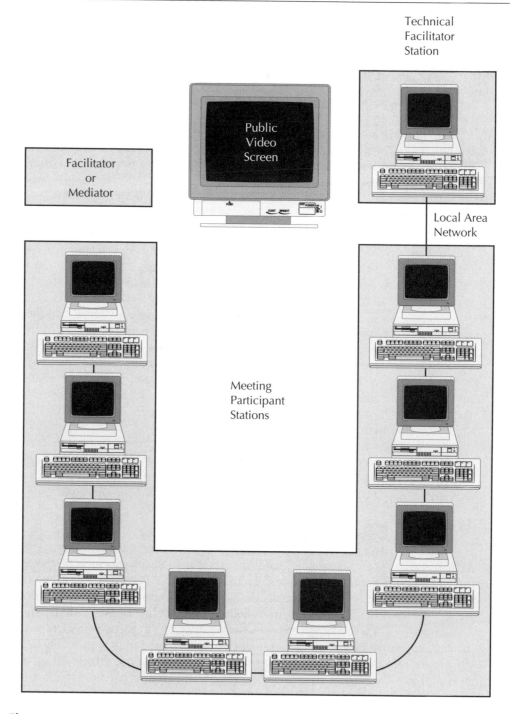

Figure 11.1   A GSS meeting environment

submitted by other group members. The GSS capacity to record information can also reduce memory and attention losses, attention blocking, and the use of incomplete information.[33] However, voiced comments and important nonverbal cues are not present and are not documented.

Anonymity is widely heralded as a GSS feature that can reduce status consciousness, pressures to conform, and evaluation apprehension. However, it may also increase free riding because it is more difficult to determine who is not doing his or her fair share.[34]

The final notable GSS capability, parallel communication, reduces interruptions and increases air time—providing equality in both access and voice. No one need wait for someone else to stop talking. However, this feature can also generate information overload and increase redundancies since, at times, no one is electronically listening to what others are electronically saying.

GSS may also improve the rationality of decision making by providing group members with step-by-step procedures that substitute for or supplement their own (possibly deficient) approaches to problem solving. Several studies have shown that GSS-driven procedures can lead to improvements in defining problems, generating alternative solutions, and improving the quality of the group's decisions.[35]

The GSS Environment: Beyond Technology

It's important to note that there are also nontechnology elements of the GSS meeting environment that may affect the nature of the group interaction process. Because GSS meetings do not take place in anyone's office, participants are not disadvantaged by having to travel to someone else's office for the meeting, perhaps finding themselves on something less than neutral turf. GSS facilities suggest by their very design and layout a concern for equality and a commitment to task. For instance, a number of meeting rooms are organized so that participants are seated at equal distances around a U-shaped table (as depicted in figure 11.1). All can see a large screen that is prominently situated at the front of the room. At times, a meeting facilitator may stand in front of the group to provide instructions or assist the group process. What is important, however, is that this kind of meeting environment promotes equitable interactions.

In traditional meeting rooms, those with higher rank or status are often advantaged, while those with lower rank, confidence, or skill are disadvantaged.

NON SEQUITUR

For instance, a group member with higher status, often the group's leader, typically elects to sit at the head of the table, giving him or her greater visual access to others (while being the focus of everyone's attention), as well as the potential for greater influence. Studies have shown that those seated in key positions will, in fact, talk more than others and will also be perceived as more influential. At the other extreme, those with high communication apprehension will invariably choose the most obscure seats, allowing them to withdraw from communication more easily and to avoid being the focus of attention. Interestingly, the GSS meeting environment neither promotes the would-be star nor provides hideouts for the apprehensive.[36]

The adoption and use of GSS and other such "Groupware" products are increasing rapidly. Many organizations have chosen to downsize, and they want to make the time spent by managers and professional staff in meetings (30 to 70 percent of their time) as productive as possible. Corporations now employ GSS to support a wide range of purposes (such as team building, strategic planning, quality control, joint applications design, and project management), and productivity gains as high as 90 percent have been reported by firms using this technology.[37]

Group Support Systems can facilitate collaborative communication, but it can't be used effectively as long as people view possessing information as a personal competitive advantage within an organization. If the corporate culture emphasizes and reinforces individual effort and ability and does not promote cooperation and information sharing, the underlying premise, or spirit, of the Groupware technology is undermined. Of course, GSS is only one type of technology organizations or communities may elect to use to assist them with problem solving.

Just as there is nothing magical about working in groups, using technology to facilitate group work may or may not be successful. Group members must be willing to experiment with the technology and to use it in constructive ways.[38]

Highlighting Technology

Supporting Community Planning

Scenario 360 from CommunityViz provides decision support software for groups involved in community planning and is being used by groups across the United States in communities of all sizes for comprehensive planning, zoning decisions, site selection and evaluation, and historic preservation

- It allows users to create two-dimensional and three-dimensional virtual representations of a community, enabling them to experiment with different land-use alternatives and visualize their impact.

- It provides a quantitative analysis tool that can measure and display various social, environmental, and fiscal impacts as users experiment with alternative scenarios.

- It is designed to make the decision-making and planning process more visual, more collaborative, and more effective.

Source: The Orton Family Foundation, "CommunityViz/Scenario 360" [online]. Available: http://www.orton.org/programs/viz/ (accessed: July 7, 2004).

Regardless of the kind of question being discussed or the organizational or technological approach chosen by your group, there are certain kinds of behaviors that group members should display throughout the discussion. We will now focus on these behaviors and suggest appropriate guidelines.

BEHAVIORAL GUIDELINES FOR DISCUSSION PARTICIPANTS

A discussion is only as good as its participants. Informed, participative members bring about an effective discussion. Uninformed, uninvolved, or unskilled interactants virtually guarantee the group's failure. In this section, we discuss some strategies we have found effective in promoting both your own success as a group member and the overall success of the group.

- *Prepare carefully for each meeting.* Every group member needs to be as knowledgeable as possible regarding the subject of discussion. It is probably inevitable that some members of your group will be better informed on certain aspects of the discussion subject than you are. But you will have expertise to contribute as well. Do your homework. Review relevant documents. Reflect on important issues the group is likely to address.

- *Approach the discussion with a group orientation.* We previously noted the importance of approaching the discussion with a desire to be a part of the *group's decision-making effort.* You should not make irrevocable judgments in advance. Rather, each person should be group oriented throughout. The point of participation in the discussion is not to satisfy your need for social approval or to gain acceptance for a personal prejudice or point of view. Each person shares some responsibility for the success or failure of the entire group. Whenever anyone allows personal ambitions to replace commitment to the objectives of the group, he or she is functioning in a manner detrimental to the group's success.

- *Participate actively.* Every group member must take an active part in the discussion and activities of the group. If you sit back silently during group meetings, you contribute nothing to the group or to your own credibility in the group or the organization. On the other hand, if you participate actively and make positive contributions to the group, you will help the group achieve its goals, improve your own standing within the group, and build an organization-wide reputation as someone who is a valued asset in group situations. Such a reputation will do much to enhance your long-term success.

- *Maintain an attitude of open-mindedness.* Closely related to a group-oriented attitude is one of open-mindedness. Group members should enter the discussion as open-mindedly as possible and strive to maintain an attitude of open-mindedness throughout the decision-making process. Encourage the expression of all points of view. State your own views with some degree of tentativeness. If others persuade you, don't hesitate to change your mind.

- *Listen carefully, constructively, and critically.* When someone else is talking, listen to that person with the intent of seeking an understanding of his or her point of view. Even if you don't agree with it, give it fair consideration. At the same time, don't hesitate to question someone whose information seems vague or whose ideas are not clearly articulated. Constructive conflict is healthy, as long as group members are able to disagree respectfully. Good group members take each other seriously, have a healthy respect for each other, are not afraid to challenge each other, and expect to be challenged in return.

- *Play several different roles.* As we discussed in chapter 10, group communication scholars have identified nearly twenty constructive roles that group members can play, ranging from information giver to harmonizer. It's easy to get in a rut and perform only one or two roles. For instance, a well informed or dominant member might primarily provide ideas and information and control the flow of the conversation. That person should develop a more balanced approach, perhaps by seeking others' ideas and offering appreciation when someone offers a good plan of action. When roles are shared in groups, everyone benefits.

- *Pay attention to nonverbal communication.* Often when we think of people working together in groups, we focus on what they say. But it is important to watch how they behave. Lack of eye contact might signal disengagement, poor preparation, or interpersonal tensions. Folded arms could suggest dissatisfaction with what others are saying or with the course of action that is being pursued. A group that meets around a table demonstrates a desire for equal participation and influence opportunity. Of course, when a group is culturally diverse, differences in cultural norms and practices will need to be taken into

---

Highlighting Ethics

Communicating Ethically in Groups

In addition to the other behavioral guidelines offered in this chapter, every group member should strive to interact ethically. Here are some guidelines:

- Show concern for others' ideas, respect for their feelings, and willingness to give them time to reflect on new information.
- Develop an attitude of being less interested in winning an argument than in achieving a consensus based on mutual understanding and respect.
- Refuse to use the group as an arena for promoting special interests or advancing your own status at the expense of others.
- Remain as eager to learn from and listen to others as to offer them your opinions and sage advice.
- Insist on accurate, complete information.
- Be willing to take extra time and put up with extra meetings for the sake of a better, more fully informed decision.
- Develop a sense of responsibility for the good of the group as a whole, while remaining mindful of the relationship between the group and the rest of the organization.
- Demonstrate the maturity to realize that other groups may have different priorities and perspectives.
- Recognize that no matter how hard this group works or how excellently it performs, other groups work hard as well and have legitimate needs to be fulfilled.

Thus, the ethical discussant is a good thinker, a good listener, a hard worker, and a responsible member of the community.

consideration. As a sensitive group member, you will want to be attuned to how the group is behaving nonverbally in addition to what they are verbalizing. If some group members seem uncomfortable or disengaged, you or others may want to take some action so that everyone is able to function constructively and have an impact.

- *Focus on matters of substance—not on personalities.* Every group member should strive to concentrate on substantive concerns. Every decision-making group has a task before it; the individuals in the group, however, are human beings who possess personalities that occasionally conflict. Severe personality clashes can destroy the socioemotional climate of the group and render the accomplishment of the group's task an impossibility.

Business Brief 11.3

Vision Engineering

A process called "vision engineering" has been used by such companies as Bridgestone/Firestone, Norsk Hydro, Sears, and U.S. Cellular to develop a meaningful organizational vision statement and a strategic plan to achieve the vision. Developed by CAP Gemini Consulting, the process begins with an executive team entering a room and finding a long table bearing about 100 stacks of cards at one end. Printed on the cards in each stack is a single fact or a demographic, social, technological, or economic trend—such as "Baby-boomers are reaching 60," "Work schedules are more flexible," or "The power of microprocessors will continue to increase." Some cards are industry specific: A beverage maker's executives found a card stating that store brands are becoming more important. All the cards hold true statements developed on the basis of the consultants' research, advice from outside experts, and industry trends the executives themselves identified. All the executives walk around the table studying the cards. Their objective is to string sets of cards together and put "headlines" on the strings. For example, cards stating "Increased use of credit cards," "Growing value of brand equity," "Rising number of Internet users," and "Ability to use technology to do specific market segmentation" might be strung together and headlined, "It's possible to bypass retailers to sell branded merchandise on the Web."

When everyone has taped a few strings and headlines to the wall, small groups debate, edit, and perhaps combine them. The groups then report to the team as a whole for another round of debate. When this phase is finished, the team should have 6 to 12 headlines, each telling a story about something happening in their business world and each a factor that should drive change.

The next phase of the exercise is for the team to figure out how each headline affects each link of their organizational chain, from research and development to customer service, for every line of business. The headlines are made into lists of threats and opportunities and lead to the final phase: a look at the capabilities and assets the company has or must develop if it is to meet the threats, take advantage of the opportunities, and ride the waves of change the future is going to bring. Thus, rather than producing a high-flown statement of vision, this process produces a cluster of opportunities, supported by a set of existing and to-be-developed assets and bounded by a realistic view of how the world is changing. As such, it avoids the "groupthink" pitfall described by one CEO, who observed, "There is a fine line between vision and hallucination."

Source: Thomas A. Stewart, "A Refreshing Change: Vision Statements That Make Sense," *Fortune*, 134, no. 6. (September 30, 1996): 195–96.

As a mature group member, you should realize that it is impossible to be equally attracted to every other member. It stands to reason that some of your fellow discussants will seem insensitive, uninformed or unintelligent, domineering, or rude from time to time. Even so, the important consideration from the viewpoint of the group's welfare is to assist *all* members, regardless of personality peculiarities or irritations, to contribute their best effort to the group's task. Figure 11.2 provides one example of an evaluation form that can be used in reacting to any group member's contribution, as well as assessing the group as a whole.

SUMMARY

Working in groups to make decisions can be satisfying when the organizational culture supports collaboration; when participants are eager to work with others; and when group members know how to plan, organize, and conduct an effective meeting. Although "participatory management" has been a buzzword for many years, getting employees involved in committee meetings can be challenging.

A small group can function effectively only under conditions where its members know something about group process and are interested in and willing to try to work together to share information and make good decisions. Understanding decision-making processes is an important first step. Groups are not always orderly and organized and do not always proceed in a step-by-step fashion. Some groups may go through distinct phases, but most are likely to proceed in less orderly ways. Being organized in a particular way may be less important than the qualities of mind, the work ethic, and the spirit with which the group approaches its task.

Underlying the issues or problems that groups address are questions of fact, conjecture, value, or policy. These questions should be articulated with simplicity and objectivity—and should possess some degree of controversiality. Although there are many different ways to organize a group's agenda, creating an agenda that is consistent with the kind of question being addressed is very helpful.

Given advances in technology, it is hardly surprising that groups in all kinds of organizations are increasingly using technological support to help them interact and achieve their goals. In particular, Group Support Systems have the capacity to assist groups by increasing each member's "talking" time, by allowing for anonymity, by providing for a collective memory or record of the meeting, and by giving the meeting structure. Using GSS does not ensure a successful group effort; members may suffer from a sense of isolation, nonverbal cues may be missed, and group members may flame. But with good intentions, training, and a collaborative culture, GSS have the potential to truly facilitate group efforts.

As with other communication skills, we assume that any organization member can *learn* to interact effectively in a small group setting. But effective group membership requires knowledge, the right kinds of attitudes (including a commitment to ethical communication), and a willingness to work at problem solving. Every group is different. Each will present special challenges. By following the principles advanced in this chapter, it is hoped, you will be well equipped to deal with difficult committee assignments and to help other group members move toward satisfying and productive outcomes.

Group Member's Name: _____

Instructor's Name: _____

Ratings should be interpreted as follows:
1 = Excellent; 2 = Good; 3 = Average; 4 = Somewhat Lacking; 5 = Poor

Individual Evaluation:

Was well prepared and knowledgeable.	1	2	3	4	5
Made specific references to information sources.	1	2	3	4	5
Contributions were concise and clear.	1	2	3	4	5
Comments were relevant to the issue being discussed.	1	2	3	4	5
Contributions were made readily and voluntarily.	1	2	3	4	5
Frequency of participation was appropriate.	1	2	3	4	5
Nonverbal communication was effective.	1	2	3	4	5
Listened carefully to other group members.	1	2	3	4	5
Seemed open-minded, willing to consider others' views.	1	2	3	4	5
Was cooperative and constructive.	1	2	3	4	5
Helped keep the discussion organized.	1	2	3	4	5
Contributed to the critical evaluation of ideas and information.	1	2	3	4	5
Was respectful and tactful in responding to others.	1	2	3	4	5
Encouraged everyone to participate.	1	2	3	4	5
Encouraged the expression of diverse points of view.	1	2	3	4	5
Assisted in leadership functions, if appropriate.	1	2	3	4	5

Comments:

Group Evaluation:

Chose a substantive question of policy, characterized by simplicity, objectivity, and controversiality.	1	2	3	4	5
Demonstrated a grasp of important issues pertaining to the discussion question.	1	2	3	4	5
Created and flexibly followed an appropriate agenda.	1	2	3	4	5
Showed evidence of having conducted good research.	1	2	3	4	5
Interacted spontaneously.	1	2	3	4	5
Interacted cooperatively and considerately.	1	2	3	4	5
Made reasonable progress toward reaching consensus.	1	2	3	4	5
Handled conflict openly and constructively.	1	2	3	4	5
Encouraged everyone to participate.	1	2	3	4	5

Comments:

Figure 11.2   Group discussion evaluation

Questions for Discussion

1. In what sense is group decision making a process rather than a procedure?
2. What are some ways (methods) of preparing for participation in a group discussion? Which seem to you to be most useful? Why?
3. What is meant by "having a group orientation"?
4. Identify each of the following discussion questions as being either a question of fact, conjecture, value, or policy. Then evaluate the merit of each as a potential discussion question, using the criteria of simplicity, objectivity, and controversiality.
   a. What should be the policy of the United States concerning gun control?
   b. What is the value of a college education?
   c. Is there a positive correlation between violence on television and the crime rate?
   d. Is having sex before marriage desirable or morally problematic?
   e. Is teenage alcoholism a serious problem in our society today?
   f. What should be our attitude toward gay rights?
5. Compare and contrast the reflective-thinking sequence, the nominal group procedure, and the question-agenda model. What are the strengths and weaknesses of each? Can you think of other potential approaches? Elaborate.
6. What are some of the advantages and disadvantages of Group Support Systems?
7. Discuss some of the behavioral characteristics of effective discussion participants. Refer to examples from your own experiences.
8. How do you assess the ethics of others in your group? How will you assess your own ethics?

Exercises

1. Take any two of the following topics and phrase them into all four types of discussion questions (fact, conjecture, value, and policy). Check each question carefully to make sure it meets the criteria of simplicity, objectivity, and controversiality.
   a. Stem cell research
   b. Pass-fail grading
   c. The Green Party
   d. Medicaid
   e. Internet pornography
   f. The minimum wage
   g. Home schooling
   h. HMOs
   i. SUVs
   j. Obesity in the United States
2. Break into groups of five to seven members each. Choose a topic of mutual interest and some controversiality and phrase it into a question for a decision-making discussion. After appropriate time for individual preparation, meet again as a group and discuss the question, attempting to reach consensus.
3. Following the above discussion, critically consider the quality of the group's decision-making efforts in terms of the problem-solving pattern used, the quality and quantity of the contributions of individual group members, and

the socioemotional variables operating within the group. Use the group evaluation form provided in figure 11.2 or generate a critique sheet of your own.

Case Application 11.1   Reynolds and Reynolds Co.

Like many companies, Reynolds and Reynolds Co., in Moraine, Ohio, was looking for ways to improve productivity without increasing costs. Its discovery: the best results come from asking workers who actually do the jobs how those jobs can be done more efficiently.

One key Reynolds and Reynolds plant, the Moraine plant, repairs computer and peripheral components, such as printers and monitors, for the company's automotive-dealer information system. While this plant is relatively small, employing 45 people, it plays a large role in the company's success. Specifically, repairing each of its own components costs Reynolds and Reynolds, on average, $35, while sending the same part outside for repairs would cost $185. Thus, with a large volume of components to be repaired, the Moraine plant saves the company nearly $8 million every year.

In spite of their substantial savings, managers believed that the Moraine plant could operate even more efficiently. Among the 45 employees, performance varied a great deal. Tension was in the air.

An initial investigation of barriers to effective performance revealed conflict between the repair functions of the Moraine plant, which worked on a quota system, and the distribution function, which tried to be responsive to the needs of customers (people at other company locations). Since each function blamed the other for any problems, a five-person task force composed of people from both areas and one from internal engineering was formed and named "ACT"—Accomplishing Communications Team. This group then conducted a 2 1/2 hour plantwide meeting of all employees, with no supervisors or managers present. While some employees expressed skepticism during the meeting about management's true intentions in launching this effort, all eventually agreed to give the new system a try.

The ACT members funneled employees' ideas to management over the next several months, including proposed revisions in the weekly work schedules (which would be drawn up by employees themselves), a plan for cross-training repair technicians, and an improved method for labeling repair parts. All these measures, and many others, were implemented, with significant cost savings to the company.

Ultimately, the approach increased productivity by nearly 40 percent, reduced the time parts wait for repairs from two weeks to 24 hours, and eliminated the need to recheck returned parts.

Source: Based on information provided by Raju Narisetti, "Bottom-Up Approach Pushes Plant's Performance to the Top," *Chicago Tribune*, November 29, 1992, sec. 7, 13.

Questions

1. What aspects of group process probably helped the Reynolds and Reynolds performance improvement effort to succeed? What factors probably impeded the effort's success?

2. What were the dangers of undertaking the effort described in this case; that is, what might have gone wrong?

3. Are there situations in which this sort of process probably should not be attempted? As a manager, what things would you consider when deciding whether or not to institute a process similar to that used by Reynolds and Reynolds?

12

Leading Group Meetings

After reading this chapter, you should be able to:

❑ Identify situations in which meetings should and should not be called

❑ List and explain factors to consider in preparing to conduct meetings

❑ Develop an effective announcement for a meeting

❑ List and explain four types of meeting leadership styles and the situations in which each is most appropriate

❑ Describe problem participants in groups and how they might be handled

❑ Identify the actions that should be taken to follow-up on group meetings

❑ Discuss the factors that impact how groups might use technology to support their meetings

One of the most common complaints we hear from supervisors, managers, and executives is that "there are too many meetings." Indeed, the higher one goes in an organization's hierarchy, the more time one is going to spend conducting or participating in meetings. It seems likely that the use of meetings in organizations and communities is going to increase rather than decrease in the future. In his book *Megatrends: Ten New Directions Transforming Our Lives*, John Naisbitt claims that "people whose lives are affected by a decision must be part of the process of arriving at that decision."[1] He goes on to argue that "whether or not we agree with the notion or abide by it, participatory democracy has seeped into the core of our value system." Already this trend is clear in the business setting. In response to a survey of management practices conducted nationwide, only 15.3 percent of all top executives and 12.3 percent of all managers said they make major decisions without consulting all their direct subordinates in meetings; all the rest used participative decision making to some extent.[2]

With this increasing emphasis on participative decision making has come an increased need for two other skills: employees and supervisors must have skills in participating in meetings and supervisors, managers, and executives must have skills in conducting meetings. James O'Toole of the Center for Effective Organizations at the University of Southern California claims that "what America will require is workers who are humane individuals, with analytical and entrepreneurial skills, who know how to work in groups, and who know how to solve problems."[3]

Preview

In keeping with this growing need, previous chapters addressed the factors influencing group participation. In this chapter, we will consider techniques for leading group meetings. Specifically, we will discuss the times at which meetings should and should not be called; how to prepare for meetings; how to announce meetings; general approaches to leading meetings; specific formats by which certain types of meetings can be run; things to do as a follow-up to a meeting; and strategies for dealing with problem participants in groups. We will also examine the ways that group leadership may be influenced by gender and consider the ways that technology may be used to support group efforts. All this should help you develop your skills in conducting group interactions in organizational and community settings.

BEFORE THE MEETING: PREPARATORY STEPS

Many of the complaints or "bad press" that meetings receive are due to their inappropriate usage. Too many meetings are held when no meeting really is needed. Conversely, too many decisions are made without a meeting when, in fact, a meeting should have occurred.

Deciding When to Call Meetings

As a first step in knowing when and when not to have a meeting, Auger suggests you keep in mind certain principles:[4] You *should* call a meeting when you need to:

- Reach a group judgment as the basis for a decision.
- Discover, analyze, or solve a problem.
- Gain acceptance from the group for an idea, program, or decision.
- Achieve a training objective.
- Reconcile conflicting views.
- Provide essential information for work guidance or for the relief of insecurities or tensions.
- Ensure equal understanding of company policy, methods, or decisions.
- Obtain immediate reactions to a problem that requires a speedy response.

You may also want to call a meeting when you want participants to feel included in the process and/or when regular meetings are a valued part of the organization's culture.

Highlighting Technology

Does E-mail Replace Meetings?

Two-thirds of executives say e-mail has cut back on the need for meetings, according to a survey by A. T. Cross Co., a maker of writing instruments. Nine out of ten say it has reduced the need for paper correspondence and improved productivity. Nevertheless, nearly half say they attend too many meetings each week; a fifth attend eleven or more.

Source: "Survey: E-mail Leads to Fewer Meetings," *San Francisco Examiner,* July 19, 1998, sec. J, 1.

On the other hand, you *should not* call a meeting when:

- Other communications, such as telephone, letter, e-mail, or memo, will produce the desired result.
- There is not sufficient time for adequate preparation by participants or the meeting leader.
- One or more key participants cannot attend.
- The meeting is not likely to produce satisfactory results because of personality conflicts or conflicts with overall management strategy.
- Expected results do not warrant spending the money it will cost to hold the meeting.

When deciding whether to call a meeting, always remember the old saying "Time is money." Meetings consume a lot of both, and you must be sure the investment is worthwhile before convening any meeting.

Preparing to Conduct Meetings

Much of the effort that goes into making a meeting successful occurs *before* the meeting happens. Only through careful planning can you be sure that the meeting will be as successful as possible. Yet research conducted by Frank suggests that preparation often is lacking: When asked, "How frequently are group meetings well planned?" 40.6 percent of the respondents in his survey of 416 organizations responded "almost never" or "sometimes."[5] To ensure thorough preparation, you should ask yourself several questions, such as:

- Have I clearly defined the purpose or purposes of the meeting?
- What are the outcomes that should emerge from this meeting? (Information? Plans to gather information? Possible courses of action? A solution to a problem? A policy statement?)
- Who should participate? As a rule, invite to the meeting people who are expected to carry out a decision to be reached at the meeting, people who possess unique information that can contribute to the meeting, people whose approval may be needed, people who have official responsibility for the matter under discussion, and people who have a personal contribution to make from a strategic standpoint (that is, whose support you want or whose opposition you want to avoid politically).
- How should people be notified of the meeting? We will talk further about methods of announcing meetings in the next section.
- How much time will the meeting probably take?
- What information, if any, do members need before the meeting?
- What follow-up, if any, will be needed after the meeting?
- What agenda will the meeting follow?
- What is the best time and place for the meeting?
- What physical arrangements need to be made for the meeting?

Although this list may seem somewhat formidable, making sure you answer these questions will help ensure that you are truly prepared for the meeting and may lead to a productive and satisfying outcome for everyone involved.

The facility or setting in which the meeting is to be held should be given careful consideration as part of the planning process. The physical location of a meeting and the equipment to be used during that meeting have a powerful impact on the meeting's success. As a result, you must plan carefully the physical facilities to be used during the session. Generally, you should consider five basic elements: task, comfort, acoustics, visibility, and interference.

Business Brief 12.1

Avoiding Meeting Pitfalls

An important element of preparing to conduct a meeting is anticipating and avoiding common meeting pitfalls. Here are seven of the most common meeting pitfalls, along with some suggestions on how to avoid them.

1. **Lack of clarity about the meeting's purpose.** Many meetings suffer from "mission creep," whereby the goal of the meeting becomes lost over time and the meeting becomes simply a regular activity (such as the weekly staff meeting that occurs whether it is needed or not). At Motorola, the opening minutes of every meeting are spent discussing its purpose, and the meeting is disbanded if the purpose cannot be clearly stated. As a first step, always ask, "What are the results this meeting should produce?"

2. **Goals that could be better accomplished by means other than a meeting.** Sometimes the best solution is to avoid meeting in the first place. To test this, write down what change a meeting is supposed to accomplish and then assess whether a meeting is the best way to reach that goal. Meetings held for the purpose of sharing information and project updates, for example, should be canceled in favor of e-mails and information-sharing software, such as Lotus Notes.

3. **Inadequate preparation.** For a meeting to function effectively, as much as possible should be decided ahead of time: the purpose, who is coming, what is to be decided, how long the meeting will last, the best meeting space, what problem-solving procedures will be used, what the agenda will be, and so on.

4. **A haphazard decision-making process.** Meetings are the forum in which team-based organizations reach many of their decisions. Yet very often there is no sense of how decisions are to be made within a group. A decision-making agenda should be selected and used as the basis for the meeting's procedures.

5. **Jumping to conclusions.** In reaching a decision, groups rarely establish criteria or standards by which solutions will be evaluated. Instead, they ignore systematic analysis in favor of the most current, dramatic, or controversial aspects of a problem. This emotional approach to selecting a solution can result in flawed meeting results and unsatisfactory problem solving.

6. **Overdeveloped egos.** Some meetings end up being not about problem solving at all. Issues may be decided not on their merits, but on the competing interests of people at the table. The meeting leader must anticipate conflicts that have little to do with the goal of the meeting and must look to create norms that curb headstrong, ego-driven acts.

7. **Insufficient follow-up.** Meetings typically end with people being assigned to carry out the conclusions. But the meeting process does not end until someone is assigned to do follow-up. Without some means of checking back and ensuring that assignments are completed, there is no way of knowing whether a meeting has been effective.

Source: Edward Prewitt, "Pitfalls in Meetings and How to Avoid Them," *Harvard Management Update* (June 1998): 9–10.

1. *Task* is a consideration of the work to be done in the meeting and of the equipment necessary to do that work. If a presentation is to be given, for example, an overhead projector, a slide projector, or laptop computer, and a screen may be needed. If participants' comments are to be solicited and discussed, a flip chart or easel pad of large sheets of paper will be needed. A blackboard also may be needed. Occasionally, videotaping equipment, such as cameras, playback units, and monitors, is used. The leader should ensure that all such equipment is at the meeting site, that spare bulbs for projectors are on hand, that electrical outlets have been located and the necessary extension cords procured, and that there are markers or chalk for use on the flip pad or blackboard.

2. *Comfort* involves several aspects of the environment. Temperature and ventilation are important. You need to determine how to control the room's temperature and ventilation, should the room become too cold, hot, or stuffy during the meeting. In all instances, speed of change is the primary concern. Any room can have its temperature or ventilation changed; the issue during a meeting is whether the change can be achieved quickly enough.

   Another aspect of comfort is the chairs: Are they padded enough or flexible enough to provide comfort for a long meeting? Are they too comfortable (creating the possibility of people's dozing off during the meeting)? Are they moveable so that people can face each other if necessary? Will desks or tables be needed? Any equipment that participants may need, such as writing tablets, pencils, or erasers, should also be set out at each person's place before the meeting begins.

3. *Acoustics*, or the ability of people to hear one another, is also an important consideration. You should be sure that sound carries well even when the room is full of people (sound always carries better in an empty room) and that the room is not overly large so that people will sit too far from one another. If necessary, obtain microphones and loudspeakers so everyone can be heard.

4. *Visibility* is also important. People should be able to see anyone who is talking, whether that person is the meeting leader or another group member. If charts, graphs, slides, PowerPoints, or other visuals are to be used, everyone must be able to see these as well. Consider the impact of any seating arrangement on group interaction. Be sure that everyone has equal access to everyone else if group discussion is to be an important part of the meeting (sitting around a circular table might be helpful in this regard) or that committee members who need to work together are seated next to one another.

5. *Interference* is one final concern. Interruptions should be prevented and background noise eliminated if at all possible. You need to investigate what things, if any, will be happening in adjoining rooms during your meeting. You also need to select a meeting location that is away from the normal work area, unless the meeting is to be very brief and informal. A "Do not disturb" notice on the door may be helpful, and participants should be told ahead of time to have messages taken for them during the meeting so interruptions will not occur. Finally, make sure that all group members have turned off their cell phones.

Highlighting Civic Engagement

Planning the Town Meeting

The Democracy 2000 Civic Engagement Project is based on the conviction that modern American communities are so complex that the conventional methods of solving problems may not work. However, if all segments of the community become actively involved in searching for solutions, a community's conflicts can be turned into agreements that win wide public support.

If you are in a leadership position and want to organize a productive town meeting, here are some guidelines to follow:

- *Assemble an organizing committee*—making sure that the organizers will be seen as neutral or represent all major shades of opinion. The more points of view the committee encompasses, the more successful the project is likely to be.

- *Define the issue or goals*—the committee will have to agree on exactly what issue to tackle and what the meeting is expected to accomplish.

- *Attract broad participation*—seek endorsements for the meeting from groups and individuals who have large followings in the community and span a wide range of opinions. Persuade them that everyone who attends the meeting will participate directly in resolving an issue they care about.

- *Maximize public and media interest*—the meeting will have the greatest impact on the community if it draws a big turnout and is covered by local media. Prepare and distribute a press kit that explains how the meeting could lead to resolving an issue that greatly concerns the community.

- *Democracy 2000 can help*—it is a nonprofit, nonpartisan organization whose mission is to help concerned citizens, community leaders, lawmakers, educators, and facilitators solve public policy problems and improve civic life. To discuss your community's needs with Democracy 2000, send an e-mail to: mailto:dem2000@igc.org.

Source: "The Civic Engagement Project: Planning an Interactive Town Meeting" [online]. Available: http://www.democracy2000.org/meetingplan.htm (accessed: May 19, 2004).

Announcing Meetings

Too often meetings fail because they are poorly announced. The wrong people show up, participants arrive unprepared, or members have to leave before the end of the meeting because no one knew how long the meeting would take. To avoid such problems, send a written announcement at least one week in advance to everyone involved in the meeting. Do not rely on telephone calls, face-to-face interactions, or even e-mail (since some people don't check their e-mail regularly). The written announcement of the meeting should say:

- *Why* the meeting is being held. Members should know what the purpose of the meeting is and what their role is to be. This gives them a chance to prepare for the meeting if necessary, and it lets them know what matters will not be part of the meeting's contents.

- *When* the meeting starts and ends. Most announcements indicate the starting time; too few say how long the meeting is expected to last. To avoid people leaving early due to other commitments, state in the announcement how long the meeting is expected to go or when it will adjourn.

Business Brief 12.2

Sample Meeting Announcement

Date: November 10, 2004
To: All Training Department Members
From: H. K. Thompson, Director of Training & Development
Re: Upcoming Department Meeting

On Friday, November 21, we will have a meeting of the Training Department, to be held in Training Room C in the Training Center, Building C. It will begin at noon and be over by 1:30 PM.

Mr. Don Johnson, Vice President of Personnel, will be present to talk about his objectives for the training function next year, and Mr. Gary Howard, Director of Employee Relations, will attend to discuss the role of Corporate Training support for in-plant locations.

The purposes of the meeting are (1) to discuss plans for the department and to choose specific programs to offer next year, (2) to review participant responses to this year's programs, and (3) to discuss any matters of concern to you. *Please bring all of your participant rating sheets to the meeting; you will be asked to present the average ratings received for each of your programs to the rest of the group.*

Our agenda is as follows:

1. Plans for next year
   a. Objectives of the Vice President—Mr. Johnson.
   b. The Role of Corporate Training for In-Plant Locations—Mr. Howard.
   c. Specific programs we should offer at Corporate facility (group suggestions).
   d. Specific programs we should offer at individual plant sites (group suggestions).
2. Program evaluations
3. Training staff's matters of concern

- *Where* the meeting is to be held. If attendees are likely to be unfamiliar with the location, a map or some description of how to find it should be included.
- *Who* is going to attend. The complete list of attendees should be provided for everyone to see. The list need not give everyone by name ("the entire training force" would be sufficient), but each attendee should know who else is coming.
- *What* is going to be considered in the meeting. An agenda or outline of the meeting's proceedings should be included. If attendees are allowed to suggest items for inclusion in the agenda, this fact also should be stated, and attendees should be told to whom their items should be sent and by what date those items should be received.

Business Brief 12.2 (above) presents a sample announcement letter. While the contents of such a letter will change from one meeting and group to the next, the basic types of information contained in this announcement should be included in every meeting notification.

LEADERSHIP STYLES

An important element of group leadership is the extent to which the leader shares power with the group members. Some leaders, for example, take total control of the meeting and decision making, simply telling everyone else what is going to happen, who is going to do what to whom, and so on. Other leaders are just the opposite: they allow a great deal of participation by the group members, both in interacting and in making decisions. How a meeting is to be conducted is something the leader must decide. We can identify four basic approaches to conducting meetings: autocratic, consultative, democratic, and laissez-faire. Some leaders combine a particular style (often the democratic or laissez-faire styles) with team-building strategies, which inspire teams to take responsibility and focus on goals that maximize outcomes.

Autocratic

Autocratic (highly directive) leadership occurs when the leader does virtually all the talking and decides everything (or virtually everything) the group will do. Meetings led by such leaders consist primarily of announcements the leader makes to the attendees, followed by any questions the attendees have for the leader. In other words, communication is almost exclusively downward and decision making is virtually nonexistent.

Generally, autocratic meetings are not really meetings but rather presentations by the group leader to the group. As we already have seen, some situations demand this sort of meeting: time may be of the essence, the group may not know enough about the topic to participate, the group may have no control over the topic so that participation would be meaningless, and so on. Whatever the case, the leader chooses to use the one-to-group setting to communicate information to the participants.

The autocratic meeting is really an exercise in public presentation. Therefore, the principles described in upcoming chapters will be of help in conducting this type of meeting. At this point, however, we can offer an agenda and some principles to follow when conducting the autocratic meeting:

I. Introduction
   A. Call the group to order.
   B. Announce the purpose of the meeting.
   C. If appropriate, explain why the meeting is being handled this way and why the group is not participating in making the decision or formulating plans.
   D. Preview the meeting agenda. List the order in which the topics will be covered, when breaks (if any) will be taken, when questions should be asked (any time; at the end of each announcement; at the end of the meeting), and when the meeting will probably end. The agenda might be written on a blackboard or flip pad at the front of the room to help keep participants oriented to the topic.

II. Presentation
   A. Announce the first topic; where appropriate, give the background of the topic, current actions or decisions, and future implications for this group.
   B. Announce the second topic; handle in the same way.
   C. Announce the third; continue through announcements.
   D. As much as possible, use visual aids: handouts, charts, graphs, overhead transparencies, and the like. Accompanying visual stimuli help participants both to understand and to remember the announcements.

III. Conclusion

   A. Ask for and answer any questions.

   B. State again any future implications the announcements have for the group.

   C. Tell the group what follow-up will occur. ("I'll send each of you a memo saying in writing what I've announced today. If you have any questions or concerns later, give me a call.")

   D. Dismiss the meeting.

The keys to successful autocratic meetings are clarity, completeness, and comprehension. The information you provide must be as clear as possible to the members. (Watch their feedback carefully for signs of puzzlement or confusion, and let them ask questions.) It must be complete, particularly if the members are to have a role in implementing the decision or if it will affect them. Finally, they must comprehend the reasoning behind the decision or the implications of the information.

Consultative

Consultative leadership encourages input from group members, although the leader still makes the final decisions. In effect, the leader "consults" with the members, asking for their thoughts and ideas concerning problems, decisions, actions, and so on. They participate in the interaction, and they have some influence over the leader's thinking. However, they have power only to the extent that they can persuade the leader to adopt their suggestions or proposals.

In consultative meetings, the leader maintains decision-making authority but asks the group to suggest alternatives, ideas, causes, and so on. At the beginning of the meeting, it is important to make this situation clear to the participants. The leader should state the problem, decision, or situation she is facing and tell the group that their ideas or suggestions are desired, but make it clear that the leader ultimately will have responsibility for the decision. Thus, while the leader promises to listen, she does not promise to do everything (or anything) the group suggests.

As an agenda for the meeting, the leader might choose to use one of those outlined in chapter 11: the reflective-thinking sequence, the question-agenda model, or the nominal group procedure. Regardless of the agenda she suggests, however, the leader will have to solicit participation from the group. Several strategies may be useful here.

First, the leader might *use an overhead question*—one asked of the group as a whole. Such a question might be, "What do you think of this?" or "What ideas do you have concerning solutions to this problem?" The problem with overhead questions, however, is that they may go over everyone's head; no one has responsibility for answering the question, so often no one answers. The silence that follows an overhead question is often deafening. If the overhead question does not produce participation or discussion, a more specific approach might prove useful.

One way to encourage participation is to *use the directed question*. That is, call on someone for an answer. Make an effort to call on someone you know to have information, whose nonverbal cues indicate he has an opinion (for example, a member who shakes his head negatively when you introduce the topic), or with whom you have spoken prior to the meeting to let her know she will be called on at the beginning of the meeting.

Directed questions should also be sufficiently open, requiring more than a yes or no response. Asking "Bill, do you agree with that?" and having Bill grunt "Uh-huh" hardly produces stimulating interaction. Ask, "What are some things you think we should do, Bill?" or "Bill, how do you feel about this issue?" Directed questions also should be passed around the group. There is a temptation to call again and again on the same member, either because he is such a good answer-giver or because you are personally acquainted with that member and feel comfortable calling on him. You must make a deliberate effort to call on different members at different times.

Finally, encourage participation by *asking redirected questions*. That is, when a group member asks you a question, redirect the question back to the group rather than immediately providing a response. For example, you might make it an overhead question: "What do all of you think of that?" Or you might direct it to another member: "Diane, how would you answer Bill's question?" Again, your purpose is to stimulate interaction among the members; conducting a question-and-answer session with individual members does not achieve active group discussion.

In larger groups, another participation-producing device is to *subdivide the group into smaller groups*, give them a topic to discuss, and have them report back a few minutes later. For example, you might divide your group of 10 into two groups of 5 members each and instruct them: "Now I want each of your groups to come up with the longest list possible of things we might do to improve the courtesy we show patients in the hospital. After about 10 minutes, I'll stop you and have you report your answers for everyone." The small group setting and specific assignment of topics are very effective in getting people to talk with one another, and this interaction will continue when the larger group is reformed later on.

At the end of a consultative meeting, one of two things should occur. First, if you have the ability and inclination to make decisions on the spot, you should do so. Tell the group which of their recommendations you will accept and which you will reject (along with reasons why you chose not to do those things), or which suggestions you will pass along to upper management and which ones seem unfeasible (again offering explanations). While some members may be disappointed that their ideas are not used, they nevertheless feel that some action will be taken based on their input, and this feeling is far more satisfying than being told, "I'll get back to you with my decision" (particularly if the leader never gets back to them).

In some situations, however, you may not have the ability or desire to make an on-the-spot commitment. Then you must use the "I'll get back to you" statement, but you also should tell them when and how you'll get back to them: "I'll send you all a memo next week telling you what I have decided" or "We'll meet again next Tuesday at this same time so I can present my decisions to you and answer any questions." Do not, under any circumstances, leave the group hanging without any feedback or follow-up.

Democratic

Democratic leadership adheres to the principle of "one person, one vote." The leader simply facilitates the meeting while group members interact, make decisions, and solve problems. In democratic meetings, decision-making power and group interaction are shared among all members. The leader has no more power in making the decision than does any other group member. However, she does control the methods used by the group, setting the agenda they will follow, controlling interaction among them, and even deciding how decisions will be made. In democratic groups, decisions can be made in several ways:

• *Consensus*. Consensus is probably the ideal method of decision making. The group simply discusses the topic until everyone agrees. In Japan and among some religious sects (such as the Quakers), decision making by consensus is rigidly followed; nothing is decided until everyone agrees. Such decision making is desirable in that everyone supports the decision arrived at by the group, but it is also disadvantageous if there are time limits. As an extreme example, the Quakers debated the issue of slavery during the nineteenth century for nearly 50 years; they finally concluded their debates (without reaching consensus) long after the Civil War was over. If your group cannot reach consensus within a reasonable time period, you should move to some other technique for making a decision.[6]

• *Group ratings or rankings*. There are mathematical techniques for arriving at compromise solutions. If, for example, two alternatives remain and the group cannot choose between them, hand everyone a sheet of paper and ask them to rate each alternative on a scale from 0 to 10 (with 0 meaning it is a totally unacceptable solution, 5 meaning the solution is largely neutral, and 10 meaning it is the perfect solution to the problem). Then collect the ratings and calculate the average rating for each alternative. If several alternatives remain, you might ask the group members individually to rank-order them (a ranking of 1 for their favorite, 2 for their second favorite, and so on). Collect the rankings, calculate the average ranking for each alternative, and select the one with the lowest number. Either ratings or rankings can help the group make a decision without there being any "winners" or "losers"; everyone's ratings or rankings had an impact on the decision.

• *Process of elimination*. Sometimes no alternative emerges as clearly the best. The strategy then might be to eliminate the worst. One technique for achieving this is called the "murder board." An alternative is written on a large sheet of paper or blackboard at the front of the room, and the group then tries to "kill" the idea by listing everything that could possibly be wrong with it. When they have run out of ideas, the next alternative is put up and subjected to the same treatment. The alternative that receives the fewest objections or has the fewest serious problems is chosen. Sometimes, however, all the alternatives are "killed"; then the group must generate new solutions to the problem.

• *Majority vote*. In small groups, the majority vote method generally should be avoided. Whenever there is a vote, someone loses. This minority may be embarrassed, resentful, angry, frustrated, and so on, and they are not likely to support the group's decision. Granted, there are times (such as when parliamentary procedure is used) when majority votes are called for, but in most meetings, some other method of decision making should be employed whenever possible.

Highlighting Diversity

Cultural Differences in Making Decisions

- Although voting on decisions is not ideal, at least Americans are accustomed to the notion of "one person, one vote" as the foundation of the U. S. government.
- Western cultures, such as the dominant U.S. culture, are grounded in an individualistic orientation that prioritizes the needs of individuals above the needs of the group—privileging individual goals, individual identity, and personal autonomy.
- Because of this individualistic orientation, Americans view voting as an individual action and abiding by the wishes of the majority as natural and appropriate.
- By contrast, Eastern cultures, such as Indonesian and Chinese cultures, are grounded in a collectivist orientation and think of the group before the individual—honoring group identify, group rights, and group harmony and collaboration.
- From this collectivist perspective, then, voting is not a viable option. Rather, group members are expected to discuss the issue until everyone can support a particular course of action.

If you are chairing a multicultural group, you will need to recognize that cultural differences can affect group processes and outcomes. Cultural diversity can be both a source of creative energy and potentially unproductive conflict. Taking the time to acknowledge and honor differences is crucial.

Source: Stella Ting-Toomey, *Communicating across Cultures* (New York: Guilford, 1999).

Laissez-Faire

Laissez-faire leadership occurs when the leader has virtually no role in the meeting. If, for example, a supervisor asks an employee to conduct the meeting while the supervisor sits at the back of the room or if the boss announces in advance that he will not attend a particular meeting so that a less inhibited discussion might occur, he is practicing laissez-faire leadership. If this leadership style is to be effective, it ought to be occasional and strategic. Since the laissez-faire leader gives away power, the group takes on both control and responsibility for its actions.

In a sense, any meeting can be a laissez-faire meeting; the leader has only to appoint a substitute leader, sit in back, and let things happen as they may, or for strategic reasons (like discouraging groupthink) not attend the meeting at all.

Team-Building Goals and Strategies

While different authors suggest different team-building strategies, they generally agree on the goals team building should achieve. First, it should cause the group members to **agree on their common goals** and objectives. It should also **sort out the roles each member will play** in working toward the goals and objectives. In addition, it should cause the group to **decide on the procedures** they will follow when working together. Finally, team building should help group members **arrive at mutually satisfactory relationships** with one another. All of these might be achieved in a single meeting lasting as long as three or four days, or they might be accomplished one at a time through a series of meetings.

Littlejohn describes one common approach to team building that requires two one-day sessions.[7] The first day is devoted to a discussion of members' perceptions of the organization and of the team members themselves. They exchange opinions and ideas about the organization as a place in which to work, and they exchange knowledge about themselves. The second day focuses on planning and goal setting. Members deal with such issues as *mission* (Why do we as a team exist?), *situation* (Where are we now?), and *strategies* (How are we going to reach our goals?). Procedures such as these ultimately achieve the goals of team building.

Several specific techniques can be used to encourage interaction and achieve team-building objectives. For instance, you might have participants individually (or in small groups) develop a list of habits or practices they think the team should develop, modify, or improve. You might have them address the question "Why do we exist as a functioning team?" Have them report their answers. Then, from the composite list produced by all groups, have the groups meet again and rank the answers according to their importance. Another interesting question members might discuss in small groups is "What would we be like if we were the 'ideal' team?" Have each group report its answers and write them on a blackboard or flip pad. Then have the groups meet again and, taking each characteristic one at a time, answer the question, "Is this us?" That is, does the overall team have that characteristic? Again, have the groups report their answers. Finally, for those characteristics where the consensus of the group is no, ask everyone, "Is this characteristic important?" If the consensus is yes, an area needing change has been identified.

The next step is to move the group toward analyzing and solving the problem. To begin, you might put the members into small groups and then assign each group one or more of the characteristics needing change. For each characteristic, have the group answer the question, "Why are we not like this now?" Have them report their answers. In doing so, they will have identified the causes of the problems confronting the team. Then, assign each small group one or more of the characteristics identified as needing change. Ask the groups to develop the longest possible list of ways the group might achieve each characteristic. Practicality should not be a concern; wild and crazy ideas should be encouraged. Have the groups report their lists of possible solutions. For each possible solution reported by a small group, ask the entire group, "Will you do this?" If the general feeling seems affirmative, ask, "How?" Record the answers as the team's action plan.

Finally, to improve relationships among group members, give each individual member enough sheets of paper so that he or she can write a message to every other individual member. Then instruct the participants to write their own name and the name of the participant to whom they are writing at the top of each page. Finally, ask them to provide information related to three statements:

- "If you were to do more of the following, it would help me to do my job better."

- "If you were to do less of or stop doing the following, it would help me to do my job better."

- "If you would continue to do the following, it would help me to do my job better."

When everyone has finished writing, have them exchange messages so that everyone has one message from every other member. Then have each member write his or her own personal action plan, listing commitments for the following statements:

- "I will keep doing the following."
- "I will do less of or stop doing the following."
- "I will continue doing the following."

These statements of personal commitment should be taped to the walls of the meeting room for everyone to see, and members should be allowed to walk around the room and read everyone else's sheet. Copies of the sheets also are kept after the meeting to serve as reminders of the pledges each member made.

In a sense, the team-building meeting is a laissez-faire meeting, but not in the stereotypic sense because the leader actively participates by asking questions, recording answers, and assigning tasks to individuals or small groups. However, all decisions are made by the group with no input from the leader or facilitator, so that all authority is delegated by the leader to them. Indeed, some executives hire consultants specializing in team building to come to the organization and conduct these meetings. In those situations, the executive exerts true laissez-faire leadership.

Business Brief 12.3

Groupthink and the War in Iraq

When weapons of mass destruction (WMD) failed to turn up in Iraq, the Senate Intelligence Committee launched an investigation to determine why the Bush administration believed such weapons existed and posed a direct threat to the United States—a belief that led the United States to launch an attack on Iraq in 2003. In their 2004 report, the committee concluded that "most major judgments about Iraq's alleged nuclear, chemical, and biological weapons programs were either overstated or were not supported by the underlying intelligence reporting."

The committee found that the intelligence community had arrived at incorrect decisions about Iraq's weapons capabilities because of several key elements of "groupthink." At the outset, intelligence agencies advising the administration did so with a bias, suffering from "a collective presumption that Iraq had an active and growing program to develop weapons of mass destruction. This groupthink dynamic led analysts and their managers to interpret ambiguous evidence as conclusive and ignore evidence that pointed to a lack of such a weapons program."

Other groupthink symptoms shown by U.S. intelligence analysts included examining few alternatives, selective gathering of information, pressure to conform within the group or withhold criticism, and collective rationalization. The intelligence community had a tendency to accept information that supported the presumption that Iraq had weapons of mass destruction, but to reject any information that contradicted that conclusion. For example, the failure of United Nations weapons inspectors to find WMD was dismissed as simply ineptitude on the inspectors' part and deceptiveness on the part of the Iraqis.

The presumption that Iraq had active WMD programs was so strong, the committee found, that formalized intelligence community mechanisms established to challenge groupthink, such as "red teams," "devil's advocacy," and other types of alternative or competitive analysis, were not utilized. As a consequence, much of the information provided or cleared by the CIA for inclusion in Secretary of State Colin Powell's February 2003 speech to the United Nations justifying war with Iraq "was overstated, misleading, or incorrect."

Source: Senate Intelligence Committee report on the war in Iraq, July 9, 2004. See MSNBC News, "Full Text: Conclusion of Senate's Iraq Report" [online]. Available: http://msnbc.com/id/5403731 (accessed: December 6, 2004).

SELECTING A LEADERSHIP STYLE

No one approach to leading a group is always best. Each situation must be examined to determine which style of leadership will be most effective. Several factors should be considered when selecting a style (and corresponding meeting agenda). First, *group expectations* are important. What sort of leadership does the group expect you to provide? Some research suggests, for example, that groups expect different leadership styles from men and women (a subject to be addressed in the next section). *Group purposes* should also be taken into account. What is the group trying to achieve? Learning, socializing, or team building require minimum leader control, while communicating specific information to the group is much more directive. *Group methods* are another consideration. Some group processes, such as brainstorming or rating problem priorities, require strict procedural control, while others, such as discussing a problem's underlying causes, can be done with virtually no leadership. *Time* is also a consideration. Participation takes time, while announcements can be given quickly. If a decision must be made at once, autocratic leadership may be required.

In choosing a leadership style, *group members' skills and maturity* should also be considered. Experienced, mature group members require less guidance and control than do new, inexperienced members. Moreover, the more people participate, the better they become at participation. Thus, gradually giving more and more participation to group members is one way of increasing the skills and maturity of the group. *The leader's own skill and confidence* are also factors to be considered. In general, directive leadership is easier to exert than consultative or democratic leadership. The latter two require skill in listening, handling conflict, controlling group interaction, and so on. Thus, as leaders become more skilled, they tend to become more participative over time.

Finally, the kind of leadership style most appropriate in a given situation will depend, in part, on the *need for group support* and the *group's interest and involvement* in the issues under discussion. Some decisions need the active endorsement of the group. In addition, participation in decision making increases the commitment of those making the decision. Simply being told what to do or how to do it minimizes commitment and motivation. And, of course, the more controversial, involving, and interesting the issue being discussed, the more the members of the group will want, and should be encouraged, to participate.

IS GENDER RELEVANT TO GROUP LEADERSHIP?

Many scholars have studied the impact of gender on group leadership. Some have reported that men are more likely than women to emerge, be viewed, or be chosen as leaders. Men frequently receive higher group contribution and influence ratings and are more likely to be liked and sought after as future group partners than are women.[8] In addition, women are more likely to use a collaborative style of leadership, with an emphasis on empowering and enabling others.[9] By contrast, men appear more likely than women to use a directive leadership style and are less inclined to share information.[10] Some small group scholars have argued that men are more likely to engage in task-oriented acts in groups while women are more inclined to perform socioemotional roles. In general, American social and cultural

Highlighting Diversity

Who Will Be Chosen as Leader?

In 1998, Virginia Valian, a professor of psychology and linguistics, published a book concerning upward mobility for women in the workplace. In this book, she reports on the following study:

- The purpose of the study was to determine whether college students would be equally likely to perceive men and women as leaders.

- She asked students to identify the leader in photos of a group sitting around a conference table.

- When the individuals in the group were all men or all women, the students overwhelmingly chose the person seated at the head of the table as the leader.

- When a man was seated at the head of the table in a mixed-sex group, students consistently selected him as the group's leader.

- However, when a woman was seated at the head of the table in a mixed-sex group, students only selected her as the group's leader half of the time.

- What can we conclude from this study?

  — People (or at least college students) seem to assume that men are more likely to be leaders than women.

  — Leader selection may have more to do with stereotypes and preconceived notions than with actual leader behaviors.

Source: Virginia Valian, *Why So Slow? The Advancement of Women* (Cambridge, MA: MIT Press, 1998).

stereotypes associate the performance of task behaviors with group leadership (in the sense of "getting the job done"). So, if women engage in fewer task behaviors than men, at least in U.S. culture, they might be less likely to be viewed as leaders.[11]

Some also cling to the stereotypical belief that women communicate in ways that are less "powerful" than men. University of Illinois communication scholar Kramerae points out that although women are perceived as speaking more "properly" than men, this sort of speech is often unrelated to the possession of power (as in the case of female school teachers and secretaries). Kramerae's research on speech stereotypes suggests that women are perceived as having "control over grammatical forms and to desire non-combative interaction, but men are perceived to have control in a more basic sense over the speech situation."[12] In general, stereotypic features of women's speech have long been viewed as "powerless"—including the use of tag questions and disclaimers (see Highlighting Diversity, which contrasts powerless and powerful speech). However, there may be a catch. Some research suggests that the same exact expressions may be viewed differently when spoken by a man than when used by a woman. For example, a man using a tag question such as, "Well, this plan looks promising to me, don't you think?" may be viewed as deferential and respectful of others' perspectives while a woman using the same expression may be seen as uncertain, lacking confidence, or even incompetent.[13] Double standards have also been associated with the use of a directive communication style. When men communicated decisively and assertively in one study, they were viewed as forceful leaders, while women were viewed as aggressive or bitchy.[14]

Highlighting Diversity

Powerless vs. Powerful Speech

Powerless	Powerful
"Well, I'm no expert in this area, but I still think we ought to. . . ."	"I think we should do this."
"This seems like it would be a pretty good idea to me."	"This is a good idea."
"We ought to adopt this plan, don't you think?"	"Let's move forward with this plan."
"I kind of like that approach."	"This is a terrific approach."
"These figures look excellent, right?"	"These figures look excellent!"
"Sounds good to me, but what do all of you think?"	"Sounds good to me!"
"Well, maybe we should consider this kind of option."	"We should pursue this option."

In spite of the real or perceived differences discussed above, many believe that *men and women are capable of performing equally effectively in leadership positions*. Several scholars have reported no significant differences between the effectiveness evaluations of male and female leaders nor in the ways that they communicate.[15] In one study, for example, subjects were more satisfied in democratically led groups, regardless of leader gender.[16] Both men and women value having the opportunity to be leaders and to exert influence. They are also equally capable of coordinating others' efforts, keeping the group on task, and producing high-quality results.[17]

Finally, some research has made the important distinction between biological sex and psychological gender, advancing the argument that the *androgynous individual* (a person possessing strengths in both the traditional masculine and the traditional feminine communication and behavioral categories) is best suited for leadership. One interesting study, for example, reported subjects' overwhelming preference for human attributes not particularly associated with either gender (such as reliability, truthfulness, and efficiency) when rating *both* the kind of person they would like to work for *and* the kind of person they would hire to supervise others. However, when the same subjects were asked to indicate whether *they* would prefer a male or a female supervisor, 82 percent selected a male.[18] These findings suggest that individuals are attempting to be fair-minded in choosing leaders, but their own personal preferences still lean in the direction of selecting males to supervise them. Over time, these kinds of reactions, attitudes, and biases are likely to change as more and more women and minorities move into leadership positions.

HANDLING PROBLEM PARTICIPANTS

As group leader, you will frequently encounter group members whose behavior is not helpful to the group. And as group leader, it will become your responsibility to deal with these people. On occasion, group pressure or some assertive group member will bring the problem participant back into line, but as a rule, the group will look to you, literally and figuratively, to take some action.

While it is impossible to anticipate every bizarre behavior that can occur in a group, we have compiled some common problem behaviors and some techniques whereby a leader can address them. Problem behaviors fall into two types: members who talk too much and prevent others from participating and members who don't talk or participate enough. Specific problem types in each category are listed next, along with some strategies you might use to deal with them.

Members Who Talk Too Much

Show-offs know a great deal about the topic and are eager to prove it. They dominate the interaction out of a desire to exhibit their in-depth knowledge, and in so doing, they prevent everyone else from talking. To deal with a show-off, you might politely interrupt with a summarizing statement and ask someone else a direct question or interrupt with an observation: "Ken, you've made some interesting points, but I want everyone to have a chance. Let's hear what Tanya thinks about this." In addition, you could assign the member some specific project, such as gathering information or developing recommendations, and then have him present it to the group for their discussion.

Quick and helpful members know all the right answers, but in providing them, they keep other members from participating. Unlike the show-off, their motive is not to exhibit skill and win approval but simply to help the group. You might manage such members by tactfully interrupting them and asking direct questions of other members, by talking about the interaction ("Juan, I really appreciate your ideas. Now let's see what someone else might contribute."), or by assigning the member a communication role, such as "idea evaluator." Before a meeting or during a break, for example, you might approach the member and say, "You really know a lot about this. Would you mind helping me evaluate the ideas that the other members contribute? We'll get their ideas, and then you indicate which seems best." Generally, the member will appreciate having such a clear and important function.

Ramblers babble incessantly during meetings and invariably take the group away from the topic and onto something else. Other group members are quick to recognize and react to this sort of person: As soon as she begins to speak, they look at each other or cast their eyes heavenward out of frustration. The leader must step in. For example, when the rambler stops for a breath, thank her, rephrase one of her statements to make it relevant to the topic, and move back to that topic with a question to the group. Alternatively, you might interrupt and ask a direct question of someone else. Finally, you could refer to the agenda or, if the topic is written on the blackboard or an easel pad, point to the board or pad and ask the member which topic she is discussing. This method is potentially embarrassing to the member, however, and could cause anger or resentment.

Arguers constantly disagree with others, try to make trouble, and seem generally hostile. Such behavior disrupts the group, and it may be motivated by any number of things: frustration at not being the leader, dislike for the other group members, general crankiness, and so on. To prevent this behavior from upsetting and frustrating the other members, the leader must deal with it relatively quickly.

You could seat the disruptive member next to you, making it easier for you to control him and to break in when arguments begin. You also might talk with the member privately and describe the behaviors you have observed. Ask the member to tell you what problems or concerns he has. Finally, if all else fails, you might privately ask the member to leave the group.

Side conversationalists insist on conducting private meetings of their own. Usually, a group will have two such problem members who will be seen whispering or muttering to each other during the meeting. Such behavior is disruptive to other members and distracts these two participants from the group proceedings. To deal with this situation, you could direct a question to one of the conversationalists: "Kim, what do you think of that?" Kim either will have to answer, which automatically brings her back into the discussion, or she will have no idea what you are talking about, and her embarrassment will keep her involved in the discussion, at least for a while. In addition, you could talk privately to the conversationalists and express your concern about their behavior. Finally, if the same two people continually converse during meetings, assign seats for the next meeting with these two members at opposite sides of the group.

Complainers blame the group's problems on things not under the control of the group: management, company policy, the economy, and so on. They would rather gripe about the evils of these things than deal with the problem the group faces. In addition, they adopt a "what's the use" attitude that may cause apathy among other group members. To manage a complainer, you might address her directly and point out that some things cannot be changed by the group. Rather, the goal of the group is to operate as best it can under the present system. Alternatively, you might ask the member for a solution to the problem: "Well, Carol, what do you think we should do about the economy?" When she answers, "We can't do anything about it," ask, "Then should we just give up and go home?" She and other members will say no, enabling you to say, "Then what should we do?" In so doing, you will bring the group back to the topic and illustrate the futility of the member's complaints.

Selfish members have a problem of their own that they want to discuss. They continually bring the group back to that problem, thus moving the group away from the topic at hand. To handle a selfish member, you could have the group discuss the member's problem. Get their opinions and recommendations, then return to the original topic. In addition, you might talk about the behavior and suggest that the member's problem be considered when the group has completed its current task: "John, you keep raising this problem. How about if we hold off on it for a while and talk about it when we have finished what we're doing?" Then deal with the member's problem when the group finishes the topic at hand. Finally, you could talk privately with the member about his problem and see if a solution can be developed outside the group.

Poor speakers lack communication skills: they speak too softly, do not speak clearly, express ideas poorly, and so on. The ideas may be good, but no one can tell because the member is inaudible or incomprehensible. To assist this sort of group member, repeat her ideas in your own words: "In other words, you're suggesting that. . . ." In addition, you may need to repeat the member's comments for everyone to hear, or ask the member to repeat her comments while she stands, faces the group, and speaks loudly. However, do not use this strategy if it is likely to embarrass the member.

Highlighting Diversity

Gender Matters

The movement by many organizations to teams has been particularly troublesome from a diversity perspective, according to Leigh Thompson, an organizational behavior professor at Northwestern University's J. L. Kellogg Graduate School of Management. "The research suggests women are viewed more harshly than men," she said. "Even people who say out loud they don't carry prejudices will revert to classic sex-role thinking in a group dynamic. In any team situation, there is an early natural status competition based on gender, age, and race."

Source: Janet Kidd Stewart, "Teams Don't Always Work," *Chicago Tribune*, July 5, 1998, sec. 13, 7.

Squabblers are two or more members who simply dislike one another and argue frequently as a result. You must be careful to distinguish between personality conflicts, which are disruptive to the group, and topic-based conflicts, which are based on real disagreements over the topic. When two members argue over several different conflicts and give off nonverbal cues indicating real dislike for each other, the leader needs to step in. For example, interrupt their argument with a direct question to one of them. This forces that member to talk to you, enabling you then to get other members involved in the interaction. Or you could summarize the comments each has made and then move on to another topic. Third, you might seat the two so that it is difficult for them to see one another. Finally, if other strategies fail, you might meet privately with the two of them, describe how their behaviors are affecting the group, and involve them in solving their own conflict.

An article in *Communication Briefings* identified a few more types of difficult group members, along with some suggested methods you might use to handle such people when they try to seize control of a meeting.[19]

- *Monopolizers* interrupt often, ramble, and repeat themselves because they enjoy hearing themselves talk. To manage them, don't argue but don't hesitate to confront them. Wait for them to take a breath and interrupt them by name. Note that they have made their point and immediately invite someone else to comment on the topic.

- *Distracters* also seek attention, and to get it they may bring up irrelevant topics that waste time. To handle such distractions, firmly halt the distracter, restate the meeting purpose, and ask the members to answer a specific question that gets them refocused on the main topic.

- *Skeptics* continually find fault with what everyone else says. To manage them, have a friendly talk with them before the meeting and firmly say what behaviors you expect. If that fails, firmly cut them off during the meeting by repeating that you want solutions, not criticisms, and then ask them to contribute.

- *Snipers* use snide comments and quips, often in quiet stage whispers, to undercut others. It may be effective to shine the spotlight on them by asking them to share their comments with everyone. Often they will decline to do so out of embarrassment and discontinue their sniping.

Certainly, there are other types of members who talk too much. However, the basic strategies described above can be applied to any member who prevents others from talking. The key is to determine the motives underlying the member's behaviors and then take action appropriate to those motives.

Members Who Do Not Talk

Uninterested members simply do not care about the group or its topic. As a result, they sit silently, perhaps looking out the window or doing something of their own (like writing notes or reading a book). To deal with this situation, you might direct a question to the member; ask for experiences as they relate to the topic. Be careful, however, to ask something the member can answer; otherwise, you add embarrassment to the apathy he is already feeling. In addition, you could assign the member specific responsibility. Have him collect information, list possible solutions, and so on. Be careful of giving that person some task vital to the group, however; the member might not come through on the task assigned. Other approaches are to meet privately with the member to discuss what the problem might be, form groups only on a voluntary basis (allowing uninterested members to leave), or seat the member in the middle of the group so that all interaction occurs around him (apathetic members usually try to sit at the back or on the fringes of the group, where they go largely unnoticed). Finally, you could play the devil's advocate: Ask the member for his opinion, and when it is given, disagree. By starting an argument with the member, you draw him into the group, and you may stir the member's interest.

Listeners are interested in the topic but prefer to listen rather than speak. They do nothing disruptive and may even provide helpful nonverbal reinforcement (head nods, attentive posture) to those who talk. But they do not contribute any ideas. To build a listener's participation, you might ask her to give an opinion whenever the member shows either agreement or disagreement nonverbally: "Susan, you seem to agree with Nancy's point. Why do you feel that way?" This sort of question is useful because you know Susan has an answer (she has been showing agreement nonverbally) and because your question draws her into the discussion. You also could direct questions to the member or, if you know something about the member, try to bring the topic around to an area in which the member has some experience. Then ask the member to recount those experiences. Finally, you could simply accept her preference to listen.

Shy group members simply are not very assertive. Nonverbal cues help you to identify them: They occasionally seem about to speak, but then some other member begins talking and they remain quiet. Directing a question to the member (be sure it is a question he can answer) can be helpful, or you might frequently ask the member for his agreement. By turning to him for approval, you increase the member's standing in the eyes of the other group members, making them more likely to involve the member as well. In addition, when the member seems to want to talk, call on him, even if it means cutting off a more assertive member who has just begun to speak.

Fearful members suffer stage fright in group situations. They are afraid of ridicule or failure, or of seeming stupid in the group's eyes. Rather than risk rejection or disapproval, they simply sit quietly. To gain a fearful member's participation,

DILBERT

DILBERT © by Scott Adams; reprinted by permission of United Feature Syndicate, Inc.

you could ask her a question that you know she can answer and then praise the answer given. In addition, you might turn frequently to the member for agreement or approval, thus building her status in the eyes of other members. Finally, you might seat the member next to you in an effort to build an association between the two of you. Your status in the group will reflect well on her.

Again, there are many other reasons why members choose not to participate. However, by controlling the overly talkative members and drawing out the non-participants, you can equalize members' contributions to the group interaction.

FOLLOW-UP

Whenever a meeting has been concluded, regardless of the style used to conduct that meeting, some follow-up must occur. At least three things need to be done: First, the group should be asked to examine their own proceedings and evaluate how effective the meeting was. Such evaluation can be done at the end of the meeting (by asking the participants to take a moment to express their thoughts in writing or to discuss briefly how well they thought the meeting went) or some time after the meeting (by distributing questionnaires about the meeting to the members and asking them to return the completed questionnaires to the leader). As a brief, informal approach to evaluating a meeting, we have found it useful to ask the participants to write their answers to three questions:

1. What part (or parts) of the meeting did you like most?

2. What part (or parts) of the meeting did you like least?

3. How might future meetings of this type be improved?

More complicated, but thorough, is the "Meeting Effectiveness Questionnaire" shown in figure 12.1. By having members complete the questionnaire, the leader can get quantitative feedback on each element of the group's proceedings. Regardless of the form and timing of feedback, groups should almost always be asked to evaluate the quality of the meeting in which they participated.

Second, the actions of the meeting should be reported to those who need to be advised. The report need not necessarily be a long set of notes or minutes but should contain enough information that those who could not attend or who will be affected by the results will know what was done and what was planned. In our view, such reports serve as useful reminders to the group participants and as notice of the group's achievements to other groups and individuals throughout the organization. Thus, we recommend that after every important meeting, a report be distributed both to the attendees and to anyone else who might have even a passing interest in the group's actions.

Circle the number that best describes how you feel about each statement below.

Key: 1 = Strongly Disagree; 2 = Disagree; 3 = Neutral; 4 = Agree; 5 = Strongly Agree

1. I understood the propose of the meeting clearly.   1   2   3   4   5

2. The persons most directly involved with the purpose of the meeting were present.   1   2   3   4   5

3. All members had the opportunity to participate by expressing their views and opinions.   1   2   3   4   5

4. I had sufficient time and information to prepare for the meeting.   1   2   3   4   5

5. The leader of the meeting kept things on track and minimized time wasted on side issues.   1   2   3   4   5

6. I understand what the results of the meeting mean for me.   1   2   3   4   5

7. I support the results of the meeting.   1   2   3   4   5

8. The leader of the meeting was open to all ideas presented.   1   2   3   4   5

9. I understood what was expected of me at the meeting.   1   2   3   4   5

10. Ideas were presented clearly and were easily understood by everyone present.   1   2   3   4   5

11. The participants seemed to want to work for the good of the group.   1   2   3   4   5

12. At the conclusion of the meeting, it was obvious to me that everyone knew what was expected of him or her.   1   2   3   4   5

13. The proper amount of time was allocated to this meeting.   1   2   3   4   5

14. The agenda or topics of the meeting were clear and easy to follow.   1   2   3   4   5

15. The meeting facilities were comfortable and appropriate.   1   2   3   4   5

16. Participation was spread evenly among the members; everyone talked about the same amount.   1   2   3   4   5

17. Conflicts between group members were resolved quickly and to everyone's satisfaction.   1   2   3   4   5

18. Decisions were made in ways that were fair to all group members.   1   2   3   4   5

19. Members dealt courteously with one another.   1   2   3   4   5

20. Each participant and all visual aids used during the meeting were easily visible to everyone.   1   2   3   4   5

In the future, we might improve similar meetings by:

Figure 12.1   Meeting effectiveness questionnaire

Third, the leader must check to be sure that commitments made during the meeting are carried out. Are people doing what they said they would do? Are they staying on schedule? Have they encountered new or unanticipated problems? Are there things the leader is committed to do for the group (such as get back to them with an answer)? In effect, the leader must monitor him or herself and the progress of the members as they do the things agreed to. Such monitoring might be achieved by speaking with members individually, asking for written progress reports, making occasional telephone calls to members, or calling another meeting.

Clearly, the work done by a group does not stop when the meeting concludes. Often, in fact, the meeting is only the beginning of the real effort. Effective, thorough follow-up is vital to the continuation of the things the group meeting began.

CONDUCTING MEETINGS VIA TECHNOLOGY

With the advent of new technology for communicating within organizations, it is not surprising to find that meetings are taking place through technological channels as well. Telephone conference calls have been commonplace for years, of course, and videoconferences are growing in popularity as well. In addition, a new technology called "spontaneous area networking" enables participants to connect their PCs instantly with others in the room and with people who are off-site. This technology allows anyone to make and record notes on "whiteboards" projected on a screen then download them to individual computers.[20]

Cybermeetings are meetings involving participants in scattered locations linked by videoconferencing equipment or e-mail. Because of decentralization, a projected increase in the number of meetings, and the incidence of crash projects that require people to interact intensely (sometimes for weeks or months), cybermeetings probably will see increasing usage. Videoconferencing equipment on desktops will eliminate the need to run to another floor, to another building, or onto a waiting jet. In addition, as we discussed in the last chapter, Group Support Systems make it possible for people to work together even if they are scattered all over the world. As groups increasingly use new technologies, some believe that new group member roles will emerge (see Highlighting Technology).

Teleconferencing is a useful way to conduct meetings involving participants across the globe. If you are involved in organizing and leading these meetings, you may want to follow these guidelines:

- Use the best equipment possible; the quality of sound varies tremendously.
- Allow individual participants ample time to learn to use their technology.
- The group should choose a conference leader and rotate that leadership.
- Written agendas should be distributed to everyone in advance, perhaps via e-mail.
- The group should decide in advance how long the conference will last.
- The conference leader should state the goals of the discussion at the beginning and review any updates since the previous teleconference.
- The leader should encourage everyone to participate, calling on particularly quiet individuals or encouraging them later with a phone call or e-mail.

Highlighting Technology

New Member Roles for High-Tech Groups

- ***The wizard.*** The primary goal of the wizard should be to help make collaborative technologies easy to use so that meeting participants aren't overwhelmed. The wizard can facilitate the use of the technology so that people weak in technology can concentrate more on the work and less on the machines.
- ***The scribe.*** Typing into technology may frustrate people who absorb information visually and verbally, and it may stifle creative thought. Using an assigned or paid scribe may help keep everyone on track.
- ***Express mail carrier.*** To encourage feedback, everyone in the group may play express mail carrier by using the anonymous remailer in the intranet (company e-mail system) to send the boss complaints, suggestions, and ideas.

Source: James Creighton and James Adams, "CyberMeeting: How to Link People and Technology in Your Organization" (AMACOM, 1998). This idea is attributed to Michael Michalko.

- The group should be sensitive to time zone differences; since someone will always be inconvenienced, it may be best to rotate the times meetings are held.
- Someone should write and e-mail to the others a brief summary of the main points covered during the conference.[21]

Ultimately, the success of any group technology depends on two factors: *accessibility* and *use*. These factors, in turn, are influenced by the management style of those in positions of leadership as well as the general culture of the organization. Employees will use a technology to communicate with team members and significant others if the technology is readily accessible and if those with whom they need to communicate routinely use it. When multiple communication channels are available, team members may need to agree on which technologies will be used when and for what purposes. In addition, if new technologies are to be empowering, team members must have some common understanding of mutual expectations and the "rules" for using such technologies. For instance, if one individual in the group fails to check her e-mail messages regularly, she may miss meetings, come poorly prepared, or simply end up being left out of many communicative exchanges with fellow group members.

Another problem associated with the use of electronic communication channels is the potential for becoming overwhelmed by junk mail. For example, groupware (which takes e-mail a step further by adding personal productivity tools and multiuser data management) forces organizations to cope with an increased flow of information. Providing employees with access to networks also tends to increase the volume and speed of communication, some of which is inevitably unwanted. David Daniels, formerly of MetLife, argues, "If e-mail is like drinking from a straw, then groupware is like drinking from a fire hose. There's definitely a risk of becoming overwhelmed by information that may be irrelevant."[22]

Depending on the circumstances, then, technology can either help or hinder group communication. In a series of experiments conducted at Carnegie Mellon University, researchers compared how small groups make decisions by using

One way that technology can be used to support group meetings is through teleconferencing. When the leader is competent and participants are given adequate time to feel comfortable with the technology, productive meetings can occur with group members scattered around the world.

computer conferences, electronic mail, and face-to-face discussion. They found that using an electronic medium caused participants to talk more frankly and more equally, with more proposals for actions generated, than the traditional meeting setting. In face-to-face group discussions, usually a few people dominated the discussion. However, they also found that the increased democracy associated with electronic interactions interfered with decision making and increased conflict. In particular, decisions made via electronic mail or computer conferences were made more slowly, and participants tended to express more extreme opinions and to vent their anger more openly (a phenomenon called "flaming") than when they sat together and talked.[23]

When groups use technology to communicate, they need to be aware that different technologies variously affect the richness and speed of group communication. While technology can assist groups in overcoming the constraints of space and time, it also demands that groups (and their leaders) learn and understand it so that they may faithfully appropriate its structures and realize its intended benefits.

SUMMARY

At one time or another, most of us find ourselves in the role of group leader in our organizations and/or in our communities. We may not be managers or administrators in the formal sense, but we are leaders in that we plan and organize meetings, call and arrange for meeting rooms, and conduct the meeting when the other members arrive. Sometimes we chair a meeting on a one-shot basis, especially if we are working with an ad hoc group. More likely, we chair an ongoing committee, which may continue for months, or even years. Our ability to manage these meetings effectively will influence many important outcomes, such as our own professional well-being. Moreover, when we lead a group to make sound decisions, we make an important contribution to the organization or community as a whole.

Whenever we find ourselves in a small group leadership position, we will function more effectively if we think carefully about the meaning of leadership, prepare carefully, follow a plan or agenda, and understand something about the principles of group dynamics discussed earlier in this book. We will need to reflect thoughtfully on the style of leadership with which we feel most comfortable and that seems most fitting for the group, task, and context. Although most group members will approach the meetings constructively, anticipating how to manage problem participants is wise. Following up on meetings is also part of the leader's job.

As you plan to work with groups, you will encounter increasingly abundant opportunities to use technological support, ranging from videoconferencing to groupware. These support systems can be constructive and empowering, so long as they are used judiciously. In addition, you are increasingly likely to chair meetings of multicultural and mixed gender groups. Such diversity can present challenges and conflicts; but if well managed, it can also become a great source of creativity and other excellent meeting outcomes.

Questions for Discussion

1. Why have meetings gained such a bad reputation in many modern organizations?
2. Why is it important to an organization or a community to have effective meetings?
3. When should you avoid calling a meeting?
4. How do the facilities in which a meeting is held affect the success of that meeting?
5. In what types of situations are autocratic meetings most desirable? Consultative meetings? Democratic meetings? Laissez-faire meetings?
6. Why should a majority vote be avoided as a decision-making device? How might the cultural composition of the group make a difference?
7. Why are team-building meetings important in an organization?
8. To what extent and in what ways is gender relevant to group leadership? Be specific.
9. As a leader, how can you judge whether a group member's actions are harmful to the group as a whole?
10. What are some of the most challenging kinds of group participants? How might you handle each?
11. What factors help determine whether technology assists or hinders group work?

Exercises

1. Write an announcement for a meeting (create your own purpose, list of attendees, and so on).

2. Conduct a mock meeting using one of these leadership approaches: autocratic, democratic, consultative, or laissez-faire. Then have members complete the "Meeting Effectiveness Questionnaire" (figure 12.1). Ask members to report on and explain their answers for each item on the questionnaire.

3. Conduct a mock meeting. At the beginning of the meeting, assign some of the problem-member roles to several group participants. Do not announce which member has which role. Assign a leader to conduct the meeting. At the meeting's end, discuss how effectively the leader handled each problem participant.

4. Choose an issue or problem that is having an adverse impact on your community (e.g., hate crimes). If you were going to organize a town meeting to address this issue, what groups would you want to have represented on the organizing committee? Why should they be involved? How would you go about motivating them to participate and obtaining media coverage for the meeting?

Case Application 12.1   Changing Graduation Requirements

For students pursuing a degree in the School of Business at the University of the Southern Pacific (USP), graduation requirements for undergraduates have remained unchanged for 10 years. Now, however, a special committee (composed of both faculty and students) has been established to examine the current requirements and likely initiate some changes.

Committee members are aware of certain widely perceived problems with the current system. Among them are the following:

- Faculty complain that even seniors cannot write well.
- Students' oral communication skills are perceived by faculty to be deficient.
- Students can obtain the business degree without having been introduced to another culture or a foreign language.
- In spite of faculty complaints about student skill deficits, grade inflation is rampant—B is considered an average grade.
- Students complain that the faculty, on the whole, are not very good at teaching. Most are more interested in their research and their graduate students.
- Students complain that too many graduate students are used as graders, discussion leaders, and even lecturers.

The committee is also working in an organizational environment that includes the following factors:

- The dean of the School of Business is concerned about dropping enrollments in business. Ten years ago, 55 percent of entering freshmen declared the intention of majoring in business. Now that figure has dropped to 30 percent.

- With globalization being an increasing reality in the business world, faculty agree that business students should be required to complete a foreign language and/or culture studies requirement. However, there are complications. First, many students currently choose business to avoid the foreign language requirement of the School of Liberal Arts and Sciences. Thus, adding that kind of new requirement to the business degree could lead to further enrollment problems.

- The state legislature (USP is a public, state-supported institution) is pressing the university to create an assessment system. If the university does not develop its own assessment system, then the legislature is threatening to create one—and mandate its use.

- Both the legislature and the newly elected president of USP's board of trustees are very concerned about the quality of teaching, including such issues as whether graduate students who teach (or help teach) are appropriately trained and supervised, how much teaching faculty do, whether faculty who teach well are rewarded appropriately, and so on.

Questions

1. Assume that you have been asked to cochair this committee. What would you do to prepare yourself and others for the first meeting?
2. What approach to conducting meetings would you use and why?
3. How would you organize an agenda for the first meeting?
4. What kinds of problems would you anticipate and how would you handle them?
5. What actions would you take to follow up on the meeting?

PART 5

PUBLIC COMMUNICATION

Public speaking, which is the best way to motivate a large group, is entirely different from private conversation. A speaker may be well informed, but if he hasn't thought out exactly what he wants to say today, to this audience, he has no business taking up other people's valuable time.

—Lee Iacocca, *Iacocca: An Autobiography*

13

Preparing and Supporting Your Speech

After reading this chapter, you should be able to:

❏ Select an appropriate speech topic based on your own interests, the interests of your audience, the demands of the situation, and your organizational affiliation

❏ Decide on your speech's purpose, in broad terms, as well as in terms of the specific audience response you are seeking

❏ Conduct research, investigating your topic by visiting the library, exploring the Internet, interviewing for information, and reflecting on your own resources

❏ Choose effective evidence to support your ideas

❏ Draw sound conclusions from the evidence you have found

Speaking in public is an increasingly common organizational communication activity. While administrators, board directors, and other executives have always made speeches, today's professional men and women of varied occupations are called on to speak with increasing regularity. Consider these examples: (1) a lawyer talks to an organization of concerned parents about the legality of textbook censorship; (2) an obstetrician informs a group of expectant mothers about alternative methods of childbirth; (3) an accountant speaks to a local Rotary Club, giving members some tips on how to file their income tax returns; (4) an educator addresses a group of fellow teachers in an effort to get them to unionize; and (5) the director of a shelter for victims of domestic violence speaks to a group of concerned citizens about the growing problem of abuse within their community. Clearly, regardless of your occupation—whether you are an educator, a social worker, a realtor, or a salesperson—you are likely to be asked to make some speeches throughout your professional life. In addition, as an engaged citizen, you may choose to or be called on to speak out, both formally and informally, in response to problems and opportunities that surround you in the workplace and in your community.

Preview

In this chapter we will address the first steps in preparing to speak. As a speaker, your first challenge is to choose an appropriate topic and to decide on your speech's purpose. Why are you speaking? What do you hope to accomplish? The next step is to investigate the topic, conducting research to find accurate and pertinent information and to assist you in forming and developing your ideas. As you discover information, you will want to select effective supporting evidence to substantiate your arguments and make them more compelling. Through judicious reasoning, you will strive to draw sound conclusions based on that evidence.

THE IMPORTANCE OF PUBLIC SPEAKING IN PROFESSIONAL AND CIVIC LIFE

Many believe that the most critical skills any prospective organizational employee can possess may be the ability to speak effectively and write clearly. Economist Peter Drucker exemplifies this view when he notes that colleges teach the *one thing* that is most valuable for the future employee to know: the ability to organize and express ideas in writing and in speaking.[1] Unfortunately, many bright young men and women graduate from college every year without having mastered these vital skills. In fact, it is often only when they are confronted with the realities of their first jobs that they recognize how often they will be asked to convey their thoughts in writing and to speak articulately—at conferences, in briefings, and during all kinds of meetings.

In addition to speaking in workplace and professional settings, everyone will encounter many opportunities to address matters of concern in the community in which he or she lives. Perhaps you are already aware of such opportunities. Does the town or city where you are attending college have a problem with homelessness? How about drugs in the schools? How many eligible students at your university vote? How accessible are restaurants and other public buildings to the

---

Highlighting Civic Engagement

The Penn State Model

- The Center for Public Speaking and Civic Engagement at Penn State University seeks to engage students in public dialogue. Among the first of its kind in the United States, the center offers students a resource to hone their public speaking skills in situations such as job interviews and conferences. The central goal, however, is to teach students how to be more active and influential in matters of civic concern—on campus, in the community or state, and in the nation and the world.

- Through participation in the center, students have learned more about how to enter local and national conversations. For example, some students became involved in:

  — Deliberations about increased parking costs and the opening of the Hooters' restaurant in State College (where Penn State is located)

  — Educational reform, presidential politics, and trade policies

- Professor J. Michael Hogan, Professor of Communication Arts and Sciences and a center faculty affiliate, points out, "We believe that *citizenship* ought to be a major component of education in the 21st century. We hope to create new spaces for public deliberation—the kind that encourages speech designed not just to defeat political adversaries but to aid citizens in their common search for understanding."

- This kind of public deliberation invites sustained public discussion in which all voices are heard and the very best decisions are made. Hogan notes that the center emphasizes the ethical responsibility of students "to speak out intelligently and thoughtfully on matters of public importance and to listen to other viewpoints."

Source: "Center for Public Speaking and Civic Engagement Aims to Involve Students in Public Dialogue" (March 2002) [online]. Available: http://www.psu.edu/ur/2002/centerpublicspeaking.html (accessed: May 21, 2004).

disabled? Is your university or your community plagued by hate crimes? These are issues that take you beyond the confines of the classroom and invite you to become involved in the affairs of the greater community at a local, state, national, or even international level. Throughout this book, we have emphasized the importance of civic engagement. When you choose to speak in public on behalf of a cause that you believe in, your *advocacy* may function as a compelling form of civic engagement.

SELECTING THE SPEECH TOPIC

If you have become involved in a community controversy, you may elect to deliver a speech or make a formal public statement. On other occasions, you may be asked or invited to make a speech. When the latter happens, you are typically faced with one of two basic situations: (1) the topic is suggested (or assigned, as in your classroom), or (2) you are told to speak about anything of your choice (perhaps within some rather broad parameters). Often, a topic is suggested that is directly related to your job. Automotive executives are asked to speak about the impact of the sharp rise in gasoline prices on their production and sales of SUVs; journalists are invited to discuss media coverage of controversial world events, such as the prison abuse scandals in Iraq; and teachers are asked to talk about how technology has impacted teaching and learning in their classrooms.

For many speakers, having to choose the speech's subject presents a challenge. Though the possible topics appear endless, no one topic may seem quite appropriate. Occasionally, speakers may panic when they can't think of a good topic, and they may be tempted to do something unethical, such as *plagiarizing* someone else's ideas. The Highlighting Ethics box on the following page defines plagiarism and offers guidelines for preventing it.

As you begin to choose your speech topic, you will want to remain committed to ethical communication throughout the speech preparation process. You can begin by approaching potential topics systematically and examining them in relationship to four perspectives: *personal, audience, situational,* and *organizational.*

Personal Perspective

Certainly the richest source of topic ideas resides within you as an individual. Begin, then, with some assessment of your personal knowledge, experiences, attitudes, and beliefs. Speeches vary in purpose; yet each is essentially a personal statement from you as a speaker to others who choose or are asked to listen. You may want to select a topic about which you already know a good deal but would like to learn more. Building on your initial interest, you may need to conduct research. After you have worked within your chosen field for some time, you will develop considerable expertise and insights into accounting, teaching, marketing, or public relations. When this happens, you may only need to reflect on what you already know and organize your thoughts into some effective, appealing strategy. Most commonly, however, both self-reflection and research will be needed.

Your personal interest in a subject may evolve from intellectual enthusiasm and curiosity as well as from firsthand experiences. If you have volunteered for many hours with the Boys and Girls Club or played soccer all through college,

Highlighting Ethics

Avoiding Plagiarism

- The speaker who plagiarizes presents ideas derived from another source as new and original. That source could be a magazine article, a book, or another student's outline.
- Temptations abound.
  - Other students may offer you their outlines.
  - Sororities and fraternities often maintain files of speech outlines and papers.
  - You may find a magazine article that seems to pretty much "say it all."
  - Material is for sale on the Internet.
- Plagiarism is *a form of unethical communication* and is considered a very serious offense.
  - It is viewed as a form of academic dishonesty by colleges and universities and can lead to severe penalties, including cheating Fs, expulsion from the university, and blocked admission to graduate and professional schools.
  - Internet sites now allow instructors to cross-check topics.
  - Some communication departments maintain files of old speech outlines, organized by topic, for instructors to consult.
- At a practical level, *it's easy to avoid plagiarizing* by following these guidelines:
  - Begin preparing your speech early—then, if you have trouble choosing a topic or finding information, you can seek assistance.
  - Pick a topic that genuinely interests you and that you will enjoy working with as you prepare your speech.
  - Conduct careful, thorough research.
  - In your speech, cite the sources you used.
  - Be sure to identify quotations for your listeners as you deliver your speech.
- *When in doubt, ask!* Your instructor can tell you if there is any problem with the way you are using information and ideas obtained from various sources.
- Avoiding plagiarism is part of *a commitment to ethical communication*—growing from your own values and character and a desire to interact with your listeners in a truthful and forthright way.

you may want to tap those experiences in choosing your speech topics. In addition, all students have had certain kinds of secondary experiences. You have read books, seen movies, and listened to lectures and speeches. You have read newspapers and news magazines, watched television, and explored the Internet. You have listened to your professors and exchanged ideas with your peers.

Sometimes conducting a *self-inventory* of your interests and experiences can be helpful in choosing a speech topic. Following are some factors to consider as you go through a thorough, thoughtful self-assessment:

- Educational background (especially anything interesting or unusual)
- Jobs held (and skills developed through jobs)
- Memorable childhood experiences

- Travel (familiar or interesting places visited)
- Special training
- Organizational affiliations
- Volunteer activities
- Hobbies and leisure activities
- Books or authors you have especially enjoyed
- People who have influenced your thinking and values (friends, writers, family members, political figures, teachers, leaders)
- Community issues/problems that concern you

The Perspective of the Audience

While your personal interests, knowledge, and experiences are crucial to topic selection, equally vital are the concerns and interests of the audience. Select a subject about which the audience has some information but would enjoy, needs to, or is eager to learn more. You will need to find ways to connect your interests and values with your listeners. No speaker can succeed without the cooperation, goodwill, and interest of his or her listeners. Choosing the speech topic is the first step in establishing that connection. Successful communication can only occur when the speaker is *audience-centered* and when reciprocal exchange occurs.

In choosing a subject, there are a number of audience-related dimensions to be considered. At the most basic level, contemplate potential subjects in relationship to the *audience's demographic characteristics*, including age, gender, socioeconomic status, and educational level. This kind of information helps you select a topic, while offering some clues as to how to handle a given topic tastefully and persuasively. For example, the topic "Health Care Options" is relevant to everyone. But if you were addressing a group of young married couples, you would likely focus on different aspects of this broad topic than if you were addressing a group of retirees.

Seeking information about the social, economic, political, and religious beliefs of the audience is also important. Such knowledge may provide insights into the needs and values of the audience. With persuasive speaking, in particular, an assessment of such values is crucial. In a classroom setting, you may conduct an audience survey to help you gauge audience values and beliefs. If you are speaking outside the classroom, you may want to get in touch with the person who invited you to speak and ask for his or her "take" on the audience. It is important to avoid making stereotypic assumptions about an audience based on minimal information. If you joined a speaker's bureau, for example, and were invited to speak to a religious organization, you would want to learn a great deal more about the nature of that organization. An audience of Unitarian Universalists is likely to take a far more liberal stance on most social issues than an audience of American Baptists, for example; and most major denominations contain both liberal and conservative branches. So, exploring the *particular* needs, values, and interests of each audience is essential.

Finally, in selecting a topic, you might consider the audience's *immediate background*. Some people share concerns and have common interests in problems simply because of the context or setting in which they find themselves. As a student enrolled in a basic business and professional communication course, you will often address your classmates. Your audience in this instance represents a diversity of religions, political views, abilities, and socioeconomic levels. But because your classmates share the bond of attending college, they have common interests. Such topics as grade inflation, the job market, the university's grading system, graduation requirements, faculty evaluation, and the university's reputation would all be potentially relevant to them.

Now that we have entered the twenty-first century, we know that audiences are increasingly diverse. No longer can we assume, for example, that a management group will be mostly male. Nor can we assume that most listeners will share the same ethnic heritage or cultural background. Pointing your listeners toward the features of your topic, proposal, or action plan that they all can connect with, regardless of their diversity, is a critical first step to your effectiveness as a public speaker.

The Situational Perspective

Every public speech is given in some context. Right now, your particular speaking context is the business and professional communication classroom. Your instructor may suggest topics that are more or less appropriate to the classroom setting. Certainly, there will be specific constraints associated with each speaking assignment. You may be asked to deliver a speech of tribute, an informative technical report, a panel presentation, or a speech of advocacy. In the future, you will speak in contexts as diverse as workshops, award ceremonies, city council meetings, and weddings. Sometimes topics will grow directly from the occasion. For instance, let us say you decide to attend a meeting of the city council because the group is discussing the proposed expansion of a shopping mall. You are opposed to the expansion, and you are there expressly to air your views on this predetermined topic. You wouldn't consider (nor would you be allowed) to speak on topics that were not on the council's planned agenda.

In every speaking situation, there will also be *time constraints*. In the classroom, you will be asked to deliver speeches as short as 3–5 minutes or as long as 10–12 minutes. In the workplace and in the community, however, speeches are far more variable in length. Professional presentations may range from 15–30 minutes (for example, ministers' sermons, luncheon speakers' presentations, and commencement addresses). If you were conducting a workshop, you might speak (in an interactive way) for several hours. Many community action panels will last for an hour or more, with speakers talking from 5–15 minutes, depending on the number of panelists and the time allotted for audience questions. Anticipating and adapting to these situational time constraints is critical. If you overstay your welcome, your listeners may turn you off (or slip out of the room). But, if you talk for 5 minutes and the audience anticipated a 20-minute presentation, you may be viewed as ill-prepared or lacking in substance.

As you begin to prepare for each speech, then, you will want to take the situational opportunities and constraints into consideration. Here are some questions you might ask yourself:

- Is a topic suggested by the theme of a conference?
- Does the type of occasion demand a particular type of speech (eulogy, toast, acceptance speech)?

- Will others be speaking on the same program? How will I position my comments relative to theirs?
- Should my topic be narrowed in scope because of limited speaking time? Should it be enlarged because of a generous time allotment?
- What other situational factors might I want to consider in this particular speaking context?

The Organizational Perspective

The final perspective from which you might consider topic selection is that of the organization you are representing. When you are called on to make a public speech, it is often because of your affiliation with a specific organization. You are the president of your sorority, the head of student government, a long-standing member of 4-H, or a member of the basketball team. In the future, you may be asked to represent your law firm, the business you work for, or the church or volunteer organization to which you belong.

In those situations, you may wonder whether you are speaking for yourself, or as an organizational representative. Sometimes, the distinction is irrelevant. On some occasions, however, you may hold views that differ in important ways from those of your organization. For instance, your church may have taken a formal stand against the ordination of homosexuals. While you agree with your church's views on *most* controversial social issues, you take strong exception to the church's stance on this one. Now, as president of the church's administrative council, you have been asked to speak about your church's position on recent social issues. How should you approach this presentation?

The process of public speaking involves **choice making** from beginning to end. One choice you might make in this situation is to decline the invitation. You may simply decide that you do not want to place yourself in an awkward situation, or that it is unfair to the church for you to represent them on this matter. Another alternative might be to accept the invitation, but approach your discussion of the social issues in an informative way—simply explaining the church's stance and outlining some of the complexities and controversies associated with each. Finally, you may discuss the church's position frankly, contrasting it with your personal views. Each of these options has practical and ethical implications.

Clearly, you need to consider the organization you are representing as you go about the task of selecting a speech topic. This does not mean that you are simply an outlet through which your organization communicates its views to the public. But the organization does create some potential constraints that ought to be recognized. As you begin to think about possible speech topics, consider the following questions:

- Is this topic of any concern to my organization?
- What is my organization's stand on the issue?
- Is its position public knowledge?
- To what extent does my opinion differ from that of the organization?
- Am I being asked to speak for myself, for the organization, or for both?
- Might I deal with the topic by sharing information but not articulating a specific point of view?
- How important is this issue to me and to my organization?

Just as the topic you choose should reflect a consideration of your interests, those of the audience, the nature of the situation, and the organization you represent, the way in which the topic is **narrowed and focused** should also reveal some sensitivity to these factors. If the general topic is pollution, for example, you might focus on the issue of noise pollution for a group of teenagers, on the practical concerns of how pollution affects our daily lives at the university for a classroom audience, and on how the automotive industry is attempting to cope with air pollution for an audience of business people. Once the topic has been selected with these considerations in mind, you are ready to think about the basic goal or purpose of your speech.

CHOOSING THE SPEECH'S PURPOSE

In many instances, the speech's purpose is virtually assigned or, at least, tactfully implied. Not long ago we were asked to make a speech as part of the opening session for a weekend-long leadership retreat. The contact person suggested to us, "Now these kids (college juniors and seniors) really want something interesting. I mean, they've been studying and listening to lectures all week; they've got finals coming up in two or three weeks. So, use a little humor, and make them laugh! I mean, I know you're both professors, but frankly the last thing we want is a lecture."

Aside from our amazement that he had bothered to seek out such dull, lifeless "professor types" to reduce this audience to giggling hysteria, we were perplexed by what he asked us to achieve. Specifically, he wanted us to introduce the audience to all of leadership theory, cite supporting research for each theory, give them practical guidelines for their own leadership behavior, and uplift them in such a way that they would feel moved to go forth with great pride in their positions and faith in themselves. Thus, we were to interest and entertain, inform and instruct, persuade and inspire—be a combination of comedian, master teacher, and evangelist! Although this example presents a rather dramatic set of public speaking demands, it is not all that different from the situations in which many speakers find themselves. In fact, most successful speeches *do* interest, inform, and persuade in varying proportions. Yet, as you choose your topic and begin the task of narrowing and focusing your speech, you should do so with some overarching purpose in mind.

To Interest

Some public speeches do little more than entertain. Often the speaker has no serious intention of being either informative or persuasive. Comedians and some after-dinner speakers deliver presentations that are geared primarily toward entertainment.

Most of us, however, rarely speak with the primary goal of entertaining our listeners. Even so, the general notion of entertainment in the sense of getting the audience to listen for intrinsic enjoyment or interest does have a critical place in effective public speaking. All too often we overlook the importance of interest. We assume that if a speech is packed full of good, factual information and well-reasoned appeals, it is sure to be a success. We fail to consider the fact that information, statistics, ideas, and presentational aids must all be related to the interests and needs of the audience. Without interest, listeners cannot learn; neither can they be moved, uplifted, inspired, or incited to action. Thus, *every speech must interest.*

It is not always easy to determine what subjects audiences will find interesting, but most audiences will respond with interest to information they perceive to be:

- *Relevant.* Nearly any audience would be interested in learning about the future of Social Security. However, a group of older listeners might find the topic especially relevant.

- *Useful.* A group of graduating college seniors is motivated to learn about the job market in a way that a group of retiring executives is not. For the seniors, the subject is useful.

- *Startling, unusual, or new.* Novelty sustains attention. The speaker who presents new insights into the economic woes (and possible recovery) of Russia, the home as the primary workplace of the future, or the scientific complexities of cloning is more likely to interest the audience than one who presents a standard treatment of legalizing marijuana, the dangers of secondhand smoke, or drinking and driving.

- *Worth knowing or repeating.* Not everyone would agree on what is worth knowing. However, speeches dealing with such topics as world peace, the economy, technology, or education are likely to be perceived as substantive and worthy of invested listening time.

- *Amusing or entertaining.* Sometimes, a speaker's primary goal is to make the audience laugh and enjoy themselves. While this goal may sound frivolous, it is one of the most difficult public speaking goals to accomplish. Speeches to entertain must be virtually perfectly attuned to the particular interests, tastes, and values of the audience.

To Inform

For most public speakers, interest is only the beginning. Much public discourse is primarily informative. Its purpose is to teach, to impart information. On occasion, you will actually present the audience with new information; at other times, you may take familiar data, information, or ideas and present a different framework, perspective, or interpretation.

Whenever you choose to give an informative speech, your major purpose is to *gain audience understanding.* Informative speeches should meet several criteria. The more they adhere to these criteria, the more likely audiences will find the information compelling.

- *Accuracy.* You will attempt to ensure accuracy in the information you present through careful observation, study, research, and critical reflection.

- *Completeness.* Including information essential to a proper understanding of the subject is necessary. Listeners will feel uneasy if they sense that your knowledge is partial or missing some vital background or insights.

- *Unity.* No audience appreciates a speech that appears to be little more than the speaker sharing some random thoughts. Your comments will seem unified to the extent that they have adherence to your thesis and follow a logical and clear progression.

- *Meaningfulness*. If the audience is asking, "So what?" then the speaker is not getting through by relating the topic to their needs, interests, and levels of understanding. Meaningful information will be seen as relevant, valuable, and useful.

Often in organizational and community settings informative speaking takes the form of oral technical reports or informative briefing. Here are some examples: (1) a floor supervisor explains to assembly-line workers the reason for a new job rotation schedule; (2) an attorney enlightens a group of citizens about the laws governing child abuse cases; (3) an electrical engineer explains to a school board the plans for wiring a new school complex; and (4) a salesperson presents figures to her department depicting the successful marketing of a new fluoride mouthwash. Informative speeches often benefit from the use of presentational aids to increase clarity and enhance understanding. Because achieving audience understanding is so important, informative speeches should be followed by a question-and-answer period.

Finally, it is important to remember that informative speeches are rarely purely informative. Many speakers transmit information to build a common ground of understanding before urging the audience to support a given point of view or to act in a specific way. The department head who speaks to her staff about potential changes in the firm's maternity/paternity leave policies may educate her listeners, but does so in such a way that her policy preference clearly emerges. In this manner, then, the speaker who disseminates information often creates the foundation for persuasion.

To Persuade

Persuasion is the final goal or purpose of public speaking. Some would argue that all communication is inherently persuasive, for even the speaker who provides factual information about specific subjects, such as how legislation is passed, how to apply for food stamps, or what the federal regulations are regarding advertising, does so with some persuasive intent of getting the audience to understand and accept the speaker's presentation of the facts. However, speeches that are explicitly persuasive fall into three basic categories: those whose purpose is to stimulate, to convince, or to actuate.

Often you will be asked to address an audience whose interests, values, feelings, and beliefs are extremely compatible with your own. In this case, your strategy may be to reinforce already existing beliefs. Thus, the **speech to stimulate** does not attempt to effect change except in the sense of changing the *degree* of listener commitment, intensifying and enhancing previously existing beliefs, attitudes, and values. Speeches that stimulate are quite common in political and religious settings.

Most of the time as a public speaker you will not find yourself in the position of addressing large groups of totally supportive listeners. More typically, you will face a mixed group: some members supportive, some negative, and many undecided. On occasion, you may encounter a totally hostile audience, but these instances are also relatively rare. When you give a **speech to convince**, you invite change—seeking to persuade the audience to accept your "take" on a problem or issue, to acknowledge the quality of your evidence and arguments. Changing people's beliefs can be challenging, particularly those that are deeply rooted in clusters of attitudes and values and that have developed in response to personal experiences and observations.

Even more challenging than convincing listeners that your "take" on an issue is right is persuading them to pursue a specific course of action. The persuasive *speech to actuate* asks for a behavioral commitment from the audience. As public speakers, we are often in positions of soliciting votes and money, requesting commitments of time and talent, or asking people to give, to share, or to show their involvement in their beliefs in some measurable way. While moving listeners to believe can be difficult, inspiring them to act is even more demanding. In the final chapter of the book, we will examine specific persuasive strategies for changing audience attitudes and moving them to action.

Specific Purposes

Once you have some basic notion of your speech's general purpose, you are ready to consider your *specific purpose*. It is not adequate to say that you want to persuade the audience regarding sound investment practices. How do you want them to respond? What is your specific goal? Once you have formulated your specific purpose, you will go on to choose evidence, draw conclusions, organize your arguments, and select a fitting delivery style. That is, your specific purpose guides many subsequent decisions you will make.

The specific purpose of your speech should be *phrased in terms of the audience response you are seeking*. It is a good practice to write out a precise purpose statement specifying what you intend to accomplish. Some examples follow:

- I want my audience to develop an interest in exploring the university's new interdisciplinary curriculum, the Liberal Arts in Management Program (LAMP).
- I want my audience to invest their savings in money market CDs.
- I want my audience to join the local union.
- I want my audience to reexamine their views toward prison reform.
- I want my audience to attend the next school board meeting and vote against closing the west-side elementary school.
- I want my audience to boycott Wal-Mart.
- I want my audience to understand the implications of recent court cases that affect disabled employees and their rights.

Writing a specific purpose statement encourages you to think concretely about what you are attempting to achieve, with the desired audience response as your particular focus. With a clearly articulated purpose, you are better able to make sound judgments about how to develop your speech. Moreover, after you have delivered your speech, thinking about the purpose you set forth to achieve can help you judge your success. In formulating your purpose statement, check it against these guidelines:

- *What is the basic purpose of the speech?* To interest, inform, stimulate, convince, or actuate? How do you hope to be interesting? What kind of audience understanding do you hope to gain? For what kind of persuasion are you aiming?

- *What is the specific audience response you are seeking?* As examples: "I want my audience to understand the differences in Eastern and Western values that cause workers to view their jobs differently"; or "I want my audience to sign up for a weekend seminar on time management."
- *Is your purpose realistic?* Can the purpose be achieved within the time limits? Is it a reasonable topic, given your knowledge of the audience's needs, interests, values, and demographic characteristics?
- *Is your purpose clear?* If your purpose is vague, both you and your audience may experience a good deal of confusion. If you say, for example, "I want to inform my audience about the need for a living wage in our community," that is about the same as saying that you are going to talk about the living wage. By contrast, the statement, "I want my audience to vote for the living wage proposal (Proposition 1688) in November" is clear about the specific kind of audience response you are seeking.

Figure 13.1 summarizes general speech purposes and criteria for assessing specific purposes.

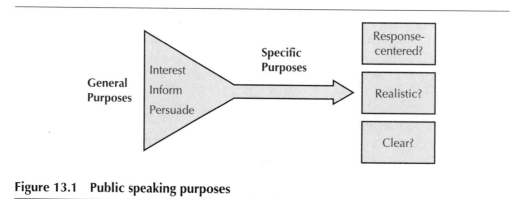

Figure 13.1   Public speaking purposes

The Speech's Thesis

Every speech should have a central idea to which every piece of information, every bit of supporting material, and every main idea is related. The *thesis statement* is a single, complete declarative sentence that embodies the idea that you want the audience to understand and/or accept in order to accomplish your specific purpose.

Let us say, for instance, that you list as your specific purpose: "I want my listeners to buy an IBM computer as their next personal computer." With the specific purpose clearly stated, you now know what you are looking for and how you will judge your own effectiveness. You can then move to stating your thesis, which might be: "The IBM computer is the best personal computer on the market." When you are gathering information and organizing your ideas, you will want to ask yourself if what you are saying *both* supports your thesis *and* advances your specific purpose. Here are some additional examples of how the specific purpose and the thesis work in tandem:

- *Specific Purpose 1:* I want my audience to become familiar with diverse options for allocating their retirement funds.
- *Thesis Statement 1:* Diverse options exist for allocating retirement funds, each possessing different risks and benefits.
- *Specific Purpose 2:* I want my audience to become convinced that our company needs a new recreational facility.
- *Thesis Statement 2:* Having a new recreational facility offers important advantages to employees and managers alike.
- *Specific Purpose 3:* I want my audience to become more committed to unionization.
- *Thesis Statement 3:* Unionization leads to an enhanced work experience for all employees.

The thesis is not the same as a preview. For instance, following from the second thesis above, the speaker might preview four specific benefits associated with the new recreational facility: enhanced organizational productivity, stress reduction for employees, a healthier work environment, and improved employer-employee relations. While the specific purpose is a guide for the speaker that is rarely shared with the audience, the thesis statement is typically advanced in the speech's introduction and may be reiterated during the conclusion. In examining your thesis statement, ask yourself:

- *Is my thesis consistent with my specific purpose?* Does it grow logically from it?
- *Is my thesis statement clear and specific?* Is it properly focused? Will listeners understand it?
- *Does my thesis statement advance the overarching concept, idea, or argument of the speech?* Is there anything I will want to address that is *not* relevant to the thesis?
- *Does the thesis avoid offering a summarizing preview* that details the speech's main points? A preview often follows the thesis statement, but is a separate step in the introduction.
- *Do I have a reasonable chance of getting my audience to consider my thesis open-mindedly*, possibly accepting it, given what I know of their attitudes, needs, and values?

Once you have selected a topic and articulated its specific purpose and thesis statement, you are ready to begin investigating the topic—discovering ideas, evidence, and information that will develop and substantiate your thesis and advance your purpose.

INVESTIGATING THE SPEECH TOPIC

When you are established in your field, you may be asked to speak about subjects that are central to your job or area of expertise. So, you will spend most of your preparation time thinking about how to organize and present ideas and information you already possess. As a business and professional communication student, however, you are less likely to rely exclusively on your own knowledge. Beyond what you already know, you will want to explore other information sources and perspectives by doing research in the library and on the Internet, as well as conducting surveys and interviews.

Taking a Personal Inventory

Before you head off to the library to start doing research or begin to surf the Net, it's wise to take stock of what you already know. Chances are that you already know something about your topic, since one of the key reasons you selected it was your interest in, experience with, and/or knowledge of the subject. Return to the list on pages 456–457, the self-inventory that you used to guide your topic selection. Again using the self-inventory as a guide, make a list of courses you've taken, relevant work experiences you've had, books you've read, your special training or skills, and other relevant factors that led you to your topic. One student, for example, selected the topic "Disabled Students and the Challenges of Getting a College Education." As she began to consider her topic, she knew that she wanted to talk about her own experiences following a serious automobile accident after which she endured over a dozen surgeries and spent several months in a wheelchair. Because of some of the problems she had encountered, she started reading widely on the subject, took a business law class that familiarized her with the laws affecting disabled students and employees, and even took a part-time job in the Office of Disabled Students at her college. Her personal reflection and knowledge growing from these experiences made a substantial foundation on which she could begin to build her speech.

Of course, not everyone will have such extensive, preexisting knowledge pertinent to the topic, but nearly everyone will have some knowledge and initial ideas on which to build. Taking the time to reflect on those impressions, experiences, and knowledge is the first step in investigating the topic.

Conducting Research

After conducting a personal inventory, gathering information through research is the next step. Doing research will allow you to expand your information base, discover fresh perspectives and ideas, and find evidence to support your views. Every speaker can benefit from doing research—even a speaker with years of topic-relevant experience. For example, if you are an advertising specialist and have been asked to speak about a new product that your company has recently unveiled, you will want to make sure your knowledge of competing products is current, and that you can give your listeners a clear sense of the effectiveness of the advertising campaign to date. If you are a student speaker with less direct experience, you will discover much of your information by conducting careful research. The research process should be as varied and comprehensive as possible.

FIELD RESEARCH: SURVEYS AND INTERVIEWS

One way of gathering information is to conduct *field research*, either by interviewing or by doing a survey. The major advantage of the *survey* is the breadth of response it provides. If you decide to conduct your own survey, you should recognize that, to be valid, the survey must be conducted on a sample representative of the population to which you want to generalize the responses. So, if you want to know what the members of your fraternity think of recently adopted antihazing legislation, you will want to make sure that you sample broadly, surveying pledges, officers, and established members who are freshmen through seniors.

Most of us are not expert pollsters or statisticians. Even so, the appropriate strategy to follow in conducting surveys is to select respondents at random and to gather relatively large samples. For an ideal survey, you would draw several samples independently from the same population to check the validity of your results. Then, if you obtained consistent results across all samples, you could reasonably assume that your data accurately reflected the general population of interest to you.

The construction of valid survey questions is a task that should be undertaken with particular care. This matter is also relevant for anyone who wants to collect information by means of interviews. In either case, one of the most common problems encountered by inexperienced researchers is the tendency to ask leading or loaded questions. These are questions that, intentionally or unintentionally, reveal your opinions or feelings. Often, they elicit a response that reinforces the questioner's prejudices rather than measuring the actual attitudes of the respondents. To be avoided, then, are such leading questions as: "Why do you think this company has adopted such an inequitable approach to dealing with male and female employees?"; "Doesn't it seem to you that the new antihazing laws are rather harsh?"; or "Why would anyone want to work for a government-funded institution these days, anyway?"

While the survey taps the views of a large number of individuals, through the *interview* it is possible to acquire greater depth of information. Whenever you want to know the reasons behind specific positions (rather than construct a profile of the views of the general population) or wish to explore the ideas of experts on a particular topic, you will probably find the interview a useful research tool.

Before seeking an interview with an expert, you need to be well prepared. In fact, it is probably wise to do some reading on your topic before approaching anyone with questions. Your interview questions should be designed to fill in gaps in your information and understanding of the topic. To prepare for an interview, here are some steps to follow:

- *Do some preliminary research* so that you can ask intelligent questions and make efficient use of the interview time.

- *Prepare a list of questions to use in the interview.* Make sure they are open, unbiased, and geared toward gathering insights you cannot gain through reading.

- *Come prepared to take notes and to listen actively*, probing and asking follow-up questions as needed.

- *Begin the interview by greeting the interviewee by name and thanking her for taking the time to talk with you.* Explain why you are interested in interviewing her.

- *Find out how much time is available for the interview and stay within those limits.* You won't want to detain a busy mayor, dean, or department head.

- Give the interviewee a sense of the sources you have already consulted and *ask if she could recommend other articles to read or others whom you should interview.*

- *At the close of the interview, thank the interviewee again,* and ask if you can get in touch, via e-mail or phone, if other questions occur to you.

If you are dealing with a controversial topic, it is usually wise to interview individuals who represent a variety of viewpoints. Suppose you were going to give a persuasive speech on the proposed construction of a new interstate highway in your state. In preparing for this speech, you might want to interview farmers and environmentalists who are strongly opposed to the project; at the same time, you will want to talk with members of the business community and political leaders who enthusiastically support the highway's construction.

While face-to-face interviews are preferable in most instances, you may also choose to conduct interviews by phone or through e-mail. If distance is an issue, or if the interviewee's schedule is already full, you may find that placing a phone call or posing your questions through e-mail to be more manageable. The great advantage of e-mail is that interviewees can respond at a time that is convenient for them (even if it's at midnight!), and they can respond in as little or as much detail as they see fit. As the interviewer, then, you can follow up with probes when anything is unclear, although follow-up requests should be kept to a minimum.

For most speeches, you cannot use interviews as your sole basis of information. Even so, in our experience, interviews tend to be underutilized as speech information sources. When you read an article about a topic, you may find yourself left with a number of unanswered questions. With an interview, however, you can probe when something is unclear. You have the opportunity to urge the interviewee to go beyond his initial statement to provide definitions or clarifying examples.

DOING RESEARCH THROUGH THE LIBRARY

Reading carefully and thoroughly on your speech topic is a vital way of gaining the information you need. The library is the place to start, and librarians are among the most helpful resources the library offers. Professional librarians are schooled in the latest information and communication technologies and systems, and they use this knowledge and skill daily. Never hesitate to ask a librarian for help.

Even though libraries and the information web that they are connected with are vast, they are increasingly user-friendly. For example, the library's catalogue of holdings is nearly always available in electronic form, accessible from computer terminals located throughout the library. You can search the holdings file for a particular subject, topic, or title. Information searches can be conducted from the library or from home via modem. Promising sources can be printed out for further exploration.

The same server that contains the catalogue may also feature various reference materials, such as encyclopedias and databases, including indexes to periodicals. There are a number of standard sources for locating reference works, such as *Basic Reference Sources, Guide to Reference Books,* and *The Guide to the Use of Libraries.* Because the sources of specific bibliographies are seemingly endless, anyone doing research should become familiar with such indexes as the *Bibliographic Index: A Cumulative Bibliography of Bibliographies and of Bibliographical Catalogues, Calendars, Abstracts, Digests, and Indexes. The Reader's Guide to Periodical Literature* is a familiar index whose citations are largely from popular magazines. Other guides to articles published in professional journals include *Applied Science and Technology Index, Psychological Abstracts, The Education Index, The International Index: Guide to Periodical Literature in the Social Sciences and Humanities,* and *Business Periodicals Index.*

If you wish to acquire information on a news event, you should begin by exploring *The New York Times Index.* On occasion, you will need materials that pertain to official government records. *The Catalogue of the Public Documents of Congress and of All Departments of the Government of the United States* is the major comprehensive index of government documents from 1893 to the present. A helpful source of information for recently published books is *Books in Print*. A less complete reference is the *Book Review Digest*, but its advantage is that it contains summaries of works cited so that you can glean some notion of the book's relevance to your particular needs. Finally, many research projects are never actually published, but much of the material they contain is indexed in *Dissertation Abstracts*.

If you are uncertain about where to go for information, and especially if no librarian is available to assist you, you might want to consult the *Guide to Information Access: A Complete Research Handbook and Directory*, published by the American Library Association.[2] This guide presents over 3,000 of the best traditional and electronic sources in the most widely researched subject categories and tells you where you can find them. It also offers guidance on research methods.

Some campuses, especially large universities, have specialized libraries for particular disciplines or special collections. For example, the School of Business may have its own library, and some find it easier to explore smaller, more specialized libraries, at least as a starting point.

USING THE COMPUTER TO CONDUCT RESEARCH

Whenever you use the computer to explore your library's holdings, you are exploring the local information network. But, you may wish to go beyond local sources, and the computer opens the door to virtually limitless information. As we noted above, you can use **e-mail** to learn more about your topic. You might also want to use the **Internet** to explore your topic. The Internet can connect you with people and information from around the world. All kinds of organizations, corporations, schools, agencies, universities, libraries, and interest and political groups have rushed to establish Internet presence. When you explore the Internet, you can find information and opinions on almost any topic imaginable—not only in textual form, but also in images, sound, and video.

Through the **World Wide Web**, you can explore speech topics and retrieve information about them. The Web is a popular network resource because Web browsing software features a graphical interface and operates like the Macintosh or Windows operating systems. To locate information for your speech topic, you can proceed in various ways: by conducting a keyword search, by exploring various links between pages and sites, or by going directly to a page for which you know the address.

Let's say, for example, that you plan to give an informative speech about Procter & Gamble's much advertised fat substitute, Olestra. Let's further assume that you have no leads on where to go for information. You'll begin with a search, choosing from among several popular Web databases, such as Yahoo! or Google (see table 13.1 for an expanded list of databases). These databases can connect you to online newspapers and magazines, agencies, and organizations. To begin your search, you might enter "Olestra" or "fat substitutes." The search engine will scan an index of sites that have titles or abundant information that matches the keywords you have supplied. In a matter of seconds, you will receive a listing of Web pages. You can scroll through it and click on any that appear promising. Once you've explored a given entry, you can return to the list and choose another entry to explore. As you investigate new sources, you will occasionally encounter

Table 13.1   Common Databases for Internet Research

AltaVista.com	GoTo.com	Lycos.com
AskJeeves.com	Google.com	MSN.com
Dogpile.com	HotBot.com	NorthernLight.com
Excite.com	iWon.com	Yahoo!.com
GO.com	LookSmart.com	

links that will give you the option of collecting other related sources that may prove relevant.

On occasion, you may want to explore the Web site of a particular organization. If you wanted to see what Procter & Gamble had done to promote its Wow chips containing Olestra, you might go directly to the P&G Web site. Or, if you wanted to do research on the causes of colon cancer, you could go directly to the American Cancer Society's Web site (www.cancer.org). Most organizations try to keep their sites labeled in predictable and easy-to-guess ways. The last three letters designate the organization's kind of Internet membership. These include the following:

.com (commercial companies)
.edu (educational institutions)
.gov (government agencies)
.mil (military institutions)
.org (nonprofit organizations)

Like other information sources, Internet sources should be carefully checked for their quality. Anyone with a minimum of skill can set up shop on the Net at very little cost. What that person chooses to put on the site is not subject to review for accuracy or fairness. While biases are sometimes obvious (as in the case of political candidates' Web pages), making judgments about source reliability is not always easy. The basic rule of thumb is: Don't take anything you find on the Net at face value. Carefully read the guidelines for evaluating Internet information listed in the Highlighting Technology box that follows. By all means, use the Internet in your research, but use it thoughtfully, critically, and together with other sources of information.

SUPPORTING THE SPEECH WITH EVIDENCE

The information you discover through your research will be used to support your ideas. Regardless of your speech's specific purpose, you will articulate several ideas, contentions, and propositions that will need to be supported with evidence. *Evidence* is the body of fact and opinion pertaining to a subject.

In most of your speeches, you will use varied kinds of evidence. Some kinds of speeches, such as technical reports, rely heavily on statistical evidence, often presented with the assistance of presentational aids. But even technical presentations can be enhanced by the use of examples, comparisons, and the opinions of experts. In general, varied evidence is an asset. Figure 13.2 illustrates the different types of evidence that may be used to support your main ideas, or *contentions*.

Highlighting Technology

Some Guidelines for Evaluating Internet Information

- *What is the source of this information, and is it credible?* You will need to know the following:
  — Names and titles or positions of the authors
  — Organizational affiliations of the authors
  — Date the page was created or updated
  — How to contact the authors
  — Did a group sponsor this page? What do you know about this group's credibility?
- *What is the purpose of the page?*
  — Some Web pages are designed to give information, while others advocate certain policies or ideologies.
  — Advocacy groups are not necessarily bad. For example, AARP (American Association of Retired Persons) tries to influence public policy affecting older Americans. Even so, wise and ethical consumers need to know that those who produced the page have an agenda that they understand.
- *How well-balanced and accurate is the content?*
  — Are a variety of viewpoints acknowledged?
  — Do the claims reflect credible evidence and balanced, well-reasoned arguments?
  — Is there any information presented that you know to be inaccurate or misleading?
- *How current is the site?*
  — Check to see how recently the site has been updated.
  — Regular updating indicates an active site.
  — A page that has been abandoned for a long time should be viewed with suspicion.

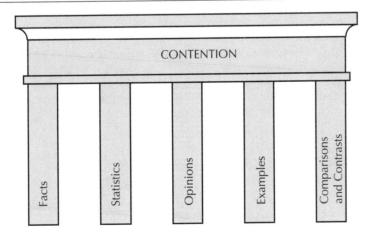

Figure 13.2   Different types of evidence that may be used to support contentions

Facts

Much of the evidence you collect will be factual; that is, it will involve relatively objective descriptions without interpretation or judgment. It is important to recognize that *facts* are not absolute truths. We make assertions about what we view as reality. If our view of reality is accurate and verifiable, then it is factual. In collecting factual information, it is important to seek reliable sources and to look through different sources to make sure you are finding consistent factual information. You ought to be able to look in more than one place and find a consistent account of how many people voted for George W. Bush in the 2004 presidential election, what the unemployment rate was for the first six months of any year, and what major factors accounted for rising oil prices in 2004. Whenever you discover inconsistencies, carefully examine your sources for bias. You may conclude that there are different approaches to explaining a particular phenomenon. If so, avoid representing such information as factual; rather, relabel it instead as a perspective, approach, or theory.

Statistics

Most public speakers use statistics as one form of factual evidence. In the business and professional world, listeners expect to be provided with statistical support. *Statistics* provide a numerical method of handling large numbers of instances. When statistics are used appropriately, they provide the most precise information about factual matters available to any public speaker.

Notice how Kathryn P. Jett uses statistics to dramatize the problem of binge drinking on campus when she addresses the Alcohol Advisory Council's Education Conference at California State University:

> A recently released report from the Harvard School of Public Health provided concrete evidence for what we already know—that binge drinking on college campuses is a serious problem. According to the Harvard study, 44% of students reported binge drinking.
>
> Other studies that measure college students binge drinking also report little or no change in the scope of the problem. The University of Michigan's Monitoring the Future Study reports that 40% of college-age students reported consuming 5+ drinks in a row within the two weeks prior to the study.
>
> Binge drinking begins as early as the 8th grade, and tends to increase throughout adolescence before gradually decreasing after about 22.
>
> Underage drinkers account for about 10% of the alcohol industry's market, which translates into about $10 billion annually. Therefore, underage drinkers are a key consumer group for the alcohol industry.[3]

By using these descriptive statistics, Jett sets the stage for the problem she wants to address. Notice, however, that she uses statistics selectively in order to not overwhelm the audience with excessive figures that might be difficult to absorb.

Statistics fall into two general categories: *descriptive* and *inferential*. A descriptive statistic states a population fact; for example, 30 percent of people living in the United States smoke cigarettes. Frequently, however, it is inconvenient or impossible to obtain descriptive data. In this instance, you can turn to inferential statistics. The collection of inferential statistics involves gathering a sample and, on the basis of that sample, reaching a conclusion about the population of interest. When Louis Harris samples a few thousand U.S. voters and predicts the election day behavior of all the voters, he is using inferential statistics. For past elections, he and other professional pollsters have done this with impressive accuracy.

It is important to remember that each inferential statistic has a confidence interval or **margin of error**. Since inferential statistics are always probabilistic in nature, you can never be certain that you have accurately described the population in question. For example, if you were to report on the basis of a survey of 1,000 assembly-line workers that 50 percent of all such workers are dissatisfied with their health insurance plans, it would be important to recognize that this particular percentage is only one of a number of different figures that might represent the workers in question. When election polls are very close, we often hear pollsters say that the election is too close to call because of the margin of error.

Another important statistical issue is **sample size and representativeness**. In general, as the size of the sample approaches the size of the population, the more confidence you can have in the accuracy of the statistic. Thus, if you want to know how workers in an organization of 3,000 employees are responding to a new incentive plan, you are more likely to reach valid conclusions if you sample the views of 300 than if you sample only 30. Moreover, your sample should be *diverse*, tapping the views of all kinds of workers, male and female, experienced and inexperienced, supervisors and subordinates. If you examine the views of only managerial personnel, or only those in a couple of departments, you may well obtain a distorted view of employees' attitudes.

When using statistics, a few **practical concerns** should be kept in mind. Statistics should be used only when they are needed and when they represent the most precise way of demonstrating a point. They should never be used simply because they sound impressive. Moreover, every attempt should be made to make the statistics as clear and personally meaningful to your listeners as possible. To say that a bond issue will cost the city $89 million sounds overwhelming, but the same figure presented as approximately $15 per taxpayer clearly makes the proposal appear manageable. So, translating statistics into audience-relevant terms can be quite helpful. Finally, seek statistics that are as recent as possible. Nothing is more useless than an outdated statistic. Figure 13.3 on the following page summarizes tests for statistical evidence.

Opinions

While evidence of fact is rooted in the notion of objectivity and suspended judgment, evidence of opinion is the application of interpretation and judgment to the known facts. There are three different types of **opinion evidence** you might use: personal testimony, lay testimony, and expert testimony.

It is probably safe to say that all speakers support their presentations with personal views from time to time. Your success in using **personal testimony** for support will largely depend on your credibility with the audience in question. If you are perceived as intelligent, accomplished in your area of endeavor, sincere and trustworthy in your motives, and fair-minded, you might rely extensively on personal testimony. This is especially true if you are speaking about an issue with which you have had years of experience.

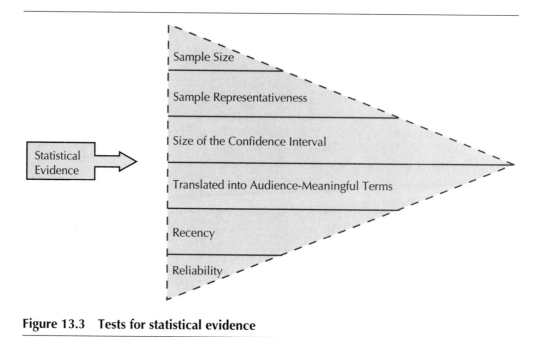

Statistical Evidence →

- Sample Size
- Sample Representativeness
- Size of the Confidence Interval
- Translated into Audience-Meaningful Terms
- Recency
- Reliability

Figure 13.3   Tests for statistical evidence

At an opening convocation at Colorado College, Congresswoman Diana DeGette delivered the keynote address in which she emphasized the value of a liberal arts education. In doing so, she shared her personal experiences and accomplishments and articulated a compelling call for civic engagement:[4]

> How do all of us craft meaningful lives with the lessons of a liberal arts education as the over-riding foundation? As incoming students, I ask you to consider what can be done for the betterment of the world in which we live. I have learned one important lesson in Congress. Armed with a quality liberal arts degree, one person truly can make a difference. . . . I soon discovered that I could draft legislation, take the issue to the floor, improve the legislation through helpful compromise, forge a lasting consensus, and steer the bill through passage and the president's signature. I could make a difference. All that was required was idealism, initiative, and imagination—a view of what could be. . . . In just my first term in Congress, I have written and passed legislation on children's health care, environmental protection, reclamation of brown fields, and other issues. . . .
>
> And I can testify to the fact that each and every one of you can also make a profound, positive difference, if you try. Many of you have already stepped forward. Some of you have become environmental activists, business owners, published writers, or recognized scholars. Most of you have already become opinion leaders.
>
> There will be a leadership vacuum in politics, business, finance, entertainment, and literature. You will be needed immediately. . . . This is your moment for preparation. Your time is now. Do everything possible to acquire the intellectual tools for leadership. The future beckons with the dawn.

Regardless of high credibility, seldom will any public speaker rely on his or her own views without incorporating other forms of support, such as statistics or examples.

Another kind of opinion evidence is *lay testimony*. Suppose you wanted to argue that most employees in your department were dissatisfied with the food being served in the company cafeteria. To support this argument you might cite the results of a poll you have taken that indicate 85 percent of all employees in your department found the food to be "extremely poor." In this case, lay opinion is good evidence because the matter being judged does not require the testimony of an expert, nor would your personal views suffice. Thus, lay testimony is useful when you want to describe the habits, attitudes, and behaviors of ordinary people. Normally, you would collect information about lay opinion by conducting a survey or by interviewing.

A third kind of opinion evidence is *expert testimony*. Most of us are not such renowned experts in our own fields that we could not profit from quoting others of greater expertise who happen to support our views. Whenever you decide to use expert testimony to support your views you need to observe a few guidelines. First, you must be concerned with the issue of actual expertise. That is, the person must be a recognized authority in the area in which he is being quoted. You should also be concerned with the expert's objectivity or fair-mindedness. It is entirely possible for an expert to be competent in a given area and yet be a poor source of testimony because of some known bias in his views. It is far better, for example, to know the views of laypersons concerning the quality of a particular brand of television set than to quote the opinion of the president of the company that manufactures them. While the president may well be an expert in electronics

When experts offer evidence, their testimony is viewed as highly credible by most members of the audience. This police officer's testimony is enhanced further by his use of reinforcing visual aids.

and quite knowledgeable about television sets in general, his views in this instance are probably influenced by self-interest. Thus, his credibility as a source is questionable.

Once you have collected some highly credible expert testimony to support your presentation, the task that still remains is to identify the expert for the audience. It is critical that the quoted expert be known and acceptable to the listeners; if she is not, then it is up to you to provide the necessary information. Assume that you are addressing a topic related to medicine; an appropriate identifying phrase might be stated as follows: "Dr. William Johnson, chief of neurosurgery at Johns Hopkins University Medical Center, has pointed out that . . ." This kind of identification is specific, precise, concise, and adequately informative.

Examples

One of the most difficult problems public speakers face is trying to make general principles or abstract notions interesting and meaningful to the audience. One of the best ways of doing this is through examples. *Examples* provide concrete frames of reference and by doing so interject life and meaning into the ideas you are communicating.

Examples can be either actual or hypothetical. They can be elaborate or brief. *Actual examples* point to real events or people. In the illustration that follows, Ingrid Newkirk, cofounder and president of PETA (People for the Ethical Treatment of Animals), offers diverse examples to demonstrate the intelligence, inventiveness, and loyalty of animals in a speech she delivered on the *Eleventh Hour* series, sponsored by the Public Broadcasting System:[5]

> There is a lot to respect and admire about animals. Our own military is still learning from dolphins, who use sonar not only to navigate, but also to stun their prey, and from bats who can find their way in total darkness. We cannot decipher animals' languages, but it is indisputable that they have them. . . . The tree frog drums his messages to others far away, while other frogs "hear" with their skin. Elephants speak to each other across many miles by using infrasound—powerful, deep rumbles at frequencies too low for us to pick up. Crows are now known not only to play (in St. Petersburg, they have worn the paint off the cathedral windows by sliding down them on their bottoms, just for fun), but to have dialects. Birds from the South of France, for example, can't understand birds of the same species from the North.
>
> Animals use tools and have their own compasses. Ants fashion boats out of leaves with which to cross rivers. Wasps make a home out of a wood and sand mixture, as we make adobe huts. . . . Rabbits and beavers construct different rooms for sleeping, for food storage, and for waste. . . . While we whine if we miss a meal or two, the emperor penguin sits for up to 45 days on the ice without one iota of food, guarding the egg that contains his successor. The tiny desert mouse rolls a stone in front of her burrow to collect the dew so she can drink water in the morning before the heat sets in. . . . As for family values, geese mate for life, and a male will risk hunters' guns to stick by his injured wife when she is shot.

Newkirk's actual examples are varied, vivid, and memorable.

The other kind of example you might want to use is hypothetical. *Hypothetical examples* are ones that might reasonably or plausibly take place, but in using them you are not referring to an actual event or person. Although hypothetical examples are concocted, they should not be unrealistic or distorted. In a classroom speech, a student used hypothetical examples to help her audience understand the experience of being disabled:[6]

> Suppose you used a wheelchair, and you were shopping for groceries one day. Your chair is partially blocking one of the aisles and a shopper comes up behind you and pushes you out of the way, much as she would an abandoned grocery cart. Later that day, another woman asks you what happened to you. You tell her that you were in a very serious automobile accident and she proceeds to lecture you on why you should have worn your seat belt.
>
> Are you having a hard time imagining that people could be so rude and unkind? If you are, you might want to give some thought to how people usually treat the disabled: like they are little children, or are stupid, or simply don't exist. I know all about these reactions from firsthand experience. Five years ago, I was in a serious automobile accident. I broke over 50 bones and spent months in rehabilitation, in casts, on crutches, and in a wheelchair. All too often, people's reactions to my disability stunned, disappointed, and angered me.

You will notice how this student firmly establishes the plausibility of her hypothetical examples. She also combines such examples with personal testimony. Speakers often use multiple kinds of evidence to reinforce their arguments.

Because examples are so easy to identify with, they can be a powerful way of supporting your ideas. Even so, they must be used with care. When we use examples, we are usually arguing that our examples represent the general principles we are discussing. Thus, one test of a good example is its *typicality*. If you were speaking on the subject of unethical behavior among corporate executives and you told the story of Enron, you would have to make sure that you didn't stereotype or overgeneralize from that example. However, if you cited numerous examples that supported your concerns, your case would be strengthened. Much depends on your thesis as well. If you are arguing that unethical executive behavior has been an increasing concern in recent years, then Enron and related examples would assist you in demonstrating your point. However, if you tried to argue that most executives are unethical based on these examples, listeners would likely question the typicality (and therefore the fairness) of your evidence.

Comparisons and Contrasts

One of the primary ways we learn is through *comparison*. We compare the known with the unknown, the more familiar with the less familiar. Whenever we encounter a new problem, we compare it with similar problems we have experienced in the past. New jobs, friends, and concepts are compared with old ones. Thus, a good way to help an audience understand what you are talking about is to compare your idea with something that they are quite familiar with or have experienced. You might compare the job of managing a company with the job of managing a family. You might discuss the architectural design you had in mind for a new municipal complex by comparing it to one in a neighboring town with which you know the audience is familiar. Or you might compare a new book with one you know they have read. By using these comparisons, you hope to enlighten your audience and make the unknown more familiar. Once the audience is more comfortable and at ease with your topic, they may become less afraid of something you are advocating.

In his speech to the conference board in New York, A. Thomas Young, former president and COO of the Martin Marietta Corporation, used the following compelling comparison in discussing ethics and breaking the law:[7]

> Whether in Washington, New York, or Peoria, most people seldom set out with the deliberate intent of breaking the law. They are drawn into it, almost as a boa constrictor defeats its prey.
>
> Most of us probably think a boa crushes its target in the powerful folds of its body. Actually, this snake places two or three coils of its body around its prey. Each time the victim exhales its breath, the boa simply takes up the slack. After three or four breaths, there is no more slack. The prey quickly suffocates.
>
> This deadly phenomenon of a victim becoming the unwitting accomplice of its own destruction is not confined to the world of reptiles. It exists in the human behavior that characterizes all walks of life anywhere on the globe. The boa we have to face—and sometimes fail to face—is following our ethical values: each lapse is another coil of the snake.

Young's comparison emphasizes his argument that if we go too far with ethical breaches, we may find ourselves unable to recover.

On occasion, you may want to inform an audience about a concept or principle by showing them its opposite. By using *contrast* rather than comparison, you are highlighting differences. This can be a compelling form of evidence when your goal is to stress the value of your advocated approach or plan in comparison to the approaches of others.

At the Democratic Convention in 2000, the Reverend Jesse Jackson addressed the delegates. Throughout his speech, he attempted to offer a vivid contrast between the Democratic and the Republican parties:[8]

> Two weeks ago, in Philadelphia, the nation was treated to a staged show—smoke, mirrors, hired acts the Republicans called inclusion. That was the inclusion illusion. In Philadelphia, diversity ended on that stage. They could not mention the words "Africa," "Appalachia," or "AIDS" once.
>
> So, it's good to be in Los Angeles, to look over this great assembly and see the real deal, the quilt with many patches that is America. There are 1,000 union workers here, 1,000 African Americans, 1,000 Latinos and Asian Americans . . . America's working families are here, headed by a Southern Baptist and an Orthodox Jew. This is America's dream team, the Democratic Party.
>
> Last week, when Al Gore chose Joe Lieberman as his running mate, he stood up for justice . . . [he] brought the sons and daughters of slaves and slave masters together with the sons and daughters of Holocaust survivors, women fighting for self-determination, [and] workers fighting for wage security and dignity.
>
> Al Gore had raised the moral chin bar. When a barrier falls to one of those locked out, it opens doors for all.
>
> On this November, there'll be two teams on the field, two plans and two directions. On the right side, the Republican team is trying to change its uniform colors. . . . But don't be fooled. Just look at the team.
>
> It's not just Bush and Cheney, but the grizzled old veterans such as Jesse Helms, and Dick Armey, and Tom DeLay, and Trent Lott, and Pat

Robertson. . . . This grizzled old team wants to take the surplus and give it away in tax breaks to benefit those who already are wealthy just to pay for their party.

But then, there's another team, the team of Gore and Lieberman . . and Gephardt, and Bonior, and Daschle, and Wellstone . . . Luis Gutierrez, Velasquez, Sanchez, Wu. This is the all-American team!

Jackson goes on to point out that, as voters approach the election, they must focus on the contrast between the two parties.

Regardless of the kind of supporting materials you select as evidence, you must be concerned about quality. In using comparisons and contrasts as evidence, remember that they are only useful or enlightening when they are justified—that is, when the events, people, or phenomena you are comparing or contrasting are similar or different enough to warrant that particular type of support.

CONSTRUCTING A PERSUASIVE ARGUMENT

When you have investigated your topic and identified the evidence you want to use in supporting your ideas, you will want to concern yourself with how you will develop your arguments. When you make an argument, you advance a claim supported by evidence, and you hope that the evidence will be judged by your listeners as relevant, sufficient, and compelling.

A *persuasive argument* consists of a claim supported by evidence grounded in a premise. A good persuasive argument must be audience centered—judged by both speaker and listeners to be sound and appealing. A persuasive argument does not prove anything absolutely, but it does make a case that seems to ring true, that seems reasonable and sensible. Of course, there will always be cultural differences in the way issues, including arguments, are perceived, as noted in Highlighting Diversity.

Highlighting Diversity

Some Research Findings

Based on research by Dr. Richard Nisbett, University of Michigan:

- Presented with weaker arguments running contrary to their own, Anglo-Americans are more likely to solidify their own opinions . . . "clobbering the weaker arguments."
- Asians, however, were more likely to modify their own position, acknowledging that even the weaker arguments had some merit.
- When asked to analyze a conflict between mothers and daughters, Anglo-American subjects quickly came down in favor of one side or the other.
- Chinese subjects were more likely to see merit in both sides, commenting, for example, "Both mothers and daughters have failed to understand each other."
- Chinese subjects expressed more liking than Anglo-Americans for proverbs containing a contradiction, like the Chinese saying "Too modest is half boastful."
- Anglo-American subjects found such contradictions "rather irritating."

Source: Erica Goode, "How Culture Molds Habits of Thought," *New York Times,* August 8, 2000, D4.

Premises

In considering an argument you are about to advance, you must be aware of the *premise*, or accepted generalization, on which your argument is built. The first test of a premise is whether it is accepted as true by the audience. What can you assume about the premises your audience would be likely to accept? Perhaps you can assume that your audience believes in fairness and justice for all, individual integrity, and respect for the individual. Yet, how do those generally accepted premises affect your speech? Perhaps you want to convince your audience that older employees in your company are being discriminated against by managers. In making this argument, you would hope that your colleagues accept the premise that no employees should be discriminated against (a fairness premise). If, however, your listeners were mostly women and many of them believed that *women* of all ages had been treated unfairly by the company, then you might have more trouble getting them to worry about the promotion problems of the older group. In this case, then, the fairness premise applies, but the listeners' *priorities* (women's rights vs. elder rights) make your specific appeal less likely to succeed. Identifying premises that resonate with the audience is a crucial step in making ideas and arguments understandable and believable.

Premises often go unarticulated. Yet, there exists a premise beneath every argument, which may or may not be acknowledged or understood. When a speaker argues that the company will save money by pursuing a particular course of action, he or she is assuming that the audience accepts the premise that saving money is desirable. But suppose the speaker is arguing that the company can no longer afford to operate its day-care center. In this case, the premise that frugality is a good thing would have to be weighed against other possible premises, such as the value of being a family-friendly organization. Depending on which premises are most salient, the speaker may or may not succeed.

Sometimes speakers will need to make the audience aware of a premise from which they may be operating. Suppose a speaker is trying to convince a student audience to vote in favor of a newly proposed campus safety fee to be assessed from each student annually. In this case, the speaker will understand that students feel they are poor, that there are already too many exorbitant fees, and that the campus is reasonably safe. Being aware of these premises, the speaker might argue that this fee is reasonable (the lowest of any other currently assessed), that it will lead to very little sacrifice (the equivalent of two cokes each week), and that the campus has become less safe over the past two years (with statistics to demonstrate the decline).

Claims

Once the premises have been examined and deemed valid, we can turn our attention to the claims being made. *Claims* are assertions put forward by a speaker as true and are supported by evidence that attests to their accuracy. In short, the strength of the claim is judged by the strength of the supporting material. There are three basic standards we can apply to help us assess the evidence for a claim.

- *The quality of the evidence should justify the audience's acceptance.* Consider the tests for evidence discussed above. Are the examples compelling, yet realistic? Are the statistics representative? Is the testimony from a respected authority?

- *The evidence presented should be relevant to the claim.* Evidence can be accurate and truthful and still not be related to the claim being advanced.
- *The evidence must be sufficient to support the claim.* Many tests of evidence focus on quality, but there is also the matter of quantity. Is there enough evidence to persuade us? Has the argument been explored in sufficient detail? Are additional examples or statistics needed?

Inductive and Deductive Reasoning

Whenever you stand before an audience and propose a particular solution as the best response to a problem, your proposal is based on some conclusion you have reached on the basis of supporting materials you have discovered. The cognitive process by which you do this is *reasoning*, the process of drawing conclusions from evidence.

Sound reasoning is not automatic. Not everyone examining the same evidence would draw the same conclusions from it. Sometimes we draw different conclusions from evidence because we are operating from different premises. Other times we are looking at different evidence, different specific examples that may lead to different perceptions. These two ways in which we reason—from particular instances to generalizable conclusions or from a general premise to specific cases—represent inductive and deductive reasoning.

INDUCTIVE REASONING

When we use *inductive reasoning*, we examine a set of specific instances or make a series of observations and proceed to draw from them a general conclusion. An example follows:

Observation 1: Jim is good at math and is majoring in business.
Observation 2: Suzanne is good at math and is majoring in business.
Observation 3: Jennifer is good at math and is majoring in business.
Conclusion: All business majors are good at math.

As you can see, we reason inductively every day, often without thinking about it. We observe a number of women, young children, doctors, accountants, and college professors, and we draw general conclusions about others who fall into these categories but whom we have not observed. This process of generalizing through inductive reasoning is one way we learn, although we must guard against stereotyping (where we completely disregard individuality, allowing our generalizations to grow into rigid categories).

Speakers who draw conclusions and advance arguments based on inductive reasoning are relying on probabilities. How sound our conclusions are will depend on how good our observations have been, whether they have been sufficient, and whether they represent a good sample of the general population. Suppose a speaker argues that when organizations offer diversity training the result is a more respectful, inclusive organizational climate. Probably she is right. But, it could be that the organizations she happened to study already had a healthy climate prior to diversity training. With inductive reasoning, we can never be absolutely certain. The best the speaker can do is convince the audience, through the weight of evidence, that the outcome is likely.

DEDUCTIVE REASONING

When we begin with a generally accepted premise and apply that premise to a specific situation, instance, or person, we are reasoning deductively. The classic example of **deductive reasoning** is the **syllogism**, which might look like this:

A. People with college educations get good jobs.
B. Peter has a college education.
C. Therefore, Peter will get a good job.

Is this a good argument? Much depends on our view of the validity of the general premise. If we can think of a number of examples of people with college degrees who have failed to gain good jobs, we may begin to counterargue. We may say, "Well, it depends on whether it's a good college." Or we might point out, "But a lot depends on what students major in." And so the premise is modified to read, "People who graduate from reputable colleges and major in business, computer science, engineering, or one of the health professions get good jobs."

The syllogism may seem a bit formal, and often, when we argue deductively, we rely on the listeners to fill in unspoken premises. This "rhetorical syllogism"—a syllogism adapted to persuasive argument—is called an **enthymeme**. We construct many arguments in our daily lives using enthymemes. For instance, "She's lazy. She never works more than is absolutely required." Here, the missing premise is "Those who are not lazy often work more than the bare minimum."

Once again, whether this argument is persuasive to the audience will depend on whether they accept the missing premise. Some listeners might ask, "Why should anyone have to work more than the minimum?" That is, there may be some disagreement about the meaning of laziness in relation to the quantity of work. In general, however, if the premises are perceived as true by the audience, then the speaker can move forward with the deductive argument.

It's important to remember that the conclusions that grow from arguments are not absolute. The audience will judge whether the case that has been made is a good one. However, when flaws in reasoning occur, arguments become unsound.

FALLACIES IN REASONING

Any claim is only as good as the evidence that supports it. Many things can go wrong during the reasoning process, leading one to draw a faulty conclusion. Following are some **fallacies** in reasoning that ought to be avoided.

• The **glittering generality** jumps to a hasty conclusion on the basis of inadequate and unrepresentative observations. This is perhaps the most common inductive fallacy. We observe a limited number of Democrats, Jews, teenagers, or salespeople and draw sweeping generalizations about others who fall into the same category.

• A **faulty analogy** compares two things, persons, events, or phenomena that are not sufficiently similar to warrant the comparison. When confronted with a proposal to create a flex-place/flex-time program, a skeptical manager remarked, "The notion of letting workers decide when and where they want to work is crazy! You might just as well talk about giving horse racing back to the horses." The inference that workers and horses are equally inept at responsible decision making is absurd. The manager could have advanced reasons for his concerns. On the basis of this dismissive analogy, however, it is impossible to discern what those reasons are.

- *Faulty causal reasoning* confuses a chronological relationship with a causal relationship. The simple fact that one event follows another in time does not necessarily mean that the first caused the second. There are often other less obvious factors that contributed to the second event. An undergraduate history student recently made a study of European war for a final term paper. He noticed that during the years immediately preceding the outbreak of recent wars there occurred an increase of armaments among the aggressive nations. On the basis of this observation, he concluded that "Increased armaments are one of the major causes of European wars." It is probably far more likely that increased armaments were the *reaction* to other causative factors, such as political upheaval or international tensions. Thus, increased armaments could reasonably be viewed as an effect rather than a cause.

- *Circular reasoning* uses arguments that go in circles, with no proof for the assertions advanced. Not long ago, one of our students informed us that a mutual acquaintance had abandoned high school teaching to go into professional theater. The remainder of our conversation went something like this: Student: "She's really a gifted actor, you know." Us: "Oh, you've seen her act?" Student: "No, but she is currently acting in New York City!" The circularity in this reasoning grows from accepting a questionable assumption: namely, that anyone who acts in New York is a gifted actor. If one were to accept this peculiar premise, then the conclusion could be viewed as logical. The difficulty here is not rooted in the deductive thought process but in an erroneous assumption that affects the process.

- *Guilt by association* judges the quality of an idea or the worth of a person or a program solely on the basis of other ideas, persons, or programs with which it is associated. An idea may be demeaned or rejected simply because it is attributed to a particular source. Suppose a speaker made the following argument: "How can we believe that this proposal is made with our best interests in mind? Mr. Johnson says that it will save us a lot of money, but Mr. Johnson belonged to an investment club in which the investors lost almost everything. One member of that club was actually indicted for fraud, and others pulled out just in time to make a lot of money—at the expense of their fellow members!" It is most likely that Mr. Johnson was not the one indicted for fraud, nor was he one of the members who pulled out, or the speaker would probably have said that. In all likelihood, Mr. Johnson was one of the unfortunate investors who lost a lot of money. But the speaker is suggesting that Mr. Johnson's plan—which is not examined for its merits—is suspect because of his former associates. Certainly this premise is open to argument.

- The *bandwagon effect* is the endorsement of ideas primarily because many other people are supporting them. When you are asked to make some judgment about a matter of physical reality, such as determining whether or not a stove is hot, it is relatively easy to decide without knowing the views of others. However, for matters involving social reality (judgments about what is considered cool, attractive, fashionable, etc.), it is often comforting to know that others support our views. Bandwagon appeals haunt us throughout our lives as we are asked to drink, smoke, eat, and enjoy because others are doing it. Knowing that other people support an idea, a product, or a lifestyle is one piece of information we might want to be aware of, but it should not be terribly persuasive taken by itself.

- The *red herring argument* attempts to throw the audience off track when a speaker does not want the quality of the argument examined. The red herring raises emotional, often irrelevant, issues aimed at gaining listeners' hasty support. A speaker once argued in favor of book censorship in the schools by asserting, "The real issue here is whether we are going to allow irresponsible and immoral administrators to expose our children to trash and filth!" Yet, perhaps those administrators who opposed censorship were deeply committed to the education of young people, but were equally committed to freedom of speech and freedom of the press. When viewed this way, the issue is not about irresponsibility or immorality, but about weighing the potentially adverse affects of such books against fundamental rights of American citizens.

The fallacies discussed above are not the only problems with reasoning you may encounter, but they are some of the more common ones. By becoming familiar with them, you will better understand the kinds of flawed arguments that can occur. Understanding these fallacies is the first step toward identifying them in the speeches of others and avoiding them in your own.

SUMMARY

Early in their careers, many people believe that they will never have to make a speech. They do not initially see why a doctor or an accountant or a police officer would need to acquire public speaking skills. After several years on the job, they develop a different view. They find themselves being asked to present their ideas or areas of expertise to others, often in a public situation. They learn that it is not enough to be a competent professional. One must also be able to communicate effectively with others—to present ideas for change persuasively, to brief new employees, and to convince others to act in civic and community settings as well.

In this chapter, we have introduced you to some of the fundamentals of public speaking: selecting an appropriate topic, choosing a purpose, framing a specific purpose in terms of the audience response you are seeking, articulating your speech's thesis, doing research, and discovering and testing evidence to support your ideas. We have also discussed the nature of argument and effective ways of reasoning so that you avoid reasoning fallacies and make sound and persuasive arguments.

Many speakers fail—not because they are stupid or lack presentational skills or experience on the job—because they have not taken the time to connect their ideas with the needs and interests of the audience or have not spoken with a clear sense of purpose so that the audience understands what they are expected to think, to believe, or to do. If audience members leave a speech scratching their heads and asking, "What does she want me to do about it?" the speaker has not been clear about her purpose, and that creates problems for everyone.

Speakers who know what they are talking about, who have gathered sound and sufficient evidence, and who have reached logical conclusions in advancing their arguments are well on the road to effective public communication in business, professional, and civic settings.

Questions for Discussion

1. To what extent should a public speaker consider his or her responsibilities as an organizational representative when speaking to an audience beyond the organization's boundary?

2. We mentioned four perspectives to be considered in selecting a topic for a public speech: personal, audience, situational, and organizational. Which of these (or which combinations of these) do you feel is generally most important? Why? What kinds of contextual factors might influence your decision?

3. What are some of the basic purposes or goals of public speaking? Provide at least one example of a topic that would work well with each basic purpose you name. Then phrase a specific purpose and a thesis statement for each topic.

4. Suppose you were making a speech on a recent tuition hike on your campus. In investigating this topic, where would you likely go to get information? How would your approach to doing research differ if you were going to talk about censorship on the Internet? Explain.

5. How will you assess the quality of information you find on the Internet?

6. What are some of the hazards of using statistics as evidence? How can these hazards be avoided?

7. Compare and contrast personal, expert, and lay testimony. What are some important considerations in using each kind of testimony as evidence?

8. How important are examples in developing persuasive arguments? What kind of examples do you feel are generally most effective? Why? What are some ways of testing examples as evidence?

9. Is there anything wrong with doing any of the following in a speech?
   a. Quoting the president of Volkswagen on the superiority of the Beetle as a safe, fuel efficient, small car
   b. Using only statistical evidence to support your point of view
   c. Relying exclusively on your own opinion to support a proposal
   d. Comparing a managerial approach at a small, private business with that at IBM

10. What is meant by a "persuasive argument"?

11. How will you determine whether your premises are good ones?

12. What is the relationship between claims and evidence?

13. Contrast inductive with deductive reasoning, defining and giving an example of each.

14. What are some of the main fallacies in reasoning that should be avoided?

15. What are some examples of issues, problems, or causes at your university or in the community that might call for you or others to become civically engaged, perhaps functioning as advocates?

Exercises

1. Find a recent (2004 and beyond) issue of *Vital Speeches of the Day,* or get on the Internet and go to: http://www.americanrhetoric.com/speechbank.htm. Select a speech that you find interesting and compelling. Read it through two or three times. Then, in a short essay, respond to these questions:

   a. What is the speaker's specific purpose and thesis? Given his or her audience, do they seem clear, reasonable, and achievable?

   b. What types of evidence does the speaker use? Which ones are the most and least effective? Explain the basis of your assessment.

   c. To what extent do the conclusions reached by the speaker seem sound and reasonable? Is there any evidence of reasoning fallacies?

2. Choose a topic you might want to use for a classroom speech. Begin to explore the topic by doing some research. Read at least three articles on the subject. Based on your reading, respond to the following in a short essay:

   a. What is your tentatively selected topic, and why did you select it?

   b. What are three pieces of evidence you found that you think you might like to use with this topic? Why do you think they will be effective?

   c. Before you consider moving forward with this topic, what additional sources will you need to consult? What kinds of evidence do you think you still need?

3. Identify an issue that is currently impacting your community or campus. Do some preliminary research. Come to class prepared to share with your instructor and fellow classmates your thoughts on the following:

   a. Why is this topic of interest to you?

   b. Why is it important for your campus or community?

   c. Based on your preliminary research, what sorts of policies, actions, and events seem to have contributed to the problem?

   d. Have you been able to identify any tentative solutions?

   e. Can you think of an audience who might benefit from hearing a presentation on this topic/problem? Try to be specific.

   f. If you were going to move forward with this topic, what would your next step be?

Case Application 13.1   Representing Your University as a Speaker

You have just been chosen to represent your college or university as a public speaker. Your audience is to be the powerful finance committee of the state legislature. You have been told to speak on any topic related to your interests and/or to higher education (so, the options are many). You are one of five students who are there to give the legislators some idea of what is on the minds of young people who attend your college. You have been asked to speak for about 8–10 minutes.

Questions

1. What topic would you choose? Why?

2. To what extent would you consider yourself a representative of the university and to what extent are you speaking just for yourself? How would your view of your role affect your communication behavior?

3. What are some of the values, demographic characteristics, and other salient factors of this audience (assuming that their profile is similar to that of your own state's legislature)?

4. Given the audience, topic, and situation, what would be your specific purpose?

5. What would be your thesis?

Case Application 13.2   Punt or Carry the Ball?

Steve Johnson is a senior scientist in the research laboratory of a prominent pharmaceutical company. For several months, the members of the executive board (of which Steve is a part) have argued fiercely about whether the firm is ready to move forward and request Food and Drug Administration (FDA) approval of a new drug to treat Alzheimer's disease. Steve has conducted a number of studies, with mixed results. In most studies, patients improved significantly (becoming more alert and showing signs of improved memory), but Steve's research also spotted some potential problems or possible side effects. Two patients developed severe anemia, and three others nearly died of high blood pressure after taking the drug for a few weeks. While the numbers were not large (since over 200 patients were tested), Steve felt that the health problems were sufficiently life-threatening to justify further investigation before going to the FDA.

After vigorous debate, the executive committee voted. Steve's views were considered with care but ultimately rejected—with a narrow majority voting to move forward with FDA approval. Almost immediately, news of the decision reached the press, precipitating considerable public interest. As an outgrowth of this interest, Steve has been asked to speak to a local service club (of which he is a lifelong member) regarding the firm's decision to take the drug to the FDA.

Questions

1. Should Steve agree to speak on this topic? Why or why not?

2. If he does speak how should he approach the speech in terms of his personal views versus the position of the organization? What strategy might he use?

3. What should be his specific purpose and thesis?

4. How might his dual allegiance to both his audience and his firm affect his presentation?

14

Organizing and Delivering the Public Speech

After reading this chapter, you should be able to:

❑ Choose an effective organizational pattern for a speech you are about to deliver; create strong transitions; and craft a compelling introduction and a memorable conclusion

❑ Create a formal outline for your speech, consistent with principles of good outlining

❑ Develop the ability to speak with confidence and to manage communication apprehension

❑ Deliver your speech using effective extemporaneous delivery

❑ Become aware of diverse styles of delivery and their associated strengths and weaknesses

❑ Craft a speech that is characterized by good oral style

❑ Devise presentational aids that support your speech by adding value to your presentation

Many speakers carefully select and focus their topics, judiciously choose a specific purpose, choose good supporting materials, and still never really experience success in their speaking endeavors. Part of their failure may be attributed to bad luck, but more commonly, a good measure of the problem is related to the way they have organized their ideas or delivered their speeches.

Preview

In this chapter, we will examine elements of effective public speaking we have not yet considered. First, we will look at speech organization, considering diverse patterns from which speakers may choose. We will also examine the steps that should be taken in introducing and concluding a speech, as well as how transitions can be used to help listeners follow the main ideas and understand their progression. Finally, we will turn our attention to the presentation of the speech, including the use of effective delivery (usually extemporaneous), the appropriate use of language (following the principles of good oral style), and the creation and use of effective presentational aids.

Organizing the Speech

Rhetorical theorists have long observed that speeches must be well structured if they are to be effective. Among the earliest to comment on the importance of organization was the Greek philosopher Plato, who wrote, "Every discourse ought to be a living creature, having a body of its own and a head and feet; there should be a middle, beginning, and end, adapted to one another and to the whole."[1] In keeping with Plato's metaphor, we will next examine the three basic parts of speeches: the introduction, the body, and the conclusion.

The Introduction

If you have ever had the experience of rising to address a room filled with chattering high school students, or excited, noisy convention folks, or even a group of contented and disinterested Rotarians following a luncheon, you are well aware of the first problem encountered by every public speaker: *gaining the attention and interest of the audience.* Every speech introduction should do this, although the manner in which it is done will vary greatly. Sometimes with serious topics about which there is great common interest, you may assume that the topic itself has captured the audience's attention. As a result, the best approach is to move directly to addressing it. This was the approach President Bush used when he spoke from Barksdale Air Force Base in the aftermath of the 9/11 terrorist attacks. He said: "Freedom itself was attacked this morning by a faceless coward. And freedom will be defended."[2]

It is more common, however, for public speakers to address audiences with mixed interest levels under less dramatic circumstances; thus, it is important to catch their attention as early as possible.

Attention-Getting Devices

Experienced speakers have found a number of introductory devices to be helpful in gaining the attention of the audience. These include: (1) establishing common ground with the audience, (2) paying the audience a deserved compliment, (3) asking a rhetorical question, (4) using humor, (5) using a narrative or illustration that leads into the subject, and (6) using an appropriate combination of these techniques. This list is not intended to be exhaustive; it merely suggests approaches that have been used successfully in the past.

Sometimes as a speaker you are separated from your audience in some significant way. You may hold a position of high status or influence, or you may have vastly different experiences or knowledge. When this is the case, you may feel it necessary to establish an early bond with the audience through the introduction. Notice how the late Neal W. O'Connor, who was chairman of the board of N. W. Ayer ABH International (an esteemed ad agency), *established common ground* with his audience, the Syracuse Press Club:[3]

> Thanks for the warmth of your welcome, a welcome back to Syracuse. One does feel old when he comes back to a place where he's been young. . . . I owe a lot to Syracuse. My father and mother both graduated from the University. Two of my father's brothers made their careers in this city. One was even president of this very hotel. I met a certain Nancy Turner, class of 1950, here. She is now Mrs. O'Connor. One of our oldest and most valued clients, the Carrier Corporation,

has made this its headquarters city. I have many good friends here whom I see all too seldom. . . . I have a great respect for Syracuse, for the city and its people.

In chapter 13, we discussed the potential significance of the speech occasion. Often the introduction is the most appropriate place to **make direct reference to either the importance of the occasion or the efforts of the audience** when praise or recognition is deserved. This was the approach used by Lewis Platt, non-executive CEO of the Boeing Company, in giving the keynote address at an international conference in Dubai, United Arab Emirates. Platt begins his speech with these words:[4]

> I am honored to be here as a keynote speaker at this important conference on global entrepreneurship. I believe that the two things (globalization and entrepreneurship) are opposite sides of the same coin. In today's world, to be an entrepreneur *is* to think globally. If you are an entrepreneur, you seek out opportunity wherever it exists, at home or abroad, and you are in the habit of looking beyond the boundaries of existing business relationships.
>
> This is my first trip to Dubai and the UAE. While I have been here for only a few hours, I am well aware of the reputation that the UAE has built as a hotbed of entrepreneurial activity and a center for global commerce within the Gulf region. I am impressed by the fact that people from more than 185 countries are living and working in the UAE. There are few if any places in the world with a more cosmopolitan mix of people.

The third attention-getting device is the **rhetorical question**. Unlike ordinary questions, rhetorical ones do not seek an outward verbal or behavioral response; rather, they are meant to stimulate thought and perhaps pique curiosity. It is not uncommon for speakers to use several rhetorical questions, pausing between each one. In the following speech introduction, Bono poses a series of rhetorical questions in addressing the 2001 Harvard graduating class:[5]

> Rock music to me is rebel music. But rebelling against what? In the 50s, it was sexual mores and double standards. In the 60s, it was the Vietnam War and racial and social inequality. What are we rebelling against now?
>
> What's your problem? What's the hole in your heart? Why are you here in Harvard Square? Why do you have to listen to me? What have you given up to get here? Is success your drug of choice? Or are you driven by another curiosity—your potential? Is missing the moment unacceptable to you? Is wasting inspiration a crime to you? It is for the musician. If this is where we find our lives rhyme, if this is our common ground, well, then, I can be inspired as well as humbled to be on this great campus. . . .

The fourth introductory device is **humor**. Several words of caution are necessary here. Humor should be used only as an introductory device when it is appropriate and tasteful. Some speakers seem to believe that every speech should begin with a joke—all too often of the standard, canned variety. Some humor can be planned in advance, but often the best kind of humor grows naturally from the speech situation and includes some references to those present or to preceding events. Moreover, some individuals are more skilled with humor than others. As a public speaker, you must honestly assess yourself with regard to this issue. There is probably no worse way to begin a speech than by telling a joke that flops. When tastefully employed, however, humor that is relevant to the topic and the occasion can serve as an extremely effective attention-getting device. In the following introduction, Richard Lamm, representing the University of Denver's Center for Public Policy and Contemporary Issues, begins his speech to the World Future Society with this humorous anecdote:[6]

> A priest was riding in a subway when a man staggered toward him, smelling like a brewery, with lipstick on his collar. He sat in the seat right next to the priest and started reading the newspaper.
>
> After a few minutes, the man turned to the priest and asked. "Excuse me, Father, what causes arthritis?"
>
> The priest, tired of smelling the liquor and saddened by the lifestyle, said roughly, "Loose living, drink, dissipation, contempt for your fellow man, and being with cheap and wicked women!"
>
> "That's amazing," said the drunk and returned to his newspaper. A while later, the priest, feeling a bit guilty, turned to the man and asked nicely, "How long have you had arthritis?"
>
> "Oh," said the man, "I don't have arthritis. I was just reading that the Pope did."
>
> The story, of course, is a lesson on assumptions.

Another attention-getting device is a *narrative* or *illustration* leading into the topic. Sometimes these devices focus on a personal experience; on other occasions, they simply recount an example or event read or remembered. They may be true to life or hypothetical, literary or historical—so long as they gain attention in a meaningful manner. In the following example, David Abney, president of UPS International, shares a parable (a narrative with a moral) in introducing his speech to a group of business leaders at the Arizona Quality Conference in Scottsdale, Arizona:[7]

> Successfully managing the ride through all the ups and downs we've had the past few years reminds me of the story of the Fox and the Hedgehog.
>
> As the parable goes, the Fox knows many things, while the Hedgehog knows one big thing. The Fox wants badly to defeat the Hedgehog. Day in and day out, the Fox circles around the Hedgehog's den, waiting for the perfect moment to pounce. Sleek, cunning, fleet of foot, and crafty—the Fox looks like a sure winner. The Hedgehog, on the other hand, is a less glamorous guy. But every time the Fox launches an offensive, the Hedgehog rolls up into a perfect little ball and sends out his coat of sharp spikes pointing outward in all directions.
>
> The game goes on and on, but despite the cunning of the Fox, the Hedgehog always wins.
>
> In commenting on this ancient parable, the essayist, Isaiah Berlin, described the Fox as "scattered and diffused, and moving on many levels." The Hedgehog, by contrast, has simplified the complex world around him into a single organizing idea . . . a basic concept that unifies and guides his life.
>
> Vince Lombardi was a hedgehog football coach.
>
> Mother Teresa was a hedgehog missionary. In fact, she one said, "Be faithful in small things because it is in them that your strength lies."
>
> In business, oftentimes, entrepreneurial companies begin life as hedgehogs. But the larger they get, the more pressure they feel to find new ways to grow. Then, the tendency is to venture away from what made them successful in the first place. Is there anything more difficult than to sustain growth, while not getting "scattered and diffused" like the Fox?
>
> How many businesses do you think manage that?
>
> Not many.

A final way to introduce a speech in an interesting and creative way is to *use several different attention-getting devices in some appropriate combination*. In fact, many excellent speakers seek to gain the audience's attention through multiple means. It is not uncommon, for example, for speakers to establish common ground with listeners, refer to the significance of the occasion, and use rhetorical questions, as in the Bono example above, or, as in the Abney example, a narrative and rhetorical questions may be used in tandem.

PROVIDING FOR AUDIENCE ORIENTATION

In addition to gaining the audience's attention, the other major function of the introduction is *orienting the audience to the speech's subject*. Although a speaker may choose to do many different things during this time of orientation (such as providing background or defining difficult or ambiguous terms), the speech's orientation phase should include four basic components: advancing the speech's thesis, justifying the topic's importance and relevance to the audience, establishing the speaker's credibility, and providing a preview. Taken together, the attention getter and the orientation phase prepare the audience for listening to the speech while engaging their interest.

- *Articulate the thesis*. One key function of the orientation phase is to articulate the speech's thesis. If your specific purpose is: "I want my listeners to volunteer at the Shalom Community Center for the poor and homeless," in the introduction to your speech you might advance this thesis: "Volunteering at Shalom is a wonderful way to lighten the burden of the poor in our community." By articulating your thesis as part of your introduction, you let the audience see the big picture. They will understand early on what your central theme, overarching point, or principal argument will be.

- *Offer justification*. In chapter 13, we stressed the importance of choosing a topic of mutual interest to both you and your listeners. Even so, during your introduction it is *critical* that you justify your topic by showing the listeners its significance—telling them why they should care. After all, you have been preparing your speech for some time and are well aware of its importance to you. The audience, however, may not focus on the topic until they begin to listen to your speech. So, those early moments are a crucial time to explain to them why the subject of your speech is relevant to them and their concerns.

For instance, a student speaker highlighted the importance of her topic in this way:[8]

> You may be wondering why you should be concerned about colon cancer. Most of us do not associate it with people our age. I know that was my attitude until my 20-year-old cousin was diagnosed with colon cancer earlier this year. When I started to do research, I learned that over 15 percent of those suffering from colon cancer are diagnosed before the age of 25. And another 20 percent will be afflicted before the age of 40. I also learned that this potentially deadly disease has stricken more and more teenagers every year since 1995.

By showing her classroom audience her topic's relevance to them, she helped motivate them to want to listen to and learn from her speech.

- *Establish your credibility*. Another part of orienting the audience entails establishing your credibility. In a sense, credibility is an ongoing issue throughout any speech, but for every speaker, the introduction represents an especially critical time to establish her or his credentials. For established professionals, this may be a less daunting task. We expect doctors to know about medicine, attorneys to know about the law, and accountants to be able to answer questions about taxes. For student speakers, however, the issue of establishing credibility is somewhat more challenging. You might establish your credibility by referring to a personal experience (for example, building several houses with Habitat for Humanity), by referring to the experiences of those close to you or about whom you care deeply (such as speaking of a friend who was injured by a drunken driver), or by demonstrating your extensive knowledge or education in a particular field or with a special subject (for example, your five years of experience playing with a jazz ensemble or your teaching assistantship in a college-level computer science class). By addressing the issue of your credibility, you are answering the audience's question: "Why should we listen to or believe you?" We will further elaborate on speaker credibility in the next chapter.

- *Give a preview.* Before moving into the body of your speech, you will complete the orientation phase by enumerating a preview. The preview introduces your major points and gives your audience a clear idea of what to expect from the remainder of your speech. In previewing, you are also signaling what you feel is most important: those things you want the audience to remember and to reflect on long after you have finished speaking. If, after enumerating your preview, you follow through with your plan, you will further enhance your credibility by demonstrating your careful organization and preparation.

The length of the introduction varies with the needs of the speech situation. Some formal speech occasions demand extensive introductory reference to the events at hand, as well as to significant persons present. Some audiences are already basically attentive; others need considerable coaxing. In general, introductions should not be too extensive, particularly in the classroom context. The introduction does, however, create an important initial impression and should be constructed with care and creativity.

The Body

The speech's body is the heart of the message. The *body* is where you present and elaborate on your major ideas. Most of your speaking time (80 percent or more) will be spent here. It is in the body of your speech that you will develop your line of thinking, elaborate on your main points, and develop your arguments. As you develop your speech, you will need to make important decisions about how you want to organize your information and ideas. There are a number of organizational patterns from which you may choose.

CHRONOLOGICAL ORDER

One commonly used pattern of arrangement is *chronological order.* You begin with a specific point in time and then move forward, or backward, depending on the nature of the subject. Chronological order may be useful with a variety of topics, as long as you are dealing with a subject involving chronological relationships. Thus, the philanthropy of Bill Gates, the development of the labor movement in the United States, the rise in homelessness as a growing problem in the United States, the evolution of the Christian Coalition as a force influencing the national political agenda, and changing perspectives on management theory are all appropriate subjects for chronological arrangement.

Spatial Arrangement

A second common pattern is *spatial arrangement*. With this pattern, you use space as your ordering principle. A speech explaining the architectural plans for a new library, a presentation describing major tourist attractions of a big city (as one travels from north to south), or a speech describing the best jazz clubs in the United States (moving from the East to the West Coast) would all be appropriate candidates for spatial organization.

Moreover, you could use spatial order to discuss any of the topics mentioned in the previous section on chronological organization simply by using a location focus rather than a time focus. For example, you might discuss Gates's contributions in several specific geographical locations (Africa, Russia, and the United States) without regard to the order in which those contributions occurred. Or you might talk of the spread of homelessness from urban centers to smaller cities and towns. These examples illustrate an important idea: *Most topics can be approached from a variety of organizational perspectives.* Your task is to make a judicious decision in choosing the most appropriate one for the particular situation in which you are speaking.

Categorical Order

One of the most common organizational patterns is *categorical order*. When you arrange your ideas categorically, you address types, forms, qualities, or aspects of the speech subject. You might discuss higher education by looking at vocational and technical institutes, community or junior colleges, four-year colleges, and universities. Similarly, you might speak about dogs according to breed; employees according gender or ethnicity; or the writings of Shakespeare in terms of type, including sonnets, histories, comedies, and tragedies.

It is often possible to look at the same subject from several categorical perspectives. You might discuss businesses according to size, type of industry, extent of family-friendly programs, degree of green orientation (showing concern for the environment), commitment to diversity, or degree of technological sophistication. Some topics clearly lend themselves to varied categorical arrangements.

Cause-and-Effect Arrangement

Whenever you choose to make an analytical speech, you may wish to consider using a *cause-and-effect arrangement*. This pattern can move from effect to cause or from cause to effect. For instance, you might use cause-and-effect order to discuss a topic such as the causes of ozone layer depletion, the effects of gang activity on communities, economic factors that lead to recession, or the factors that contribute to trusting employer-employee relationships.

When using causal arrangement, keep in mind that a chronological relationship does not necessarily equal a causal relationship. One event following another may represent chance as easily as cause. You may want to review our discussion of faulty causal reasoning in chapter 13. In addition, whenever you look at a given effect to seek its causes, you must continually guard against oversimplification. The quest for the single cause is often doomed to failure. Finally, sometimes cause-and-effect order is incorporated as part of an overall problem-solution pattern. Within the structure of a problem-solution speech, you will analyze the problem (effect) in terms of contributing causes.

PROBLEM-SOLUTION PATTERN

The *problem-solution pattern* is one of the most frequently used by public speakers. Typically, we associate this kind of pattern with persuasive speaking, although it is possible to discuss a problem and inform the audience of proposed solutions without taking a stand on the best solution. Most of the time, however, when you choose a problem-solution pattern of organization, you will take a position on your preferred solution, the one you hope the audience will adopt. You might propose solutions to such problems as credit card fraud, the rise in eating disorders among college students, the underrepresentation of African Americans among lawyers, or regulating drugs obtained through the Internet.

Depending on the problem and your assumptions about the audience's prior knowledge, you might spend more or less time discussing the nature of the problem and its contributing causes. In situations where the audience is well versed on the problem, you might only briefly describe it and spend most of your speaking time exploring viable solutions.

MOTIVATED SEQUENCE PATTERN

One potentially effective approach to organizing a problem-solution speech is the *motivated sequence*.[9] This pattern is organized around five steps: (1) arouse, (2) dissatisfy, (3) gratify, (4) picture, and (5) move. Using this pattern, you first concern yourself with capturing the audience's attention. The next task is to demonstrate the nature of the problem, depicting the difficulties, tensions, or tragedy of a specific situation of immediate concern. Next, you link your recommended solution with the problem so that the audience can understand and accept the proposal as a viable, appealing solution to the problem. The accepting audience is more than one who understands how the solution can work. They must, instead, be able to *visualize* the results. Finally, you conclude your speech with appeals and challenges that reflect an understanding of the audience's needs and values and that are designed to move them to accept the solution you have advanced with enthusiasm and commitment.

The motivated sequence encourages a detailed consideration of a proposed solution. It is best suited to those topics that combine emotional with logical appeals. So, if you were addressing the problem of HMO abuses, the motivated sequence might work quite well, but it would likely be less effective if you were proposing a solution to the problem of inadequate recreational facilities in the community.

ALTERNATIVE PATTERNS OF ORGANIZATION

In addition to the traditional organizational patterns examined above, other options exist. Due to cultural backgrounds or personal preference, some speakers may prefer less direct and more organic patterns of organization.[10] For instance, a speech may be organized around telling one or more stories, using a *narrative pattern*. The speaker may begin by introducing a theme, such as the idea that the best business leaders are highly ethical. Then, various stories would be shared to illustrate and reinforce the speaker's thesis. Or, a speaker might pay tribute to a single person by sharing an extended narrative of the person's life. The speech is a continuous narrative with various internal stories drawn out and emphasized.

Each would relate to an overarching theme, perhaps by demonstrating how the person being honored lived a life of courage.

If the speaker wants to build in a sense of drama or climax within a narrative pattern, he or she may choose to use a *spiraling narrative*. For instance, the speaker might give the speech of tribute described by sharing stories that build in intensity. The person's simple acts of courage might be shared first, moving to more unusual acts, and perhaps culminating with uncommon acts of valor. Again, each would be united by the general theme. When delivered effectively, narrative patterns can contribute to a powerful, engaging presentation. See Highlighting Diversity for an extended illustration of another common narrative pattern.

GENERAL GUIDELINES FOR ORGANIZING THE SPEECH

Given the wide variety of organizational patterns from which you can choose, a few general principles should be kept in mind. First, select your organizational pattern carefully. The way you present your ideas and information should be *strategic*, designed to enhance the chance that you will elicit the audience response you are seeking. If you are talking to an audience about a technical area in which they have little background and experience, you have to devote a good portion of your speech to educating them—giving them information they need so that they can understand what you want them to do.

Second, give some thought to *symmetry* and *balance*. Normally, you would develop each of your main points so that each idea is given equal emphasis. But, if you decide that one idea is clearly more controversial, complex, or important than the others, you may consciously decide to devote more time to that idea. Again, what is important is that the decision be strategic.

Finally, be aware of *primacy and recency effects*. Although researchers have not been able to agree on whether arguments are more memorable and persuasive if they are placed first (primacy) or last (recency), they do agree that those two positions are the most powerful—and that information or arguments embedded in the middle of a message are less likely to have the same impact.[11]

Highlighting Diversity

The Exemplum as an Alternative Organizational Pattern

For hundreds of years, communication educators have used a narrative pattern of organization called the exemplum. Five elements are included:

- State a quotation or a proverb.
- Identify and explain the author or source of the proverb or quotation.
- Rephrase the proverb in your own words.
- Share a story that illustrates the quotation.
- Apply the quotation or proverb to the audience.

In short, the speaker using this pattern builds the speech around a quotation that is developed through a narrative. This pattern can be especially useful for inspirational or motivational speeches that elaborate on a shared value, such as integrity.

Source: J. R. McNally, "Opening Assignments: A Symposium," *Speech Teacher* 18 (1969): 18–20.

Transitions as Bridges

A final vital aspect of speech organization is the *transition*, the bridge connecting one idea with another. Good transitions are critical to the coherence and continuity of the speech. Each major idea needs to be rounded off and related to that which follows. Too many speakers believe that they can move magically from one main point to another. Thus, they concentrate on remembering the main concepts in the speech while paying little attention to the problem of moving smoothly from point to point. Many basically well-structured speeches have been seriously hindered by poor transitions.

Sometimes transitions can be relatively brief. For example, "Now that we've considered the basic dimensions of the problem, let's attempt to analyze its causes." On other occasions, an entire paragraph may be needed to maintain the flow of thought or demonstrate the nature of the relationships involved.

Speakers can sometimes employ *rhetorical questions as transitional devices*. Some examples are: "But what do we really mean by the term 'team player'?"; "How do you think a well-educated person would approach this kind of complex problem?"; "What, then, are the ways we can best prepare our employees for the kinds of technological changes that are about to occur?"

If a preview is used at the beginning of the speech, it may be necessary only to use *signposts* subsequently, saying "first, second, and finally," in moving from point to point. Rarely, would any speaker want to rely exclusively on this manner of transition, however.

Internal summaries can also be useful as transitions. With the internal summary, you usually review the points already covered, and you may even preview the ideas or approaches to follow; for example, "Now that we've looked at some of the major dimensions of our economic plight, let's move on to consider some ways of improving the situation."

Unfortunately, transitions are often ignored by speakers. Without the skillful use of transitions, speeches seem incoherent. One of the best ways to ensure that audiences perceive the unity and interrelatedness of your ideas is to make these relationships clear through good transitions. In sum, transitions can create bonds by revealing the speech's main ideas as integral parts of a coherent whole.

The Conclusion

We've all heard speakers who pause slightly near the end of their speech and then mumble, "Well, I guess that's all I have to say. I sure appreciate your attention. [Further pause.] Thank you." Some might call this a conclusion, but we would contend that the speaker did not conclude; he or she simply stopped. The specific purpose of a conclusion will vary from speech to speech, but the general purpose is to bring the speech to a strategic close—thus creating a final impact. We turn now to a consideration of some specific concluding devices.

CHALLENGING YOUR LISTENERS

One common method of concluding persuasive speeches is with a *challenge*. You may challenge the audience to act, to believe, to meet the need, to demonstrate concern, or even to live a different kind of life. When newspaper columnist and author, Anna Quindlen, delivered the commencement address at Mount

Holyoke College in 1999, she introduced her speech by sharing her desire to be "perfect"; to fit a mold for which she was not well suited became like "always caring a backpack filled with bricks on my back." In her conclusion, she refers again to the backpack in offering this compelling challenge:[12]

> Most commencement speeches suggest that you take up something or other: the challenge of the future, a vision of the twenty-first century. Instead, I'd like you to give up. Give up the backpack.
>
> Give up the nonsensical and punishing quest for perfection that dogs too many of us through too much of our lives. . . .
>
> Begin to say no to the Greek chorus that thinks it knows the parameters of a happy life when all it knows is the homogenization of human experience. Listen to that small voice from inside you that tells you to go another way. George Eliot wrote, "It is never too late to be what you might have been." It is never too early, either. And it will make all the difference in the world. Take it from someone who has left the backpack full of bricks far behind.
>
> Every day feels light as a feather.

SUMMARIZING YOUR IDEAS

A second concluding device useful with informative as well as persuasive discourse is the *summary*. In summarizing, you may repeat the main points in a straightforward, almost literal fashion; or you may choose to restate the major ideas in different, and often more concise, phraseology. Summaries are often used in conjunction with another concluding device. A student used the following summary, followed by a rhetorical question, to conclude his speech on the Liberal Arts and Management Program (LAMP), a new interdisciplinary curriculum at Indiana University:[13]

> In short, the Liberal Arts and Management Program is an excellent alternative to a traditional college degree. Indiana is one of only a few schools offering this interdisciplinary degree (so, it's a unique opportunity). It combines a broad education in the liberal arts and sciences with a substantial cluster of business courses (giving you the best of both worlds). And, you have a lot of contact with your professors because LAMP is small, with several courses team-taught by faculty from the liberal arts and business. At a time when business leaders are calling for more liberally educated employees, why not look into LAMP?

ENDING WITH A QUOTATION

Yet another concluding device is the *quotation*. Quoted material can take the form of expert testimony, poems, songs, or striking, memorable slogans. Quotations should be pertinent and meaningful; they *must* be brief. In his speech to the nation on October 1, 1979, President Jimmy Carter concluded with a striking quotation:[14]

> The struggle for peace—the long, hard struggle to bring weapons of mass destruction under the control of human reason and human law—is the central drama of our age.
>
> At another time of challenge in our nation's history, President Abraham Lincoln told the American people: "We shall nobly save, or meanly lose, the last best hope of earth."
>
> We acted wisely then, and preserved the union. Let us act wisely now, and preserve the world.

McDonaldization in Society
By an Indiana University Undergraduate Student

Specific Purpose: I want my audience to gain an understanding of the meaning and impact (both positive and negative) of McDonaldization on society.

Introduction

  I. *Attention-Getting Device*

    When I was in the first grade, my idea of a good time on Saturday was to get my older brother to take me to McDonald's for lunch. I loved the playland, the Happy Meals, and the ice cream cones. How about you? Did you used to frequent McDonald's when you were a child? Do you still like it?

  II. *Orientation Phase*

    Of course, McDonald's is only one example of the global fast-food industry. Yet, because it's the first and the largest, McDonald's tends to symbolize the others and their pervasive impact on the world.

    Credibility

    I have studied business here at IU for three years. I have had summer jobs working at McDonald's and Wendy's. Last year I read an intriguing book by the noted economist, Ritzer, *The McDonaldization of Society*, which caused me to see my business knowledge and experiences in a new light.

    Justification

    Ritzer (1996) points out that the principles of the fast-food restaurant are coming to dominate more and more sectors of our society. The success of McDonaldization is apparent as Americans spent more than $110 billion on fast food in the year 2000 (Schlosser, 2001). Ritzer argues that *no one* escapes the influence of McDonaldization, even those who do not eat fast food.

    Thesis

    Because McDonaldization is so much a part of our lives, it is important to understand its impact on our society.

    Enumerated Preview

    I'd like to begin today by sharing some of the history of McDonald's. Then I'll go on to discuss the basic principles of McDonaldization. I'll conclude by examining the pros and cons of this phenomenon and looking at possible alternatives.

Transition: Let's begin by looking briefly at McDonald's history.

Body

  III. McDonald's is the first U.S. fast-food chain to gain real international prominence (McDonald, 1997).

    A. Ray Kroc began franchising McDonald's in 1955 and there are now over 14,000 outlets.

    B. You can find McDonald's all over the world: in France, China, Russia, and Japan (Cohon, 1999).

Transition: But "McDonaldization" extends far beyond one fast-food chain. What are its underlying principles?

  IV. The basic principles of McDonaldization are efficiency, calculability, predictability, and control—based on turn-of-the-century rules of bureaucracy (Taylor, 1911; Weber, 1947).

    A. Efficiency is at the heart of McDonaldization.

Figure 14.1   Sample outline of an informative speech

C. The dehumanizing effect of McDonaldization is evident as more and more jobs are becoming monotonous, boring routines which require little thinking or creativity (Harrisburg, 1987).

Transition: It almost seems that McDonaldization is so pervasive, especially in our society, that other ways of creating organizations might be difficult to imagine. Yet, there are other possibilities.

VII. In an *Atlantic Monthly* article, Barber describes alternatives to such a McDonaldized way of life.

A. Companies such as Southwest Airlines have bucked the trend of predictability by having spontaneous and creative pilots and service attendants who play games, joke with passengers, and create an overall unique atmosphere where several surprises may arise.

B. Ben and Jerry's ice cream has taken several measures to avoid becoming McDonaldized.

1. They use an abundance of ingredients in each flavor.

2. Employees do not wear uniforms and are encouraged to be spontaneous.

C. The recent popularity of bed and breakfast operations indicates a desire by many Americans to try something new and receive personal attention.

Conclusion

VIII. *Summary*

The process of McDonaldization can perhaps best be summarized by considering two contrasting theories. "In a rapidly changing, unfamiliar, and seemingly hostile world, there is comfort in the comparatively stable, familiar, and safe environment of a McDonaldized system" (Ritzer, 12). The opposite point of view argues that a McDonaldized environment offers a dehumanizing setting which increases the gap between rich and poor, and creates fewer jobs involving creativity, rather more monotonous tasks.

Concluding Device

Perhaps most of us want the best of both worlds: creativity with some predictability, quantitative as well as qualitative measures of success, and some measure of control in a larger context of individual empowerment. Understanding McDonaldization is one step toward thinking through what we really value.

Bibliography*

Albright, M. (1995, January 15). Inside job: Fast-Food chains serve a captive audience. *St. Petersburg Times*, p. 1 H.

Barber, B. (1992, March). Jihad vs. McWorld. *Atlantic Monthly*, 53–63.

Cohon, G. (1999). *To Russia with fries.* Toronto: McClelland & Stewart.

Herzberg, F. (1987). One more time: How do you motivate employees? *Harvard Business Review*, 65,109–17.

Jaques, E. (1990) In praise of hierarchy. *Harvard Business Review*, 68, 127–33.

McDonald, R.J. (1997). *The complete hamburger: The history of America's favorite sandwich.* New York: Birch Lane Press.

Ritzer, G. (1995). *Expressing America: A critique of the global credit card society.* Thousand Oaks, CA: Pine Ridge Press.

Ritzer, G. (1996). *The McDonaldization of society.* San Diego, CA: New Delhi.

Schlosser, E. (2001). *Fast food nation.* Boston: Houghton Mifflin.

Taylor, F. (1911). *Principles of scientific management.* New York: Harper & Row.

Vidal, J. (1997). *McLibel: Burger culture on trial.* New York: New Press.

Weber, M. (1947). *The theory of social and economic organization.* New York: Oxford University Press.

*Note: This bibliography follows the style manual of the APA (American Psychological Association), 5th edition, published in 2001.

Highlighting Civic Engagement

Keyword Outline for a Speech to Actuate

The keyword outline that follows is based on a speech whose purpose is to persuade the audience to become involved with Habitat for Humanity.

I. Introduction
   A. Story of single parent domestic abuse survivor
   B. Personal participation in Habitat builds
   C. Show relevance
   D. Thesis
   E. Preview

II. What is Habitat for Humanity?
   A. Nonprofit Christian housing ministry
   B. Started in the U.S. in 1976 by Millard Fuller
   C. Eliminating world-wide poverty housing
   D. Makes adequate housing a matter of conscience and action

III. Where is Habitat?
   A. All fifty states in the U.S.
   B. Nearly 100 other countries
   C. Over 2,200 total affiliates
   D. Local Habitat building 50th house

IV. How does the Habitat system work?
   A. Selection criteria for homeowners
      1. Need
      2. Ability to repay no-interest mortgage
      3. Willingness to put in "sweat equity" hours
   B. Builds modest homes
      1. About 1,100 square feet
      2. Low mortgage payments—under $300 per month
   C. House payments revert to a "Fund for Humanity"
      1. More houses built

V. How can you get involved?
   A. Find local affiliate
   B. Gifts from the heart (financial and food donations)
   C. Global village—Habitat volunteer vacation
   D. Women's build
   E. Campus chapters and programs
   F. Jimmy Carter's Work Project (distribute handouts)

VI. Conclusion
   A. Revisit personal story
   B. Summarize
   C. Appeal for action

As is typical of keyword outlines, this one's development is much sketchier than its full-sentence equivalent would be. The use of phrases and single words is appropriate and should assist with an extemporaneous style of delivery.

DELIVERING THE SPEECH

However well organized you might be, the actual delivery of the speech is of paramount importance. Many intelligent, well-intentioned, and well-prepared speakers have failed to move their listeners simply because of an inability to present the speech directly, spontaneously, and emphatically. To deliver any speech effectively, speakers must approach the situation with some measure of confidence; yet stage fright remains a nearly universal phenomenon.

Developing Confidence

The term *stage fright* originated in the theater, but most people do not have to participate in a dramatic production to experience this unfortunate malady. Quaking limbs, quivering voices, and dry mouths are only a few of the dreaded symptoms. It is a paradox of human nature that most of us desire attention, but when we receive attention in the form of an audience, we respond with some measure of fear. Essentially, it is a fear of personal failure, for we expose a good deal of ourselves through our public expression of attitudes and ideas.

Even so, many speakers lack confidence because they hold a number of erroneous notions about stage fright, or what is more commonly known today as *communication apprehension.*[17] Among these fallacious assumptions are: (1) the speaker is virtually alone in experiencing anxiety in public speaking; (2) only beginners experience apprehension; (3) everyone in the audience can tell exactly how frightened a speaker is; and (4) stage fright is always debilitating for the speaker. Let us consider each in turn.

- *Anxiety in public speaking is not an uncommon occurrence.* In fact, only rarely do public speakers experience no anxiety before or during the actual delivery of their speeches. One study demonstrated that 77 percent of all experienced speakers admitted to some communication apprehension on each speaking occasion.[18] Of course, "experienced" speakers are not necessarily synonymous with "great" speakers. Yet, historically, some of the most eloquent orators of all time were besieged by stage fright, including Cicero, Abraham Lincoln, and Winston Churchill. Clearly then, communication apprehension is not infrequent, nor is it experienced by only the small and insignificant. Business Brief 14.1 dramatizes this point.

- *Normally, communication apprehension decreases as we gain experience as public speakers.* It is not uncommon for students in basic public speaking courses to experience fairly intense anxiety during their first speech performance. As public speaking becomes a part of their normal classroom activities, however, they grow to greet future assignments with greater confidence.

- *Speakers frequently overrate the accuracy with which listeners can judge the extent of their nervousness.* Even if there are no overt physical reactions to anxiety, we often assume that the audience can see through our smiles and calm appearance to the turmoil and uncertainty lurking beneath.[19] Once again, studies do not support this assumption. Listeners, including college speech teachers, are notoriously poor at judging the level of anxiety in speakers. The typical tendency is to underrate communication apprehension, attributing greater confidence to the speaker than he or she claims to feel. In fact, it is not uncommon for speakers to

---

Business Brief 14.1

Stage Fright in the Business World

The *Wall Street Journal* published an interesting article focusing on the fear of public speaking in the business world. The article reported that:

> In this garrulous, smooth-talking world, many executives and professionals are afflicted with what specialists call presentation phobia, or stage fright. A far cry from butterflies in the stomach, it's sometimes severe enough to slow careers to a stop.
>
> The fear can strike not only the chief executive facing a hall of shareholders but also the manager asked to "say something about yourself" at a staff meeting. Bert Decker of Decker Communications, a San Francisco consulting firm, estimates that "roughly half the business population" labors under (some) form of the anxiety and tries to avoid speaking in public.
>
> But as treatment becomes more effective and widely available, more people are getting help. "Of the full range of anxiety disorders," says Charles Melville, an Atlanta psychiatrist, "people can most predictably overcome a fear of public speaking."

Source: Jolie Solomon, "Executives Who Dread Public Speaking Learn to Keep Their Cool in the Spotlight," *Wall Street Journal,* May 4, 1990, 133.

---

believe they "acted nervous," while audience members will comment on the degree to which the speakers seemed completely in control and self-assured!

- Earlier in this section we referred to stage fright as an "unfortunate malady." While this represents a commonly held view, in truth, *communication apprehension is a hindrance to your performance only if it is severe or uncontrolled.* A number of psychological studies have demonstrated that moderate anxiety *can be an asset* in performance, whether you are taking an examination or giving a speech.[20] You should welcome some anxiety as a possible stimulus for a better presentation. Whenever you become anxious before giving a speech, you get an extra shot of adrenaline. Unfortunately, this increased source of energy may manifest itself in shaking hands and other signs of nervousness. Yet that same energy can be channeled into positive behaviors that may enhance the effectiveness of your presentation. Moderate tension can provide a creative edge, a more dynamic style of delivery, a more animated presentation. Besides, if you didn't care about your speech, why would you become anxious? We may feel nervous in part because we *do* care and want to do well. When viewed from this perspective, communication apprehension becomes a tool for creating a more involving presentation as well as being a sign of speaker concern and engagement.

- Finally, there is perhaps no better way to control anxiety than to *know that you are well prepared* for the speech event.[21] When you have carefully analyzed your audience, engaged in thorough research, strategically structured the organizational pattern of the speech, and practiced the delivery of the speech, and when you are committed to the ideas therein, you are in an excellent position to control your anxiety. Without such diligent preparation, however, some apprehension may be well founded.

Styles of Delivery

There are three major styles of speech delivery: impromptu, manuscript, and extemporaneous. Each type of delivery may be appropriate, or even necessary, depending on the speech situation.

IMPROMPTU SPEAKING

Impromptu speeches are essentially off-the-cuff; they are delivered without preparation, other than perhaps a few minutes to organize your thoughts. As you function in professional and social groups and organizations, you are often called upon to articulate a point of view, make a brief report, or explain a procedure. More often than not, requests for these speeches arise directly within the meeting when someone needs information.

While impromptu speaking is a common occurrence in daily organizational life, you should never elect to give an impromptu speech when you are asked in advance to make a speech. By definition, impromptu speaking excludes the opportunity for research, audience analysis, arranging a strategic plan, and practicing delivery. As a result, you have minimal control over most crucial speech variables.

SPEAKING FROM A MANUSCRIPT

In manuscript speaking, you write the speech out word for word and read the manuscript to the audience. The use of the manuscript is not infrequent among business and professional speakers. In fact, manuscripts are sometimes required when the speaking occasion is especially important. In the political world, manuscript speaking is widespread. Nearly all major presidential addresses are delivered with the assistance of a manuscript. If poorly handled, however, the manuscript can become a most deadly form of delivery.

Common problems associated with manuscript speaking are limited eye contact, poor oral style, difficulties associated with reading, and inflexibility. Unless speakers practice frequently before delivering the manuscript, they are apt to become bogged down in the manuscript itself during the presentation. We have all seen speakers who are glued to their manuscripts, looking up only sporadically or failing to look up at all. Without eye contact, a sense of directness and involvement cannot be effectively communicated.

What might be some advantages of speaking from a manuscript? When properly used, the manuscript speech provides the opportunity for maximum speaker control. Time limitations are important and often overlooked by public speakers. By using a manuscript, you can plan precisely with regard to time, again leaving some room for "during delivery" alterations. The potential for excellence in language usage is also great with the use of the manuscript. Descriptive passages can be created with attention to color, precision, simplicity, and figurative elements. Precise verbs can be chosen and incorporated throughout the speech. The manuscript speech can become a work of art as long as you are constantly aware of the need for maintaining a conversational quality. Finally, because you will present the speech pretty much as you have practiced it, you are likely to face the speaking occasion with an enhanced sense of confidence.

EXTEMPORANEOUS SPEAKING

The final style of delivery is extemporaneous. Many individuals confuse impromptu and extemporaneous speaking, believing that a speaker does little to prepare for an extemporaneous speech. On the contrary, extemporaneous delivery requires a great deal of preparation. The extemporaneous speech is carefully prepared, thoroughly outlined, practiced but not memorized, and delivered from speaking notes (typically in the form of a keyword outline). When speaking extemporaneously, you commit key ideas to memory, but precise words, specific phrases, and particular examples vary during practice sessions as well as during the actual presentation of the speech.

When you speak extemporaneously, you can place your outline either on four-by-six-inch note cards or on full sheets of paper, depending on the particulars of the speech situation. If you plan a great deal of bodily movement, including perhaps the use of a chalkboard, it is probably best to use note cards. On the other hand, papers are entirely appropriate if they are placed on the podium and left there; in fact, they allow you to see a larger portion of the speech at one glance. When used properly, with plenty of practice, the notes for extemporaneous speaking have the potential for allowing maximum flexibility, directness, and spontaneity. Your notes serve as a reminder of strategies planned and ideas developed; but you should be able to deviate from them whenever the situation invites it. As an extemporaneous speaker, you can make structural alterations, clarify or elaborate with additional examples or illustrations, and omit unnecessary remarks because you are creating the speech as you deliver it.

This is not to imply that extemporaneous speakers can do no wrong. There are times when they flounder, groping for the precise words they need (and times when they never find them); they may ramble or use too many examples, especially of a personal nature. With appropriate criticism and guidance, however, these problems usually decrease as the speaker gains experience. Perhaps the greatest advantage of extemporaneous delivery is that it requires total involvement on the part of the speaker.

Characteristics of Effective Delivery

In discussing the three major styles of delivery, we have alluded to the basic qualities of effective delivery. In general, public speakers are most effective when their delivery is characterized by spontaneity, directness, flexibility, and involvement.

- *Spontaneity* is particularly important in the use of gestures and bodily movement. Neither should be planned in advance; they should emerge naturally from the speech, as a kind of enlarged conversation. Both gestures and bodily movement should reinforce the spoken words so that movement does not consist of aimless wandering around the room. As a general rule, you ought to gesture whenever you feel like it, making some attempt to adjust the size of the gesture to the size of the room (a small classroom versus a 5,000-seat auditorium).

  You may also choose to make some spontaneous changes in content as you speak. You may decide that you want to allude to comments a previous speaker has made or that you need to define a term or provide an additional example as you move through your speech. These sorts of spontaneous changes reflect the fact that you are attuned to the audience and are attempting to adapt to their needs and interests as you go.

- *Directness* is another critical quality of effective delivery. Probably the best way to communicate directly with listeners is to *establish eye contact* with them as we speak. In U.S. culture, when a communicator cannot or does not look us in the eye, we often respond negatively.[22] When we look directly at others, we are attempting to show our willingness to communicate, and we may convey a sense of integrity as well. Of course, as Highlighting Diversity emphasizes, there are many cultural variations in practices and reactions to eye contact.

Directness can also be demonstrated through appropriate vocal qualities. You should speak loudly enough to be heard—but not so loudly that you blast listeners from the room. Some speakers talk with an overly projected, artificial vocal quality, leaving the impression of a dramatic production rather than a speaking occasion. On the other hand, no one cares to listen to a monotone. Ideas are best communicated directly to audiences by speakers who employ vocal variety and expressiveness.

- *Flexibility* is a third quality of effective delivery. To be a flexible speaker, you must be alert to information, responses, and other stimuli that might indicate a need for change in your planned strategy and choice of words. Speakers who insist on delivering the speech precisely as they have practiced it often fail to meet important needs of audience members. They are not responsive to boredom, confusion, or hostility. Thus, they say what they want to say, but the listeners cannot, will not, or do not receive the message. Once again, the most effective public speakers are usually those who are especially responsive to audience feedback. Clearly, spontaneity and flexibility are closely related.

- *Involvement* is the final important delivery characteristic. It is imperative that you sound and appear concerned about your communicated message. Involvement is a total delivery concept, including eye contact, movement, word choice, and facial expression. The audience will believe that you are committed to your ideas when you reinforce your words with appropriate nonverbal and inflectional emphasis. The speaker who says "I couldn't believe in this more" in a deadpan manner without communicating an image of total commitment might

Highlighting Diversity

Acknowledging Cultural Differences in Eye Contact and Gaze

- In Japan, meeting participants often look down or close their eyes while others are talking. By doing so, they show their attentiveness to and even agreement with the speaker.

- African Americans, Native Americans, Chicanos, and Puerto Ricans often avoid eye contact as a nonverbal sign of recognition and respect for an authority-subordinate relationship.

- In some Far Eastern cultures, it is considered rude to look into another person's eyes while interacting with him or her.

- For Arabs, the eyes are a key to a person's being; looking deeply into another person's eyes allows one to see another's soul.

- In U.S. culture, we clearly place ourselves at a disadvantage if we do not use our eyes to communicate a sense of directness, openness, and candor.

Sources: Edward T. Hall and M. R. Hall, *Understanding Cultural Differences* (Yarmouth, ME: Intercultural Press, 1990); and Carolyn Calloway-Thomas, Pamela J. Cooper, and Cecil Blake, *Intercultural Communication: Roots and Routes* (Boston: Allyn & Bacon, 1999).

as well say, "I couldn't care less about this"; certainly the latter is more likely the meaning the audience will perceive.

The key to developing the kind of effective delivery described above is to *be well prepared* and to practice your speech. Preparing a substantive presentation and feeling a genuine commitment to your message are essential. However, the final step involves *practicing aloud*, several times, until you feel comfortable with your notes and your speech's content and confident in your ability to deliver your speech with competence and conviction. For some speakers, only two or three practice sessions are needed; for others, many more are necessary. As you gain experience as a public speaker, you will learn what works for you.

Responding to Questions

Every public speaker should be prepared to answer audience questions, usually following the presentation. There are situations in which the speaker encourages listeners to interrupt her during the speech whenever they have a question, when something is unclear, or when they simply wish to relate a personal view. The typical procedure, however, is for the speaker to present her ideas without interruption, and then to entertain questions during a forum period following the speech.

No speaker should underestimate the importance of responding meaningfully to listeners' questions. In a sense, the *question-and-answer* or *forum period* is simply an extension of the more formally structured presentation, for the skill with which questions are answered will be a major determinant of listeners' overall response to the speech. The forum period represents yet another opportunity for you to reinforce important ideas, build your credibility, provide additional interesting information, and even deal with aspects of the topic untouched by the speech itself.

To manage the question-and-answer period procedurally, you may want to follow these guidelines:

- *Demonstrate your desire to interact with the audience.* You may want to move out from behind the podium, or sit on the edge of a table. Listen carefully and respectfully to each question posed. Ask for clarification if you do not understand what is asked. Sometimes, audience members are reluctant to ask questions. Show patience, actively invite their participation, and even consider asking questions yourself. For instance, you might ask, "I know that many of you work for companies that provide flex-time options. You know what my take is on flex-time, but I'd love to learn more about your feelings and experiences."

- *All listeners should be able to hear and understand questions that are posed.* It may be helpful to have the questioning audience member rise and state his question; if the room is especially large, you may simply repeat the question before answering it.

- *No one questioner should be allowed to dominate the forum period, nor should you pursue irrelevant questions for long.* If an irrelevant issue is raised or a question is so technical that you suspect only a few listeners are interested in hearing the response, you might ask the person who raised the inquiry to talk with you following the forum period.

- *Never attempt to fake your way through a difficult question.* It is best to admit that you do not have that kind of experience or perhaps never uncovered that kind of data during your research. While continual responses of "I don't know" damage your credibility, a single admission of ignorance tends to humanize you and give you a positive mark for openness. You can then offer to look into the question posed and get in back in touch with the questioner (usually by obtaining her e-mail address).

- *Know how much time is available for answering questions.* Just as you should be aware of how long you are expected to speak, it is equally important to know how much time is allocated out of your speaking time for questions, and don't go beyond the allocated time. Time limits vary greatly, but whatever they are, they should be respected.

Following the question-and-answer period, you will probably need some additional time to interact informally with some listeners. Try to arrange your schedule so that you can afford to stay and chat with those who have additional ideas to share or questions to ask. These informal exchanges may lead to more formal alliances later on, as you exchange cards or e-mail addresses with audience members, setting the stage for sustained contact.

LANGUAGE: STRIVING FOR GOOD ORAL STYLE

When we speak of good *oral* style, we are really stressing the fact that speaking and writing are not the same. Speakers who read from a written text often sound stuffy or overly formal. In listening to them, we may feel that their remarks really do not speak to us directly.

Differences between Oral and Written Styles

Generally speaking, in contrast to written prose style, when we employ good oral style, we use:

- *More personal pronouns* (we, ours, I, mine, you, yours)
- *More simple sentences* (with some variety)
- *Shorter sentences* (assisting audience comprehension)
- *More rhetorical questions* (gaining and sustaining the audience's attention by challenging them to think)
- *More repetition of words, phrases, and sentences* (intentionally repeating key ideas, colorful phrases, or slogans that we want the audience to remember and ponder after the speech is over)
- *More simple, familiar words* (knowing that good speeches must be instantly intelligible)
- *More contractions* (giving the speech a natural, conversational quality)
- *More figurative language* (using words and phrases that are pleasing to the ear and stimulating the audience's imagination; also making abstract ideas concrete, adding color and life to the speech, and reinforcing key ideas)[23]

Choosing Words

One of your main goals as a public speaker is to be clear. One way of achieving clarity is to choose your words with great care, paying attention to their concreteness, simplicity, preciseness, and appropriateness.

CONCRETE WORDS

Concrete words are usually preferable to abstract words for effective speaking. Concrete words point to real events or objects that help the audience associate with your topic, description, or objectives. As your words become more and more concrete, the pictures you paint in the minds of your audience tend to become clearer and clearer.

Concrete words appeal to the senses. They point to something the listeners can hear, touch, see, taste, or feel: lemon, motorcycle, boots, tea, roses, picnic table, the howl of a wolf, the smell of freshly perked coffee. Whenever you must deal with a relatively abstract concept in your speaking, you can make it clearer and more concrete by providing specific illustrations and examples.

SIMPLE WORDS

Besides being concrete, your words should also be simple. Simplicity is related to clarity. When you use simple words, you avoid being vague, pretentious, or verbose. But simplicity is not the same as simplemindedness. In fact, many great speakers of the past, including Winston Churchill and Franklin Roosevelt, were masters of simplicity.

Although simple words are usually familiar ones as well, there are some phrases that have become clichés. Thus, in striving for simplicity and familiarity, you should avoid using such clichés as: "it goes without saying," "in the final analysis," "few and far between," "easier said than done," "all in all," "last but not least," or "clear as crystal." These are only a few examples of expressions that were probably amusing and interesting at one time but are now stale from overuse.

PRECISE WORDS

Concreteness and simplicity in word choice work in tandem with precision. Although we often speak of synonyms, rarely do we find any two words that have *exactly* the same meaning. If you looked up the following five words, you would soon discover that while each has to do with being poor, they still represent subtly different shades of meaning: *destitute, impoverished, bankrupt, impecunious,* and *needy.*

Precise words are accurate. Rather than using the verb *walked,* for instance, you might describe the *way* a person walked by using such verbs as *staggered, ambled, strutted, sauntered, waddled,* or *raced.* By selecting the best word in each case, you also eliminate unnecessary modifiers, such as, "walked *slowly*" or "walked *drunkenly.*" Thus, precise language is usually compact.

ETHICAL WORDS

Using words or language that the audience considers offensive or tasteless will not get the desired response. But, more than that, *knowingly* using such language suggests that the speaker lacks concern or respect for the audience. As in any communication situation, mutual respect is the hallmark of ethical communication. As ethical speakers, we will also want to **avoid sexist language**—or any language that is demeaning to any group, culture, or individual. We are not just

Highlighting Ethics

Avoiding Sexist Language

- **Speak in the plural whenever possible.** If you say, "Managers are usually genuinely interested in their employees' well-being. . . . *They* try to motivate," you don't have to worry about portraying the manager as a man or a woman. The more you use the plural, the more gender-neutral your language will tend to be.

- **Switch to "he or she" when you must use a singular subject.** You might say, "An employee who chooses the HMO health plan will have to work within an approved provider network. *He or she* will want to make sure that. . . ." This approach works well as long as you don't overdo it.

- **Eliminate gender inflections.** Any of us can learn to say "chairperson" rather than "chairman," "mail carrier" in place of "mailman," and "server" instead of "waitress."

- **Avoid using gender markers.** It is always inappropriate to highlight a person's gender (or sexual orientation) when referring to his or her profession. Eliminate expressions such as "my female dentist," "that lesbian tennis player," or "the woman manager." Of course, the same rule applies to racial or ethnic markers; equally offensive is "that Hispanic doctor" or "that black lawyer."

- **Don't hesitate to use gender-specific pronouns when they are appropriate.** If you are referring to a person who is part of a group, all of whom are either males or females, you should refer to that person with an accurate pronoun. For instance, a former president of the United States would be "he" because we have had no female presidents. Similarly, a mother is "she," as is a Buddhist nun.

talking about being "politically correct." We are talking about the speaker's attitude toward the listeners and toward others in society. The Highlighting Ethics box (above) offers some guidelines for avoiding sexist language.

Using language that may be perceived as sexist, racist, or offensive in some way will present some real problems, whatever the speaker's intentions or level of awareness. When, during the 1992 presidential race, Ross Perot addressed a nearly all African American audience and referred to them as "you people," he was poorly received by his audience, and his comment was repeated countless times by the press, as well as his opponents. In short, whatever the speaker's intentions or attitudes, audience perceptions of appropriateness, ethics, and good taste are paramount.

Constructing Sentences

As you choose your words carefully and begin to place them into sentences, some additional guiding principles are useful.

KEEP SUBJECTS AND VERBS CLOSE TOGETHER

First, construct each sentence so that the subject and the verb are close together. This increases the intelligibility of the sentence. It is also a practical characteristic of daily conversation; therefore, it sounds more natural. Consider the following sentence, in which subject and verb have been separated:

"This plan, which has been tested in other companies like our own and has resulted in enormous profits, is worthy of your support."

To place the subject and the verb together and thus increase the sentence's intelligibility, you might create two separate sentences, as follows:

"This plan is worthy of your support. It has been tested in companies like our own and has resulted in enormous profits."

KEEP SENTENCES SHORT

Another important guideline is to use short, active sentences. Short sentences are easier for audiences to follow and comprehend. Supposedly, a "standard" sentence is made up of seventeen words.[24] Even so, some variety is essential. Longer sentences can be clear when they are properly constructed. In writing sentences, you should avoid needless repetition, unnecessary modifiers, and circumlocutions, such as *"The reason why* I think this plan will work is because. . . ."

- *Use the active voice.* One of the best ways to delete unnecessary words is to *use the active voice* whenever possible. Compare the following:

  — Much dissatisfaction with this new rotation schedule has been expressed by line workers. (passive voice)

  — Line workers have expressed much dissatisfaction with this new rotation schedule. (active voice)

  Sometimes the passive voice is unclear because it is wordy, but often it is intrinsically unclear. For example, "This product was chosen because it met governmental standards. . . ." What this sentence does not tell us is who did the choosing. Depending on the issue being discussed, that might be very important information.

- *Use only necessary modifiers.* There are two kinds of modifiers in the English language, those that comment and those that define. Commenting modifiers include *very, most,* and *definitely.* These modifiers tell us nothing new; instead, they try to boost the meaning of the word they modify. Yet, if your words are selected carefully, with a concern for precision, they should be able to stand alone without the assistance of modifiers that simply try to make their meaning more emphatic. Of course, some modifiers are essential; they tell us something we need to know. Depending on whether a plan is described as "innovative," "costly," "sensible," or "outdated," we will and should respond differently. Defining modifiers provide information that the noun standing alone cannot convey.

Good oral style, then, is the kind of style you will use as you deliver your speech extemporaneously. By doing so, you will sound natural and conversational. Because listeners will respond positively to language they find understandable and memorable, you enhance the chances of communicating effectively when you use good oral style.

USING PRESENTATIONAL AIDS

In every speaking situation, communicating information clearly, concretely, and concisely is an overarching goal. One way of doing this is through the use of presentational aids. When chosen wisely and prepared with care, presentational aids can go a long way toward enhancing the speech and making ideas and information more accessible to listeners.

When you use presentational aids, you reinforce your ideas by letting your audience see them as well as hear about them. If you design and use your aids well, you also enhance your credibility and make your ideas and information more memorable and compelling. A number of options exist.

Depicting Statistics

In most speaking situations, you will find yourself using statistics as support from time to time. Presentational aids can often help you to present statistical information clearly and concisely.

GRAPHS

One common method for presenting statistical summaries is by a graph. A graph is a representation of numbers by geometric figures drawn to scale. Speakers often use graphs to make statistical information more vivid and to depict relationships. Three of the more familiar and useful kinds of graphs are line, bar, and pie graphs. *Line graphs* are especially useful for depicting comparative relationships through time. Many business and professional presentations focus on information relating to time-based trends—for example, comparing gross or net profits, production, or wages. As a result, the line graph is one of the more useful tools of the presentational speaker. Figure 14.2 presents an example of a line graph depicting net profits for a period of thirty years.

It is possible to place more than one curve on a single graph, but it may be at the expense of clarity. Moreover, you should recognize that a trend can be dis-

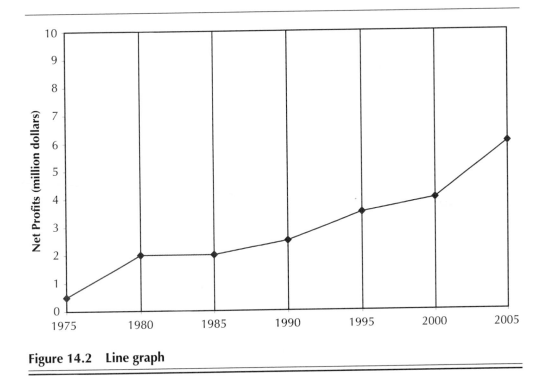

Figure 14.2   Line graph

torted simply by compressing or elongating the space allotted to time periods while keeping the other dimension of the graph constant. The ethical speaker will not knowingly distort a trend simply to dramatize a particular point.

Another kind of commonly used graph is the *bar graph*. These graphs usually depict quantity. Thus, a simple bar graph literally uses bars to indicate amounts and is well suited to presenting comparative statistics. Figure 14.3 depicts comparisons of worker productivity, focusing on seven time periods.

Bar graphs are particularly useful as visual aids in that they can be made large enough for the audience to see and easily understand the point being made. As with the line graph, it is possible to depict a number of different statistical comparisons simultaneously on the same bar graph, often through the use of different colors or shadings. Once again, however, simplicity should be sought to avoid confusion.

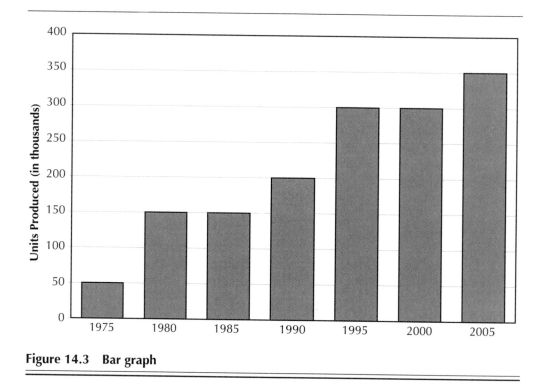

Figure 14.3   Bar graph

The final graph that is commonly used to depict statistics is the *pie graph*. The pie graph is useful for showing numerical distribution patterns. In particular, you may want to depict how a total figure breaks down into different parts. For instance, if you wanted to depict the student population at your university according to race or ethnicity, you might use a pie graph, such as the one shown in figure 14.4.

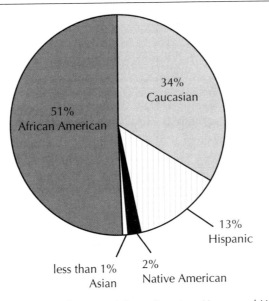

Source: Derived from U.S. Conference of Mayors, *A Status Report on Hunger and Homelessness in America's Cities* (Washington, DC: U.S. Conference of Mayors, 2002), 97.

Figure 14.4   Pie graph

Traditional Presentational Aid Options

THE CHALKBOARD OR WHITEBOARD

Probably the simplest and most basic aid is the chalkboard. Using this allows you to put diagrams and sketches on the board as an explanation unfolds. If you are counting on using a chalkboard or whiteboard, however, you had better check in advance to make sure the room has one. The chalkboard is a convenient and potentially effective means of depicting important data. Moreover, moving to and from the board may help you manage any communication apprehension you are experiencing.

Of course, the chalkboard has its limitations. Because it is so familiar to most audiences, it tends to be less interesting or less impressive than other forms of presentational aids. But if your handwriting is legible, if you are working on a clean board, and if you can practice so that you do not lose contact with the audience while you write, then the chalkboard may be a sensible choice of visual support. You may also want to consider preparing the board in advance and covering it with a screen, to be lifted at the appropriate moment.

POSTER BOARD DRAWINGS

Other visual aids can be prepared in advance and brought with you to the speaking event. For example, if you want to use color or a sophisticated design, you may elect poster board drawings as a presentational aid. These can be prepared in advance and can be as professional and impressive as budget and talent will allow. Poster boards are not without their disadvantages, however. They are clumsy to transport and handle. They require some sort of special equipment to display (such as a tripod or tape). In addition, in some professional settings, a poster board drawing would simply seem out of place. While you might prepare and use a poster board if you were speaking to students in an elementary school classroom (or even in your own classroom), you would probably be less inclined to use this kind of presentational aid if you were making a presentation at IBM.

FLIPCHARTS

A flipchart is essentially an oversized writing tablet. Using this method, you would place drawings or lists on the chart and display them on a convenient frame (such as a tripod) that facilitates movement from one drawing to the next. Flipcharts are commonly used in business, conference, and workshop settings. In these contexts, speakers use flipcharts to record ideas generated during discussions or brainstorming. Flipchart pages can also be torn from the tablet and taped onto walls as a way of organizing small group activities.

HANDOUTS

On occasion, you may decide to prepare copies of handouts to aid the audience's comprehension. Handouts are especially useful when you are referring to extensive lists of figures, such as budgetary statements in the context of a technical report. You can also use handouts to outline essential information to which the audience can refer during subsequent decision-making sessions. By using handouts, you reduce the need for the audience to take notes. Thus, listeners can devote greater attention to your ideas. The handout also serves as an outline for you, potentially assisting you in your organization and delivery.

When using handouts, you should pass them out at the moment you plan to discuss them (not in advance) and make sure that copies are available for everyone. In addition, if you are using multiple handouts, you may want to use varied colors so that listeners can easily find the information that is of interest to them. You might point out, for example, that the blue handout contains the budget, the green one has important names and contact information, and the yellow one sketches an agenda for a proposed conference.

MODELS

Some speeches call for a model as a visual aid. An architect, for example, will likely need to use a three-dimensional model of a proposed apartment building so that the audience will have a precise picture of the structure he envisions. A nurse who wants her listeners to gain an understanding of the immune system might use a model of the human anatomy to help explain the various parts of the system and how they function. One major advantage of these models is the clarity and precision with which they allow you to demonstrate your ideas.

OBJECTS

You can also use actual objects as presentational aids. Assume that a speaker is proposing the adoption of a new line of toys aimed at fostering creativity and teaching certain critical concepts, such as numbers and spatial relationships. Assume further that samples of these toys exist. What better way to persuade the audience of the uniqueness and value of the toys than by displaying and demonstrating them?

TRANSPARENCIES AND OVERHEAD PROJECTORS

Overhead projectors are useful for displaying detailed or complex information on a large screen. These projectors are commonly found in classrooms and meeting rooms. They allow the speaker to project lists, figures, charts, graphs, and other information onto a large screen. Transparencies can look professional and be easily created by computer. They are easy to transport and use.

However, certain principles should be observed when using an overhead projector. Here are some tips:

- The transparencies should be as simple and readable as possible. Avoid crowding too much information onto a single transparency. Adjust the font size to the room size. In a typical classroom or business meeting room, an 18–20 point font should be adequate.
- When ready to use the projector, check to make sure that it is properly focused and that you have placed the transparency properly on the projector (so that you can read from it directly).
- Avoid standing between audience members and the projected image. You can point to the transparency with a pencil, or you may prefer to use a pointer and point to the screen as you discuss specific parts of the image.
- When unveiling a list, do so one point at a time to focus the audience's attention.
- When you move to the screen, make sure you continue to speak to the audience, rather than delivering your comments to the screen.
- When moving from one transparency to the next, try to accomplish the switch quickly and smoothly to avoid blinding the audience with a bright white light between slides.

When used appropriately, the overhead projector is one of the most effective presentational aids available to you. Given its widespread use, you will want to become adept at using it.

SLIDES

Slides are particularly useful for showing pictures or delivering presentations that must be repeated in the future. For maximum effectiveness, plan your slide presentation in advance to maintain a relatively steady pace. As you show each new slide, allow a moment of silence so the audience has an opportunity to grasp its contents, then describe and discuss what they are viewing. In addition, avoid turning your back to the audience and talking to the screen; glance at the screen to determine what the slide is showing and then speak directly to the audience as you provide added information.

Computer-Assisted Options

Audiences are becoming increasingly accustomed to speakers using professional and polished presentational aids. This expectation is especially salient in the business and professional world. It is hard to imagine a business professional rushing to make an important speech with a pile of posterboard drawings under one arm! More realistically, speakers in professional contexts will use transparencies, models, and perhaps flipcharts (especially in workshop settings). Moreover, speakers are increasingly using presentational software and electronic presentation systems to make sophisticated and professional-looking presentational aids.

There are two major ways that computers can assist you in preparing presentational aids. Ideally, you will use a computer to create *and* present your graphics. If you have used a laptop to prepare your graphics, you will then take it to the meeting where you are speaking and use it, together with a portable screen, to display your visuals. Or, using computers that may not be portable, you can still use a software package (such as PowerPoint, Appleworks, or Astound) to create slides and to incorporate images, sound, and even video clips into your presentation. You then save your presentation on a disk and take it with you to a room equipped with a computer and large screen to be used during your presentation.

Obviously, not everyone will have access to this sort of equipment. Nevertheless, you can still use your computer to generate presentational aids—to construct a graph, table, or other visual display that you want to print out and use as a black-and-white or full-color transparency with an overhead projector. Certainly, in a classroom setting, these sorts of aids will be very well received and will give your presentation a professional air. The following are some guidelines for preparing and using computer-generated graphics:

- *Seek out workshops to help you master the software.* You can probably pick up a lot on your own by simply experimenting, but if you can take a short course or workshop, you may learn more quickly and be more likely to discover a wider array of options available to you. Check on whether your campus offers workshops and make the time to attend one.

- *Master the basics.* A good place to begin is by creating graphics that can be used on the overhead projector. You might start by generating a list of main ideas to be discussed in your speech, or you might construct a simple graph or chart. Remember that fonts should be at least 18 point to be visually accessible to audience members. To further enhance their visibility, use bold letters and fonts that are plain and easy to read.

- *Emphasize content.* Fancy technology is no substitute for strong content. Even the most dazzling PowerPoint presentation will fail if the ideas and information in the speech are weak or lacking in substance. If your PowerPoint display fails, you should still feel confident that the ideas you are conveying are worth listening to.

- *Simplicity is the rule.* Your graphics should be designed so that they are simple, uncluttered, and consistent. Most software will allow you to add all sorts of

DILBERT

DILBERT © by Scott Adams; reprinted by permission of United Feature Syndicate, Inc.

peripheral elements, such as shading and background patterns, as well as movement and highlighting. Even so, you will want to avoid anything that is distracting. Avoid the temptation to have a new main point come flying or spinning onto the screen. Stay away from backgrounds that are glitzy. Remember, computer-generated graphics, like other presentational aids, should support your speech, not distract from it or take undue attention away from you, the speaker.

- *Use the technology to full advantage.* Once you have mastered the basics and have had some experience using computer-generated graphics, you may want to become more creative. If your topic lends itself to such options, you might download images from the Internet to be made into slides to accompany your presentation. In displaying a bar graph, show the audience one bar at a time to simplify the statistics and focus the audience's attention on the point you are making. And, of course, experiment with color—choosing color schemes that are vivid, tasteful, and professional.

- *Always have multiple backups!* If you have your graphics on your laptop, save a backup file onto a floppy disk. Always make overheads that could be used in case the screen or computer you've been promised isn't there. As a final backup, prepare handouts in case there are electrical problems or other kinds of equipment failure. The more sophisticated our presentational aids, the greater our tendency to count on them for our speech's effectiveness. This is a mistake. No matter how wonderful your computer-generated graphics may be, you should be able to make your presentation with more traditional means of presentational support and still communicate effectively.

Once you have learned to prepare and present computer-generated presentational aids, you will probably rarely use more traditional aids.

Practical Considerations

Regardless of the type of presentational aid you choose to use, whether you are using a simple, low-tech chalkboard or PowerPoints presented via your laptop computer, here are some general guidelines you should follow:

- *Use presentational aids only when they are justified.* Some speakers try to jazz up their speeches by using presentational aids throughout. But unnecessary visuals can annoy or distract an audience as easily as persuade them. Presentational aids should be used to clarify, to make points more concrete, or to demonstrate something that is difficult to describe without them.

- *Don't hesitate to use presentational aids that are needed.* You cannot tell an audience what a proposed budget is "like." To be clear and complete, you must present it in detail visually, usually by providing a handout. Similarly, it would be foolish to describe a building plan, a surgical procedure, or an automobile design without presentational aids.

- *Your presentational aids should be large enough so that each member of the audience can see and decipher them with ease.* Any presentational aid that cannot be seen is actually a hindrance and would best be omitted entirely.

- *Your presentational aids should be clear and, if possible, colorful.* Your writing or printing should be neat and clear. Whatever color scheme you choose, your presentational aid should enhance clarity and be pleasing to the eye.

- *Keep your presentational aids simple.* The inclusion of many complicated details will serve only to distract the audience and obscure the point being made. In general, it is best to illustrate only the essentials, with one concept featured with each diagram, overhead, or chart. Remember: graphics software packages can lead you astray. Don't let your graphics upstage you.

- *Consider the needs of each audience member in presenting your presentational aids.* Position presentational aids high enough so that those in the front of the room do not obstruct the view of those in the back. If you are showing an object, for example, and if the speaking context permits, you might want to walk into the audience, showing the object to listeners as you talk about it.

- *Do not inadvertently obscure the view of your presentational aid by standing in front of it.* Speakers often project their own images onto screens, blocking the transparencies they are projecting. Speakers who use chalkboards may do the same thing—partially hiding what they are writing on the board—and, at the same time, talk to the board rather than to their listeners.

- *Direct the audience's attention to the relevant portion of your presentational aid by pointing to it as you discuss it.* In this way, you can help the audience follow your remarks. You can point by using your finger or, with large visual aids, a pointer. Speakers using PowerPoint presentations can direct the audience's attention to each point by having each one appear at the crucial moment.

- *Usually, presentational aids should be displayed only when they are being discussed during your speech.* When you are finished with them, remove them from view. When presentational aids are randomly displayed at the beginning of the presentation or left in view after they have functioned as aids, you are inviting the audience to continue to look at the visual while ignoring you and your message.

- *Practice with presentational aids prior to the presentation.* Make sure you are comfortable with the equipment. Equally important, be sure you can move smoothly from your notes at the podium to the visual aid and back again without losing either your composure or your sense of directness with the audience.

Presentational aids are potentially useful and compelling supporting devices. Not every speaker should use them, but most presentations would benefit from their skillful use. The careful preparation of presentational aids is simply one way for the speaker to demonstrate a concern for clarity, precision, and audience interest. When properly prepared and presented, presentational aids should, as their name suggests, *aid* audience comprehension. Furthermore, by using them, you are communicating the message that you have cared enough to prepare carefully and to consider the welfare of your audience.

SUMMARY

Deciding *how* to present ideas and information is a significant challenge for every public speaker. To begin, organizing your speech into a form well suited to the audience's needs and your specific purpose represents a major strategic choice. You have many patterns to choose from—ranging from the chronological to the problem-solution. You may want to experiment with different organizational patterns by outlining different approaches you might take. By creating a formative outline, you put your ideas down on paper and examine the way your speech is developing. Later, you will develop a formal outline to reflect your final speech plan (including an introduction, body, and conclusion) and to give your instructor insights into your organizational strategy. Finally, you will use a key-word outline to assist you in delivering your speech extemporaneously.

For most public speaking contexts, the extemporaneous style of delivery is best (although you may, on occasion, speak impromptu or from a manuscript). Extemporaneous delivery allows you to be direct with your audience, as well as flexible, spontaneous, and involved. In general, these qualities will serve you well as you speak within your organization, as a spokesperson for your organization, or as a citizen speaking on behalf on some community cause or social issue in which you deeply believe. Through extemporaneous delivery, you are also more likely to use conversational language, so that your sentences are not stilted and your word choice is simple and appropriate. As you speak with increasing frequency and as you work to improve over time, your oral style will continue to improve. Of course, whatever your delivery style, your language should reflect the utmost concern for ethics—always avoiding sexist, racist, or any kind of language the audience might perceive as offensive or inappropriate.

Finally, using carefully prepared presentational aids is an excellent way to enhance your speech. With presentational aids, you can highlight your main ideas, depict statistics, picture things that otherwise have to be imagined, and show the audience that you prepared well for your presentation. Almost any speech can benefit from the use of at least one presentational aid. As with other aspects of your speech, presentational aids will be more effective if they are prepared well in advance (using the criteria discussed in this chapter) and if you practice using them before you deliver your speech. Modern technologies allow for the creation and use of computer-generated graphics, and listeners are increasingly accustomed to seeing them used. Exploring the potential of such technologies is crucial for all speakers.

Questions for Discussion

1. What are some of the elements of an effective speech introduction? Be specific. What are some methods of gaining the audience's attention? Cite examples whenever possible.

2. What are some speech topics that would be well suited to each of the following patterns of organization? Provide at least three examples for each pattern.

   a. Chronological order

   b. Spatial order

   c. Categorical order

   d. Cause-and-effect order

   e. Problem-solution order

   f. The motivated sequence

   g. Narrative pattern

3. Discuss the basic characteristics of good speech conclusions. What are some specific devices that might be used to conclude speeches? Examples?

4. Compare and contrast the formative, the formal, and the keyword outline. How is each useful to a speaker?

5. Refute or defend the following: "Stage fright is a nearly universal phenomenon." Cite evidence to support your position. What are some strategies for developing confidence as a public speaker?

6. Compare and contrast impromptu and extemporaneous speaking. What are the conditions under which each is appropriately used?

7. If given the choice, would you elect to speak extemporaneously or from a manuscript? Why? How would you prepare for the mode of delivery you have chosen?

8. What are some problems you might anticipate with regard to answering questions after a speech? How might you cope with each? Again, be specific.

9. List some of the differences between oral and written styles. What happens when a public speaker violates the "rules" of good oral style?

10. What are some of the characteristics of good word choice and sound sentence structure? Cite examples of each quality you name.

11. List several guidelines for the effective use of presentational aids.

12. What are some ways in which computer-generated graphics might be especially helpful in supporting a speech? What are some pitfalls to avoid?

Exercises

1. Choose *one* of the following topics. Assume that you have been assigned to speak on this chosen topic to your classroom audience. What would your specific purpose be? Your thesis? Compose a good introduction and a good conclusion. Choose a tentative strategy of organization for the body, and sketch out an outline. Explain the reasoning behind your choices.
   a. Grade inflation
   b. College majors that lead to jobs
   c. Affirmative action
   d. AmeriCorps
   e. HMOs
   f. Working in teams in the professional world
   g. Ethics in advertising
   h. Weight training
   i. Low carb diets
   j. The future of Social Security

2. Select a topic of your choice and deliver it to the classroom audience using extemporaneous delivery. Try to capitalize on the qualities of effective delivery outlined in this chapter. Ask your instructor to make a videotape of your speech so that you can later watch yourself and gain from self-analysis. Ask the audience to focus specifically on your delivery and tell you how it might be improved.

3. Choose another speech topic and develop it into a manuscript speech. Be sure to guard against composing it like an essay rather than a speech and practice it several times so that you can overcome some of the problems associated with manuscript speaking. Then follow the same procedure in delivering the speech outlined above. Which mode of delivery do you prefer? Or would your preference depend on the context, the topic, and so forth?

4. After each of your speeches, allow the audience to ask you questions. In answering, make every effort to follow the guidelines established in this chapter. After the question-and-answer period, ask the class to evaluate that part of your presentation as well. To what extent, for example, did your responses to questions contribute to your clarity, credibility, and perceived responsiveness?

5. Go on the Internet to the following Web site: www.americanrhetoric.com/speechbank.htm. Click on "Top 100 Speeches." Choose any one of those top speeches that are of interest to you, print up a transcript of the speech, and then, following the transcript, view the speech on the Internet. As you view the speech, consider the effectiveness of the speaker's oral style. Mark specific instances where either word choice or sentence structure is especially good or bad. Also consider the speaker's delivery (especially in terms of spontaneity, involvement, directness, and flexibility). Then write a brief (2–3 pages) speech analysis in which you discuss the extent to which the speaker developed her or his speech using good oral style and delivered it effectively.

Case Application 14.1   Analyzing a Speech Outline— a Call for Civic Engagement

In April 2004, a student in an honors public speaking class at Indiana University delivered a persuasive speech on the topic of Teach for America. The class was a service-learning section of public speaking, with an emphasis on civic engagement.

Carefully read the outline that follows and respond to the questions posed at the end.

Teach for America and the Education Gap
By Melody Kanney

Specific Purpose: To inform the audience about the education gap and to persuade them to apply to Teach for America or related education programs.

Thesis: Teach for America is an effective program in closing the education gap, and only with the help of students like you can these programs continue.

I. Arouse

As university students, you probably don't think much about the unequal and poor quality education that many children across the country are currently receiving.

The reality is that students in lower-income inner city or rural school districts are being robbed of an adequate education.

The students in these areas are often taught in old, dilapidated buildings that do not meet acceptable standards.

The facilities and equipment are outdated, making it hard for students in these low-income school districts to keep up with the greatly advantaged schools in the surrounding suburban communities.

They also face family and peer pressures that can take the focus away from school work.

Racial issues continue to plague school districts as well.

After the 1954 *Brown v. Board of Education* Supreme Court decision allowing African American youth to attend white schools, many whites began to quickly move away from cities and into the suburbs.

These suburban communities grew increasingly wealthy and were able to invest a lot of money in their schools.

By contrast, the plummeting number of factory jobs in the inner cities caused a strong economic decline and the re-segregated city schools grew worse.

The effects of this downward education spiral have become very hard to overcome.

An article in the January 2004 issue of *Good Housekeeping* highlighted the effective efforts of teachers who work with disadvantaged students.

One of these teachers, Michelle Osborn, a sixth-grade teacher in rural Louisiana, said of her students, "You hear stories about students in these schools lacking intelligence and motivation—that isn't true. But they don't have access to technology and other resources, so they're at a disadvantage."

Transition: You may be wondering to yourself, "What difference do some new computers, better school buildings, more experienced teachers, and funding make?" Well, the effects these things can have on education can go far beyond the school walls.

II. Dissatisfy

Statistics supporting the education gap are discouraging.

1. Nine-year-olds in low-income areas are three grade levels behind their peers in higher income areas.
2. Later in life, these children are seven times less likely to graduate from college, according to the Teach for America organization Web site.
3. The March 2004 issue of *U.S. News and World Report* states that African Americans on average start kindergarten academically behind whites, and the effects of this ripple not only into high school, but beyond.

Transition: Educational differences in blacks and whites are continually influenced by family income and parents' attitudes, but the most important factor concerning school learning, regardless of race, is the quality of teachers, according to this *U.S. News* article.

4. A recent study by the National Commission on Teaching and America's Future found that "in every subject area, students in high-poverty schools are more likely than other students to be taught by teachers without even a minor in the subjects they are teaching."
5. A 2002 publication of the National Association of State Boards of Education clarified that what students need most from teachers are:
   a. high standards
   b. a challenging curriculum
   c. extra help
   d. sufficient knowledge of the subject area they are teaching

Transition: In light of all these immense problems, what can be done? What possible solutions might we pursue?

III. Gratify

A. Teach for America is a wonderful solution.

    1. A Princeton undergraduate, Wendy Kopp, wrote her senior thesis about America's need for an organization that would allow outstanding college graduates to teach in underresourced and disadvantaged inner-city schools to lessen the education gap.

    2. The program became known as Teach for America, and for the past 15 years, it has had a significant impact on lower-income school systems throughout the United States.

    3. Currently the president of the organization, Kopp was recently honored with a Child's Champion Award in the November 2003 issue of *Child Magazine*. In the article, she explains, "The quality of education you receive has so much to do with your chance in life. There are children who go on to college because of a teacher they had in elementary school."

    4. There is much evidence of the program's success.

        a. To date, the program has helped more than 10,000 young adults work with 1.5 million students.

        b. Teach for America is now at work in 22 major cities across the United States.

        c. With the increased applicant interest in the program and continued financial support, the effects of this amazing program will continue to grow.

    5. Here's how the program works.

        a. The Teach for America organization lets graduates of colleges and universities, like you and me, apply for positions in inner-city schools that so badly need our help.

        b. You don't have to have any teaching experience at all.

        c. By looking through the applications, recommendations, and conducting a rigorous interview day, Teach for America is able to select the candidates that they think will best teach, inspire, and relate to the students in these problem areas.

        d. My best friend was accepted this spring and, after an intense summer training institute over the summer, will soon be teaching high school English in the under-funded districts of Houston, Texas.

        e. Upon acceptance, new corps members live for two years in a city they highly prefer and teach students who otherwise would be at an extreme educational disadvantage.

    6. The Teach for America program is sustainable.

        a. Sixty-percent of Teach for America alumni choose to remain in some facet of education after their two years.

        b. It only costs Teach for America $9,500 to recruit, select, train, and support each corps member.

Transition: What if you feel you can't teach or you are not chosen for this program?

For those of us who are unable to participate in this amazing program, there is much that can still be done.

1. We can contribute toward or participate in programs with related goals, such as AmeriCorps (which originally oversaw Teach for America), Careers in the Common Good, and The New Teacher Project.
2. We can vote for educational reforms in funding and equal standards when the issues are presented in upcoming elections.
3. We can volunteer in local schools or tutoring programs to help those who struggle with their education.
    a. For example, here in Bloomington, two of my roommates tutor in the JAMS program, in which they help juvenile offenders who have started life out on the wrong foot.

Transition: So what exactly can one individual do to help fix these problems that are affecting schools across the United States? Well, the truth is, a lot.

IV. Picture

A. Take a moment to think of a teacher you've had who has inspired you to pursue education on a higher level. Think about how much you admired that instructor, and how much they influenced your direction in life.
B. Now imagine yourself in that person's shoes, teaching students just like you—or better still, teaching students less fortunate than any of us.
C. Imagine a world where all children in the school system are given equal opportunities and are able to move beyond the economic and societal situations into which they were born.
D. Think of schools with modern equipment and technology, cooperative communities, and knowledgeable, passionate teachers. Don't all children deserve this?

V. Move to Action

A. If you have an interest in helping to improve the lives of future generations of children by giving them more opportunities in life, I urge you all to apply to Teach for America as you approach your college graduation in the coming years.
B. Search out new sources of information regarding the education gap, and see what you can take part in or create to close this gap. All children deserve the same opportunities that many of us have had—why not work to prepare these individuals for the best future possible?
C. Just think of the impact you could have if you were a part of this prestigious program!
D. The effort it takes to participate in this program is well worth the long-lasting, positive effects you could potentially have on the lives of so many deserving children.

Questions:

1. What organizational pattern does the speaker use? Given her specific purpose, is this pattern appropriate? Why/why not? Can you think of a better way to organize this speech?

2. How would you assess the quality of her introduction and conclusion? Be specific.

3. What do you think of the quality of her transitions? Do they contribute to a sense of flow and coherence?

4. Using the formal outline on pages 502–505 as a point of comparison, critically assess the quality of Melody's outline. How might it be improved?

5. Does her language reflect good oral style? If so, in what ways? If not, how could it be improved?

6. What are some ways that this speaker might incorporate presentational aids into this presentation? Why do you think the aids you suggest would be helpful?

7. Does Melody make a compelling case for becoming involved with Teach for America? Might you be interested in pursing this opportunity? Why/ why not?

15

Special Persuasive Speaking Applications

After reading this chapter, you should be able to:

❑ Comprehend the diversity of special presentations you might be asked to make in business, professional, and civic settings

❑ Understand the basic principles of audience analysis—including common needs and values, as well as differences among listeners

❑ Establish and sustain your credibility as you deliver a persuasive speech

❑ Use emotional appeals to move audiences ethically and effectively

❑ Develop persuasive strategies for using evidence

❑ Create and deliver a proposal presentation to a small group audience

❑ Prepare and deliver a sales presentation to a group of perspective clients

A few years ago, a group of professionals from a prominent eastern manufacturing firm approached us, asking us to teach them how to make good oral presentations. The group was quite diverse, composed of, among others, a 21-year-old college intern working in sales as part of his field experience for a degree in marketing, a 30-year-old woman who had just moved into a supervisory position, and a 50-year-old upper-level manager who had been with the company for more than 25 years. Besides their differences in age and status within the firm, their speaking needs also varied. The young man wanted to know how to make better persuasive presentations to customers; the woman was interested in learning how to present concise, informative reports to her newly acquired staff; and the senior manager needed to learn how to make high-quality public presentations to promote the company at conferences around the world. In addition, several of them were actively involved in nonprofit, community-based organizations. In spite of the differences in their speaking needs, they all had two things in common: Not a single person in the group (nine in all) had ever studied public speaking, nor had they anticipated doing any public speaking when they started their careers.

In many ways, these individuals are typical. Most people assume they will rarely, if ever, make oral presentations after they graduate from college. Yet, as we noted earlier, public speaking is common in business, professional, and community settings. Often, the situations that matter most to us when we speak are those in which we are giving persuasive speeches, functioning as advocates for some proposal, product, service, or cause in which we believe.

Preview

In this chapter, we expand our examination of persuasive speaking, first by looking at audience values, needs, and interests—with a concern for both commonalities and diversity. Next, we focus on how persuasive speakers can establish and maintain credibility and use emotional appeals and evidence in ethical and appealing ways. Finally, we turn our attention to two special kinds of public presentations commonly delivered in business, professional, and civic life: the proposal presentation and the sales presentation.

PERSUASIVE SPEAKING: BASIC PRINCIPLES

Without the ability to communicate persuasively, most organizations could not survive, and most professionals would find their ability to solve problems and achieve upward mobility severely hampered. Managers must communicate persuasively whenever they talk to the public about the quality of their firm or product. Supervisors endeavor to convince employees that they should strive for excellence. Any worker who has a bright idea is immediately confronted with the problem of selling it to others. Salespersons are regularly required to approach customers or potential clients and persuade them to purchase their products or services. Finally, as members of volunteer organizations, we are all regularly confronted with opportunities to persuade our fellow citizens to take some action or make some change in programs, policies, or ways of doing things.

In our discussion of speech purposes in chapter 13, we suggested that accomplishing a persuasive purpose can be challenging. The persuasive speaker typically sets out to convince an audience to work harder, consider a product innovation, vote for some new policy or procedure, or invest their time or money in some worthy endeavor. Most listeners can absorb information without feeling threatened; but they often squirm when asked to think creatively, spend money, cast a vote, or invest their valuable time in some specific way. To be a successful persuasive speaker, then, you must begin by thoroughly acquainting yourself with your audience and their needs and values.

Analyzing the Audience

Every audience can be described and analyzed according to basic demographic characteristics, as we discussed in chapter 13. Some audiences are mostly male, others are basically youthful, mostly well educated, or rather well-to-do. Thus, you will want to consider the basic listener characteristics of age, gender, socioeconomic status, culture, and educational level, as well as religious and political beliefs. If you wanted, for instance, to convince a group of supervisors in your organization that sexual harassment was a problem, you would need to consider both your gender and your listeners' gender before formulating a persuasive plan. If you were a woman addressing a group of male supervisors on this subject, your approach should be designed to minimize defensiveness.

Understanding audience motivation is one key to successful persuasive speaking. When the audience is culturally diverse, the speaker will want to appeal to such basic human values as fairness, tolerance, and respect for life. While cultural differences must be respectfully acknowledged, discovering common ground is equally vital.

ACKNOWLEDGING DIVERSITY: SEEKING A COMMON FOCUS

Of course, since audiences are increasingly diverse, assessing their interests, predispositions, and values can be a complex undertaking. In making the persuasive speech on sexual harassment mentioned above, for instance, you would likely be talking to female as well as male supervisors. Moreover, your listeners might possess different sexual orientations. One way of approaching this subject might be to argue that sexual harassment represents (above all else) an abuse of power. Whoever is in the more powerful position, then, must be particularly vigilant—sensitive to the way(s) that their verbal and nonverbal behavior might be perceived by others in less powerful positions in the organization or in society. By using this kind of strategy, you are helping listeners focus on the one thing they have in common (regardless of gender or sexual orientation): they are all in positions of authority. If you can help the audience to focus on this common concern, you will likely connect with them and make an effective persuasive presentation.

When you are speaking to a group of listeners who are culturally diverse, you will need to be sensitive to differences in their values, cultural orientations, and worldviews that are likely to influence the way they respond to you and your message. Highlighting Diversity contrasts U.S. values with those of others.

When reflecting on cultural differences, it is critical that we avoid *ethnocentrism*—that is, assuming that *our* cultural values, beliefs, and ways of doing things are superior to those of others. At the same time, however, once those differences have been respectfully recognized, we need to find a way to establish

Highlighting Diversity

How U.S. Values Contrast with Those of Other Cultures

The Washington International Center shares a list of U.S. values with international visitors to help them understand U.S. culture. Here are some of the values they particularly emphasize:

- *Personal control of the environment*—not influenced by fate. Many people in the United States think that people who believe in fate are backward, primitive, or naive. Those from other cultures may believe that Americans overestimate their degree of control.

- *Positive view of change*—linked to development, improvement, progress, and growth. Many traditional cultures, by contrast, consider change disruptive and value stability, continuity, and a rich and ancient heritage.

- *Time valued as a commodity*—valued, borrowed, spent, and saved. It is of utmost importance. To those from other cultures, Americans may seem more concerned with accomplishing goals than in developing deep interpersonal relationships.

- *Equality*—a cherished value. Americans say that all people are "created equal." Yet, seven-eighths of the world feel quite differently. To them, rank, status, and authority are more desirable—even if they personally find themselves at the bottom of the social order. Class and authority are, for them, associated with security and certainty.

- *Individualism*—unique in the United States, and therefore, precious and wonderful. Even though Americans join groups, they still consider themselves individualistic.

- *Privacy*—sometimes physically apart from others. Privacy is hard for people from other cultures to understand, as many are far more group oriented. Some don't even have a word in their language for privacy, which may be associated with loneliness and isolation from the group.

- *Future oriented*—life will get better. As a result of hope in the future, Americans tend to devalue the past. Yet, the past is highly revered by those of other cultures and is associated with tradition and wisdom.

- *Directness, openness, and honesty*—forthright, frank, and direct communication style. Other cultures are more indirect and subtle and may view Americans as overly blunt.

Source: Ohio State University Extension Fact Sheet: Family and Consumer Sciences, "Appreciating Other Cultures" (no date given) [online]. Available: http://www.ohioline.osu.edu/shy-fact/5000/5202.html (accessed: June 15, 2004).

common ground, as public speakers and as human beings. In his book, *Shared Values for a Troubled World*, Rushworth M. Kidder, former president of the Institute for Global Ethics, argues for the existence of a global code of ethics based on widely shared values. Those values are *love, truthfulness, fairness, freedom, unity, tolerance, responsibility,* and *respect for life.*[1] If Kidder's assessment is correct, then appealing to these basic values should resonate with listeners of many cultures. Other scholars argue that, in addition to some common values, diverse audience members also share certain fundamental needs. Once those needs are understood, they can be used by speakers to motivate listeners to act.

UNDERSTANDING LISTENER MOTIVATION

Psychologist Abraham Maslow contends that individuals are motivated by *unfulfilled* personal needs, some of which are more basic to existence than others.

He argues, for example, that audience members must be physically comfortable and secure before you can appeal to their higher needs for love, esteem, and belonging.[2] Anyone who has been forced to attend a lecture before lunch without the benefit of breakfast is well aware of the learning distraction created by hunger pains! While it is difficult to help people learn when their basic needs are unsatisfied or poorly understood, it is virtually impossible to stimulate their thinking, change their beliefs, or move them to act under such circumstances.

Habits as Motives

Although there are many sources of human motivation, for many audience members *habits* serve as motives. They will prefer, now and in the future, what they have known and felt comfortable with in the past. But individuals vary greatly in the rigidity of their response patterns. At one extreme are the persons who are comfortable only with the status quo. They are cautious, conservative, and low in risk-taking in nearly all circumstances. These individuals are invariably opposed to any idea that involves risk. They may not think the present system perfect, but they take considerable consolation in the knowledge that they are accustomed to it. "Creative," "innovative," and "new" are words that automatically elicit negative responses from these persons. At the opposite end of the habit continuum are those who are consistently flexible, open-minded, and ever responsive to change. These individuals may be instantly attracted to an idea or moved to purchase a product simply because it carries the label "new" or "improved."

When you look at your audience, then, you might consider their habits. Are your listeners a traditional group who seem inclined to let things drift along, without taking risks or initiating change? Or are they a bunch of eager beavers who want to move forward, rise to the challenge, and live life on the "cutting edge"? More likely than not, they will be diverse in their habits (yet another dimension of audience diversity), and your task will be to calm the nerves of the reluctant without boring those who are eager to throw caution to the wind.

Personal Needs as Motives

Habits are only one perspective from which to consider human motivation. Every individual has needs that must be satisfied for the person to live and function happily and productively in society. When personal needs go unfulfilled, they create voids, distress, weakness, and other kinds of physical and psychological discomfort. Earlier we referred to the human motivation research of Maslow that identified a hierarchy of human needs (See figure 15.1). Beginning at the bottom of the needs hierarchy, they are:[3]

- *Physiological needs*—health and well-being
- *Safety*—personal security, freedom from fear of the unknown
- *Love and belonging*—the social need of knowing that one is regarded warmly and belongs comfortably to groups that are significant to him or her
- *Esteem*—moving beyond being accepted to being respected and held in high regard
- *Self-actualization*—finding one's niche; striving for ultimate personal fulfillment

Some audience members will listen to a persuasive speech with the aim of endorsing the best solution or making the best decision for the welfare of the organization or greater community. But while organizational representatives,

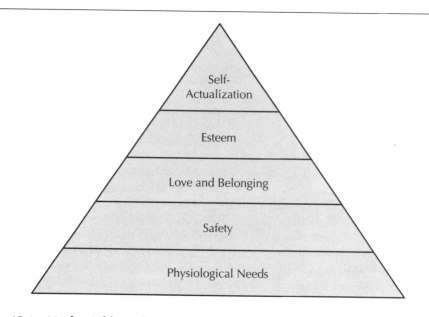

Figure 15.1   Maslow's hierarchy of personal needs

executives, and managers are "organization men and women" in one sense, they are at the same time human beings with personal needs and motives. Thus, it is critical to consider the diversity of their needs. Audience members who are insecure about their own capabilities, are uncertain of their acceptance within the department, or believe that they are held in low esteem present a different type of persuasive problem than listeners who are completely confident, affectionately regarded by all, or respected as talented, innovative leaders.

Not all writers believe that the needs identified by Maslow are the most telling. McClelland argues, for instance, that all needs are socially acquired. He identifies three major sets of personal needs:[4]

- *Need for achievement*—being driven to succeed, being extremely hardworking, and desiring feedback
- *Need for power*—having the ability to make subordinates feel inspired to excel
- *Need for affiliation*—having the desire to be with others, to belong, and to interact socially.

The audience members with strong achievement needs may be listening to your speech from the perspective of "What's in it for me?" They may wonder whether the change you are proposing would give them an opportunity to use their abilities and to excel. Their motivation is very different from that of people who are more affiliative and, hence, concerned with how the proposed change might affect the organization's social environment. As you construct your persuasive strategy, you need to consider the motivational bent of each audience member so that you can make your presentation as compelling as possible. Again, you might consider some cultural differences, as listeners from Eastern cultures likely have a stronger need for affiliation in general than those from Western cultures (who are more likely to emphasize the need to achieve).[5]

The Need to Contribute as a Motive

The final set of important motivating factors is externally directed. Many professional people have a genuine concern for the welfare of the organization as a whole. Ideas they perceive as enhancing the position of the organization and the community will receive their hearty support. Secure in their personal and professional positions within the organization, they are committed to advancing the goals of the institution, as well as rendering public service. Drucker addresses this notion in his book, *The Effective Executive*, in which he points to "commitment to contribution" as a characteristic of many successful high-level managers.[6] See Business Brief 15.1 on the following page for an illustration of a leader whose desire or need to contribute is clear and compelling. In this instance, the leader is motivated by a desire to contribute substantively to society. Such sentiments often involve a widening of the listener's perspective to include not only his or her own specialty or department, but the processes, purposes, and goals of the entire organizational family.

The desire to make a lasting contribution often takes us even beyond the boundaries of our own organizations, with the hope that we can make a difference in the community, the state, the nation, or the world in which we live. This commitment to contributing invites us to focus on problems in our communities, to move *beyond* ourselves and our places of work, to reach out to the poor, the disabled, the abused, and the homeless. In other words, this internal urge to give back—to function as an engaged citizen—may function as a powerful motive for many listeners. Highlighting Civic Engagement presents a brief portion of a persuasive speech that calls on the members of the audience to volunteer.

Highlighting Civic Engagement

A Persuasive Speech

Remarks of Governor Judy Martz, given at the State Capitol, Helena, Montana, October 27, 2002

When you leave tonight, I ask that you consider committing your time and efforts to your local community. Commit yourself to making your community and state a better place.

President Bush, early in his administration, urged every American to dedicate 4,000 hours to their country and fellow man.

I urge you, not only to give the 4,000 hours, but also to be selective with your time and ensure your community and country are a stronger place because you serve. I also urge you to ask, persuade, and entice your friends to join you. . . .

The United States is a strong nation. . . . We are stronger because we volunteer. We are stronger because we engage our friends and neighbors for the betterment of our communities. And through that strength, we will continue to serve as role models as we build a lasting legacy for our children and grandchildren.

Source: Judy Martz, "Award for Civic Engagement" (October 27, 2002) [online]. Available: http://www.discoveringmontana.com/gov2/css/speeches.asp?ID=47 (accessed: June 11, 2004).

Business Brief 15.1

The Boss Who Made a Lasting Contribution

Aaron Feuerstein, chief executive officer (CEO) of Malden Mills, a textile company located in Lawrence, Massachusetts, is considered a hero by most of his employees. Always known as demanding but fair, Feuerstein found that his leadership was put to the test in December 1995 when a catastrophic fire nearly destroyed the company's manufacturing plant. Employees were convinced that their jobs were gone. That was before Feuerstein announced that he would keep all of his 3,000 employees on the payroll for a month while he started rebuilding the 90-year-old family business. In January, he announced that he would pay them for a second month. In February, he said he would pay them for a third month. By March, most of the employees had returned to work full-time. In the meantime, Feuerstein had paid out several million dollars to give his employees a chance.

What sets this CEO apart? His own words are revealing. When asked how he differed from his fellow CEOs, he said, "The fundamental difference is that I consider our workers an asset, not an expense." He believes that his job goes beyond just making money for shareholders, even though the only shareholders of Malden Mills are Feuerstein and his family.

His philosophy is clear. Feuerstein asserts:

> I have a responsibility to the workers, both blue-collar and white-collar. I have an equal responsibility to the community. It would have been unconscionable to put 3,000 people on the streets and deliver a death blow to the cities of Lawrence and Methuen. Maybe on paper our company is worth less to Wall Street, but I can tell you, it's worth more. We're doing fine.

Before the fire, the plant produced 130,000 yards a week. A few weeks after the fire, it was up to 230,000 yards. Feuerstein notes, "Our people became very creative. They were willing to work 25 hours a day."

A deeply religious man whose command of biblical Hebrew is impeccable, Feuerstein often quotes Hillel, the first-century Talmudic scholar; for example, "in a situation where there is not a righteous person, try to be a righteous person." And again, "Not all who increase their wealth are wise."

Malden Mills stands out in the Lawrence area, once a thriving center for the textile industry. Business after business left Lawrence in search of lower labor costs. Those companies that stayed downsized, laying off hundreds of workers in attempts to stay profitable. According to Feuerstein:

> That goes straight against the American Dream. You work hard and should make a good living and have a good retirement. I could get rid of all the workers who earn $15 an hour and bring in a contract house that will pay their laborers $7 an hour. But that breaks the spirit and trust of the employees. If you close a factory because you can get work done for $2 an hour elsewhere, you break the American Dream.

Source: Michael Ryan, "They Call Their Boss a Hero," *Parade Magazine* (September 8, 1996): 4–5. Even though Malden Mills continued to struggle and later declared bankruptcy, it successfully emerged from bankruptcy protection in October of 2003. Now under new leadership, Aaron Feuerstein maintains his position as chairman of the board and president (nonexecutive). He has been recognized around the world for his high standards of corporate responsibility. See "Malden Mills Successfully Emerges from Chapter 11" (October 17, 2003) [online]. Available: http://www.polartec.com/contentmgr/showdetails.php/id/755 (accessed: June 16, 2004).

This, then, is yet another dimension of human motivation that you need to consider as a persuasive speaker. A proposal for change that aims to improve the quality of a specific company product, ensure a safer environment for the public, or create, in general, a better, more harmonious society would have great intrinsic appeal to a group of listeners who are motivated by external, other-oriented concerns. Figure 15.2 illustrates the need to contribute as a factor influencing listener motivation.

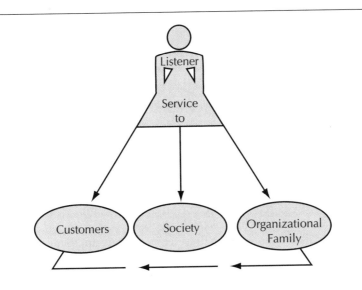

Figure 15.2   Factors influencing human motivation

Often the key to gaining support for an idea or plan does not reside in a rational justification of the idea or solution, but in one's ability to comprehend the forces within the audience that predispose them to believe and behave in predictable ways. Such knowledge makes it possible to create a persuasive strategy that will relate the virtues of the plan to the motives already present within the listeners.

Building Credibility

Think of the last time someone tried to sell you something and failed. Why didn't you buy? Perhaps you simply didn't have the money, but beyond that, the would-be persuader may have "turned you off" in some way. Maybe the salesperson seemed deceptive and you worried that the product wasn't as great as he claimed. Or perhaps you asked some questions the person couldn't answer, and so you grew to doubt whether he knew what he was talking about. Possibly his personal style was offensive. Maybe he came on too strong, or at the other extreme, seemed to be more interested in going to lunch than in making the sale. In short, he may have done something that caused you to view him as lacking credibility. He might have been selling a marvelous product, perhaps the exact kind of self-cleaning microwave oven you have always wanted. But because you were unimpressed with him as a person and a communicator, you decided to keep on looking.

FACTORS CONTRIBUTING TO CREDIBILITY

What is true for the salesperson in this case is true for any public speaker with a persuasive purpose. Thousands of years ago, Aristotle pointed out that the speaker's *ethos* or *credibility* is her or his most powerful source of influence.[7] Even the most carefully constructed and soundly supported speech will fail if the speaker is viewed as low in credibility. Most researchers agree that several factors combine to influence listener perceptions of speaker credibility.[8] In general, if audiences perceive speakers to be **competent, trustworthy, objective,** and **enthusiastic** they will view them as highly credible. Of course, these dimensions are interrelated. Listeners have little regard for the sincere speaker who is not terribly well versed. Nor will they tolerate the bright but deceptive speaker. Objectivity is important in that listeners, while recognizing that a persuasive speaker has taken a stand, still want to believe that she has given fair consideration to more than one point of view. Listeners also prefer to feel that the speaker would still be willing to hear opposing views. Finally, most listeners find it easier to be convinced by a persuasive speaker who is genuinely enthusiastic and dynamic than by one who is either too pushy or too bland.

What can you do to enhance your credibility as a public speaker? First, you must recognize that even before you begin to speak, your listeners will likely have some impression of your credibility. If, for example, you are known within your organization as an expert on nutrition and you are speaking on the need for a balanced diet, the audience's perception of your credibility should be quite positive. Even if the audience knows nothing about you, however, they will begin to assess your credibility as soon as they see you. Your appearance counts. The way you dress is important, as is the way you walk, sit, smile, and shake hands. Looking professional, suiting your attire to the occasion, and appearing neatly groomed are also essential.

If you are in a rather formal public speaking situation, your listeners will also gain some impression of your credibility from the remarks of the person who introduces you. If you know you are to be introduced, you might send your introducer pertinent information several days beforehand—information geared, in part, toward enhancing your credibility. Avoid sending a long, detailed resume. Introducers often have trouble picking out the crucial information.

GUIDELINES FOR ESTABLISHING CREDIBILITY

You can also do things during your speech to alter your perceived credibility. Credibility building is a process that unfolds as you share your thoughts with the audience. Here are some techniques you might try:

- *Establish common ground with the audience*. In general, audiences enjoy listening to speakers with whom they believe they have something in common. If you once worked in a department like theirs, say so. Whenever you can demonstrate values, concerns, or aspirations that you and your audience hold in common, you help your credibility.

- *Build trust*. Normally, trust building is a process that evolves only over time. Even so, you can often establish yourself as a trustworthy source of information on a particular subject by techniques such as self-disclosure (admitting that you were terribly out of shape before joining the company's fitness program) or by establishing your individuality (speaking as an executive who once viewed most administrators as incompetent).

- If appropriate, *reinforce your status.* If your introducer does the job well, you may not have to do this. If not, however, *tasteful* references to your experience, education, or position are entirely appropriate. Mention your experience with politics, working at summer camps, and so forth as you address each of these subjects. Obvious name-dropping and repeated references to a prestigious award or position must be avoided.

- *Support your views with evidence.* We have already discussed the importance of using evidence. In general, the better your evidence, the more the audience will perceive you as credible. In the next section, we will discuss specific ways to use evidence that are designed to enhance your persuasiveness.

- *Strive for good delivery.* We have already discussed principles of effective delivery in detail. Here let us simply note that persuasive speakers who deliver their speeches fluently and with apparent confidence, who sound sincere and committed to their ideas, will go a long way toward establishing themselves as trustworthy, competent, and enthusiastic communicators.

- If appropriate, *use presentational aids.* Such aids are not necessary for every speech. If they make sense and if you want to take the time to prepare them, however, they can add color and interest to your presentation. Using handouts or computer-generated graphics highlighting your main points and key statistics will influence the audience to perceive you as well organized. The presence of any carefully prepared presentational aid suggests that you went to some effort to prepare for the presentation and implies you took the task seriously.

There is no standard way to build your credibility. Each topic, audience, and speech situation presents its own set of obstacles to be overcome. No speaker is equally credible on every topic he addresses. In some instances, your credibility may be almost automatic. In others, you may want to consider using all the credibility-building devices listed above. In most speaking situations, even highly credible speakers attempt to nurture their images by establishing common ground, using evidence, and striving for excellent delivery. To be an effective and persuasive speaker, your credibility can never be too high.

Appealing to Audience Emotions

As a persuasive speaker, you often want to get your audience excited about some cause, move them to action, or help them to become less complacent. You will have difficulty achieving those goals on the basis of logical appeals alone. You may decide then to use some *emotional appeals* (or what the Greeks called *pathos*) designed to make your listeners feel sad, happy, angry, sympathetic, compassionate, or proud. To get people to act, to move them to change some policy, you often have to move their hearts as well as their heads.

CONCERN FOR ETHICS

If your persuasive goal is to move your listeners to action, be sure to use emotional appeals in ways that are ethical. You should always build your persuasive speech on a firm foundation of strong evidence and sound reasoning. Any attempt to get listeners to act in hasty, unthinking ways is clearly unethical. Discerning listeners will not be moved by a speaker's emotional appeals in the absence of substantiating evidence. Johannesen suggests eleven commandments of ethical communication to guide you as you prepare your speech.[9]

1. Do not use false, fabricated, misrepresented, distorted, or irrelevant evidence to support arguments or claims.

2. Do not intentionally use unsupported, misleading, or illogical reasoning.

3. Do not represent yourself as informed or as an "expert" on a subject when you are not.

4. Do not use irrelevant appeals to divert attention or scrutiny from the issue at hand. Avoid, for instance, "smear" attacks on an opponent's character or appeals to hatred or bigotry.

5. Do not ask your audience to link your idea or proposal to emotion-laden values, motives, or goals to which it is actually not related.

6. Do not deceive your audience by concealing your real purpose, by concealing self-interest, by concealing the group you represent, or by concealing your position as an advocate of a viewpoint.

7. Do not distort, hide, or misrepresent the number, scope, intensity, or undesirable features of consequences or effects.

8. Do not use "emotional appeals" that lack a supporting basis of evidence or reasoning, or that would not be accepted if the audience had time and opportunity to examine the subject themselves.

9. Do not oversimplify complex, gradation-laden situations into simplistic two-valued, either-or, polar views or choices.

10. Do not pretend certainty where tentativeness and degrees of probability would be more accurate.

11. Do not advocate something in which you do not believe yourself.

Once you have presented convincing arguments, you can use emotional appeals to kindle your audience's feelings, engage their beliefs, and move them to action. Keep in mind, however, that ethical speaking demands that we treat our listeners as we ourselves would like to be treated when we are audience members.

WAYS TO APPEAL TO LISTENER EMOTIONS

Speakers can appeal to audience emotions in a number of ways: One of the most common ways of appealing to listeners' emotions is through the use of an *emotionally moving story or illustration*. Discussing basic facts about pay inequity, crowded student housing, or alcoholism among workers is not enough. You need to use specific examples. In this way, the emotional appeal grows from the content of the speech itself.

Sometimes *your language can* also *evoke emotional responses*. You might describe a competitor, for instance as "profit-driven," "dishonest," or "power hungry." Or you might describe the philosophy of your own company as "fair-minded," "consumer-oriented," or "loyal to the American tradition of progress." You must be careful if you choose to move your audience in this way, however. Sometimes this technique is simply too obvious. This is especially true if the moving phrases are not developed or supported later in the speech. Thus, stirring words, phrases, and slogans must be used tastefully, ethically, and with restraint.

Perhaps the most powerful source of *emotional appeal is your sincerity, commitment, and conviction as a persuasive speaker.* You cannot move an audience simply by using the right words and plugging in colorful examples. Audiences are amazingly good at detecting insincerity or apathy. If you are feeling the emotions you wish to arouse in your audience, then everything you say and the way you say it will reinforce your commitment and hopefully convey a compelling message.

Strategies for Using Evidence

We suggested earlier that persuasive speakers are more likely to be successful if they support their views with evidence. Together with pathos and ethos, *logos*, or *logical appeals* made through the use of sound evidence and reasoning, is a critical part of effective persuasive speaking. In this section, we want to elaborate on the relationship between persuasiveness, the organization of evidence, and credibility.

USE SUFFICIENT EVIDENCE

First, you need to assess your own credibility in the eyes of the audience. If you are not well known to your audience, or if audience members are hostile to your position or in any way question your authority or motives, you should plan to use abundant evidence. Only those speakers with the highest credibility can make unsubstantiated assertions and still be persuasive.

Equally important, no one has high credibility with all audiences. When you present a proposal, your credibility may be extremely high with those who know you well or those who would benefit from the plan you are advocating. However, for those audience members who perceive themselves to be in competition with you, the ones who have never worked with you or even heard of you, or those who are hostile toward anyone who advocates change, your credibility may be less clearly established. Since most of us are rarely in speaking situations where our credibility is uniformly high with all audience members, the safest strategy is to use evidence to enhance our persuasiveness.

USE EVIDENCE THAT IS "NEWS"

Another factor you might want to consider in gathering evidence is whether the audience has heard it before. Using evidence with which the audience is familiar does little to enhance your persuasive impact. If the audience already knows that "professors at this university are paid about $5,000 a year less than those at other Big Ten institutions," they have probably either accepted this evidence as true or rejected it as false. In either case, you have persuaded no one. In short, evidence with which the audience is not familiar is more persuasive than evidence to which they have already been exposed.[10]

USE EVIDENCE THAT PROMOTES ENDURING
SUPPORT AND IS RESISTANT TO COUNTERINFLUENCE

Using evidence also plays an important part in long-term attitude change. That is, whenever you are in a position of arguing for some principle of enduring value, something that you want the audience to think about over an extended period of time, or something about which they do not have to act immediately, you will be more persuasive if you substantiate your ideas with supporting evidence.

In addition, if you know that listeners will be exposed to opposing arguments after listening to you, you can make them more resistant to counterinfluence by using evidence.[11] Suppose, for instance, that you were participating in a public forum on the drug problem in your community, and the event has been organized as a debate. You might speak first, arguing that more money should be devoted to drug education in the elementary and secondary schools. Following your presentation, others might argue that a better way to use resources is to create a drug patrol squad to patrol the schools and to hire more police. In this situation, and others like it, you will have a better chance of being persuasive as you compete with other speakers if your ideas are supported with first-rate evidence.

Acknowledge Both Sides of the Argument

Another issue you need to consider is whether you should acknowledge opposing points of view. That is, should you simply present arguments to support your ideas, or should you devote some time to discussing opposing arguments? Most plans, however well conceived, have both advantages and disadvantages. A brilliant idea is expensive. Creating a new division may cause some established departments to be trimmed. Most innovations are accompanied by some risk. Obviously, it is more pleasurable and easier to discuss the strengths of your ideas than to address potential risks or weaknesses. Even so, in most situations, you will be more persuasive if you set forth your own arguments and acknowledge opposing points of view.[12] The only exception might be when you are speaking to an audience that already agrees with you. But when you talk with those who are opposed or ambivalent, those who are bright and well educated, or those who have already heard opposing arguments you should present both sides. Since most audiences fall into at least one of these categories, the latter is the preferred route.

Present Supporting Evidence First

Once you have decided to present both supporting and opposing arguments, the next concern is how best to arrange them. Should you begin by attacking the opposition or by presenting arguments supporting your own point of view? Usually, the latter course of action is preferable.[13] When listeners are exposed to a speaker's case, they often move in the direction of the speaker's arguments. Once this has happened, they are more likely to stick with the speaker and listen to his or her reasons for opposing other positions. If, by contrast, the speaker begins by pointing to flaws in the opposing arguments (and especially if those arguments are appealing to some audience members), listeners may react defensively by moving closer to the opposition and becoming more resistant or more closed to the speaker's arguments even before they hear them.

Establish Common Ground before Voicing Disagreement

Whenever you have to argue against an audience's beliefs, the best approach is to begin by establishing some substantive common ground. Talk about some things both you and the audience hold dear. Suppose you are arguing in favor of increasing property taxes to gain funding for education in your community, and you know that your audience has opposed such increases in the past. You might begin by acknowledging your *mutual* commitment to the welfare of the children of the community and the quality of education within the school corporation.

Then you can begin to develop your arguments. Not only is establishing common ground an attention-getting device, but an early affirmation of commonly held values tends to increase the audience's assessment of your credibility as a speaker and makes them more open to hearing your claims.[14]

PROPOSAL PRESENTATIONS

Assume for a moment that you have worked in an organization for several years. Throughout your professional experience, you have learned to communicate effectively, articulating your ideas while listening respectfully to the views of others. Your experience, competence, and interpersonal skills have led you into important group experiences within the organization; you presently belong to several influential committees. But now you find yourself in a slightly different position: you have been asked to present one of your creative marketing concepts to the board of directors, and you must develop a proposal for the board's consideration.

Or, suppose you have worked for two years as the executive director of a homeless shelter. This particular shelter is housed in the basement of a church, and the church has recently acquired some additional property and resources to build a new facility. You feel strongly that the church basement is no longer an adequate space for your community's growing poor and homeless population. You would like very much to see the new facility include a space for a new, larger homeless shelter—so that services in health care, after-hours day care, and weekend meals can be added to the shelter's current programs. You are to meet with the shelter's board to advance your proposal. The board consists of several members of the community, shelter volunteers, and key members of the church.

In both of these situations, you are functioning as a kind of "public" speaker in that you will face an audience and defend a course of action. But the board is not a typical audience; you are not facing the general public but rather a small group with considerable decision-making power and a good deal of status. Your success in this kind of situation depends as much on your understanding of the dynamics of this small group audience as it does on the quality of the proposal you put forth.

Defining the Proposal Presentation

Proposal presentations are developed by some member of an organization, sometimes at a superior's request, and delivered to a small group of decision makers. Occasionally, these presentations are made to small groups of peers, but more often they are delivered to superiors. On occasion, the speaker is not personally acquainted with most members of the audience; she may know them only by reputation. At other times, the speaker may be asked to present a proposal to a small group of high-level executives with whom she consults nearly every day. In either case, proposal presentations require special preparation and practice since those listening are organizational representatives or community leaders with great demands on their time and energies.

Preparing for the Presentation

Those who present proposals usually convey a lot of information. They may explain, for example, the meaning of consumer trends or report statistics on the rise in homelessness. Explaining and reporting are crucial speaker functions in this context, but the presentational speaker acts largely as a *persuader* in that he supports a specific proposal in the presence of decision makers who have the power to accept or reject it.

To be persuasive, proposal presentations must be solution focused and audience centered. Presentational speakers are almost invariably proponents of change, agents of innovation. Successful presentational speaking begins with a proposal worth presenting, but it is equally critical that the speaker engage in painstaking preparation, focusing on an analysis of the audience as members of the organizational structure, as individuals, and especially as decision makers within a small group.

KNOW THE ORGANIZATION

As you approach the creation of a proposal presentation, you should recognize that the organization offers a highly structured environment for communication interaction. To varying degrees, all of the formal and informal channels and constraints discussed in chapter 2 will be operant. For example, presenting a proposal is typically an experience in upward communication. Those to whom you communicate in this context possess both power and status; they are successful leaders who can accept or reject your proposal. In the case of the homeless shelter director offered earlier, for example, you are speaking to the very group who hired you and who have the authority to replace you. Thus, when you function as a presentational speaker it is important for you to guard against the tendency to distort information, a common upward communication problem.[15]

Another important aspect of the organizational context is the increasing trend toward specialization. Along with the knowledge explosion came the organizational tendency to seek individuals with increasing depths of expertise.[16] Such depth, however, is often accompanied by considerable narrowness of focus. As a result, the expert who is called on to make a presentation to a small group of decision makers faces the task of relating her or his expert knowledge to the understanding and needs of the larger group. In addition, organizations have competing needs. As the homeless shelter director, you are aware that the church has a number of other priorities. While your expertise and interest is in homelessness, you understand that many board members are equally concerned with programs for youth, international missions programs, and the need for a remodeled church kitchen. While the problem of audience adaptation is not unique to presentational speakers, the often critical nature of the proposal being presented and the complexities associated with upward communication heighten its importance.

KNOW THE IMMEDIATE AUDIENCE

It is only on rare occasions that public speakers know their audiences personally. In this sense, you usually have an advantage in a presentational speaking situation. Often, particularly in smaller organizations, you will know all of the decision makers on a daily working basis. Even if you lack firsthand knowledge, belonging to the organization is an asset, for this allows you access to the information needed to analyze your audience judiciously.

UNDERSTAND THE DYNAMICS OF THE GROUP

Small group audiences are different from the audiences faced by most public speakers. They have a dynamic quality, possessing psychological bonds, goals, and norms for interacting and decision making. You may want to review chapters 10, 11, and 12 for a detailed consideration of small group communication.

A general understanding of group dynamics allows you to focus on more specific, in-depth knowledge of the particular group in question. For instance, it is important to discover which members of the group function as its leaders. Many assume that the appointed leader is the person to whom arguments should be directed. However, small group research has shown us that appointed leaders may or may not lead the group in a significant sense.[17] What we need to know is which group members *consistently* influence the group. Appeals should be aimed at the most influential individuals.

Equally important is an understanding of how power and status are distributed within the group. Most decision-making groups consist of persons with rather high status within the organization. We might be tempted to assume automatically that a vice president would have more power than a floor supervisor. But, it is more important to identify the *functionally powerful* figures within the group, since high status and power are not invariably associated. Once you have engaged in careful audience analysis, you are ready to plan a fruitful strategy of organization.

ORGANIZE THE PROPOSAL

Whenever you make a speech, it is important that your remarks be clearly organized. Like other speeches, the elements of the proposal should be arranged in such a way that they reveal some purposive design. Although different proposals will use different persuasive strategies, several general principles of arrangement take on particular significance because of the organizational context in which proposals are presented. In this sense, then, all proposals should be arranged in accordance with the principles of unity, coherence, emphasis, completeness, and conciseness.

- The principles of **unity** and **coherence** are closely related. We usually say that a speech is unified when we can discover a central theme to which each element of the message logically relates. In the context of a proposal presentation, the central purpose is to get the decision-making group to accept and support a given course of action. In a unified presentation, every major subdivision relates to and supports that basic action-oriented theme. This unity is strengthened by the coherence of the arguments as well. Coherence here means that the parts of the message are logically interrelated.

- Another basic quality of a well-arranged presentation is **emphasis**. It is not possible for audiences, even highly skilled decision makers, to digest and remember everything a speaker says. Thus, it is critical that presentations be constructed so that the most important ideas and data are stressed. There are many strategies for emphasizing information. Audiences tend to pay more attention to those arguments they hear first and last.[18] One strategy, then, is to place the strongest arguments early and late in the speech, with less essential ideas in the middle. You can employ a certain amount of repetition as a means of emphasis, although not at the expense of conciseness. Finally, using presentational aids is an effective method of visualizing and stressing critical ideas and statistics.

- The fourth characteristic of a well-organized presentation is **completeness**. Complete presentations are comprehensive—they address the crucial issues relating to the central theme. The notion of completeness does not imply that you say everything there is to say about a given topic. Rather, it suggests that you present the proposal as completely as possible given the constraints of time and the needs, understanding, and interests of the audience.

- Of course, the need to address issues completely and comprehensively must be weighed against the final organizational goal of *conciseness*. Organizational decision makers need complete information on which to base their decisions. Because of the demands on their time, it is crucial that a complete picture be created in the most concise manner possible. Effective presentations are filled with pertinent information and compelling arguments, but they are never wastefully wordy or unduly repetitious.

Patterns of Arrangement for the Presentation

As we pointed out in the previous chapter, every effective public presentation should have an introduction, a body, and a conclusion. But there are some special patterns of organization that are especially well suited to proposal presentations: the scientific problem-solving pattern, the state-the-case-and-prove-it pattern, and the motivated sequence. We discussed the motivated sequence in chapter 14; you may want to reread it to refresh your memory. Like the motivated sequence, the patterns presented here could be used with any speech whose goal is to get the audience to take some concrete action.

SCIENTIFIC PROBLEM-SOLVING PATTERN

The first pattern, *scientific problem solving*, is based on John Dewey's reflective-thinking system.[19] This pattern of organization is most often effective in discussing a relatively complicated problem—especially if the audience is largely ignorant of the facts or if audience resistance or hostility is anticipated. Through the scientific approach to problem solving, you lead the audience through a systematic series of steps involving:

- defining the problem (including an understanding of current policies, if any)
- exploring the problem (examining causes and effects)
- articulating criteria to be used in judging the quality of any proposed course of action
- enumerating and evaluating representative solutions
- selecting the best solution

There are a number of advantages to this pattern of organization. When handled effectively, this strategy contributes to your image as an open, fair-minded communicator. You encourage the audience to examine the problem along with you and to consider a variety of possible solutions—not just the particular one you are advocating. With such an approach, members of the audience may feel that they have participated in selecting the best alternative. It is difficult to maintain hostility in the face of such a disarmingly open approach to problem solving.

When the audience is poorly informed, this inductive development of the topic provides a natural framework for the communication of essential information. As a speaker, you do not assume that the audience is already familiar with the problem, its causes, and potential remedies. Rather, you assume that you possess important information that, when shared with the audience, will allow you and the audience together to discover the best alternative. In this sense, then, the scientific pattern of problem solving creates a feeling of audience participation and has the potential for bringing the speaker and listeners closer together. Educating the audience has become the vehicle of persuasion.

STATE-THE-CASE-AND-PROVE-IT PATTERN

Another pattern of organization useful for presentational speaking is the *state-the-case-and-prove-it* pattern. This is a relatively simple arrangement entailing the straightforward development of a central thesis with supporting arguments. Normally, each supporting element begins with a contention or topic sentence, followed immediately by substantiating material. Typically, the pattern consists of:

- a short introduction (in which you briefly acknowledge a known problem);
- your thesis statement;
- a series of contentions or arguments (with appropriate elaboration and support);
- a concluding summary during which you repeat the thesis, summarize your case, and call for action.

Whereas the scientific problem-solving pattern is an *inductive* approach to organization, the state-the-case-and-prove-it pattern is *deductive*. You begin with a general conclusion and, by advancing specific arguments to support it, attempt to show that your conclusion or proposed course of action is justified. The speech, then, is one of proof and reinforcement.

The state-the-case-and-prove-it pattern is useful in situations that differ considerably from those that call for the scientific problem-solving approach. Specifically, the state-the-case-and-prove-it pattern is appropriate for organizing the discussion of familiar, much argued topics of controversy. When the audience is familiar with a particular problem and has perhaps heard it discussed many times before, there is no need for the speaker to explore it gradually and comprehensively. The appropriate strategy is to state one's position clearly and to systematically support it.

During the introduction of a state-the-case-and-prove-it presentation, you usually acknowledge that the audience is familiar with the problem. Then you explain your reason for reopening a discussion of the issue. It may be that new information has been accumulated or that recent events have modified a previously satisfactory or stable situation. For example, perhaps a large plant's closing has led to a sudden rise in the number of impoverished households in the community; this, in turn, has led to a greatly enhanced demand for the services and resources of the homeless shelter and a steady increase in the homeless population. As the shelter director, you will want to clarify and demonstrate the seriousness of this new state of affairs when you address the board.

Throughout the presentation, you must clearly state the relevance of each supporting element to the general thesis you are advocating. In the conclusion, highlight the significance and value of your arguments, encouraging the audience to reflect on the quality of the proof presented. Then, ask them to support your proposal.

The state-the-case-and-prove-it pattern is solution heavy. The speaker's goal is to persuade the audience to support his or her particular solution. The challenge, then, is to help listeners realize that the proposed course of action is the one they want to pursue. (See figure 15.3.)

Delivering Your Proposal

Because of the relatively intimate communication environment in which proposals are presented, effective conversational delivery is crucial. Here are some guidelines to follow:

• *Use extemporaneous delivery.* You will likely be delivering your presentation in a boardroom environment, perhaps standing (or even seated) at the end of a con-

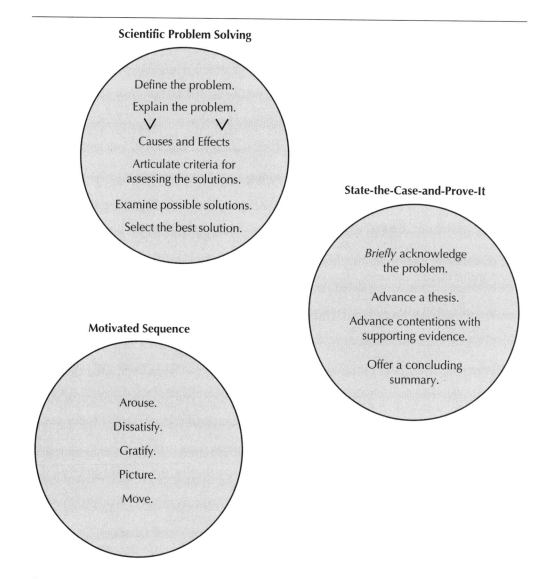

Figure 15.3   Organizational patterns for proposal presentation

ference table. You must be direct, flexible, and spontaneous. Your eye contact should include everyone in the room, and you should move and gesture as naturally as possible.

- *Use presentational aids.* When presenting proposals, visuals help the audience follow you, remember your arguments, and picture your plan. Make sure your aids look professional and that you can use them with ease. Check the room in advance to make sure that the equipment you need is there. Consider using computer-generated graphics (see chapter 14). Handouts are often helpful as you present data for decision makers to ponder and act on.

- *Respect time limits.* This group is probably meeting for some time, and you are only a part of their agenda. If your presentation takes more time than they anticipated, listeners may resent being put off their schedule. Leave ample time for questions.

- *Know the group's culture.* Your presentational style should fit in with the group's culture and norms as much as possible. They may prefer a presentation that is highly interactive, allowing for questions along the way, or they may want a brief presentation, followed by an extensive question-and-answer period. The more you know about their expectations and preferences, the more easily you will be able to connect with them and deliver your proposal presentation effectively.

SALES PRESENTATIONS

The key to success for any organization is sales: Unless someone can sell the organization's services or products to someone else, that organization simply will not survive. Unlike proposal presentations, sales presentations occur between an organization and its environment (such as an individual customer or another organization) rather than within the organization. Sales speakers act as representatives for themselves, their organization, and their organization's products or services.

Like the proposal presentation, the sales presentation typically is given before a small group. Groups to which sales presentations are made may take many forms, depending on the product or service being sold and the organization of which the group is a part. As consultants, for example, the authors have found themselves trying to sell their consulting services to groups of top-level university administrators; members of the personnel department of a major airline; a nursing task force consisting of staff nurses and first-level nursing supervisors; a vice president of engineering and his immediate staff; the vice president of human resources, director of training, director of labor relations, and training manager of a major insurance company; and the entire middle management group (approximately 10 people) of a small manufacturing firm. In situations like these, success depends on your knowledge of your own product or service; an understanding of the organization to which you are selling; and sensitivity to the characteristics, needs, and biases of the group to which you are speaking directly.

Preparing for the Sales Presentation

As in any speaking situation, the most important work occurs before the actual presentation takes place. Careful preparation significantly enhances your chances for success; poor preparation virtually guarantees failure. In planning your sales presentation, you need to: (1) gain information about your audience and the speaking situation; (2) use that information to outline your presentation; and (3) prepare supporting materials (such as presentational aids) to use during the presentation.

GAINING INFORMATION

Typically, you will not be acquainted with the group to whom you are selling. However, you will probably have some contact with at least one member of that group, if only to schedule your presentation. During that initial contact, try to learn as much of the following information as you can:

- *Who will make the decision* concerning purchase of the service or product?

- *Who will be attending the meeting?* Learn how many people are coming (so you know what to expect and how many copies of handout materials you need to bring) and what positions these people hold.

- *If the decision maker is not scheduled to be part of that meeting, why not?* Typically, meetings that do not include the decision maker are not very productive for the sales presenter.

- *How long is the meeting to last?* Obviously, you will need to tailor your presentation to fit the time limitations.

- *Why is this organization considering purchasing this service or product?* In other words, what are their needs? Some needs-analysis questions can be extremely helpful, enabling you to show specifically how your service or product will help this organization.

- *What criteria will be used to make the decision?* Occasionally, this information is not known by the person making the arrangements with you, but if you can get it you will know what to emphasize in your remarks.

- *What physical arrangements or equipment are or can be available?* Be sure to ask for any room arrangement you prefer and for any equipment (such as an overhead projector or a videotape player) you need.

Obtaining this sort of information and then using it to shape your presentation will enable you to provide an efficient, effective view of your service or product.

ORGANIZING THE PRESENTATION

In the preceding section, we considered several organizational patterns for proposal presentations. Any of these patterns might be appropriate for a sales presentation as well. However, there is another pattern that we find equally, if not more, effective. This pattern parallels the procedures followed during a sales interview and is called the *Introduction-Need-Presentation-Close (INPC) model*. Following this model, the *introduction* phase should:

1. *Identify who you are and what organization you represent.* In a brief statement, give your name and title in your organization, your organization's name, how long your organization has been in this business (if appropriate), your organization's specialties or notable achievements, and some customers who use your products or services. This information helps the group to feel that they are dealing with an experienced, reputable organization and sales representative.

2. *Briefly state the purpose of your presentation:* to ask some questions of the group (if you have a need and desire to do so), to describe your product or service, and then answer any questions they might have.

3. *Establish the climate for the presentation.* Experience shows that informal, extemporaneous presentations are more effective in sales situations. To create such a climate, you might make a statement like, "I intend to be fairly informal in my remarks, so please feel free to ask questions whenever you like. And I'll ask you any questions that I have as well." This statement encourages two-way communication between you and the group, and it provides a more relaxed atmosphere for everyone.

The *need* portion of the presentation is important as well. Obviously, some need must exist; otherwise it is unlikely that you would have been asked to make this presentation in the first place. To establish the need, you might simply address a question to the group as a whole, such as, "Why are you considering this service or product now?" The group spokesperson or leader probably would provide an answer, looking to other group members for support. However, since this approach might make you seem unprepared, it probably would be better simply to describe the organization's needs as you see them, based on your preparatory conversations. Finally, you could describe typical needs you have found in other similar organizations. By watching audience reactions to the typical needs you describe, you probably will be able to determine which needs are present here.

Presentation of your product or service occurs once the needs have been established. Typically, this presentation will consist of three steps:

1. Provide an overview of what the product is and how it works or of how the service is performed (taking the group through a step-by-step sequence).

2. Describe particularly important features of your product or service as they respond to the group's needs.

3. Explain the benefits of your product or service to the group or their organization.

The *close* in a sales presentation is a bit complicated. Typically, the group will need to meet after you have left to make their decision. Indeed, they also may have met with other sales representatives or have such meetings scheduled in the near future, so that they need to consider the competitors' services or products as well. In short, it is highly unlikely that the group will be able or willing to make a decision while you are there. Therefore, asking for their decision would be inappropriate and potentially embarrassing. Instead, the close of a sales presentation should:

1. *Summarize the benefits* you illustrated when you tied the features of your product or service to the organization or group's needs. It is these benefits that should cause the group to select your product or service, and you must make sure they are understood and remembered.

2. *Reiterate why the group should choose you and your organization.* Refer to the information you provided during the introduction about your organization's experience and reputation. Many products and services are very similar; the unique qualifications of your organization may be the determining factor that gets you the sale.

3. *Ask for questions*. If the group has asked questions during your presentation, there may be few or none at this point. Our experience, however, has been that many questions are asked and that this is one of the most important elements of the sales presentation. The questions you are asked reveal those things that the group found most important (or the most difficult to understand). Consequently, they are things that you need to stress again. The questions may also reveal the individual biases or preferences of the members, allowing you to direct your remarks even more specifically to their concerns. By handling questions effectively, you not only maintain the positive impression you have created up to this point, but advance your cause significantly. When preparing for the presentation, try to anticipate questions the group might ask and have answers ready. Figure 15.4 depicts the INPC model.

PREPARING SUPPORTING MATERIALS

The presentation phase of the presentation often benefits significantly from the use of presentational aids. As discussed in chapter 14, aids such as chalkboards, flipcharts, overhead transparencies, models, and varied computer-generated graphics add clarity and interest to the presentation. As a rule, every sales presentation should be accompanied by some form of presentational aid (and usually, more than one). In preparing for the presentation, develop aids that are professional in appearance, neat, and communicative and that add to the credibility of your organization and your product or service.

Delivering the Sales Presentation

We have already noted some elements involved in delivering the sales presentation:

- It should be delivered extemporaneously.
- It should be somewhat informal in tone.
- It should involve the use of presentational aids.
- It should allow for questions and answers.

In addition, we should note that the characteristics of effective delivery presented in chapter 14 apply here as well. An effective sales presentation is characterized by a delivery that is spontaneous, direct, flexible, and involving.

The Wizard of Id
by Brant Parker and Johnny Hart

By permission of John L. Hart FLP and Creators Syndicate, Inc.

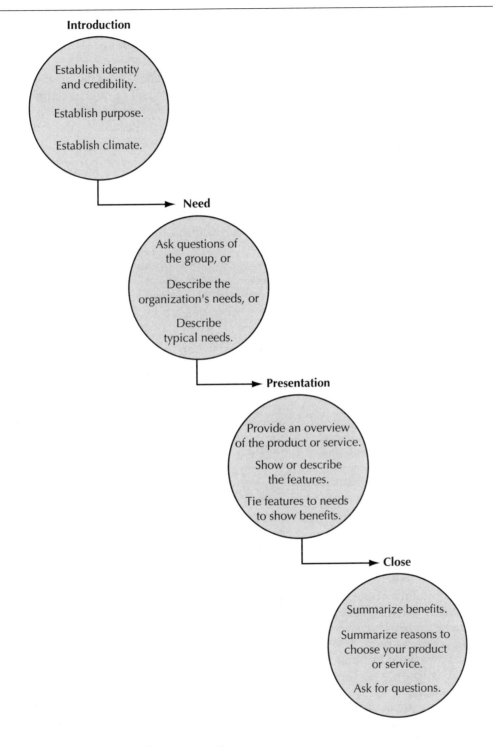

Figure 15.4   The INPC sales presentation

Particularly important in a sales presentation are the elements of *spontaneity and flexibility*. As you present your introduction, need, presentation, and close, you must be sensitive to feedback (verbal and nonverbal) from the audience and must adjust to that feedback appropriately. Sometimes the feedback and adjustment are obvious: Someone interrupts your presentation to ask a question, and you adjust by giving an answer. More often, however, feedback and adjustment are subtle, requiring extreme sensitivity and flexibility on your part. In this section, we will consider briefly how to read reactions, interpret them, and adjust to them.

NONVERBAL BEHAVIORS

While knowledge of your product is important, perhaps even more important is knowledge of people. You need to understand the people to whom you talk. You need to know how to read their feelings and reactions accurately and what to do about the things you perceive. With this ability, you are almost certain to be successful. Without it, success will be very difficult to achieve.

At the outset, you must remember one important fact: words often tell very little about how a person feels. We express most of our feelings with our eyes, gestures, and voice. Research suggests that only about 7 percent of the feelings we convey are expressed through our words. Another 38 percent (roughly) are expressed through the tone of voice we use—rate of speech, voice inflection, pitch, volume, and so on. Finally, our face, eyes, and gestures account for about 55 percent of the feelings we convey.[20] (See chapter 5 for further discussion of nonverbal communication.)

To read people accurately, then, you must become skillful at noticing quick changes in the eyes and face. These changes may be incredibly fast, lasting only a quarter to a half of a second. But if you are observant, you can perceive changes as specific as enlargement of someone's pupils (often a sign of interest), as well as general changes in body posture.

While you speak, the group members are constantly sending messages about their feelings and reactions. Most informative are the eyes: if someone likes you or is interested in your presentation, her or his eyes will seem to brighten as the muscles around the eyes tense. On the other hand, if the person wishes you would go away, the muscles around the eyes may be relaxed, with the face drooping slightly. More than any other factor, the eyes reveal what the mind is thinking.

There are two important dangers in trying to read body language. First, you cannot assume that specific actions have particular meanings. Folded arms may mean rejection, but they also may mean that the individual is cold or is just comfortable in that position. Second, you should not try to keep track of so many actions that you lose your concentration. But if you are able to focus on some general body language groupings, then you might be able to use nonverbal cues to your advantage.

There are five basic groups of nonverbal (and occasionally, verbal) cues that indicate how a person is feeling, together with our suggestions for how to handle each:

Group 1

- *Approval*. Nonverbal cues may indicate positive acceptance of you and your claims. Signs of approval include leaning forward toward you, maintaining eye contact, changes in vocal inflection (an animated voice), frequent gestures, a pleasant, smiling expression, frequent head nods, raised eyebrows, willing responses to your questions, and vocal indications of agreement ("Uh-huh," "Yeah," and so on). Sometimes a customer will express approval verbally as well, using approval statements such as, "That sounds good" or "I really like that." Such verbal and nonverbal expressions should indicate to you that the customer likes what you are saying and accepts the feature, benefit, or proof you have offered.

- *Handling approval.* When you see signs of approval, what do you do? First, consider closing. If the meeting has gone on for some time, with the group agreeing with or showing interest in the features and benefits you described, you may ask for questions at this point. However, if it is still very early in the meeting, you may decide closing is premature. Instead, you might reinforce the approval.

Sales usually are the result of a series of agreements. If the group seems to be approving, try to get the members to make an open commitment, saying that they agree with a benefit you have described. For example, you might ask the entire group, "You seem to feel that the cases in this book are particularly good. Is that right?" Such reinforcement makes these small battles you have won more memorable and more influential when you try to win the entire war later on. Finally, move on to another point.

Group 2

- *Confusion.* While describing features or benefits, you may perceive signs of puzzlement. Yet, many people will choose not to ask questions, either because they do not wish to appear uninformed or stupid or because they do not want to prolong the meeting. It is important that you be sensitive to these signs and respond to them appropriately. Nonverbal signs of confusion or lack of understanding include a slight scowl or frown, narrowing of the eyes, tilting the head to one side, raising the eyebrows, or pursing the lips. Verbally, a confused person might ask to have a point repeated, give a response that is "off the wall," ask for an explanation, or give vocal cues such as, "Huh?" or "What?" It is important to pick up such signs. Understanding must be achieved if the group is to be convinced to buy what you are selling.

- *Handling confusion.* When you perceive confusion, review what you just said, but in a different way. Say something like, "Let me go over that again, because it's important." Give the group another chance to follow your thinking. Alternatively, you might note that others often find this point confusing and again ask for a reaction. For example: "It seems like a lot of people have trouble understanding this. Am I explaining it all right?" Finally, you might simply respond to the reaction. If someone is reluctant to indicate confusion or lack of understanding, your question may prompt the person to admit confusion and tell you what specifically is unclear. However, if the person's reluctance to indicate confusion stems from a desire to get the meeting over with, he or she may insist that everything is perfectly clear, even though it's not. Therefore, you might review the point one more time and then move on.

Group 3

- *Skepticism.* Sometimes listeners find it difficult to believe what you are saying. After all, they may have been subjected to dozens of sales calls from representatives and may have heard the same claims repeated by each. It is only natural for them to be a little suspicious of the things you (and all the other reps) say. Common nonverbal signs of skepticism include: raising one eyebrow, tilting the head backward, tilting the head forward and peering out from under the eyebrows, shifting from an open posture to one that is more closed (perhaps by folding the arms or crossing legs), frowning or scowling, narrowing the eyes, looking away from you, or shaking the head.

Some verbal signs of skepticism include, "Do you really expect me to believe that . . . ?" and "Well, I rather doubt that. . . ." Each of these statements suggests that your points are not being accepted and that you will need to take some action to convince the group.

- *Handling skepticism.* When you perceive skepticism, you first might ask about the behaviors you have observed: "You seem skeptical about this. Do you have some reservations about what I'm saying?" This question invites the group members to state openly any concerns they might have—concerns that otherwise might go unspoken and unanswered. Then respond appropriately to stated reservations and invite the group to raise any other reservations in their minds. Finally, to handle persistent skepticism, you must offer some sort of proof for what you have claimed. Continue to provide proof until the group accepts the validity of your point or it becomes clear that someone is expressing a personal objection rather than skepticism about a particular feature. When such an objection emerges, handle it as you would any other objection.

Group 4

- *Indifference.* When customers see sales representatives frequently, it becomes easy for them to adopt an attitude of indifference. They have sat through countless presentations, most of which make the same claims and use the same buzz words. They have become jaded, adopting an unspoken attitude of "All right, so tell me how *your* product or service is better than all the others." The more experienced they are, the more likely they are to adopt such an indifferent attitude.

Several nonverbal cues convey indifference, including "hanging" facial muscles, a slumped or overly relaxed posture, an expressionless face, a posture that leans away from you, a tapping or wiggling foot, heavy sighs, frequent changes of posture (squirming), drumming the fingers or tapping with some object, and providing very little response to your questions. In addition, the group may simply agree with everything you say, giving no direct expression of indifference but at the same time giving you nothing to go on. To get a sale, you have to motivate them before they will have any interest in the features and benefits you describe.

- *Handling indifference.* When you see indifference, stop selling and ask questions designed to uncover needs. The specific question you ask to identify needs is determined by the reason for the group's indifference. If the group sees no need for your product, ask questions for background information. For example:

    "Tell me about your work."
    "What things need to be improved?"

If the organization has a self-developed procedure, ask about the procedure to see if there might be any problems. For example:

"What have you liked best about that procedure?"
"What things would you improve if you could?"
"What problems have you had?"

If the client is satisfied with a competitor, ask about the competing product or service to identify possible problems. For example:

"What do you like most about . . . ?"
"What complaints have employees offered?"

Often, customers do not want to express their lack of interest. They know you will try to give answers, and rather than taking the time to hear your answers, they decide to suffer through the presentation in silence, ask for a brochure, and let you leave. You cannot afford this type of treatment; you have invested time to put yourself in front of this group and a meaningful conversation is important. By urging them to talk to you, you are more likely to uncover some needs that can be met or some problems that can be answered, and in so doing increase the chances of getting a sale.

Group 5

• *Objections*. Several nonverbal cues, when shown in combination, often indicate objections to you and your product or service: folded arms, crossed legs, clenched fists or tense hands, posture turned away from you (with shoulders at an angle), frowns, tight lips or facial grimace, avoidance of eye contact, flat voice with very little variance in volume or pitch, and very short answers to your questions. Verbal objections generally show clear disagreement with your arguments or focus on perceived disadvantages of your product.

During your presentation, people are likely to raise complaints, objections, questions, and other roadblocks to a potential sale. Much of your effectiveness throughout the sales call will be determined by how well you deal with the objections that come up. While each client and each situation is different, there are some common reasons why objections are raised and, in some cases, why a particular client seems to be more resistant than others.

Some clients raise objections because they simply want more information or because they don't know what they want or need. Rather than resisting your sales effort, they are expressing an objection to receive assurance on some doubtful point or because they have not properly understood your presentation. For example, they might object because not enough benefits are apparent yet. Indeed, this is the reason for most objections, and once a client sees enough benefits, there is no longer a reason to object.

On the other hand, some clients raise objections based on hidden motives: to show you that they are intelligent, clever, and not an easy sale; because they are tired of seeing the parade of sales representatives knocking at their door; as a stalling tactic to avoid making a decision at this time; because they already have made up their minds but do not want to say no to your face; or because they are resistant to change.

There are many other reasons, of course, why clients raise objections to your claims. Most objections reflect legitimate concern or curiosity about the content and features of your product or service. And each objection gives you an opportunity to exercise your skills as a sales representative.

- *Handling objections*. There are four basic strategies for dealing with objections a client raises. First, you could **meet the objection directly**. This sort of approach handles the objection in an assertive manner, supported by specific evidence. It requires that you be well organized and thoroughly familiar with the features of your product or service.

Second, you could **sidestep the objection**. If an objection does not seem to be a major concern in the client's mind, you can simply avoid it. But be careful; while sidestepping an objection avoids wasting time discussing trivial matters, you must judge carefully whether the objection is trivial or not. If you sidestep an objection that really is important to the client, you may lose the sale.

Minimizing the objection is a third approach that strives to reduce the impact of objections. You can implement this approach verbally and/or nonverbally. To minimize an objection verbally, you first might remind the client of benefits he has already accepted—benefits that might outweigh the objection that has been raised. In reviewing those benefits, first begin with some introductory phrase, such as:

> "Remember some of the things we have talked about."
> "Look at the big picture for a second."

Then summarize the benefits already agreed to. However, if there are no benefits to review or if the list does not seem to outweigh the objection, then you need to ask questions to uncover needs. In other words, you start the need and presentation steps over again in an effort to build a case for your product. Eventually, you hope to compile a list of agreed-to benefits that will outweigh this objection.

Nonverbal reactions can be used to minimize objections, although they must be used carefully. Raising your eyebrows in surprise, for example, indicates your amazement that such an objection would even be raised. Similarly, frowning or shaking your head indicates that, in your opinion, a minor point has been raised. A heavy sigh, shrugging your shoulders, and turning your head away are other signals that you do not view this matter to be important. The biggest danger in using nonverbal cues to minimize objections is that you may anger the client. The issue may indeed be very important in the client's mind, and your sigh or shrug may be perceived as offensive. For that reason, minimizing objections nonverbally should be used very carefully and only occasionally.

Giving in to an objection is appropriate when you just cannot win the point. For instance, it would probably be futile to try to sell a communication textbook to a college professor who has just written her own or to attempt to sell someone an IBM computer when she is the devoted and delighted owner of a new Macintosh.

When there is no way of overcoming an objection or the objection indicates a legitimate preference for a competitor, you may have to give in. But there still may be other ways to get a sale. For example, you might suggest the client use one of your other products or services on a trial basis, admit this one problem but try to counter with other more important advantages, or simply move to other needs the client has. For instance, the professor in the example above likely teaches several classes, and perhaps you have other books that can meet her needs. Giving in on an objection does not mean giving up.

By watching for, interpreting, and responding to feedback from the client group, you add significantly to the effectiveness of your sales presentation. Certainly, there may be other groups of nonverbal and verbal cues that indicate specific reactions or feelings. For our purposes, however, the groups listed above are most relevant, and it is these you should look for and try to read and treat effectively when making a presentation.

Ethics and Civic Engagement

Normally, when we think of sales presentations, we imagine individuals who represent organizations speaking on behalf of those organizations' products or services. Some may worry that a salesperson will say or do anything to get the sale—even if it means exaggerating a product's attributes or omitting a product's deficiencies. Clearly, this kind of exaggeration or distortion is unethical. Equally important is questioning the inherent worth, goodness, or quality of any product or service that is being sold—as well as the conditions that surround its production. What if the milk someone sells you contains a dangerous additive? How do you feel about buying clothing that was made in sweatshops? Are you comfortable using hair spray that was tested on animals? Do you want to shop at a store that offers low prices but fails to provide fair wages and benefits to its employees? You may want to reflect on these questions as a thoughtful consumer of advertising and a critical listener of any presentation that is designed to sell you a product, service, or idea. Return to chapter 1 and revisit the ethical perspectives presented there.

Highlighting Civic Engagement and Ethics

Consumer Activism

- *The Course:* C223 Business and Professional Communication
- *The Assignment:* The Advocacy Speech Assignment
- *The Description:* This assignment provides you with an opportunity to engage in consumer activism by asking your peers to boycott a product or company that threatens public safety or violates ethical standards. Alternatively, you may propose changing a national or state law that regulates the practices of businesses or other professional organizations.
- *Basic Requirements:*

  7–8 minutes in length

  Deliver extemporaneously, using speaking notes

  Orally cite *at least* five sources

  Use good oral style

  Organize your speech so that it concludes with a specific and compelling call to action

  Prepare a formal outline with an appended bibliography of 8–10 sources

Acknowledgment: This assignment was originally created by George LaMaster, a doctoral student in the Department of Communication and Culture at Indiana University in 2001 (and now Assistant Professor of Communication at Marian College in Indianapolis, Indiana).

To ensure that they consider the ethical implications of the products they are asked to purchase, students who take the business and professional communication course at Indiana University are encouraged to become thoughtful, discerning consumers of communication, as well as engaged citizens. One assignment that invites this kind of orientation is described in the Highlighting feature that follows.

This kind of speaking assignment provides a different slant on a sales presentation. Both the boycotting presentation and the sales presentation are persuasive speeches to actuate. But while the sales presentation promotes a product or service, the boycotting speech assignment asks the speaker to examine existing products with a critical eye and to demand responsible, ethical behavior on the part of the audience as consumers and the organizations as manufacturers and employers. This kind of public speaking reinforces critical thinking and a concern for civic engagement.

SUMMARY

This concluding chapter has introduced you to two of the specific kinds of persuasive speaking contexts you are likely to encounter as you move into jobs requiring professional training and perhaps some managerial responsibility. Often, these presentations are delivered to very important people—board members, upper-level managers, potential customers—in short, people who can make the difference in your professional opportunities and the success of your organization.

Because both sales and proposal presentations are specific kinds of persuasive speeches, it is important to understand the basic nature of persuasion. Among other things, you must consider audience members' sources of motivation as well as their needs and values. Equally crucial is being seen as credible (that is, as trustworthy, competent, fair-minded, and dynamic) in the eyes of the audience. Knowing how to appeal to audience emotions (within an ethical framework) and how to use evidence in ways that advance arguments and make listeners resistant to counterinfluence attempts is also critical to effective persuasive speaking.

Although we have suggested specific concerns and techniques that may be useful in special public communication contexts, we also want to emphasize that *the underlying principles of effective public speaking are quite similar across situations.* That is, in every speech situation, you must prepare carefully, know your material or product, carefully analyze the audience (acknowledging, among other things, cultural differences), clearly and strategically organize your remarks, and present your ideas or information using effective (usually extemporaneous) delivery. And *each* time you prepare to give a speech, whether in professional or civic settings, you must not lose sight of the transactional nature of communication. When you deliver public speeches, you still exchange roles of sender and receiver. You hope to influence others' ideas and decisions, but as you watch and hear others react to your thinking and arguments, you are often influenced as well.

That is, in public speaking, as in other communication contexts, you participate in a dynamic process in which all participants share control. Moreover, public speaking requires the highest concern for responsible, ethical communication.

Questions for Discussion

1. Discuss some of the basic elements influencing human motivation. How significant do you consider each of these elements? Can you think of other motivational factors to add to the factors considered in the book?

2. List some differences and commonalities in values you might anticipate when you speak to audiences who are culturally diverse.

3. What are some of the ways in which organizations (and their leaders) demonstrate their "commitment to contribution"? Cite specific examples.

4. What are some things you can do as a speaker to establish your credibility with listeners?

5. How important are emotional appeals in persuasive speaking? What are some specific ways of appealing to audience emotions?

6. How can you use evidence most persuasively? Be specific.

7. In what ways might a small group audience differ from a traditional public speaking audience? How might the differences affect your preparation as a speaker?

8. Explain the following: unity, coherence, emphasis, completeness, and conciseness. In what ways might these qualities of organization be particularly relevant for speakers who are preparing proposal presentations?

9. Under what circumstances (topic, audience, personal point of view) would you elect to use the following patterns of organization? Why?

   a. Scientific problem solving

   b. State-the-case-and-prove-it pattern

   c. Motivated sequence

10. You are talking to the person who has invited you to make a sales presentation. What kinds of questions should you ask to gain information you need?

11. Briefly describe the INPC model of organization. How does it differ from (and how is it similar to) the patterns of organization referred to in question 9?

12. Reading and responding to listener reactions when giving a sales presentation are crucial. Name at least two reactions you might look for and describe how you might handle each.

Exercises

1. In a 250-word typed essay, respond to the following: Choose an organization to which you have belonged for at least one year (for instance, a sorority, a church, a volunteer organization, or a speech or accounting club). Now assume that you have been asked to present a proposal to this group's executive board. You have come up with a proposal—presenting a plan or course of action for this group to endorse. For example, you might want your fraternity to sponsor a dance marathon to raise money for cancer research.

   With a specific group in mind, analyze your "audience." Consider your small group audience both as individuals and as a dynamic, interacting whole. Be specific in terms of their habits, needs, and other motives. What are their similarities? In what ways are they diverse? What cultural differences among audience members can you identify? Which listeners are the most powerful or most respected?

Based on your analysis, what specific things will you do to enhance the chances that they will accept your proposal (in terms of preparation, organization, and presentation)? Justify your choices.

2. Select a product or service with which you have had some experience and that impresses you very much. Prepare and deliver a four- to five-minute sales presentation to your classmates in which you attempt to sell them the product. Prepare at least three presentational aids and follow the INPC model of organization. As you deliver your presentation, pay particular attention to listener reactions.

Following your presentation, respond to listener questions following the guidelines for handling confusion, skepticism, and so on as discussed in the text.

When you are finished, ask your classmates to complete the following form:

Name of speaker:_____

Product or service:_____

Indicate below how likely you are to buy this product or service:

Extremely likely ____ Somewhat likely ____ Undecided ____

Somewhat unlikely ____ Extremely unlikely ____

Briefly explain the basis for your reactions:

Collect the forms, read through them, and decide what changes you would make if you were to give this sales presentation a second time to the same or a very similar audience.

3. After doing some careful research on companies and products that you consider questionable or unethical, complete the boycotting speech assignment described on page 563 in the Highlighting Civic Engagement and Ethics box. Deliver your speech to your classmates. Then, ask them to complete the following assessment form:

Name of speaker:_____

Name of product, service, or organization to be boycotted:

_____

Indicate below how likely you are to boycott this product or organization:

Extremely likely ____ Somewhat likely ____ Undecided ____

Somewhat unlikely ____ Extremely unlikely ____

Briefly explain the basis for your reactions:

Case Application 15.1   Making Strategic Choices in Preparing and Presenting a Proposal

James Goodman is a computer analyst in an automobile manufacturing organization. His boss has asked him to present a proposal advocating the purchase of a new, expensive, and fairly controversial computer for the organization. The small group to which Goodman is to make the presentation is composed of: (1) the vice president for research and development (young, innovative, flexible, liberal); (2) the director of finance (middle-aged, rigid, conservative, in favor of the status quo); (3) the supportive boss who made the request; (4) the director of data analysis (young, brilliant, cautious, conservative); and (5) the president (near retirement, moderate on most issues, listens mostly to the advice of the vice presidents in the organization).

Questions

1. Given the expense of the computer, the controversiality concerning its worth, and the nature of the audience, what strategy should Goodman adopt?
2. What assumptions might he make about the dynamics of this particular small group?
3. What pattern of arrangement would be most appropriate? Why?
4. What are some lines of argument that might be especially effective?
5. How should Goodman use evidence to be most persuasive?

Case Application 15.2   Selling Good Food

Susan West works for Healthy Options, a food service organization that provides healthy food alternatives to more traditional foods. The organization emphasizes low-fat, low-cholesterol, high-fiber diets and promotes vegetarianism.

Susan's job is to try to sell this food service to colleges and universities throughout the United States. Currently, she is scheduled to make a sales presentation to the director of food services and his administrative staff at a large public university located in the South. She has studied the food services this university currently offers students and has found numerous fast-food options, along with dorm menus that feature the influence of Southern cooking (including fried chicken, biscuits and gravy, and heavy desserts).

Susan's persuasive challenge appears substantial.

Questions

1. What additional information should Susan obtain before planning her presentation?
2. What are some of the biggest objections that Susan will have to be prepared to address? How can she best present her evidence and ideas to deal with those objections?

3. How might she organize her presentation? Why would this pattern likely be effective?

4. Should Susan use emotional appeals? If so, what kinds would be most moving? If not, why not?

5. How might Susan deliver her sales presentation so that her listeners are most likely to be receptive, or at least open, to considering Healthy Options alternatives?

Appendix
Parliamentary Procedure

Generally speaking, the larger the group, the more difficult it is for the group's leader to control the meeting. In very large group meetings, such as stockholders' meetings or meetings of legislative bodies, the leader frequently chooses to use a very structured format to ensure orderly communication. Perhaps the most commonly used large group format is parliamentary procedure.

BASIC PRINCIPLES OF PARLIAMENTARY PROCEDURE

The rules of parliamentary procedure were not developed by any single person or group of people. Rather, they evolved over hundreds of years through the experiences of thousands of self-governing assemblies. They have become somewhat complicated over time, but their basic principles have rarely changed. If you understand the principles, the rules make more sense and are easier to apply. These principles include:

- *The majority rules*. Obviously, this is a democratic approach to group communication. Rarely can total agreement be reached on any issue. To have some basis for action in cases where disagreement occurs, the principle is followed that the preferences of the majority are carried out.

- *The rights of the minority are protected*. The majority cannot be granted unlimited power. Every member of the assembly has individual rights, regardless of whether he or she happens to agree with the majority. These rights include the right to a secret ballot, the right to nominate for office, and the protection of the constitution and bylaws of the organization. As leader you must ensure that these rights are protected and that no one is steamrollered by the majority.

- *Business must be accomplished*. Meetings are held to bring about some action. The group welcomes free presentation of all the facts and opinions on any problem under discussion, but the discussion cannot consume an entire meeting, nor should it get in the way of getting things done.

569

- *Feelings must be respected*. We must be careful not to lose sight of individual feelings as we conduct the group's business and control its interaction. Just as courtesy is important in all our social relationships, so too must it be maintained in large group meetings.

Obviously, these four principles will contradict one another at times; for example, the rights of a minority may interfere with the rapid accomplishment of the group's business or with the rule of the majority. As group leader or chairperson, you must do all you can to maintain a balance among these principles. The rules of parliamentary law have been developed to help you achieve such a balance.

The Order of Business

The order of business used by a large group will vary somewhat. However, a typical group agenda includes the following elements:

1. *Call to order*. After determining that a quorum (the minimum number needed to transact business, usually a simple majority of the total membership) is present, the chairperson gets the attention of the group (often by rapping a gavel on the podium) and says, "The meeting will please come to order."

2. *Opening ceremonies*. Many groups open their meetings with a prayer, pledge of allegiance, song, and so on. If such a ceremony is used by this group, the chairperson next would say, "Let us open our meeting by. . . ."

3. *Roll call*. If a roll call is desired to determine who is in attendance, the chairperson says, "The secretary will please call the roll." Occasionally, he or she might add, "Members will answer to their names by . . . ," stating the way in which members should respond to their names.

4. *Reading of the minutes*. The chairperson next says, "The secretary will read the minutes of the last meeting." When the minutes have been read, he or she then asks, "Are there any corrections or additions to the minutes?" If none are offered, the chairperson states, "The minutes stand approved as read." If corrections are offered (and agreed to by the chairperson and the assembly), the secretary is instructed to make the necessary changes. Then the chairperson states, "The minutes stand approved as corrected."

5. *Reports*. After the reading of the minutes, the chairperson typically calls on the chairpersons of standing and special committees to make reports to the group. If there are no objections, the report is accepted by the group (not endorsed but filed for future reference). If any proposed action grows from a committee report, it is introduced later under "new business."

6. *Unfinished business*. The chairperson says, "We now will consider any unfinished business." Anything left over or postponed from the previous meeting may be discussed and voted on at this time.

7. *New business*. The chairperson says, "We will now consider any new business." As a rule, this portion of the meeting consumes most of the time spent by the group.

8. *Program*. Occasionally, the group has some program (such as a speaker, film, or presentation) planned as part of the meeting. When no more new business is forthcoming, the chairperson asks, "Is there any further new business

to come before this meeting? If not, will the chairperson of the program committee (or other member in charge of the program) please take charge of the program planned for this meeting." The chairperson and secretary may then sit in the audience for the program.

9. *Miscellaneous, announcements, and so on*. Before adjourning, the chairperson may ask if there are any announcements to be made, notes to be read, or other routine matters not requiring group action. Some groups do this earlier in the meeting, following the reading of the minutes.

10. *Adjournment*. One of two procedures may be used to adjourn a meeting. If the meeting always adjourns at a fixed time and that time arrives, the chairperson may say, "The meeting is adjourned." If not, the chairperson may ask, "Is there a motion to adjourn?" In the latter case, some member of the group says, "I move we adjourn." This motion must be seconded by another group member, and it cannot be discussed. The motion is put to a vote, and the result announced: "The motion is adopted; the meeting is adjourned." In the highly unlikely event that the motion to adjourn is defeated, the chairperson would announce the vote and call for any additional new business on the assumption that the majority had something else they want to do before closing the meeting.

Taking Action: Introducing and Managing Motions

In large group settings where parliamentary procedure is used, the purpose of the meeting generally is to decide on various courses of action. Possible courses of action are suggested by the group members, who do so in the form of *motions* for discussion by the group. One such motion, as we already have seen, is the motion to adjourn—a suggestion that the meeting be terminated and everyone leave. Almost all decisions made by the group are handled in a similar fashion: A member suggests a course of action (that is, he or she states a motion), the group considers it, and ultimately a decision to adopt or reject that motion is made. The real "work" involved in leading a large group meeting is handling the members' motions and ensuing discussion while preserving the four principles we stated earlier. Several steps are followed in handling motions offered by members.

1. *The member obtains the floor*. The member rises, calling out, "Mister (or Madam) Chairperson." In smaller or more informal groups, the member might remain seated and address the chair. The member should not rise without addressing the chair if he or she wants to obtain the floor. The chairperson then recognizes the member by saying the member's name, nodding in the member's direction, or in some other way referring to the member. The member should not speak until receiving recognition from the chair.

2. *The member states the motion* by saying, "I move that we . . . ," thus suggesting the action she wants the group to take. The motion should be as complete as possible so that no unnecessary amendments need be made, but it should not be overly long and complicated. Long motions should be submitted in writing.

3. *The motion is seconded*. For a motion to be considered, it must be supported by at least one other group member. The person giving the second need not rise;

he or she only needs to call out, "Second" or "I second the motion." If no one seconds the motion, the chairperson may ask, "Is the motion seconded?" If still no one seconds the motion, the chairperson states, "The motion is lost for lack of a second." If a second is given, the chairperson then states the motion to the group by saying, "It has been moved and seconded that we. . . ." Then the chair calls for discussion: "Is there any discussion on the motion?"

4. **Members discuss the motion.** Several points should be kept in mind here. Each member who wants to speak must first obtain the floor (be recognized by the chairperson), just as if a new motion were being offered. Discussion must be confined to the motion at hand, and the one who offered the motion typically is given first opportunity to discuss it. Usually, people are recognized as they stand and address the chair; however, if someone rises and interrupts the previous speaker, he or she is ruled out of order and not given the floor. If many people desire to speak, the chair tries to "alternate the floor," first recognizing someone in favor of the motion and then recognizing someone against it, giving each position a turn to speak. Any member who has already spoken once is not recognized until all members wanting to express themselves for the first time have done so. Finally, the chair does not offer her or his opinions on the motion; his or her job is simply to keep order.

5. **The chair determines that the discussion is finished.** When members stop rising to request recognition, the chairperson asks, "Is there any further discussion?" If some is offered, the chair repeats the question later. When no further discussion is offered, she or he proceeds to the next step, restating the motion. He or she might say, "If there is no further discussion, we are ready to vote. The question is on the motion to. . . ."

6. **The members vote on the motion.** This can occur in several ways. Frequently, the group uses a **voice vote**, where the chairperson says, "As many as are in favor of the motion say aye (pronounced "I"); those opposed say no." If the number of ayes clearly is larger than the number of nos, or vice versa, the decision is announced. The group also can vote by **raising hands or by standing** to show support for or opposition to the motion. If the motion requires a two-thirds majority, standing or hand-raising votes should be taken to enable the chairperson to count the votes. Members can request this type of vote by calling, "Division," or by saying, "I call for a division of the house." Then the chairperson must request that a standing vote be taken. Finally, a group can **vote by secret ballot or by general consent**. In the latter case, the chairperson says, "If there is no objection, we will . . ." (stating the action that the motion requires). The chairperson then pauses to allow members to object. If no one does, the motion is considered to be passed by unanimous approval; if an objection is offered, a vote is taken by voice, show of hands, standing, or ballot.

7. **The chairperson has a right to vote whenever her or his vote will change the outcome.** However, the chairperson may not want to reveal her or his opinions and thus may choose not to vote except in the case of a secret ballot. However, if the chairperson's vote will either create or break a tie, he or she may want to vote openly. A tie vote defeats a motion (majority rule means that half of those voting plus one must support the motion). By creating a tie with her or his

vote, the chairperson would defeat a motion; by breaking a tie, the chairperson would carry the motion.

8. *The chairperson announces the result of the vote after the vote is taken.* If there is no doubt of the result, the chairperson says, "The ayes have it; the motion is carried" or "The nos have it; the motion is defeated." Then the chairperson indicates the effect of this vote. He or she says, "We will therefore . . ." (stating the action that the motion requires the group to take). Finally, the chairperson moves to the next piece of business. If a main motion was voted on, the chairperson asks, "Is there any further business to come before us?"

Types of Motions

There are different types of motions that group members can offer, and these must be handled in different ways. So far, we have primarily discussed main motions, motions that bring a subject before the group for consideration and action. However, other types of special motions require unusual handling. To be effective, the chairperson must be able to answer several questions in his or her own mind whenever a motion is offered and to then take appropriate action. These questions include:

- What type of motion is it?
- Which motions may it displace in receiving the attention of the group, and which motions may displace it?
- Does it require a second? May it be discussed?
- What vote does it require: majority or two-thirds?

MAIN MOTIONS

To help you understand the types of motions you or other group members might make, we will consider some special motions that commonly occur. The first group are all considered *main motions*.

- *The motion to take a matter "off the table."* When some motion has been tabled or "placed on the table," discussion of that motion has been suspended temporarily. A member can bring the matter to the attention of the group again by moving that the original motion be taken off the table and considered by the group.
- *The motion to reconsider action previously taken.* This motion can be offered only by someone who voted in favor of the original motion, and its effect is to place the original motion before the group again as though a vote never had been taken. It is important to note, however, that a motion to reconsider is appropriate only for matters the group can undo; things that cannot be changed should not be reconsidered. This motion is also appropriate only during the same meeting in which the original motion was passed or during the next meeting the group holds.
- *The motion to repeal or rescind an action previously taken.* This motion is similar to the preceding but is used in later meetings when the motion to reconsider is no longer appropriate. It can be offered by any member, and its effect is to reverse the action previously taken.

SUBSIDIARY MOTIONS

A second group of motions are *subsidiary motions*, which are applied to main motions to get them in proper shape so the group can take action on them. They include:

- *The motion to amend.* When the group does not like the wording of the main motion, they may change that wording by amending the motion. The group may add words, remove words, or substitute words; however, they can do only one of these things at a time (that is, they cannot simultaneously add some words, remove others, and substitute for still others). The maker of the main motion does not need to approve these changes; the majority vote of the group determines whether the main motion is amended. To amend a motion, a member rises, addresses the chair, and says, "I move we amend the motion by adding (removing, substituting) the words . . . after the words . . . so that the motion will read. . . ." This motion requires a second before it can be considered. The group may also want to amend the amendment, and this is moved in the same way. The process cannot be carried any further, however (that is, you cannot amend an amendment to an amendment). The voting order is (a) amendment to the amendment, (b) amendment, and (c) motion.

- *The motion to refer to a committee.* The group may want to have some committee handle a matter rather than devoting time to the matter in this meeting. Thus, a member might rise, address the chair, and say, "I move we refer this motion to . . ." or "I move that a . . . committee be created to handle this matter."

- *The motion to postpone to a particular time.* A member might rise, gain recognition, and say, "I move that we postpone consideration of this matter until our next meeting" or "I move that we postpone consideration of this matter for 10 minutes." A specific time must be stated, and it may not be beyond the next regular meeting of the group.

- *The motion to put an end to discussion and vote at once.* If this motion is made and passed by two-thirds of the group, it immediately stops discussion and brings about an immediate vote on the matter before the group. To make such a motion, a member rises, is recognized, and says, "I move that we put an end to discussion on this matter." An alternative way of stating this motion is, "I move the previous question."

- *The motion to lay a matter on the table.* Like the motion to postpone consideration, this motion delays consideration of the matter at hand; however, it does not state any time limit. The person offering the motion simply says, "I move that this matter be laid on the table." If the motion is seconded and supported by a majority vote, discussion of the matter stops until the matter is taken off the table at some future time. If not seconded or supported by a majority vote, the motion to table is defeated and discussion on the original matter continues.

INCIDENTAL MOTIONS

Incidental motions make up the third motion group. They are offered during the course of a meeting when an unusual situation arises that needs immediate action by the group. These may be offered at virtually any time, and they must be decided on before discussion returns to the matter at hand. Some common incidental motions are:

- *A point of order.* When anyone makes a mistake in parliamentary law, any member may rise without being recognized and say, "Mister (or Madam) Chairman, I rise to a point of order." The chairperson then will say, "State your point of order." The member then explains the error that was made. Usually, the chair will rule on the matter by stating, "Your point of order is well taken" (then making the necessary changes) or "Your point of order is not well taken" (with no changes being made).

- *An appeal from the decision of the chair.* Whenever the chairperson makes a decision that a member believes is wrong (including a decision on a point of order), the member may rise and say, "I appeal from the decision of the chair." If this motion is seconded, the member has a right to explain his or her position, the chair may defend himself or herself, and other members may speak on the matter. A vote is then taken, and the decision of the majority is followed no matter what the chairperson may think. A tie vote serves to uphold the chairperson's decision since it is assumed the chairperson would vote for himself or herself.

- *A motion to suspend the rules.* This is done so that some procedure or motion normally out of order can be used or discussed. Rules may be suspended only for a specific purpose and for the limited time necessary to accomplish the proposed action. Many rules cannot be suspended, such as basic rules governing a quorum, voting requirements, or voting methods. For the most part, only procedural rules are suspended. The motion to suspend the rules requires a two-thirds majority for adoption.

- *A motion to object to the consideration of some matter.* This allows the group to avoid the discussion of an issue because it is viewed as embarrassing, unnecessarily contentious, frivolous, or inopportune. This motion also requires a two-thirds majority for adoption. The only time the motion to object is in order is immediately after the objectionable motion has been stated by the presiding officer. If discussion of the motion has begun, it is too late to object to its consideration.

- *A parliamentary inquiry.* This motion's purpose is simply to seek advice from the chairperson. This advice usually focuses on issues such as the appropriate parliamentary procedure to follow in making a particular motion. Whenever a group member is uncertain about how to refer some matter to a committee, how to word a motion properly, or how to nominate a candidate for office, he or she might conduct a parliamentary inquiry. Like other special motions designed to maintain the rules, the parliamentary inquiry may interrupt a speaker, although the chairperson may choose to hold her or his reply until the person who has the floor has concluded.

PRIVILEGED MOTIONS

The final group of motions, *privileged motions*, are of such importance that they can be made at almost any time. They include:

- *The motion to adjourn.* This motion is for closing the meeting or sometimes, strategically, for terminating the discussion of a particular question. This motion may not interrupt a speaker, but it is in order at any time. As we pointed out earlier, it is neither amendable nor debatable, and it must be put to an immediate vote.

- *The motion to recess the group.* Unlike the motion to adjourn, the motion to recess the group is intended to temporarily disband the meeting. Recesses are occasionally needed to obtain additional information, to discuss voting procedures, to rest, or to count votes. The motion to recess may interrupt any business other than the process of voting. It may not interrupt a speaker.

- *The question of privilege.* This motion requires that the presiding officer deal with some situation affecting the welfare of the organization's members, such as fire, offensive remarks, or poor acoustics. The question of privilege is unusual in that it needs no second, and it can interrupt both business and speaker. The presiding officer may decide the matter or may submit it to a vote of the group.

This list is not intended to be exhaustive; rather, it highlights major motions that are often used in formal business meetings in diverse organizational and community settings.

Maintaining Precedence

As we said earlier, the chairperson must know not only the types of motions, but their *precedence*—that is, what motions may displace other motions. One motion may replace another already before the house if the new motion has sufficient power or precedence to do so. It is important that you know which motions have which levels of precedence. If one motion is under consideration and another is made, you must decide whether the new motion is appropriate for consideration or whether consideration of the new motion should be denied until discussion of the original motion is completed.

To help you keep track of precedence, the chart in table 1 lists types of motions in order of precedence. It also indicates whether each motion requires a second from another group member, whether discussion of the motion is allowed, whether the motion can be amended, and what level of voting support (simple majority or two-thirds) is needed.

Table 1   Order of Precedence of Motions

Types of Motions[a]	Requires Second?	May Be Discussed?	May Be Amended?	Vote Needed
Privileged:				
To fix the time of the next meeting	Yes	No	Yes	Majority
To adjourn	Yes	No	No	Majority
To recess	Yes	No	Yes	Majority
Question of privilege	No	No	No	Chair[e]
Incidental:				
An appeal from the decision of the chair	Yes	Yes[b]	No	Majority
A point of order	No	No	No	Chair[e]
To suspend the rules	Yes	No	No	Two-thirds
To object to consideration	No	No	No	Two-thirds
Parliamentary inquiry	No	No	No	Chair[d]

Table 1   Order of Precedence of Motions *(continued)*

Types of Motions[a]	Requires Second?	May Be Discussed?	May Be Amended?	Vote Needed
Subsidiary:				
To lay on the table	Yes	No	No	Majority
To put an end to discussion (to move the previous question)	Yes	No	No	Two-thirds
To limit debate	Yes	No	Yes	Two-thirds
To postpone to a certain time	Yes	Yes	Yes	Majority
To refer to a committee	Yes	Yes	Yes	Majority
To amend a motion	Yes	Yes[b]	Yes	Majority
To postpone indefinitely	Yes	Yes	No	Majority
Main:				
An ordinary main motion	Yes	Yes	Yes	Majority
To take a matter off the table	Yes	No	No	Majority
To reconsider action previously taken	Yes[c]	Yes[b]	No	Majority
To repeal or rescind action previously taken	Yes[c]	Yes	Yes	Majority[d]

[a] Listed in order of precedence from highest to lowest, a second motion cannot be considered unless it has higher precedence than the motion already before the group.

[b] May be discussed, unless it applies to an undebatable question.

[c] Opens the main motion to discussion as well.

[d] If prior notice is given that such a motion is forthcoming, a majority is needed; if no such notice is given, a two-thirds vote is needed.

[e] Requires only chairperson's decision; a majority vote is needed if appealed from chair.

SUMMARY

Even though most opportunities to lead groups occur in the context of smaller committee meetings, on certain occasions you may be elected to a leadership position that requires you to conduct business meetings involving much larger groups of people. These sorts of meetings necessitate the use of parliamentary procedure. Although the rules of parliamentary procedure may seem complicated at first, most can be learned with relative ease as you use them over time. The rules of parliamentary procedure are all based on important underlying principles, such as the right of all members to have their views aired. That's why, for instance, limiting or restricting discussion requires the support of two-thirds of the organization's members. Other important motions grow from such principles as turn taking, the right of the majority to prevail, and the right of the minority to be protected. Most chairpersons have the support of a parliamentarian so that parliamentary questions can be resolved as expediently and judiciously as possible. Even so, the more you know about parliamentary procedure, the more smoothly and successfully you will be able to chair each meeting.

Our purpose here is simply to acquaint you with basic decisions you will have to make when conducting large group meetings under these rules. For a more detailed and complete understanding of parliamentary procedure, you should consult one of the many excellent books devoted to that topic.[1]

Notes

CHAPTER 1

[1] James Toedtman, "Enron's Kenneth Lay Defiant," *The Oregonian*, July 9, 2004, sec. B, 1.

[2] Bruce Japsen, "TAP Workers' Trial Nears End," *Chicago Tribune*, July 5, 2004, sec. 4, 1.

[3] Erin McClam, "Jury Convicts Cable Company Founder, Son," *The Oregonian*, July 9, 2004, sec. B, 2.

[4] James Miller, "Sales Scandals Rattle Newspaper Business," *Chicago Tribune*, June 20, 2004, sec. 5, 1

[5] Mark Harrington, "Ex-Symbol CEO Waiting out Charges in Sweden," *Chicago Tribune*, July 4, 2004, sec. 5, 2.

[6] Aviva Brandt, "Archdiocese Files for Bankruptcy Protection," *The Register-Guard*, July 7, 2004, 1, 6.

[7] Jennifer Schramm, "A Return to Ethics?" *HR Magazine*, July 2003, 144.

[8] "Americans Still Furious about Corporate Scandals," *USA Today*, January 13, 2004, sec. A, 15.

[9] Schramm.

[10] Robert D. Putnam, *Bowling Alone: The Collapse and Revival of American Community* (New York: Simon & Schuster, 2000).

[11] Ibid., 414.

[12] LaRue Tone Hosmer, *The Ethics of Management* (Homewood, IL: Richard D. Irwin, 1987), 106.

[13] Lawrence J. Flynn, "The Aristotelian Basis for the Ethics of Speaking," *Speech Teacher* 6 (1957): 179–87.

[14] Christine Dugas, "Putnam Targets Its Cutthroat Culture." *USA Today*, April 15, 2004, sec. B, 1–2.

[15] See Richard L. Johannesen, "The Emerging Concept of Communication as Dialogue," *Quarterly Journal of Speech* 57 (1971): 373–82; John Stewart, "Foundations of Dialogic Communication," *Quarterly Journal of Speech* 64 (1978): 183–201; Richard L. Johannesen, *Ethics in Human Communication*, 5th ed. (Prospect Heights, IL: Waveland Press, 2002; and Linda Ellinor and Glenna Gerard, *Dialogue: Rediscover the Transforming Power of Conversation* (New York: John Wiley & Sons, 1998).

[16] Vance Packard, *The Hidden Persuaders* (New York: McKay, 1957).

[17] John K. Galbraith, *The New Industrial State* (Boston: Houghton Mifflin, 1967).

[18] Judith Crown, "BP Might Soften Amoco's Emissions Stance," *Crain's Chicago Business*, November 16, 1998, 9.

[19] John Heileman, "Gearing Ourselves for Globalization," *Business 2.0*, January/February 2004, 34–35.

[20] Jagdish Bhagwati, *In Defense of Globalization* (New York: Oxford University Press, 2004).

[21] Lisa Takeuchi Cullen Wilson, "Wal-Mart's Gender Gap," *Time*, July 5, 2004, 44.

[22] Corrie L. Fishel, "Civil Rights Agencies Urge Employers to Guard Against Discrimination," *Mosaics*, January 2002, 2.

[23] *Federal Register* 45, no. 219 (November 10, 1980).

[24] Brenda Paik Sunoo, "After Everything Else—Buy Insurance," *Workforce* 77 (October 1998): 45–50.

[25] Jane Spencer, "Shirk Ethic: How to Fake a Hard Day at the Office." *Wall Street Journal*, May 15, 2003, sec. D, 1.

[26] Ibid.

[27] Nancy Flynn, *The ePolicy Handbook* (AMACOM, 2001).

[28] Eilene Zimmerman, "When Employee Surveillance Crosses the Line," *Workforce* (February 2002): 38–45

[29] Ibid.

[30] Ibid.

[31] "Whistle-blower Says He Made 'Moral Call,'" *Chicago Tribune*, August 7, 2004, sec. 1, 4.

[32] Gary M. Wederspahn, "Exporting Corporate Ethics," *Global Workforce* 2, no. 1 (January 1997): 29.

[33] Alan Kors and Harvey Silvergate, *The Shadow University: The Betrayal of Liberty on America's Campuses* (Free Press, 1998).

[34] "Political Correctness and the Cowing of Academia," *USA Today*, November 12, 1998.

[35] Charles M. Madigan, "Free Speech: Do Americans Really Believe in It?" *Chicago Tribune*, July 4, 2004, sec. 2, 1–4.

[36] Christopher K. Bart, "Sex, Lies and Mission Statements," *Business Horizons* 40, no. 6 (November-December, 1997).

[37] Clinton McLemore, *Street-Smart Ethics* (Westminster: John Knox Press, 2003).

[38] Ibid.

[39] Samuel Greengard, "50% of Your Employees Are Lying, Cheating & Stealing," *Workforce* (October 1997): 44–53.

[40] McLemore.

[41] Ibid.

[42] Harry Wessel, "Keeping in Step with the Boss," *Chicago Tribune*, June 18, 2003, sec. 6, 1–4.

[43] Ibid.

[44] Tim Talevich, "Carly Unplugged," *The Costco Connection* (June 2004): 18–19.

CHAPTER 2

[1] Amitai Etzioni, *Modern Organizations* (Englewood Cliffs, NJ: Prentice-Hall, 1964).

[2] Bill Coplin, "For New Graduates, 'Soft Skills' are the Secret Weapon in Job Hunt," *USA Today*, June 10, 2004, sec. A, 15.

[3] Vincent J. Schodolski, "Med Students Now Must Learn People Skills Too," *Chicago Tribune*, July 18, 2004, sec. 1, 9.

[4] "As You Climb the Ladder, Style Counts," *Management Review* 76 (May 1987): 9.

[5] W. O. Underwood. "A Hospital Director's Administrative Profile," *Hospital Administration* 9 (1963): 37–39.

[6] "Hot Jobs for the 21st Century" [online]. Available: http://www.dol.gov/wb/factsheets/hotjobs03.htm (accessed November 29, 2004).

[7] Everett Rogers and Rehka Agarwala-Rogers, *Communication in Organizations* (New York: Free Press, 1976), 6.

[8] Peter Drucker, *The Practice of Management* (New York: Harper & Row, 1959), 92.

[9] Herbert A. Simon, *Administrative Behavior*, 2d ed. (New York: Macmillan, 1958), xvi.

[10] Linda L. Putnam, "The Interpretive Perspective," in *Communication and Organization: An Interpretive Approach*, ed. L. L. Putnam and M. E. Pacanowsky (Beverly Hills: Sage, 1983), 45.

[11] Alex Bavelas and Dermot Barrett, "An Experimental Approach to Organizational Communication," *Personnel* 27 (1951): 368.

[12] Thomas J. Peters and Robert H. Waterman, Jr., *In Search of Excellence* (New York: Harper & Row, 1982), 124.

[13] Raymond G. Smith, *Speech Communication: Theory and Models* (New York: Harper & Row, 1970), 14.

[14] See Charles Conrad and Marshall Scott Poole, *Strategic Organizational Communication in a Global Economy*, 6th ed. (Belmont, CA: Thomson Wadsworth, 2005), 2–14.

[15] Thomas W. Hourihan, "Help Employees to Understand Their Benefits," *Personnel Administrator* 28 (April 1983): 92–98.

[16] Diana Knude, "A Narrow Net," *San Francisco Examiner*, August 19, 1999, J-1.

[17] Betty Sosnin, "Digital Newsletters 'E-volutionize' Employee Communications," *HR Magazine* (May 2001): 99–107

[18] "What Employees Want to Know," *Communication Briefings* (December 1993): 3.

[19] "How to Keep Good Workers," *Communication Briefings* (July 1993): 5.

[20] Bob Nelson, *1001 Ways to Reward Employees* (New York: Workman, 1994); and Bob Nelson, *1001 Ways to Energize Employees* (New York: Workman, 1997).

[21] David J. Dee, "So What's the Small Idea," *The Costco Connection*, June 2004, 17

[22] William H. Read, "Upward Communication in Industrial Hierarchies," *Human Relations* 15 (1962): 3–15; and Patricia Hayes Andrews and Richard T. Herschel, *Organizational Communication: Empowerment in a Technological Society* (Boston: Houghton Mifflin, 1996), 108–13.

[23] Alan G. Robinson and Dean M. Schroeder, *Ideas Are Free: How the Idea Revolution is Liberating People and Transforming Organizations* (San Francisco: Berrett-Koehler, 2004), 24.

[24] Frank Corrado, *Getting the Word Out* (Homewood, IL: Business One Irwin, 1993).

[25] Terrence E. Deal and Allen A. Kennedy, *Corporate Cultures* (Reading, MA: Addison-Wesley, 1982).

[26] Thomas J. Peters and Robert H. Waterman, Jr., *In Search of Excellence* (New York: Harper & Row, 1982), 121–22.

[27] Gordon Allport and Leo Postman, *The Psychology of Rumor* (New York: Henry Holt, 1947).

[28] Keith Davis, "The Care and Cultivation of the Corporate Grapevine," in *Readings in Interpersonal and Organizational Communication*, 3d ed., ed. R. C. Huseman et al. (Boston: Holbrook Press, 1973), 131–36.

[29] Lev Grossman, "Meet Joe Blog," *Time*, June 21, 2004, 67–70.

[30] John Naisbitt, *Megatrends: Ten New Directions Transforming Our Lives* (New York: Warner Books, 1982).

[31] Samuel Greengard, "Increase the Value of Your Intranet," *Workforce* 76 (March 1997): 88.

[32] Jim Barksdale, "The Next Step: Extranets," *Columns: The Main Thing* [online]. Available: http://wpnetscape.com/comprod/columns/mainthing/extranets.html (accessed November 29, 2004).

[33] Sherwood Ross, "Job Interviews on Video: The Electronic Handshake," *Chicago Tribune*, May 24, 1998, sec. 6, 21.

[34] "Help Your Online Resume Stand out," *Chicago Tribune*, May 30, 2004, sec. 6, 1.

[35] Patrick Kiger, "Lessons from a Crisis: How Communication Kept a Company Together," *Workforce*, November 2001, 28–34.

[36] Samuel Greengard, "Storing, Shaping and Sharing Collective Wisdom," *Workforce* 77 (October 1998): 82–88.

[37] Ibid.

[38] "Your Job," *Chicago Tribune*, March 19, 1998, sec. 6, 5.

[39] Joanne Cleaver, "Can You Hear Me Now?" *Chicago Tribune*, May 28, 2003, sec. 6, 1–2.

[40] Chris Serb, "You Never Call: Health Plans Overlook an Easy Step to Keeping Seniors Satisfied," *Hospitals and Health Networks* 72 (October 22, 1998): 32–33.

CHAPTER 3

[1] Terrence E. Deal and Allen A. Kennedy, *Corporate Cultures* (Reading, MA: Addison-Wesley, 1982); and Deal and Kennedy, *The New Corporate Cultures* (Reading, MA: Perseus Books, 1999). For another insightful perspective on organizational culture, see Ann T. Jordan, *Business Anthropology* (Prospect Heights, IL: Waveland Press, 2003).

[2] Richard Stone, *The Healing Art of Storytelling* (New York: Hyperion Press, 1996), 4.

[3] Lee G. Bolman and Terrence E. Deal, *Reframing Organizations: Artistry, Choice and Leadership* (San Francisco: Jossey Bass, 1997).

[4] Frederick Taylor, *Scientific Management* (New York: Harper & Row, 1911).

[5] Douglas McGregor, *Professional Manager* (New York: McGraw-Hill, 1967).

[6] Rensis Likert, *New Patterns of Management* (New York: McGraw-Hill, 1961); and Rensis Likert, *The Human Organization* (New York: McGraw-Hill, 1967).

[7] David Greising, "Memo to Times: Leadership Style Can Be Blinding." *Chicago Tribune*, May 18, 2003, sec. 5, 1.

[8] Robert Blake and Jane Mouton. *The Managerial Grid* (Houston: Gulf, 1964).

[9] Paul Hersey, Kenneth H. Blanchard, and R. K. Hambleton, *Contracting for Leadership Style: A Process and Instrumentation for Building Effective Work Relationships* (Columbus: Ohio State University Center for Leadership Studies, 1977); Paul Hersey and Kenneth H. Blanchard, "Life Cycle Theory of Leadership," *Training and Development Journal* 23 (1969): 26–34; and Paul Hersey and Kenneth H. Blanchard, *Management of Organizational Behavior: Utilizing Human Resources*, 3d ed. (Englewood Cliffs, NJ: Prentice-Hall, 1977).

[10] Richard Tanner Johnson and William G. Ouchi, "Made in America (Under Japanese Management)," *Harvard Business Review* 52 (September–October 1974): 61–69; and William G. Ouchi, *Theory Z: How American Business Can Meet the Japanese Challenge* (New York: Addison-Wesley, 1981), 76.

[11] See, for example: Charles Heckscher, *White Collar Blues* (New York: Basic Books, 1995); and Jennifer Laabs, "The New Loyalty," *Workforce* 77 (November 1998): 35–39.

[12] Edward E. Lawler, *High-Involvement Management: Participative Strategies for Improving Organizational Performance* (San Francisco: Jossey-Bass, 1986), 3.

[13] David L. Bradford and Allan R. Cohen, *Power Up: Transforming Organizations through Shared Leadership* (New York: John Wiley and Sons, 1998).

[14] Janet Kidd Stewart, "Teams Don't Always Work," *Chicago Tribune*, July 5, 1998, sec. 13, 7

[15] "Jeans Therapy: Levi's Factory Workers Are Assigned to Teams, and Morale Takes A Hit," *Wall Street Journal*, May 20, 1998, 1

[16] Brian Dumaine, "Who Needs a Boss?" *Fortune* 7 (May 1990): 52–60.

[17] Marcus Buckingham and Curt Coffman, *First, Break All The Rules* (New York: Simon and Schuster, 1999).

[18] Stephen R. Covey, *The 7 Habits of Highly Effective People* (New York: Simon and Schuster, 1989).

[19] Stephen R. Covey, *Principle-Centered Leadership* (New York: Summit Books, 1990).

[20] Ken Blanchard and Michael O'Connor, *Managing By Values* (San Francisco: Berrett-Koehler, 1997).

[21] George Labovitz and Victor Rosansky, *The Power of Alignment* (New York: John Wiley and Sons, 1997).

[22] See, for example, James O'Toole, *Leading Change: The Argument for Values-Based Leadership* (New York: Ballentine Books, 1995); Joseph V. Quigley, *Vision: How Leaders Develop It, Share It, & Sustain It* (New York: McGraw-Hill, 1993); and Eric Harvey and Alexander Lucia, *Walking the Talk Together* (Dallas: Performance, 1998).

[23] Robert S. Kaplan and David P. Norton, *The Balanced Scorecard* (Boston: Harvard Business School Press, 1996).

[24] Thomas J. McCoy, *Creating an "Open Book" Organization* (New York: American Management Association, 1996).

[25] John Case, *Open-Book Management* (New York: HarperCollins, 1995).

[26] Karl Albrecht and Ron Zemke, *Service America!* (Homewood, IL: Dow Jones-Irwin, 1985).

[27] Karl Albrecht, *At America's Service* (Homewood, IL: Dow Jones-Irwin, 1988).

[28] Richard C. Whiteley, *The Customer Driven Company* (Reading, MA: Addison-Wesley, 1991); and Richard C. Whiteley and Diane Hessan, *Customer Centered Growth* (Reading, MA: Addison-Wesley, 1996).

[29] Fred Wiersema, *Customer Intimacy* (Santa Monica, CA: Knowledge Exchange, 1996).

[30] Robin L. Lawton, *Creating a Customer-Centered Culture* (Milwaukee, WI: ASQC Press, 1993).

[31] Peter M. Senge, *The Fifth Discipline* (New York: Doubleday, 1990).

[32] Gifford and Elizabeth Pinchot, *The End of Bureaucracy & the Rise of the Intelligent Organization* (San Francisco: Berrett-Koehler, 1993).

[33] Ben Nagler, "Recasting Employees Into Teams," *Workforce* 77 (January 1998): 101–06.

[34] Al Neuharth, *Confessions of an S.O.B.* (New York: Doubleday, 1989).

[35] Allan Sloan, "The Hit Men," *Newsweek*, February 26, 1996, 44–48.

[36] Ibid.

[37] Gary Strauss, Tom Lowry, and David Henry, "Sagging Profits Sink Iron-fisted Chairman," *USA Today*, June 16, 1998, 1

[38] "Villains? Heck No. We're Like Doctors." *Newsweek*, February 26, 1996, 49.

[39] Del Jones, "Explosive CEOs Passé, but Are Nice Ones Here to Stay," *USA Today*, May 22, 2000, sec. B, 6.

[40] William George, *Authentic Leadership* (San Francisco: Jossey-Bass, 2003).

[41] Christine Dugas, "Putnam Targets Its Cutthroat Culture." *USA Today*, April 15, 2004, sec. B, 1–2.

[42] Thomas J. Peters and Robert H. Waterman, Jr., *In Search of Excellence* (New York: Harper & Row, 1982).

[43] Steve Powers, "Leadership Lessons for 2004," *Business 2.0*, January/February 2004, 32.

[44] Alan Farnham, "In Search of Suckers," *Fortune* 7 (October 1996): 119–26.

[45] Carol Kleiman, "Workplace Moves to Metrosexual Mode," *Chicago Tribune*, July 27, 2004, sec. 3, 2.

[46] Lois Frankel, *Nice Girls Don't Get the Corner Office* (New York: Warner Business Books, 2004).

[47] Shari Coudron, "Be Cool: Cultivating a Cool Culture Gives HR a Staffing Boost," *Workforce* 77 (April 1998): 50–61.

[48] Ibid., 60.

[49] Robert Tannenbaum, Irving R. Weschler, and Fred Massarik, *Leadership and Organization: A Behavioral Science Approach* (New York: McGraw-Hill, 1961), 11

50 Anita Thompson, "A Look at Leadership," *The Costco Connection* (March 2004): 16–17.

51 Warren Bennis and Robert J. Thomas, *Geeks and Geezers* (Boston: Harvard Business Press, 2002), 28.

52 Rob Kaiser, "'Been There, Done That' Kind of Advice for Charlie Bell," *Chicago Tribune*, April 12, 2004, sec. 3, 1.

53 Michael Medved, "Good Teamwork Outshines Superstar Systems," *USA Today*, August 8, 2001, 13A.

54 "The Manager's Intelligence Report," by Lawrence Ragan Communications, November 1999.

55 Katherine Yung, "New Corporate Climate: Faster, Better, Cheaper," *Chicago Tribune*, April 6, 2004, sec. 3, 4.

56 Ibid.

57 Laura Stack, "Employees Behaving Badly," *HR Magazine* (October 2003): 111–16.

58 Tom Terez, "When Fear Strikes the Workplace," *Workforce* (August 2001): 24

59 Martin Miller, "Reining in the Rage," *The Arizona Republic*, February 23, 2004, sec. E, 1.

60 Charlene Marmer Solomon, "Managing Virtual Teams," *Workforce* (June 2001): 60–65.

61 Ibid.

62 Susan J. Wells, "Telecommuting to Work," *HR Magazine* (October 2001): 35–45.

63 AFL-CIO, "Executive Pay Watch" [online]. Available: http://www.aflcio.org/corporateamerica/paywatch/ (accessed November 26, 2004).

64 Del Jones, "What Do These 3 Photos have in Common?" *USA Today*, December 10, 2003, sec. B, 1–2

65 Ed Ruggero and Dennis Haley, *The Leader's Compass: Set Your Course for Leadership Success* (New York: Warner Business Books, 2003).

66 Jones, 2.

67 Larry Donnithorne, *The West Point Way of Leadership: From Learning Principled Leadership to Practicing It* (New York: Prometheus Books, 2003).

68 Ibid.

69 Katherine Sopranos, "Who's Afraid of the Big Bad Boss," *Chicago Tribune*, June 21, 1998, sec. 6, 1.

70 Lisa Bertagnoli, "Feeling Burned by a Dragon Boss?" *Chicago Tribune*, December 11, 2002, sec. 6, 1.

71 Benedict Casey, "Fear in the Workplace: The Bullying Boss," *The New York Times*, June 22, 2004, D1–4.

72 David L. Weiner, *Power Freaks: Dealing with Them in the Workplace or Anyplace* (New York: Prometheus Books, 2002).

73 Patrick Dorin, *The Dragon Complex: Strategies for Identifying and Conquering Workplace Abuse* (Boston: Cypress, 2002).

74 Ibid., D4.

75 Kim Girard, "The Fine Art of Sucking Up," *Business 2.0* (April 2003): 112.

CHAPTER 4

1 William P. Sullivan, "Have You Got What It Takes to Get to the Top?" *Management Review* 72 (April 1983): 7–11.

2 Jonathan Alter, "The Art of the Closing Argument," *Newsweek*, July 19, 2004, 27.

3 Blake Morrison, "What You Won't Hear the Pilot Say," *USA Today*, September 27, 2000, sec. A, 1–2.

4 William Johnson, *People in Quandaries* (New York: Harper & Row, 1946); and Alfred Korzybski, *Science and Sanity* (Lancaster, PA: Science Press, 1951).

5 D. Bourland, "The Semantics of Non-Aristotelian Language," *General Semantics Bulletin* 35 (1968): 60–63.

6 Gary Blake and Robert Bly, *The Elements of Business Writing* (New York: Longman, 1991).

7 Nathan Bierma, "Plain English Campaign Keeps It Simple for 25 Years," *Chicago Tribune*, July 22, 2004, B2.

8 Eileen Ambrose, "Biz-speak," *Chicago Tribune*, July 4, 2004, sec. 3, 5.

9 For example, see Theodore Bernstein, *The Careful Writer* (New York: The Free Press, 1965); *The Chicago Manual of Style*, 15th ed. (Chicago: University of Chicago Press, 2003); William Strunk, Jr. and E. B. White, *The Elements of Style*, 4th ed. (New York: Allyn & Bacon, 1999); Richard Alanham, *Revising Prose* (New York: Allyn & Bacon, 1999); Joseph M. Williams, *Style: Toward Clarity and Grace* (Chicago: University of Chicago Press, 1995); Mark Turner, *The Literary Mind* (London: Oxford University Press, 1998); and Terri Brooks, *Wordsworth* (Prospect Heights, IL: Waveland Press, 2000).

10 Adapted from: John Clayton, "The Ten Principles of Good Business Writing," *Harvard Management Communication Letter* 3, no. 9 (September 2000): 8–9.

11 Strunk and White, 55.

[12] Nancy L. Breuer, "The Power of Storytelling," *Workforce* (December 1998): 36–41.

[13] "Avoid These Common Mistakes When Using E-Mail to Manage People," *Motivational Manager* (July 1998): 2.

[14] Nancy Flynn, *The ePolicy Handbook* (New York: AMACOM, 2001).

[15] J. Gibb, "Defensive Communication," *Journal of Communication* 11 (1961): 141–48; and Sharon Ellison, *Don't Be So Defensive* (Kansas City: Andrews McMeel, 1998).

[16] Erving Goffman, *Encounters* (Indianapolis: Bobbs-Merrill, 1961).

[17] S. Palmer, *Understanding Other People* (New York: Crowell, 1955).

[18] A. Fleishman, "How to Sabotage a Meeting," *ETC.* 24 (1967): 341–44.

[19] Robin Dunbar, *Grooming, Gossip and the Evolution of Language* (Boston: Harvard University Press, 1996), 14.

[20] Robert L. Genua, *Managing Your Mouth* (New York: AMACOM, 1992).

[21] Samuel Greengard, "Gossip Poisons Business." *Workforce* (July 2001): 24–28

[22] Annette Simmons, *A Safe Place for Dangerous Truths: Using Dialogue to Overcome Fear and Distrust at Work* (New York: ANACOM, 1999), 74.

[23] Noa Davenport, Ruth Distler Schwartz, and Gail Pursell Elliott, *Mobbing: Emotional Abuse in the American Workplace* (Ames, IA: Civil Society, 2002), 132.

[24] Genua, 146.

[25] Anna Quindlen, "A Foul Mouth and Manhood," *Newsweek*, July 12, 2004: 24–29.

[26] Gibb.

[27] Wendy Leebov, *Practical Assertiveness for Health Care Professionals* (Chicago: American Hospital Association, 1991).

[28] Stephanie Armour, "Cash or Critiques: Which Is Best?" *USA Today*, December 16, 1998, sec. B, 4.

[29] Dale Dauten, "Recognition Is Caffeine for Employee's Soul," *Arizona Republic*, March 5, 2002, sec. 3, 2.

[30] David Cottrell and Eric Harvey, *The Manager's Communication Handbook* (Dallas: The Walk the Talk Company, 2003), 28–29.

[31] Gary Topchik, *Managing Workplace Negativity* (New York: AMACOM, 2001).

[32] Muriel Solomon, *What Do I Say When . . . ?* (Englewood Cliffs, NJ: Prentice-Hall, 1988).

[33] Jonathan Turley, "The Lost Art of the Apology," *Chicago Tribune*, July 18, 2004, sec. 2, 9.

CHAPTER 5

[1] Suzette Haden Elgin, *The Gentle Art of Verbal Self-Defense at Work* (Paramus, NJ: Prentice Hall Press, 2000), 44.

[2] Daniel Goleman, *Emotional Intelligence* (New York: Bantam Books, 1995).

[3] Michael Maas, "In Offices of the Future . . . The Productivity Value of Environment," *Management Review* 72 (March 1983): 16–20.

[4] Brenda Paik Sunoo, "Redesign for a Better Work Environment," *Workforce* (February 2000): 39–46.

[5] Fred I. Steele, *Physical Settings and Organizational Development* (Reading, MA: Addison-Wesley, 1973).

[6] Sunoo, 44.

[7] Judith Nemes, "Turning down the Noise Levels," *Crain's Chicago Business*, March 29, 1999, SR5.

[8] Michael B. McCaskey, "The Hidden Messages Managers Send," in *Harvard Business Review on Effective Communication* (Boston: Harvard Business School, 1999), 119–44.

[9] Sunoo, 44.

[10] Thomas J. Allen, "Communication Networks in R&D Laboratories," *R&D Management* 1 (1970): 14.

[11] Sunoo, 42.

[12] Simon Brown, *Practical Feng Shui* (London: Ward Lock, 1997).

[13] Edward T. Hall, *The Silent Language* (Garden City, NJ: Doubleday, 1959).

[14] D. W. Stacks and J. K. Burgoon, "The Persuasive Effects of Violating Spatial Distance Expectations in Small Groups" (paper presented at the Southern Speech Communication Association, Biloxi, MS, 1979).

[15] Judee K. Burgoon, "Spatial Relationships in Small Groups," in *Small Group Communication: Theory and Practice*, 8th ed., ed. R. Y. Hirokawa and others (Los Angeles: Roxbury, 2003), 89–90.

[16] Albert Mehrabian, "Inference of Attitude from the Posture, Orientation, and Distance of a Communicator," *Journal of Consulting and Clinical Psychology* 32 (1968): 308.

[17] M. Lefkowitz, Robert Blake, and Jane Mouton, "Status Factors in Pedestrian Violation of Traffic Signals," *Journal of Abnormal and Social Psychology* 51 (1955): 704–06.

[18] John T. Malloy, *Dress for Success* (New York: Warner Books, 1978).

[19] Wendy Bounds, Rebecca Quick, and Emily Nelson, "Every Day Is Casual at Work," *San Francisco Chronicle*, August 29, 1999, sec. C, 1.

[20] Ibid.

[21] Sue Fox, with Perrin Cunningham, *Business Etiquette for Dummies* (New York: Hungry Minds, Inc., 2001), 50.

[22] Peter Andersen, "Nonverbal Communication in the Small Group," in *Small Group Communication: A Reader*, 5th ed., ed. R. Cathcart and L. Samovar (Dubuque, IA: Wm. C. Brown, 1988), 334–35.

[23] Mehrabian.

[24] James W. Neuliep, *Intercultural Communication: A Contextual Approach* (Boston: Houghton Mifflin, 2000), 236–41.

[25] Nathan Bierma, "Hand Gestures May Expand, Express Unspoken Thoughts," *Chicago Tribune*, August 5, 2004, sec. 5, 2.

[26] Susan Goldin-Meadow, *Hearing Gestures: How Our Hands Help Us Think* (Cambridge, MA: Harvard University Press, 2003).

[27] Susan Goldin-Meadow and David McNeill, *Hand and Mind: What Gestures Reveal About Thought* (Chicago, IL: University of Chicago Press, 2000), 97.

[28] Albert Mehrabian and M. Williams, "Nonverbal Concomitants of Perceived and Intended Persuasiveness," *Journal of Personality and Social Psychology* 13 (1969): 37–58.

[29] Andersen, 337.

[30] Ibid.

[31] Paul Ekman, *Emotions Revealed: Recognizing Faces and Feelings to Improve Communications and Emotional Life* (New York: Henry Holt, 2004), 84–112.

[32] Kimberlee Roth, "One Look Says It All: How Expressions Speak Volumes," *Chicago Tribune*, May 23, 2004, sec. 13, 1–2.

[33] Goleman, *Emotional Intelligence*; and Daniel Goleman, *Working with Emotional Intelligence* (New York: Bantam, 1998).

[34] Howard M. Rosenfeld, "Instrumental Affiliative Functions of Facial and Gestural Expressions," *Journal of Personality and Social Psychology* 4 (1966): 65–72; and Mehrabian and Williams.

[35] See, for example: "What Your Face Reveals and Conceals," *Harvard Management Communication Letter* 3, no. 6 (June 2000): 8–9; Daniel McNeill, *The Face* (New York: Little, Brown and Co., 1998); Mark L. Knapp and Judith A. Hall, *Nonverbal Communication in Human Interaction* (Fort Worth, TX: Harcourt Brace, 1996); and Paul Ekman and Erika Rosenberg, *What the Face Reveals* (New York: Oxford University Press, 1998).

[36] Elgin, 127.

[37] Ashley Montagu, *Touching: The Human Significance of the Skin* (New York: Columbia University Press, 1971).

[38] J. T. Auer, *The Joy of Selling* (Toronto: Stoddard, 1992), 45–51.

[39] Kenneth Blanchard and Spencer Johnson, *The One Minute Manager* (New York: Morrow, 1982).

[40] Nancy Henley, *Body Politics: Power, Sex, and Nonverbal Communication* (Englewood Cliffs, NJ: Prentice-Hall, 1977).

[41] See Daniel Canary and Tara Emmers-Sommer, *Sex and Gender Differences in Personal Relationships* (New York: Guilford Press, 1997); and Diana Ivy and Phil Backland, *Exploring Genderspeak: Personal Effectiveness in Gender Communication* (New York: McGraw-Hill, 1999).

[42] William Gudykunst, *Cross-Cultural and Intercultural Communication* (Thousand Oaks, CA: Sage, 2003).

[43] M. H. L. Hecker, "Speaker Recognition: An Interpretive Survey of the Literature," *ASHA Monographs*, no. 16 (Washington, DC: American Speech and Hearing Association, 1971).

[44] Howard Giles and Richard Y. Bourhis, "Voice and Racial Categorization in Britain," *Communication Monographs* 43 (1976): 108–14; Norman J. Lass and others, "Speaker Sex Identification from Voiced, Whispered and Filtered Isolated Vowels," *Journal of the Acoustical Society of America* 59 (1976): 675–78; Joel R. Davitz, *The Communication of Emotional Meaning* (New York: McGraw-Hill, 1964); and Mark Snyder, "Self-Monitoring of Expressive Behavior," *Journal of Personality and Social Psychology* 30 (1974): 526–37.

[45] Andersen, 340.

[46] Richard E. Porter and Larry A. Samovar, "Communication in the Multicultural Group," in *Small Group Communication: Theory and Practice*, 8th ed., ed. R. Y. Hirokawa and others (Los Angeles: Roxbury, 2003), 230–38.

[47] Jonathan Alter, "In the Time of Tolerance," *Newsweek*, March 30, 1998, 44.

[48] "A Powerful Tool: Your Voice," *Costco Connection* (June 2004): 9.

[49] Judy Artunian, "Phone Etiquette Pays in Business," *Chicago Tribune*, May 5, 2003, sec. 6, 3.

[50] See Neuliep, 122–27.

CHAPTER 6

[1] John Naisbitt, *Megatrends: Ten New Directions Transforming Our Lives* (New York: Warner Books, 1982), 45.

[2] Jeffrey S. Nielsen, *The Myth of Leadership* (Palo Alto, CA: Davies-Black, 2004), 6.

[3] Jonathan Alter, "The Layered Lives We Lead," *Newsweek*, August 23, 2004, 29.

[4] William Haney, *Communication and Organizational Behavior* (Burr Ridge, IL: Richard D. Irwin, 1967), 56.

[5] From David C. Thomas and Kerr Inkson, *Cultural Intelligence* (San Francisco: Berrett-Koehler, 2004), 109.

[6] See, for example: Timothy Leary, *Interpersonal Diagnosis of Personality* (New York: Ronald, 1957); William C. Schutz, *FIRO: A Three-Dimensional Theory of Interpersonal Behavior* (New York: Holt, Rinehart & Winston, 1958); William C. Schutz, *The Interpersonal Underworld* (Palo Alto, CA: Science and Behavior Books, 1966); and Robert F. Bales, *Personality and Interpersonal Behavior* (New York: Holt, Rinehart & Winston, 1971).

[7] Ronald B. Adler and Neil Towne, *Looking Out/Looking In*, 10th ed. (Belmont, CA: Wadsworth, 2002).

[8] Ellen Berscheid and Elaine H. Walster, *Interpersonal Attraction*, 2nd ed. (Reading, MA: Addison-Wesley, 1978). Also see Judy C. Pearson and others, *Human Communication* (Boston: McGraw-Hill, 2003).

[9] John Daly, "Homophily-Heterophily and the Prediction of Supervisor Satisfaction" (paper presented at the annual meeting of the International Communication Association, Portland, Oregon, April 1976).

[10] Thomas M. Rand and Kenneth N. Wexley, "Demonstration of the Effect: 'Similar to Me,' in Simulated Employment Interviews," *Psychological Reports* 36 (1975): 535–44; and Charles J. Stewart and William B. Cash, *Interviewing: Principles and Practices*, 9th ed. (Boston: McGraw-Hill, 2000), 223–56.

[11] David Landy and Elliott Aronson, "Liking for an Evaluator as a Function of His Discernment," *Journal of Personality and Social Psychology* 9 (1968): 133–41.

[12] John R. P. French and Bernard Raven, "The Bases of Social Power," in *Group Dynamics*, ed. D. Cartwright and A. Zander (New York: Harper & Row, 1960), 259–68.

[13] Irwin Altman and Dalmas Taylor, *Social Penetration: The Development of Interpersonal Relationships* (New York: Holt, Rinehart & Winston, 1973); and Charles R. Berger, *Communication and Social Influence Processes* (East Lansing: Michigan State University Press, 1995).

[14] See, for example: Michael L. Hecht, "Satisfying Communication and Relationship Labels: Intimacy and Length of Relationship as Perceptual Frames of Naturalistic Conversation," *Western Journal of Speech Communication* 48 (1984): 201–16; and Mark L. Knapp and A. L. Vangelisti, *Interpersonal Communication and Human Relationships*, 4th ed. (Boston: Allyn & Bacon, 2000).

[15] See, for example: Albert Mehrabian, *Public Places and Private Spaces* (New York: Basic Books, 1976).

[16] W. Barnett Pearce, *Interpersonal Communication: Making Social Worlds* (New York: HarperCollins, 1994), 87–94.

[17] Marsha Houston Stanback and W. Barnett Pearce, "Talking to 'The Man': Some Communication Strategies Used by Members of 'Subordinate' Social Groups," *Quarterly Journal of Speech* 67 (1981): 21–30.

[18] Charles M. Rossiter and W. Barnett Pierce, *Communicating Personally* (New York: Bobbs-Merrill, 1975); and J. Stewart, *Bridges not Walls* (Boston: McGraw Hill, 2002).

[19] Dale Carnegie, *How to Win Friends and Influence People*, rev. ed. (New York: Simon & Schuster, 1981; originally 1936).

[20] Wendy Leebov, *Positive Co-Worker Relationships in Health Care* (Chicago: American Hospital, 1990).

[21] Edward J. Hegarty, *How to Talk Your Way to the Top* (West Nyack, NY: Parker, 1973).

[22] Arlene Yerys, "How to Get What You Want through Influential Communication," *Management Review* 71 (June 1982): 12–18.

[23] Chuck Green, "Just Shy of a Promotion," *Chicago Tribune*, September 24, 2003, sec. 6, 1–4; and Jared Sandberg, "How to Work the Crowd in Your Office Travels, in 25 Words or Less," *Wall Street Journal*, August 13, 2003, sec. B, 1.

[24] Frank Stagnaro, "The Benefits of Leveling with Employees: ROLM's Experience," *Management Review* 71 (July 1982): 16–20.

[25] Rossiter and Pierce.

[26] Samuel Culbert, *Interpersonal Process of Self-Disclosure: It Takes Two to See One* (Washington, DC: NTL Institute for Applied Behavioral Science, 1967).

[27] Joseph Luft, *Group Processes: An Introduction to Group Dynamics* (Palo Alto, CA: National Press Books, 1970).

[28] Rafael Steinberg, *Man and the Organization* (New York: Time-Life Books, 1975).

[29] Rossiter and Pierce.

[30] Stephen R. Covey, *The 7 Habits of Highly Effective People* (New York: Simon & Schuster, 1989).

[31] Suzette Haden Elgin, *The Gentle Art of Verbal Self-Defense at Work* (Paramus, NJ: Prentice Hall Press, 2000).

[32] Ibid., 44.

[33] Madelyn Burley-Allen, "Listen Up," *HR Magazine* (November 2001): 115–20.

[34] Donald T. Campbell, "Systematic Effort on the Part of Human Links in Communication Systems," *Information and Control* (1958): 334–69.

[35] Erving Goffman, *Interaction Ritual* (New York: Doubleday, 1967); and Stephen W. Littlejohn, *Theories of Human Communication*, 7th ed. (Belmont, CA: Wadsworth, 2002).

[36] "'Listening' Errors Prove Costly for Firms," *San Jose Mercury News*, March 14, 1984, 1F.

[37] Andrew D. Wolvin and Carolyn Gwynn Coakley, *Listening*, 2d ed. (Dubuque, IA: Wm. C. Brown, 1985); and J. Brownell, *The Skills of Listening-Centered Communication* (paper presented at the National Communication Association Convention, Miami, FL, 2003).

[38] Natasha Josefowitz, "Getting through to the Unreachable Person," *Management Review* 71 (March 1983): 48–50.

CHAPTER 7

[1] Chester Bernard, *The Functions of the Executive* (Cambridge, MA: Harvard University Press, 1950), 14.

[2] Bernard Berelson and Gary A. Steiner, *Human Behavior: An Inventory of Scientific Findings* (New York: Harcourt Brace Jovanovich, 1964), 588.

[3] Theodore Herbert, *Dimensions of Organizational Behavior* (New York: Macmillan, 1976), 347.

[4] William Evan, "Conflict and Performance in R&D Organizations," *Industrial Management Review* 7 (1965): 35–46.

[5] Rensis Likert, *New Patterns of Management* (New York: McGraw-Hill, 1961).

[6] Lewis M. Killian, "The Significance of Multiple-Group Membership in Disaster," *American Journal of Sociology* 57 (1952): 309–14.

[7] Many books have addressed the need for communities to handle conflicts constructively. See, as examples, Daniel Yankelovich, *Coming to Public Judgment: Making Democracy Work in a Complex World* (Syracuse, NY: Syracuse University Press, 1991); *Civic Index: Measuring Your Community's Civic Health* (Washington, DC: The National Civic League, 2003); and Linda Ellinor and Glenna Gerard, *Dialogue: Rediscover the Transforming Power of Conversation* (New York: John Wiley & Sons, 1998).

[8] See, for example, Christina Baldwin, *Calling the Circle: The First and Future Culture* (New York: Bantam Books, 1998).

[9] Paul Martin DuBois and Jonathan Hutson, *Bridging the Racial Divide: A Report on Interracial Dialogue in America* (Brattleboro, VT: Center for Living Democracy, 1997), 64.

[10] From Kare Anderson, *Getting What You Want: How to Reach Agreement and Resolve Conflict Every Time* (New York: Penguin Books, 1993).

[11] "How to Deal with Conflict," *Communication Briefings* 15, no. 1 (1998): 1.

[12] Robert R. Blake and Jane S. Mouton, *The Managerial Grid* (Houston, TX: Gulf, 1964).

[13] J. Hall and W. H. Watson, "The Effects of a Normative Intervention on Group Decision-Making Performance," *Human Relations* 23 (1970): 299–317.

[14] Gregory B. Northcraft, Margaret A. Neale, and Linda K. Stroh, *Organizational Behavior: A Management Challenge*, 3rd ed. (Mahwah, NJ: Lawrence Erlbaum Associates, 2001).

[15] David A. Whetton and Kim S. Cameron, *Developing Management Skills*, 2d ed. (New York: HarperCollins, 1991).

[16] Joseph E. McGrath, *Groups: Interaction and Performance* (Englewood Cliffs, NJ: Prentice-Hall, 1984); also see Joseph E. McGrath and Andrea B. Hollingshead, *Groups Interacting with Technology* (Thousand Oaks, CA: Sage, 1994) for an excellent review of the research.

[17] Roger Fisher and William Ury, "Getting to Yes," *Management Review* 48 (1982): 16–21.

[18] Ann Douglas, *Industrial Peacemaking* (New York: Columbia University Press, 1962).

[19] Deborah M. Kolb, *The Mediators* (Cambridge, MA: MIT Press, 1995).

[20] Marshall Scott Poole, M. Holmes, and G. DeSanctis, "Conflict Management in a Computer-Supported Meeting Environment," *Management Science* 8 (1991): 926–53; also see Patricia Hayes Andrews and Richard T. Herschel, *Organizational Communication: Empowerment in a Technological Society* (Boston: Houghton Mifflin Company, 1996), 235–68.

[21] J. A. Savage, "Unions Cutting Bargain with High-Technology 'Devil'" *Computerworld* 24, no. 1 (July 23, 1990): 115.

[22] Mark Estes, "Adversaries Find Common Ground," *Workforce* 76, no. 3 (March 1997): 97.

CHAPTER 8

[1] Charles J. Stewart and William B. Cash, *Interviewing: Principles and Practices*, 9th ed. (Boston: McGraw-Hill, 2000), 11.

[2] See Jeanne Tessier Kahn and Jo Switzer Young, *Interviewing Art and Skill* (Boston: Allyn & Bacon, 1995); and Robert W. Eder and Michael M. Harris, eds., *The Employment Interview Handbook* (Thousand Oaks, CA: Sage, 1999).

[3] Stewart and Cash, 240.

[4] See Donald W. Klopf, *Intercultural Encounters* (Englewood, CO: Morton, 1998); and Julia T. Wood, *"But I Thought You Meant . . . Misunderstandings in Human Communication* (Mountain View, CA: Mayfield, 1998).

[5] Robert W. Eder and Michael M. Harris, "Employment Interview Research: Historical Update and Introduction," in *The Employment Interview Handbook*, ed. R. W. Eder and M. M. Harris (Thousand Oaks, CA: Sage, 1999), 1–27.

[6] See Barbara F. Okun, *Effective Helping: Interviewing and Counseling Techniques* (Pacific Grove, CA: Brooks/Cole, 1997).

[7] See James C. Hansen, *Counseling: Theory and Practice.* (Boston: Allyn & Bacon, 1994).

[8] For an excellent discussion of types and uses of questions can be found in Stanley L. Payne, *The Art of Asking Questions* (Princeton, NJ: Princeton University Press, 1980).

[9] Craig D. Tengler and Frederic M. Jablin, "Effects of Question Type, Orientation, and Sequencing in the Employment Screening Interview," *Communication Monographs* 50 (1983): 245–63.

[10] Ibid., 262–63.

[11] James M. Lahiff, "Interviewing for Results," in *Readings in Interpersonal and Organizational Communication*, ed. R. C. Huseman, C. M. Logue, and D. L. Freshley, 3d ed. (Boston: Holbrook Press, 1973), 335.

[12] Douglas McGregor, "An Uneasy Look at Performance Appraisal," *Harvard Business Review* 58 (1957): 66–71.

[13] Randall Brett and Alan J. Fredian, "Performance Appraisal: The System Is Not the Solution," *Personnel Administrator* 26 (1981): 61–68; and James W. Smitter, ed. *Performance Appraisal: State of the Art in Practice* (San Francisco: Jossey-Bass, 1998).

[14] James M. Lahiff, "Interviewing for Results," in *Readings in Interpersonal and Organizational Communication*, 3d ed., ed. R. C. Huseman, C. M. Logue, and D. L. Freshley (Boston: Holbrook Press, 1973); and Emanuel Kay, Herbert H. Meyer, and John R. P. French, "The Effect of Threat in a Performance Appraisal Interview," *Journal of Applied Psychology* 49 (1965): 311–17.

[15] See Terry R. Lowe, "Eight Ways to Ruin a Performance Review," *Personnel Journal* 65 (1986): 60–62 for a discussion of these and other problems with appraisal interviews.

[16] Judith Hale, *The Performance Consultant's Fieldbook: Tools and Techniques for Improving Organizations and People* (San Francisco: Jossey-Bass, 1998).

[17] Roger Kaufman and others, *The Guidebook for Performance Improvement: Working with Individuals and Organizations* (San Francisco: Jossey-Bass, 1998).

[18] Brett and Fredian, 63–68.

[19] For a more detailed consideration of employee performance appraisal, see Elaine F. Gruenfeld, *Performance Appraisal: Promise and Peril* (Ithaca, NY: Cornell University Press, 1981); Robert Hargrove, *The Art of Masterful Coaching* (San Francisco: Jossey-Bass, 1998); as well as books by Smitter and Kaufman noted above.

[20] Guvenc G. Alpander, "Training First-Line Supervisors to Criticize Constructively," *Personnel Journal* 59 (1980): 216–21.

21 Arnold B. Kanter, *The Complete Book of Interviewing: Everything You Need to Know from Both Sides of the Table* (New York: Times Books, 1995).

22 See advice given in Benedict Carey, "Fear in the Workplace: The Bullying Boss," *New York Times*, June 22, 2004, D6.

CHAPTER 9

1 Joseph A. Raelin, "First-Job Effects on Career Development," *Personnel Administrator* 28 (August 1983): 71–92.

2 See Renee Ruhnow, Robert M. Noe, Randall Odom, and Stanley Adamson, "Interviews: A Look at Their Reliability and Validity," *HR Focus* (February 1992): 13; and Robert W. Eder and Michael M. Harris, "Employment Interview Research: Historical Update and Introduction," in *The Employment Interview Handbook*, ed. R. W. Eder and M. M. Harris (Thousand Oaks, CA: Sage, 1999), 1–27.

3 Mark V. Roehling, James E. Campion, and Richard D. Arvey, "Unfair Discrimination Issues," in *The Employment Interview Handbook*, 49–67; and George E. Gerken, "Preconception-Misconception, or Why Do We Interview Ineffectively," *Manage* (October 1993): 34–35.

4 See Patricia R. Bergeson, *The Americans with Disabilities Act (ADA): Practical Considerations for Employers* (Chicago: Pope, Ballard, Shepard & Fowler, 1991); and Phillip M. Perry, "Your Most Dangerous Legal Traps When Interviewing Job Applicants," *Law Practice Management* (March 1994): 50–56.

5 See American Psychological Association, "Sources of Additional Information on Personnel Assessment" [online]. Available: http://www.hr-guide.com/data/6369.htm (accessed December 5, 2004); Equal Employment Opportunity Commission, "Uniform Guidelines" [online]. Available: www.uniformguidelines.com.html (accessed December 7, 2004); Mark V. Roehling, James E. Campion, and Richard D. Arvey; and Phillip M. Perry.

6 Carol Kleiman, "From Genetics to Honesty, Firms Expand Employee Tests, Screening," *Chicago Tribune*, February 9, 1992, sec. 8, 1; and Patrick H. Raymark, Mark J. Schmit, and Robert M. Guion, "Identifying Potentially Useful Personality Constructs for Employee Selection," *Personnel Psychology* 50 (1997): 723–36.

7 Eric Rolfe Greenberg, "Workplace Testing: Results of a New AMA Survey," *Personnel* 65 (April 1988): 36–44; R. M. Guion, *Assessment, Measurement, and Predictions for Personnel Decisions* (Mahwah, NJ: Erlbaum, 1997).

8 See Steven M. Ralston and Robert Brady, "The Relative Influence of Interview Communication Satisfaction on Applicants' Recruitment Decisions," *Journal of Business Communication* 31 (1994): 61–77.

9 "The Center for Integrity in Business: Social Impact Management" [online]. Available: http://www.spu.edu/depts/sbe/cib/social_impact_cib.htm (accessed June 17, 2004).

10 H. L. Sheppard and H. Belitsky, *The Job Hunt: Job-Seeking Behavior of Unemployed Workers in a Local Economy* (Baltimore, MD: Johns Hopkins University Press, 1971); and "No Job Openings? Set up an Interview Anyway," *Chicago Tribune*, August 16, 1998, Jobs Section, 6.

11 See John R. Cunningham, *The Inside Scoop: Recruiters Tell College Students Their Secrets in the Job Search* (New York: McGraw-Hill, 1998), 45–58.

12 Richard N. Bolles, *The 2004 What Color Is Your Parachute? A Practical Manual for Job-Hunters and Career Changers* (Berkeley, CA: Ten Speed Press, 2004).

13 See, for example, A. B. Kanter, *The Essential Book of Interviewing: Everything You Need to Know from Both Sides of the Table* (New York: Times Books, 1995); and Martin Yate, *Knock 'Em Dead: The Ultimate Job Seeker's Handbook*, 17th ed. (Avon, MA: Adams Media, 2004).

14 Howard M. Sherer, "Effective Entry-Level Organizational Communication as Assessed through a Survey of Personnel Recruiters" (PhD dissertation, Indiana University, 1984).

15 Harold D. Janes, "The Cover Letter and Résumé," *Personnel Journal* 48 (1969): 732–33.

16 It is important to note that the length of the resume will partly be determined by the employee's background (a mid-career applicant is likely to have a longer resume); and some employers, including those who hire college professors, expect to see resumes that are quite lengthy. Like everything else, the resume must be adapted to the context.

17 David C. Gilmore and others, "Impression Management Tactics," in *The Employment Interview Handbook*, ed. R. W. Eder and M. M. Harris (Thousand Oaks, CA: Sage, 1999), 321–36.

18 Steven M. Ralston, "The Relative Effectiveness of Interviewee Communication Behavior, Job Application and Job Description upon Simulated Personnel Selection Decisions" (PhD dissertation, Indiana University, 1986).

[19] Lois J. Einhorn, Patricia H. Bradley, and John E. Baird, Jr., *Effective Employment Interviewing: Unlocking Human Potential* (Glenview, IL: Scott, Foresman, 1982).

[20] Lois J. Einhorn, "An Inner View of the Job Interview: An Investigation of Successful Communicative Behaviors," *Communication Education* 30 (1981): 217–28.

CHAPTER 10

[1] Robert F. Bales, *Interaction Process Analysis: A Method for the Study of Small Groups* (Cambridge, MA: Addison-Wesley, 1950).

[2] Clovis R. Shepherd, *Small Groups* (Scranton, PA: Chandler, 1964).

[3] See Gay Lumsden and Donald Lumsden, *Communicating in Groups and Teams: Sharing Leadership*, 3d ed. (Belmont, CA: Wadsworth, 2000).

[4] Brian Dumaine, "The Trouble with Teams," *Fortune* (September 5, 1994): 65–70.

[5] R. Wellins, W. Byham, and J. Wilson, *Empowered Teams* (San Francisco, CA: Jossey-Bass, 1991), 3.

[6] See David A. Whetton and Kim S. Cameron, *Developing Management Skills*, 5th ed. (New York: HarperCollins, 2000).

[7] Jon R. Katzenbach and Douglas K. Smith, "The Discipline of Teams," *Harvard Business Review* 71 (1993): 111–20.

[8] J. Billington, "The Three Essentials of an Effective Team," *Harvard Management Update* 2 (January 1997): 3–8.

[9] Dumaine, 67.

[10] Katzenbach and Smith, 116.

[11] See E. Salas and others, "The Effect of Team Building on Performance: An Integration," *Small Group Research* 30 (1999): 309–29.

[12] See John Gribas and Cal W. Downs, "Metaphoric Manifestations of Talking 'Team' with Team Novices," *Communication Studies* 53, no. 2 (Summer 2002): 112–28.

[13] As quoted in Lumsden and Lumsden, 74.

[14] E. E. Lawler and S. A. Mohrman, "Quality Circles after the Fad," *Harvard Business Review* 63 (1985): 65–71; and Robert E. Cole, *How American Business Learned to Play the Quality Game* (New York: Oxford University Press, 1999).

[15] G. W. Meyer and R. G. Stott, "Quality Circles: Panacea or Pandora's Box?" *Organizational Dynamics* 13 (1985): 34–50.

[16] Ibid.

[17] Thomas S. Foster, *Managing Quality: An Integrative Approach* (Upper Saddle, NJ: Prentice Hall, 2001).

[18] Cynthia Stohl, "Quality Circles and Changing Patterns of Communication," *Communication Yearbook* 9 (Beverly Hills, CA: Sage, 1986), 483–510.

[19] Melissa K. Marcello and Robert Perrucci, "Small Groups and Civic Engagement—All about Me?" *The Communitarian Network* 10, no. 3 (Summer 2000) [online]. Available: http://www.gwu.edu/~ccps/rcp/rcp_smallgroups.html (accessed May 19, 2004).

[20] See "Business Strengthening America" [online]. Available: http://www.bsanetwork.org/about.html (accessed: July 1, 2004) for a description of a campaign "to mobilize the business community to support effective service and civic engagement by every American."

[21] For additional reading on dialogue and democratic deliberation, see Daniel Yankelovich, *The Magic of Dialogue: Transforming Conflict into Cooperation* (New York: Simon & Schuster, 1999); and Benjamin Barber, *A Place for Us: How to Make Society Civil and Democracy Strong* (New York: Hill and Wang, 1998).

[22] Frederick Taylor, *Scientific Management* (New York: Harper & Row, 1911).

[23] Solomon E. Asch, "Studies of Independence and Conformity: A Minority of One against a Unanimous Majority," *Psychological Monographs* 70 (1956).

[24] Edgar Schein, *Process Consultation, Volume II* (Reading, MA: Addison-Wesley, 1987), 67.

[25] George Cheney, "On the Various and Changing Meanings of Organizational Membership: A Field Study of Organizational Identification," *Communication Monographs* 50 (1983): 342–62.

[26] Asch.

[27] Carolyn W. Sherif, Muzafer Sherif, and Roger E. Nebergall, *Attitude and Attitude Change: The Social Judgment-Involvement Approach* (Philadelphia, PA: Saunders, 1965).

[28] Patricia Hayes Andrews, "Ego-Involvement, Self-Monitoring, and Conformity in Small Groups: A Communicative Analysis," *Central States Speech Journal* 36 (1985): 51–61.

[29] Stanley Schachter, "Deviation, Rejection, and Communication," *Journal of Abnormal and Social Psychology* 46 (1951): 190–207.

[30] K. Phillip Taylor, "An Investigation of Majority Verbal Behavior toward Opinions of Deviant Group Members in Group Discussions of Policy" (unpublished doctoral dissertation, Indiana University, 1969).

[31] Carl L. Thameling and Patricia Hayes Andrews, "Majority Responses to Opinion Deviates: A Communicative Analysis," *Small Group Research* 23 (1992): 475–502.

[32] John R. Wenburg and William Wilmot, *The Personal Communication Process* (New York: John Wiley, 1973).

[33] Dennis S. Gouran and Patricia Hayes Andrews, "Determinants of Punitive Responses to Socially Proscribed Behavior: Seriousness, Attribution of Responsibility, and Status of Offender," *Small Group Behavior* 15 (1984): 524–44.

[34] E. P. Hollander, "Conformity, Status, and Idiosyncrasy Credit," *Psychological Review* 65 (1958): 117–27.

[35] Phillip K. Tompkins, *Organizational Communication Imperatives: Lessons of the Space Program* (Los Angeles: Roxbury, 1993).

[36] Patricia Hayes Bradley, C. Mac Hamon, and Alan M. Harris, "Dissent in Small Groups," *Journal of Communication* 26 (1976): 155–59. Also see M. Sean Limon and Franklin J. Boster, "The Impact of Varying Argument Quality and Minority Size on Influencing the Majority and Perceptions of the Minority," *Communication Quarterly* 49 (Fall 2001): 350–65.

[37] Thameling and Andrews, 480–500; and Renee Meyers and others, "Majority-Minority Influence: Identifying Argumentative Patterns and Predicting Argument-Outcome Links," *Journal of Communication* 50 (2000): 3–30.

[38] For a more extended discussion of social pressure and conformity, see Patricia Hayes Andrews, "Group Conformity," in *Small Group Communication: Theory and Practice*, 7th ed., ed. R. S. Cathcart, L. A. Samovar, and L. D. Henman (Madison, WI: Brown and Benchmark, 1996), 225–35.

[39] Kenneth D. Benne and Paul Sheats, "Functional Roles of Group Members," *Journal of Social Issues* 4 (1948): 41–49.

[40] Ibid.

[41] Michael E. Mayer, "Behaviors Leading to More Effective Decisions in Small Groups Embedded in Organizations," *Communication Reports* 11 (Summer 1998): 123–32.

[42] John R. P. French and Bernard Raven, "The Social Bases of Power," in *Studies in Social Power*, ed. D. Cartwright (Ann Arbor, MI: Institute for Social Research, 1959), 65–84.

[43] Dennis S. Gouran and Randy Y. Hirokawa, "Counteractive Functions of Communication in Effective Group Decision-Making," in *Communication and Group Decision-Making*, ed. R. Y. Hirokawa and M. S. Poole (Beverly Hills, CA: Sage, 1986), 81–90.

[44] Gouran and Andrews.

[45] See Tompkins; and Jacob Hurwitz and Alvin Zander, "Some Effects of Power in the Relations among Group Members," in *Group Dynamics*, ed. D. Cartwright and A. Zander (New York: Harper & Row, 1960), 483–92.

[46] Peter Drucker, *Effective Decisions* (Effective Executive Series, 1968).

[47] Shepherd, 67.

[48] William Foster Owen, "Metaphor Analysis of Cohesiveness in Small Discussion Groups," *Small Group Behavior* 16 (1985): 415–24.

[49] Marvin E. Shaw, "Group Composition and Group Cohesiveness," in *Small Group Communication: A Reader*, 6th ed., ed. R. S. Cathcart and L. A. Samovar (Dubuque, IA: Wm. C. Brown, 1992), 214–20.

[50] Leonard Berkowitz, "Group Standards, Cohesiveness, and Productivity," *Human Relations* 7 (1954): 509–19.

[51] Irving Janis, *Groupthink*, 2d ed. (Boston: Houghton Mifflin, 1982), 3.

[52] See Larry Browning, "Interpreting the *Challenger* Disaster: Communication under Conditions of Risk and Reliability," *Industrial Crisis Quarterly* 2 (1988): 211–27; Dennis S. Gouran, Randy Y. Hirokawa, and Amy E. Martz, "A Critical Analysis of Factors Related to Decisional Processes Involved in the *Challenger* Disaster," *Central States Speech Journal* 37 (1986): 119–35; and Tompkins.

[53] Steve M. Alderton and Larry Frey, "Effects of Reactions to Arguments on Group Outcomes," *Central States Speech Journal* 34 (1983): 88–95; and David R. Seibold and Renee A. Meyers, and Sunwolf "Communication and Influence in Group Decision-Making," in *Communication and Group Decision-Making*, 2nd ed., ed. R. Y. Hirokawa and M. S. Poole (Beverly Hills, CA: Sage, 1996), 242–68.

[54] Janis.

[55] Ibid., 9.

56 Rebecca Cline, "Detecting Groupthink: Methods for Observing the Illusion of Unanimity," *Communication Quarterly* 38 (1990): 112–26.

57 Janis, 197–98.

58 See Cline, pp. 120–26; Irving Janis, "Vigilant Problem Solving," in *Crucial Decisions: Leadership in Policymaking and Crisis Management*, ed. I. Janis (New York: Free Press, 1989), 89–117; and Dennis S. Gouran, "Leadership as the Art of Counteractive Influence in Decision-Making and Problem-Solving Groups," in *Small Group Communication: Theory and Practice*, 8th ed., ed. R. Y. Hirokawa and others (Los Angeles: Roxbury, 2003), 172–83.

CHAPTER 11

1 J. Richard Hackman, "Why Teams Don't Work," in *Theory and Research in Small Groups*, ed. R. S. Tindale and Associates (New York: Plenum Press, 1998), 246.

2 Keith Davis, *Human Behavior at Work* (New York: McGraw-Hill, 1972). Note, however, that the distinction can be made between conjunctive tasks (which require pooling information), at which groups excel, and disjunctive tasks, at which individuals can work quite well alone. Also see J. Richard Hackman, *Groups that Work (and Those that Don't): Creating the Conditions for Effective Teamwork* (San Francisco: Jossey-Bass, 1990).

3 Stephen L. Ross, "Creative Problem Solving," in *Organizational Communication*, 2d ed., ed. S. D. Ferguson and S. Ferguson (New Brunswick, NJ: Transaction Books, 1988), 481–88; Sunwolf, "Getting to 'GroupAha!': Provoking Creative Thought Processes in Task Groups," in *New Directions in Group Communication*, ed. Larry R. Frey (Thousand Oaks, CA: Sage, 2002), 154–70; and Warren Bennis and P. W. Biederman, *Organizing Genius: The Secrets of Creative Collaboration* (Reading, MA: Addison-Wesley, 1997).

4 Norman R. F. Maier, "Assets and Liabilities in Group Problem-Solving: The Need for an Integrative Function," *Psychological Review* 74 (1967): 239–49; and John Kao, *Jamming: The Art and Discipline of Business Creativity* (New York: HarperBusiness, 1997).

5 C. C. Manz and H. P. Sims, *Business without Bosses: How Self-Management Teams Are Building High-Performing Companies* (New York: John Wiley, 1993).

6 Dennis S. Gouran and Randy Y. Hirokawa, "Effective Decision Making and Problem Solving in Groups: A Functional Perspective," in *Small Group Communication: Theory and Practice*, 8th ed., ed. R. Y. Hirokawa and others (Los Angeles: Roxbury, 2003), 27–38.

7 See research by Poole and Roth; in particular, Marshall Scott Poole and J. Roth, "Decision Development in Small Groups V: Test of a Contingency Model," *Human Communication Research* 15 (1988): 549–89.

8 Dennis S. Gouran, *Discussion: The Process of Group Decision Making* (New York: Harper and Row, 1974), 66–80.

9 Robert F. Bales and Fred L. Strodtbeck, "Phases in Group Problem-Solving," *Journal of Abnormal and Social Psychology* 46 (1951): 485–95; and M. McCollom, "Re-evaluating Group Development: A Critique of Familiar Models," in *Groups in Context: A New Perspective on Group Dynamics*, ed. J. Gillette and M. McCollom (Lanham, MD: University Press of America, 1995), 133–54.

10 Bales and Strodtbeck.

11 B. W. Tuckman and M. A. C. Jensen, "Stages of Small-Group Development," *Group and Organizational Studies* 2 (1977): 419–27.

12 Thomas M. Schiedel and Laura Crowell, "Idea Development in Small Groups," *Quarterly Journal of Speech* 50 (1964): 140–45.

13 Marshall Scott Poole, "Decision Development in Small Groups I: A Comparison of Two Models," *Communication Monographs* 50 (1983): 1–24; and Marshall Scott Poole, "A Multiple Sequence Model of Group Decision Development," in *Small Group Communication: Theory and Practice*, 8th ed., ed. R. Y. Hirokawa and others (Los Angeles: Roxbury, 2003), 76–82.

14 Marshall Scott Poole and J. Roth, "Decision Development in Small Groups IV: A Typology of Group Decision Paths," *Human Communication Research* 15 (1988): 323–56; Marshall Scott Poole and Carolyn Baldwin, "Developmental Processes in Group Decision Making," in *Communication and Group Decision Making*, ed. R. Y. Hirokawa and M. S. Poole (Thousand Oaks, CA: Sage, 1996), 215–41.

15 Connie Gersick, "Revolutionary Change Theories: A multiple-level Explanation of the Punctuated Equilibrium Paradigm," *Academy of Management Review* 16 (1991): 10–36; and Connie Gersick, "Time and Transition in Work Teams: Toward a New Model of Group Development," in *Small Group*

Communication: Theory and Practice, 8th ed,. ed. R. Y. Hirokawa and others (Los Angeles: Roxbury, 2003), 59–75.

16 Randy Y. Hirokawa and R. Pace, "A Descriptive Investigation of the Possible Communication-Based Reasons for Effective and Ineffective Group Decision Making," *Communication Monographs* 50 (1983): 363–79.

17 Randy Y. Hirokawa, "Group Communication and Problem-Solving Effectiveness: An Investigation of Group Phases," *Human Communication Research* 9 (1983): 291–305.

18 See Randy Y. Hirokawa and K. Rost, "Effective Group Decision-Making in Organizations," *Management Communication Quarterly* 5 (1992): 267–88; Randy Y. Hirokawa, Larry Erbert, and Anthony Hurst, "Communication and Group Decision-Making Effectiveness," in *Communication and Group Decision-Making*, 2nd ed., ed. R. Y. Hirokawa and M. S. Poole (Thousand Oaks, CA: Sage, 1996), 269–300; and Gouran and Hirokawa.

19 See Charles Conrad and Marshall Scott Poole, *Strategic Organizational Communication: Into the Twenty-First Century*, 5th ed. (Fort Worth, TX: Harcourt Brace, 2001).

20 M. D. Cohen, J. G. March, and J. P. Olson, "A Garbage Can Model of Organizational Choice," *Administrative Science Quarterly* 17 (1972): 1–25.

21 Poole and Roth, 549–89.

22 P. C. Nutt, "Types of Organizational Decision Processes," *Administrative Science Quarterly* 29 (1984): 414–50.

23 John Dewey, *How We Think* (Boston: Heath, 1910).

24 See Dennis S. Gouran, *Making Decisions in Groups: Choices and Consequences* (Prospect Heights, IL: Waveland Press, 1982).

25 Alex F. Osborn, *Applied Imagination*, rev. ed. (New York: Scribner, 1957); Isa N. Engleberg and Dianna R. Wynn, *Working in Groups: Communication Principles and Strategies*, 2nd ed. (Boston: Houghton Mifflin, 2000), 199–200.

26 Donald C. Mosley and Thad B. Green, "Nominal Grouping as an Organization Development Intervention Technique," *Training and Development Journal* (March 1974): 30–37.

27 Frederic M. Jablin, David R. Seibold, and Rich L. Sorenson, "Potential Inhibiting Effects of Group Participation on Brainstorming Performance," *Central States Speech Journal* 28 (1977): 113–21; Frederic M. Jablin, "Cultivating Imagination: Factors That Enhance and Inhibit Creativity in Brainstorming Groups," *Human Communication Research* 7 (1981): 245–58; and Sunwolf.

28 Jay F. Nunamaker and others, "Electronic Meeting Systems to Support Group Work," *Communications of the ACM* 34 (1991): 40–61; and Gerardine DeSanctis and Peter Monge, "Communication Processes for Virtual Organizations," *Organization Science* 10, no. 6 (1999): 693–703.

29 R. Brent Gallupe, Gerardine DeSanctis, and Gary Dickson, "The Impact of Computer-Based Support on the Process and Outcomes of Group Decision Making," *MIS Quarterly* 12 (1988): 277–98; and Patricia Hayes Andrews and Richard T. Herschel, *Organizational Communication: Empowerment in a Technological Society* (Boston: Houghton Mifflin, 1996), 223–30.

30 Suzanne Herrick-Walker, "The Effect of Group Decision Support Systems on Decision-Making Groups Containing High Communication Apprehensives: Satisfaction, Participation, and Productivity" (unpublished master's thesis, Indiana University, 1991).

31 See Andrews and Herschel, 221–30.

32 Jay Nunamaker and others, "Group Support Systems Research: Experience from the Lab and Field," in *Group Support Systems: New Perspectives*, ed. L. M. Jessup and J. S. Valacich (New York: Macmillan, 1993), 78–96; and Marshall Scott Poole and Gerardine DeSanctis, "Structuration Theory in Information Systems Research: Methods and Controversies," in *The Handbook of Information Systems Research*, ed. M. E. Whitman and A. B. Woszczynski (Hershey, PA: The Idea Group, 2004), 206–49.

33 Alan R. Dennis and others, "Information Technology to Support Electronic Meetings," *Management Information Systems Quarterly* 12, no. 4 (December 1988): 591–624; Gerardine DeSanctis, Marshall Scott Poole, and Gary W. Dickson, "Teams and Technology: Interactions over Time," in *Research on Managing Groups and Teams: Technology*, vol. 3, ed. M. A. Neale and others (Stamford, CT: JAI Press, 2000), 1–27.

34 Nunamaker and others, "Group Support Systems Research," 78–96; and Alain Pinsonneault and Nelson Heppel, "Anonymity in Group Support Systems Research: A New Conceptualization, Measure, and Contingency," *Journal of Management Information Systems* 14, no. 3 (Winter 1998): 89–108.

35 Gallupe, DeSanctis, and Dickson; and Craig Scott, "New Communication Technologies and Teams," in *Small Group Communication: Theory and Practice*, 8th ed., ed. R. Y. Hirokawa and others (Los Angeles: Roxbury, 2003), 134–47.

[36] Richard T. Herschel and Patricia Hayes Andrews, "Empowering Employees in Group Work: A Case for Using Group Support Systems," *Information Strategy: The Executive's Journal* 9 (1993): 36–42.

[37] David Kirkpatrick, "Here Comes the Payoff from PCs," *Fortune* 23 (March 1992): 93–100; Anika Luthra and Kevin Desouza, "Intelligence Sharing in Virtual Teams: Managing Organizational Effects of Technology," *Journal of Competitive Intelligence and Management* 1, no. 3 (Winter 2003): 1–11.

[38] Susan R. Feather, "The Impact of Group Support Systems on Collaborative Learning Groups Stages of Development," *Information Technology, Learning, and Performance Journal* 17, no. 2 (Fall 1999): 23–34.

CHAPTER 12

[1] John Naisbitt, *Megatrends: Ten New Directions Transforming Our Lives* (New York: Warner Books, 1982), 159.

[2] Allan Cox, *The Cox Report on the American Corporation* (New York: Delacorte, 1982), 136.

[3] Perry Pascarella, *The New Achievers: Creating a Modern Work Ethic* (New York: Free Press, 1984), 106.

[4] B. Y. Auger, "Staff Meetings: Energy Waste or Catalyst for High Performance," *Data Management* 20 (May 1980): 39–41.

[5] Allan D. Frank, "Trends in Communication: Who Talks to Whom?" *Personnel* 62 (December 1985): 41–47.

[6] For example, see William G. Dyer, *Team Building: Issues and Alternatives* (Reading, MA: Addison-Wesley, 1977); and D. R. Ilgen, "Teams Embedded in Organizations: Some Implications," *American Psychologist* 54 (1999): 129–39.

[7] Robert F. Littlejohn, "Team Management: A How-To Approach to Improved Productivity, Higher Morale, and Longer Lasting Job Satisfaction," *Management Review* 71 (January 1982): 23–28.

[8] Patricia Hayes Andrews, "Sex and Gender Differences in Group Communication: Impact on the Facilitation Process," *Small Group Behavior* 23, no.1 (1992): 74–94; and Nina M. Reich and Julia T. Wood, "Sex, Gender, and Communication in Small Groups," in *Small Group Communication: Theory and Practice*, 8th ed., ed. R. Y. Hirokawa and others (Los Angeles: Roxbury, 2003), 218–29.

[9] Alice Eagly and B. Johnson, "Gender and Leadership Style: A Meta-analysis," *Psychological Bulletin* 108 (1990): 233–56; Joyce K. Fletcher, Judith V. Jordan, and Jean Baker Miller, "Women and the Workplace: Applications of a Psychodynamic Theory," *American Journal of Psychoanalysis* 60 (2000): 243–61.

[10] Elizabeth J. Natalle, "Gendered Issues in the Workplace," in *Gendered Relationships*, ed. J. T. Wood (Mountain View, CA: Mayfield, 1996), 253–74.

[11] See Andrews, 74–94.

[12] Cheris Kramerae, *Men and Women Speaking* (Rowley, MA: Newbury House, 1981), 92.

[13] Patricia Hayes Bradley, "The Folk-linguistics of Women's Speech: An Empirical Investigation," *Communication Monographs* 48 (1981): 73–90.

[14] D. Butler and F Geis, "Nonverbal Affect Responses to Male and Female Leaders: Implications for Leadership," *Journal of Personality and Social Psychology* 58 (1990): 48–59.

[15] B. Wilkins and P. Andersen, "Gender Differences and Similarities in Management Communication," *Management Communication Quarterly* 5 (1991): 6–35; Gary Powell, *Women and Men in Management* (Newbury Park, CA: Sage, 1993); and Reich and Wood, 225–27.

[16] E. Kushell and R. Newton, "Gender, Leadership Style, and Subordinate Satisfaction: An Experiment," *Sex Roles* 14 (1986): 203–09.

[17] Fletcher, Jordan, and Miller, 250–61.

[18] A. Cann and W. D. Siegfried, "Sex Stereotypes and the Leadership Role," *Sex Roles* 17 (1987): 401–8.

[19] "Manage Meeting Malcontents," *Communication Briefings* 17, no. 4 (November 1998): 1.

[20] Mildred Culp, "Cyber Meetings: Showing Off the Latest Way of Showing Up," *Chicago Tribune*, May 24, 1998, sec. 6, 21.

[21] Charlene Marmer Solomon, "Make the Most of Teleconferencing," *Global Workforce* 3, no. 6 (November 1998): 14.

[22] N. Wreden, "Regrouping for Groupware," *Beyond Computing* 2 (March/April, 1993): 52–55; and Jessica Lipnack and Jeffrey Stamps, *Virtual Teams: People Working across Boundaries with Technology*, 2d ed. (New York: John Wiley & Sons, 2000).

[23] Lee Sproull and Sara Kiesler, "Computers, Networks, and Work," *Scientific American* 256 (September 1991): 116–23; and Craig R. Scott, "Communication Technology and Group Communication," in *The Handbook of Group Communication Theory and Research*, ed. L. R. Frey, D. S. Gouran, and M. S. Poole (Thousand Oaks, CA: Sage Publications, 1999), 432–72.

CHAPTER 13

1 Peter Drucker, "How to Be an Employer," *Fortune* (May 5, 1952), 126.

2 Sandy Whiteley, ed., *The American Library Association Guide to Information Access: A Complete Research Handbook and Directory* (New York: Random House, 1994).

3 Kathryn P. Jett, "Binge Drinking" (April 2002) [online]. Available: http://www.adp.cahwnet.gov/director/kpj_speech_041202.shtml (accessed May 30, 2004).

4 Diana DeGette, "The Value of a Liberal Arts Education" (August 1998) [online]. Available: http://www.gos.sbc.edu/d/degette.html (accessed May 19, 2004).

5 Ingrid Newkirk, "Address to the *Eleventh Hour*" (April 2001) [online]. Available: http://www.gos/sbc.edu/n/newkirk.html (accessed May 19, 2004).

6 This speech extract is based on a presentation given in a class at by Holly Baxter, a doctoral student in the Department of Speech Communication at Indiana University.

7 A. Thomas Young, "Ethics in Business," *Vital Speeches of the Day* 58 (1992): 726–27.

8 Jesse Jackson, "Remarks at the Democratic National Convention" (August 2000) [online]. Available: http://www.cnn.com/ELECTION/2000/conventions/democratic/transcripts/u060815.html (accessed May 27, 2004).

CHAPTER 14

1 Irwin Edmond, *The Works of Plato* (New York: Simon & Schuster, 1928), 309.

2 George W. Bush, "Freedom Itself Was Attacked This Morning" (September 11, 2001) [online]. Available: http://www.americanrhetoric.com/speeches/gwbush911barksdale.htm (accessed June 1, 2004).

3 Neal W. O'Connor, "The Freedom to Communicate: An Advertising Man Re-reads the First Amendment," *Vital Speeches of the Day* 42 (1976): 179.

4 Lewis Platt, "Accepting Risk—Daring Greatness: An Entrepreneurial Credo" (March 20, 2004) [online]. Available: http://www.boeing.com/news/speeches/2004/platt_040320.html (accessed May 19, 2004).

5 Bono, "2001 Harvard Commencement Address" (June 12, 2001) [online]. Available: http://www.americanrhetoric.com/speeches/bonoharvardcommencement.htm (accessed May 31, 2004).

6 Richard Lamm, "Unexamined Assumptions: Destiny, Political Institutions, Democracy and Population," *Vital Speeches of the Day* 64 (September 15, 1998): 712.

7 David Abney, "The Hedgehog's Lemonade Recipe" (November 20, 2003) [online]. Available: http://www.pressroom.ups.com/execforum/speeches/speech/text/0,1403,498,00.html (accessed: June 1, 2004).

8 This speech was delivered by a business and professional communication student at Indiana University in the spring of 1999.

9 This pattern was originally introduced by Alan H. Monroe in *Principles and Types of Speech* (New York: Scott, Foresman, 1935) and has been refined in later editions; see, for example, Raymie McKerrow, Bruce E. Gronbeck, Douglas Ehninger, and Alan H. Monroe, *Principles and Types of Speech Communication*, 14th ed. (New York: Longman, 2000).

10 See Karen Zediker, *Rediscovering the Tradition: Women's History with a Relational Approach to the Basic Public Speaking Course*, paper presented at the Western States Communication Association, Albuquerque, New Mexico, 1993. This paper reviews the work of Christine Jorgensen-Earp, who argues that these patterns are often used by women and ethnic speakers.

11 See James C. McCroskey, *An Introduction to Rhetorical Communication*, 8th ed. (Boston: Allyn and Bacon, 2001).

12 Anna Quindlen, "Commencement Speech" (May 23, 1999) [online]. Available: http://www.gos.sbc.edu/q/quindlen.html (accessed May 19, 2004).

13 This speech was delivered by a student in the LAMP program at Indiana University during the fall semester, 1999.

14 Jimmy Carter, "U.S. Response to Soviet Military Force in Cuba," *Vital Speeches of the Day* 42 (1979–80): 4.

15 Martin Luther King, Jr., "I Have a Dream," in *American Rhetorical Discourse*, 3d ed., Ronald F. Reid and James F. Klumpp (Long Grove, IL: Waveland Press, 2005), 843.

16 Robert C. Purcell, "Values for Value: Integrity and Stewardship," *Vital Speeches of the Day* 64 (October 1, 1998): 766.

[17] A great deal of research has addressed the issue of communication apprehension. Some articles include: Joe Ayres and Tim S. Hopf, "Visualization: The Next Generation," *Communication Research Reports* 8 (1991): 133–40; Ralph R. Behnke and Chris R. Sawyer, "Milestones of Anticipatory Public Speaking Anxiety," *Communication Education* 48 (1999): 165–72; Behnke and Sawyer, "Public Speaking Anxiety as a Function of Sensitization and Habituation Processes," *Communication Education* 53 (2004): 164–73; and Amy M. Bippus and John A. Daly, "What Do People Think Causes Stage Fright? Naive Attributions about the Reasons for Public Speaking Anxiety," *Communication Education* 48 (1999): 63–72.

[18] John A. Daly and others, *Avoiding Communication: Shyness, Reticence, and Communication Apprehension*, 2d ed. (Cresskill, NJ: Hampton Press, 1997); and James C. McCroskey, "Oral Communication Apprehension: A Summary of Recent Theory and Research," *Human Communication Research* 4 (1977): 79–96.

[19] For an interesting discussion of how students with high communication apprehension often assume that the audience is overly critical, see Marianne Martini, Ralph R. Behnke, and Paul E. King, "The Communication of Public Speaking Anxiety: Perceptions of Asian and American Speakers," *Communication Quarterly* 40 (1992): 279–88; and Russell F. Proctor II, and others, "Approach, Avoidance, and Apprehension: Talking with High CA Students about Getting Help," *Communication Education* 43 (1994): 312–21.

[20] See Joe Ayres and Tim Hopf, *Coping with Speech Anxiety* (Norwood, NJ: Ablex, 1993), 5–21.

[21] Other ways of managing stage fright include systematic desensitization, visualization, and cognitive restructuring. See Joe Ayres and Tim S. Hopf, "Visualization: A Means of Reducing Anxiety," *Communication Education* 34 (1985): 318–23; Peter Desberg, *No More Butterflies: Overcoming Stagefright, Shyness, Interview Anxiety, and Fear of Public Speaking* (Oakland, CA: New Harbinger, 1996); and Virginia P. Richmond and James C. McCroskey, *Communication: Apprehension, Avoidance, and Effectiveness*, 5th ed. (Boston: Allyn & Bacon, 1998).

[22] For a classic work on nonverbal communication, see Edward T. Hall, *The Silent Language* (Garden City, NY: Doubleday, 1959). More recent works include Edward T. Hall, *The Dance of Life* (New York: Doubleday, 1983); and Mark Knapp and J. Hall, *Nonverbal Communication in Human Interaction*, 5th ed. (Belmont, CA: Wadsworth, 2002).

[23] See Jane Blankenship, *A Sense of Style* (Belmont, CA: Dickenson, 1968), pp. 112–24. For books focusing on written style, especially in a business context, see David H. Lynch, *Business Writer's Guide*, 4th ed. (New York: McGraw-Hill, 2000); and Diana Roberts Wienbroer and others, *Rules of Thumb for Business Writers* (New York: McGraw-Hill, 2000).

[24] Rudolph Flesch, *The Art of Plain Talk* (New York: Harper & Brothers, 1946), 38.

CHAPTER 15

[1] Rushworth M. Kidder, *Shared Values for a Troubled World: Conversations with Men and Women of Conscience* (San Francisco: Jossey-Bass, 1994). This book reports on in-depth interviews with moral leaders of many cultures.

[2] Abraham Maslow, *Motivation and Personality* (New York: Harper & Row, 1954).

[3] Ibid.

[4] David C. McClelland and David H. Burnham, "Power Is the Great Motivator," *Harvard Business Review* 73 (1995): 126–39.

[5] U.S. Peace Corps, "Culture Matters" (no date given) [online]. Available: http://www.languageand-culture.com/lcw_eng/about_culture/about_culture_cultural.html (accessed: June 16, 2004).

[6] For an extensive discussion of transformational leadership, as well as other leadership theories, see Peter F. Drucker, *The Effective Executive* (New York: Harper & Row, 1967); also see Peter G. Northouse, *Leadership: Theory and Practice*, 2d ed. (Thousand Oaks, CA: Sage, 2000); and Michael Z. Hackman and Craig E. Johnson, *Leadership: A Communication Perspective*, 4th ed. (Long Grove, IL: Waveland Press, 2004).

[7] See *The Rhetoric of Aristotle*, trans. George Kennedy (New York: Oxford University Press, 1992).

[8] Jack L. Whitehead, "Factors of Source Credibility," *Quarterly Journal of Speech* 54 (1968): 59–63.

[9] Richard L. Johannesen, *Ethics in Human Communication*, 5th ed. (Prospect Heights, IL: Waveland Press, 2002), 31–32.

[10] James C. McCroskey, *An Introduction to Rhetorical Communication*, 7th ed. (Boston: Allyn and Bacon, 1997), 87–107.

[11] For an excellent review of this research, see John C. Reinard, "The Empirical Study of the Persuasive Effects of Evidence: The Status after 50 Years of Research," *Human Communication Research* 15 (1988): 3–59.

[12] Mike Allen, "Comparing the Persuasive Effects of One- and Two-Sided Messages," in *Persuasion: Advances through Meta-Analysis*, ed. M. Allen and R. W. Preiss (Cresskill, NJ: Hampton Press, 1997), 87–98.

[13] Michael Burgoon and Judee K. Burgoon, "Message Strategies in Influence Attempts," in *Communication Behavior*, ed. G. J. Hanneman and W. J. McEwen (Reading, MA: Addison-Wesley, 1975), 149–65.

[14] Ibid., 158.

[15] Janet Fulk and S. Mani, "Distortion of Communication in Hierarchical Relationships," in *Communication Yearbook 9*, ed. M. L. McLaughlin (Newbury Park, CA: Sage, 1986), 483–510.

[16] See, for example, P. G. Clampitt, *Communicating for Managerial Effectiveness* (Newbury Park, CA: Sage, 1991); and Alvin Toffler, *Powershift* (New York: Bantam Books, 1990).

[17] See Patricia Hayes Andrews and Richard T. Herschel, *Organizational Communication: Empowerment in a Technological Society* (Boston: Houghton Mifflin, 1996), 170–79.

[18] See McCroskey, 203.

[19] John Dewey, *How We Think* (Boston: Heath, 1910).

[20] See Virginia P. Richmond and James C. McCroskey, *Nonverbal Behavior in Interpersonal Relations*, 3d ed. (Boston: Allyn & Bacon, 1995); and James W. Neuliep, *Intercultural Communication: A Contextual Approach* (Boston: Houghton Mifflin, 2000), 231–66.

APPENDIX

[1] For example, see General Henry M. Robert and others, *Robert's Rules of Order Newly Revised*, 10th ed. (Boulder, CO: Perseus Books Group, 2000); John E. Baird, Sr., *A Guide to Conducting Meetings* (New York: Abingdon Press, 1965); and Alice Sturgis, *Sturgis Standard Code of Parliamentary Procedure*, 4th ed. (Falls Church, VA: Higher Education, 2000). In addition, the American Legal Publishing Corporation released *Robert's Rules of Order Newly Revised* on CD-ROM (May 2004). For further information, visit their Web site at http://www.amlegal.com/rorassociation.htm.

Name Index

Subject Index